ADOLESCENCE

Fourth Edition

A·D·O·L·E·S·C·E·N·C·E

John W. Santrock

*University of Texas
at Dallas*

Wm. C. Brown Publishers

Book Team

Editor *Michael Lange*
Developmental Editor *Carla Aspelmeier*
Art Editor *Gayle A. Salow*
Photo Editor *Mary Roussel*
Permissions Editor *Vicki Krug*
Visuals Processor *Andé Meyer*

 Wm. C. Brown Publishers

President *G. Franklin Lewis*
Vice President, Publisher *George Wm. Bergquist*
Vice President, Publisher *Thomas E. Doran*
Vice President, Operations and Production *Beverly Kolz*
National Sales Manager *Virginia S. Moffat*
Advertising Manager *Ann M. Knepper*
Marketing Manager *Kathy Law Laube*
Production Editorial Manager *Colleen A. Yonda*
Production Editorial Manager *Julie A. Kennedy*
Publishing Services Manager *Karen J. Slaght*
Manager of Visuals and Design *Faye M. Schilling*

Cover photo © David W. Hamilton/The Image Bank

Cover and interior design: Terri W. Ellerbach

The credits section for this book begins on page 637, and is considered an extension of the copyright page.

Library of Congress Catalog Card Number: 89–50280

Cloth ISBN 0–697–11154–7

Paper ISBN 0–697–05950–2

Printed in the United States of America by Wm. C. Brown Publishers, 2460 Kerper Boulevard, Dubuque, IA 52001

10 9 8 7 6 5 4 3 2

To Tracy and Jennifer, who, as they have matured, have helped me to appreciate the marvels of adolescent development.

Brief Contents

Table of Contents

I

The Nature of Adolescent Development

CHAPTER

1

Introduction

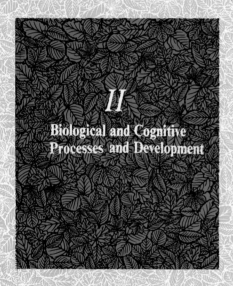

II

**Biological and Cognitive
Processes and Development**

Cognitive Development and Social Cognition

Information Processing and Intelligence

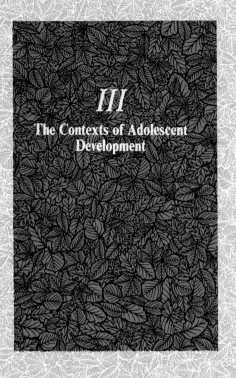

III

The Contexts of Adolescent Development

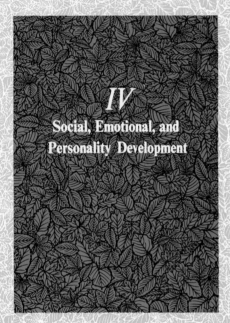

IV

Social, Emotional, and
Personality Development

CHAPTER

10

The Self and Identity

Prologue: Groucho Marx: Developing an
    Identity 364

14

Achievement, Careers, and Work

V
Disturbances, Stress,
and Health

Preface

T welve years ago I agreed to write the first edition of *Adolescence.* My oldest daughter, Tracy, was 12 years old and just embarking on the fascinating, complex, long journey of making the transition from child to adult. Now twelve years later, *Adolescence* and Tracy have moved through a number of changes. Both have been an important part of my life during the last dozen years. Both are special.

When I wrote the first edition of *Adolescence,* I wanted to put together a book that would portray the scientific study of adolescent development in an interesting and scientific manner. The fourth edition of *Adolescence* continues my effort to both inform and excite the reader. Because ours is a field of rapidly changing knowledge with extensive research on adolescence being conducted throughout the world, the second and third editions of *Adolescence* represented substantial changes from their predecessors. The fourth edition of *Adolescence* continues the tradition of extensive research updating.

The Research System

Beginning with the first edition and continuing through the present edition, *Adolescence* is above all else an extremely up-to-date presentation of research in the three primary domains of development: biological, cognitive, and social processes. Research on biological, cognitive, and social processes continues to dominate the core of *Adolescence.* This core includes both classic and leading edge research. *Adolescence* includes an abundance of recent references, including more than 200 from 1989 alone. Adolescent psychology is expanding on many frontiers and I have attempted in each chapter to capture the excitement of these new discoveries as well as the classic studies that are the foundation of the discipline.

One of the most important changes in the fourth edition is the greatly expanded coverage of the ethnic and cultural worlds of adolescents. Adolescents' ethnic and cultural worlds are emphasized throughout the text, in a separate chapter on culture, and in a new feature called THE CULTURAL WORLDS OF ADOLESCENTS, which appears one or more times in each chapter. Among the topics of these boxed inserts are "A black student's view of public schools," "An international perspective on abortion trends," "How Soviet adolescents view nuclear war," "Annie and Tony's disagreement about Spanish," and "The American Indian's quest for identity: Isn't it enough just to be?"

Among the new contents of the fourth edition of *Adolescence* are an entire chapter devoted to sexuality and an entire chapter devoted to stress and health. Each of these topics is of immense importance to today's adolescents. This expanded coverage in separate chapters also recognizes the burgeoning research and interest in both of these areas of psychology. Much more extensive space is devoted to school dropouts, minority group adolescents, music videos, gender roles, sexually transmitted diseases, adolescent pregnancy, work, the transition from school to work, crack cocaine, stress, nutrition, and exercise.

The Writing System

In addition to continuing the strategy of providing extensive research updating and coverage of leading edge research, I asked myself what else I could do to improve the fourth edition of *Adolescence*. After some self-searching, the answer was: improve the writing style of the book. Those familiar with earlier editions of the book will notice this change after only a few minutes. To accomplish the goal of improving the book's writing style, I went over the book thoroughly—adding, subtracting, integrating, and simplifying. I examined alternative ways of presenting ideas and asked my students to provide feedback on which strategies were most effective. Virtually every sentence, every paragraph, every section of the book were rewritten with these goals uppermost in my mind.

Most authors with successful editions of a book only make cosmetic changes in the fourth edition. Why spend so much time rewriting, adding, subtracting, integrating, and simplifying the fourth edition? While the third edition was perceived as a solid scientific overview of adolescence, over the course of three editions the book had become excessively long in places and the rhythm and flow of the writing needed to be fine-tuned. Also, each time a concept is introduced, I have been careful to follow it with a comprehensible definition and either research examples, personal examples, or both. Noticeable in the fourth edition of *Adolescence* is an increased use of examples taken from the lives of adolescents as they experience their world.

The Learning System

A substantial change in the third edition of *Adolescence* was the introduction of extensive pedagogy. A carefully designed, refined learning system has been built into the fourth edition of *Adolescence*. Critical to this framework are the CONCEPT TABLES that appear several times in each chapter. They are designed to activate the student's memory and comprehension of major topics or key concepts that have been discussed to that point. This allows the student to get a handle on complex concepts and ideas and to understand how key concepts are interrelated. Concept tables provide a visual picture, or cognitive framework, of the most important information in each section.

In addition, PROLOGUES—imaginative, high-interest pieces focused on a topic related to the chapter's content—open each chapter of *Adolescence*. Nine of the 17 prologues in the fourth edition are new. For example, Chapter 1 opens with "Today's Adolescents: The Best of Times and the Worst of Times," Chapter 11 opens with "Mary Smith of 1955 and Tracy McKinley of 1990," and Chapter 12 opens with "The Mysteries and Curiosities of Adolescent Sexuality." PERSPECTIVE ON ADOLESCENT DEVELOPMENT boxes appear several times in each chapter. A brief glimpse through any chapter reveals their special appeal. Seventeen new boxes have been written for the fourth edition of *Adolescence*. They include in Chapter 5, "Analytical Ann, Insightful Todd, and Street-Smart Art," in Chapter 8, "The 'Shopping Mall' High School," in Chapter 9, "The Dreams and Struggles of John David Guitierrez," in Chapter 12, "Angela, Michelle, and Stephanie: Three Adolescent Mothers," in Chapter 14, "The Life and Career Paths of Joanne and Joan," in Chapter 15, "Frog and Dolores," and in Chapter 16, "Daily Hassles and Daily Uplifts in the Lives of Young Adolescents."

At the end of each chapter, a detailed SUMMARY in outline form provides a helpful review. KEY TERMS are boldfaced in the text, listed with page references at the end of each chapter, and defined in a page-referenced glossary at the end of the book. An annotated list of SUGGESTED READINGS also appears at the end of each chapter. Finally, at the book's end, a brief EPILOGUE encourages students to look back over what they have read during the course and to examine their own adolescence and the role adolescence plays in life's human cycle.

Ancillaries

Wm. C. Brown Publishers and the ancillary team have worked together to produce an outstanding integrated teaching package to accompany *Adolescence*. The authors of the teaching supplements are all experienced teachers of the adolescence course. The supplements have been designed to make it as easy as possible to customize the entire package to meet the unique needs of individual professors and students.

The key to this package is the INSTRUCTOR'S MANUAL prepared by Michael G. Walraven of Jackson Community College. In addition, a comprehensive TEST ITEM FILE has been prepared by Gregory Fouts, University of Calgary. Each test item is referred to both text page and learning objective, and is identified as factual, conceptual, or applied.

A TRANSPARENCY SET consisting of 40 acetate transparencies developed new for this edition of *Adolescence,* have been designed to help in classroom teaching and lecture organization.

A STUDENT STUDY GUIDE by Michael G. Walraven includes the following for each chapter: page-referenced learning objectives, a chapter overview, key terms exercise, guided review, student test questions, and a set of questions that go "beyond the text," asking students to think critically about issues raised in the chapter and to apply chapter material to real-life circumstances.

wcbTestPak is a computerized system that enables you to make up customized exams quickly and easily. Test questions can be found in the Test Item File, which is printed in your instructor's manual or as a separate packet. For each exam you may select up to 250 questions from the file and either print the test yourself or have **wcb** print it.

Printing the exam yourself requires access to a personal computer—an IBM that uses 5.25- or 3.5-inch diskettes, an Apple IIe or IIc, or a Macintosh. TestPak requires two disk drives and will work with any printer. Diskettes are available through your local **wcb** sales representative or by phoning Educational Services at 319–588-1451. The package you receive will contain complete instructions for making up an exam.

If you don't have access to a suitable computer, you may use **wcb**'s call-in/mail-in service. First determine the chapter and question numbers and any specific heading you want on the exam. Then call Pat Powers at 800–351-7671 (in Iowa, 319–589-2953) or mail information to: Pat Powers, Wm. C. Brown Publishers, 2460 Kerper Blvd., Dubuque, IA 52001. Within two working days, **wcb** will send you via first-class mail a test master, student answer sheet, and an answer key.

WCB QuizPak, the interactive self-testing, self-scoring quiz program, will help your students review text material from any chapter by testing themselves on an Apple IIe, IIc, or Macintosh, or an IBM PC. Adopters will receive the QuizPak program, questions disks, and an easy-to-follow user's guide. QuizPak may be used at a number of workstations simultaneously and requires only one disk drive.

Acknowledgments

A project of this magnitude requires the efforts of many people. I owe special thanks to my editor, Michael Lange, and to my senior developmental editor, Sandra Schmidt. They both have contributed in many ways to the fourth edition of *Adolescence*—through their ideas, organizational talents, and writing skills. Carla Aspelmeier, production editor, spent long hours copyediting and overseeing the book's production. Terri Ellerbach, designer, provided creative touches that make the book extremely attractive. Vicki Krug efficiently obtained permissions. Special thanks go to Michael G. Walraven, Jackson Community College, who prepared the Instructor's Manual and Student Study Guide, and to Gregory Fouts, University of Calgary, who prepared the Test Item File. Thanks also go to Toosje Tyssen, who cheerfully and competently prepared the book's glossary.

I have benefitted extensively from the ideas and insights of many colleagues. I would like to thank the following individuals for their feedback on earlier editions of *Adolescence:*

Fredda Blanchard-Fields, Louisiana State University
James A. Doyle, Roane State Community College
Richard M. Ehlenz, Lakewood Community College
Martin E. Ford, Stanford University
Gregory T. Fouts, University of Calgary
Charles L. Fry, University of Virginia
Beverly Jennings, University of Colorado–Denver
Emmett C. Lampkin, Scott Community College
Royal Louis Lange, Ellsworth Community College
Daniel K. Lapsley, University of Notre Dame
Susan McCammon, East Carolina University
Joseph G. Marrone, Siena College
Vern Tyler, Western Washington University

I would like to also thank the reviewers of the first edition of *Adolescence:* Frances Harnick, University of New Mexico, Indian Children's Program, and Lovelace-Bataan Pediatric Clinic; Robert Bornstein, Miami University; Toni E. Santmire, University of Nebraska; and Lynn F. Katz, University of Pittsburgh; and of the second edition: Martin E. Ford, Stanford University; B. Jo Hailey, University of Southern Mississippi; June V. Irving, Ball State University; Alfred L. Karlson, University of Massachusetts–Amherst; E. L. McGarry, California State University–Fullerton; John J. Mirich, Metropolitan State College; Anne Robertson, University of Wisconsin–Milwaukee; Douglas Sawin, University of Texas; and Carolyn L. Williams, University of Minnesota.

I also express considerable gratitude to the following instructors who provided in-depth reviews of chapters from the current edition of *Adolescence:*

Frank Ascione, Utah State University
Fredda Blanchard-Fields, Louisiana State University
Gregory Fouts, University of Calgary
Charles Fry, University of Virginia
William Gnagey, Illinois State University
Dick E. Hammond, Southwest Texas State University
Joline Jones, Worcester State College
Daniel Lapsley, University of Notre Dame
Royal Lange, Ellsworth Community College
Daniel Lynch, University of Wisconsin–Oshkosh
Ann McCabe, University of Windsor

A final note of thanks goes to my family—Mary Jo, my wife, and Tracy, 23, and Jennifer, 20, whose love and companionship I cherish.

About the Author

John W. Santrock received his Ph.D. from the University of Minnesota in 1973. He taught at the University of Georgia and currently is Professor of Psychology and Human Development at the University of Texas at Dallas. Professor Santrock is a member of the editorial board of *Developmental Psychology.* His research on father custody is widely cited and is used in expert witness testimony to promote flexibility and alternative considerations in custody disputes. The research involves videotaped observations in different contexts, extensive interviews, and standardized tests. He recently completed an NIMH grant to study family and peer relations in stepmother and stepfather families. He has authored or co-authored six other highly successful texts, including *Psychology,* 2nd ed., *Child Development,* 4th ed., and *Life-Span Development,* 3rd ed. Professor Santrock also is a professional tennis coach.

ADOLESCENCE

The Nature of Adolescent Development

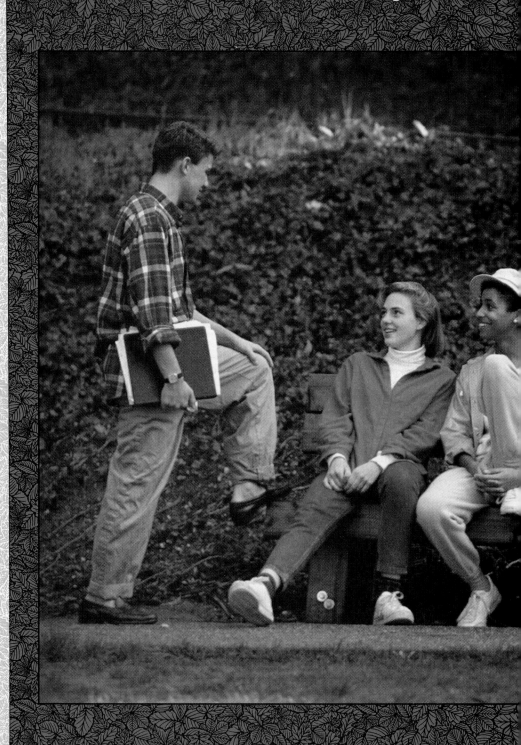

A few years ago it oc-
curred to me that when I
was a teenager, in the early
Depression years, there
were no teenagers! The
teenager has sneaked up on
us in our own lifetime, and
yet it seems he has always
been with us. . . . The
teenager had not yet been
invented, though, and there
did not yet exist a special
class of beings, bounded in
a certain way—not quite
children and certainly not
adults.

P. Musgrove, Youth and Social Order,
Copyright © 1964.

Brian Jordan is 10 years old and in the fifth grade. He is 4 feet, 7 inches tall and weighs 70 pounds. Kim Krane sits next to him at school and has started to show an interest in him. Last week at recess she even grabbed him on the playground and kissed him in front of his two best friends. Was Brian ever embarrassed! His buddies still tease him about it. He told Kim to never try to kiss him again. She just giggled and told him he was cute. What has happened to Kim? Last year when she was in the fourth grade she didn't have very much interest in boys, but now she is starting to look at them in a different light.

Looking at Kim, we can easily tell that she is showing some signs of puberty—her breasts are developing noticeably and she has started to wear a training bra, although she has not had her first period yet. Brian has not started puberty yet—he has no pubic or facial hair, his voice hasn't changed, and his height and weight have shown only very gradual increases during the last several years. When Kim kissed him, she even had to bend down because she is 4 inches taller than Brian and she outweighs him by 15 pounds. Nonetheless, Brian still feels he is a lot stronger than Kim and he is more physically aggressive than she is—that is, other than when it comes to making passes at somebody.

Cognitively, both Brian and Kim are what psychologists call concrete thinkers—that is, much of their thought is about their actual experiences, and they don't yet think very abstractly. Many of their thoughts are about momentary, concrete experiences. For example, they are incapable of imagining a community or a society radically different from the one they now live in.

When we look at Kim and Brian's relationships with their parents and peers, we find that while they sometimes have ideas that differ from those of their parents, there doesn't seem to be much parent-child conflict. Both Kim and Brian have shown an interest in spending more time with their peers in the last several years, and much of that time is spent with same-sex peers, although Kim has already started to show a stronger opposite-sex interest. The culture Brian and Kim live in is suburban, southern, American, and middle-class. Both Brian and Kim are achievement-oriented and do well in school, although Kim's parents feel she has started to daydream too much lately and Brian's parents sometimes feel he is not serious enough about school.

When we enter the lives of Brian and Kim at the age of 13, we find that some significant changes have occurred. Gradually, over the last year, Brian has entered puberty. He now has some pubic hair, his voice is getting deeper, and he is 5 feet, 1 inch tall and weighs 95 pounds. Last week he woke up somewhat surprised because he had his first wet dream.

Also last week, he went to an eighth-grade boy–girl party at one of his best friend's homes. At this time, Brian is showing a strong interest in the opposite sex. Unfortunately, the girl he likes doesn't seem to like him as much as he likes her. Every time he tries to talk to her she abruptly walks away—he thinks maybe it is because he is so short.

Kim, at the age of 13, is much further into puberty than Brian. She had her first period 16 months ago, and her breasts are almost fully developed. She no longer is interested in Brian—instead she is trying to interest the captain of the junior high football team, a ninth grader, in asking her to the homecoming dance. So far, she hasn't been successful, but she is working on it. Last night, for example, one of her girl friends called the boy on the phone and told him how much Kim likes him.

Cognitively, there are several changes that seem to have just begun for Brian and Kim. They have started to think in more abstract ways, not always relying on concrete experiences for generating thoughts, and they are more organized problem solvers than they were in the fifth grade. Both seem to be somewhat egocentric—for example, they often think that people are looking at them. The other day, Kim walked into a restaurant with her parents and said, "Oh, no, my hair. What can I do?" When her parents asked what was the matter, she replied, "Everybody is looking at me—look at this hair, it just won't stay down."

Kim had just walked by a mirror at the entrance of the restaurant and checked her appearance.

Brian and Kim and their parents all agree that parent–adolescent conflict seems to be greater than when Brian and Kim were in the fifth grade. Brian's parents say that he just doesn't seem to want to listen to them anymore, and Kim's mother says that she has a hard time taking the rude comments Kim makes about her. Both Brian and Kim have shown a stronger push for independence from their parents than they did three years ago, and their parents seem to be having a little bit of a tough time accepting it—their parents seem to want them to conform to their adult standards. Nonetheless, the parent–adolescent conflict we find between Brian and Kim and their parents has not even come close to the point of being pathological; it has just increased in the last year or so.

While Brian and Kim had shown some increased interest in peers during the latter part of the elementary school years, now they seem to want to spend just about all of their free time with their peers. Indeed, they spend a lot of time during the week thinking about what they can do with their friends on the weekends.

At the age of 17 Brian and Kim are seniors, and both have already sent in their applications to several colleges and universities. Brian finally began to grow as much as he wanted to; by the time he was 15 he was 5 feet, 11 inches tall and weighed 135 pounds. Since then he hasn't grown any more but he has put on 10 more pounds. Brian is now more muscular than he was in the eighth grade, and girls no longer are taller than he is—to his relief. Kim is still 5 feet, 1 inch tall, but she has gained 15 pounds and now weighs 115 pounds. Both Brian and Kim think a lot about their bodies, but it doesn't preoccupy their thoughts as much as when they were in the eighth grade. Both Brian and Kim have come close to having sexual intercourse with the people they are going steady with, but so far they have not. Kim says that it is getting harder and harder to refrain from having sex with Bob, whom she has been dating for about 14 months now.

Cognitively, both Brian and Kim, at the age of 17, are more advanced thinkers than they were in the junior high school years. Their thoughts have become even more abstract and they engage more frequently in extended speculation about what their lives are going to be like in the future, their ideals and goals, and about what an idealistic world would be like. As part of their concern for the future, they have begun to think much more seriously about the kinds of occupations they are going to pursue. Kim is debating whether she will get married after high school or pursue a college degree. Recently, she has entertained the possibility of doing both. Brian is not sure what he wants to do with his life, but it's not because he hasn't thought about it. He has continued to do well in school and has a job in a brokerage office as a "gofer," running errands for the brokers.

Both Brian and Kim feel their relationships with their parents have cooled down somewhat from earlier adolescence, and both seem to think more independently from both their parents and their peers. Still, they retain close ties to both their parents and their peers, spending more and more time with their friends but still being monitored and influenced by their parents. An overriding concern for both Brian and Kim is the development of an identity, developing a sense of who they are, what they are all about, and what they are going to do with their lives.

You have just been introduced to Brian Jordan and Kim Krane. In some ways they are like all adolescents, and yet in other ways each is like no other adolescent. One of the goals of this book is to point out the communalities, exceptions, and individual variations in adolescent development. Brian and Kim are but two of the more than dozen adolescents you will be introduced to at the beginning of each section of this book. As you read the descriptions of adolescents in the part openers, keep in mind that there is a great deal of individual variation as well as some common themes among adolescents.

Introduction

Whatever is formed for long duration arrives slowly to its maturity.

Samuel Johnson,
The Rambler, *1750.*

Today's Adolescents: The Best of Times, The Worst of Times

I t is both the best of times and the worst of times for adolescents. Their world possesses powers and perspectives inconceivable 50 years ago: computers, longer life expectancies, the entire planet accessible through television, satellites, air travel. So much knowledge, though, can be chaotic and dangerous. School curricula have been adapted to teach new topics: AIDS, adolescent suicide, drug and alcohol abuse, incest. The hazards of the adult world—its sometimes fatal temptations—descend upon children and adolescents so early that their ideals may become demolished.

Crack, for example, is far more addictive and deadly than marijuana, the drug of an earlier generation. Strange fragments of violence and sex flash out of the television set and lodge in the minds of youth. The messages are powerful and contradictory. Rock videos suggest orgiastic sex. Public health officials counsel safe sex. Oprah Winfrey and Phil Donahue conduct seminars on lesbian nuns, exotic drugs, transsexual surgery, serial murders. Television pours a bizarre version of reality into the imaginations of adolescents.

Every stable society transmits values from one generation to the next. That is civilization's work. In today's world, there is a special concern about the nature of values being communicated to adolescents. Today's parents are raising adolescents in a world far removed from the era of Ozzie and Harriet 30 years ago when two of three American families consisted of a father who was the breadwinner, a mother, and the children and adolescents they were raising. Today fewer than one in five families fits that description. Phrases such as "quality time" have found their way into the American vocabulary. Absence is a motif in the lives of many adolescents. It may be an absence of authority and limits, or of emotional commitment (Morrow, 1988).

Growing up has never been easy. In many ways, the developmental tasks of today's adolescents are no different than the adolescents of Ozzie and Harriet's world. Adolescence is not a time of rebellion, crisis, pathology, and deviance. A far more accurate vision of adolescence is of a time of evaluation, a time of decision making, a time of commitment, a time of carving out a place in the world. Most of the problems of today's youth are not with the youth themselves. What adolescents need is access to a range of legitimate opportunities and to long-term support from adults who care deeply about them.

Each of us has memories of our adolescence—of relationships with parents, peers, and teachers, and of ourselves. This book is a window to the journey of adolescence. The transition from being a child to being an adult is told in words that I hope stimulate you to think about where you have been, where you are, and where you are going in life. You will see yourself and others as adolescents and be motivated to reflect on how the adolescent years influence who we and others are. *Adolescence* is about life's rhythm and meaning, about turning mystery into understanding, and about weaving together a portrait of one of life's most important developmental periods.

*I*n this first chapter, we evaluate the following questions: What do parents, educators, and scientists want to know about adolescents? What is the history of interest in adolescents? Could adolescence possibly be a sociohistorical invention? What are the periods and processes of development? How can we define adolescence? How extensively is adolescence influenced by maturation and by experience? Is development more continuous or more discontinuous?

What Do Parents, Educators, and Scientists
Want to Know about Adolescents?

What do you think parents would like to know about their adolescents' development? What do teachers and scientists want to know about adolescents? They all would like to know the most effective ways adults can deal with adolescents.

You have lived through adolescence. I once was an adolescent. No one else experienced adolescence in quite the same way you or I did—your thoughts, feelings, and actions during your adolescent years, like mine, were unique. But we also encountered and handled some experiences in the same ways during adolescence. In high school, we learned many of the same skills that other students learned and grew to care about the same things others cared about. Peers were important to us. And, at one time or another, we probably felt that our parents had no idea what we were all about.

Not only did we feel that our parents misunderstood us, but our parents felt that we misunderstood them. Parents want to know why adolescents have such mercurial moods—happy one moment, sad the next. They want to know why their teenagers talk back to them and challenge their rules and values.

BLOOM COUNTY   by Berke Breathed

They want to know what parenting strategies will help them rear a psychologically healthy, competent adolescent who will become a mature adult. Should they be authoritarian or permissive in dealing with their adolescents? And what should they do when their adolescents increasingly rely on peers to influence their decisions—sometimes peers who have backgrounds and standards the parents detest? Parents worry that their adolescent will have a drinking problem, a smoking problem, take drugs, have sexual intercourse too early, or do poorly in school. They want to know if the situations they are encountering with their adolescents are unique, or if other parents are experiencing the same difficulties and frustrations with their youth.

Educators, as well as parents, have a strong interest in trying to understand adolescents. Adolescents spend a large part of their day at school. What is the best way to teach English to a 13-year-old or biology to a 16-year-old? What can educators change about the nature of today's schools that will foster the development of social as well as intellectual competence in adolescents? What can they do in our schools to direct adolescents toward careers that best suit their abilities and desires? And teachers want to know the best strategies for instructing adolescents—for example, should they be more directive or let students be more active in classroom decision making?

Scientists, as well as parents and educators, are interested in adolescents. They want to know how biological heritage and individual environments influence adolescent behavior. Do the genes the adolescents inherited some 15 years before still influence how they act, feel, and think? What aspects of family life, peer interaction, school experiences, and cultural standards cause adolescents to become responsible or irresponsible socially?

In answer to these and other questions, scientists develop theories about adolescents. These theories help them to explain why adolescents behave in particular ways, whether they will behave the same way in other circumstances, and what their behavior will be like in the future.

Foremost among the interests of scientists who study adolescents is finding out if there is something unique about adolescents that sets them apart from children and adults. Does the 15-year-old think differently than the 8-year-old? Does the 16-year-old interact differently with her parents than the 10-year-old? Does the 17-year-old view himself differently than the 23-year-old? Do adolescents have problems that are not found at other points in development? (For example, consider premarital sex and delinquency.)

Scientists are not only interested in what ways adolescents are different from children and adults, but intrigued by how adolescents might be similar to them. Further, in thinking about similarities, scientists are interested in how all adolescents might be similar to each other in some ways and yet different in others.

In their concern for developing a clear demarcation between the child and the adolescent, and between the adolescent and the adult, scientists have debated whether it is appropriate to describe adolescence as a *stage* of development. Does the child's biological, social, and cognitive functioning undergo dramatic transformations at the onset of adolescence and does something similar occur at the end of adolescence? Or, by contrast, is the child's progress to adolescence smooth (or devoid of abrupt transition) and the adolescent's change to adulthood likewise? Interest in evaluating the unique and stagelike properties of adolescence has led scientists to study youth in a variety of environmental circumstances—adolescents from different historical time periods are compared, as are adolescents who grow up in very different cultures.

Now that we have considered the interests that parents, educators, and scientists have in adolescents, we turn our attention to a historical perspective on adolescence. You will discover that a scientific interest in adolescence developed rather late in history.

Historical Perspective

We begin by studying how adolescents were perceived by the early Greeks, then turn to perceptions of adolescents in the Middle Ages and the Enlightenment. The lives of adolescents in the early years of America are examined, and the time period of 1890–1920 is given special attention. Further developments in adolescents' lives in the twentieth century are evaluated and the nature of stereotyping adolescents is investigated.

The Greeks

An interest in adolescence can be found in early Greece. Both Plato and Aristotle commented about the nature of youth. In *The Republic* (fourth century B.C./1968 trans.), Plato described three facets of human development (or as he called it, the "soul"): desire, spirit, and reason. According to Plato, reason, the highest of the facets, does not develop in childhood, but rather first appears in most individuals at about the age period we call adolescence today. Plato argued that since reason does not mature in childhood, the education of children should focus on music and sports. But the onset of rational thought in adolescence requires a change in the educational curricula—at that point, in Plato's view, sports and music should be replaced by science and mathematics.

Plato believed that in the early years of childhood, character, not intellect, should be developed. Even though Plato stressed the importance of early experience in the formation of character, he nonetheless pointed out that experiences in later years could modify character. Arguments about the importance of early experience in human development are still prevalent today. Do the first few years of life determine the adolescent's or adult's personality? Are later experiences in adolescence just as important in forming and shaping personality as experiences in the early years?

For Aristotle (fourth century B.C./1941 trans.), the most important aspect of the age period we call adolescence is the development of the ability to choose. This self-determination becomes the hallmark of maturity in Aristotle's view.

Aristotle viewed the individual at the onset of youth as unstable and impatient, lacking the self-control to develop into a mature person.

Aristotle was one of the first individuals to provide specific time periods for stages of human development. He defined three stages: infancy, the first seven years of life; boyhood, age seven to puberty; and young manhood, puberty to age 21. According to Aristotle, then, from puberty to age 21, youth need to replace their lack of self-control with self-determination. This view of adolescence is not unlike some of our current views, as we use labels like independence, identity, and career choice.

The Middle Ages and the Enlightenment

Society's view of adolescence changed considerably during the Middle Ages. From the time of Aristotle and Plato through the sixteenth century, knowledge about human development actually took a step backward. It was during this time period that the view of the child as a miniature adult was dominant. Children and adolescents were believed to entertain the same interests as adults. And, since they were simply miniature adults, they were treated as such, with strict, harsh discipline. In the Middle Ages neither the adolescent nor the child was given status apart from the adult (Muuss, 1989).

During the eighteenth century Jean Jacques Rousseau offered a more enlightened view of adolescence. Rousseau, a French philosopher, did more than any other individual to restore the belief that a child is not the same as an adult. In *Emile* (1762, 1962 trans.) Rousseau argued that treating the child like a miniature adult is not appropriate and is potentially harmful. Rousseau believed that children up until the age of 12 or so should be free of adult restrictions and allowed to experience their world naturally, rather than having rigid regulations imposed on them.

Rousseau, like Aristotle and Plato, believed that development in childhood and adolescence occurs in a series of stages. From Rousseau's perspective, the four stages of development are

> *Infancy* (the first four to five years). The infant is much like an animal with strong physical needs, and the child is hedonistic (dominated by pleasure and pain).
>
> *Savage* (5 to 12 years). During this time, sensory development is most important. Sensory experiences such as play, sports, and games should be the focus of education. Like Aristotle, Rousseau argued that reason had not developed by the end of this time period.
>
> *Stage 3* (12 to 15 years). Reason and self-consciousness develop during this stage, along with an abundance of physical energy. Curiosity should be encouraged in the education of 12–15-year-olds by providing a variety of exploratory activities. According to Rousseau, *Robinson Crusoe* is the book to read during this stage of human development because it includes insightful ideas about curiosity and exploratory behavior.

The Nature of Adolescent Development

Stage 4 (15 to 20 years). The individual begins to mature emotionally during this time period—interest in others replaces selfishness. Virtues and morals also appear at this point in development.

Rousseau, then, helped to restore the belief that development is stratified, or subject to distinct phases. But his ideas about adolescence were speculative. Other individuals in the nineteenth and twentieth centuries had to bridge the gap between the ideas of philosophers and the empirical approach of scientists.

Adolescence in the Early Years of America

Have adolescents of different eras always had the same interests? Have adolescents always experienced the same kind of academic, work, and family environments as they do today? Today's adolescents spend far more time in school than at work, in structured rather than unstructured environments, and in sessions with their agemates than did their counterparts of the 1800s and early 1900s. Let's look more closely at two time periods in the history of America and discover what adolescence was like in each time as described by Joseph Kett (1977) in his book *Rites of Passage*.

The Early Republic, 1790–1840

The migration of young people from the farms to urban life began during this time. School opportunities became a reality, and career choices grew more varied. However, increasing disorderliness and violence characterized the society.

Work apprenticeships took up much of the day for many adolescent boys, with some apprentices beginning as early as the age of twelve, others as late as 16 or 17. Some children left home to become servants even at the age of eight or nine. Many adolescents remained dependent on their families while they engaged in apprentice work experiences. Ages 20–25 were then usually filled with indecision. But as in most eras, there were exceptions to this generalization—for example, the man Francis Lieber wrote about in his diary:

Story from real life. I arrived here in October, 1835.
In January, 1836, W ____ and another student were expelled from college on account of a duel. Since that time W ____ has:
First: Shot at this antagonist in the streets of Charleston.
Second: Studied (?) law with Mr. DeSaussure in Charleston.
Third: Married.
Fourth: Been admitted to the Bar.
Fifth: Imprisoned for two months in the above shooting.
Sixth: Become father of fine girl.
Seventh: Practiced law for some time.
Eighth: Been elected a member of the legislature. Now he is only twenty-two years old. What a state of society this requires and must produce . . . (Perry, 1882, as described in Kett, 1977).

The most important period within this time frame was the era from 1880 to 1900. A gap in economic opportunities developed between lower-class and middle-class adolescents. Middle-class parents were pressed into selecting child-rearing orientations that would ensure the successful placement of their youth in jobs. These child-rearing practices encouraged the adolescent to become passive and conform to societal standards.

To capitalize on the new jobs created by the industrial revolution, youth had to stay in school longer and even go on to college. Delay of gratification and self-restraint became behaviors that were encouraged by parents who saw that going to school longer and studying harder meant greater returns for their adolescents in the future.

While college was becoming more of a reality for many youth, it mainly was open to middle-class, but not lower-class, adolescents. Similarly, the youth groups that developed as part of school and church activities were essentially middle-class in nature.

The conformity to adult leadership in most of the youth groups coincided with the general orientation toward adolescents at this time in America: adults know what is right; do what they tell you, and you'll get somewhere someday.

The Age of Adolescence

The end of the nineteenth century and the early part of the twentieth century represented an important period in the invention of the concept we now call adolescence. And there were subsequent changes adolescents experienced later in the twentieth century that influenced their lives in substantial ways.

The Turn of the Century

Between 1890 and 1920 a number of psychologists, urban reformers, educators, youth workers, and counselors began to mold the concept of adolescence. At this time, young people, especially boys, no longer were viewed as decadent problem causers, but instead were seen as increasingly passive and vulnerable—qualities previously associated only with the adolescent female. When G. Stanley Hall's book on adolescence was published in 1904, it played a major role in restructuring thinking about adolescents. Hall was saying that while many adolescents appear to be passive, they are experiencing considerable turmoil within.

Norms of behavior for adolescents began to be developed by educators, counselors, and psychologists. The storm-and-stress concept that Hall had created influenced these norms considerably. As a result, adults attempted to impose conformity and passivity on adolescents in the 1900–1920 period. Examples of this conformity can be observed in the encouragement of school spirit, loyalty, and hero worship on athletic teams.

G. Stanley Hall

Historians label G. Stanley Hall (1844–1924) the father of the scientific study of adolescence. Hall's ideas were published in the two-volume set *Adolescence* in 1904. (For a sample of what the first academic text on adolescence was like, read Perspective on Adolescent Development 1.1.)

Charles Darwin, the famous evolutionary theorist, had a tremendous impact on Hall's thinking. Hall applied the scientific, biological aspects of Darwin's views to the study of adolescent development. He believed that all development is controlled by genetically determined physiological factors. Environmental influences on development were minimized in his view, especially in infancy and childhood. Hall did acknowledge that the environment accounts for more change in development during adolescence than in earlier age periods. Thus, Hall believed—as we do today—that at least during adolescence, heredity interacts with environmental influences to determine the individual's development.

Like Rousseau, Hall subscribed to a four-stage approach to development: infancy, childhood, youth, and adolescence. Adolescence is the period of time from about 12 to about 23 years of age, or when adulthood is achieved. Hall saw adolescence as the period of *Sturm und Drang,* which means storm and stress. This label was borrowed from the German writings of Goethe and Schiller, who wrote novels full of idealism, commitment to goals, revolution, passion, and feeling. Hall sensed there was a parallel between the themes of the German authors and the psychological development of adolescents.

According to Hall, the adolescent period of storm and stress is full of contradictions and wide swings in mood and emotion. Thoughts, feelings, and actions oscillate between humility and conceit, goodness and temptation, and happiness and sadness. One moment the adolescent may be nasty to a peer, yet in the next moment be extremely nice to her. At one time he may want to be left alone, but shortly thereafter desire to cling to somebody. In sum, G. Stanley Hall views adolescence as a turbulent time charged with conflict (Ross, 1972), a perspective labeled the **storm and stress view** of adolescence.

Hall's view also had implications for social development and education (White, 1985). Hall conceived of development as a biological process directed toward a series of possibilities of social organization. As children moved into adolescence they were thought to be capable of entering progressively more complicated and powerful social arrangements. In the terminology of today, Hall might be called a "sociobiological developmentalist." Hall's analysis of the adolescent years also led him to believe that the time to begin strenuously educating such faculties as civility, scientific thinking, and morality is after the age of 15. However, Hall's developmental vision of education rested mainly on highly speculative theory rather than empirical data. While Hall believed systematic methods should be developed to study adolescents, his research efforts usually resorted to the creation of rather weak and unconvincing questionnaires. Even though the quality of his research was suspect, Hall is a giant

Adolescence, 1904

Hall's two-volume set, published in 1904, included the following chapters:

Volume I

Chapter

1   Growth in Height and Weight
2   Growth of Parts and Organs During Adolescence
3   Growth of Motor Power and Function
4   Diseases of Body and Mind
5   Juvenile Faults, Immoralities, and Crimes
6   Sexual Development: Its Dangers and Hygiene in Boys
7   Periodicity
8   Adolescence in Literature, Biography, and History

Volume II

9   Changes in the Sense and Voice
10 Evolution and the Feelings and Instincts Characteristic of Normal Adolescence
11 Adolescent Love
12 Adolescent Feelings toward Nature and a New Education in Science
13 Savage Public Initiations, Classical Ideals and Customs, and Church Confirmations
14 The Adolescent Psychology of Conversion
15 Social Instincts and Institutions
16 Intellectual Development and Education
17 Adolescent Girls and their Education
18 Ethnic Psychology and Pedagogy, or Adolescent Races and their Treatment

G. Stanley Hall

Hall's strong emphasis on the biological basis of adolescence can be seen in the large number of chapters on physical growth, instincts, and evolution. His concern for education also is evident, as is his interest in religion.

in the history of understanding adolescent development. It was he who began the theorizing, the systematizing, and the questioning that went beyond mere speculation and philosophy. Indeed, we owe the scientific beginnings of the study of adolescent development to Hall.

The Inventionist View of Adolescence

In the quote that opens Part 1, A. K. Cohen comments about the teenager sneaking up on us in our own lifetime. At a point not too long ago in history,

Further insight into Hall's concept of adolescence can be gleaned from his preface to the volumes:

> Development (in adolescence) is less gradual and more saltatory, suggestive of some ancient period of storm and stress when old moorings were broken and a higher level attained. . . . Nature arms youth for conflict with all the resources at her command—speed, power of shoulder, biceps, back, leg, jaw—strengthens and enlarges skull, thorax, hips, makes man aggressive and prepares woman's frame for maternity. . . .
>
> Sex asserts its mastery in field after field, and works its havoc in the form of secret vice, debauch, disease, and enfeebled heredity, cadences the soul to both its normal and abnormal rhythms, and sends many thousand youth a year to quacks, because neither parents, teachers, preachers, or physicians know how to deal with its problems. . . . The social instincts undergo sudden unfoldment and the new life of love awakens. . . . Youth awakes to a new world and understands neither it nor himself. . . .
>
> Never has youth been exposed to such dangers of both perversion and arrest as in our land and day. Urban life has increased temptations, prematurities, sedentary occupations, and passive stimuli, just when an active, objective life is most needed. Adolescents' lives today lack some of the regulations they still have in older lands with more conservative traditions. . . . (Volume I, pp. xi, xiii, xv)

Hall's preoccupation with the evils of adolescence are threaded throughout the texts. This is nowhere more clear than in his comments about masturbation:

> One of the very saddest of all the aspects of human weakness and sin is [masturbation]. . . . Tissot, in 1759, found every pupil guilty. . . . Dr. G. Bachin (1895) argued that growth, especially in the moral and intellectual regions, is dwarfed and stunted [by masturbation]. Bachin also felt that masturbation caused gray hairs, and especially baldness, a stooping and enfeebled gait. . . .
>
> Perhaps masturbation is the most perfect type of individual vice and sin . . . it is the acme of selfishness.
>
> Prominent among predisposing causes are often placed erotic reading, pictures, and theatrical presentations. . . . Schiller protests against trousers pockets for boys, as do others against feather beds, while even horseback riding and the bicycle have been placed under the ban by a few extremist writers.
>
> . . . The medical cures of masturbation that have been prescribed are almost without number: bromide, ergot, lupin, blistering, clitoridectomy, section of certain nerves, small mechanical appliances, of which the Patent Office at Washington has quite a collection. Regimen rather than special treatment must, however, be chiefly relied on. Work reduces temptation, and so does early rising. . . . Good music is a moral tonic. . . . (Volume I, pp. 411–471)

Clearly, our current beliefs about masturbation differ substantially from those of Hall's time. As indicated in the overview of chapters in Hall's volumes, he wrote about many other aspects of adolescence in addition to sex and masturbation. His books are entertaining as well as informative. You are encouraged to look up his original work in your library and compare his comments with those made about adolescence in this text. ᶾ

Source: G. S. Hall, *Adolescence* (2 vols.), New York: Appleton, 1904.

the teenager had not yet been invented. Social and historical conditions have led a number of writers to argue that adolescence has been "invented" (Elder, 1975; Field, 1981; Finley, 1985; Hill, 1980; Lapsley, Enright, & Serlin, 1985; Lapsley & Rice, 1988). While adolescence clearly has biological foundations, nonetheless social and historical occurrences have contributed to the acceptance of adolescence as a transitional time between childhood and adulthood—this is the **inventionist view.** We have discussed many of these circumstances in our overview of the historical background of adolescence.

They include the decline in apprenticeship; increased mechanization during the industrial revolution, including upgraded skill requirements of labor and specialized divisions of labor; the separation of work and the home; the writings of G. Stanley Hall; the increased use of child guidance tracks; changes in fertility patterns and family structure; urbanization; the appearance of youth groups such as the YMCA and Boy Scouts; and age-segregated schools.

The role of schools, work, and economics have figured prominently in the current flourish of interest in the historical invention of adolescence. Some contributors argue that the institutionalization of adolescence was a by-product of the cultural motivation to create a system of compulsory public education. From this view, secondary schools are seen mainly as vehicles for transmitting intellectual skills to youth (e.g., Callahan, 1962; Cremin, 1961; Stedman & Smith, 1983). However, others argue that the primary purpose of secondary schools has been to deploy youth within the economic sphere and to serve as an important cog in the authority structure of the culture.

Daniel Lapsley, Robert Enright, and Ronald Serlin (1985) adopt the latter stance. They believe that American society "inflicted" the status of adolescence on its youth, and argue that the history of child-saving legislation is actually the history of the origins of adolescence. By developing laws for youth, the adult power structure placed young people in a submissive position in the authority hierarchy of our culture. It is a location that restricts their options, encourages dependency, and makes their move into the world of work more manageable.

The period of 1890–1920 is now considered the age of adolescence—the time when adolescence was invented. It was during this time period that a great deal of compulsory legislation was enacted (Tyack, 1976). In virtually every state there were laws excluding youth from most employment and requiring them to attend secondary school. Extensive enforcement provisions administered by the state characterized most of this legislation.

Two clear changes resulted from such legislation—decreased employment and increased school attendance by youth. From 1910 to 1930 there was a dramatic decrease in the number of 10–15-year-olds who were gainfully employed, dropping about 75% in this time frame (Table 1.1). Between 1900 and 1930 there also was a tremendous increase in the number of high school graduates (Table 1.2). Approximately 600% more individuals graduated from high school and there was approximately a 450% increase in enrollment in high schools during this historical period.

Just as school and work figured prominently in the invention of adolescence, historical changes continued to accompany the lives of adolescents during more recent times.

TABLE 1.1   *Percentage of Males and Females, Aged 10–15, Who Were Gainfully Employed in Selected States 1910–1930[1]*

States	1910		1920		1930		% Decline 1910–1930[2]	
	M	F	M	F	M	F	M	F
New Hampshire	10.2	7.1	4.4	2.3	1.4	1.2	−86	−83
Vermont	10.3	3.2	4.8	1.8	2.6	1.0	−75	−69
Massachusetts	11.3	8.6	10.0	7.1	2.3	2.0	−82	−77
Rhode Island	15.5	13.2	14.3	12.6	3.1	3.0	−81	−77
Connecticut	11.7	8.3	9.0	7.1	3.2	2.8	−76	−66
New York	8.4	5.5	5.5	3.9	1.9	1.3	−77	−76
New Jersey	11.0	8.0	8.3	6.9	2.2	2.4	−80	−70
Pennsylvania	15.1	7.8	6.7	4.5	2.0	2.1	−86	−74
Delaware	23.3	8.6	7.9	3.8	2.6	1.4	−88	−70
Maryland	21.1	10.2	10.0	5.0	4.7	2.5	−77	−75
Virginia	33.2	10.6	12.7	3.6	7.3	2.0	−78	−81
North Carolina	57.5	34.1	21.7	11.5	15.1	7.2	−74	−79
South Carolina	58.2	45.4	28.7	20.1	23.0	13.6	−60	−70

[1]Source: *Abstract of the 15th Census of the United States, 1930.* (In Lapsley, Enright, & Serlin, 1985).
[2]Calculation of Lapsley & others, 1985.

Further Changes in the Twentieth Century

During the three decades from 1920 to 1950, adolescents gained a more prominent status in society as they went through a number of complex changes. The lives of adolescents took a turn for the better in the 1920s, but moved through difficult times in the 1930s and 1940s. In the 1920s, the Roaring Twenties atmosphere rubbed off on adolescents. Passivity and conformity to adult leadership was replaced by increased autonomy and conformity to peer values. Adults began to model the styles of youth, rather than vice versa. If a new dance came in vogue, the adolescent girl did it first and her mother learned it from her. Prohibition was the law of the time, but many adolescents drank heavily. More permissive attitudes toward the opposite sex developed, and kissing parties were standard fare. Short skirts even led to a campaign by the YWCA against such abnormal behavior (Lee, 1970).

Just when adolescence was getting to be fun, the Great Depression arrived in the 1930s, followed by World War II in the 1940s. Economic and political concerns of a serious nature replaced the hedonistic adolescent values of the 1920s. Radical protest groups that were critical of the government increased in number during the 1930s, and World War II exposed adolescents to another serious, life-threatening event. Military service provided travel and exposure to other youth from different parts of the United States. This experience promoted a broader perspective on life and a greater sense of independence.

TABLE 1.2   *Percentage of Growth in High School Graduation, 1870–1940*

Year	% Change
1870	
1880	50
1890	83
1900	116
1910	64
1920	112
1930	101
1940	83

Source: Series H598–681, *Historical Statistics of the United States.*

(a) *The Roaring Twenties was a time when adolescents began to behave more permissively. Adults began to model the styles of youth. Adolescent drinking increased dramatically. (b) In the 1940s, many youth served in World War II. Military service exposed many youth to life-threatening circumstances and allowed them to see first-hand the way people in other countries live. (c) In the 1950s, many youth developed a stronger orientation toward education. Television was piped into many homes for the first time. One of the 50s fads, shown here, was seeing how many people could squeeze into a phone booth. (d) In the late 1960s, many youth protested U.S. participation in the Vietnam War. Parents became more concerned about adolescent drug use as well. (e) In the 1970s and 1980s, much of the radical protest of youth quieted down. Today's adolescents are achievement-oriented, more likely to be working at a job, experiencing adult roles earlier, showing more interest in equality of the sexes, and heavily influenced by the media.*

(a)

(b)

(c)

(d)

(e)

The Nature of Adolescent Development

By 1950, the developmental period we refer to as adolescence had come of age—not only did it possess physical and social identity, but legal attention was paid to it as well. Every state had developed special laws for youth between the ages of 16 and 18 or 20. Adolescents in the 1950s have been described as the silent generation (Lee, 1970). Life was much better for adolescents in the 1950s than it had been in the 1930s and 1940s. The government was paying for many individuals' college educations through the GI bill, and television was beginning to invade most homes. Getting a college degree, the key to a good job, was on the minds of many adolescents during the 1950s—so were getting married, having a family, and settling down to the life of luxury displayed in television commercials.

While the pursuit of higher education persisted among adolescents in the 1960s, it became painfully apparent that many black adolescents not only were being denied a college education, but were receiving an inferior secondary education as well. Racial conflicts in the form of riots and "sit-ins" were pervasive, with college-age adolescents among the most vocal participants.

The political protest of adolescents reached a peak in the late 1960s and early 1970s, when millions of adolescents violently reacted to what they saw as unreasonable American participation in the Vietnam war. As parents watched the 1968 Democratic presidential nominating committee, they not only saw political speeches in support of candidates but their adolescents fighting with the police, yelling obscenities at adults, and staging sit-ins.

Parents became more concerned in the 1960s about teenage drug use and abuse than in past eras. Sexual permissiveness in the form of premarital sex, cohabitation, and endorsement of previously prohibited sexual conduct also increased.

By the mid-1970s, much of the radical protest of adolescents had abated and was replaced by increased concern for an achievement-oriented, upwardly mobile career to be attained through hard work in high school, college, or a vocational training school. Material interests began to dominate adolescent motives again, while ideological challenges to social institutions seemed to become less central. The women's movement involved the greatest amount of protest in the 1970s. If you carefully read the descriptions of adolescents in America in earlier years, you noticed that much of what was said pertained more to adolescent males than females. The family and career objectives of adolescent females today would barely be recognized by the adolescent females of the 1890s and early 1900s. Later in the text much more will be said about the increased participation of adolescent females in the work force, including the impact this movement has had on the family and on the female adolescent's relationships with males.

What are adolescents like today? Think back to when you were 12, 13, 14, or 15 years of age. Then think about the adolescents you know today. In what ways are they similar to or different from what you were? I asked this question in a recent class, querying students about how today's adolescents might be different from the adolescents of 10–20 years earlier. A summary of their responses is presented in Table 1.3.

TABLE 1.3 *Today's Adolescents*

In a class discussion, students commented on how they think today's adolescents are different from the adolescents of approximately 10–20 years ago. Today's adolescents are perceived to be:

1. More achievement-, money-, and college-oriented.
2. Growing up earlier, experiencing things earlier, being pushed into adult life-styles sooner.
3. More likely to be working at a job.
4. More financially dependent on parents for a longer period of time.
5. Using alcohol more (especially females).
6. Showing more interest in equality of the sexes.
7. Growing up in a greater variety of family structures—for example, more adolescents now live in divorced and working-mother families.
8. Reacting to authority differently. In the late 1960s and early 1970s, the rebelliousness of adolescents seemed to be politically motivated and directed at the government, while the rebelliousness now has taken the form of more open, overt confrontation with parents and school authorities. Also, the rebelliousness of the 1960s and 1970s seemed to be directed more toward attaining peace and showing a concern for others.
9. More aware of their rights. School dress codes and physical punishment by school officials are not as common as they were. Adolescents have discovered they have certain rights and that they are no longer completely at the mercy of adults.
10. More interested in physical fitness.
11. More influenced by the media, which expose them to a world beyond their immediate families, schools, and neighborhoods. The media also carry more open messages about sexuality.
12. More sexually permissive.
13. More preoccupied with self.

We have described some important sociohistorical circumstances experienced by adolescents, and we have described how society viewed adolescents at different points in history. As we see next, caution needs to be exercised in generalizing about the adolescents of any era.

Stereotyping Adolescents

It is very easy to stereotype a person, groups of people, or classes of people. A **stereotype** is a broad category that reflects our impressions about people, including ourselves. The world is extremely complex—every day we are confronted with thousands of different configurations of stimuli. The creation of stereotypes is one way we simplify this complexity. We simply assign a label to a group of people (for example, "youth are promiscuous") and we then have much less to consider when we think about this set of people. Once we assign these labels, however, it is very difficult to abandon them—even in the face of contradictory evidence.

Stereotypes about the interests, behaviors, and emotions of adolescents abound: "They say they want a job, but when they get one, they don't want to work"; "They're all lazy"; "They're all sex fiends"; "They're all into drugs, every last one of them"; "Kids today don't have the moral fiber of my generation"; "The problem with adolescents is that they have it too easy"; "They're a bunch of smart-alecks";—and so it goes.

A study by Daniel Yankelovich (1974) indicates that many such stereotypes about youth are false. Yankelovich compared the attitudes of adolescents with those of their parents about different values, life-styles, and codes of personal conduct. There was little or no difference in the attitudes of the adolescents and their parents toward self-control, hard work, saving money, competition, compromise, legal authority, and private property. There was a substantial difference between the adolescents and their parents when their attitudes toward religion were sampled (89% of the parents said that religion was important to them, compared to only 66% of the adolescents). But note that a majority of the adolescents still subscribed to the belief that religion is important. Other researchers also have found that many of the ideas the layperson has about adolescents are based on stereotypes (Hill, 1983; Youniss & Smollar, 1985). Some of the stereotypes about adolescents are based on the visible, rebellious adolescents of the 1960s and 1970s. One expert on adolescence labeled the stereotyping of adolescents as stressed, rebellious, and incompetent the **adolescent generalization gap** rather than the generation gap, meaning that widespread generalizations about adolescents have developed based on information about a limited group of adolescents (Adelson, 1979).

An investigation by Daniel Offer and his colleagues (1988) further documents that the vast majority of adolescents are competent human beings without deep emotional turmoil. The self-images of adolescents around the world were sampled—the United States, Australia, Bangladesh, Hungary, Israel, Italy, Japan, Taiwan, Turkey, and West Germany. A healthy self-image characterized at least 73% of the adolescents studied. They appeared to be moving toward adulthood with a healthy integration of previous experiences, self-confidence, and optimism about the future. While there were some differences in the adolescents, they were happy most of the time, they enjoyed life, they perceived themselves as able to exercise self-control, they valued work and school, they expressed confidence about their sexual selves, they expressed positive feelings toward their families, and they felt they had the capability to cope with life's stresses. Not exactly a storm and stress portrayal of adolescence.

Some of the readiness to assume the worst about adolescents may involve the short memories of adults. With little effort, most adults can remember behavior of their own that stretched—even shocked—the patience of their elders. In matters of taste and manners, young people of every generation have seemed radical, unnerving, and different from adults—different in how they look, how they behave, the music they enjoy, their hairstyles, and the clothing they choose. But it is an enormous error to confuse the adolescent's enthusiasm for trying on new identities and enjoying moderate amounts of outrageous behavior with hostility toward parental and societal standards. Acting-out and boundary-testing are time-honored ways in which adolescents move toward accepting, rather than rejecting, parental values. I remember when my oldest

How Do Soviet Adolescents View Nuclear War?

How do Soviet children feel about the threat of nuclear war? Eric Chivian and his colleagues (1985) went to the Soviet Union and questioned 347 boys and girls from 9–17 years of age to find out. The researchers had been told before they went to Russia that Soviet youth would know little about nuclear war. The opposite was true. Soviet children were very aware of the consequences of nuclear war. Said one 13-year-old Russian boy, "The entire Earth will become a wasteland. All buildings will be destroyed. All living things will perish—no grass, no trees, no greenery." The Soviet youths were pessimistic about the chances of surviving a nuclear war. Only 3% thought that they and their families would survive one, compared to 16% of a similar group of American youth. But Soviet youth were more optimistic than American youth about the possibility of avoiding nuclear war. Only 12% of the Soviet youth thought a nuclear war would occur in their lifetime compared to 38% of the American youth. Soviet children are active in trying to prevent nuclear war. They sign petitions to send to NATO; they belong to international friendship clubs. The researchers asked the Soviet youth at the end of the interview if they had any messages for American children. One said, "I wish that they would struggle and fight against nuclear war." Another commented, "We are the same type of people they are. We also want peace." ⟨⟨

daughter was in her first year of high school. My wife was certain that she was going to waste— she detested her taste in clothes and hairstyle, didn't like her friends, didn't care for the boys she was dating, thought she was underachieving in school, and was frightened by some of her escapades. Just this month, Tracy graduated from college and observers would be hard pressed to find vestiges of the earlier so-called "immaturity." Her values are similar to her parents and her mother no longer worries as much about her ability to become a competent adult.

It does little good, and can do considerable disservice, to think of adolescence as a time of rebellion, crisis, pathology, and deviation. Far better, and far more accurate, is a vision of adolescence as a time of evaluation, a time of decision-making, a time of commitment as youth carve out their place in the world. How competent they will become often depends on their access to a range of legitimate opportunities and to the long-term support of adults who deeply care about them (William T. Grant Foundation Commission on Work, Family and Citizenship, 1988).

Historical Perspective on Adolescence

Concept	Processes/Related Ideas	Characteristics/Description
Early history	The Greeks	Plato argued that reason emerges in adolescence and that childhood experiences influence adolescence. Aristotle believed that the ability to choose is an important aspect of adolescence, that self-determination is the hallmark of adolescent maturity, and that development has three stages.
	The Middle Ages and the Enlightenment	In the Middle Ages, knowledge about adolescents moved a step backwards; children became adults, not adolescents. In the eighteenth century, Rousseau described a more enlightened view of adolescence. He proposed four stages of development. Reason and self-consciousness were thought to develop at 12–15 years of age and emotional maturity was thought to replace selfishness at 15–20 years of age.
Adolescence in America	The early years	In the eighteenth and most of the nineteenth century, work apprenticeships took up most of the adolescent male's life. Little has been written about adolescent females during this period.
	The age of adolescence	Between 1890 and 1920 a cadre of psychologists, urban reformers, youth workers, and counselors began to mold the concept of adolescence. G. Stanley Hall's book *Adolescence* in 1904 marked the beginning of the scientific study of adolescence. Hall is known for his storm and stress view of adolescence and the belief that biology plays a prominent role in development.
	The inventionist view	A number of scholars argue for an inventionist view of adolescence. They believe that legislation ensured the dependency of youth and made their move into the economic sphere more manageable.
	Further developments in the twentieth century	Adolescents gained a more prominent status in society from 1920 to 1950. By 1950, the developmental period we call adolescence had come of age. It possessed physical and social identity. During the 1960s and early 1970s, adolescent rebelliousness came to the forefront in American society. Much of the radical protest has abated, but today's adolescents face many other issues.
Stereotyping adolescents	Its nature	A stereotype is a broad category reflecting our impressions about people. Many stereotypes about adolescents are inaccurate. It is not unusual for widespread generalizations about adolescents to be based on a limited group of highly visible adolescents.

A summary of main ideas related to a historical perspective on adolescent development is presented in Concept Table 1.1. Now that we have studied at length the historical interest in adolescents, we turn our attention to a number of issues that confront theorists and researchers as they investigate adolescent development.

The Nature of Development

Each of us develops in certain ways like all other individuals, in other ways like some other individuals, and in other ways like no other individuals. Most of the time our attention is directed at an individual's uniqueness. But developmentalists are drawn to adolescents' communalities as well as their idiosyncrasies. As children and as adolescents, all human beings travel some common paths. Each of us—Leonardo Da Vinci, Joan of Arc, George Washington, Martin Luther King, Jr., your author, and you—walked at about the age of one, talked at about the age of two, engaged in fantasy play as a child, and became much more independent as an adolescent.

Just what do we mean when we speak of an adolescent's development? We use the term **development** to mean a pattern of movement or change that begins at conception and continues throughout the life cycle. Most development involves growth, although it can consist of decay (as in death). The pattern of movement is complex because it is the product of several processes—biological, cognitive, and social.

Biological, Cognitive, and Social Processes

Biological processes involve changes in the individual's physical nature. Genes inherited from parents, the development of the brain, height and weight gains, motor skills, and the hormonal changes of puberty all reflect the role of biological processes in development. Chapter 3 provides detailed coverage of biological processes in adolescent development.

Cognitive processes involve changes in the adolescent's thought, intelligence, and language. Memorizing a poem, solving a math problem, and imagining what it would be like to be a movie star all reflect the role of cognitive processes in the adolescent's development. Chapters 4 and 5 focus on the nature of cognitive processes in adolescent development.

Social processes involve changes in the adolescent's relationships with other people, emotions, and personality. Talking back to parents, an aggressive attack on a peer, development of assertiveness, and an adolescent's joy at the senior prom all reflect the role of social processes in adolescent development. Parts 3 and 4 provide extensive coverage of social processes in adolescent development.

Remember as you read about biological, cognitive, and social processes that they are intricately interwoven. You will read about how social processes shape cognitive processes, how cognitive processes promote or restrict social processes, and how biological processes influence cognitive processes. While it is helpful to study the different processes involved in adolescent development in separate chapters and sections of the book, keep in mind that you are studying the development of an integrated human adolescent who has only one mind and one body (see Figure 1.1).

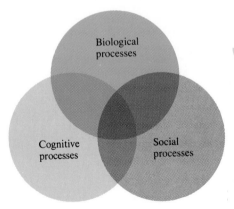

Figure 1.1   Changes in development are the result of biological, cognitive, and social processes. These processes are interwoven in the development of the individual through the human life cycle.

Periods of Development

For the purposes of organization and understanding, we commonly divide development into the periods of childhood, adolescence, and adulthood. However, the childhood period has been subdivided into prenatal, infancy, early childhood, and middle and late childhood by developmentalists. Adolescence has been divided into early and late adolescence, and a period called youth identifies the transition between adolescence and adulthood. Further, developmentalists describe adulthood in terms of early, middle, and late periods. Let's briefly look at these periods to learn some of their main characteristics. Approximate age bands are placed on the periods to provide a general idea of when a period first appears and when it ends.

The **prenatal period** is the time from conception to birth. It is a time of tremendous growth—from a single cell an organism complete with a brain and behavior capabilities is produced in approximately a nine-month period.

Infancy extends from birth to 18 or 24 months. Infancy is a time of extreme dependence upon adults. Many psychological activities are just beginning—language, symbolic thought, sensorimotor coordination, and social learning, for example.

Early childhood, which extends from the end of infancy to about 5 or 6 years, roughly corresponds to the period in which the child prepares for formal schooling. The early childhood years sometimes are called the preschool years. During this time the young child learns to become more self-sufficient and to care for herself, develops school readiness skills (following instructions, identifying letters), and spends many hours in play and with peers. First grade typically marks the end of this period.

Middle and late childhood extends from about 6 to 11 years of age, approximately corresponding to the elementary school years. Sometimes this period is called the elementary school years. The fundamental skills of reading, writing, and arithmetic are mastered. Formal exposure to the larger world and its culture takes place. Achievement becomes a more prominent theme in the child's world and self-control increases.

Our major interest in this book is the development of adolescents. However, as our developmental timetable suggests, considerable development and experience have occurred before the individual reaches adolescence. No boy or girl enters adolescence as a blank slate with only a genetic blueprint determining thoughts, feelings, and behaviors. Rather, the combination of a genetic blueprint, adolescence experiences, and childhood experiences determine the course of adolescent development. Keep in mind this point about the continuity of development between childhood and adolescence. More about the issue of continuity and discontinuity in development appears shortly.

Can we define adolescence? It is not an easy task because we need to consider not only age but sociohistorical influences as well. Remember our earlier discussion of the increased interest in the inventionist view of adolescence, the belief that a number of forces came together to produce the period of development we now call adolescence. With such limitations in mind, we define **adolescence** as the period of transition between childhood and adulthood. Keeping in mind that there may be cultural and historical limitations on the age band of adolescence, we can say that in America and in most cultures today adolescence begins at roughly 10–13 years of age and ends at 18–22 years of age. This period consist of biological, cognitive, and social changes ranging from the development of sexual functions to abstract thinking capabilities to independence.

There is an increasing tendency to describe adolescence in terms of early and late periods. **Early adolescence** encompasses most pubertal change and roughly corresponds to the middle school or junior high school years. **Late adolescence** refers to approximately the latter half of the second decade of life. Investigators are increasingly sensitive to the distinction between early and late adolescence. Researchers now are more likely to control for or investigate the age of adolescents than in past years, and more care is being taken to specify that the results of an investigation may or may not generalize to all ages of adolescents (Hamburg & Takanishi, 1989).

Today, developmentalists do not believe that change ends with adolescence (Hetherington, Lerner, & Perlmutter, 1989; Santrock, 1989). Remember in our definition of development we described development as a life-long process. Kenneth Kenniston (1970) suggests that adolescents do notabruptly move into the period of adulthood. Rather, they are faced with a complex world of work that involves many specialized tasks. Many older adolescents and young adults must spend an extended period of time training in technical institutes, colleges, and postgraduate centers. For many individuals, this situation creates an extended sense of economic and personal "temporariness." Their earning levels are low and sporadic and they may change residences frequently. Marriage and a family are put off until later. This period may be as short as 2–4 years, although it is not unusual for it to last 8–10 years. Kenniston calls this period **youth,** which is entered as early as 17 or 18 years of age or as late as 21 or 24 years of age. The period can last through the late 20s.

Early adulthood usually begins in the late teens or early 20s and lasts through the 30s. It is a time of establishing personal and economic independence. Career development takes on an even more important role than in late adolescence. For many young adults, selecting a mate, learning to live with someone else in an intimate way, and starting a family take up a great deal of time. Probably the most widely recognized marker of entry into adulthood is the occasion when the young individual takes a more or less permanent, full-time job. It usually happens when individuals finish school—high school for

The Nature of Adolescent Development

some, college for others, postgraduate training for yet others. Clear-cut patterns of determining when an individual has left adolescence or youth and entered adulthood are not easy to pin down. One of every 4 adolescents does not finish high school and many students who finish college cannot find a job. Further, if we consider economic independence as an adulthood criterion, such independence is more often a long, gradual process rather than an abrupt one. Increasingly, college graduates return to live with their parents as they attempt to get their feet on the ground economically.

As can be seen, defining when adolescence ends is not an easy task. It has been said that adolescence begins in biology and ends in culture. This means that the marker for entry into adolescence is determined by the onset of pubertal maturation and that the marker for entry into adulthood is determined by cultural standards and experiences. As we will discover in Chapter 3, defining entry into puberty is not an easy task either. For boys, is it the first whisker or the first wet dream? For girls, is it the enlargement of breasts or the first period? For boys and girls, is it a spurt in height? We usually can tell when a boy or girl is in puberty, but its actual onset often goes unnoticed.

Keep in mind also that **middle adulthood** is important in understanding adolescence. This period of development is entered roughly at 35–45 years of age and exited at some point between 55 and 65 years of age. This period is salient in the lives of adolescents because their parents either are about to enter this adult period or are already in it. Middle adulthood is a time of increased concern about transmitting values to the next generation, enhanced interest in one's body, a changing time perspective, and a changing career perspective. In Chapter 6 we will study how both the maturation of adolescents and the maturation of parents contribute to an understanding of parent-adolescent relationships.

Eventually the rhythm and meaning of life's human cycle wend their way to **late adulthood,** which lasts from approximately 60 or 70 years of age until death. It is a time of adjustment to decreasing strength and health and to retirement and reduced income. Reviewing one's life and adapting to social roles are prominent features of late adulthood, as are lessened responsibility, increased freedom, and grandparenthood.

The periods of development are shown in Figure 1.2 along with the processes of development—biological, cognitive, and social. As can be seen in Figure 1.2, the interplay of biological, cognitive, and social processes produces the periods of development in life's human cycle.

Maturation and Experience

We can think of development as produced not only by the interplay of biological, cognitive, and social processes but also by the interplay of maturation and experience. **Maturation** is the orderly sequence of changes dictated by the genetic blueprint we each have. According to the maturational view, just as a

Figure 1.2   Processes and periods of
life-span development. The unfolding of
the life-cycle's periods of development is
influenced by the interplay of biological,
cognitive, and social processes.

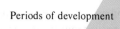
Periods of development

Late
adulthood

Middle
adulthood

Early
adulthood

Adolescence

Processes of development

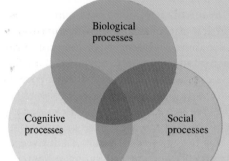
Biological
processes

Cognitive
processes

Social
processes

Middle
and late
childhood

Early
childhood

Infancy

Prenatal
period

sunflower grows in an orderly way—unless flattened by an unfriendly environment—so does the human grow in an orderly way. The range of environments can be vast, but the maturational approach argues that the genetic blueprint produces communalities in our growth and development. We walk before we talk, speak one word before two words, grow rapidly in infancy and less so in early childhood, experience a rush of sexual hormones in puberty after a lull in childhood, reach the peak of our physical strength in late adolescence and early adulthood and then decline, and so on. The maturationists acknowledge that extreme environments—those that are psychologically barren or hostile—can depress development, but they believe basic growth tendencies are genetically wired into the human.

By contrast, other psychologists emphasize the importance of experiences in development. Experiences run the gamut from the individual's biological environment—nutrition, medical care, drugs, and physical accidents—to the social environment—family, peers, schools, community, media, and culture.

The debate about whether development is influenced primarily by maturation or by experience is another version of the **nature-nurture controversy** that has been a part of psychology throughout its history. The "nature" proponents claim that biological and genetic factors are the most important determinants of development; the "nurture" proponents claim that environment and experience are more important.

Ideas about the nature of development have been like a pendulum, swinging between nature and nurture. Today we are witnessing a surge of interest in the biological underpinnings of development, probably because the pendulum had swung too far in the direction of thinking that development was due exclusively to environmental experiences (Hinde & Gorebel, 1989; Savin-Williams, 1987). While nature has grown in popularity recently, all psychologists today believe that both nature *and* nurture are responsible for development; the key to development is the interaction of nature and nurture rather than either factor alone (Plomin, 1989). For example, an individual's cognitive development is the result of heredity-environment interaction, not heredity or environment alone. Much more about the importance of heredity-environment interaction appears in Chapter 3.

Yet another way to analyze the nature of development is to consider the roles of life time, social time, and historical time (Neugarten & Datan, 1973; Neugarten & Neugarten, 1986). **Life time** refers to our biological timetable. Chronological age is often used as an indicator of life time, but chronological age is at best only a rough indicator of an individual's position in a number of physical and psychological dimensions. Because from early infancy on, individual differences are a major factor in development. Age is also not a good index of many forms of psychological and social behavior, unless there is accompanying knowledge of the particular society in which the individual lives. An obvious example compares a girl in the United States who attends school with a same-aged girl in a rural village in the Near East who is the mother of two children.

Social time refers to the social determinants of development, those related to a culture's standards. For example, preliterate societies use "rites of passage" to mark the transition from one age status to the next, such as the passage from youth to maturity and to marriage (Van Gennep, 1969). However, only a rough parallel exists between social time and life time in many societies. There are different sets of age expectations and age statuses in different societies.

Historical time refers to the timing of major historical events in the individual's life. Wars and depressions often act as historical watersheds—that is, major turning points—in the social system. Significant historical events affect levels of education, fertility patterns, sexual mores, labor participation patterns, and so on (Caspi & Elder, 1989; Elder & Caspi, in press). Historical time is involved in the emergence of the concepts of childhood, adolescence, and life-span development themselves. Childhood as a distinct phase of life did not emerge until the seventeenth and eighteenth centuries. The concept of adolescence did not emerge until the beginning of the twentieth century. Middle age as a life cycle period did not emerge until even more recently in the twentieth century, linked to increased longevity of our population.

The importance of historical time in understanding adolescence fits with the inventionist view of adolescence discussed earlier in the chapter. Remember that in the inventionist view youth were systematically removed from meaningful roles in the adult society. Their dependence was prolonged and cultural childhood was imposed on biologically mature individuals. A recent analysis of the content of the oldest continuing journal in developmental psychology (*Journal of Genetic Psychology—Pedagogical Seminary*) provided further evidence of history's role in the perception of adolescents (Enright & others, 1987). Four historical periods—the depressions of the 1890s and 1930s, and the two world wars—were evaluated. During the depression periods, scholars talked about the psychological immaturity of youth and their educational needs. In contrast, during the world wars scholars did not describe youth as immature, but rather underscored their importance as draftees and factory workers.

In sum, many different aspects of maturation and experience, nature and nurture, life time, social time, and historical time are involved in the adolescent's development. The biological features of adolescence—those involving the pubertal changes of hormones, sexual maturation, and a height and weight spurt—represent adolescence's universality. The sociohistorical dimensions of adolescence—acquiring adult social status or being deprived of it—are more varied. Some cultures get this over rather quickly; others—such as the American culture—drag it out over many years. Some cultures, especially primitive ones, have uniform criteria for adult social status; others (again, for example, the American culture) have no uniform criteria. Much more about cultural variations in adolescence appears in Chapter 9, where we describe the pubertal rites of primitive cultures and a number of cross-cultural and ethnic comparisons of adolescents.

Continuity and Discontinuity

Think about your development for a moment. Did you gradually grow to become the person you are, not unlike the slow, cumulative growth of a seedling into a giant oak? Or did you experience sudden, distinct changes in your growth, not unlike the way a caterpillar changes into a butterfly? (see Figure 1.3). For the most part, developmentalists who emphasize experience have described development as a gradual, continuous process; those who emphasize maturation have described development as a series of distinct stages. In Chapter 2, you will read about several prominent stage theories of development.

Some developmentalists emphasize the **continuity of development,** stressing a gradual, cumulative change from conception to death. A child's first word, while seemingly an abrupt, discontinuous event, is viewed as the result of weeks and months of growth and practice. Puberty, while also seemingly an abrupt, discontinuous occurrence, is viewed as a gradual process occurring over several years.

Other developmentalists emphasize the **discontinuity of development,** stressing distinct stages in the life span. Each of us is described as passing through a sequence of stages in which change is qualitatively rather than quantitatively different. As the oak moves from seedling to giant oak, it is *more* oak—its development is continuous. As the caterpillar changes to a butterfly, it is not just more caterpillar. It is a *different kind* of organism—its development is discontinuous. At some point, a child moves from not being able to think abstractly about the world to being able to. At some point, an adult moves from an individual capable of reproduction to one who is not. These are qualitative, discontinuous changes in development, not quantitative, continuous changes.

Another form of the continuity-discontinuity issue is whether development is best described by *stability* or *change* (Bornstein & Krasnegor, 1989). Will the shy child who hides behind the sofa when visitors arrive be the wallflower at college dances, or will this child become a sociable, talkative individual? Will the fun-loving, carefree adolescent have difficulty holding down a nine-to-five job as an adult, or become a straight-laced, serious conformist? The **stability-change issue** basically addresses the degree to which we become older renditions of our early existence or whether we can develop into someone different than we were at an earlier point in development. One of the reasons

Figure 1.3   Continuity and discontinuity in development: Is development more like a seedling gradually growing into a giant oak or a caterpillar suddenly becoming a butterfly?

Negative Emotional and Behavioral States in Childhood and Adjustment in Adolescence

The issue of continuity–discontinuity raises the possibility that problems and disturbances appearing to surface in adolescence may have their origin in childhood. It may be that adolescence only increases the intensity of problems that have emerged earlier for some individuals. A continuity view of adolescent development argues that we should not only look at what is happening in the adolescent's life for clues to his or her adjustment, but also delve into the childhood background of the adolescent.

One widely known investigation that addresses the continuity issue in regard to adolescent adjustment is the New York Longitudinal Study (Chess & Thomas, 1977, 1984; Thomas, Chess, & Birch, 1968; Thomas & Chess, 1977). This investigation now has spanned almost thirty years. One recent report from this large scale study (Lerner & others, 1988) focused on the extent to which information about negative emotional states and behavioral characteristics (such as aggression, anxiety, noncompliance, depression) in childhood is related to adjustment during the adolescent years. One hundred thirty-three white, middle-class children were rated on these negative characteristics from infancy to adolescence. Measures of family, peer, and personal adjustment also were obtained.

The most intriguing results from this investigation revealed how early negative emotional behaviors in the years 1–6 were highly related to adolescent adjustment

Negative emotional states in the years one through six were related to adolescent adjustment in the New York Longitudinal Study.

adult development was so late in being studied was the predominant belief for many years that nothing much changes in adulthood; the major changes were believed to take place in childhood, especially during the first five years of life. Today most developmentalists believe that some change is possible throughout the life span, although scholars disagree, sometimes heatedly, about just how much change can take place and how much stability there is. More about the

In the New York Longitudinal Study, children who showed high rates of aggressive behavior at 1–6 years of age, had poor family adjustment during adolescence.

pattern of findings is consistent with the findings of other research, suggesting that aggressive adolescents have difficulty adjusting to parents and anxious, shy, or otherwise introverted adolescents often have problems with friendships and peer relationships (Parker & Gottman, 1987). What is important about these findings is the long-term prediction of adolescent adjustment by emotional behavior problems in the *early* part of childhood and the lack of additional prediction of adolescent adjustment by later childhood characteristics. This lack of additional predictability of adolescent adjustment by later childhood characteristics and adjustment was likely related to the fact that aggression and anxiety were relatively stable over the 1–12-year age range in the New York Longitudinal Study. One interpretation of these data is that negative emotional behaviors often emerge in the early part of childhood, are carried through the childhood years into adolescence, and influence the nature of adjustment during adolescence. These findings clearly point to the importance of a continuity view of adolescent development, and the attendant theme that experiences and development during the childhood years should not be ignored in our evaluation of the adjustment and social competence of adolescents. We believe, however, that experiences throughout childhood and adolescence are important determinants of adolescent development. The story told by the recent New York Longitudinal Study simply instructs us not to ignore early childhood characteristics and experiences in our attempt to chart the manner in which adolescents construct a vision of reality and social maturity.

problems with parents and peers. This pattern was specific to the type of emotional difficulty—aggression predicting poor family adjustment in adolescence and anxiety predicting peer adjustment problems. Subsequent emotional difficulties in the 7–12-year age range did not provide added accuracy in predicting parent and peer adjustment in adolescence. School adjustment problems in adolescence, however, were best predicted by aggressive behaviors in the 7–12-year age range. The overall

issue of continuity–discontinuity in development is presented in Perspective on Adolescent Development 1.2.

At this point we have discussed a number of ideas about the nature of development. A summary of these ideas is presented in Concept Table 1.2. In the next chapter we turn our attention to the scientific orientation in studying adolescent development, discussing the theories and methods used by developmentalists who conduct research with adolescents.

The Nature of Development

Concept	Processes/Related Ideas	Characteristics/Description
What is development?	Its nature	Development is a pattern of movement or change that begins at conception and continues throughout the human life cycle. It can involve growth or decline.
Biological, cognitive, and social processes	Biological	Changes in the individual's physical nature.
	Cognitive	Changes in the individual's thought, intelligence, and language.
	Social	Changes in relationships with other people, emotions, and personality.
Periods of development	Prenatal and infancy	Prenatal lasts from conception to birth, a time of dramatic growth. Infancy lasts from birth to about two years of age and is a time of considerable dependence on adults as well as the emergence of many abilities.
	Early childhood and middle and late childhood	Early childhood lasts from about 2–5 years of age and also is known as the preschool years. Self-sufficiency increases as do school-readiness skills. During middle and late childhood, from about 6 to 10 or 11 years of age, academic skills are mastered and there is formal exposure to the larger world. This period also is called the elementary school years.
	Adolescence	The transition from childhood to adulthood, involving physical, cognitive, and social changes. It is entered roughly at 10–13 years and exited at 18–22 years of age. There is an increasing tendency to define adolescence in terms of early and late periods. It has been said that adolescence begins in biology and ends in culture.

Summary

I. The Greeks

Plato argued that reason emerges in adolescence and that childhood experiences influence adolescence. Aristotle believed that the ability to choose is an important aspect of adolescence, that self-determination is the hallmark of adolescent maturity, and that development has three stages.

II. The Middle Ages and the Enlightenment

In the Middle Ages, knowledge about adolescence moved a step backwards; children were thought of as adults, not adolescents. In the eighteenth century, Rousseau described a more enlightened view of adolescence. He proposed four stages of development. Reason and self-consciousness were thought to develop at 12–15 years of age, and emotional maturity was thought to replace selfishness at 15–20 years of age.

III. The Early Years in America

In the eighteenth and most of the nineteenth century, work apprenticeships took up most of the adolescent male's life. Little has been written about adolescent females during this period.

Concept	Processes/Related Ideas	Characteristics/Description
	Youth	Kenniston proposed this period as a transition between adolescence and adulthood. It is a period of temporariness and can last as long as 8–10 years.
	Adulthood	Divided into early, middle, and late periods. Early adulthood covers roughly the third and fourth decades of life and involves themes of career development and intimacy. Taking a more or less permanent job has been a common marker for entrance into adulthood, but this criterion does not always hold up. Middle adulthood is especially important in our study of adolescence because most parents of adolescents are in this period. Late adulthood is the final period of the human life cycle.
Issues in adolescent development	Maturation and experience	Development is influenced by the interaction of maturation and experience. The debate of whether development is primarily due to maturation or to environment is another version of the nature-nurture controversy. Life time, social time, and historical time also are considerations. Ideas about historical time mesh with the inventionist view of adolescence. The biological features of puberty represent adolescence's universal nature, while sociocultural features are less uniform.
	Continuity and discontinuity	Some developmentalists describe development as continuous (gradual, cumulative change); others describe it as discontinuous (abrupt, sequence of stages). Another form of the continuity-discontinuity issue is whether development is best described by stability or by change.

IV. The Age of Adolescence and the Inventionist View

Between 1890 and 1920 a cadre of psychologists, urban reformers, youth workers, and counselors began to mold the concept of adolescence. G. Stanley Hall's book *Adolescence,* in 1904, marked the beginning of the scientific study of adolescence. Hall is known for his storm and stress view of adolescence and the belief that biology plays a prominent role in development. A number of scholars argue for an inventionist view of adolescence. They believe that legislation ensured the dependency of youth and made their move into the economic sphere more manageable.

V. Further Developments in the Twentieth Century

Adolescents gained a more prominent status in society from 1920 to 1950. By 1950, the developmental period we call adolescence had come of age. It possessed physical and social identity. During the 1960s and the early 1970s, adolescent rebelliousness came to the forefront in American society. Much of the radical protest has abated, but today's adolescents face many other issues.

VI. Stereotyping Adolescents

A stereotype is a broad category reflecting our impressions about people. Many stereotypes about adolescents are inaccurate. It is not unusual for widespread generalizations about adolescents to develop based on a limited group of highly visible adolescents.

VII. What Is Development?

Development is a pattern of movement or change that begins at conception and continues throughout the human life cycle. It can involve growth or decline. Development involves the interaction of biological, cognitive, and social processes.

VIII. Periods of Development—Childhood

Prenatal development lasts from conception to birth, a time of dramatic growth. Infancy lasts from birth to about 2 years of age and is a time of considerable dependence on adults as well as the emergence of many abilities. Early childhood lasts from about 2–5 years of age and also is known as the preschool years. Self-sufficiency increases, as do school-readiness skills. During middle and late childhood, from about 6–10 or 6–11 years of age, academic skills are mastered and there is formal exposure to the larger world. This period also is called the elementary school years.

IX. Adolescence and Youth

Adolescence is the transition between childhood and adulthood, involving physical, cognitive, and social changes. It is entered roughly at 10–13 years and exited at 18–22 years of age. There is an increasing tendency to define adolescence in terms of early and late periods. It has been said that adolescence begins in biology and ends in culture. Kenniston proposed that youth is a period of transition between adolescence and adulthood. It is a period of personal temporariness and can last as long as 8–10 years.

X. Adulthood

Adulthood is divided into early, middle, and late periods. Early adulthood covers roughly the third and fourth decades of life and involves themes of career development and intimacy. Taking a more or less permanent job has been a common marker for entrance into adulthood, but this criterion does not always hold up. Middle adulthood is especially important in our study of adolescence because most parents of adolescents are in this period. Late adulthood is the final period of the human life cycle.

XI. Issues in Adolescent Development

One important issue involves maturation and experience. Development is influenced by the interaction of maturation and experience. The debate about whether development is primarily due to maturation or to environment is another version of the nature-nurture controversy. Life time, social time, and historical time also are considerations. Ideas about historical time mesh with the inventionist view of adolescence. The biological features of puberty represent adolescence's universality, while sociocultural features are less uniform. Some developmentalists describe development as continuous (gradual, cumulative change); others describe it as discontinuous (abrupt, sequence of stages). Another form of the continuity-discontinuity issue is whether development is best described by stability or by change.

Key Terms

storm and stress 15
inventionist view 17
stereotype 22
adolescent generalization
   gap 23
development 26
biological processes 26
cognitive processes 26
social processes 26
prenatal period 27
infancy 27

early childhood 27
middle and late
   childhood 27
adolescence 28
early adolescence 28
late adolescence 28
youth 28
early adulthood 28
middle adulthood 29
late adulthood 29
maturation 29

nature-nurture
   controversy 31
life time 31
social time 32
historical time 32
continuity of
   development 33
discontinuity of
   development 33
stability-change issue 33

Suggested Readings

Developmental Psychology, Child Development, Journal of Youth and Adolescence,
   and *Journal of Early Adolescence.*
   The chances are excellent that your library will have one or more of these
   research journals that either focus exclusively on adolescents or include many
   articles about adolescents. Take some time to leaf through issues of the
   journals published within the last several years to obtain a glimpse of the
   research issues that interest the scientists who study adolescents.

Elder, G. H. (1980). Adolescence in historical perspective. In J. Adelson (Ed.),
   Handbook of adolescent psychology. New York: Wiley.
   An intriguing portrayal of how historical time influences the nature of
   adolescent development.

Hill, J. P. (1980). *Understanding early adolescence: A framework.* Chapel Hill,
   N.C.: University of North Carolina.
   This booklet provides an excellent overview of the nature of development in
   early adolescence. Written by John Hill, one of the leading scholars in
   adolescent development.

Kett, J. F. (1977). *Rites of passage.* New York: Basic Books.
   Kett describes in great detail three major historical phases in the way the
   adolescent has been dealt with in the United States. The nature of adolescence
   from 1790 to the present is discussed.

Lee, C. B. T. (1970). *The campus scene: 1900–1970.* New York: McKay.
   Lee's book is an excellent, entertaining description of late adolescent
   development and college life. The author makes many comparisons between
   peer interaction and parent-adolescent interaction in different decades of the
   twentieth century.

Ross, D. (1972). *G. Stanley Hall: The psychologist as prophet.* Chicago: University
   of Chicago Press.
   This is an intriguing biographical sketch of the father of adolescent
   psychology, G. Stanley Hall.

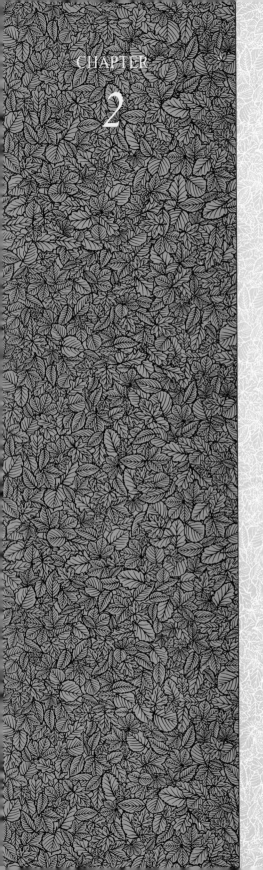

Theories and Methods

There is nothing quite so practical as a good theory.

Kurt Lewin

41

The Youths of Erikson and Piaget

*E*rik Erikson and Jean Piaget, whose theories we will address in this chapter, have developed extraordinary insights about the nature of adolescent development. The lives of theorists and their experiences have a major impact on the content of their theories. The search for understanding human behavior includes an examination of one's own behavior.

Erik Erikson's theory emphasizes the development of identity in adolescence. What was Erikson's experience with identity as he was growing up? History shows us that Erikson was born June 15, 1902, near Frankfurt, Germany, to Danish parents. Before Erik was born, his parents separated and his mother left Denmark to live in Germany, where she had some friends. At age three, Erik became ill, and his mother took him to see a pediatrician named Homberger. Erik's mother fell in love with the pediatrician, married him, and gave young Erik the middle name of his new stepfather—Homberger.

Erik attended primary school between the ages of 6 and 10, and then the *Gymnasium* (high school) from age 11 to age 18. He studied art and a number of languages rather than science courses like biology and chemistry. Erik did not

Erik Erikson (b. 1902)

like the formal atmosphere of his school, and this was reflected in his grades. At age 18, rather than going to college, the adolescent Erikson wandered through the continent, keeping notes about his experiences in his personal diary. After a year of travel through Europe, he returned to Germany and enrolled in art school, became dissatisfied, and enrolled in another. Then he began to give up his

Jean Piaget, famous Swiss psychologist and the architect of cognitive developmental theory.

sketching and eventually traveled to Florence, Italy. Robert Coles (1970) vividly describes Erikson at this time,

> To the Italians he was not an unfamiliar sight: the young, tall, thin Nordic expatriate with long, blond hair. He wore a corduroy suit and was seen by his family and friends as not odd or "sick" but as a wandering artist who was trying to come to grips with himself, a not unnatural or unusual struggle. (p. 15)

Jean Piaget's theory, on the other hand, emphasizes cognitive development. Piaget was born August 9, 1896, in Neuchâtel, Switzerland. Jean's father was an intellectual type who taught young Jean to think systematically. Jean's mother also was bright, and strongly religious. His father maintained an air of detachment from his mother, who was described by Jean as prone to frequent outbursts of neurotic behavior. In his autobiography, Piaget (1952) explained why he chose to study cognitive rather than social development:

> I started to forego playing for serious work very early. Indeed, I have always detested any departure from reality, an attitude which I relate to my mother's poor mental health. It was this

disturbing factor which at the beginning of my studies in psychology made me keenly interested in psychoanalytic and pathological psychology. Though this interest helped me to achieve independence and to widen my cultural background, I have never since felt any desire to involve myself deeper in that particular direction, always much preferring the study of normalcy and of the workings of the intellect to that of the tricks of the unconscious. (p. 238)

At the age of 22, Piaget went to work in the psychology laboratory at the University of Zurich. There he was exposed to the insights of Alfred Binet, who developed the first intelligence test. By the time Piaget was 25, his experience in varied disciplines had helped him to see important links between philosophy, psychology, and biology.

These experiences of Erikson and Piaget are examples of how theorists' own experiences and behavior influence their thinking. Perhaps Erikson's own wanderings and search for self contributed to his theory of adolescent identity development. And perhaps Piaget's own intellectual experiences with his parents and schooling contributed to his theory of logical thinking in adolescence.

*I*n this chapter, we study two key ingredients of the scientific approach to adolescent development—theories and methods. According to Henri Poincaré, "Science is built of facts the way a house is built of bricks, but an accumulation of facts is no more science than a pile of bricks a house." Science *does* depend upon the raw material of facts or data, but as Poincaré indicated, science is more than facts. The nature of theory illustrates Poincaré's point.

What Is a Theory?

Theories are general beliefs that help us explain the data or facts we have observed and to make predictions. A good theory has **hypotheses.** Hypotheses are assumptions that can be tested to determine their accuracy. For example, a theory of adolescent depression would explain our observations of depressed adolescents and predict why adolescents get depressed. We might predict that adolescents become depressed because they fail to focus on their strengths and dwell extensively on their weaknesses. This prediction would help to direct our observations by telling us to look for exaggerations of weaknesses and under-estimations of strength and skills.

Erikson's and Piaget's theories are but two of the many theories you will read about in this chapter. We begin by describing psychoanalytic theories of adolescent development, one of which is Erikson's. Then we turn to cognitive theories of adolescent development, one of which is Piaget's. Our third group of theories to be discussed is behavioral, social learning. The diversity of theories makes understanding adolescent development a challenging under-taking. Just when you think one theory has the correct explanation of adolescent development, another theory will crop up and make you rethink your earlier conclusion. To keep from getting frustrated, remember that adolescent development is complex and multifaceted. No single theory has been able to ac-count for all aspects of adolescent development. Each theory contributes an important piece to the puzzle of adolescent development. While the theories sometimes disagree about certain aspects of adolescent development, much of their information is *complementary* rather than contradictory. Together they let us see the total landscape of adolescent development in all its richness.

Psychoanalytic Theories

For psychoanalytic theorists, adolescent development is primarily unconscious (beyond awareness) and is made up of structures of thought heavily colored by emotion. Psychoanalytic theorists believe that behavior is merely a surface characteristic and that to truly understand an adolescent's development, we have to look at the symbolic meanings of behavior and the deep inner workings of the mind. Psychoanalytic theorists also stress that early experiences with parents and underlying sexual tension shape the adolescent's development. These characteristics are highlighted in the psychoanalytic theory of Sigmund Freud (Looney & Blotcky, 1989; Nichtern, 1989).

Freud's Theory

Loved and hated, respected and despised, for some the master, for others misdirected—Sigmund Freud, whether right or wrong in his views, has been one of the most influential thinkers of the twentieth century. Freud was a medical doctor who specialized in neurology. He developed his ideas about psychoanalytic theory from his work with patients with mental problems. He was born in 1856 in Austria and he died in London at the age of 83. Most of his years were spent in Vienna, though he left the city near the end of his career because of Nazi anti-Semitism.

Sigmund Freud

The Structure of Personality

Freud (1924) believed that personality has three structures: the id, the ego, and the superego. One way to understand the three structures is to consider them as three rulers of a country (Singer, 1984). The id is king or queen, the ego is prime minister, and the superego is high priest. The id is an absolute monarch, owed complete obedience; it is spoiled, willful, and self-centered. The id wants what it wants right now, not later. The ego as prime minister has the job of getting things done right; it is tuned into reality and is responsive to society's demands. The superego as high priest is concerned with right and wrong; the id may be greedy and needs to be told that nobler purposes should be pursued.

The **id** is the reservoir of psychic energy and instincts that perpetually press us to satisfy our basic needs—food, sex, and avoidance of pain, for example. In Freud's view, the id is completely unconscious, beyond our awareness; it has no contact with reality. The id works according to the **pleasure principle;** that is, it *always* seeks pleasure and avoids pain. Freud believed the id is the only part of personality present at birth; even in adults the id acts like a selfish infant, demanding immediate gratification.

It would be a dangerous and scary world if our personalities were all id. As the young child develops, he learns that he cannot eat 26 popsicles; sometimes he is not allowed to eat even one. He also learns that he has to use the toilet instead of his diaper. As the child experiences the demands and constraints of reality, a new structure of personality is being formed—the **ego.** The ego abides by the **reality principle;** it tries to bring the individual pleasure within the boundaries of reality. Few of us are cold-blooded killers or wild wheeler-dealers; we take into account obstacles to our satisfaction that exist

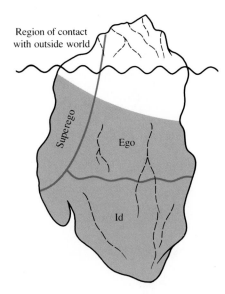

Region of contact
with outside world

Superego

Ego

Id

Figure 2.1   This rather odd-looking
diagram illustrates Freud's belief that
most of personality's important thoughts
occur beneath the level of conscious
awareness. Whereas the ego and
superego are partly conscious and partly
unconscious, the id is completely
unconscious, just like the large,
submerged part of an iceberg.

in our world. We recognize that our sexual and aggressive impulses cannot go unrestrained. The ego helps us to test reality—to see how far we can go without getting into trouble and hurting ourselves.

While the id is completely unconscious, the ego is partly conscious. It houses our higher mental functions—reasoning, problem solving, and decision making, for example. For this reason, the ego is referred to as the executive branch of personality; like an executive in a company, it makes the rational decisions that help the company succeed.

The id and the ego have no morality. They do not take into account whether something is right or wrong. This is left to the third structure of personality, the **superego,** which is referred to as the moral branch of personality. Think of the superego as what we often refer to as our "conscience." Like the id, the superego does not consider reality; it doesn't deal with what is realistic, only with whether the id's sexual and aggressive impulses can be satisfied in moral terms. You probably are beginning to sense that both the id and the superego make life rough for the ego. Your ego might say, "I will only have sex occasionally and be sure to take the proper precautions because I don't want the intrusion of a child in the development of my career." But your id is saying, "I want to be satisfied; sex is pleasurable." And your superego is at work too, saying "I feel guilty about having sex."

Freud considered personality to be like an iceberg: most of personality exists below our level of awareness, just as the massive part of the iceberg is beneath the surface of the water. Figure 2.1 illustrates this analogy.

Defense Mechanisms

How does the ego resolve the conflict between its demands for reality, the wishes of the id, and the constraints of the superego? In Freud's view, the conflicting demands of the personality structures produce anxiety. For example, when the ego blocks the pleasurable pursuits of the id, an inner anxiety is felt. This diffuse, distressed state develops when the ego senses that the id is going to cause some harm to the individual. The anxiety alerts the ego to resolve the conflict by means of **defense mechanisms,** which protect the ego and reduce the anxiety produced by the conflict.

Freud thought that the most powerful and pervasive defense mechanism is **repression;** it works to push unacceptable id impulses out of our awareness and back into our unconscious mind. Repression is the foundation from which all other defense mechanisms work; the goal of every defense mechanism is to *repress* or push threatening impulses out of awareness. Freud said that our early childhood experiences, many of which he believed were sexually laden, are too threatening and conflictual for us to deal with consciously. We reduce the anxiety of this conflict through the defense mechanism of repression.

Among the other defense mechanisms we use to protect the ego and reduce anxiety are sublimation, reaction formation, and regression. **Sublimation** occurs when a socially useful course of action replaces a distasteful one. For example, an individual with strong sexual urges may turn them into socially approved behavior by becoming an artist who paints nudes. **Reaction formation** occurs when we express an unacceptable impulse by transforming it into its opposite. For example, an individual who is attracted to the brutality of war becomes a peace activist. Or an individual who fears his sexual urges becomes a religious zealot. **Regression** occurs when an individual behaves in a way that characterized a previous developmental level. When anxiety becomes too great for us, we revert to an early behavior that gave us pleasure. For example, a woman may run home to her mother every time she and her husband have a big argument.

Two final points about defense mechanisms need to be understood. First, they are unconscious—we are not aware we are using them to protect our ego. Second, when used in moderation or on a temporary basis, defense mechanisms are not necessarily unhealthy. For example, the defense mechanism of denial can help an individual cope with impending death. For the most part, though, we should not let defense mechanisms dominate our behavior and prevent us from facing reality's demands. More about defense mechanisms and adolescent development appears in Perspective on Adolescent Development 2.1.

The Development of Personality

As Freud listened to, probed, and analyzed his patients, he became convinced that their problems were the result of experiences early in life. Freud believed that we go through five stages of psychosexual development and that at each stage of development we experience pleasure in one part of the body more than others. He called these body parts **erogenous zones** because of their pleasure-giving qualities.

Freud thought that our adult personality was determined by the way conflicts between these early sources of pleasure—the mouth, the anus, and then the genitals—and the demands of reality were resolved. When these conflicts are not resolved, the individual may become fixated at a particular stage of development. **Fixation** is closely linked with the defense mechanism of regression. Fixation occurs when an individual's needs are under- or overgratified. For example, a parent may wean a child too early, be too strict in toilet training the child, punish the child for masturbation, or smother the child with warmth. We will return to the idea of fixation and how it may show up in an adult's personality, but first we need to learn more about the early stages of personality development.

The Role of Defense Mechanisms in Adolescent Adjustment: The Views of Peter Blos and Anna Freud

For Peter Blos (1962, 1989), one of the most well accepted contemporary psychoanalytic theorists who studies adolescents, regression during adolescence is not defensive at all but rather an integral part of puberty. Such regression, according to Blos, is inevitable and universal. The nature of this regression may vary from one adolescent to the next. It may involve childhood autonomy, compliance, and cleanliness, or it may involve a sudden return to the passiveness that characterized the adolescent's behavior during infancy or early childhood. Blos believes that intrafamilial struggles during adolescence reflect the presence of unresolved conflicts from childhood.

An excellent example of how the psychoanalytic theorist works in tying together adolescent feelings with childhood experiences rests in the work of Joseph Adelson and Margery Doehrman (1980). When their patient, John, was 16 he entered a group therapy session with other adolescents. At this time he was recovering from severe depression following the break-off of a serious relationship with a girlfriend. It was the girl's mother who referred John to the clinic, sensing that John's depression was severe, just as she had earlier detected that his dependency on her daughter was acute. John was a handsome, intelligent, articulate adolescent and a leader at school, hardly the type of person you would think might be deeply and severely depressed.

After a series of sessions with John, it became apparent that he kept most girls at a distance, particularly when they seemed to want to get seriously involved or to "mother" him. On the other hand, he was attracted to

What might be the focus of psychoanalytic theorists such as Peter Blos and Anna Freud if they analyzed the dating relationships of this adolescent couple?

During the first 12 to 18 months of life, the activities that bring the greatest amount of pleasure center around the mouth; in the **oral stage** of development, chewing, sucking, and biting are chief pleasure sources. These actions reduce the infant's tension.

The period from about 1½ years to 3 years of life is called the **anal stage** because the child's greatest pleasure involves the anus, or the eliminative functions associated with it. In Freud's view, the exercise of the anal muscles reduces tension.

girls who were either aloof or tomboyish. It gradually became clear that John's relationships with girls were characterized by a wish to reestablish a union with his mother and that he had an intense fear of that wish. He was attracted to girls who were standoffish, but once he established a relationship with one of them, he would sink into an uncontrollable dependency upon her, to the point of being enthralled by such dependency.

To some degree, then, John's attachments to girls represented a wish to become reunited with his mother. What was John's relationship with his mother like in adolescence? He was often abusive toward her; he complained that she nagged at him all the time; but in truth he was frightened by his regressive feelings toward her, according to Adelson. The regressive feelings came out clearly in group therapy when his intelligent participation would be replaced by sarcasm and then scorn whenever he seemed to be drawn to the "maternal" females in the group. This was particularly true with the woman therapist, who was seen as the group's "mother."

Although some psychoanalytic writers, like Blos, consider regression a normal part of adolescent development, for individuals like John the reappearance of unresolved conflicts from early childhood requires therapy. For most individuals, however, the conflicts are not so serious that therapy is warranted. Thus, the intensity and persistence of the regression determine whether it is a healthy or unhealthy part of adolescent development.

Anna Freud (1958, 1966) has developed the idea that defense mechanisms are the key to understanding adolescent adjustment. She believes that the problems of ad-olescence are not to be unlocked by understanding the id, or instinctual forces, but instead are to be discovered in the existence of "love objects" in the adolescent's past, both oedipal and preoedipal. She argues that the attachment to these love objects, usually parents, is carried forward from the infant years and merely toned down or inhibited during the latency years. During adolescence, these pregenital urges may be reawakened, or worse, newly acquired genital (adolescent) urges may combine with the urges that developed in early childhood.

Anna Freud goes on to describe how adolescent defense mechanisms are used to ward off these infantile intrusions. Youth may withdraw from their attachment and identification with their parents and suddenly transfer their love to others—to parent substitutes, to leaders who represent ideals, or to peers. Or, rather than transferring the attachment to someone else, adolescents may reverse their feelings toward the attachment figure—replacing love with hate or dependence with rebellion. Finally, the instinctual fears may even generate unhealthy defensive solutions—for example, the adolescent may withdraw within himself, which could lead to gradiose ideas of triumph or persecution; or regression could occur. Thus, from Anna Freud's perspective, a number of defense mechanisms are essential to the adolescent's handling of conflicts.

The **phallic stage** of development occurs approximately between the ages of 3 and 6; its name comes from the word *phallus,* a symbolization of penis. During the phallic stage, pleasure focuses on the genitals as the child discovers that self-manipulation is enjoyable.

In Freud's view, the phallic stage has special importance because it is during this period that the **Oedipus complex** appears. This name comes from a story in Greek mythology, in which Oedipus, the son of the King of Thebes,

Freud said we go through five stages of psychosexual development. In the oral stage (a), pleasure centers around the mouth. In the anal stage (b), pleasure focuses on the anus—the nature of toilet training is important here. In the phallic stage (c), pleasure involves the genitals—the opposite-sex parent becomes a love object here. In the latency stage (d), the child represses sexual urges—same-sex friendship is prominent. In the genital stage (e), sexual reawakening takes place—the source of pleasure now becomes someone outside the family.

(a)

(b)

(c)

(d)

(e)

The Nature of Adolescent Development

unwittingly kills his father and marries his mother. In the Oedipus complex, the young child develops an intense desire to replace the parent of the same sex and enjoy the affections of the opposite-sexed parent. How is the Oedipus complex resolved? At about 5 to 6 years of age, children recognize that their same-sex parent might punish them for their incestuous wishes. To reduce this conflict, the child identifies with the same-sex parent, striving to be like him or her. If the conflict is not resolved, though, the individual may become fixated at the phallic stage. Table 2.1 reveals some possible links between adolescent and adult personality characteristics and fixation, sublimation, and reaction formation involving the phallic stage, as well as the oral and anal stages.

TABLE 2.1 *Possible Links Between Adult Personality Characteristics and Fixation at Oral, Anal, and Phallic Stages*

Stage	Adult Extensions	Sublimations	Reaction Formations
Oral	Smoking, eating, kissing, oral hygiene, drinking, chewing gum	Seeking knowledge, humor, wit, sarcasm, being a food or wine expert	Speech purist, food faddist, prohibitionist, dislike of milk
Anal	Notable interest in one's bowel movements, love of bathroom humor, extreme messiness	Interest in painting or sculpture, being overly giving, great interest in statistics	Extreme disgust with feces, fear of dirt, prudishness, irritability
Phallic	Heavy reliance on masturbation, flirtatiousness, expressions of virility	Interest in poetry, love of love, interest in acting, striving for success	Puritanical attitude toward sex, excessive modesty

From *Introduction to Personality* by E. Jerry Phares. Copyright © 1984 Scott, Foresman and Company. Reprinted by permission.

In the **latency stage,** occurring between approximately 6 years of age and puberty, the child represses all interest in sexual urges, showing more interest in developing intellectual and social skills. This activity channels much of the child's energy into emotionally safe areas and aids the child in forgetting the highly stressful conflicts of the phallic stage.

The **genital stage,** which occurs from puberty on, is a time of sexual reawakening; the source of sexual pleasure now becomes someone outside of the family. Freud believed that unresolved conflicts with parents reemerge during adolescence. When resolved, the individual is capable of developing a mature love relationship and functioning independently as an adult.

Because Freud explored so many new and uncharted regions of personality and development, it is not surprising that many individuals thought his views needed to be replaced or revised. One of these individuals, whose theory has become a prominent perspective on adolescent development, was Erik Erikson.

Erikson's Theory

Like Freud, Erikson (1950, 1968) stresses the importance of early family experiences and unconscious thought. However, he believes Freud shortchanged culture's role in personality development. For example, both Freud and Erikson describe changes that take place during adolescence. For Freud, these changes are primarily sexual in nature. For Erikson, the changes involve the

Phases of the life cycle	1	2	3	4	5	6	7	8
Late adulthood								Integrity vs. despair
Middle adulthood							Generativity vs. stagnation	
Young adulthood						Intimacy vs. isolation		
Adolescence					Identity vs. identity confusion			
Middle and late childhood				Industry vs. inferiority				
Early childhood			Initiative vs. guilt					
Infancy		Autonomy vs. shame, doubt						
Infancy	Trust vs. mistrust							

Figure 2.2   Erikson's eight stages of the life cycle.

development of an identity. Erikson believes it is during adolescence that individuals begin a thorough search for who they are, what they are all about, and where they are going in life. As part of this search for an identity, the adolescent often experiments with a variety of roles—some sexual, others ideological, and yet others vocational.

Erikson says that Freud was wrong in thinking that developmental change does not occur in adulthood. And Erikson says that humans have the potential to solve their conflicts and anxieties as they develop, painting a more optimistic picture of development than Freud's pessimistic view of the id's dominance. For Erikson, the **epigenetic principle** guides our development through life's human cycle. This principle states that anything that grows has a ground plan, out of which the parts arise, each having a special time of ascendency, until all of the parts have arisen to form a functioning whole.

In Erikson's theory, eight stages of development unfold as we go through the life cycle. He called these *psychosocial stages* (in contrast to Freud's psychosexual stages). The eight stages are shown in Figure 2.2. Each stage consists of a unique developmental task that confronts the individual with a crisis that must be faced. For Erikson, the crisis is not a catastrophe but a turning point of increased vulnerability and enhanced potential. The more successful the individual resolves the crises, the healthier development will be.

Erikson's first psychosocial stage: trust vs. mistrust.

Second stage: autonomy vs. shame and doubt.

Third stage: initiative vs. guilt.

Fourth stage: industry vs. inferiority.

Fifth stage: identity vs. identity confusion.

Sixth stage: intimacy vs. isolation.

Seventh stage: generativity vs. stagnation.

Eighth stage: integrity vs. despair.

The first stage, **trust vs. mistrust,** corresponds to the oral stage in Freud's theory. An infant depends almost exclusively on parents, especially the mother, for food, sustenance, and comfort. Parents are the primary representative of society to the child. If parents discharge their infant-related duties with warmth, regularity, and affection, the infant will develop a feeling of trust toward the world, a trust that someone will always be around to care for one's needs. Alternatively, a sense of mistrust develops if parents fail to provide for the infant's needs in their role as caregivers.

The second stage, **autonomy vs. shame and doubt,** corresponds to Freud's anal stage. The infant begins to gain control over eliminative functions and motor abilities. At this point, children show a strong push for exploring their world and asserting their will. Parents who are encouraging and patient allow the child to develop a sense of autonomy, but parents who are highly restrictive and impatient promote a sense of shame and doubt.

The third stage, **initiative vs. guilt,** corresponds to Freud's phallic stage and the preschool years. The child's motor abilities continue to expand, and mental abilities also become more expansive and imaginative. Parents who allow the child to continue to explore the world's unknowns and encourage symbolic thought and fantasy play promote initiative in their child; restrictive, punitive parents promote guilt and a passive reception of whatever the environment brings.

The fourth stage, **industry vs. inferiority,** corresponds to Freud's latency stage and the elementary school years. At this time, the child becomes interested in how things work and how they are made. Achievement becomes a more salient part of the child's life. If parents and teachers make work and achievement an exciting and rewarding effort, the child develops a sense of industry; if not, the child develops a sense of inferiority.

The fifth stage, **identity vs. identity confusion,** corresponds to the adolescent years. At this time, individuals are faced with finding out who they are, what they are all about, and where they are headed in life. Adolescents are confronted with many new roles and adult situations—vocational and romantic, for example. Parents need to allow the adolescent to explore many different roles and different paths within a particular role. If the adolescent explores such roles in a healthy manner and arrives at a positive path to follow in life, then a positive identity will be achieved. If an identity is pushed on the adolescent by parents, if the adolescent does not adequately explore many roles, and if a positive future path is not defined, then identity confusion reigns.

The sixth stage, **intimacy vs. isolation,** corresponds to the early adulthood years. Early adulthood brings a stronger commitment to an occupation and the opportunity to form intimate relationships with others. Erikson described intimacy as finding oneself yet losing oneself in another. If the young adult forms healthy friendships and an intimate close relationship with another individual, intimacy will be achieved; if not, then isolation will result.

The seventh stage, **generativity vs. stagnation,** corresponds to the middle adulthood years. A chief concern of adults is to assist the younger generation

An Eskimo Girl's Search for Cultural Identity

Mary is an Eskimo girl who has just turned 13. She lives in a small Arctic village. She sympathizes with those who yearn for the old days and ways, but she wants more. She is an expert on rock music, has a stereo set, wonders when she will go to the city, dance in a dance hall. At school one day, she challenged the teacher to describe what "culture" means. The teacher began describing what the Eskimo culture is like. Mary didn't like the teacher's response. According to Mary, "she was talking like she *thought* an Eskimo talks, or like she thought that we all *should* talk. Even my grandfather doesn't talk like that. He likes the electricity the white people brought to our village; and he likes to listen to my stereo; and he likes to go on a ride in a snowmobile. He says that if he was younger he'd learn how to ride a motorcycle. . . . The teachers are white and they come here from Chicago and New York. They all say the same things to us. . . . My parents and my grandfather and my aunts and uncles keep telling me that I shouldn't speak my mind to people; instead, I should ask them what they believe and what they want, and be friendly with them. But it's hard for me to pretend I like a person if I don't really like her. . . . My grandfather says a lot of white people who come here would like to see us living in igloos. He jokes that he is going to build an igloo and go live in it, and then he will be the teacher's hero. I'm not sure he would know how to build one! (Coles, 1977).

in developing and leading useful lives—this is what Erikson meant by *generativity.* The feeling of having done nothing to help the next generation is *stagnation.*

The eighth and final stage, **integrity vs. despair,** corresponds to late adulthood. In the later years of life, we look back and evaluate what we have done with our life. Through many different routes the older individual may have developed a positive outlook in each of the previous stages of development. If so, the retrospective glances will reveal a picture of a life well spent, and the individual will feel a sense of satisfaction—integrity will be achieved. If the older adult resolved one or more of the earlier stages negatively, the retrospective glances may yield doubt or gloom—the despair Erikson talks about.

Erikson does not believe the proper solution to a stage crisis is always completely positive in nature. Some exposure or commitment to the negative end of the individual's bipolar conflict is sometimes inevitable—you cannot trust all people under all circumstances and survive, for example. Nonetheless, in the healthy solution to a stage crisis, the positive resolution dominates.

Evaluating the Psychoanalytic Theories

While psychoanalytic theories have become heterogeneous, they nonetheless share some core principles. Our development is determined not only by current experiences but by experiences from early in our life. That early experiences are important determinants of personality and that we can better understand personality by examining it developmentally are principles that have withstood the test of time. The belief that environmental experiences are mentally transformed and represented in the mind likewise continues to receive considerable attention. Psychoanalytic theorists forced psychologists to recognize that the mind is not all consciousness; our minds have an unconscious portion that influences our behavior. The emphasis of psychoanalytic theorists on the importance of conflict and anxiety requires us to consider the dark side of our existence, not just its bright side. Adjustment is not always easy, and the adolescent's inner world often conflicts with the outer demands of reality.

However, the main concepts of psychoanalytic theories have been difficult to test. Inference and interpretation are required to determine whether psychoanalytic ideas are accurate. Researchers have not successfully investigated such key concepts as repression in the laboratory. Much of the data used to support psychoanalytic theories comes from patients' reconstruction of the past, often the distant past, and is of doubtful accuracy. Other data come from clinicians' subjective evaluations of clients; in such cases it is easy for clinicians to see what they expect because of the theory they hold. Some psychologists object that Freud overemphasized sexuality and the unconscious mind. The psychoanalytic theories also provide a model of the child that is too negative and pessimistic. Children are not born into the world with only a bundle of sexual and aggressive impulses; their compliance with the demands of external reality does not always conflict with their biological needs.

Cognitive Theories

Exploring the human mind has been regarded with a mystical awe throughout most of human history. Now 10,000 years after the dawn of civilization, a new understanding of the mind is flourishing. Mind is a complex term but primarily it is our cognitive activity—perception, attention, memory, language, reasoning, thinking, and the like. Whereas psychoanalytic theories emphasize unconscious thoughts, cognitive theories emphasize conscious thoughts. The developing individual is perceived as rational and logical, capable of using the mind to effectively interact with and control the environment. The cognitive theory that has dominated the study of development is the masterpiece of Jean Piaget.

Piaget's first cognitive developmental stage: sensorimotor.

Second stage: preoperational.

Piaget's Theory

Jean Piaget was a child genius. At the age of 10, he wrote an article about a rare albino sparrow, which was published in the *Journal of the Natural History of Neuchâtel*. The article was so brilliant that the curators of the Geneva Museum of Natural History, who had no idea the article had been written by a 10-year-old, offered young Piaget a job at the museum. Piaget continued to live in Switzerland as an adult and became one of the most influential forces in child development in the twentieth century. It was said of Piaget following his death at the age of 84 in 1980 that we owe him the present field of cognitive development (Flavell, 1980). What was the theory of this giant in developmental psychology?

Piaget's theory will be covered in greater detail as we discuss cognitive development in adolescence later in the book. Here we briefly present the main ideas. Piaget (1952, 1954) stressed that the child actively constructs his own cognitive world; information is not just poured into his mind from the environment. Two processes underlie the individual's construction of the world; organization and adaptation. To make sense of our world, we organize our experiences. For example, we separate important ideas from less important ideas. We connect one idea to another. But we not only organize our observations and experiences; we *adapt* our thinking to include new ideas because additional information furthers understanding. Piaget (1954) believed that we adapt in two ways: assimilation and accommodation.

Assimilation occurs when we incorporate new information into our existing knowledge. **Accommodation** occurs when we adjust to new information. Suppose that a 16-year-old girl wants to learn how to type. Her parents buy her a typewriter for her birthday. She has never had the opportunity to use a typewriter. From experience and observation, however, she realizes that a typewriter is to be placed on a table, that it has keys to be punched, and that paper must be inserted into it. Since she realizes each of these things, she sets the typewriter on the table, inserts the paper, and begins to type—incorporating her behavior into a conceptual framework that already exists (assimilation). But as she begins to strike some of the keys, she makes several mistakes. So, she begins to type more slowly. Soon she realizes that she has to get someone to help her learn to type efficiently or take a class in typing at her high school. These adjustments show her awareness of the need to slightly alter her concept of typing (accommodation).

Piaget also believed that we go through four stages in understanding the world. Each of the stages is age-related and consists of distinct ways of thinking. It is the *different* way of understanding the world that makes one stage more advanced than another; knowing *more* information does not make the child's thinking more advanced in the Piagetian view. This is what Piaget meant when he said that the child's cognition is *qualitatively* different in one stage compared to another. Here are brief descriptions of Piaget's four stages of cognitive development.

The Nature of Adolescent Development

In the **sensorimotor stage,** which lasts from birth to about 2 years of age, the infant constructs an understanding of the world by coordinating sensory experiences (such as seeing and hearing) with physical, motoric actions—hence the term *sensorimotor.* At the beginning of this stage, the newborn has little more than reflexive patterns with which to work; at the end of the stage, the 2-year-old has complex sensorimotor patterns and is beginning to operate with primitive symbols.

In the **preoperational stage,** which lasts from approximately 2 to 7 years of age, the child begins to represent the world with words, images, and drawings; symbolic thought goes beyond simple connections of sensory information and physical action. But while preschool children can symbolically represent the world, according to Piaget, they still cannot perform **operations,** that is, mental operations that are reversible. This is why Piaget (1967) said children 2 to 7 years of age are in the preoperational stage of thought.

In the **concrete operational stage,** which lasts from approximately 7 to 11 years of age, children can use operations—they can mentally reverse the liquid from one beaker to another and understand that the volume is the same even though the beakers are different in height and width. Logical reasoning replaces intuitive thought as long as the principles can be applied to specific or *concrete* examples. Concrete operational thinkers need objects and events present to reason about them. For example, they cannot imagine the steps necessary to complete an algebraic equation, which is far too abstract at this stage of development.

In the **formal operational stage,** which appears between the ages of 11 and 15, the adolescent moves beyond the world of actual, concrete experiences and thinks in abstract and more logical terms. As part of thinking more abstractly, adolescents develop images of ideal circumstances. They may think about what an ideal parent is like and compare their parents with this ideal standard. They begin to entertain possibilities for the future and are fascinated with what they can be. In solving problems, adolescents are more systematic, developing hypotheses about why something is happening the way it is; then they may test these hypotheses in a deductive fashion.

Piaget's stages are summarized in Table 2.2. A comparison of Piaget's stages with Freud's and Erikson's stages is presented in Figure 2.3. Notice that only Erikson's theory describes changes during the adult years. And remember that Piaget's theory stresses conscious thought while the psychoanalytic theories of Freud and Erikson stress unconscious thought.

The Information Processing Approach

The **information processing approach** is concerned with how individuals process information about their world—how information enters our mind, how it is stored and transformed, and how it is retrieved to perform such complex activities as problem solving and reasoning. A simple model of cognition is

Third stage: concrete operational.

Fourth stage: formal operational.

TABLE 2.2 *Piaget's Stages of Cognitive Development*

Stage	Description	Age Range
Sensorimotor	The infant progresses from reflexive instinctual action at birth to the beginning of symbolic thought. The infant constructs an understanding of the world by coordinating sensory experiences with physical actions.	Birth to 2
Preoperational	The child begins to represent the world with words and images; these words and images reflect increased symbolic thinking and go beyond the connection of sensory information and physical action.	2 to 7
Concrete operational	The child now can reason logically about concrete events and can mentally reverse information.	7 to 11
Formal operational	The adolescent reasons in more abstract, idealistic, and logical ways.	11 to 15

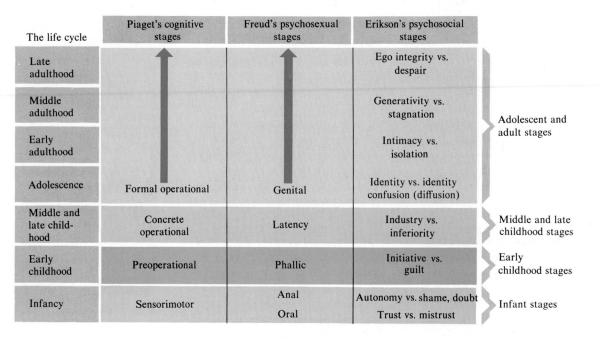

Figure 2.3   A comparison of Piaget's, Freud's, and Erikson's stages.

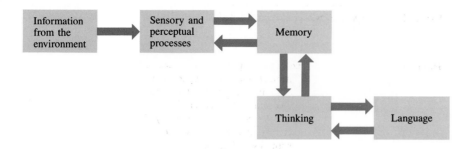

Figure 2.4   A model of cognition.

shown in Figure 2.4. Cognition begins when information from the world is detected through sensory and perceptual processes. Then information is stored, transformed, and retrieved through the processes of memory. Notice in our model that information can flow back and forth between memory and perceptual processes. For example, we are good at remembering the faces we see, yet at the same time our memory of an individual's face may be different from how the individual actually looks. Keep in mind that our information processing model is a simple one, designed to illustrate the main cognitive processes and their interrelations. We could have drawn other arrows—between memory and language, between thinking and perception, and between language and perception, for example. Also, it is important to know that the boxes in the figure do not represent sharp, distinct stages in processing information. There is continuity and flow between the cognitive processes as well as overlap.

By the 1940s, serious challenges confronted the claim of behaviorists that organisms learn primarily through environment-behavior connections. The first successful computer suggested that machines could perform logical operations. This indicated that some mental operations might be modeled by computers, and possibly computers could tell us something about how cognition works. Cognitive psychologists often use the computer to help explain the relation between cognition and the brain. The physical brain is described as the computer's hardware and cognition as its software (see Figure 2.5). The ability to process information has highlighted psychology's cognitive revolution since the 1950s.

The information processing approach raises important questions about changes in cognition across the life span. One of these questions is: Does processing speed increase as children grow older and decrease as adults grow older? The idea of speed of processing is an important aspect of the information processing approach. Many cognitive tasks are performed under real time pressure. For example, at school we have a limited amount of time to add and subtract and take tests; at work we have deadlines for completing a project. There is a good deal of evidence that processing speed is slower in younger children than in adolescents, and slower in elderly adults than in young adults. But the causes of these differences have not been determined. Although some causes might be biological in origin, they might reflect differences in knowledge about or practice on a task (Salthouse, 1988; Santrock & Bartlett, 1986).

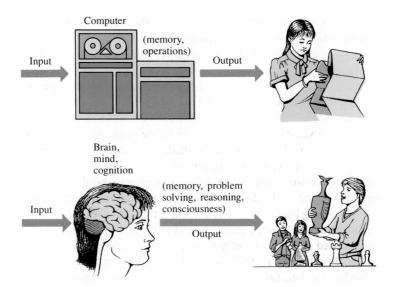

Figure 2.5   Computers and cognition: an analogy.

Evaluating the Cognitive Theories

Both Piaget's cognitive-developmental theory and the information processing approach contribute in important ways to our knowledge about life-span development. Today, researchers enthusiastically evaluate the accuracy of Piaget's theory. Through such examination, some of Piaget's ideas have remained unscathed while others are being modified (Beilin, 1989 a, b).

The information processing approach has opened up many avenues of research, offering detailed descriptions of cognitive processes and sophisticated methods for studying cognition (Klahr, 1989 a, b). The cognitive theories provide an optimistic view of human development, ascribing to children and adults the ability and motivation to know their world and to cope with it in constructive ways.

Like all theories the cognitive theories have their weaknesses. There is skepticism about the pureness of Piaget's stages and his concepts are somewhat loosely defined. The information processing approach has not yet produced an overall perspective on development. Both the Piagetian and information processing approaches may have underestimated the importance of the unconscious mind and environmental experiences, especially family experiences, in determining behavior.

Behavioral and Social Learning Theories

Tom, who is 15 years old, is going steady with Ann, who is 14. Both have warm, friendly personalities and they enjoy being with each other. Psychoanalytic theorists would say that their warm, friendly personalities derive from long-standing relationships with their parents, especially their early childhood experiences. They also would argue that the reason for their attraction to each other is unconscious; they are unaware of how their biological heritage and early life experiences have been carried forward to influence their personality in adolescence.

Psychologists from the behavioral and social learning perspective would observe Tom and Ann and see something quite different. They would examine their experiences, especially their most recent ones, to understand the reason for their attraction. For example, Tom would be described as rewarding Ann's behavior, and vice versa. No reference would be made to unconscious thoughts, the Oedipus complex, defense mechanisms, and so on.

Behaviorists believe we should examine only what can be directly observed and measured (Baer, 1989; Bijou, 1989). At approximately the same time Freud was interpreting his patients' unconscious minds through their early childhood experiences, behaviorists such as Ivan Pavlov and John B. Watson were conducting detailed observations of behavior in controlled laboratory circumstances. Out of the behavioral tradition grew the belief that development is observable behavior, learned through experience with the environment. The two versions of the behavioral approach that are prominent today are the view of B. F. Skinner and social learning theory.

B. F. Skinner, famous American psychologist who has been one of the main theorists responsible for the behavioral view.

Skinner's Behaviorism

During World War II, B. F. Skinner constructed a rather strange project—a pigeon-guided missile. A pigeon in the warhead of the missile operated the flaps on the missile and guided it home by pecking at an image of a target. How could this possibly work? When the missile was in flight, the pigeon pecked the moving image on the screen. This produced corrective signals to keep the missile on its course. The pigeons did their job well in trial runs, but top Navy officials just could not accept pigeons piloting their missiles during a war. Skinner, however, congratulated himself on the degree of control he was able to exercise over the pigeons.

Following the pigeon experiment, Skinner (1948) wrote *Walden Two,* a novel in which he presented his ideas about building a scientifically managed society. Skinner envisioned a utopian society that could be engineered through behavioral control. Skinner viewed existing societies as poorly managed because individuals believe in myths such as free will. He pointed out that humans are no more free than pigeons; denying that our behavior is controlled by environmental forces is to ignore science and reality, he argued. In the long run, Skinner said, we would be much happier when we recognized such truths, especially his concept that we could live a prosperous life under the control of positive reinforcement.

Skinner did not need the mind, conscious or unconscious, to explain development. For him, development was the individual's behavior. For example, observations of Sam reveal that his behavior is shy, achievement-oriented, and caring. Why is Sam's behavior this way? For Skinner, rewards

A Behavioral Contract for Billy

Following is a typical conversation between 17-year-old Billy and his father:

> *Father* Where have you been?
>
> *Billy* Do I have to tell you about everything I do?
>
> *Father* What do you think this place is—a motel? I pay for your clothes, your car, your food, your money for dates, and God knows what else!
>
> *Billy* Why don't you just get rid of me and kick me out, then?
>
> *Father* How could you get a job? Your grades are pitiful! And you hang around with a bunch of bums and creeps.
>
> *Billy* I suppose you're so perfect—what about last week when your buddies came over and you all got drunk! You're a great model for me!

Billy and his father were on a collision course. Eventually things grew so bad that Billy's parents decided that they needed to see a counselor to get some help with Billy.

The counselor was a behaviorist who first talked with each of the family members separately, trying to get them to pinpoint Billy's problems. At first, the father described Billy as a bum, stupid, and lazy. And initially, Billy said that his father was cold, impatient, and a middle-class

and punishments in Sam's environment have shaped him into a shy, achievement-oriented, and caring individual. Because of interactions with family members, friends, teachers, and others, Sam has *learned* to behave in this fashion.

Since behaviorists believe that development is learned and often changes according to environmental experiences, it follows that rearranging experiences can change the individual's development. For the behaviorist, shy behavior can be changed into outgoing behavior; aggressive behavior can be shaped into docile behavior; lethargic, boring behavior can be turned into enthusiastic, interesting behavior.

Skinner describes the way in which behavior is controlled in the following way. The individual *operates* on the environment to produce a change that will lead to a reward (Skinner, 1938). Skinner chose the term *operants* to describe the responses that are actively emitted because of the consequences for the individual. The consequences—rewards and punishments—are *contingent,* or depend on the individual's behavior. For example, an operant might be pressing a lever on a machine that delivers a candy bar; the delivery of the dullard. One of the first steps a behaviorist takes is to get the conflicting parties to specify in concrete, behavioral terms what such global constructs like "middle-class dullard" and "impatient" mean. For example, the behaviorist got Billy to specify some behavioral referents for the word "impatient," such as: "As soon as I walk in the door ten minutes late, he doesn't even ask questions anymore, he just yells at me and shoves me in the corner."

After lengthy discussions with the family, the therapist was able to get Billy and his parents to agree on some behaviors they would like to see changed in each other. She also was able to get them to agree to sign a **behavioral contract** that spelled out what everybody needed to do to help Billy and his father change their behavior toward each other.

Billy agreed to (1) not come in after 11:00 P.M. on weeknights and midnight on weekends; (2) look for a part-time job so he could begin supporting himself to some degree; and (3) not call his father insulting names. In return, Billy's father agreed to (1) not yell at Billy, but, if angry about something to ask Billy in a low tone of voice to explain what had happened; (2) not criticize teenagers, particularly Billy's friends; and (3) give Billy a small sum of money each week for gas and dates—but only until Billy obtained a job, at which time Billy would start paying his own expenses.

The counselor encouraged Billy and his father to agree to a point system for each of these three behavioral areas. If they failed to meet the standards they had agreed to, they lost points; if they met the standards, they gained points. The points could be transferred into money at the end of each week. Both Billy and his father agreed that Billy's mother could keep track of the number of points earned each day to assess their progress. If the system began to break down or if disputes about the system needed to be settled, the participants could discuss the problem at the weekly meeting with the counselor. The points of conflict and contingencies might change as the situation improved or worsened. The behavioral therapist would monitor the system and change the contract accordingly.

candy bar is contingent on pressing the lever. In sum, **operant conditioning** is a form of learning in which the consequences of behavior lead to changes in the probability of that behavior's occurrence.

More needs to be said about reinforcement and punishment. **Reinforcement** (or reward) is a consequence that increases the probability a behavior will occur. By contrast, **punishment** is a consequence that decreases the probability a behavior will occur. For example, if someone smiles at you and the two of you continue talking for some time, the smile has reinforced your talking. However, if someone you meet frowns at you and you quickly leave the situation, the frown has punished your talking with the individual. Information about how the consequences of the adolescent's behavior can be used to help the adolescent become better adjusted is described in Perspective on Adolescent Development 2.2.

Social Learning Theory

Some psychologists believe the behaviorists basically are right when they say development is learned and is influenced strongly by environmental experiences. But they believe Skinner went too far in declaring that cognition is

Albert Bandura

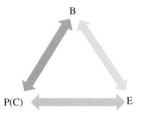

Figure 2.6 Bandura's model of the reciprocal influence of behavior, personal and cognitive factors, and environment. P(C) stands for personal and cognitive factors, B for behavior, and E for environment. The arrows reflect how relations between these factors are reciprocal rather than unidirectional. Examples of personal factors include intelligence, skills, and self-control. Albert Bandura, *Social Foundations of Thought and Action: A Social Cognitive Theory,* © 1986, P. 24. Reprinted by permission of Prentice-Hall, Inc., Englewood Cliffs, N.J.

unimportant in understanding development. **Social learning theory** is the view of psychologists who emphasize behavior, environment, *and* cognition as the key factors in development.

The social learning theorists say we are not like mindless robots, responding mechanically to others in our environment. And we are not like weathervanes, behaving like a Communist in the presence of a Communist or like a John Bircher in the presence of a John Bircher. Rather, we think, reason, imagine, plan, expect, interpret, believe, value, and compare. When others try to control us, our values and beliefs allow us to restrict their control.

Albert Bandura (1977, 1986, 1989) and Walter Mischel (1973, 1984) are the main architects of the contemporary version of social learning theory that was labeled **cognitive social learning theory** by Mischel. Bandura believes much of our learning occurs by observing what others do. Through observational learning (also called modeling or imitation) we cognitively represent the behavior of others and then possibly adopt this behavior ourselves. For example, a boy may observe his father's aggressive outbursts and hostile interchanges with people; when observed with his peers, the young boy's style of interaction is highly aggressive, showing the same characteristics as his father's behavior. Or, a young female adopts the dominant and sarcastic style of her boss. When observed interacting with one of her subordinates, the young woman says, "I need this work immediately if not sooner; you are so far behind you think you are ahead!" Social learning theorists believe we acquire a wide range of such behaviors, thoughts, and feelings through observing others' behavior; these observations form an important part of our development.

Social learning theorists also differ from Skinner's behavioral view by emphasizing that we can regulate and control our own behavior. For example, another young female executive who observed her boss behave in a dominant and sarcastic manner toward employees found the behavior distasteful and went out of her way to be encouraging and supportive toward her subordinates. Someone tries to persuade you to join a particular social club on campus and makes you an enticing offer. You reflect about the offer, consider your interests and beliefs, and make the decision not to join. Your *cognition* (your thoughts) leads you to control your behavior and resist environmental influence in this instance.

Bandura's (1986, 1989) most recent model of learning and development involves behavior, the person, and the environment. As shown in Figure 2.6, behavior, cognitive and other personal factors, and environmental influences operate interactively. Behavior can influence cognition and vice versa; the person's cognitive activities can influence the environment; environmental influences can change the person's thought processes; and so on.

Let's consider how Bandura's model might work in the case of a college student's achievement behavior. As the student diligently studies and gets good grades, her behavior produces positive thoughts about her abilities. As part of her effort to make good grades, she plans and develops a number of strategies to make her studying more efficient. In these ways her behavior has influenced her thought and her thought influenced her behavior. At the beginning of the semester, her college made a special effort to involve students in a study skills program. She decided to join. Her success, along with that of other students who attended the program, has led the college to expand the program next semester. In these ways, environment influenced behavior, and behavior changed the environment. The expectations of the college administrators that the study skills program would work made it possible in the first place. The program's success has spurred expectations that this type of program could work in other colleges. In these ways, cognition changed the environment, and the environment changed cognition. Expectations are an important variable in Bandura's model.

Like the behavioral approach of Skinner, the social learning approach emphasizes the importance of empirical research in studying development. This research focuses on the processes that explain development—the social and cognitive factors that influence what we are like as people.

Evaluating the Behavioral and Social Learning Theories

The behavioral and social learning theories emphasize that environmental experiences determine development. These approaches have fostered a scientific climate for understanding development that highlights the observation of behavior. Social learning theory emphasizes both environmental influences and cognitive processes in explaining development; this view also suggests individuals have the ability to control their environment.

Criticisms of the behavioral and social learning theories are sometimes directed at the behavioral view alone and at other times at both approaches. The behavioral view has been criticized for ignoring the importance of cognition in development and placing too much importance on environmental experiences. Both approaches have been described as being too concerned with change and situational influences on development, not paying adequate tribute to the enduring qualities of development. Both views are said to ignore the biological determinants of development. Both are labeled as reductionist, which means they look at only one or two components of development rather than at how all of the pieces fit together. And critics have charged that the behavioral and social learning theories are too mechanical. By being overly concerned with several minute pieces of development, say the detractors, the most exciting and rich dimensions of development are missed.

An Eclectic Approach to Adolescent Development

Which of these approaches—psychoanalytic, cognitive, or behavioral, social learning—is the best way to view adolescent development? There is no single indomitable theory that offers all the answers (Miller, 1989). Each theory contributes to the science of adolescent development, but no single theory provides a complete description and explanation of adolescent development. For

Theories of Adolescent Development

Concept	Processes/Related Ideas	Characteristics/Description
What are theories?	Their nature	General beliefs that help us to explain what we observe and to make predictions. A good theory has hypotheses, which are assumptions that can be tested.
Psychoanalytic theories	Freud's theory	Freud said that our personality has three structures—id, ego, and superego—which conflict with each other. Most of our thoughts are unconscious in Freud's view and the id is completely unconscious. The conflicting demands of personality structures produce anxiety; defense mechanisms, especially repression, protect the ego and reduce anxiety. Freud was convinced that problems develop because of childhood experiences. He said we go through five psychosexual stages—oral, anal, phallic, latency, and genital. During the phallic stage, the Oedipus complex is a main source of conflict.
	Erikson's theory	Erikson developed a theory that emphasizes eight psychosocial stages of development: trust vs. mistrust, autonomy vs. shame, doubt, initiative vs. guilt, industry vs. inferiority, identity vs. identity confusion, intimacy vs. isolation, generativity vs. stagnation, and integrity vs. despair.
	Evaluating the psychoanalytic theories	Strengths are an emphasis on the past, the developmental course of personality, mental representation of environment, unconscious mind, and emphasis on conflict. Weaknesses are the difficulty in testing main concepts, lack of an empirical data base and overreliance on past reports, too much emphasis on sexuality and the unconscious mind, and a negative view of human nature.
Cognitive theories	Piaget's theory	Piaget's theory is responsible for the field of cognitive development. He believes we are motivated to understand our world and use the processes of organization and adaptation (assimilation, accommodation) to do so. Piaget says we go through four cognitive stages: sensorimotor, preoperational, concrete operational, and formal operational.
	The information processing approach	Is concerned with how we process information about our world. Includes how information gets into our mind, how it is stored and transformed, and how it is retrieved to think and solve problems. The development of the computer promoted this approach—the mind as an information processing system was compared to how

these reasons, the three major approaches to adolescent development are presented in this text in an unbiased fashion. As a result, you can view the field of adolescent development as it actually exists—with different theorists drawing different conclusions about the nature of adolescent development.

There are many other theories of adolescent development we have not mentioned in this chapter. Other theories will be woven into the discussion of adolescent development in the remainder of the book. For example, in Chapter

been discarded and others revised. Theories are an integral part of understanding adolescent development. They will be weaved through our discussion of adolescent development in the remainder of the book.

Collecting Information about Adolescent Development—Methods

Systematic observations can be conducted in a number of ways. For example, we can watch adolescents' behavior in the laboratory or in a more natural setting such as a school, a home, or the neighborhood. We can question adolescents using interviews and surveys, develop and administer standardized tests, conduct case studies, or carry out physiological research. To help you understand how developmentalists use these methods, we will continue our theme of drawing examples from the study of adolescent aggression.

Observation

Sherlock Holmes chided Watson, "You see but you do not observe." We look at things all the time, but casually watching adolescents interacting with their parents is not scientific observation. Unless you are a trained observer and practice your skills regularly, you may not know what to look for, you may not remember what you saw, what you are looking for may change from one moment to the next, and you may not communicate your observations effectively.

For observations to be effective, we have to know what we are looking for, whom we are observing, when and where we will observe, how the observations will be made, and in what form they will be recorded. That is, our observations have to be made in some *systematic* way. Consider aggression. Do we want to study verbal or physical aggression, or both? Do we want to study younger adolescents or older adolescents, or both? Do we want to evaluate them in a university laboratory, at school, at home, in the neighborhood, or at all of these locations? A common way to record our observations is to write them down, using shorthand or symbols. However, tape recorders, video cameras, special coding sheets, and one-way mirrors are used increasingly to make observations more efficient.

When we observe, frequently it is necessary to *control* certain factors that determine adolescent behavior but are not the focus of our inquiry. For this reason some researchers like to observe adolescent behavior in a **laboratory,** that is, a controlled setting in which many of the complex factors of the "real world" are removed. For example, Albert Bandura (1965) brought children into the laboratory and had them observe an adult repeatedly hit a plastic, inflated Bobo doll about three feet tall. Bandura wondered to what extent the children would imitate the adult's aggressive behavior. The children's imitation of the adult model's aggression was pervasive.

Conducting laboratory research, though, has some disadvantages. First, it is virtually impossible to conduct without the participants knowing that they are being studied. Second, the laboratory setting may be *unnatural* and therefore cause *unnatural* behavior. Individuals usually show less aggressive behavior in the laboratory than in a more familiar setting, such as in a park or at home. They also show less aggression when they are aware that they are being observed. Third, some aspects of adolescents' lives are difficult if not impossible to reproduce in the laboratory. Certain types of stress are difficult (and unethical) to investigate in the laboratory—for example, recreating the circumstances that stimulate marital conflict or a parent yelling at an adolescent. In **naturalistic observation,** then, developmentalists observe behavior in real-world settings and make no effort to manipulate or control the situation. Naturalistic observations have been conducted at hospitals, schools, parks, homes, malls, dances, and other contexts (e.g., Bronfenbrenner, 1989; Cairns & Cairns, in press; Csikszentmihalyi & Larson, 1984; Montemayor & Flannery, 1989; Savin-Williams, 1987).

Interviews and Questionnaires

Sometimes the best and quickest way to get information from adolescents is to ask them for it. Psychologists use interviews and questionnaires to find out about the experiences and attitudes of adolescents. Most **interviews** are conducted face to face, although they may take place over the telephone. An experienced interviewer knows how to put adolescents at ease and get them to open up. A competent interviewer is sensitive to the way adolescents respond to questions and often probes for more information.

Interviews are not without their problems. Perhaps the most critical of these problems is the response set of "social desirability," in which adolescents or adults tell the interviewer what they think is socially desirable rather than what they truly think or feel. When asked about conflict in their families, adolescents and their parents may not want to disclose that arguments have been frequent in recent months. Skilled interviewing techniques and questions to eliminate such defenses are critical in obtaining accurate information.

Psychologists also question adolescents and adults using questionnaires or surveys. A **questionnaire** is similar to a highly structured interview except that adolescents read the question and mark their answer on the paper rather than verbally responding to the interviewer. One major advantage of questionnaires is that they can be given to large numbers of individuals easily. Questions on surveys should be concrete, specific, and unambiguous, and an assessment of the authenticity of the replies should be made (Agnew & Pyke, 1987; Sax, 1989).

Case Studies

A **case study** is an in-depth look at an individual. Case studies are used when the unique aspects of an individual's life cannot be duplicated, either for practical or ethical reasons, yet they have implications for understanding development. A case study provides information about an individual's hopes, fears, fantasies, traumatic experiences, family relationships, health, or anything that will help the psychologist understand the adolescent's development. One case study involves a 16-year-old who had damage to the right side of the brain that left him with an inability to express himself emotionally. Another case study involves Genie, a child who was raised almost in complete isolation from

The Nature of Adolescent Development

the age of 20 months to the age of 13. Genie is proof of human resilience in learning language, although she never learned to ask questions and did not understand much grammar (Curtiss, 1978).

Standardized Tests

Standardized tests require that the adolescent answer a series of written or oral questions. Two distinctive features of standardized tests are (1) that the adolescent's answers usually are tallied to yield a single score, or a set of scores, that reflects something about the adolescent, and (2) that the adolescent's score is compared to the scores of a large group of similar adolescents to determine how the adolescent responded *relative* to others. Scores often are described in percentiles. For example, perhaps an adolescent scored in the 92nd percentile of the Stanford-Binet Intelligence Test. This method informs us how much lower or higher the adolescent scored than the large group of adolescents who had taken the test previously.

To continue our look at how different measures are used to evaluate aggression, consider the Minnesota Multiphasic Personality Inventory (called the MMPI), which includes a scale to assess delinquency or antisocial tendencies. The items on this scale ask adolescents to respond whether they are rebellious, impulsive, and have trouble with authority figures. This part of the MMPI might be given to adolescents to determine their delinquent and antisocial tendencies.

Physiological Research

Psychologists also can use physiological methods to obtain information about adolescent development. Increased research into the biological basis of adolescent development has produced some intriguing insights. For example, researchers recently discovered that higher concentrations of some hormones are associated with aggressive behavior in male adolescents. More about this research appears in Chapter 3 (Inoff-Germain & others, 1988; Susman & others, 1987).

Multimeasure, Multisource, Multicontext Approach

Methods have their strengths and weaknesses. Direct observations are extremely valuable tools for obtaining information about adolescents. But there are some things we cannot observe in adolescents—their moral thoughts, their inner feelings, the arguments of their parents, how they acquire information about sex, and so on. In such instances, other measures such as interviews, questionnaires, and case studies may be valuable. Because every method has limitations, many investigators have increasingly turned to the use of multiple measures in assessing adolescent development. For example, a researcher might ask adolescents about their aggressive or delinquent behavior, check with their friends, observe them carefully at home and in the neighborhood, interview their parents, and ask teachers about the adolescents. Researchers hope that the convergence of multimeasure, multisource, and multicontext information provides a more comprehensive and valid assessment of adolescent development.

Figure 2.7   Examining the correlation between permissive parenting and adolescent self-control. This figure illustrates that an observed correlation between two events cannot be used to conclude that one event causes a second event. It could also be that the second event causes the first, or that a third event causes the correlation between the first two events.

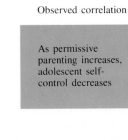

Observed correlation

As permissive parenting increases, adolescent self-control decreases

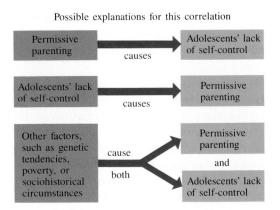

Possible explanations for this correlation

Permissive parenting → *causes* → Adolescents' lack of self-control

Adolescents' lack of self-control → *causes* → Permissive parenting

Other factors, such as genetic tendencies, poverty, or sociohistorical circumstances → *cause both* → Permissive parenting *and* Adolescents' lack of self-control

Strategies for Setting Up Research Studies

How can we determine if early maturation is related to an adolescent's self-image? How can we determine if lack of parental supervision in the after-school hours is associated with increased peer influence? How can we determine if listening to rock music lowers an adolescent's grades in school? When designing a research study to answer such questions, the investigator must decide whether to use a correlational or an experimental strategy.

Correlational Strategy

One goal of adolescent development research is to describe how strongly two or more events or characteristics are related. When a researcher has this goal, a **correlational strategy** is used. This is a beneficial strategy because the more strongly two events are correlated (related, associated), the more we can predict one from the other. For example, if we find that as parents use more permissive ways to deal with their adolescents the adolescents' self-control decreases, it does not mean that the parent style caused the lack of self-control. It could mean that, but it also could mean that the adolescents' lack of self-control stimulated parents to simply throw up their arms in despair and give up trying to control the obstreperous adolescents' behavior. And it also could mean that other factors might be causing this correlation, such as genetic background, poverty, and sociohistorical conditioning. (A few decades ago a permissive parenting strategy was widely advocated, but today it is no longer in vogue.) Figure 2.7 portrays these possible interpretations of correlational data.

Researchers often use a **correlation coefficient** to describe the degree of association between two variables. The correlation coefficient ranges from −1.00 to +1.00. A negative number means an inverse relation. For example, today we often do find a *negative* correlation between permissive parenting and adolescent self-control. And we often find a *positive* correlation between a parent's involvement and monitoring of an adolescent's life and the adolescent's self-control. The higher the correlation coefficient (whether positive or negative), the stronger the association between the two variables. A correlation of −.40 is a stronger correlation than +.20 because we disregard the positive or negative nature of the correlation in determining the correlation's magnitude.

Experimental Strategy

The **experimental strategy** allows us to determine the causes of behavior precisely. The psychologist accomplishes this task by performing an **experiment,** which is a carefully regulated setting in which one or more of the factors believed to influence the behavior being studied is manipulated and all others are held constant. If the behavior under study changes when a factor is manipulated, we say that the manipulated factor causes the behavior to change. Experiments are used to establish cause and effect between events, something correlational studies cannot do. *Cause* is the event being manipulated and *effect* is the behavior that changes because of the manipulation. Remember that in testing correlation, nothing is manipulated; in an experiment, the researcher actively changes an event to see the effect on behavior.

The following example illustrates the nature of an experiment. The problem to be studied is whether a course in time management affects adolescent grades in school. We decide that to conduct the experiment we need one group of adolescents who will take the course in time management and one that will not. We randomly assign the adolescents to these two groups. *Random assignment* greatly reduces the probability that the two groups will differ on such factors as intelligence, social class, alertness, health problems, and so on.

The subjects who take the time management course are called the **experimental group,** that is, the group whose experience is manipulated. The subjects who do not take the time management course are the **control group,** that is, a comparison group treated in every way like the experimental group except for the manipulated factor. The control group serves as a baseline against which the effects found in the manipulated condition can be compared.

After the adolescents in the experimental group have taken the time management course, the grades of the two groups are compared. When we analyze the results, we discover that the experimental group adolescents made higher grades. We conclude that the time management course increased the grades of its participants.

In an experiment, the manipulated, or influential, factor is called the **independent variable.** The label *independent* is used because this variable can be changed independently of other factors. In the time management study, the time management course was the independent variable. The experimenter manipulated the nature of the course (content, length, instructor, and so on) independently of all other factors. In an experiment, the research determines what effect the independent variable has on the **dependent variable.** The label *dependent* is used because this variable depends on what happens to the subjects in the experiment. In the time management study, the dependent variable was the adolescents' grades in school. The adolescents' grades depended on

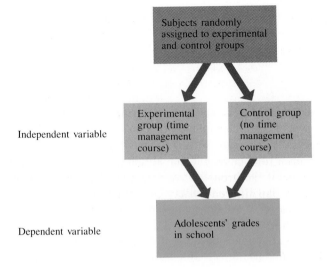

Figure 2.8   Principles of the experimental strategy applied to the effects of time management instruction on adolescents' grades in school.

the influence of the independent variable (whether or not a time management course was taken). An illustration of the nature of the experimental strategy, applied to the time management study, appears in Figure 2.8.

It might seem as if we should always choose an experimental strategy over a correlational strategy, since the experimental strategy gives us a better sense of one variable's influence over another. Yet there are three instances when a correlational strategy might be preferred: (1) when the focus of the investigation is so new that we have little knowledge of which factors to manipulate (e.g., factors associated with AIDS); (2) when it is physically impossible to manipulate the variables (e.g., suicide); and (3) when it is unethical to manipulate the variables (for example, determining the link between parenting strategies and adolescent competence).

Time Span of Inquiry

A special concern of developmentalists is the time span of a research investigation. Studies that focus on the relation of age to some other variable are common in the field of adolescent development. We have several options: we can study different children and adolescents of different ages and compare them; we can study the same children and adolescents as they grow older over time; or we can use some combination of these approaches. We consider each of these in turn.

Cross-Sectional Approach

In the **cross-sectional approach,** children and adolescents are compared all at one time. In a typical study of adolescent memory, learning, or peer group interaction, we might test a group of 8-year-olds, a group of 12-year-olds, and a group of 16-year-olds with some procedure designed to elicit information about each of these topics. Notice that the children and adolescents tested are of different ages, were born at different times, may have experienced different types of parenting and schooling, and been influenced by different trends and fads in dress, television, and learning materials.

A cross-sectional design is valuable because it can be conducted in a relatively short period of time. This enables us to get an answer to an important question quickly. Most research in adolescent development is cross sectional in nature. However, you may already have anticipated some problems with cross-sectional research. One problem is that since different groups of children and adolescents are tested, it is not "logical" to talk about how "individual" children and adolescents have changed over time. We can only draw inferences about how the groups of children and adolescents differed. A second problem is that group differences may have many sources, only some of which are due to normative features of their development over the age periods in question. For example, the different parenting and school practices in effect when each group of individuals was very young could explain some of the differences. Such differences, linked to when the children were born and grew up, are commonly called **cohort effects,** that is, those effects due to an individual's time of birth or generation but not to age.

Longitudinal Approach

The second option is to examine the same group of children or adolescents over some extended period of time. This option is called the **longitudinal approach.** In a typical longitudinal study of the same topics discussed earlier under the cross-sectional approach, we might structure a test that we administer to children and adolescents when they are 8, 12, or 16 years old. In this example the same children would be studied over an 8-year time span, allowing us to examine patterns of change within each individual child or adolescent. One of the great values of the longitudinal approach is its evaluation of how individual children and adolescents change as they grow up.

Fewer longitudinal than cross-sectional studies are conducted because they are so time consuming and costly. A close examination of the longitudinal approach reveals some additional problems. (1) Since children or adolescents are examined over a long period of time, some of them drop out because they lose interest or move away and cannot be recontacted by the investigator. A fairly common finding is that the remaining adolescents represent a slightly biased sample, in that they tend to be psychologically better or superior to those who have dropped out on almost every dimension the investigator thinks to check out (e.g., intelligence, motivation, and cooperativeness). (2) With repeated testing, individual adolescents may become "testwise," which may increase their ability to perform "better" or "more maturely" the next time the investigator interacts with them. (3) Finally, although cohort effects may not be obvious in a longitudinal approach, they may exist. A group of adolescents born at a particular time may look like they are changing and developing as a result of general maturation. But in fact, some of the change may be due to special experiences the adolescents encountered that were not encountered by adolescents a decade earlier. For example, consider the rather rapid introduction of microcomputers into the lives of children and adolescents during the 1980s. The computer vocabulary and skill development of children and adolescents growing up in the 1970s was virtually nonexistent. By comparison, the skills of children and adolescents growing up in the 1990s makes them look like budding Albert Einsteins with computers (Santrock & Yussen, 1989).

Sequential Approach

Developmentalists also combine the cross-sectional and longitudinal approaches in their effort to learn more about adolescent development. The combined cross-sectional, longitudinal design is called the **sequential approach.** In most instances, this approach starts off with a cross-sectional study that includes children and adolescents of different ages. A number of months or years after the initial assessment, the same children and adolescents are tested again—this is the longitudinal aspect of the design. At this later time, a new group of children and adolescents is assessed at each age level. The new groups at each level are added at a later time to control for changes that might have taken place in the original group of children and adolescents. For example, some may drop out of the study or retesting might improve their performance. The sequential approach is complex, time consuming, and expensive, but it does provide information that is not possible to obtain from the cross-sectional or longitudinal approaches alone. The sequential approach has been especially beneficial in calling attention to cohort effects in development (Baltes, 1973; Kertzer & Schaie, 1989; Nesselroade & Baltes, 1984; Schaie, 1977).

At this point we have covered many ideas about the science base of adolescent development. The main points of our discussion of methods are listed in Concept Table 2.2.

Ethics in Research on Adolescent Development

When Pete and Ann, two 19-year-old college students, agreed to participate in an investigation of dating couples, they did not consider that the questionnaire they filled out would get them to think about issues that might lead to conflict in their relationship and possibly end it. One year after this investigation (Rubin & Mitchell, 1976), nine of the ten participants said that they had discussed their answers with their dating partner. In most instances the discussions strengthened their relationship. But in some cases, the participants used the questionnaire as a springboard to discuss problems or concerns previously hidden. One participant said, "The study definitely played a role in ending my relationship with Larry." In this circumstance, the couple had different views about how long they expected to be together. She anticipated that the relationship would end much sooner than Larry thought. Discussion of their answers to the questions brought the long-term prospects of the relationship out in the open, and eventually Larry found someone who was more interested in marrying him.

Methods

Concept	Processes/Related Ideas	Characteristics/Description
Scientific method	Its Steps	A series of procedures to obtain accurate information. Its steps involve identifying and analyzing a problem, collecting data, drawing conclusions, and revising theory.
Ways of collecting information—measures	Observation	A key ingredient in adolescent development research that includes laboratory and naturalistic observation.
	Interviews and questionnaires	Used to assess perceptions and attitudes. Social desirability is a special problem with their use.
	Case studies	Provides an in-depth look at an individual. Caution in generalizing is warranted.
	Standardized tests	Designed to assess an individual's characteristics relative to those of a large group of similar individuals.
	Physiological research	Focus is on the biological dimensions of the adolescent.
	Multimeasure, multisource, multicontext approach	Researchers increasingly are studying adolescents using different measures, obtaining information from different sources, and observing children in different contexts.
Strategies for setting up research studies	Correlational strategy	Describes how strongly two or more events or characteristics are related. It does not allow causal statements.
	Experimental strategy	Involves manipulation of influential factors, the independent variables, and measurement of their effect on the dependent variables. Subjects are randomly assigned to experimental and control groups in many studies. The experimental strategy can reveal the causes of behavior and tell us how one event influenced another.
Time span of inquiry	Cross-sectional approach	Individuals of different ages are compared all at one time.
	Longitudinal approach	The same individuals are studied over a period of time, usually several years or more.
	Sequential approach	A combined cross-sectional, longitudinal approach that evaluates cohort effects in development.

At first glance, you would think that a questionnaire on dating relationships would have any substantial impact on the participants' behavior. But psychologists increasingly recognize that considerable caution must be taken to ensure the well-being of the participants in a psychological study. Today colleges and universities have review boards that evaluate the ethical nature of research conducted at their institutions. Proposed research plans must pass the scrutiny of an ethics research committee before the research can be initiated. In addition, the American Psychological Association (APA) has developed guidelines for the ethics of its members.

The code of ethics adopted by APA instructs researchers to protect their subjects from mental and physical harm. The best interests of the subjects need to be kept foremost in the researcher's mind. All subjects, if they are old enough, must give their informed consent to participate in the research study. This requires that subjects know what their participation will entail and any risks that might develop. For example, subjects in an investigation of the effects of divorce on adolescent development should be told beforehand that interview questions might stimulate thought about issues they might not anticipate. The subjects should also be informed that in some instances a discussion of the family's experiences might improve family relationships, while in other instances it might bring up issues that bring the adolescent unwanted stress.

Summary

I. What Are Theories?

Theories are general beliefs that help us to explain what we observe and to make predictions. A good theory has hypotheses, which are assumptions that can be tested.

II. Psychoanalytic Theories

Freud's and Erikson's theories are two main psychoanalytic theories of adolescent development. Freud said that our personality has three structures—id, ego, and superego—that conflict with each other. Most of our thoughts are unconscious in Freud's view and the id is completely unconscious. The conflicting demands of personality structures produce anxiety; defense mechanisms, especially repression, protect the ego and reduce anxiety. Freud was convinced that problems develop because of childhood experiences. He said we go through five psychosexual stages—oral, anal, phallic, latency, and genital. During the phallic stage, the Oedipus complex is a main source of conflict. Erikson developed a theory that emphasizes eight psychosocial stages of development: trust vs. mistrust, autonomy vs. shame, doubt, initiative vs. guilt, industry vs. inferiority, identity vs. identity confusion, intimacy vs. isolation, generativity vs. stagnation, and integrity vs. despair.

III. Evaluating the Psychoanalytic Theories

Strengths are an emphasis on the past, the developmental course of personality, mental representation of the environment, unconscious mind, and emphasis on conflict. Weaknesses are the difficulty in testing main concepts, lack of an empirical data base and overreliance on past reports, too much emphasis on sexuality and the unconscious mind, and a negative view of human nature.

IV. Cognitive Theories

Piaget's cognitive developmental theory and the information processing view are the two main cognitive theories. Piaget's theory is responsible for the field of cognitive development. He believes we are motivated to understand our world and use the processes of organization and adaptation (assimilation and accommodation) to do so. Piaget says that we go through four cognitive stages: sensorimotor, preoperational, concrete operational, and formal operational. The information processing approach is concerned with how we process information about our world. It focuses on how information gets into our mind, how it is stored and transformed, and how it is retrieved to think and solve problems. The development of the computer promoted this approach—the mind as an information processing system is compared to how a computer processes information. The information processing approach raises questions about development, among them the rise and decline of the speed of processing information.

V. **Evaluating the Cognitive Theories**

Both the Piagetian and the information processing approaches have made important contributions to understanding adolescent development. They have provided a positive, rational portrayal of adolescents as they develop, although they may underestimate the power of unconscious thought and environmental experiences. The purity of Piaget's stages has been questioned and the information processing approach has not yet produced an overall perspective on development.

VI. **Behavioral and Social Learning Theories**

The two main approaches in this theoretical orientation are Skinner's behaviorism and social learning theory. Skinner's behaviorism emphasizes that cognition is not important in understanding development. In Skinner's view, development is observed behavior, which is determined by the rewards and punishments in the environment. In social learning theory, the environment is an important determinant of behavior, but so are cognitive processes. We have the capability of controlling our own behavior through thoughts, beliefs, and values. Bandura's emphasis on observational learning exemplifies the social learning approach, as does his model of the reciprocal influences of behavior, person (cognitive), and environment. The contemporary version of social learning theory is called cognitive social learning theory.

VII. **An Eclectic Approach to Adolescent Development**

Each of the theories described has a number of strengths and weaknesses, but no single theory is capable of explaining the complexity of adolescent development. For this reason, an eclectic approach to adolescent development is followed in this book.

VIII. **Evaluating the Behavioral and Social Learning Theories**

The strengths of both theories include emphases on environmental determinants and a scientific climate for investigating development, as well as a focus on cognitive processes and self-control in social learning theory. The behavioral view has been criticized for taking the person out of development and for ignoring cognition. These approaches have not given adequate attention to biological processes and to development as a whole.

IX. **Scientific Method**

The scientific method is a series of procedures to obtain accurate information. Its steps involve identifying and analyzing a problem, collecting data, drawing conclusions, and revising theory.

X. **Ways of Collecting Information—Measures**

Observation, interviews and questionnaires, case studies, standardized tests, and physiological research are the main ways developmentalists collect information. Observation is a key ingredient in adolescent development research. It includes laboratory and naturalistic observation. Interviews and questionnaires are used to assess perceptions and attitudes. A special problem with their use is respondents telling interviewers what they think is socially desirable rather than what they really think. Case studies provide an in-depth look at an individual. Caution in generalizing is warranted. Standardized tests are designed to assess an individual's characteristics relative to those of a large group of similar individuals. In physiological research the focus is on the biological dimensions of the adolescent. Researchers increasingly are studying adolescents using different measures, obtaining information from different sources, and observing adolescents in different contexts.

XI. Strategies for Setting Up Studies

The two main strategies are correlational and experimental. The correlational strategy describes how strongly two or more events or characteristics are related. It does not allow causal statements. The experimental strategy involves manipulation of influential factors, the independent variables, and measurement of their effect on the dependent variables. Subjects are randomly assigned to experimental and control groups in many studies. The experimental strategy can reveal the causes of behavior and tell us how one event influenced another.

XII. Time Span of Inquiry

The three time spans are cross-sectional, longitudinal, and sequential. In the cross-sectional approach, individuals of different ages are compared all at one time. In the longitudinal approach, the same individuals are studied over a period of time, usually several years or more. The sequential approach is a combined cross-sectional, longitudinal approach that evaluates cohort effects in development.

Key Terms

theories 44
hypotheses 44
id 45
pleasure principle 45
ego 45
reality principle 45
superego 46
defense mechanisms 46
repression 46
sublimation 47
reaction formation 47
regression 47
erogenous zones 47
fixation 47
oral stage 48
anal stage 48
phallic stage 49

Oedipus complex 49
latency stage 52
genital stage 52
epigenetic principle 53
trust versus mistrust 55
autonomy versus shame
    and doubt 55
initiative versus guilt 55
industry versus
    inferiority 55
identity versus identity
    confusion 55
intimacy versus isolation
    55
generativity versus
    stagnation 55

integrity versus despair
    56
assimilation 58
accommodation 58
sensorimotor stage 59
preoperational stage 59
operations 59
concrete operational
    stage 59
formal operational stage
    59
information processing
    approach 59
operant conditioning 65
reinforcement 65
punishment 65

The Nature of Adolescent Development

Suggested Readings

Achenbach, T. (1978). *Research in developmental psychology: Concepts, strategies, and methods*. New York: Free Press.
    A well-written introduction to research in developmental psychology with examples of different strategies and designs.
Adelson, J., & Doehrman, M. J. (1980). The psychodynamic approach to adolescence. In J. Adelson (Ed.), *Handbook of adolescent psychology*. New York: Wiley.
    An up-to-date, authoritative overview of contemporary psychoanalytic views, including those of Blos and Anna Freud.
Cowan, P. A. (1978). *Piaget with feeling: Cognitive, social, and emotional dimensions*. New York: Holt, Rinehart, & Winston.
    Cowan's book is an excellent interpretation of Piaget, particularly in discussing the relevance of Piaget's ideas about adolescence to the social dimensions of the adolescent's world.
Erikson, Erik. (1968). *Identity: Youth and crisis*. New York: Norton.
    This is Erikson's most detailed work on adolescents. Exciting reading, with many insights into the lives of individual adolescents that apply to the lives of all adolescents.
Miller, P. H. (1989). Developmental theories of adolescence. In J. Worrell & F. Danner (Eds.), *The adolescent as decision maker*. New York: Academic Press.
Muuss, R. E. (1989). *Theories of adolescence* (5th ed.). New York: Random House.
    This book provides a broad overview of theories of adolescence, including those discussed in this chapter, a number of European theories, as well as others.
Patterson, G. R. (1982). *Coercive family processes*. Eugene, OR: Castalia Press.
    Patterson, a leading social learning theorist, describes in fine-grained manner the nature of family interaction and how it can become destructive in childhood and adolescence.
Vasta, R. (Ed.) (1989). *Six theories of child development: Revised formulations and current issues*. Greenwich, CT: JAI Press. *A very recent overview of major developmental theories by leading experts, including Bandura.*

Biological and Cognitive Processes

and Development

B arbara Henson is 10 years old and is in the fifth grade at a suburban elementary school. She is 4 feet, 6 inches tall and weighs 75 pounds. Her mother has to prod her to take care of her appearance at times—she doesn't keep her hair clean and sometimes goes two days without washing her face. Barbara often spends her after-school hours playing with several girl friends in her neighborhood. In cognitive terms, she interprets her world in a very concrete manner—her use of imagery has become an effective memory tool, and her attention to tasks has improved in recent years, but she still seems to need objects and events to be present to think and reason about them. Her thought is characterized by what she is experiencing and what is happening to her.

When we look at Barbara at the age of 12 we find that some remarkable changes have gradually taken place over the last two years. She is now a seventh grader and has undergone a growth and weight spurt—she presently is 5 feet, 3 inches tall and weighs 110 pounds. She looks at her mother at eye level now, rather than having to look up at her. Within the last six months, Barbara has shown much more concern about her physical appearance. She has started to wash her face daily and washes and brushes her hair frequently. Two months

ago, Rodney, a boy in her class at school, called and asked her to go to a school party with him. Barbara not only spends more time thinking about Rodney than she would have at age 10, but finds that boys are gradually starting to take over more and more of her thoughts and play a more important part in her life. Barbara had her first period six months ago, but since then she has experienced it only twice. She recently has started to spend more time in front of the mirror, looking at her body, checking over every inch of it. She has also started to worry more about how others perceive her body— sometimes she feels embarrassed about it, and at other times she feels proud that she is "developing." In the cognitive area, Barbara has just started to engage in more abstract speculation—her thoughts about what other people are thinking about her are a part of this changing cognitive orientation. She has also begun to reason more about things, people, and events that are not immediately present.

At the age of 15, Barbara is in the 10th grade, in her first year at the senior high school in her town. She has grown only one inch since she was 12, and she has been able to keep her weight at 110 pounds. She and her friend Ashley jog two to three miles several times a week. When they go jogging, Barbara likes to take her St. Bernard dog along—her parents say she does it to get attention from boys, but Barbara swears it's to keep the dog in shape. Barbara spends a lot of time now on her appearance. Her mother says that if she spent as much time studying as brushing her hair she would be making straight A's. Barbara's figure is more shapely now than when she was twelve, and she takes a great deal of pride in keeping her body toned up. Her period is occurring on a more regular basis now. Her interest in boys remains strong and she enjoys the admiring stares she gets from some of them when she walks down the hall at her school, although she could do without the "sleazy" comments some make. She has finished first-year algebra, and her problem-solving ability has become more organized—she used to just go ahead and solve a problem without thinking about alternative strategies.

At the age of 18, Barbara has just graduated from high school and is getting ready for her first year of college. She hasn't grown any since she was 15. Her weight has given her problems on a couple of occasions, but she recently has gotten back into her running schedule and is down to 115 pounds. For a while her body image wasn't very good, but she is starting to feel better about herself again. The biological and hormonal changes in her body during the last four to five years have not been nearly as great as they were during her junior high school years. And, while she still shows a concern about her body and her appearance, the concern doesn't preoccupy her thoughts quite as much as during early adolescence. Something Barbara has noticed is that at certain times of the month she seems to be more moody than at others—often the moodiness increases several days before her period occurs. Nonetheless, her menstrual cycle has become an accepted part of her existence, and most of the time it does not involve much pain or bother for Barbara.

Cognitively, Barbara sometimes engages in more abstract speculation about herself, others, and the world than when she was 15. Her thoughts are also even more organized than when she was 15— she manages her time better, thinks through problems in more detailed ways, and doesn't jump to conclusions as quickly as she did earlier in her adolescence. Her vocabulary has increased, and her more sophisticated reasoning skills have now taken her to the point where she can often come up with solutions that are just as intelligent or more intelligent than those of her parents, something that she has learned to moderate somewhat so she won't make her parents feel too bad.

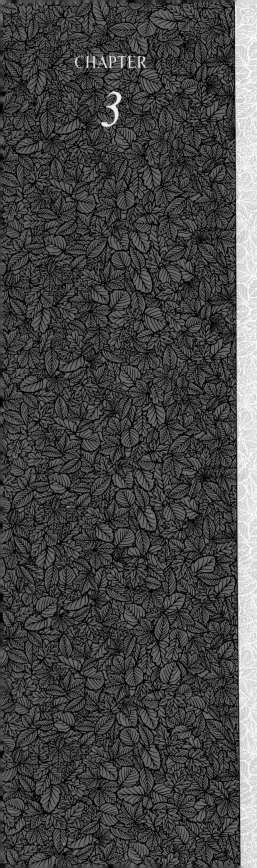

Biological Processes and Physical Development

I think that what is happening to me is so wonderful and not only what can be seen on my body, but all that is taking place inside. I never discuss myself with anybody; that is why I have to talk to myself about them.

Anne Frank, Diary of a Young Girl, 1947

Puberty's Mysteries and Curiosities

I am pretty confused. I wonder whether I am weird or normal. My body is starting to change but I sure don't look like a lot of my friends. I still look like a kid for the most part. My best friend is only 13 but he looks like he is 16 or 17. I get nervous in the locker room during PE class because when I go to take a shower I'm afraid somebody is going to make fun of me since I'm not as physically developed as some of the others.

Robert, age 12

I don't like my breasts. They are too small and they look funny. I'm afraid guys won't like me if they don't get bigger.

Angie, age 13

I can't stand the way I look. I have zits all over my face. My hair is dull and stringy. It never stays in place. My nose is too big. My lips are too small. My legs are too short. I have four warts on my left hand and people get grossed out by them. So do I. My body is a disaster!

Ann, age 14

I'm short and I can't stand it. My father is six feet tall and here I am only five foot four. I'm 14 already. I look like a kid and I get teased a lot, especially by other guys. I'm always the last one picked for sides in basketball because I'm so short. Girls don't seem to be interested in me either because most of them are taller than I am.

Jim, age 14

The comments of these four adolescents in the midst of pubertal change underscore the dramatic upheaval in our bodies following the calm, consistent growth of middle and late childhood. Young adolescents develop an acute concern about their bodies. Columnist Bob Greene (1988) recently dialed a party line called Connections in Chicago to discover what young adolescents were saying to each other. The first thing the boys and girls asked—after first names—was physical descriptions. The idealism of the callers was apparent. Most of the girls described themselves as having long blonde hair, being 5 feet, 5 inches tall, and weighing about 110 pounds. Most of the boys described themselves as having brown hair, said they lifted weights, were 6 feet tall, and weighed 170 pounds.

*P*uberty's changes are perplexing to adolescents as they go through them. But while these changes bring forth doubts, questions, fears, and anxieties, most of us survive them quite well. Our journey through puberty's fascinating moments explores its nature and its psychological dimensions. But first we evaluate the contributions of heredity to adolescent development.

Genetic Influences on Adolescent Development

When we observe and talk with adolescents, it is easy to forget that genetic influences are still important some 10–20 years after conception. No matter what the species, there must be some mechanism for transmitting characteristics from one generation to the next. Each adolescent carries a genetic code inherited from his or her parents. The genetic codes of all adolescents are alike in one important way—they all contain the human genetic code. Because of the human genetic code, a fertilized human egg cannot grow into an eel, an egret, or an elephant.

The Nature of Genes

We each began life as a single cell weighing 1/20 millionth of an ounce! This tiny piece of matter housed our entire genetic code—the information about whom we would become. These instructions orchestrated growth from that single cell to an adolescent made of trillions of cells, each containing a perfect replica of the original genetic code. Physically the hereditary code is carried by biochemical agents called genes and chromosomes. Aside from the obvious physical similarity this code produces among adolescents (e.g., in anatomy, in brain structure, and in organs), it also accounts for much of the psychological sameness (or universality) among us.

The special arrangement of chromosomes and genes each adolescent has inherited makes her or him unique. This arrangement or configuration is called the individual's **genotype.** On the other hand, all the observed and measurable characteristics of the adolescent are called the individual's **phenotype.** Phenotypical characteristics may be physical, as in height, weight, eye color, and skin pigment; or they may be psychological, as in intelligence, creativity, identity, and moral character.

Identical phenotypical characteristics may be produced by different genotypes. For example, three unrelated adolescents may each have a measured IQ of 110 but have vastly different genes for intelligence. In such a case, the adolescents have different genetic makeups but the same IQ. The opposite is also possible. Differences in phenotypical characteristics may be produced by the same genotype. For example, identical twins with different IQs are a not uncommon finding. Thus, different IQs may be produced by identical genetic makeups.

What is the relation between genotype and phenotype? That is, to what extent does heredity determine what each individual becomes in life? Hardly any characteristics of the adolescent are solely the result of a particular genetic code. Virtually all of the adolescent's psychological characteristics are the result of the interaction between the adolescent's inherited code and environmental influences. So when someone asks you whether you believe some trait of an adolescent (e.g., aggressiveness, shyness, activity level, intelligence, and so on) is inherited or the product of environment, a safe answer is "both."

Some Genetic Principles

Genetic determination is a complex affair and much is unknown about the way genes work. But a number of genetic principles have been discovered, among them polygenically inherited characteristics, reaction range, and canalization.

Few psychological characteristics are the result of the actions of single gene pairs. Most are determined by the interaction of many different genes. This is the principle of **polygenic inheritance.** There are as many as 50,000 or more genes and so a staggering number of possible combinations of these. Traits produced by this mixing of genes are said to be polygenically determined.

For each genotype, a range of phenotypes can be expressed. Imagine that we could identify all of the genes that would make an adolescent introverted or extraverted. Would measured introversion-extraversion be predictable from knowledge of the specific genes? The answer is no, because even if our genetic model was adequate, introversion-extraversion is a characteristic shaped by experience throughout life. For example, a parent may push an introverted child into social situations and encourage the child to become more gregarious.

To understand the case of introversion in an adolescent, think about a series of genetic codes that predispose the adolescent to develop in a particular way and imagine environments that are responsive or unresponsive to this development. For example, the genotype of some adolescents may predispose them to be introverted in an environment that promotes a turning inward of personality, yet in an environment that encourages social interaction and outgoingness these adolescents may become more extraverted. However, it would be unlikely for the adolescent with this introverted genotype to become a strong extravert. The term **reaction range** is used to describe the range of phenotypes for each genotype, suggesting the importance of the environment's restrictiveness or enrichment (see Figure 3.1).

Sandra Scarr (1984) explains reaction range in the following way. Each of us has a range of potential. For example, an individual may be shorter than average. No matter how well fed the individual is, an individual with "short" genes will never be taller than average. Scarr believes that characteristics such as intelligence and introversion work the same way. That is, there is a range within which the environment can modify intelligence, but intelligence is not completely malleable. Reaction range gives us an estimate of how malleable intelligence is.

Biological and Cognitive Processes and Development

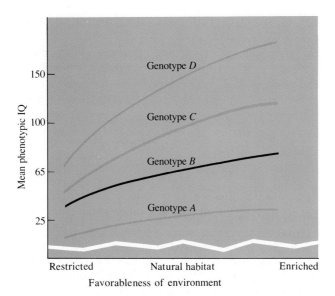

Figure 3.1 Hypothetical set of reaction ranges of intellectual development of several genotypes under environmental conditions that range from poor to good. Although each genotype responds favorably to improved environments, some are more responsive to environmental deprivation and enrichment than others.

Genotypes, in addition to producing many phenotypes, may show the opposite track for some characteristics—those that are somewhat immune to extensive changes in the environment. These characteristics seem to stay on track—a particular developmental course—regardless of the environmental assaults on them (Waddington, 1957). **Canalization** is the term used to describe the narrow path or developmental course that certain characteristics take. Preservative forces act to protect or buffer an individual from environmental extremes. For example, Jerome Kagan (1984) points to his research on Guatemalan infants who had experienced extreme malnutrition as infants, yet showed normal social and cognitive development in childhood.

Methods Used by Behavior Geneticists

Behavior genetics is concerned with the degree and nature of behavior's hereditary basis. Behavior geneticists assume that behaviors are jointly determined by the interaction of heredity and environment. To study heredity's influence on development, behavior geneticists often use either the adoption study or the twin study.

In the **adoption study,** researchers compare correlations between adolescents' characteristics and those of their biological and adoptive parents. Adopted adolescents share half their genes with each biological parent, but do not share an environment with them. In contrast, they share an environment with their adopted parents but not their genes.

In the **twin study,** identical (**monozygotic**) twins and fraternal (**dizygotic**) twins are compared. Identical twins are born when a fertilized egg divides into two parts that then develop into two separate embryos. Since the twins come

from the same fertilized egg, they share all of their genes. In contrast, fraternal twins develop when a woman's ovaries release two eggs instead of one and each egg is fertilized by different sperm. Fraternal twins share the same womb but they are no more alike genetically than any two siblings, and they may be of different sexes. By comparing groups of identical and fraternal twins, psychologists capitalize on the basic knowledge that identical twins are genetically more similar than fraternal twins. Several problems, though, crop up when the twin study method is used. Adults may stress the similarities of identical twins more than those of fraternal twins. And identical twins may perceive themselves as a "set" and play together more than fraternal twins. If so, observed similarities in identical twins could be environmentally influenced.

The concept of **heritability** is used in many adoption and twin studies. Heritability is a statistical estimate of the degree to which physical, cognitive, and social characteristics among individuals are due to their genetic differences. It is measured by the use of correlational statistical procedures. The highest degree of heritability is 1.00. A heritability quotient of .80 suggests a strong genetic influence, one of .50 a moderate genetic influence, and one of .20 a much weaker but nonetheless perceptible genetic influence.

Although heritability values may vary considerably from one study to the next, it is possible to determine the average magnitude of a particular characteristic's quotient. For some kinds of mental retardation the average heritability quotient approaches 1.00. That is, the environment makes almost no contribution to the characteristic's variation. This is not the same as saying the environment has no influence. The characteristic could not be expressed without the environment.

The heritability index is not a flawless measure of heredity's influence on development. It is only as good as the information fed into it and the assumptions made about genetic-environmental interaction. First, it is important to consider how varied the environments are that are being sampled. The narrower the range of the environments, the higher the heritability index; the broader the range of environments, the lower the heritability index. Another important consideration is the validity and reliability of the measure being used in the investigation. That is, what is the quality of the measures? The weaker the measure, the less confidence we have in the heritability index. A

TABLE 3.1 *Dimensions and Clusters of Temperament in Chess and Thomas's Research*

Temperament Dimension	Description	Temperament Cluster		
		Easy Child	*Difficult Child*	*Slow-to-Warm-Up Child*
Rhythmicity	Regularity of eating, sleeping, toileting	Regular	Irregular	
Activity level	Degree of energy movement		High	Low
Approach-withdrawal	Ease of approaching new people and situations	Positive	Negative	Negative
Adaptability	Ease of tolerating change in routine plans	Positive	Negative	Negative
Sensory threshold	Amount of stimulation required for responding			
Predominant quality of mood	Degree of positive or negative affect	Positive	Negative	
Intensity of mood expression	Degree of affect when pleased, displeased, happy, sad	Low to moderate	High	Low
Distractibility	Ease of being distracted			
Attention span/ persistence				

final consideration is that the heritability index assumed that heredity and environment can be separated; information can be quantitatively added together to arrive at a discrete influence for each. In reality, heredity and environment interact. Their interaction is lost when the heritability index is computed.

Temperament

To see how heredity works in determining one human characteristic, we evaluate information about temperament. Some adolescents are extremely active, moving their arms, legs, and mouths almost incessantly. Others are more tranquil. Some adolescents show a strong curiosity for exploring their environment for great lengths of time. Others show less curiosity. Some adolescents respond warmly to people. Others are much more shy. All of these behavioral styles represent an individual's temperament.

Alexander Chess and Stella Thomas (Chess & Thomas, 1977; Thomas & Chess, 1987; Thomas, Chess, & Birch, 1970) define temperament broadly in terms of an individual's behavioral style. They developed nine dimensions of temperament that fall into three clusters. The nine dimensions are rhythmicity of biological functions, activity level, approach to or withdrawal from new stimuli, adaptability, sensory threshold, predominant quality of mood, intensity of mood expression, distractibility, and persistence-attention span. The three temperament clusters are easy, difficult, and slow-to-warm-up. Table 3.1 lists the nine different temperaments, their description, and the three temperament clusters. The table also shows which of the nine dimensions were critical in spotting a cluster and what the level of responsiveness was for a critical feature. A blank space indicates that the dimension was not strongly related to a cluster.

Other researchers suggest different basic dimensions of temperament. Arnold Buss and Robert Plomin (1987) believe that individuals differ on the following basic dimensions of temperament:

Emotionality is the tendency to be distressed. It reflects the arousal of the individual's sympathetic nervous system. Buss and Plomin believe that individuals are labeled "easy" or "difficult" based on their emotionality.

Sociability is the tendency to prefer the company of others to being alone. It matches up with the tendency to respond warmly to others.

Activity involves tempo and vigor of movement. Some adolescents walk fast, are attracted to high-energy games, and jump or bounce around a lot. Others are more placid.

A number of scholars, including Chess and Thomas, conceive of temperament as a stable characteristic of newborns that comes to be shaped and modified by later experiences (Thomas & Chess, 1987; Goldsmith & others, 1987). This raises the question of heredity's role in temperament. Twin and adoption studies have been conducted to answer this question (DeFries & others, 1981; Plomin 1987; Plomin, DeFries, & McClearn, in press). The researchers found a heritability index in the range of .50 to .60, suggesting a moderate influence of heredity on temperament. However, the strength of the association usually declines as infants develop through childhood and adolescence. This supports the belief that temperament becomes more malleable with experience. Alternatively, it may be that as the child becomes older, behavioral indicators of temperament are more difficult to spot. The biological basis of the temperament of inhibition or shyness and its developmental course recently has been charted by Jerome Kagan (1987a,b) and Stephen Suomi (1987). To learn more about how stable our tendency to be shy is and how much it can be modified, turn to Perspective on Adolescent Development 3.1.

Heredity-Environmental Interaction and Development

Both genes and environment are necessary for an organism—from amoeba to human—to even exist. Heredity and environment operate—or cooperate—together to produce an adolescent's intelligence, temperament, height, weight, ability to pitch a baseball, career interests, and so on. No genes, no organism; no environment, no organism (Scarr, 1989; Scarr & Weinberg, 1980; Weinberg, 1989). If an attractive, popular, intelligent girl is elected president of her senior class in high school, would we conclude that her success is due to environment or to heredity? Of course it is both. Because the environment's influence depends on genetically endowed characteristics, we say that the two factors *interact*. (Plomin, 1989).

Biological and Cognitive Processes and Development

Born To Be Shy?

Each of you has seen a shy toddler—the one who clings to a parent and only reluctantly ventures into an unfamiliar place. Faced with a stranger, the shy toddler freezes, becomes silent, and stares fearfully. The shy toddler seems visibly tense in social situations; parents of such children often report they always seem to have been that way.

Despite parents' comments that shy children and adolescents seem to have been shy virtually from birth, psychologists have resisted the notion that such characteristics are inborn, focusing instead on the importance of early experiences. Both the research of Jerome Kagan with extremely shy children and the research of Stephen Suomi with "uptight" monkeys support the belief that shyness is a part of an individual's basic temperament.

Kagan (1987, 1989), collaborating with Steven Resnick and Nancy Snidman, followed the development of extremely inhibited and uninhibited 2–3-year-old children until their early adolescent years. They evaluated the children's heart rates and other physiological measures as well as observing their behavior in novel circumstances. By early adolescence, the very inhibited children no longer behaved exactly as they did when they were 2, but they still revealed the pattern of very inhibited behavior combined with intense physiological responsiveness to mild stress. Very uninhibited children typically speak within the first minute when they are observed in a social situation, but very inhibited children will sometimes wait as long as 20 minutes before they say anything.

Suomi (1987) has discovered that uptight monkeys, like Kagan's inhibited children, do not easily outgrow their intense physiological response to stress and their frozen behavioral responses to social situations. Even in adolescence—which is 4–5 years of age in monkeys—those who

Many adolescents who are shy also were shy as young children.

were uptight at birth continued to respond in intense ways to stress, but at this point they became hyperactive. As adults, they seemed to regress in the face of stress, revealing the shy, inhibited behavior seen in infancy.

Kagan says that the proper environmental context can change the tendency to be shy. But if parents let their child remain fearful for a long time, it becomes harder to modify the shyness. Kagan discovered that 40% of the originally inhibited children—mainly boys—became much less inhibited by 5½ years, while less than 10% became more timid. Based on parent interviews, parents helped their children overcome their shyness by bringing other children into the home and by encouraging the child to cope with stressful circumstances.

Modification of shyness can be extreme in some cases. Some shy individuals even become performers. Celebrities such as Johnny Carson, Carol Burnett, Barbara Walters, and Michael Jackson have strong tendencies toward shyness, but showed that they could overcome heredity's influence (Asher, 1987).

But as we have seen, developmentalists probe further to determine more precisely the influence of heredity and environment on development. What do we know about heredity-environment interaction? According to Sandra Scarr and Kenneth Kidd (1983), we know that literally hundreds of disorders appear because of genetic miscodings. We know that abnormalities in chromosome number adversely affect the development of physical, intellectual, and behavioral features. We know that genotype and phenotype do not map onto each other in one-to-one fashion. We know that it is very difficult to distinguish between genetic and cultural transmission. There usually is a familial concentration of a particular disorder, but familial patterns are considerably different than what would be precisely predicted from simple modes of inheritance. We know that when we consider the normal range of variation, the stronger the genetic resemblance the stronger the behavioral resemblance. This holds more strongly for intelligence than personality or interests. The influence of genes on intelligence is present early in children's development and continues through the late adulthood years. We also know that being raised in the same family accounts for some portion of intellectual differences among individuals, but common rearing accounts for little of the variation in personality or interests. One reason for this discrepancy may be that families place similar pressures on their children for intellectual development in the sense that the push is clearly toward the highest level; but they do not direct their children toward similar personalities or interests, in which extremes are not especially desirable. That is, virtually all parents would like their children to have above-average intellect, but there is much less agreement about whether a child should be highly extraverted.

What do we need to know about the role of heredity-environmental interaction in development? Scarr and Kidd (1983) commented that we need to know the pathways by which genetic abnormalities influence development. We need to know more about genetic-environmental interaction in the normal range of development. For example, what accounts for the difference in one individual's IQ of 95 and another individual's IQ of 125? The answer requires a polygenic perspective and information about cultural and genetic influences.

We also need to know about heredity's influence across the entire life cycle. For instance, puberty is not an environmentally produced accident (Rowe & Rodgers, 1989); neither is menopause. While puberty and menopause can be influenced by such environmental factors as nutrition, weight, drugs, health, and the like, the basic evolutionary and genetic program is wired into the species. It cannot be eliminated, nor should it be ignored. This genetic perspective gives biology its appropriate role in our quest to better understand human development through the life cycle. Next, we consider other dimensions of biology's role in adolescent development and evaluate some general features of physical growth in adolescence.

General Features of Physical Growth in Adolescence

There are many aspects to the adolescent's physical growth. Among those that have been given the most attention are height and weight, skeletal growth, reproductive functions, and hormonal changes. What is the nature of growth curves for such bodily characteristics? What factors influence these growth curves? We consider each of these questions in turn.

Biological and Cognitive Processes and Development

Four Developmental Growth Curves

The developmental growth curves for physical development in general, for the reproductive organs, for the brain and head, and for the lymphoid glands are shown in Figure 3.2. Most skeletal and muscular components of growth, such as height and weight, follow the general curve, as do organs like the liver and kidneys. This growth curve changes gradually in the beginning, but rises dramatically at about age 12, characterizing what is commonly referred to as the adolescent growth spurt.

However, the growth curve for the reproductive organs changes even more dramatically than the general curve for height and weight. The prepubertal phase of reproductive development is fairly dormant, but the adolescent phase of the curve is even more precipitous than the general height and weight curve. Why is there a difference in the growth curves for height and weight as compared to reproductive functions? The answer lies in an analysis of glandular and hormonal influences. The glands and hormones that control height and weight are not the same ones that regulate reproductive functions. The development of the skeletal and muscular systems, along with that of most organs, is controlled by the pituitary and thyroid glands. On the other hand, the growth of the reproductive organs is regulated by the sex hormones (androgens and estrogens), which show marked increases in activity at the onset of adolescence.

A third growth curve represents the development of the skull, eyes, and ears, which mature sooner than any other parts of the body. At any point during childhood, the head is in general more advanced developmentally than any other aspect of the body. And the top parts of the head, the eyes and brain, grow faster than the lower portions, such as the jaw.

Some biologists (Epstein, 1974, 1978) and educators (Toepfer, 1979) argue that the brain does not grow in the relatively smooth, continuous fashion illustrated in Figure 3.2. These same individuals argue that just as there is a height, weight, and sexual spurt that characterizes puberty, so too there is a spurt in brain growth. Brain growth spurts are said to occur between 2 and 4, 6 and 8, 10 and 12, and 14 and 16 years of age. During these spurts, the brain is believed to increase from 5%–10% in size. Since cell formation in the brain is essentially complete at birth, these growth spurts are not due to new cells being formed but to growth within the cells that have already formed.

The scientists who stress brain growth spurts also believe that these growth spurts affect the brain's synapses (the points of contact between axons, or sending connectors, and dendrites, or receiving connectors). During the growth spurts, the axons and dendrites lengthen. This view of brain development, which emphasizes stages or spurts of brain growth, is called **brain-growth periodization.** For more information about the importance of the brain in adolescent development and the nature of brain spurts, read Perspective on Adolescent Development 3.2.

Figure 3.2 Growth and maturity of body systems as a percentage of total postnatal growth.

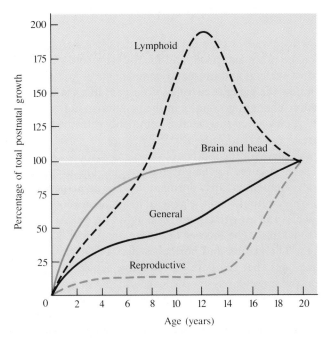

The fourth type of growth pattern is very different from the first three. The lymphoid tissues of the tonsils, adenoids, appendix, and lymph nodes reach a developmental peak before the onset of adolescence, and then decline, presumably under the influence of increases in sex hormones.

Factors That Influence Growth Curves

What are the factors that influence growth curves? At the present time we know that at least four mechanisms are responsible (Damon, 1977): target-seeking or self-stabilizing factors, maturity gradients, feedback regulation, and body mass. Concerning *target-seeking or self-stabilizing factors,* in cases where growth has been stunted by disease or poor nutrition, the individual's growth often catches up with its original path after the negative conditions have been removed. This regulatory force likely has a genetic basis.

Concerning *maturity gradients,* we know that these factors are present in different regions of the body. For example, the head is always more advanced developmentally than the trunk, and the trunk is always more advanced developmentally than the limbs.

Concerning *feedback regulation,* biological structures adapt to feedback. For example, the secretions of the pituitary gland influence various other glands, such as the thyroid and the sex glands; the pituitary secretions adjust to the levels of hormones in the other glands. When the other glands' secretions reach appropriate levels, the pituitary regulates its output to continue the equilibrium that has developed.

Biological and Cognitive Processes and Development

Heredity and General Dimensions of Physical Growth

Concept	Processes/Related Ideas	Characteristics/Description
The nature of genes	Genes, chromosomes, genotypes, and phenotypes	Each adolescent carries a genetic code that was inherited from his or her parents. Physically the hereditary code is carried by biochemical agents called genes and chromosomes. Genotype refers to the special configuration of genes each individual has. Phenotype refers to all the observed and measurable characteristics of the individual.
	Some genetic principles	Genetic transmission is complex but some principles have been worked out, among them polygenic inheritance, reaction range, and canalization.
	Methods used by behavior geneticists	Behavior genetics is the field concerned with the degree and nature of behavior's hereditary basis. Among the most important methods developed by behavior geneticists are the twin study and the adoption study. The concept of heritability is used in many of the twin and adoption studies. The heritability index is not without its flaws.
Temperament and the nature of heredity-environmental interaction	Temperament	Refers to behavioral style. Chess and Thomas developed nine temperament dimensions and three temperament clusters. Temperament is influenced strongly by biological factors in infancy but becomes more malleable with experience. Introversion-extraversion is moderately influenced by heredity.
	Heredity-environment interaction and development	No genes, no organism; no environment, no organism. Because the environment's influence depends on genetically endowed characteristics, we say that the two factors interact.
General dimensions of physical growth	Four growth curves	Include a general growth curve, consisting of most aspects of skeletal and muscular growth; a reproductive curve; a curve for the brain and head; and a curve for lymphoid tissues. Some biologists argue that brain growth occurs in spurts; others disagree.
	Factors influencing growth curves	Include target-seeking or self-stabilizing factors, maturity gradients, feedback regulation, and body mass.

Concerning *body mass,* Rose Frisch and Roger Revelle (1970) argue that the body has built-in sensors that detect when a certain mass is reached. These detectors then trigger the growth spurt that occurs at the onset of puberty. For young girls, a body weight approximating 106 ± 3 pounds triggers menarche (the first menstruation) and the conclusion of the pubertal growth spurt. Body mass predicts the approximate time female adolescents experience menarche in many different cultures.

At this point we have discussed a number of ideas about heredity and about general features of growth in adolescence. A summary of these ideas is presented in Concept Table 3.1.

The Adolescent's Brain, Brain Spurts, Cognitive Development, and Education

"As long as the brain is a mystery, the universe, the reflection of the structure of the brain, will also be a mystery."

Santiago Ramón y Cajal

We don't know very much about what probably is the most important physical structure in the adolescent's development—the brain. As we discuss the adolescent's cognitive growth and development later in this section, we will discover that the manner in which the adolescent processes information about himself or herself and the world is a hallmark of cognition in adolescence. The underlying hardware or machinery that makes this information processing possible is made up of the brain and nervous system. If you think for one moment that the brain is an unimportant aspect of the adolescent's development, consider the following examples of the awesome magnitude and complexity of the brain. There are some 10–20 billion neurons (nerve cells) in the adolescent's brain. The average nerve cell has been described as being as complex as a small computer, each one having as many as 15,000 physical connections with other cells (Kolb and Whishaw, 1988). At times the adolescent's brain may be lit up with as many as a quadrillion connections!

The nerve cells in a canary's brain are exactly the same as those in a frog's brain. The reason frogs croak and canaries sing is that the nerve cells are organized differently in the two brains. The adolescent's own gift of speech is present because human nerve cells are organized in ways that permit language processing.

Given that the adolescent's brain is different than a canary's or a frog's, is it any different than a child's? We know precious little information about this important question, yet neuroscientific research over the course of the next 100 years may well develop some important keys for our understanding the maturation of the brain and thought as individuals move from childhood through the adolescent years.

According to Epstein's view of brain spurts, what should the nature of this young adolescent's education be like? How has Epstein's view been criticized?

One biologist, Herman Epstein (1974, 1980) proposed a simple hypothesis: When boys and girls move into one of Piaget's cognitive developmental periods, their brains reveal an unusual amount of growth as well. How does Epstein measure brain growth? He has called on two methods—growth of the head, particularly its circumference, which is closely linked to brain size, and evaluation of electrical waves through use of the electroencephalograph (EEG). These brain waves are influenced by cognitive activities like thinking and problem solving.

With regard to the circumference of the head, children appear to experience growth at three points in development: at approximately the time of the onset of Piaget's concrete operational period about 6–7 years of age, the onset of the formal operational period (about 10–12 years of age), and at a second time in the formal operational period (about 14–16 years of age). With regard

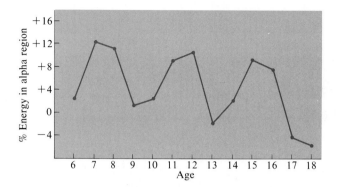

Figure 3.A   Spurts of electrical activity in the brain according to age.

to electrical waves, as shown in Figure 3.A, spurts in electrical activity of the brain coincide with increases in the circumference of the head.

Do the head circumference and electrical activity data document important changes in Piaget's stages of concrete and formal operational thought? Epstein argued that they did. Not only did Epstein suggest that the brain data indicated underlying changes in Piaget's stages, but he and others (e.g., Toepfer, 1979) argued that the brain data had implications for how children and adolescents should be educated. For example, based primarily on the head circumference and brain wave data, it was publicized that adolescents between the ages of 12 and 14 are likely to be incapable of learning new skills because this age span reflects little or no growth of the brain. It also was emphasized that adolescents can only consolidate earlier learned skills during this time period, so middle and junior high schools should not attempt to teach new learning skills during this age span.

Did the Epstein data warrant such generalizations and implications for the education of adolescents? Quite clearly they did not! The Epstein data described infor-

mation about the nature of brain growth and included no measures of cognitive or educational skills. More recent research (e.g., McCall & others, 1983) has revealed that no correlation exists between spurts in head growth and cognitive changes when cognitive skills are actually measured in concert with head growth. Yet another investigation (Lampl & Emde, 1983) focused on whether growth spurts in head circumference, as well as other types of growth, such as height and weight, actually correspond to certain developmental growth periods, like 6–7 years of age, 10–12 years of age, and so forth. Each boy and girl in the study did show growth spurts, but the growth spurts were not consistently related to developmental time periods.

In sum, there do seem to be some periods of development when brain growth is particularly rapid. The degree to which these brain spurts are closely linked with rapid growth in cognitive skills, such as those associated with the onset of Piagetian stages, has not been fully documented. Also, it clearly has not been discovered that adolescents should be taught only to consolidate skills learned at an earlier time because their brain growth is slow at a particular point in development. It also should be noted that the measures of the brain are extraordinarily crude and global. Many neuroscientists believe the most important changes in the brain occur at a more micro level than was assessed in the Epstein studies. These scientists argue that we will understand the mysteries of the brain, including the adolescent's brain, only by studying neurological development at the biochemical, cellular level. So far our knowledge of changes at the biochemical level in adolescents is zero because such research has not been conducted. So, while changes in the brain of adolescents represent a frontier of important knowledge about adolescent development, we are very naive about what kinds of change actually go on in the brains of adolescents.   ≥•

Puberty

Comedian Bill Cosby once remarked that the problem with his teenage son was not that he grew, but that he did not know when to stop growing. The adolescent growth spurt takes place in puberty.

The Boundaries and Determinants of Puberty

Puberty can be distinguished from adolescence. For most of us puberty has ended long before adolescence is exited, although puberty is the most important marker of adolescence's beginning. What is puberty? **Puberty** is a rapid change to physical maturation involving hormonal and bodily changes that take place primarily during early adolescence.

Imagine a toddler displaying all the features of puberty—a 3-year-old girl with fully developed breasts or a boy just slightly older with a deep male voice. That is what we would see by the year 2250 if the age at which puberty arrives kept getting younger at its present pace. In Norway, **menarche**— the girl's first menstruation—occurs at just over 13 years of age, compared to 17 years of age in the 1840s. In the United States—where children mature up to a year earlier than children in European countries—the average age of menarche has been declining an average of about 4 months per decade for the past century (see Figure 3.3). Fortunately, however, we are unlikely to see pubescent toddlers, since what has happened in the past century is special. The best guess is that it is the result of a higher level of nutrition and health. The available information suggests that menarche began to occur earlier at about the time of the Industrial Revolution, a period associated with increased standards of living and advances in medical science (Petersen, 1979).

Genetic factors also are involved in puberty. Puberty is not simply an environmental accident. As indicated earlier, while nutrition, health, and other factors affect puberty's timing and variations in its makeup, the basic genetic program is wired into the nature of the species (Scarr & Kidd, 1983).

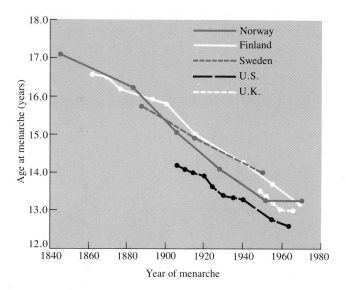

Figure 3.3 Age (median) at selected northern European countries and the United States from 1845 to 1969.

Another key factor in puberty's occurrence is body mass, which was mentioned earlier (Frisch & Revelle, 1970). Remember that menarche occurs at a relatively consistent weight in girls. A body weight approximating 106 ± 3 pounds can trigger menarche and the end of the pubertal growth spurt. And for menarche to begin and continue, fat must make up 17% of the girl's body weight. Both teenage anorexics whose weight drops dramatically and female athletes in certain sports (such as gymnastics) may become amenorrheic (absence or suppression of menstrual discharge).

In summary, puberty's determinants include nutrition, health, heredity, and body mass. So far our discussion of puberty has emphasized its dramatic changes. Keep in mind, though, that puberty is not a single, sudden event. We know when a young boy or girl is going through puberty, but pinpointing its beginning and its end is difficult. Except for menarche, which occurs rather late in puberty, no single marker heralds puberty. For boys, the first whisker or first wet dream are events that could mark its appearance, but both may go unnoticed.

Hormonal Changes

Behind the first whisker in boys and behind the widening of hips in girls is a flood of **hormones,** powerful chemical substances secreted by the endocrine glands and carried through the body by the bloodstream. The key to understanding the endocrine system's role in pubertal change is the **hypothalamic-pituitary-gonadal axis** (Nottelman & others, 1987). The **hypothalamus** is a structure in the higher portion of the brain, and the pituitary is the body's master gland. It is located at the base of the brain. Its designation as the master gland comes from its ability to regulate a number of other glands. The term

Figure 3.4   Hormone levels by sex and pubertal stage for testosterone and estradiol.

Source: E. D. Nottelmann, et al., "Hormone Level and Adjustment and Behavior during Early Adolescence," May 1985, page 38. Paper presented at the annual meeting of the American Association for the Advancement of Science, Los Angeles, CA.

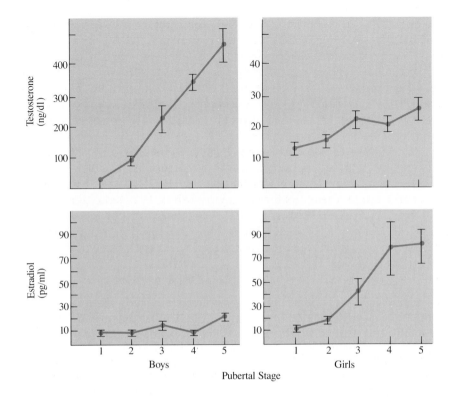

gonadal refers to the sex glands—the testes in males and the ovaries in females. How does this hormonal sysem work? While the pituitary gland monitors endocrine levels, it is regulated by the hypothalamus. The pituitary gland sends a signal via **gonadotropin** (a hormone that stimulates the testes or ovaries) to the appropriate gland to manufacture the hormone. Then the pituitary gland, through interaction with the hypothalamus, detects when the optimal level is reached and responds by maintaining gonadotropin secretion (Petersen & Taylor, 1980).

There are two main general classes of sex hormones that are important in understanding pubertal development—androgens and estrogens. **Androgens** mature primarily in males, and **estrogens** mature mainly in females. Current research, however, has been able to pinpoint more precisely which androgens and estrogens play the most important roles in pubertal development. For example, **testosterone** appears to assume an important role in the pubertal development of males. Throughout puberty, increasing testosterone levels are clearly linked with a number of physical changes in boys: development of external genitals, increase in height, and voice changes (Fregly & Luttge, 1982). In females, **estradiol** is likely the most important hormone responsible for pubertal development. The level of estradiol increases throughout puberty and then varies in women across their menstrual cycle. As estradiol level rises, breast and uterine development occur and skeletal changes appear as well (Fregly and Luttge, 1982). As shown in Figure 3.4, in one study (Nottelmann

Biological and Cognitive Processes and Development

& others, 1987) testosterone levels were found to increase eighteen fold in boys, but only twofold in girls across the pubertal period. For girls in the same study, there was an eightfold increase in estradiol, but the increase for this hormone in boys was only twofold. Note that both testosterone and estradiol are present in the hormonal makeup of both boys and girls, but that testosterone is dominant for boys while estradiol is stronger in girls. It should be mentioned that testosterone and estradiol are part of a complex hormonal system and that each hormone is not solely responsible for pubertal change. Nonetheless, their strong association with the physical changes of puberty suggests that they play a very important role in the pubertal process.

The same influx of hormones that puts hair on a male's chest and imparts curvature to a female's breast may contribute to psychological adjustment in adolescence. In one study of 108 normal boys and girls ranging in age from 9 to 14, a higher concentration of testosterone was present in boys who rated themselves more socially competent (Nottelmann & others, 1987). In another investigation of 60 normal boys and girls in the same age range, girls with higher estradiol levels expressed more anger and aggression (Inoff-Germain & others, 1988).

Before we leave the discussion of hormones and puberty, one additional aspect of the pituitary gland's role in development needs to be described. Not only does the pituitary gland release gonadotropins that stimulate the testes and ovaries, but through its interaction with the hypothalamus, it also secretes hormones that either directly lead to growth and skeletal maturation, or produce such growth effects through interaction with the **thyroid gland,** located in the neck region (Styne, 1988). Remember we earlier commented that the pituitary gland often is viewed as the master gland because of its interconnections with so many other glands. Here we have seen the role of the pituitary gland in sending hormones to the sex glands, the testes and ovaries, and to the thyroid gland.

An overview of the location of the major endocrine glands and their functions is shown in Figure 3.5. Now that we have studied the important role of the endocrine system in pubertal development, we turn our attention to the external physical changes that characterize puberty.

Physical Changes

Among the most noticeable physical changes during puberty are increases in height and weight, and sexual maturation.

Height and Weight

As indicated in Figure 3.6, the growth spurt for girls occurs approximately 2 years earlier than for boys. The growth spurt for girls begins at approximately 10½ years of age and lasts for about 2 years. During this time girls increase in height by about 3½ inches per year. The growth spurt for boys begins at about 12½ years of age and also lasts for about 2 years. Boys usually grow about 4 inches per year during this time frame (Faust, 1977; Tanner, 1970).

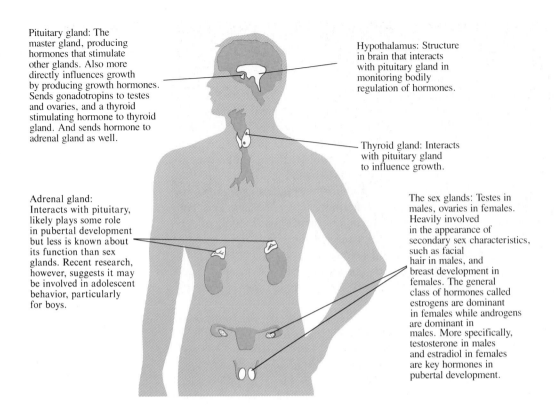

Pituitary gland: The master gland, producing hormones that stimulate other glands. Also more directly influences growth by producing growth hormones. Sends gonadotropins to testes and ovaries, and a thyroid stimulating hormone to thyroid gland. And sends hormone to adrenal gland as well.

Hypothalamus: Structure in brain that interacts with pituitary gland in monitoring bodily regulation of hormones.

Thyroid gland: Interacts with pituitary gland to influence growth.

Adrenal gland: Interacts with pituitary, likely plays some role in pubertal development but less is known about its function than sex glands. Recent research, however, suggests it may be involved in adolescent behavior, particularly for boys.

The sex glands: Testes in males, ovaries in females. Heavily involved in the appearance of secondary sex characteristics, such as facial hair in males, and breast development in females. The general class of hormones called estrogens are dominant in females while androgens are dominant in males. More specifically, testosterone in males and estradiol in females are key hormones in pubertal development.

Figure 3.5   The major endocrine glands involved in pubertal change.

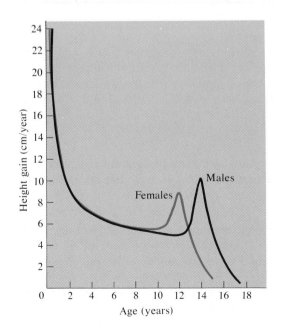

Figure 3.6   Typical individual growth curves for height in boys and girls. These curves represent the height of the typical boy and girl at any given age.

Biological and Cognitive Processes and Development

The adolescent height spurt occurs on the average two years earlier for girls than boys and is quite noticeable in this dance setting.

Boys and girls who are shorter or taller than their peers before adolescence are likely to remain so during adolescence (Tanner, 1970). In our society, there is a stigma attached to short boys. At the beginning of the adolescent period, girls tend to be as tall or taller than boys their age, but by the end of the junior high years most boys have caught up or, in many cases, even surpassed girls in height. And even though height in the elementary school years is a good predictor of height later in adolescence, there is still room for the individual's height to change in relation to the height of his or her peers. As much as 30% of the height of late adolescents is unexplained by height in the elementary school years (Tanner, 1970).

The rate at which adolescents gain weight follows approximately the same developmental timetable as the rate at which they gain height. Marked weight gains coincide with the onset of puberty. During early adolescence, girls tend to outweigh boys, but by about age 14, just as with height, boys begin to surpass girls (Faust, 1977; Tanner, 1970).

Sexual Maturation

Think back to the onset of your puberty. Of the striking changes that were taking place in your body, what was the first change that occurred? Researchers have found that male pubertal characteristics develop in this order: increase in penis and testicle size, appearance of straight pubic hair, minor voice change, first ejaculation (which usually occurs through masturbation or a wet dream), appearance of kinky pubic hair, onset of maximum growth, growth of hair in armpits, more detectable voice changes, and growth of facial hair (Faust, 1977; Garrison, 1968). Three of the most noticeable areas of sexual maturation in boys are penis elongation, testes development, and growth of

Figure 3.7   Normal range and average age of development of sexual characteristics in males.

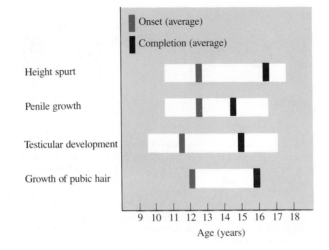

facial hair. The normal range and average age of development for these sexual characteristics, along with height spurt, is shown in Figure 3.7. Figure 3.8 shows the typical course of male sexual development during puberty.

What is the order of appearance of physical changes in females? First, either the breasts enlarge or pubic hair appears. Later hair will appear in the armpits. As these changes occur, the female grows in height and her hips become wider than her shoulders. Her first menstruation comes rather late in the pubertal cycle. Initially her menstrual cycles may be highly irregular. For the first several years she may not ovulate every menstrual cycle. In some instances it is not until 2 years after her period begins that she becomes fertile. No voice changes comparable to those in pubertal males take place in pubertal females. By the end of puberty, the female's breasts have become more fully rounded. Two of the most noticeable aspects of the female's pubertal change are pubic hair and breast development. Figure 3.9 shows the normal range and average age of development of these sexual characteristics as well as information about menarche and height gain. Figure 3.10 shows the typical development of pubic hair and breasts during puberty.

Individual Variation

The pubertal sequence may begin as early as 10 years of age or as late as 13½ for most boys. It may end as early as 13 years or as late as 17 years for most boys. The normal range is wide enough that given two boys of the same chronological age, one may complete the pubertal sequence before the other one has begun it. For girls, the age range of the first menstrual period is even wider. Menarche is considered to be within a normal range if it appears between the ages of 9–15 (Hill, 1980; Brooks-Gunn, 1988).

Biological and Cognitive Processes and Development

 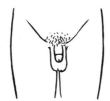   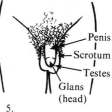

1.
No pubic hair. The testes, scrotum, and penis are about the same size and shape as those of a child.

2.
A little soft, long, lightly colored hair, mostly at the base of the penis. This hair may be straight or a little curly. The testes and scrotum have enlarged, and the skin of the scrotum has changed. The scrotum, the sack holding the testes, has lowered a bit. The penis has grown only a little.

3.
The hair is darker, coarser, and more curled. It has spread to thinly cover a somewhat larger area. The penis has grown mainly in length, the testes and scrotum have grown and dropped lower than in stage 2.

4.
The hair is now as dark, curly, and coarse as that of an adult male. However, the area that the hair covers is not as large as that of an adult male; it has not spread to the thighs. The penis has grown even larger and wider. The glans (the head of the penis) is bigger. The scrotum is darker and bigger because the testes have gotten bigger.

5.
The hair has spread to the thighs and is now like that of an adult male. The penis, scrotum, and testes are the size and shape of those of an adult male.

Psychological Dimensions of Puberty

A host of psychological changes accompany an adolescent's pubertal development. Imagine yourself as you were beginning puberty. Not only did you probably think of yourself differently, but your parents and peers probably began acting differently toward you. Maybe you were proud of your changing body, even though you were perplexed about what was happening. Perhaps your parents no longer perceived you as someone they could sit in bed with and watch television or as someone who should be kissed goodnight. Among the intriguing questions about puberty's psychological dimensions posed by developmentalists are the following. What parts of their body image are adolescents preoccupied with the most? What are the psychological dimensions of menarche and the menstrual cycle? What are the psychological consequences of early and late maturation? How complex is on-time and off-time in pubertal development? Are the effects of pubertal timing exaggerated? Let's look further at each of these questions.

Body Image

One thing is certain about the psychological aspects of physical change in adolescence—adolescents are preoccupied with their bodies and develop individual images of what their bodies are like. Perhaps you looked in the mirror on a daily or sometimes even hourly basis to see if you could detect anything different about your changing body. Preoccupation with one's body image is strong throughout adolescence, but it is especially acute during puberty, a time when adolescents are more dissatisfied with their bodies than in late adolescence (Hamburg, 1974; Wright, 1989).

Figure 3.8   Different stages of male sexual development: the growth of pubic hair, testes, scrotum, and penis.

Figure 3.9 Normal range and average age of development of sexual characteristics in females.

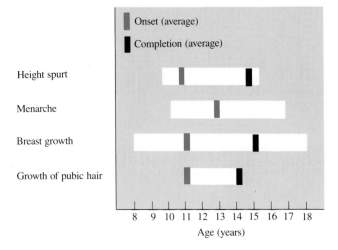

THE CULTURAL WORLDS OF ADOLESCENTS 3.1

Female Circumcision

There are two main types of female circumcision. The milder form is practiced in 20 countries, mostly in East, West, and Central Africa. All or part of the clitoris, and sometimes the internal vaginal lips, are removed. In the second, more radical type of operation, all of the external genitalia are removed and the outer lips sewn shut, leaving just a tiny opening, which urine and menstrual discharge can pass through. In Mali, Sudan, and Somalia, the majority of the females undergo this radical procedure. In Africa alone, more than 75 million females are circumcised. Female circumcision also is practiced in some areas of the Middle East and southeastern Asia. One of the main goals of the operation is to ensure that sex is linked with procreation rather than enjoyment. In many cultures, the female circumcision is carried out as part of the ceremonial ritual signaling membership in the adult community. An increasing number of African women are trying to eliminate female circumcision. In some countries, their efforts are meeting with some success. For example, in Sudan, a survey of female high school students indicated that while 96% had been circumcised, more than 70% strongly recommended that their younger sisters, and young girls in general, should not be circumcised (Kenyatta, 1965; Pugh, 1983; Taylor, 1985).

Biological and Cognitive Processes and Development

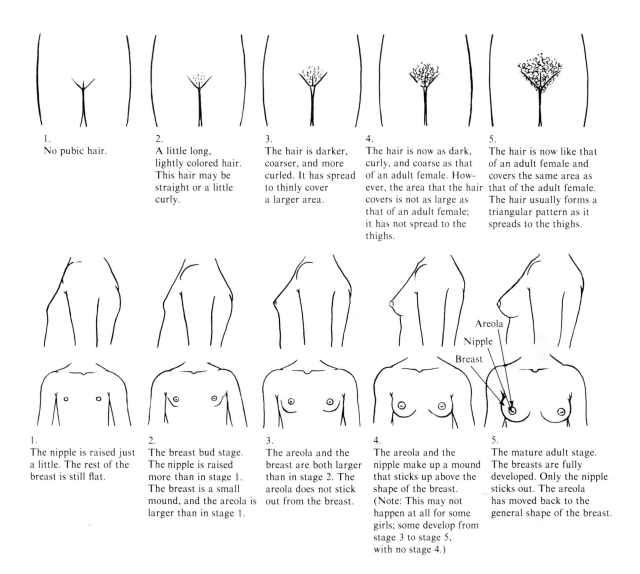

1.
No pubic hair.

2.
A little long, lightly colored hair. This hair may be straight or a little curly.

3.
The hair is darker, coarser, and more curled. It has spread to thinly cover a larger area.

4.
The hair is now as dark, curly, and coarse as that of an adult female. However, the area that the hair covers is not as large as that of an adult female; it has not spread to the thighs.

5.
The hair is now like that of an adult female and covers the same area as that of the adult female. The hair usually forms a triangular pattern as it spreads to the thighs.

1.
The nipple is raised just a little. The rest of the breast is still flat.

2.
The breast bud stage. The nipple is raised more than in stage 1. The breast is a small mound, and the areola is larger than in stage 1.

3.
The areola and the breast are both larger than in stage 2. The areola does not stick out from the breast.

4.
The areola and the nipple make up a mound that sticks up above the shape of the breast. (Note: This may not happen at all for some girls; some develop from stage 3 to stage 5, with no stage 4.)

5.
The mature adult stage. The breasts are fully developed. Only the nipple sticks out. The areola has moved back to the general shape of the breast.

Figure 3.10   Different stages of female sexual development: pubic hair and breast growth.

Being physically attractive and having a positive body image is associated with an overall positive conception of one's self. In one investigation, girls who were judged as being physically attractive and who generally had a positive body image had higher opinions of themselves in general (Lerner & Karabenick, 1974). In another investigation, breast growth in girls 9–11 years old was associated with a positive body image, positive peer relationships, and superior adjustment (Brooks-Gunn & Warren, in press).

Was there a part of your body you were preoccupied with the most during puberty? In one study, boys and girls did not differ much in their preoccupation with various body characteristics (Lerner & Karabenick, 1974). For

both males and females, general appearance, the face, facial complexion, and body build were thought to be the most important characteristics in physical attractiveness. Ankles and ears were thought to be the least important.

Menarche and the Menstrual Cycle

The onset of puberty and menarche have often been described as "main events" in most historical accounts of adolescence (e.g., Rousseau, 1762; Hall, 1904; A. Freud, 1958; Erikson, 1968). Basically, these views suggest that pubertal change and events such as menarche produce a different body that requires considerable change in self-conception, possibly producing an identity crisis. Only within the last decade has there been empirical research directed at understanding the female adolescent's adaptation to menarche and the menstrual cycle (Brooks-Gunn, 1987, 1988; Brooks-Gunn & Ruble, 1982; Grief & Ullman, 1982).

In one investigation (Brooks-Gunn & Ruble, 1982) of 639 girls, a wide range of reactions to menarche were unveiled. Most of the reactions, however, were quite mild, as girls described their first period as a little upsetting, a little surprising, or a little exciting and positive. In this study, 120 of the fifth and sixth grade girls were telephoned to obtain more personal, detailed views of their experience with menarche. The most frequent theme of the girls' responses was positive, namely, that menarche was an indicator of their maturity. Other positive aspects to menarche included reports that they now could

Biological and Cognitive Processes and Development

have children, were experiencing something that made them more like adult women, and now were more like their friends. The most frequent negative aspects of menarche reported by the girls were its hassle, having to carry supplies around, and its messiness. A minority of the girls also indicated that menarche involved physical discomfort, produced behavioral limitations, and created emotional changes.

Questions also were asked about the extent to which the girls communicated with others about the appearance of menarche, the extent to which the girls were prepared for menarche, and how the experience was related to early/late maturation. Virtually all of the girls told their mothers immediately, but most of the girls did not tell anyone else about menarche, with only 1 in 5 informing a friend. However, after two or three periods had occurred, most girls had talked with girlfriends about menstruation. Girls not prepared for menarche indicated more negative feelings about menstruation than those who were more prepared for its onset. Girls who matured early had more negative reactions than average or late maturing girls. In summary, menarche initially may be disruptive, particularly for early maturing and unprepared girls, but it typically does not reach the tumultuous, conflicting proportions described by some early theoreticians.

Early and Late Maturation

Some of you entered puberty early, others late, and yet others on time. When adolescents mature earlier or later than their peers, might they perceive themselves differently? In the California Longitudinal Study some years ago, it was reported that early maturing boys perceived themselves more positively and had more successful peer relations than their late maturing counterparts (Jones, 1965). The findings for early maturing girls were similar but not as strong as for boys. When the late maturing boys were studied in their 30s, however, they had developed a stronger sense of identity than the early maturing boys (Peskin, 1967). Possibly this occurred because the late maturing boys had more time to explore life's options or because the early maturing boys continued to focus on their advantageous physical status instead of career development and achievement.

More recent research, though, confirms that at least during adolescence, it is advantageous to be an early maturing rather than a late maturing boy (Blyth, Bulcroft, & Simmons, 1981; Petersen, 1987a; Simmons & Blyth, 1987). Roberta Simmons and Dale Blyth (1987) studied more than 450 individuals for 5 years, beginning in the 6th grade and continuing through the 10th grade, in Milwaukee, Wisconsin. Students were individually interviewed and achievement test scores and grade point averages were obtained. The presence or absence of menstruation and the relative onset of menses were used to classify girls as early, middle, or late maturers. The peak rate of growth in height was used to classify boys according to these categories.

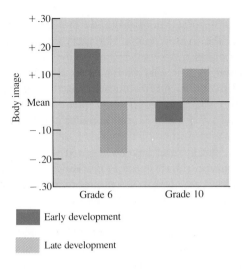

Figure 3.11 Early and late maturing adolescent girl's perceptions of body image in early and late adolescence.

Early development

Late development

Somewhat surprisingly, there were fewer significant relationships between pubertal development and psychological and social development than was anticipated. However, the significant findings that did occur reveal some interesting patterns:

Self-concept. Early-maturing boys had a higher level of self-esteem than middle- or late-maturing boys in the seventh grade, but there were no differences in the ninth and tenth grades.

Body Image. One of the most important tasks of adolescence is to incorporate dramatic physical changes into a positive body image. Students were asked to report how satisfied they were with their height, weight, figure development (for girls) and muscular development (for boys). Early maturers were less satisfied with their bodies than were late maturers, and early maturers were less satisfied with their weights at all grade levels. When weight was controlled, the significant differences between early and late maturers disappeared, suggesting that weight, not early maturation, was the culprit.

For the girls, a complex pattern developed in regard to satisfaction with figure development. In the sixth grade, the more developed, menstruating girls showed greater satisfaction with their figures than late-maturing girls did. But by the 9th and tenth grades, the pattern was reversed. When all the girls had developed, it was the late maturers who were the most satisfied with their figures. Thus, by the 9th and 10th grades early maturers were less satisfied with their heights, weights, and figures than were late maturers (Figure 3.11).

Biological and Cognitive Processes and Development

One possible reason for this pattern of findings is that by the 9th and 10th grades early maturers are usually shorter and stockier and late maturers are often taller and thinner. Possibly the late-maturing females in the 9th and 10th grades more closely approximate the American ideal of feminine beauty—tall and slim, with a figure. Also, after enduring a number of years of being undeveloped, late maturing girls may feel a sense of pride and relief that they are now developing. For early maturing girls, having a developed figure is nothing new.

Maturation seemed to have less influence on the body images of boys, although when differences appeared, they invariably favored early rather than late maturers. These differences seemed to be more pronounced in early adolescence.

Opposite-sex Popularity.   In the sixth and seventh grades, girls who had reached menarche reported that they were more popular with boys and dated more than girls had who had not reached menarche. In the 10th grade, early-maturing girls said they were dating more than their late-maturing counterparts. Note that opposite-sex behavior is the first category in which early maturing girls seem to have an advantage.

Independence.   Early-maturing girls also seem to have more independence than late-maturing girls. Girls who had reached menarche in the sixth or seventh grades reported that they were more likely to be allowed to take the bus home alone, more likely to be left alone when their parents were gone, more likely to babysit, and more often perceived to be making their own decisions. By the 10th grade, however, such differences seemed to have disappeared.

Academic Behavior.   In the sixth and seventh grades, early-maturing girls were less likely to have good grades and scored lower on achievement tests than their peers. These effects did not appear in the later adolescent years. Whether they are long-lasting is difficult to determine, though, since a number of the early-maturing girls dropped out of the study.

Complexity of On-Time and Off-Time in Development

Being on-time or off-time in terms of pubertal events is a complex affair. For example, the dimensions may involve not just biological status and pubertal age, but also chronological age, grade in school, cognitive functioning, and social maturity (Petersen, 1987b). Adolescents may be at risk when the demands of a particular social context don't match the adolescents' physical and behavioral characteristics (Lerner, 1987). Dancers whose pubertal status develops on time are one example. In general peer comparisons, on-time dancers should not show adjustment problems. However, they do not have the ideal characteristics for the world of dancers. That is, the ideal characteristics of dancers are generally those associated with late maturity—a thin, lithe body build. The dancers, then, are on-time in terms of pubertal development for their peer group in general, but there is an asynchrony to their development in terms of their more focused peer group—dancers.

A special concern about being off-time in pubertal development focuses on health care. To learn more about the implications for health care of being off-time in pubertal development, read Perspective on Adolescent Development 3.3.

Are Puberty's Effects Exaggerated?

Some researchers have begun to question whether puberty's effects are as strong as once was believed (Brooks-Gunn & Warren, 1989; Lerner, 1988; Petersen, 1987a). Have the effects of early and late maturation been exaggerated? Puberty affects some adolescents more strongly than others, and some behaviors more strongly than others. Body image, dating interest, and sexual behavior are quite clearly affected by pubertal change. The recent questioning of puberty's effects suggests that if we look at overall development and adjustment in life's human cycle, puberty and its variations have less dramatic effects for most individuals than is commonly thought. For some young adolescents the transition through puberty is stormy, but for most it is not. Each period of life's human cycle has its stresses. Puberty is no different. It imposes new challenges resulting from emerging developmental changes, but the vast majority of adolescents weather these stresses nicely. In thinking about puberty's effects, also keep in mind that the world of adolescents involves not only biological influences on development, but also cognitive and social or environmental influences. As with all periods of human development, these processes work in concert to produce who we are in adolescence. Singling out biological changes as the dominating change in adolescence may not be a wise strategy.

While extreme early or late maturation may be risk factors in development, we have seen that the overall effects of early or late maturation are often not great. Not all early maturers will date, smoke, and drink, and not all late maturers will have difficulty in peer relations. In some instances, the effects of grade in school are stronger than maturational timing effects (Petersen & Crockett, 1985). Because the adolescent's social world is organized by grade rather than pubertal development, this finding is not surprising. However, this does not mean that maturation has no influence on development.

Biological and Cognitive Processes and Development

Pubertal Timing and Health Care

What can be done to identify off-time maturers who are at risk for problems? Many boys and girls whose development is extremely early or extremely late are likely to come to the attention of a physician—such as a boy who has not had a spurt in height by the age of 16 or a girl who has not menstruated by the age of 15. Girls and boys who are early or late maturers but well within the normal range are less likely to be taken to a physician because of their maturational status. Nonetheless, these boys and girls may have fears and doubts about being normal that they do not raise unless the physician, counselor, or some other health care provider takes the initiative. A brief discussion outlining the sequence and timing of events and the large individual variations in them may be all that is required to reassure many adolescents who are maturing off-time.

Health care providers may want to discuss the adolescent's off-time development with parents as well as the adolescent. Information about the peer pressures occurring with off-time development can be beneficial. Especially helpful to early maturing girls is a discussion of peer pressures to date and to engage in adultlike behavior at early ages. The transition to middle school or junior high school, or to high school, may be more stressful for girls and boys who are in the midst of puberty than for those who are not (Brooks-Gunn, 1988).

If pubertal development is extremely late, a physician may recommend hormonal treatment. In one investigation of extended pubertal delay in boys, hormonal treatment worked to increase height, dating interest, and peer relations in several boys, but there was little or no improvement in other boys (Lewis, Money, & Bobrow, 1977).

In sum, most early and late maturing individuals weather puberty's challenges and stresses competently. For those who do not, discussions with sensitive and knowledgeable health care providers and parents can improve the coping abilities of the off-time maturing adolescent.

Rather, we are reminded that we always need to evaluate puberty's effects within the larger framework of interacting biological, cognitive, and social contexts (Brooks-Gunn, 1988; Lerner, Lerner, & Tubman, 1989).

At this point we have discussed a number of ideas about the nature of puberty. A summary of these ideas is presented in Concept Table 3.2.

Puberty

Concept	Processes/Related Ideas	Characteristics/Description
Boundaries and Determinants	Their nature	Puberty is a rapid change to physical maturation involving hormonal and bodily changes that take place primarily during early adolescence. Its determinants include nutrition, health, heredity, and body mass.
Hormonal changes	Hypothalamic-pituitary-gonadal axis	The endocrine system is made up of endocrine glands and their secretions. The secretions of these ductless glands are called hormones, powerful chemicals that regulate organs. The hypothalamic-pituitary-gonadal axis is an important aspect of the complex hormonal system that contributes to pubertal change.
	Androgens and estrogens	Testosterone, a member of the general class of hormones known as androgens, plays a key role in the pubertal development of males. Estradiol, a member of the general class of hormones known as estrogens, plays a key role in the pubertal development of females. Recent research has documented a link between hormonal levels and the adolescent's behavior.
	Pituitary and thyroid glands	The pituitary gland also stimulates growth, either through the thyroid gland, or more directly through growth hormones.
Physical changes	Height and weight	The growth spurt for boys occurs about 2 years later than for girls, with 12½ being the average age of onset for boys and 10½ being the average age of onset for girls.
	Sexual maturation	A predominant feature of pubertal change. Includes a number of changes in physical development for both boys (such as penile growth, testicular development, and pubic hair) and girls (such as pubic hair and breast growth).

Summary

I. The Nature of Genes

Each adolescent inherits a genetic code from his or her parents. Physically the hereditary code is carried by biochemical agents called genes and chromosomes. Genotype refers to the special configuration of genes each individual has. Phenotype refers to all the observed and measurable characteristics of the individual. Genetic transmission is complex, but some general principles have been worked out, among them polygenic inheritance, reaction range, and canalization. Behavior genetics is the field concerned with the degree and nature of behavior's hereditary basis. Among the most important methods developed by behavior geneticists are the twin study and the adoption study. The concept of heritability is used in many of the twin and adoption studies. The heritability index is not without its flaws.

Concept	Processes/Related Ideas	Characteristics/Description
	Individual maturation	Extensive within a wide normal range. The normal range is wide enough that given two boys of the same chronological age, one may complete the pubertal sequence before the other has begun it.
Psychological dimensions	Body image	Adolescents show considerable interest in their body image. Young adolescents are more preoccupied and less satisfied with their body image than late adolescents are.
	Menarche and the menstrual cycle	Menarche is the girl's first period. Menarche and the menstrual cycle produce a wide range of reactions in girls. Those who are not prepared or who mature early have more negative reactions.
	Early and late maturation	Early maturation favors boys at least during adolescence. As adults, though, late maturing boys achieve more successful identities. The results for girls are more mixed than for boys.
	On-time and off-time	Being on-time or being off-time in pubertal development is complex. Adolescents may be at risk when the demands of a particular context and the adolescent's physical and behavioral characteristics are mismatched.
	Are puberty's effects exaggerated?	Recently some scholars have expressed doubt that puberty's effects on development are as strong as once believed. It is important to keep in mind that adolescent development is influenced by an interaction of biological, cognitive, and social factors, rather than being dominated by biology. While extreme early or late maturation may place an adolescent at risk, the overall effects of early and late maturation are not great. This is not the same as saying puberty and early or late maturation have no effect on development. They do, but puberty's changes always need to be considered in terms of the larger framework of interacting biological, cognitive, and social factors.

II. Temperament

This refers to behavioral style. Chess and Thomas developed nine temperament dimensions and three temperament clusters. Temperament is influenced strongly by biological factors in infancy but becomes more malleable with experience. Introversion-extraversion is moderately influenced by heredity.

III. Heredity-Environment Interaction

No genes, no organism; no environment, no organism. Because the environment's influence depends on genetically endowed characteristics, we say that the two factors interact.

IV. General Dimensions of Physical Growth

These include a general growth curve, consisting of most aspects of skeletal and muscular growth; a reproductive curve; a curve for the brain and head; and a curve for lymphoid tissues. Some biologists argue that brain growth occurs in spurts; others disagree. Factors that influence growth curves include target-seeking or self-stabilizing factors, maturity gradients, feedback regulation, and body mass.

V. Boundaries and Determinants of Puberty

Puberty is a rapid change to physical maturation involving hormonal and bodily changes that take place primarily in early adolescence. Puberty's determinants include nutrition, health, heredity, and body mass.

VI. Hormonal Changes

The endocrine system is made up of endocrine glands and their secretions. The secretions of these ductless glands are called hormones, powerful chemicals that regulate organs. The hypothalamic-pituitary-gonadal axis is an important aspect of the complex hormonal system that contributes to pubertal change. Testosterone, a member of the general class of hormones known as androgens, plays a key role in the pubertal development of males. Estradiol, a member of the general class of hormones known as estrogens, plays a key role in the pubertal development of females. Recent research has documented the link between hormonal levels and the adolescent's behavior. The pituitary gland also stimulates growth, either through the thyroid gland, or more directly through growth hormones.

VII. Physical Changes

The growth spurt for boys occurs about 2 years later than for girls, with 12½ being the average age of onset for boys and 10½ being the average age of onset for girls. Sexual maturation is a predominant feature of pubertal change. It includes a number of changes in physical development for both boys (such as penile growth, testicular development, and pubic hair) and girls (such as pubic hair and breast growth). There is extensive individual variation within a wide normal range for puberty's changes. The normal range is wide enough that given two boys of the same chronological age, one may complete the pubertal sequence before the other has begun it.

VIII. Psychological Dimensions

Adolescents show considerable interest in their body image. Young adolescents are more preoccupied and less satisfied with their body image than late adolescents are. Menarche is the girl's first period. Menarche and the menstrual cycle produce a wide range of reactions in girls. Those who are not prepared or who mature early have more negative reactions. Early maturation favors boys at least during adolescence. As adults, though, late-maturing boys achieve more successful identities. The results for girls are more mixed than for boys. Being on-time or being off-time in pubertal development is complex. Adolescents may be at risk when the demands of a particular context and the adolescent's physical and behavioral characteristics are mismatched.

IX. Are Puberty's Effects Exaggerated?

Recently some scholars have expressed doubt that puberty's effects are as strong as once believed. It is important to keep in mind that adolescent development is influenced by an interaction of biological, cognitive, and social factors, rather than being dominated by biology. While extreme early or late maturation can place an adolescent at risk, the overall effects of early and late maturation are not great. This is not the same thing as saying puberty and early or late maturation have no effect on development. They do, but puberty's changes always need to be considered in terms of the larger framework of interacting biological, cognitive, and social factors.

Key Terms

genotype 91	monozygotic 93	hypothalamus 105
phenotype 91	dizygotic 93	gonadal 106
polygenic inheritance 92	heritability 94	gonadotropin 106
reaction range 92	puberty 104	androgens 106
canalization 93	menarche 104	estrogens 106
behavior genetics 93	hormones 105	testosterone 106
adoption study 93	hypothalamic-pituitary-	estradiol 106
twin study 93	gonadal axis 105	thyroid gland 107

Suggested Readings

Adams, G. R., Montemayor, R., & Gullotta, T. P. (Eds.). (1989). *Biology of adolescent behavior and development*. Newbury Park, CA: Sage.
An excellent, very recent portrayal of issues involved in the biological basis of adolescent development.

Brooks-Gunn, J. (1988). Antecedents and consequences of variations in girls' maturational timing. In M. D. Levine & E. R. McAnarney (Eds.), *Early adolescent transitions*. Lexington, MA: Lexington Books.
An authoritative review of what we know about the young adolescent girl's pubertal transitions.

Journal of Youth and Adolescence, 1985, Vol. 14, Nos. 3, 4.
These two issues of this research journal have been devoted to the study of maturational timing in adolescence, including many insights into how puberty is experienced.

Lerner, R. M., & Foch, T. T. (Eds.). (1987). *Biological-psychological interaction in early adolescence*. Hillsdale, NJ: Erlbaum.
Includes articles on a wide range of topics related to pubertal changes and their effects on development.

McCoy, K., & Wibbelsman, C. (1987). *The teenage body book*. Los Angeles, CA: The Body Press.
An award winning book for youth. Includes extensive questions adolescents have about their bodies and the answers to those questions.

Scarr, S., & Kidd, K. K. (1983). Developmental behavior genetics. In P. H. Mussen (Ed.), *Handbook of child psychology* (Vol. 2, 4th ed.). New York: Wiley.
A thorough treatment of heredity's influence on development.

Cognitive Development
and Social Cognition

Our life is what our thoughts make it.

Marcus Aurelius, Meditations,
2nd Century B.C.

125

Sandy's Personal Fable

When you were an adolescent, you not only thought about numbers and words but spent a great deal of time thinking about social matters. As part of this thinking, you probably showed a heightened interest in being unique as well as being indestructible. In early adolescence, our ideas often are filled with idealistic notions and hypothetical possibilities. And at this point in development, our thoughts reveal an increased ability to step outside of ourselves and anticipate what the reactions of others will be in imaginative circumstances. To retain a sense of personal uniqueness and to preserve the feeling of being perceived in a positive way by others, adolescents may construct a personal fable—a story about themselves. In the following description, Sandy develops a personal fable about a handsome boy named Bob:

> Bob was important to me before I really knew him at all. It began when my mother invited him to a dance at the end of my ninth grade year. I didn't see much of him at the dance because I was actively pursuing someone else, and my brother's friends from prep school were being very nice to me as little sister. Afterwards, however, he asked me out a couple of times. We didn't get along particularly well or ill, weren't particularly attracted or repelled; but then I went away to school.

At school, I found that everyone else had someone "on the outside" to talk about, and, in most cases, to correspond with or even to visit and have visit them. My problem was that I had never been able to bear any of the boys who had shown a great interest in me, probably because I didn't like myself and thought there had to be something basically wrong with anyone who did. Consequently, I had nothing remotely approaching an outside attachment and little hope of forming a spectacular one at school. Still, I was determined to keep up with the competition, so I made up a relationship with Bob. This had the advantage of being based in fact. I had gone out with him and he was real. Also, he was in school in England, which explained why he never showed up and, to some extent, why he didn't write, since he would have had to ask his parents to find out from my parents where I was. Then, too, his not having shown much interest in me meant that I didn't despise him. This made it easier for me to represent myself as being madly in love with him.

After a few days I had the other girls convinced, and after a few months I believed it myself.

(From G. W. Goethals and D. S. Klos, Experiencing Youth. Copyright 1970 Little, Brown & Company. Scott, Foresman and Company, Glenview, IL)

*I*n this chapter, we explore the fascinating world of the adolescent's thoughts. In Chapter 2, you were introduced briefly to Jean Piaget's theory of cognitive development. More than any other theory, it is Piaget's theory that has had the most to say about the way adolescents think differently than children. We begin by describing Piaget's ideas about concrete and formal operational thought, evaluate whether Piaget's ideas adequately explain adolescent cognition, and then turn to the intriguing world of the adolescent's thoughts about social matters.

Piaget's Theory and Adolescent Cognition

To learn about Piaget's theory of cognitive development, we review and expand on some of the basic ideas presented in Chapter 2, focusing in greater detail on the two stages of thought that Piaget believed primarily characterize the way adolescents think—concrete operational and formal operational.

An Overview of Piaget's Theory and Concrete Operational Thought

Piaget's theory is one of the most well known, most widely discussed views of adolescent development. Piaget stressed that adolescents are motivated to understand their world because doing so is biologically adaptive. To understand their world adolescents use the processes of organization and adaptation (assimilation and accommodation). Piaget believed that individuals develop through four stages: sensorimotor, preoperational, concrete operational, and formal operational. Let's now examine in greater detail these last two stages.

Remember that, according to Piaget, concrete operational thought takes place approximately between the ages of 7 and 11 and is made up of **operations**—mental actions that are reversible. The concrete operational thinker can mentally reverse liquid from one beaker to another and understand that the volume is the same even though the beakers differ in height and width. In Piaget's most famous task, an individual is presented with two identical beakers, each filled with the same amount of liquid (see Figure 4.1). The individual is asked if these beakers have the same amount of liquid, and the individual usually says yes. Then, the liquid from one beaker is poured into a third beaker, which is taller and thinner than the first two (see Figure 4.1). The individual is then asked if the amount of liquid in the tall, thin beaker is equal to that which remains in one of the original beakers. Concrete operational thinkers answer "yes" and justify their answers appropriately. Preoperational thinkers (usually children under the age of about 7) often answer "no" and justify their answers in terms of the differing height and width of the beakers. This example reveals the ability of the concrete operational individual to decenter and coordinate several characteristics (such as height and width) rather than focusing on a single property of an object (such as height).

Figure 4.1 The beaker task is used by developmentalists to determine whether an individual can think in concrete operational ways.

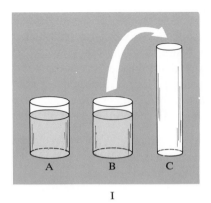
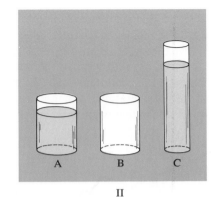

This ability to recognize that the length, number, mass, quantity, area, weight, and volume of objects and substances do not change through transformations that alter their appearance Piaget called **conservation.** An important aspect of conservation is that individuals do not conserve all quantities on all tasks simultaneously. The order of their mastery is number, length, liquid quantity, mass, weight, and volume. Piaget used the term **horizontal décalage** to describe how conservation of *different forms* of quantity does not appear at the same time developmentally. For example, an 8-year-old child may know that a long stick of clay can be rolled back into a ball but not understand that the ball and stick weigh the same. At about 9 years of age the child will recognize that the ball and the stick weigh the same. Eventually at about 11–12 years of age the child will understand that the clay's volume is unchanged by rearranging it. Children initially master tasks in which the dimensions are more salient and visible, and only later master those not as visually apparent, such as volume.

Many of the concrete operations identified by Piaget focus on the way individuals reason about the properties of objects. One important skill that characterizes the concrete operational thinker is the ability to classify or divide things into different sets or subsets and to consider their interrelations. An example of the concrete operational thinker's classification skills involves a family tree of four generations (see Figure 4.2) (Furth & Wachs, 1975). This family tree indicates that the grandfather (A) has three children (B, C, & D), each of whom has three children (E through J), and that one of these children (J) has three children (K, L, & M). An individual who comprehends the classification can move up and down a level (vertically), across a level (horizontally), and up and down and across (obliquely) within the system. The concrete operational thinker understands, for example, that person J can simultaneously be father, brother, and grandson.

While concrete operational thought is more advanced than preoperational thought, it has limitations. The main limitation is that concrete operational thought focuses on the world that is directly observable, the *concrete* world. Concrete operational thinking fares much better with the real, perceived world than with abstract, hypothetical circumstances. For example,

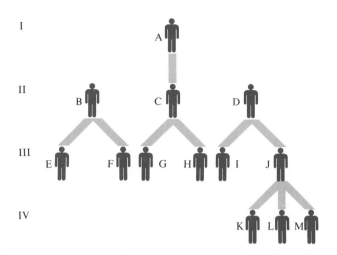

Figure 4.2 Piaget believed that concrete operational thinkers can classify things into different sets or subsets and consider their interrelations. In this family tree of four generations, children who are concrete operational thinkers can move vertically, horizontally, and obliquely within the system

concrete operational thinkers are capable of understanding such mathematical operations as addition and subtraction, which involve being able to mentally reverse numbers, but they are not capable of imagining the steps necessary to complete an algebraic equation, which involves more abstract concepts.

The Characteristics of Formal Operational Thought

What are the characteristics of formal operational thought? Most significantly, adolescent thought is more abstract than child thought. Adolescents are no longer limited to actual, concrete experiences as anchors for thought. They can conjure up make-believe situations, events that are strictly hypothetical possibilities or purely abstract propositions, and try to reason logically about them.

The abstract quality of the adolescent's thought at the formal operational level is evident in the adolescent's verbal problem-solving ability. While the concrete operational thinker would need to see the concrete elements A, B, and C to be able to make the logical inference that if A = B and B = C, then A = C, the formal operational thinker can solve this problem merely through verbal presentation.

Another indication of the abstract quality of the adolescent's thought is his or her increased tendency to think about thought itself. One adolescent commented, "I began thinking about why I was thinking what I was. Then I began thinking about why I was thinking about why I was thinking about what I was." If this sounds abstract, it is, and it characterizes the adolescent's enhanced focus on thought and its abstract qualities.

Accompanying the abstract nature of formal operational thought in adolescence is thought full of idealism and possibilities. While children frequently think in concrete ways, or in terms of what is real and limited, adolescents begin to engage in extended speculation about ideal characteristics—qualities they desire in themselves and in others. Such thoughts often

Adolescent thought is different than child thought. One way it is different is that adolescents begin to think about thought itself. The adolescent girl shown here might be thinking, "Why am I thinking about Bob the way I'm thinking about Bob?"

lead adolescents to compare themselves and others in regard to such ideal
standards. And during adolescence, the thoughts of individuals are often fantasy flights into future possibilities. It is not unusual for the adolescent to
become impatient with these newfound ideal standards and become perplexed
over which of many ideal standards to adopt.

Adolescents also are more likely than children to think in hypothetical
deductive ways and reason in more logical fashion about problems, according
to Piaget. It is sometimes said that the adolescent's thought is more like a
scientist's than a child's, meaning that the adolescent often entertains many
possibilities and tests many solutions in a planned way when having to solve
a problem. This kind of problem solving has been called **hypothetical-
deductive reasoning.** Basically this means that in solving a problem, an individual develops hypotheses or hunches about what will be a correct solution
to the problem, and then in a planned manner tests one or more of the hypotheses, discarding the ones that do not work. (See Table 4.1 for one example
of hypothetical-deductive reasoning.) Jerome Bruner and his associates have
used a modification of the familiar game Twenty Questions in extensive work
on cognitive skills (Bruner, 1966). The adolescent is given a set of 42 colorful
pictures displayed in a rectangular array (six rows of seven pictures each) and
is asked to determine which picture the experimenter has in mind (that is,

TABLE 4.1   *An Exemplary Task of Hypothetical-Deductive Reasoning*

A common task for all of us is to determine what can logically be inferred from a statement made by someone else. Young children are often told by teachers that if they work hard, they will receive good grades. Regardless of the empirical truth of the claim, the children may believe that good grades are the result of hard work, and that if they do not get good grades, they did not work hard enough. (Establishing the direction of the relationship between variables is an important issue).

Children in late concrete operations, too, are concerned with understanding the relations between their behavior and their teachers' grading practices. However, they are beginning to question the "truths" of their childhood. First, they now know that there are four possible combinations if two variables are dichotomized (work hard—not work hard; good grades—not good grades).

Behavior	*Consequences*
1. Work hard	good grades
2. Work hard	not good grades
3. Not work hard	good grades
4. Not work hard	not good grades

Two combinations are consistent with the hypothesis that [a student's] hard work is necessarily related to good grades: (1) they work hard and get good grades, (4) they do not work hard and do not get good grades. When the presumed "cause" is present, the effect is present; when the cause is absent, the effect is absent. There are also two combinations that do not fit the hypothesis of a direct relation between hard work and good grades: (2) they work hard and do not get good grades, and (3) they get good grades without working hard.

The adolescent's notion of possibility allows him or her to take this analysis of combinations one important step further. Each of the four basic combinations of binary variables may be true or it may not. If 1, 2, 3, or 4 are true alone or in combination, there are 16 possible patterns of truth values.

1 or 2 or 3 or 4 is true		4 patterns
1–2 or 1–3 or 1–4 or 2–3 or 2–4 or 3–4 are true		6 patterns
1–2–3 or 1–2–4 or 1–3–4 or 2–3–4 are true		4 patterns
All (1–2–3–4) are true		1 pattern
All are false		1 pattern
	Total	16 patterns

The list is critically important because each pattern leads to a different conclusion about the possible relation between two variables. (Table 4.1 from *Piaget with Feeling,* Philip Cowan, copyright © 1978 Holt, Rinehart & Winston, Inc., reprinted by permission of the publisher.)

---

which is "correct"). The person is allowed to ask only questions to which the experimenter can reply yes or no. The object of the game is to select the correct picture by asking as few questions as possible. The person who is a deductive hypothesis tester formulates a plan to propose and test a series of hypotheses, each of which narrows the field of choices considerably. The most effective plan consists of a "halving" strategy. (*Q:* Is it in the right half of the array? *A:* No. *Q:* Okay; is it in the top half? And so on.) Used correctly, the halving strategy guarantees the questioner the correct solution in seven questions or less, no matter where the correct picture is located in the array. Even if he is using a less elegant strategy than the optimal "halving" one, the deductive hypothesis tester understands that when the experimenter answers no to one of his guesses, several possibilities are immediately eliminated.

By contrast, the concrete thinker may persist with questions that continue to test some of the same possibilities that previous questions should have eliminated. For example, the child may have asked whether the correct picture

Culture and Formal Operational Thought

The ability to think in scientific ways—to develop hypotheses, systematically evaluate possible solutions, and deduce a correct answer to a difficult problem—is an important dimension of formal operational thought. A majority of adolescents in the United States do not think in formal operational ways when presented with scientific reasoning problems, and in developing countries an even smaller percentage of individuals do so (Neimark, 1982). In one cross-cultural investigation including the countries of the United States, Germany, Austria, and Italy, only 7% of the eighth-grade students reasoned in formal operational ways (Karplus, 1981). In one Italian group, the adolescents did especially well. Closer observation revealed that these adolescents had been with the same outstanding teacher for 3 years, indicating the role education may play in improving formal operational thought. According to observers, in many third-world, developing countries formal operational thought in the form of scientific thinking is a rare occurrence. ❧

was in row 1 and received the answer no, but later asks whether the correct picture is *x,* which is in row 1.

Thus, formal operational thinkers test their hypothesis with judiciously chosen questions and tests. Often a single question or test will help them to eliminate an untenable hypothesis. By contrast, concrete operational thinkers often fail to understand the relation between a hypothesis and a well chosen test of it—stubbornly clinging to the idea despite clear, logical disconfirmation of it.

According to Piaget (1972), the nature of adolescent reasoning can be explained by the characteristics of formal operational thought, especially the ability to reason about what is possible and hypothetical as opposed to what is real, and the ability to reflect on one's own thoughts. These features of formal operational thought are believed to be responsible for a number of typical adolescent characteristics—a focus on internal life, a preoccupation with life plans, a future orientation, and an interest in developing an ideological perspective.

Formal operational thought has been conceptualized as occurring in two phases. In the first phase, the increased ability to think in a hypothetical way produces unconstrained thoughts with unlimited possibilities. This early formal operational thought submerges reality (Broughton, 1983). What is real is overwhelmed. What is ideal and possible dominate. During the middle years of adolescence, an intellectual balance is restored. Adolescents now test out the products of their reasoning against experience and a consolidation of formal operational thought takes place.

Biological and Cognitive Processes and Development

Piaget's (1952) early writings seemed to indicate that the onset and consolidation of formal operational thought is completed during early adolescence, from about 12–15 years of age. Later, Piaget (1972) concluded that formal operational thought is not achieved until later in adolescence, between approximately 15 and 20 years of age.

Piaget's concepts of assimilation and accommodation help us to understand the two different phases of formal operational thought. Remember from Chapter 2 that *assimilation* occurs when adolescents incorporate new information into their existing knowledge; *accommodation* occurs when adolescents adjust to new information. During early adolescence, there is an excess of assimilation as the world is perceived too subjectively and idealistically. In the middle years of adolescence, an intellectual balance is restored, as the individual accommodates to the cognitive upheaval that has taken place. In this view, the assimilation of formal operational thought marks the transition to adolescence; the accommodation marks a later consolidation of thought (Lapsley, 1989).

Individual Variation in Adolescent Cognition

Piaget's theory emphasizes universal and consistent patterns of formal operational thought. His theory does not adequately account for the unique, individual differences that characterize the cognitive development of adolescents. These individual variations in adolescents' cognitive development have been documented in a number of investigations (Bart, 1971; Neimark, 1982; Kaufmann & Flaitz, 1987).

Some individuals in early adolescence are formal operational thinkers; others are not. A review of formal operational thought investigations revealed that only about 1 of every 3 eighth-grade students is a formal operational thinker (Strahan, 1983). Some investigators find that formal operational thought increases with age in adolescence (Arlin, 1984; Martorano, 1977); others do not (Strahan, 1987). Many college students and adults do not think in formal operational ways either. For example, investigators have found that from 17% to 67% of college students think in formal operational ways (Elkind, 1961; Tomlinson-Keasey, 1972).

Many young adolescents are at the point of consolidating their concrete operational thought, using it more consistently than in childhood. At the same time, many young adolescents are just beginning to think in a formal operational manner. By late adolescence, many adolescents are beginning to consolidate their formal operational thought, using it more consistently. And there often is variation across the content areas of formal operational thought, just as there is in concrete operational thought in childhood. A 14-year-old adolescent may reason at the formal operational level when it comes to analyzing algebraic equations but not do so with verbal problem solving or when reasoning about interpersonal relations.

Formal operational thought is more likely to be used in areas in which adolescents have the most experience and knowledge (Carey, 1988; Flavell, 1985). Children and adolescents gradually build up elaborate knowledge through extensive experience and practice in various sports, games, hobbies, and school subjects such as math, English, and science. The development of expertise in different domains of life may make possible high-level, developmentally mature-looking thought. In some instances, the sophisticated reasoning of formal operational thought may be responsible. In other instances, however, the thought may be largely due to the accumulation of knowledge that allows more automatic, memory-based processes to function. Some developmentalists are wondering if the acquisition of knowledge could account for all cognitive growth. Most, however, argue that *both* cognitive changes in such areas as concrete and formal operational thought *and* the development of expertise through experience are at work in understanding the adolescent's cognitive world. More about knowledge's role in the adolescent's thinking appears in the next chapter.

One recent proposal argues that a better understanding of Piaget's theory of formal operational thought can be achieved by considering the distinction between "knowing that" and "knowing how" (Byrnes, 1988a,b). The argument is that reasoning takes place in two basic forms: "knowing that" and "knowing how." "Knowing that" has been called conceptual knowledge or declarative knowledge (Hiebert & LeFevre, 1987; Mandler, 1983). It consists of networks of the core concepts in a given domain, such as biology or physics. "Knowing how" is simply a representation of the steps an individual should follow in order to solve a problem. It has been referred to as procedural knowledge (Anderson, 1985). For example, in the domain of physics "knowing that" would consist of understanding the relation between the core concepts of "force" and "mass." In contrast, "knowing how" would consist of understanding how to solve introductory physics test problems using formulas and the like.

The argument by James Byrnes (1988a, 1988b) is that Piaget's theory of formal operations can be better understood if it is recast as "knowing that." However, Daniel Keating (1988, in press) argues that Piaget's theory is actually about "knowing how," and that considering his view of formal operations in terms of "knowing that" is a misinterpretation. The lively debate about Piaget's theory of formal operations is likely to continue as experts strive to determine just exactly what Piaget meant by formal operational thought and search for the true nature of adolescent cognitive development.

Beyond Formal Operational Thought

Some critics of Piaget's theory argue that specialized thinking about a specific skill represents a higher stage of thought than formal operational thought. Piaget did not believe this was so. For him, the change to reasoning about a special skill (such as the kind of thinking engaged in by a nuclear physicist or a medical researcher) is no more than window dressing. A nuclear physicist may think in ways that an adolescent cannot think, but the adolescent and the nuclear physicist differ only in their familiarity with an academic field of inquiry. They differ in the content of their thought, not in the operations they bring to bear on the content (Piaget, 1970).

Biological and Cognitive Processes and Development

Some developmentalists believe that the absolute nature of adolescent logic and buoyant optimism diminish in early childhood. According to Gisela Labouvie-Vief (1982, 1986), a new integration of thought takes place in early adulthood. She thinks the adult years produce pragmatic constraints that require an adaptive strategy of less reliance on logical analysis in solving problems. Commitment, specialization, and channeling energy into finding one's niche in complex social and work systems replace the youth's fascination with idealized logic. If we assume that logical thought and buoyant optimism represent the criteria for cognitive maturity, we would have to admit that the cognitive activity of adults is too concrete and pragmatic. But from Labouvie-Vief's view the adult's understanding of reality's constraints reflects maturity, not immaturity.

Even Piaget (1967) detected that formal operational thought may have its hazards:

> With the advent of formal intelligence, thinking takes wings and it is not surprising that at first this unexpected power is both used and abused. . . . Each new mental ability starts off by incorporating the world in a process of egocentric assimilation. Adolescent egocentricity is manifested by a belief in the omnipotence of reflection, as though the world should submit itself to idealistic schemes rather than to systems of reality. (pp. 63–64)

Our cognitive abilities are very strong in early adulthood, and they do show adaptation to life's pragmatic concerns. Less clear is whether our logical skills actually decline. Competence as a young adult probably requires doses of both logical thinking skills and pragmatic adaptation to reality. For example, when architects design a building, they logically analyze and plan the structure but understand the cost constraints, environmental concerns, and the time it will take to get the job done effectively.

Cognitive change in adulthood also involves wisdom, which like a good wine may get better with age. **Wisdom** is broad interpretive knowledge. It involves understanding the limits and conditions of life and living—mortality, health, physical capacity, emotional range, social constraints, and personal talents. And it involves the accumulation of life-long experience in dealing with one's own life tasks and observing others deal with theirs (Baltes & others, 1988; Erikson, 1980; Smith, Dixon, & Baltes, in press). One tangible sign of wisdom is sound or good judgment in conducting one's own life. This practical knowledge system takes years to develop. Developmentalists believe that it may not reach its peak until the late adulthood years.

Piaget's Theory and Adolescent Education

Piaget's theory has been widely applied to education, although more extensively with children than adolescents. Piaget was not an educator and never pretended to be. But he did provide a sound conceptual framework from which to view educational problems. What principles of Piaget's theory of cognitive development can be applied to education? David Elkind (1976) described two.

First, the foremost issue in education is *communication*. In Piaget's theory, the adolescent's mind is not a blank slate. To the contrary, the adolescent has a host of ideas about the physical and natural world. Adolescents come to school with their own ideas about space, time, causality, quantity, and number. We need to learn to comprehend what adolescents are saying and to respond to their ideas. Second, adolescents are by nature knowing creatures. The best way to nurture this motivation for knowledge is to allow the adolescent to spontaneously interact with the environment. Educators need to ensure that they do not dull the adolescent's eagerness to know by providing an overly rigid curriculum that disrupts the adolescent's own rhythm and pace of learning.

Why have applications to adolescent education lagged behind applications to children's education? Adolescents who are formal operational thinkers are at a level similar to their teachers and to the authors of textbooks. In Piaget's model, it is no longer necessary to pay attention to qualitative changes in cognition. Also, the structure of education itself undergoes considerable change between elementary and secondary levels. For children, the basic focus of education is the classroom. Children may be involved with, at most, several teachers during the day. In secondary schools, the focus shifts to subject matter divisions of curriculum. Each teacher sees a student for 45–60 minutes a day in connection with one content area (English, history, math, for example). Thus, both teachers and texts may become more focused on the development of curriculum than on the developmental characteristics of students. And when teachers *are* concerned about students' developmental characteristics in adolescence, they pay more attention to social-personality dimensions than to cognitive dimensions (Cowan, 1978).

One main argument that has emerged from the application of Piaget's theory to education is that instruction may too often be at the formal operational level even though the majority of adolescents are not actually formal operational thinkers. That is, the instruction may be too formal and too abstract. Possibly it should be less formal and more concrete. Perspective on Adolescent Development 4.1 describes a comparison of two teaching formats with different cognitive orientations—one a more formal curriculum, the other a more concrete curriculum. The available data suggest that adolescents construct a view of the world on the basis of observations and experiences and that education should take this into account when developing a curriculum for adolescents (Burbules & Linn, 1988; Carey, 1986; Danner, 1989; Linn, 1987).

Language Development

An important aspect of the adolescent's cognitive development involves language. Piaget (1952) believed that cognition always directs language. Among the significant language changes that occur during adolescence, many of which are related to Piaget's view of cognitive development, are those pertaining to words and concepts, prose and writing, and pragmatics, each of which we consider in turn.

Biological and Cognitive Processes and Development

Piaget's Theory and the Teaching of Science

Consider a curriculum area that virtually every adolescent is exposed to during the junior high and high school years—science. Most science courses (or at least the majority of units taught in each of them) follow a reasonably formal, straightforward lecture format. Classifications of animals and plants are memorized through exposure to the teacher's lecture and the text.

Some educational experts believe that this format is not the best way to teach science, particularly for students who have not yet reached the stage of formal operational thought. Instead, they believe that improved learning and advances in cognitive development are more likely to occur when adolescents observe and collect organisms from their natural habitats and then relate them to various subjects covered in the course. In this manner, the adolescent is forced to restructure his or her concrete way of thinking about the world and logically categorize events and objects in more formal, logical ways.

One investigation was specifically designed to test whether the more formal lecture method or the hands-on experience of student participation was superior at promoting cognitive development (Renner & others, 1976). Students in junior high school science courses were taught using either the formal lecture method or the hands-on, participatory method. In the formal classes, the students used standard textbooks, read and recited from the books, and learned concepts about the scientific method. In the experimental, hands-on classes, the junior high science students were given considerable experience in solving laboratory problems and there was extensive open inquiry and student-directed investigations. There also was a considerable amount of structure in the hands-on strategy with precise expectations and careful directions being given. The students in both types of classes were tested on Piaget's concrete and formal operational tasks both before and after participation in the classes.

In applying what we know about the development of adolescent thought, special consideration has been given to the best way adolescents can be taught science. How have Piaget's ideas been applied to teaching science in secondary schools?

Junior high students who were taught in the hands-on, participatory way advanced their formal operational thought more than their counterparts who were taught in a more standard format. It is important to note that the use of concrete materials did not interfere with the transition to formal operational thought, but actually seemed to enhance the move.

Piaget's ideas even have been applied in this manner at the college level. For example, in one investigation in the area of humanities, curriculum designed to enhance the transition from concrete to formal operational thought with college freshmen was successful, with 21 of 22 students beginning the year at the concrete level moving to the formal operational level by the end of the term (Wideck, Knefelkamp, & Parker, 1975).

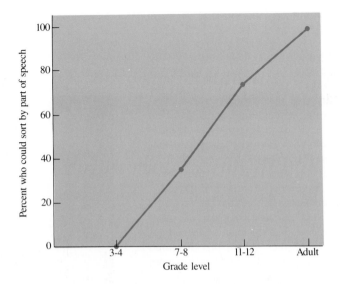

Figure 4.3   Percentage of subjects by different ages who could sort words by parts of speech.

Based on J. M. Anglin, The Growth of Word Meaning, *Copyright © 1970 The MIT Press, Cambridge, MA.*

Adolescents are more sophisticated in their ability to understand words and their related abstract concepts (Fischer & Lazerson, 1984). The understanding of grammar is a case in point. While children can learn the definition of a part of speech, such as what a noun is, and can become fairly adept at imitating model sentences in English workbooks, a true understanding of grammar seems not to appear until adolescence. With the increase in abstract thinking, adolescents seem to be far superior to children in analyzing the function of a word in a sentence.

For instance, in one research study, elementary school children, adolescents, and adults were asked whether they knew what nouns, verbs, adjectives, and prepositions were (Anglin, 1970). Since parts of speech are taught in most schools by the third grade, it was not surprising that most of the people, including the third- and fourth-graders, gave correct definitions. However, when the people were required to sort words (such as during, flower, dead, poor, cry, listen, and white) according to parts of speech, none of the elementary school children could do this task. As shown in Figure 4.3, many of the adolescents and adults were successful at this task.

Another aspect of language that increases during adolescence that is related to words and concepts is **metaphor.** A metaphor is an implied comparison between two ideas that is conveyed by the abstract meaning contained in the words used to make the comparison. A person's faith and a piece of glass may be alike in that both can be shattered easily. A runner's performance and a politician's speech may be alike in that both are predictable. Concrete thinkers have a difficult time understanding such metaphorical relations. Consequently, many elementary school-aged children are puzzled by the meanings of parables and fables (Elkind, 1976).

Yet another aspect of language that reveals an increased understanding during adolescence is **satire,** which refers to a literary work in which irony, derision, or wit in any form is used to expose folly or wickedness. Caricatures

Biological and Cognitive Processes and Development

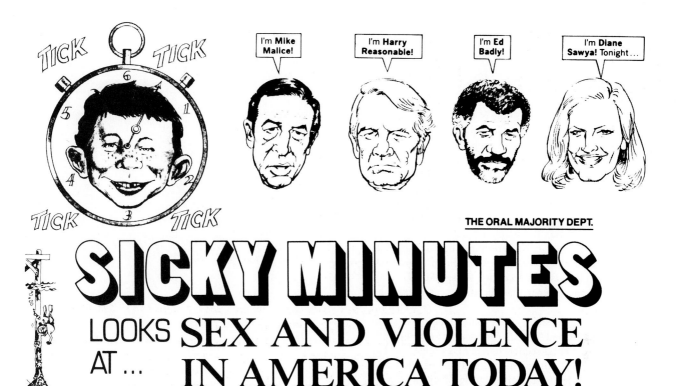

Figure 4.4   Excerpt from Mad Magazine.

are an example of such satire. During adolescence, satire often takes on rhythmical qualities. Junior high school students may make up satirical labels for teachers, such as "The walking wilt Wilkie and wilking machine" or "The magnificent Manifred and his manifest morbidity." They also substantially increase their use of nicknames that are satirical and derisive—"Stilt," "the refrigerator," "spaz" are three such examples. The satire of *Mad* magazine also is more likely to be understood by adolescents than children (Figure 4.4). This magazine relies on double meaning, exaggerations, and parody to highlight absurd circumstances and contradictory happenings. Such complexities in the use of language and caricature are lost on children, but begin to find an audience in adolescents.

The written language of adolescents is often very different from their spoken language (Bereiter & Scardamalia, 1982; Fischer & Lazerson, 1984; Olson, 1977). When adolescents talk with each other they typically are face to face so they can monitor the listener's interest and understanding. When an adolescent writes, however, no other person is present. Therefore, the writer must create an abstract idea of what his or her audience is like. Further, in spoken communication it is usually a much shorter time before a reply is given by the other person, while in written communication it may be necessary to write a number of paragraphs without interruption or a response.

Detecting Deception and Sarcasm

To comprehend the full meaning of a speaker's message, an adolescent needs to be sensitive to the speaker's belief and purpose. In most instances, people say what they believe. However, such conversational sincerity may be broken, and it may be broken for different reasons. Consider a circumstance in which a swimmer, after diving into a pool, comes up to the surface and says, "Come on in. The water is warm." The statement may be sincere or deliberately false. To distinguish between these possibilities, the listener must determine the facts and the speaker's belief about the facts. In addition to whether the statement is sincere or deceptive, the speaker also may try to signal the listener that the statement is false by using sarcasm.

To test the possibility that understanding the sincerity, deception, and sarcasm in a speaker's message follows a developmental sequence, Amy Demorest and her colleagues (1984) studied 6-, 9-, and 13-year-olds and adults. The subjects were given stories about a conversation between two people containing sincere, deceptive, or sarcastic statements (see Table 4.A for what the conversations between the story characters were like). The subjects' ability to identify speaker belief and communicative purpose in sincere, deceptive, and sarcastic re-

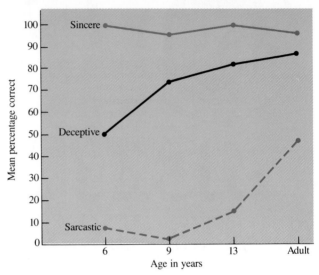

Figure 4.A   Children's, adolescents', and adults' understanding of whether a conversation involves sincerity, deception, or sarcasm.

marks was assessed. As shown in Figure 4.A, all of the six-year-old children took remarks as sincere by assuming that a speaker's belief and purpose are in line with

As can be seen, writing is a complex aspect of language and communication, and it is not surprising that children are very poor at writing (Hunt, 1970; Scardamalia, Bereiter, & Goelman, 1982). An organization of ideas is very important in writing—logical thought processes help the writer provide a hierarchical organization for the reader, letting him or her know which ideas are more general, which are more specific, as well as those that are more important than others (Englert, Stewart, & Hiebert, 1988). Not only has it been found that children are very poor at organizing their ideas ahead of time before they write, but they also have considerable difficulty detecting the most salient points in a prose passage (Brown & Smiley, 1977).

While many adolescents are not yet Pulitzer Prize winning novelists, they do seem to be more capable of distinguishing more general points from more specific points as they write. And, they seem better than children at highlighting important points to be made as they write. With their increased logical thought, the sentences adolescents string together make more sense than

TABLE 4.A *Three Versions of Character Conversations Designed to Be Sincere, Deceptive, or Sarcastic*

Versions

Sincere . . . . Jay needed to get his hair cut. A new barbershop had just opened in town. Jay went to the new barbershop for a haircut. *Jay got the best haircut he had ever had. It was just the right length.* Jay walked home from the barbershop. He saw Mike walking down the street. Mike noticed Jay's new haircut. He crossed the street to speak to Jay. Mike said to Jay, "That new haircut you got looks terrific."	Deceptive . . . *Jay got the worst haircut he had ever had. It was so short that his ears seemed to stick out.* He [Mike] put his arm around Jay's shoulders and smiled at Jay. Sarcastic . . . *Jay got the worst haircut he had ever had. It was so short that his ears seemed to stick out.* He [Mike] laughed and pointed to Jay's head.

(From Amy Demorest, et al., "Words Speak Louder than Actions: Understanding Deliberately False Remarks" in *Child Development,* 55, 152–153, 1984. Copyright 1984 The Society for Research in Child Development, Inc., Chicago, IL. Reprinted by permission of the publisher and the author.)

his or her statement. By nine years of age though, children are able to appreciate the deliberate deception of the speaker; however, at this age deception and sarcasm are both seen as deceptive. Finally, at some point between 13 years of age and adulthood, adolescents become capable of better appreciating that a speaker's purpose may also be out of line with his or her statement. That is, it is during adolescence that sarcasm and deception are distinguished. When sarcasm is detected, the listener gives more weight to the speaker's behavior than to his or her statement.

those of children. Further, their essays are more likely to include an introduction, several paragraphs that represent a body of the paper, and concluding remarks (Fischer & Lazerson, 1984).

Pragmatics refers to the rules of conversation. There is no doubt that most adolescents are much better conversationalists than children. Such rules allow adolescents to convey intended meanings and to "get along" with those they are talking to. The domain of pragmatics is broad. It covers such things as (a) taking turns in discussions, instead of everyone talking at once; (b) using questions to convey commands (Why is it so noisy in here?), (c) using words like "the" and "a" in ways that enhance understanding (He is *the* living end! or He is not just *a* person.), (d) using polite language in appropriate situations (when a guest comes to the house), and even (e) telling stories that are interesting, jokes that are funny, and lies that convince. To learn more about the ability of children and adolescents to detect when someone is lying as well as when sarcasm is being used, read Perspective on Adolescent Development 4.2.

Piagetian Contributions and Criticisms

Piaget was a genius at observing children and adolescents, and some of his insights are surprisingly easy to verify. Piaget showed us some important things to look for in development, including the shift from concrete operational to formal operational thought. He also showed us how we must make our experience fit our cognitive framework, yet simultaneously adapt our cognitive orientation to experience. Piaget also revealed how cognitive change is likely to occur if the situation is structured to allow gradual movement to the next higher level.

Piaget's theory, however, has not gone uncriticized (Gelman & Baillargeon, 1983; Kuhn, 1988; Lapsley, 1989; Overton, 1989; Small, 1990). First, Piaget conceived of stages as unitary structures of thought, so his theory assumes considerable synchrony in development. That is, various aspects of a stage should emerge at about the same time. However, formal operational concepts do not always appear in synchrony. For example, idealism may be more full blown at one point, hypothetical-deductive reasoning at another. Second, small changes in procedures involving Piagetian tasks sometimes have significant effects on an adolescent's thoughts. Third, in some cases adolescents can be trained to reason at a higher level. This poses a special problem for Piaget's theory, which argues that such training only works on a superficial level and is ineffective unless the individual is at a transitional point. Fourth, some cognitive abilities emerge earlier than Piaget envisioned, others later. As we have seen, hypothetical-deductive reasoning does not appear as frequently in early adolescence as Piaget originally believed.

At this point we have discussed many ideas about Piaget's theory of cognitive development. A summary of these ideas is presented in Concept Table 4.1. Now we turn our attention to the social side of cognition.

Social Cognition

In recent years we have witnessed a flourish of interest in how individuals reason about social matters. For many years the field of cognitive development focused more heavily on nonsocial phenomena such as logic, number, words, and the like. Now there is lively interest in how adolescents reason about their social world as well (Bruner & Bornstein, in press; Newman, Griffin, & Cole, 1989; Rogoff, 1989; Wertsch, 1989). We will discuss social cognition's nature, egocentrism and perspective taking, implicit personality theory, social cognitive monitoring, whether Piaget's theory adequately explains the adolescent's social cognition, and the discussion of social cognition in the remainder of the text.

Biological and Cognitive Processes and Development

Piaget's Theory and Adolescent Cognition

Concept	Processes/Related Ideas	Characteristics/Description
Overview and concrete operational thought	Overview	Piaget's widely acclaimed theory stresses biological adaptation through organization and assimilation and accommodation. Piaget argued that individuals move through four stages of cognitive development. Adolescents are likely to be either concrete operational or formal operational thinkers.
	Concrete operational thought	For Piaget, it takes place between approximately 7 and 11 years of age. It is made up of operations and involves reasoning about objects' properties. Conservation and classification skills are characteristics. It is limited by the inability to reason abstractly about objects.
Characteristics of formal operational thought	Their nature	Abstractness and idealism, as well as hypothetical-deductive reasoning, are highlighted in formal operational thought. Formal operational thought involves the ability to reason about what is possible and hypothetical, as opposed to what is real, and the ability to reflect on one's own thoughts. Formal operational thought occurs in two phases—an assimilation phase in which reality is overwhelmed (early adolescence) and an accommodation phase in which intellectual balance is restored through a consolidation of formal operational thought (middle years of adolescence).
Individual variation	Its extent	It is extensive and Piaget did not give this adequate attention. Many young adolescents are not formal operational thinkers but rather are consolidating their concrete operational thought.
Beyond formal operational thought	Adult cognitive changes	Many life-span developmentalists believe Piaget was incorrect in thinking that formal operational thought is the highest form of cognition. They argue that more pragmatic, specialized thought takes place in early adulthood and that wisdom may increase throughout the adult years.
Piaget and adolescent education	Its nature	Piaget's theory has been applied to children's education much more than to adolescent education. Applications to adolescent education often follow the belief that instruction is too formal and abstract for adolescents.
Language	Relation to cognitive changes	Adolescents develop more sophisticated cognitive strategies for handling words and concepts, prose and writing, and pragmatics.
Piagetian contributions and criticisms	Evaluating Piaget's theory	Piaget was a genius at observing children and adolescents. He showed us some important things to look for and mapped out some general cognitive changes. Criticisms focus on such matters as stages, which are not as unitary as he believed and do not follow the timetable he envisioned.

Social Cognition's Nature

Social cognition focuses on how individuals conceptualize and reason about the social world—the people they watch and interact with, relationships with those people, and the groups in which they participate. Social cognition also involves how individuals reason about themselves and others (Flavell, 1985). Two views have promoted interest in social cognition: the cognitive developmental view and social information processing.

The Cognitive Developmental View

The cognitive developmental view of social cognition is based primarily on the theories of Jean Piaget (1952) and Lawrence Kohlberg (1969, 1976), as well as the research and thinking of John Flavell (1981, 1985; Flavell & others, 1968). They believe an individual's social thoughts can be understood better if his or her maturational development is considered.

Kohlberg, in particular, has promoted the role of cognitive developmental theory in understanding different facets of social development. He is known primarily for his contributions to understanding moral development, but he also has expanded Piaget's ideas to account for many social phenomena, not just morality. For example, Kohlberg has applied a cognitive developmental perspective to gender roles, role-taking abilities, peer relations, attachment, and identity.

Like Piaget, Kohlberg believes that biological maturation and environmental experiences interact to produce the individual's stage of thought. Kohlberg says that adolescents attempt to attain intellectual balance or equilibrium. These attempts are influenced by moment-to-moment interactions with people and events in the world. In reaching a new stage of thinking, individuals are able to balance past impressions about the world and themselves with currently incoming information. Hence, adolescents who have achieved a stable sense of identity ("I know who I am and where I am going") can handle ostensible threats to their identity ("You aren't working hard enough—you play around too much") without being intellectually blitzed. Over a reasonably long period of time, the balance that has been achieved in a particular stage of thought is disrupted because maturing adolescents gain cognitive abilities that enable them to perceive inconsistencies and inadequacies in their thinking. Just as scientists who are confronted with unexplained events and outcomes must reformulate their theories to explain them, so individuals must shift their former ways of thinking to account for new discrepancies. When individuals are able to balance new information with past impressions, they have reached a new stage in thinking.

Hence, children in elementary school may categorize the identities of themselves and others along a limited number of dimensions—even just one or two, such as "He is a boy, and I am a girl." But as they grow into adolescence, children begin to realize that different people are characterized by traits other than just gender. They recognize, for example, that someone's introverted, quiet style of interaction may shape his/her personal identity just as much or more than his/her "maleness" or "femaleness."

Kurt Fischer (1980; Fischer, Hand, & Russell, 1983) refers to this ability of the adolescent to coordinate two or more abstract ideas as the stage of **abstract relations,** and argues that it appears in most adolescents from about 14 to 16 years of age. For example, at the age of 16, the individual may be able to coordinate the abstraction of conformity with the abstraction of individualism in thinking about his or her personality or the personality of others. Consider the adolescent girl who sees herself as a conformist at school, where she dresses in conventional ways and behaves according to the rules of the school, but views herself as an individualist in social relationships, choosing unconventional friends and wearing unusual clothes in their company. By piecing together these abstractions, she likely views herself as being a different kind of person in the two contexts and senses that in some ways she is a contradictory person.

Thus, from the cognitive developmental perspective, adolescence involves a great deal of change in how individuals think and reason about themselves and others. Later in our discussion of social cognition, we will describe the nature of egocentrism and perspective taking in adolescence—two topics that also have been part of the cognitive developmental view of social cognition in adolescence. Now, however, we describe a second conceptual perspective on adolescent social cognition, that of social information processing.

Social Information Processing

Two converging conceptual developments have led to the belief that a better understanding of the adolescent's social cognition can come from viewing such cognition in terms of **social information processing.** First, when Walter Mischel (1973) introduced the view called cognitive social learning theory, he included a number of cognitive processes that serve as important mediators between experiences with the social world and the adolescent's behavior. Mischel spoke of the importance of plans, memory, imagery, and other mechanisms as highly significant contributors in how individuals process information about themselves and their social world. At the same time, a perspective that was to become the dominant view in cognitive science was maturing, the view known as information processing, which was initially described in Chapter 2 and will be discussed in much greater detail in Chapter 5. Scientists interested in studying social cognition have drawn heavily from the information processing perspective in their focus on social memories, social problem solving, social decision making, and so forth. Keep in mind, however, that the information processing perspective is not a developmental perspective. So there is nothing in this view that would tell us about how adolescents might process information about themselves and their social world differently than children do. Nonetheless, the information processing view has been valuable in informing us of the importance of many cognitive factors in the adolescent's processing of social information and will continue to provide an important framework for studying social cognition in the decades ahead.

Egocentrism and Perspective Taking

Two important aspects of thinking about the self and others that develop in adolescence are egocentrism and perspective taking.

Egocentrism

"Oh my gosh! I can't believe it. Help! I can't stand it!" Tracy desperately yells. "What is wrong? What is the matter?" her mother asks. Tracy responds, "Everyone in here is looking at me." The mother queries, "Why?" Tracy says, "Look, this one hair just won't stay in place," as she rushes to the rest room of the restaurant. Five minutes later she returns to the table in the restaurant after she has depleted an entire can of hair spray. During a conversation between two 14-year-old girls, the one named Margaret says, "Are you kidding, I won't get pregnant." And, 13-year-old Adam describes himself, "No one understands me, particularly my parents. They have no idea of what I am feeling."

These comments of Tracy, Margaret, and Adam represent the emergence of egocentrism in adolescence. David Elkind (1967, 1976, 1978) believes two types of thinking represent the emergence of this unique kind of **egocentrism in adolescence**—the imaginary audience and the personal fable—and that underlying this egocentric thought is the emergence of formal operational thought.

Tracy's comments and behavior reflect the **imaginary audience** phenomenon. This is the belief that others are as preoccupied with the adolescent's behavior as he or she is. Attention-getting behavior, so common in early adolescence, may reflect this interest in an imaginary audience, that is the desire to be noticed, visible, and "on stage." An adolescent may think that others are as aware of a small spot on his trousers as he is, possibly knowing or thinking that he has masturbated. The adolescent girl, walking into her eighth grade classroom, thinks that all eyes are riveted on her complexion. So, particularly during early adolescence, individuals see themselves as constantly on stage, believing they are the main actors and all others are the audience.

The comments of Margaret and Adam reflect a second aspect of adolescent egocentrism called the **personal fable.** This construction refers to the adolescent's sense of personal uniqueness and indestructibility. Their sense of personal uniqueness makes them feel that no one can understand how they really feel. For example, an adolescent girl thinks that her mother can in no way sense the hurt she feels because her boyfriend broke up with her. Another aspect of the personal fable involves the belief that one is indestructible. As part of their effort to retain this sense of personal uniqueness, adolescents often craft a story about the self that is not true. For reasons likely tied to an emerging interest in idealism and the ability to think in more abstract and hypothetical ways, young adolescents often get caught up in a mental world far removed from reality, one that may entail the belief that things just can't or won't happen to them and that they are omnipotent and indestructible.

Many adolescent girls spend long hours in front of the mirror depleting cans of hair spray, tubes of lipstick, and jars of cosmetics. How might this behavior be related to changes in adolescent cognitive and physical development?

There has been a flourish of research interest in the phenomenon of adolescent egocentrism in recent years (e.g., Adams & Jones, 1981; Damon & Hart, 1982; Elkind, 1985; Elkind & Bowen, 1979; Enright, Shukla, & Lapsley, 1980; Gray & Hudson, 1984; Lapsley, 1985; Lapsley, in press; Lapsley & others, 1986; Lapsley & Murphy, 1985; Selman, 1980; Stephenson & Wicklund, 1983; Walker, 1980; Wicklund, 1979). Much of the thrust of this research interest has focused on Elkind's conceptualization of egocentrism. Issues focus on such matters as what the components of egocentrism really are, the nature of self-other relationships in adolescence, and why egocentric thought emerges in adolescence. While Elkind (1985) continues to argue that egocentrism and the adolescent's construction of an imaginary audience come about because of formal operational thought, others believe that interpersonal understanding is involved (Lapsley, 1985; Lapsley & Murphy, 1985; Lapsley & Rice, 1988). The imaginary audience may be due both to the ability to think hypothetically (formal operations) and to the ability to step outside of one's self and anticipate the reactions of others in imaginative circumstances (perspective taking). Robert Selman's view on perspective taking provides a context for understanding egocentric thought. As part of our discussion of perspective taking, Selman's theory will be outlined.

Perspective Taking

Role taking and **perspective taking** are both terms used to describe an individual's ability to infer and adopt the perspective of another (Flavell, 1985; Shantz, 1983). Investigators are often not only interested in the cognitive changes involved in perspective taking, but also want to know about the way perspective taking is related to other aspects of development, such as empathy (showing feeling for another) and moral judgment.

The most widely acclaimed theory of perspective taking has been developed by Robert Selman (1976, 1980). Selman assumes that perspective taking skills increase with age, at least into adolescence. In his view, perspective taking involves five levels:

Level *0* The egocentric, undifferentiated stage
Level *1* The differentiated and subjective perspective-taking stage
    (ages 5–9)
Level *2* Reciprocal and recursive role-taking stage
Level *3* Simultaneous role-taking stage
Level *4* The in-depth and societal perspective-taking stage

Selman (1980) has shown how these stages of perspective taking can be applied to four areas of individual and social development: individual concepts; friendship concepts; peer group concepts; and parent-child concepts. At level 0, children are capable of recognizing the relation of subjective states of self and other, but frequently they are not distinguished. At level 1, children comprehend that even in similarly perceived circumstances the self and other's perspective may be either the same or different. But the child shows no concern for the unique psychological lives of people. At level 2, children can reflect on their own thoughts and feelings from someone else's perspective—that is, they can put themselves in another person's shoes and see themselves the way the other person sees them. At level 3, the recursive nature of reciprocal perspectives develops, and the individual begins to think "He thinks that I think that she wants. . . ." Also, at this level, the adolescent can move to a third-party position to understand the mutuality of various human perspectives. Finally, at level 4, the highest level in Selman's model, perspectives among individuals form a network or system, and generalized concepts of society's viewpoints are developed (legal, moral, and so forth). At this level, there is a belief that the mutuality of individuals occurs not only at superficial levels of shared expectations, but also at deeper levels of unverbalized feelings and values.

Selman's research has shown strong support for the sequential nature of perspective taking, although there is considerable overlap in the age at which children and adolescents reach the perspective-taking stages. In one investigation, 60% of the 10-year-old children were at level 2 perspective taking, the remaining children at levels 1 and 3 (Selman & Byrne, 1974). This means that at the threshold of adolescence, 80% are likely to be no higher than level 2 in social perspective taking. In another investigation, only 6 of 28 individuals aged 10–13 were at level 3 or higher, with 78% of the early adolescents no higher than level 2 (Byrne, 1973). Level 3 was not firmly present until about the age of 16. Selman (1980) acknowledges considerable overlap in the age ranges he applies to the development of interpersonal understanding—for example, level 2 (6 years 9 months to 15 years 10 months), level 3 (11 years 3 months to 20+ years). It is the attainment of level 3 perspective taking that some researchers believe accounts for the imaginary audience and personal fable dimensions of adolescent egocentrism (Lapsley, 1985, 1989).

The relation between the self and another individual is complex. Most major developmental theorists believe that development changes in self-other relationships are characterized by movement from egocentrism to perspectivism (Shantz, 1983), but the considerable overlap in the age range at which various levels of perspective taking emerge make generalizations about clearcut stages difficult (Lapsley, 1989).

Implicit Personality Theory

Another dimension of social cognition that changes during adolescence is the ability of adolescents to think like a personality theorist in interpreting their own or another's personality (Barenboim, 1981, 1985). **Implicit personality theory** refers to the lay person's conception of personality. How do the implicit personality theories of adolescents come to resemble the way personality theorists in the field of psychology conceptualize personality? First, when adolescents are given information about another person, they consider previously

Biological and Cognitive Processes and Development

acquired information and current information, not relying solely on the concrete information at hand like children do. Second, adolescents are more likely
to detect the situational or contextual variability in their and others' behavior,
rather than thinking that they and others always behave consistently. Third,
rather than merely accepting surface traits as a valid description of another
person or themselves, adolescents begin to look for deeper, more complex, even
hidden causes of personality.

In the following comments obtained in one developmental investigation
of how individuals perceive others (Livesley & Bromley, 1973), we can see
how the development of an implicit personality theory proceeds:

> Max sits next to me, his eyes are hazel and he is tall. He hasn't got a very big
> head, he's got a big pointed nose. (p. 213; age seven years, six months)
>
> He smells very much and is very nasty. He has no sense of humor and is
> very dull. He is always fighting and he is cruel. He does silly things and is
> very stupid. He has brown hair and cruel eyes. He is sulky and eleven years
> old and has lots of sisters. I think he is the most horrible boy in the class. He
> has a croaky voice and always chews his pencil and picks his teeth and I think
> he is disgusting. (p. 217; age nine years, eleven months)
>
> Andy is very modest. He is even shyer than I am when near strangers
> and yet is very talkative with people he knows and likes. He always seems
> good tempered and I have never seen him in a bad temper. He tends to
> degrade other people's achievements, and yet never praises his own. He does
> not seem to voice his opinions to anyone. He easily gets nervous. (p. 221; age
> fifteen years, eight months)
>
> . . . she is curious about people but naive, and this leads her to ask too
> many questions so that people become irritated with her and withhold
> information, although she is not sensitive enough to notice it. (p. 225; young
> adult)

Social Cognitive Monitoring

As part of their increased awareness of themselves and others, which includes
both internal thoughts and external behavior, adolescents monitor their social
world more extensively. Consider the circumstance of the following adolescent. Bob, a 16-year-old, feels that he does not know as much as he wants or
needs to know about Sally, another 16-year-old. He also wants and needs to
know more about Sally's relationship with Brian, a 17-year-old. In his effort
to learn about Sally, Bob decides that he wants to know more about the groups
that Sally belongs to—her student council friends, the clique she belongs to,
and so forth. Bob thinks about what he already knows of all these people and
groups, and decides he needs to find out how close he is to his goal of understanding them by taking some appropriate, feedback-producing action. What
he discovers by taking that action will determine his social-cognitive progress
and how difficult his social-cognitive task is. Notice that the immediate aim
of this feedback-producing action is not to make progress toward the main
goal, but to monitor that progress.

The Adolescent's Cognitive Monitoring of the Social World

An individual's ability to monitor and make sense of his social thoughts seems to increase during middle childhood and adolescence. An important aspect of social cognition is the individual's development of conscious self-awareness. Flavell (1981) believes that developing differentiated thoughts about oneself is a gradual process. Statements such as "I think I am not easily fooled by others" or "I tend to give people the benefit of the doubt" evidence the development of such self- and social awareness. And although the child may distinguish only between succeeding or failing to learn something he or she wants to know about someone else, the adolescent may understand the more complex notion that what has been learned may be either accurate or inaccurate. Acquiring this latter distinction can serve as the basis for still further development in monitoring social thought. For example, later in development the individual may recognize that the accuracy of social thought is difficult to assess and that knowledge of certain aspects of the self or of others may actually decrease accuracy. For instance, prejudice, intense emotions, or mental or physical illness might produce inaccurate perceptions of oneself and

Think about your social world when you were 8–9 years old. Now think about it when you were 15–16 years old. Just as these 15–16-year-olds at Crossgates Shopping Mall in Albany, New York, when you were an adolescent you undoubtedly spent more time monitoring your social world than when you were a child.

There are a number of cognitive monitoring methods that adolescents engage in on virtually a daily basis. A student may meet someone new and quickly think, "It's going to be hard to really get to know this guy." Another adolescent may check incoming information about an organization (school, club, group of friends) to determine if it is consistent with the adolescent's impressions of the club or the group. Still another adolescent may question someone or paraphrase what that person has just said about her feelings to ensure that he has understood them correctly. Perspective on Adolescent Development 4.3 presents further details of John Flavell's ideas on the importance of cognitive monitoring of social matters during adolescence.

Piaget's Theory and Social Cognitive Change

Can Piaget's theory explain the many social cognitive changes that characterize adolescent development? Some critics of Piaget's approach believe it cannot (Blasi & Hoeffel, 1974; Broughton, 1977; Lapsley, 1989). They argue others. While some forms of social-cognitive knowledge do not develop until later, other aspects of this awareness may emerge quite early in development, according to Flavell. Thus, a young child may be entirely able to recognize that a friend is not thinking clearly about people because she is upset or in a bad mood.

Individuals also learn to evaluate the social behavior of others and to recognize when this behavior is not accompanied by social thought. Flavell argues that in the early years of development, the child attributes no social cognitions to others. Later on, the child may automatically assume that others' social thoughts always coincide with their social behavior. For example, the child may assume that helpful actions reflect an intent to help and harmful actions the intent to harm. Still later, the child may think that both types of actions portray either no intent at all or an incongruent one, such as a helpful action performed unintentionally for purely selfish reasons, or even with an intent to achieve ultimate harm.

Flavell goes on to talk about the implications of children's and adolescents' ability to monitor their social cognitions as an indicator of their social maturity and competence:

> In many real-life situations, the monitoring problem is not to determine how well you understand what a message means but rather to determine how much you ought to believe it or do what it says to do. I am thinking of the persuasive appeals the young receive from all quarters to smoke, drink, commit aggressive or criminal acts, have casual sex without contraceptives, have or not have the casual babies that often result, quit school, and become unthinking followers of this year's flaky cults, sects, and movements. (Feel free to revise this list in accordance with *your* values and prejudices.) Perhaps it is stretching the meanings of . . . cognitive monitoring too far to include the critical appraisal of message source, quality of appeal, and probable consequences needed to cope with these inputs sensibly, but I do not think so. It is at least conceivable that the ideas currently brewing in this area could some day be parlayed into a method of teaching children (and adults) to make wise and thoughtful life decisions as well as to comprehend and learn better in formal educational settings. (Flavell, 1979, p. 910)

that formal possibility is abstract and theoretical, perceiving the real as a special case of the possible. Subjective possibility is concrete, perceiving the possible as an extension of the real. Formal operational thought approaches problems deductively by seeking the underlying causal structure and then deducing the specific case. Concrete operations is inductive and consists of making extrapolations from relevant prior experience. Formal operational thought is adaptive if the causal structure is known and the deductive rules are correctly followed. Concrete operations is adaptive if the adolescent has a rich and varied social history from which to make the appropriate inductions. What this means is that the kinds of possibilities that concern the typical adolescent—ideological orientation, life plans, social and political commitments, for example—cannot be adequately explained by formal operational thought. The possibilities that spring forth from social life do not require an understanding of perfect logical reasoning in a formal manner, but something else, such as motivation, imagination, desire, and creativity. Rather than formal operational thought producing social cognitive change in adolescence, rich and varied social experiences and communication may be sufficient.

Social Cognition

Concept	Processes/Related Ideas	Characteristics/Description
Social cognition's nature	What is social cognition?	Refers to the way people conceptualize and reason about their social world, including the relation of their selves to others.
	Two major views	The cognitive developmental view is based on the ideas of Piaget, Kohlberg, and Flavell. Social thoughts are influenced by the individual's maturational status. The social information processing view is based on cognitive social learning theory and the information processing perspective.
Egocentrism and perspective taking	Egocentrism	Elkind proposed that adolescents, especially young adolescents, develop an egocentrism that involves both the construction of an imaginary audience—the belief that others are as preoccupied with my behavior as I am—and a personal fable—a sense of personal uniqueness and indestructibility. Elkind believes that egocentrism appears because of formal operational thought. Others argue that perspective taking also is involved.
	Perspective taking	Adolescents are more sophisticated at perspective taking than children, but there is considerable overlap in the age at which individuals reach higher levels of perspective taking. Selman's model has served as the basis for thinking about perspective taking in adolescence.
Implicit personality theory and social cognitive monitoring	Implicit personality theory	Refers to the public's or lay person's conception of personality. The implicit personality theories of adolescents are closer to those of scientists who study personality than are children's. Adolescents are more likely to consider the past and present, contextual factors, and deeper causes.
	Social cognitive monitoring	Adolescents engage in much more sophisticated social cognitive monitoring than children do.
Piaget's theory and social cognitive changes	An evaluation	Critics of Piaget's approach argue that formal operational thought does not adequately explain the nature of social cognitive change in adolescence. The inductive aspect of concrete operational thought and a rich and varied social life may be sufficient.
Social cognition in the remainder of the text	Its nature	Interest in social cognition has blossomed and we will study it throughout the text in chapters on intelligence, families, peers, the self and identity, and moral development.

Social Cognition in the Remainder of the Text

Interest in social cognition has blossomed and the approach has infiltrated many different aspects of the study of adolescent development. In the next chapter, we investigate the topic of social intelligence. In our discussion of families in Chapter 6, the emerging cognitive abilities of the adolescent will be evaluated in concert with parent-adolescent conflict and parenting strategies. In our description of peer relations in Chapter 7, the importance of social knowledge and social information processing in peer relations is highlighted. In our overview of the self and identity in Chapter 10, social cognition's role in understanding the self and identity will be explored. And in our evaluation of moral development in Chapter 13, considerable time will be devoted to discussing Kohlberg's theory, which is a prominent aspect of the study of social cognition in adolescence.

At this point we have described many different aspects of social cognition. A summary of these ideas is presented in Concept Table 4.2. In the next chapter we continue our discussion of adolescent cognition, evaluating the nature of information processing and intelligence.

Summary

I. Overview and Concrete Operational Thought
Piaget's widely acclaimed theory stresses biological adaptation through organization and through assimilation and accommodation. Piaget argued that individuals move through four stages of cognitive development. Adolescents are likely to be either concrete operational or formal operational thinkers. Concrete operational thought takes place between 7 and 11 years of age. It is made up of operations and involves reasoning about the properties of objects. Conservation and classification skills are characteristics. It is limited by the inability to reason abstractly about objects.

II. The Characteristics of Formal Operational Thought
Abstractness and idealism, as well as hypothetical-deductive reasoning, are highlighted in formal operational thought. Formal operational thought involves the ability to reason about what is possible and hypothetical, as opposed to what is real, and the ability to reflect on one's own thoughts. Formal operational thought occurs in two phases—an assimilation phase in which reality is overwhelmed (early adolescence) and an accommodation phase in which intellectual balance is restored through a consolidation of formal operational thought (middle years of adolescence).

III. Individual Variation
It is extensive and Piaget did not give this adequate attention. Many young adolescents are not formal operational thinkers but rather are consolidating their concrete operational thought.

IV. Beyond Formal Operational Thought
Many life-span developmentalists believe Piaget was incorrect in thinking that formal operational thought is the highest form of cognition. They argue that more pragmatic, specialized thought takes place in early adulthood and that wisdom increases throughout the adult years.

V. Piaget's Theory and Education
Piaget's theory has been applied to children's education much more than to adolescent education. Applications to adolescent education often follow the belief that instruction is too formal and abstract for adolescents.

VI. Language
Adolescents develop more sophisticated cognitive strategies for handling words and concepts, prose and writing, and pragmatics.

VII. Evaluating Piaget's Theory

Piaget was a genius at observing children and adolescents. He showed us some important things to look for and mapped out some general cognitive changes. Criticisms focus on such matters as stages, which are not as unitary as he believed and do not follow the timetable he envisioned.

VIII. Social Cognition's Nature

Social cognition refers to the way people conceptualize and reason about their social world, including the relation of the self to others. Two major views of social cognition are the cognitive developmental view—based on the ideas of Piaget, Kohlberg, and Flavell—and social information processing—based on the ideas of cognitive social learning theory and the information processing perspective.

IX. Egocentrism and Perspective Taking

Elkind proposed that adolescents, especially young adolescents, develop an egocentrism that involves the construction of an imaginary audience—the belief that others are as preoccupied with my behavior as I am—and a personal fable—a sense of personal uniqueness and indestructibility. Elkind believes that egocentrism appears because of formal operational thought. Others argue that perspective taking is responsible. Adolescents are more sophisticated at perspective taking than children, but there is considerable overlap in the age at which individuals reach higher levels of perspective taking. Selman's model has served as the basis for thinking about adolescent perspective taking.

X. Implicit Personality Theory and Social Cognitive Monitoring

Implicit personality theory refers to the lay person's conception of personality. The implicit personality theories of adolescents are closer to those of scientists who study personality than are children's. Adolescents are more likely to consider the past and the present, contextual factors, and deeper causes. Adolescents engage in much more sophisticated social cognitive monitoring than children do.

XI. Piaget's Theory and Social Cognitive Changes

Critics of Piaget's approach argue that formal operational thought does not adequately explain the nature of social cognitive change in adolescence. The inductive aspect of concrete operational thought and a rich and varied social life may be sufficient.

XII. Social Cognition in the Remainder of the Text

Interest in social cognition has blossomed and we will study it throughout the text in chapters on intelligence, families, peers, the self and identity, and moral development.

Key Terms

operations 127
conservation 128
horizontal décalage 128
hypothetical-deductive
    reasoning 130
wisdom 135
metaphor 138

satire 138
pragmatics 144
social cognition 144
abstract relations 145
social information
    processing 145

egocentrism in
    adolescence 146
imaginary audience 146
personal fable 146
perspective taking 147
implicit personality
    theory 148

Suggested Readings

Elkind, D. (1976). *Child development and education.* New York: Oxford University
    Press.
    An excellent easy-to-read introduction to the implications of Piaget's ideas for
    educators. Practical examples are given for approaching classroom teaching
    from the Piagetian perspective.
Flavell, J. H. (1985). *Cognitive development* (2d ed.). Englewood Cliffs, NJ:
    Prentice-Hall.
    An outstanding statement of the major contemporary ideas about cognitive
    development by one of the leading scholars in the field. Although inspired by
    Piaget's work, Flavell goes well beyond it, offering new insights, critical
    evaluation, and reflections about his own original research, including many
    ideas about social cognition.
Ginsburg, H., & Opper, S. (1988). *Piaget's theory of intellectual development* (3rd
    ed.). Englewood Cliffs, NJ: Prentice-Hall.
    One of the best explanations and descriptions of Piaget's theory.
Lapsley, D. K. (1989). Continuity and discontinuity in adolescent social cognitive
    development. In R. Montemayor, G. Adams, & T. Gullota (Eds.), *Advances in*
    adolescent research (Vol. 2). Orlando, FL: Academic Press.
    An excellent critique of Piaget's ideas on social cognitive change and extensive
    coverage of contemporary ideas on adolescent social cognition.
Selman, R. L. (1981). What children understand of intrapsychic processes: the child
    as a budding personality theorist. In E. K. Weber and E. Weber (Eds.),
    Cognitive and affective growth. Hillsdale, NJ: Erlbaum.
    This article contains Selman's account of how he thinks the adolescent forms
    a theory of personality. Includes an overview of his ideas about role taking.
Shantz, C. U. (1983). The development of social cognition. In P. H. Mussen (Ed.),
    Handbook of child psychology (Vol. 3, 4th ed.). New York: Wiley.
    Carolyn Shantz, one of the pioneers of research on contemporary issues in
    social cognition, provides a very detailed and critical appraisal of the
    information on social-cognitive development.

CHAPTER

5

Information Processing and Intelligence

The mind is an enchanting thing.

Marianne Moore, Collected Poems, 1951

157

Reading *Martina*

Barbara Smith is a sixth-grade student at a middle school. Her favorite activity is tennis, so her mother recently bought her a book entitled, *Martina,* which is about tennis star Martina Navratilova's life. Barbara finished reading the first 11 pages of the book. She placed it on the table in the hall as she left for tennis practice. Her 8-year-old sister, Nancy, saw Barbara leave the book on the table. She grabbed the book and started to read it. Nancy finished the entire book in 12 minutes. In that 12 minutes she read several sentences in different chapters as she leafed rapidly through the book. She also studied each of the book's photographs and read some of their captions.

After Barbara returned from tennis practice, she showered, ate, and then read another chapter in *Martina,* which Nancy had returned to its place on the table. She sat quietly for 30 minutes and read the next 18 pages of the book. A few of the words were difficult but Barbara got the idea of what Martina's family background was like and how she started to play tennis in her native country of Czechoslovakia. She especially noted how Martina's father spent long hours playing tennis with her and how she dreamed of being a star.

Nancy, Barbara's younger sister, walked by her room just as she was finished reading for the evening. Nancy asked, "Did you like the book? I did." Barbara replied, "You are too little to understand it. Shrimps can't read this kind of book." Their mother heard them begin to argue and ran upstairs to intervene. She asked Nancy what the book was about. Nancy said, "A tennis player. I can't remember her name, though." Barbara laughed and said, "She doesn't know very much, does she?" The mother reprimanded Barbara for teasing Nancy, then walked out into the hall with Nancy and told her not to worry about what Barbara said.

The next day the mother went to Barbara's room while Barbara was at tennis practice and picked up the book about Martina. She sat down and skimmed the book in about one hour, forming a general idea of the book. As she read, she made mental notes and developed many concepts about Martina's life on and off the tennis court.

When we read, we process information and interpret it. So reading serves as a practical example to introduce the topic of information processing in adolescence. To read effectively, adolescents have to perceive and attend to a complex set of visual symbols—words. Note that Barbara and her mother attended more to words and sentences, while Nancy attended more to pictures. Another process in reading is holding the information we process in memory. Note that after about one hour of reading, the mother was able to get the gist of the entire book and hold the book's themes in her memory. But Barbara was able to cover only several chapters of the book in this time frame and at this point her memory of what the book is about is much more impoverished than her mother's (Santrock & Yussen, 1989).

*T*he study of adolescents' information processing is concerned with basic processes such as attention, memory, and thinking. In the first part of this chapter, we consider these processes and other aspects of information processing. In the second part of the chapter we discuss the nature of intelligence in adolescence.

Information Processing

Information processing is at once a framework for thinking about adolescent development and a facet of that development. As a framework, information processing includes certain ideas about how adolescent minds work and the best methods for studying this. As a facet of development, different aspects of information processing change as children make the transition through adolescence to adulthood. For example, changes in attention and memory are essentially changes in the way individuals process information. In the discussion that follows we will review some basic ideas about the information processing approach first discussed in Chapter 2 and compare the information processing approach with other cognitive orientations. Then we will describe the nature of attention, memory, and cognitive monitoring in adolescence. To conclude our discussion of information processing, we evaluate its application to adolescent education.

The Information Processing Perspective

Remember that in Chapter 2 we described the basic nature of the information processing approach. Information processing is concerned with how individuals analyze the many sources of information in the environment and make sense of these experiences. Information processing includes how information gets into adolescents' minds, how it is stored and transformed, and how it is retrieved to think and solve problems. The development of the computer promoted this approach—the mind as an information processing system has been compared to the computer as an information processing system. The information processing system raises questions about development, among them changes in the way we process information as we make the transition from childhood to adulthood.

How does the information processing perspective differ from other perspectives we have discussed? Let's think about how the information processing perspective differs from the behavioral perspective (Chapter 2) and the Piagetian cognitive developmental perspective (Chapters 2 and 4). The behavioral approach focuses on behaviors and the events in the environment that change these behaviors. Traditional principles of behaviorism and learning do little to explain what is going on in the adolescent's mind, although in recent years cognitive social learning theory has emphasized some cognitive processes. Piagetian theory, in contrast, has much to say about the adolescent's

The manner in which an adolescent goes about solving an algebraic equation provides an excellent example of the role information processing plays in the adolescent's cognitive world. Describe how attention, perception, memory, thinking, and problem solving are wrapped up in the adolescent's ability to solve an algebraic equation.

mind. For example, Piaget described the adolescent's thoughts as more abstract, idealistic, and logical than the child's. But the Piagetian description is somewhat general—it does not tell us much about how the adolescent reads or solves math problems. It leaves out some important details about how the adolescent's mind actually works on specific kinds of tasks like solving algebraic equations and writing long essays.

The information processing perspective tries to correct some of the shortcomings of traditional behaviorism or learning theory and Piagetian cognitive developmental ideas. It describes mental processes and offers details about how these processes work in concrete situations. Where possible, these descriptions include analyses of all the steps necessary to complete some task, the specific mental processes needed to complete these steps, and precise estimates of how "hard" or "how long" the mind has to work to execute these steps (Klahr, 1989).

Let's examine how an adolescent's mind might work in processing information about an algebraic equation. An event (S) occurs in the environment. Suppose the event is the appearance of the following algebraic equation on the chalkboard in school: "$2x + 10 = 34$. Solve for x." This event contains information that a person can detect and understand. Success in detecting and making sense of it depends on how completely and efficiently the information is processed. Development can be equated with becoming more skillful and efficient at information processing. Once the processing is complete, the person produces an observable response (R). In this model, then, cognitive activity refers to the flow of information through the different steps of processing.

Consider how a well-seasoned algebra student engages cognition. The teacher writes the equation on the board (S). The student looks up and notes that something has been written on the board (*attention*). This "something" is then determined to be a series of numbers, letters, and signs, and—at a higher level of identification—two simple statements: (1) "$2x + 10 = 34$" and (2) "Solve for x" (*perception*). The student must preserve the results of this perceptual analysis over a period of time (*memory*), even if only for the brief interval needed to write the problem on a worksheet.

The student then begins to elaborate on the product of perception and memory (*thinking*). This level of analysis can be described best with an imaginary mental soliloquy (though, of course, the reasoning might take an altogether different track or even a nonverbal form): "Let's see. It's an equation—x is the unknown, and I'm supposed to figure out the value of x. How do I do that?" The final level of analysis (*problem solving*) addresses the question: "How do I do that?" Problem solving then takes the following form: "Okay, $2x + 10 = 34$. First, I have to collect the unknown on one side of the equation and the known values on the other side. To do this, I'll leave the $2x$ where it is—on the left. Then I'll subtract 10 from each side to remove the 10 from the left. This leaves $2x = 24$. Now I have to express the equation as

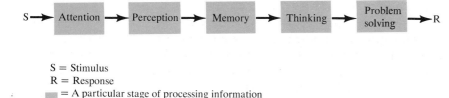

S = Stimulus
R = Response
■ = A particular stage of processing information
■→■ = Consecutive stages of processing information
in a left-to-right direction

'$x =$ something,' and it's solved. How do I do this? I know! Divide each side by 2 and that will leave $1x$, or x, on the left side. Now I have $x = 12$. That's the answer!" A summary of the processes used in solving the algebraic equation is presented in Figure 5.1.

Figure 5.1 is a necessarily oversimplified representation of information processing that omits a great deal and does not indicate the many routes that the flow of information may take. For example, each hypothetical step (e.g., perception) may overlap with other steps (e.g., memory) or be composed of several substeps. Neither of these features is captured in the diagram, whose purpose is to focus on the basic elements of information processing. In many instances the processing of information is dynamic and simultaneous, and many different models of how this processing takes place have been developed. You may remember that in Chapter 2 we described another simplified model of information processing to give you a sense of the basic processes involved in adolescent cognition.

Information processing psychologists may try to write a computer program to represent the steps needed to solve a problem. Indeed, information processing psychologists sometimes rely on computers to tell them something about the way adolescent cognition works. **Artificial intelligence,** the branch of computer science devoted to creating computers capable of handling complicated tasks that require some "thinking," has been given special attention. Since true "thinking" is usually considered to be a human activity, when computers play chess, solve math problems, create designs, guide industrial robots, and "see" enemy aircraft approaching, the computer thought is dubbed "artificial." What is artificial about it? Computers do not have human brains and a central nervous system. So, physically, computers operate differently than people. Human beings also do not think in strictly logical fashion. They are intuitive and emotional, even when working on the logical types of problems in physics and math. Debate continues as to whether computers will ever achieve the powers of human thought (Boden, 1989; Grawbard, 1988). Some computer scientists believe computers have already accomplished this goal. Critics argue that the highest forms of human intelligence have not been created and simply cannot be modeled in a machine. More about this fascinating issue appears in Perspective on Adolescent Development 5.1.

"Ask If the Computer Ever Eats Breakfast"

Without exactly trying to settle the computer-human debate, Richard Lehrer and Steven Yussen (1988) recently studied children, adolescents, and adults to discover what ideas these everyday "experts" have about the similarities and differences between human thought and the "thought" of computers. Individuals in the 3rd, 5th, 8th, 11th/12th grades, and university students were asked to respond to a series of questions, such as the following: "What is intelligence?"; "Are computers and people intelligent in the same way, or are they different?"; "People often think about what they are doing. For example, they think about whether they are solving a problem correctly or not. Do computers think about what they are doing like people do?"; "People have different feelings. They sometimes feel happy, sad, excited, bored, tired. . . . Do computers have feelings like these?" and "What question could you ask where you would be sure to get a different (kind of) answer from a person and a computer?"

The elementary school children frequently cited physical differences between people and computers. Their responses included the following: "Computers can't see!"; "Ask if it ever eats breakfast. A computer will have to say no. But a person will have to say yes"; and "Ask if it swims." Although these children generally regarded computers as non-feeling things, they did believe that computers could feel certain emotions such as "excited" and "tired." The children explained that a computer might get excited if it figured out a hard problem and might get tired if it was on for a long time.

The adolescents and college students were more likely to distinguish between computers and humans on the basis of internal, mental properties. For example, they frequently mentioned the extraordinary speed and memory capacities of computers (e.g., "Computers can do things much faster than people." "If you gave it a problem like 3,688 times 4,266, a computer could get it right."). They also commented on the computer's lack of flexibility in problem solving and the stereotyped responses it would give to a question. And, they strongly stated that in no way could a computer experience an emotion.

The concept of differences between natural and artificial intelligence is interpreted in different ways by children and adolescents. It is important to note that any one set of ideas about this distinction is not necessarily the correct one. Rather this concept, like many others, changes with development and experience.

Attention and Memory

While the bulk of research on information processing has been conducted with children and adults, the information processing perspective is important in understanding adolescent cognition. As we saw in the example of the adolescent solving an algebraic equation, attention and memory are two important cognitive processes.

Attention

Two ways adolescents can use attention are selective attention and divided attention. In **selective attention,** the adolescent has the problem of ignoring some stimuli while focusing on others more relevant to his or her interests or goals. For example, the adolescent may need to ignore the blaring television while studying for an exam. Researchers have found that adolescents are superior to children at selective attention (Higgins & Turnure, 1984; Sexton & Geffen, 1979).

In other situations, adolescents may be called on to handle two or more information channels at once. This is a problem in **divided attention** for the adolescent. For example, while listening to the teacher the adolescent may also want to hear what a friend in the next row is whispering. Following the content of both messages simultaneously is not an easy task. In an interesting investigation (Schiff & Knopf, 1985), 9- and 13-year-olds viewed displays showing a set of visual symbols (e.g., *, &, =, +, $) in the center and some letters (e.g., A, G, M, P, Y) in the corners. The adolescents were much better than children at dividing their attention in that they (a) detected whether the symbols at the center included a certain target symbol, and (b) remembered the letters shown in the corners. Other types of divided attention have been shown to improve with development as well (Guttentag, 1984).

Memory

There are few moments when adolescents' lives are not steeped in memory. Memory is at work with each step adolescents take, each thought they think, and each word they utter. **Memory** is the retention of information over time. It is central to mental life and to information processing. To successfully learn and reason, adolescents need to hold on to information and to retrieve the information they have tucked away. In **short-term memory,** adolescents retain recently encountered information or information retrieved from long-term memory for a brief time, usually 15 to 30 seconds. In **long-term memory,** adolescents retain information for an indefinite period of time and the information can be used over and over again.

A common way to assess short-term memory is to present a list of items to remember, which is often referred to as a memory span task. If you have taken an IQ test, you probably were asked to remember a string of numbers or words. You simply hear a short list of stimuli—usually digits—presented at a rapid pace (one per second, for example). Then you are asked to repeat the digits back. Using the memory span task, researchers have found that short-term memory increases extensively in early childhood and continues to increase in older children and adolescents, but at a slower pace. For example, in one investigation, memory span increased by 1½ digits between the ages of 7 and 13 (Dempster, 1981) (see Figure 5.2). Keep in mind, though, memory span's individual differences, which is why IQ and various aptitude tests are used.

How might short-term memory be used in problem solving? In a series of experiments, Robert Sternberg (1977; Sternberg & Nigro, 1980; Sternberg & Rifkin, 1979) attempted to answer this question by giving third-grade, sixth-grade, ninth-grade, and college students analogies to solve. The main differences occurred between the younger (third and sixth grade) and older (ninth grade and college) students. The older students were more likely to complete the information processing required to solve the analogy task. The children, by contrast, often stopped their processing of information before they had considered all of the necessary steps required to solve the problems. Sternberg

Figure 5.2   Developmental differences (solid line) and individual differences, expressed as ranges (dashed lines), in digit span.

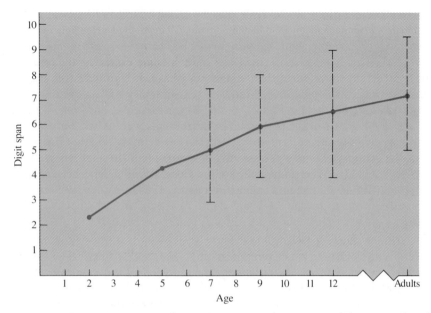

believes that incomplete information processing occurred because the children's short-term memory was overloaded. Solving problems such as analogies requires individuals to make continued comparisons between newly encoded information and previously coded information. Sternberg argues that adolescents probably have more storage space in short-term memory, which results in fewer errors on problems like analogies.

In addition to more storage space, are there other reasons adolescents might perform better on memory span tasks and in solving analogies? While many other factors may be involved, information processing psychologists believe that changes in the speed and efficiency of information processing are important, especially the speed with which information can be identified.

Long-term memory increases substantially in the middle and late childhood years and likely continues to improve during adolescence, although this has not been well documented by researchers. If we know anything at all about long-term memory, it is that it depends on the learning activities engaged in when learning and remembering information (Siegler, in press). Most learning activities fit under the category of **strategies.** These activities are under the learner's conscious control (Buchel, 1988). They sometimes are also called control processes. There are many of these activities but one of the most important is *organization,* the tendency to group or arrange items into categories.

Cognitive Monitoring

Attention and memory may occur rather quickly as adolescents examine information or attempt to complete some task. Adolescents may devote little effort and complete the new activity quickly. By contrast, a variety of activities

Biological and Cognitive Processes and Development

occur over an extended period of time and require mobilization of considerable cognitive resources on the part of adolescents. When adolescents read, write, and solve math problems, the activity usually takes place over an extended period of time. And when adolescents encounter some difficulty or lapse of attention, they must overcome the temporary hiatus and get back on track. Problem solving and cognitive monitoring are involved in adolescents' ability to guide and control their activities (Voss, 1989). More about problem solving, including creativity in solving problems, appears later in the chapter in our discussion of intelligence. Here we focus on cognitive monitoring.

Cognitive monitoring is the process of taking stock of what one is currently doing, what will be done next, and how effectively the mental activity is unfolding. When adolescents engage in an activity like reading, writing, or solving a math problem, they are repeatedly called on to take stock of what they are doing and what they plan to do next (Baker & Brown, 1984; Bereiter & Scardamalia, 1982). In Chapter 4, we indicated the importance of social cognitive monitoring in understanding the way adolescents solve social problems. Here we underscore the importance of cognitive monitoring in solving problems in the nonsocial aspects of intelligence—reading, writing, math, and so on. For example, when adolescents begin to solve a math problem—especially one that might take a while to finish—they must figure out what kind of problem they are working on and what is a good approach to solving it. And once they undertake a problem solution, they need to check on whether the solution is working or whether some other approach needs to be taken.

What evidence is there that children and adolescents need advice to help them monitor their cognitive activities? Plenty! (e.g., Garner, 1987; Mayer, 1987). Parents, teachers, and peers can serve as important cognitive monitoring models and also can interact with adolescents in ways to improve their cognitive monitoring. In one strategy, cognitive monitoring is placed in the hands of peers. That is, instead of adults telling adolescents what to do and checking their performance, this chore is performed by other adolescents.

Reading continues to play a powerful role in adolescents' lives, just as it did when they were children. In the last decade, considerable interest has developed in the process of cognitive monitoring as an important aspect of reading. What do we mean by cognitive monitoring?

Information Processing and Education

When you were in school, did teachers work with you on improving your information processing skills, such as memory? Did any of your teachers work with you on your reading skills after the first and second grade? Did any of your teachers discuss with you ways in which cognitive monitoring could enhance your learning? If you are like most individuals, you spent little or no time in school improving these important processes involved in our everyday intellectual encounters with the world.

Why is it important to have an educational goal of improving the information processing skills of adolescents? Think for a moment about yourself and the skills necessary for you to be successful in adapting to your environment and for improving your chances of getting a good job and having a successful career. To some extent, knowledge itself is important; more precisely, content knowledge in certain areas is important. For example, if you plan to become a chemical engineer, a knowledge of chemistry is required. Our schools have done a much better job of imparting knowledge than in instructing students how to process information.

Another important situation in your life where instruction in information processing would have helped you tremendously was when you took the SAT or ACT test. SAT cram courses are popping up all over the United States, in part because schools have not done a good job of developing information processing skills. For example, is speed of processing information important on the SAT? Most of you probably felt that you did not have as much time as you would have liked to handle difficult questions. Are memory strategies important on the SAT? You had to read paragraphs and hold a considerable amount of information in your mind to answer some of the questions. And you certainly had to remember how to solve a number of math problems. Didn't you also have to remember the definitions of a large number of vocabulary words? And what about problem solving, inferencing, and understanding? Remember the difficult verbal problems you had to answer and the inferences you had to make when reasoning was required?

The story of information processing is one of attention, perception, memory (especially the control processes in memory), thinking, and the like. These information processing skills become even more crucial in education when we consider that we are now in the midst of a transition from an industrial to a postindustrial, information society, with approximately 65% to 70% of all workers involved in services. The information revolution in our society has placed strain on workers who are called on daily to process huge amounts of information in a rapid fashion, to have efficient memories, to attend to relevant details, to reason logically about difficult issues, and to make inferences about information that may be fuzzy or unclear. Students graduate from high school, college, or postgraduate work and move into jobs requiring information processing skills, yet they have had little or no instruction in improving these skills.

At this time, we do not have a specified curriculum of information processing that can be taught in a stepwise, developmental fashion to our nation's children and adolescents. We also do not have the trained personnel for this instruction. Further, some information processing experts believe that processes such as attention and memory cannot be trained in a general way. Rather, they argue that information processing is domain- or content-specific. That is, we should work on improving information processing skills that are specific to math or specific to history. They do believe, though, that an infusion of the information processing approach into all parts of the curriculum would greatly benefit adolescents (Glazer & Bassok, 1989).

Researchers are beginning to study the importance of information processing skills for school learning. Ellen Gagne (1985) provided a menu of information processing skills that need to be given attention when instructing adolescents in specific content areas—reading, writing, math, and science, for example. Her review concludes that successful students—those who get better grades and higher achievement test scores—are better at information processing skills such as focusing attention, elaborating and organizing information, and monitoring their study strategies. As yet, though, we do not know the extent to which these information processing skills can be taught. Nonetheless, in one investigation, Gagne and her colleagues demonstrated that adolescents can be taught how to elaborate so that information can be remembered more efficiently. Elaboration refers to more extensive processing. Getting adolescents to think of examples of the concept is a good way to improve memory of the concept. So is getting adolescents to think about how the concept relates to themselves. Other experts in cognitive psychology also believe that information processing skills can be taught. For example, Joan Baron and R. J. Sternberg (1987) stress that we need to teach adolescents to think in less irrational ways. Adolescents need to be more critical of the first ideas that pop into their minds. They should be taught to think longer about problems and to search in more organized ways for evidence to support their views.

At this point we have discussed numerous ideas about information processing. A summary of these ideas is presented in Concept Table 5.1. Now we turn our attention to another way of analyzing the adolescent's cognition. We will discover that the study of adolescent intelligence has involved an emphasis on individual differences, knowledge, and intelligence tests.

Intelligence

Robert Sternberg recalls being terrified of taking IQ tests as a child. He says that he literally froze when the time came to take such tests. When he was in the sixth grade, he was sent to take an IQ test with the fifth graders and still talks about how embarrassing and humiliating the experience was. Sternberg recalls that maybe he was dumb, but he wasn't *that* dumb. He finally overcame his anxieties about IQ tests and performed much better on them. Sternberg became so fascinated with IQ tests that he devised his own at the age of 13 and began assessing the intellectual abilities of his classmates until the school psychologist scolded him. Later in our discussion of intelligence you will discover that Sternberg recently has developed a provocative theory of intelligence. Our exploration of intelligence focuses on the following questions: What is intelligence? How is intelligence measured? Does intelligence have one or many faces? Can aptitude and achievement tests be distinguished? What are some of the major controversies and issues involving intelligence? What are the extremes of intelligence like? We consider each of these in turn.

Information Processing

Concept	Processes/Related Ideas	Characteristics/Description
The information processing perspective	Overview	Information processing is concerned with how individuals analyze the many sources of information in the environment and make sense of these experiences. It includes how information gets into the mind, how it is stored and transformed, and how it is retrieved to think and solve problems.
	Comparison with other approaches	Traditional principles of behaviorism and learning do little to explain what is going on in the mind. Piaget's cognitive developmental theory provides a general outline of changes in cognition but leaves out some important details about the steps involved in analyzing information. The information processing perspective tries to correct some of these deficiencies.
	Computer analogies	Information processing psychologists may write a computer program to represent the steps needed to solve a problem. Information processing psychologists sometimes rely on computers to tell them how the human mind works—an area referred to as artificial intelligence.
Attention and memory	Attention	Two ways adolescents can use attention are selective attention and divided attention. Adolescents are more superior in using these two forms of attention than children.
	Memory	The retention of information over time. Can be divided into short-term memory—information held for about 15–30 seconds—and long-term memory—information held indefinitely. Strategies, or control processes, improve adolescent memory, especially organization. Increases in storage space, as well as speed and efficiency of information processing, are likely involved in the adolescent's superior memory when compared to the child's memory.
Cognitive monitoring	Its nature	The process of taking stock of what one is doing currently, what will be done next, and how effectively mental activity is unfolding. Parents, teachers, and peers can be effective sources for improving the adolescent's cognitive monitoring.
Information processing and education	applications	The information processing perspective needs to be applied more widely to the education of adolescents. This is especially true as we move further into the information age. Researchers are working on a menu of information processing skills that can be taught, but as yet we do not have a stepwise, developmental curriculum of information processing.

What Is Intelligence?

Intelligence is a possession that most adolescents value highly, yet it is an abstract concept with few agreed upon referents. We would agree upon referents for such characteristics as adolescent height, weight, and age, but would be

Biological and Cognitive Processes and Development

less certain to agree on referents for something like an adolescent's size. Size is a more *abstract* notion than height or weight. We can only estimate an adolescent's size from a set of empirical measures of height and weight. Measuring an adolescent's intelligence is much the same as measuring the adolescent's size, though *much more* abstract. That is, we believe an adolescent's intelligence exists, but we do not measure an adolescent's intelligence directly. We cannot peel back the adolescent's scalp and observe the adolescent's intellectual processes in action. The only way we can study these intellectual processes is *indirectly* by evaluating the intelligent acts the adolescent generates. For the most part, psychologists have relied on intelligence tests to provide an estimate of the adolescent's intelligence.

Throughout much of Western civilization's history, intelligence has been described in terms of knowledge and reasoning (Kail & Pellegrino, 1985). Today, most of us view intelligence in a similar light. In one investigation, individuals were asked to judge which of 250 behaviors were typical of an intelligent individual (Sternberg & others, 1981). Both experts (psychologists researching intelligence) and lay individuals (people of varying backgrounds and education) judged the behaviors similarly. The two groups agreed that intelligence can be divided into two main dimensions. The first is *verbal ability,* reflected in such behaviors as "displays a good vocabulary," "reads with high comprehension," "is knowledgeable about a particular field of knowledge," and "displays curiosity." The second is *problem solving skills,* reflected in such behaviors as "reasons logically and well," "is able to apply knowledge to problems at hand," and "makes good decisions."

In addition to believing that intelligence involves verbal ability and problem solving skills, psychologists who study intelligence also emphasize individual differences in intelligence and the assessment of intelligence. **Individual differences** are the stable, consistent ways adolescents are different from each other. The history of the study of intelligence has focused extensively on individual differences and their assessment. We can talk about individual differences in the adolescent's personality or any other domain of development, but it is in the area of intelligence that the most attention is given to individual differences. For example, an intelligence test will tell us whether an adolescent can reason better than most others who have taken the test. Psychologists have a name for the field that involves the assessment of individual differences—**psychometrics.**

Earlier we said that intelligence often is defined as verbal ability and problem solving skills. But we also said that intelligence is an abstract concept that is difficult to define. Intelligence also may be defined as the ability to learn from and adapt to the experiences of everyday life. If we were to settle on a definition of adolescent intelligence based on these criteria, it would be that **intelligence** is verbal ability, problem solving skills, and the ability to learn from and adapt to the experiences of everyday life. As we discuss the most widely used adolescence intelligence tests and the nature of intelligence, you will discover that experts still debate what intelligence is.

The Binet and Wechsler Tests

The two most widely used individual intelligence tests with adolescents are the Binet and Wechsler tests, each of which we consider in turn.

The Binet Tests

In 1904, the French Ministry of Education asked psychologist Alfred Binet to devise a method that would determine which students did not profit from typical school instruction. School officials wanted to reduce overcrowding by placing those who did not benefit from regular classroom teaching in special schools. Binet and his student Theophile Simon developed an intelligence test to meet this request. The test is referred to as the 1905 Scale and consisted of 30 different items ranging from the ability to touch one's nose or ear when asked to the ability to draw designs from memory and define abstract concepts.

Binet developed the concept of **mental age (MA),** which is an individual's level of mental development relative to others. Binet reasoned that a mentally retarded child would perform like a normal child of a younger age. He developed norms for intelligence by testing 50 nonretarded children from 3 to 11 years of age. Children suspected of mental retardation were given the test and their performance was compared with children of the same chronological age in the normal sample. Average mental-age scores (MA) correspond to chronological age (CA), which is age from birth. A bright child has an MA above CA, a dull child has an MA below CA.

The term **intelligence quotient (IQ)** was devised in 1912 by William Stern. IQ consists of a child's mental age divided by chronological age multiplied by 100:

$$IQ = \frac{MA}{CA} \times 100$$

If mental age is the same as chronological age, then the individual's IQ is 100; if mental age is above chronological age, the IQ is more than 100; if mental age is below chronological age, the IQ is less than 100. Scores noticeably above 100 are considered above average; those noticeably below are considered below average. For example, a 6-year-old child with a mental age of 8 would have an IQ of 133 while a 6-year-old child with a mental age of 5 would have an IQ of 83.

Over the years extensive effort has been expended to standardize the Binet test, which has been given to thousands of children and adults of different ages, selected at random from different parts of the United States. By administering the test to large numbers of individuals and recording the results, it has been found that intelligence measured by the Binet approximates a **normal distribution** (see Figure 5.3). This type of distribution is symmetrical, with a majority of cases falling in the middle of the possible range of scores and few scores appearing towards the ends of the range.

The many revisions of the Binet test in the United States are called the Stanford-Binet tests (Stanford University is where the revisions were done). Many of the revisions were carried out by Lewis Terman, who applied Stern's

Biological and Cognitive Processes and Development

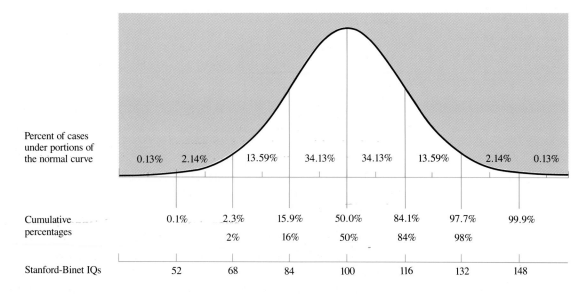

Percent of cases under portions of the normal curve	0.13%	2.14%	13.59%	34.13%	34.13%	13.59%	2.14%	0.13%

Cumulative percentages	0.1%	2.3%	15.9%	50.0%	84.1%	97.7%	99.9%	
		2%	16%	50%	84%	98%		

Stanford-Binet IQs	52	68	84	100	116	132	148

IQ concept to the test, developed extensive norms, and provided detailed, clear instructions for each problem appearing on the test.

The current Stanford-Binet is given to individuals from the age of 2 through adulthood. It includes a wide variety of items, some requiring verbal responses, others nonverbal responses. For example, items that characterize a 6-year-old's performance on the test include the verbal ability to define at least six words such as "orange" and "envelope," and the nonverbal ability to trace a path through a maze. Items that reflect the average adult's intelligence include defining such words as "disproportionate" and "regard," explaining a proverb, and comparing idleness and laziness.

The fouth edition of the Stanford-Binet was published in 1985 (Thorndike, Hagan, & Sattler, 1985). One important addition to this version is the analysis of the individual's responses in terms of four content areas: verbal reasoning, quantitative reasoning, abstract/visual reasoning, and short-term memory. A general composite score also is obtained to reflect overall intelligence. The Stanford-Binet continues to be one of the most widely used individual tests of intelligence.

The Wechsler Scales

Besides the Stanford-Binet, the most widely used individual intelligence tests with adolescents are the **Wechsler scales,** developed by David Wechsler. They include the Wechsler Adult Intelligence Scale—Revised (WAIS-R), which is given to older adolescents and adults, and the Wechsler Intelligence Test for Children—Revised (WISC-R), which can be given to children and adolescents aged 6 to 16 (Wechsler, 1949, 1955, 1974, 1981).

The Wechsler scales not only provide an overall IQ score, but the items are grouped according to 11 subscales, 6 of which are verbal and 5 of which are nonverbal. This allows the examiner to obtain separate verbal and nonverbal IQ scores and to see quickly the areas of mental performance in which

Figure 5.3 The normal curve and Stanford-Binet IQ scores (Sattler, 1982). The distribution of IQ scores approximates a normal curve. Most of the population falls in the middle range of scores. Notice that extremely high and extremely low scores are very rare. Slightly more than two-thirds of the scores fall between 84 and 116. Only about 1 in 50 individuals has an IQ of more than 132 and only about 1 in 50 individuals has an IQ of less than 68.

Figure 5.4 The subtests of the WISC-R and examples of each subtest.

VERBAL SUBTESTS

General Information

The child is asked a number of general information questions about experiences that are considered normal for children in our society.

For example, "Name the days of the week."

Similarities

The child must think logically and abstractly to answer a number of questions about how things are similar.

For example, "In what way are boats and trains the same?"

Arithmetic Reasoning

Problems measure the ability of the child to do arithmetic mentally, including addition, subtraction, multiplication, and division.

For example, "If oranges are $1.20 per dozen, how much does one orange cost?"

Vocabulary

To evaluate word knowledge, the child is asked to define a number of words. This subtest measures cognitive functions such as concept formation, memory, and language.

For example, "What does the word 'afraid' mean?"

Comprehension

This subtest is designed to measure the judgment and common sense of the child.

For example, "Why do people buy life insurance?"

Digit Span

This subtest primarily measures attention and short-term memory. The child is asked to repeat numbers forward and backward.

For example, "I am going to say some numbers and I want you to repeat them backwards:

4   7   5   2

PERFORMANCE SUBTESTS

Picture Completion

A number of drawings are shown, each with a significant part missing. Within a period of several seconds, the child must differentiate essential from nonessential parts of the picture and identify which part is missing. This subtest measures visual alertness and the ability to organize information visually.

For example, "I am going to show you a picture with an important part missing. Tell me what is missing."

Picture Arrangement

A series of pictures out of sequence are shown to the child, who is asked to place them in their proper order to tell an appropriate story. This subtest evaluates how the child integrates information to make it logical and meaningful.

For example, "The pictures below need to be placed in an appropriate order to tell a meaningful story."

172

Figure 5.4   (*continued*)

Object Assembly

The child is asked to assemble pieces into something. This subtest measures visual-motor coordination and perceptual organization.

For example, "When these pieces are put together correctly, they make something. Put them together as quickly as you can."

Block Design

The child must assemble a set of multi-colored blocks to match designs the examiner shows. Visual-motor coordination, perceptual organization, and the ability to visualize spatially are measured.

For example, "Use the four blocks on the left to make the pattern on the right."

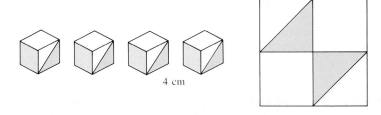

4 cm

Coding

This subtest evaluates how quickly and accurately a child can link code symbols and digits. The subtest assesses visual-motor coordination and speed of thought.

For example, "As quickly as you can, transfer the appropriate code symbols to the blank spaces."

Code

Test

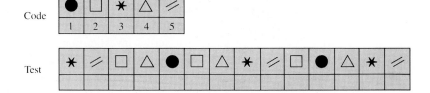

the individual is below average, average, or above average. The inclusion of a number of nonverbal subscales makes the Wechsler test more representative of verbal *and* nonverbal intelligence; the Binet-Simon test includes some nonverbal items but not as many as the Wechsler scales. The subscales of the Weschler Intelligence Scale for Children—Revised (WISC-R) are shown in Figure 5.4, along with examples of each subscale.

Does Intelligence Have a Single Nature?

Is it more appropriate to think of intelligence as an adolescent's general ability or as a number of specific abilities? Long before David Wechsler analyzed intelligence in terms of general and specific factors (giving the child an overall IQ but also providing information about specific subcomponents of intelligence), Charles Spearman (1927) proposed that intelligence has two factors. Spearman's **two-factor theory** argued that individuals have both general intelligence, which he called *g,* and a number of specific intelligences, which he called *s.* Spearman believed that these two factors could account for an individual's performance on an intelligence test.

However, some factor approaches abandoned the idea of a general intelligence and searched for specific factors only. L. L. Thurstone (1938) proposed a **multiple-factor theory of intelligence.** Thurstone consistently came up with 6 to 12 abilities when analyzing large numbers of intelligence test responses. He called these factors primary mental abilities. The seven primary mental abilities that most often appeared in Thurstone's analysis were verbal comprehension, number ability, word fluency, spatial visualization, associative memory, reasoning, and perceptual speed.

One recent classification, developed by Howard Gardner (1983, 1989), also includes seven components of intelligence, although they are not the same as Thurstone's seven factors. By turning to Perspective on Adolescent Development 5.2, you can read about Gardner's seven frames of mind. Clearly, there is disagreement about whether intelligence is a general ability or a number of specific abilities, and if there are specific abilities, disagreement about just what those are (Carroll, 1989).

Disagreement characterizes the approaches to intelligence for two primary reasons (Kail & Pellegrino, 1985). First, there are many ways to analyze the same data. Different apparent solutions, which produce different psychological interpretations, can be obtained from the same data. Second, the data obtained in separate studies differ. The critical data for interpreting whether intelligence is a general ability or a number of specific abilities involve correlation—recall our discussion of correlation in Chapter 2. The pattern of correlations depends on the group tested (e.g., adolescents, armed service recruits, or criminals), the total number of tests administered, and the specific tests included in the battery. The outcome of the studies is that the abilities thought to make up the core of intelligence may vary across investigations. Despite these inconsistencies, evidence suggests that intelligence is *both* a general ability and a number of specific abilities.

Aptitude and Achievement Tests

Psychologists distinguish between an **aptitude test,** which predicts an individual's ability to learn a skill or what the individual can accomplish with training, and an **achievement test,** which measures what has been learned or what skills have been mastered. However, the distinction between the two types of tests

Bird to Beethoven—Seven Frames of Mind

A blond-haired 13-year-old boy springs into motion during a junior high basketball game in the small town of French Lick, Indiana. Grabbing a rebound, he quickly dribbles the ball the length of the court, all the while processing the whereabouts of his five opponents and four teammates. He throws the ball to an open teammate who scores on an easy layup. Years later the young boy had become a 6-foot 9-inch superstar for the Boston Celtics. His name—Larry Bird. Is there intelligence to Bird's movement and perception of the spatial layout of the basketball court?

Now we turn the clock back 200 years. Another 13-year-old boy is playing a piano at a concert hall in front of a large audience. The young adolescent is Ludwig von Beethoven, whose musical genius was evident at a young age. Did Beethoven have a specific type of intelligence, one we might call musical intelligence?

Bird and Beethoven are different types of individuals with different types of abilities. Howard Gardner (1983), in his book *Frames of Mind,* argues that Bird's and Beethoven's talents represent two of seven intelligences that we possess. Beyond the verbal and mathematical intelligences tapped by such tests as the SAT and most traditional intelligence tests, Gardner thinks that we have the ability to spatially analyze the world, movement skills, insightful skills for analyzing ourselves, insightful skills for analyzing others, and musical skills.

Gardner believes that each of the seven intelligences can be destroyed by brain damage, that each involves unique cognitive skills, and that each shows up in exaggerated fashion in both the gifted and *idiots savants* (individuals who are mentally retarded but who have unbelievable skill in a particular domain, such as drawing, music, or computing). I remember vividly an individual from my childhood who was mentally retarded but could instantaneously respond with the correct day of the week (say Tuesday or Saturday) when given any date in history (say June 4, 1926, or December 15, 1746).

Critics of Gardner's approach point out that we have geniuses in many domains other than music. There are outstanding chess players, prize fighters, writers, politicians, physicians, lawyers, preachers, and poets, for example; yet we do not refer to chess intelligence, prize-fighter intelligence, and so on.

(a) *Larry Bird, NBA superstar of the Boston Celtics. Howard Gardner believes Bird's movement skills and spatial perception are forms of intelligence.* (b) *Ludwig van Beethoven. Gardner also argues that musical skills, such as those shown by Beethoven are a form of intelligence.*

Most of us labored through a test like the SAT toward the end of our high school years. How is the SAT both an aptitude test and an achievement test?

is sometimes blurred. Both tests assess the individual's current status, both include several types of questions, and both produce results that usually are highly correlated. It is important to remember that the test's *purpose,* not its *content,* determines whether it is an aptitude or an achievement test.

The Scholastic Aptitude Test (SAT), taken each year by more than 1 million high school seniors, measures some of the same abilities as intelligence tests. However, it does not yield an overall IQ score; rather it provides separate scores for verbal and mathematical ability. The SAT is similar to the original Binet in that it was developed to predict success in school. The SAT has the ingredients of both an aptitude test and an achievement test. It is an achievement test in the sense that it measures what adolescents have learned in terms of vocabulary, reading comprehension, algebraic skills, and so on. It is an aptitude test in the sense that it is used to predict adolescents' performance in college. While the SAT is widely used to predict success in college, it is only one of many pieces of information that determines whether a college admits a student. High school grades, the quality of the student's high school, letters of recommendation, individual interviews with the student, and special circumstances in the student's life that might have impeded academic ability are taken into account along with SAT scores (Dyer, 1987). In recent years controversy has developed over whether private coaching can raise a student's SAT scores. The student's verbal and mathematical abilities, which the SAT taps, have been built up over years of experience and instruction. Research shows that private coaching on a short-term basis does not substantially raise SAT scores. On the average, researchers find that SAT-preparation courses raise the students' scores only 15 points on the SAT's 200 to 800 scale (Kulik, Bangert-Drowns, & Kulik, 1984).

Biological and Cognitive Processes and Development

Controversies and Issues in Intelligence

Intelligence has been one concept of psychology that seems to attract controversy. Among the most controversial issues involving intelligence are those related to heredity-environment determinants, racial differences, cultural biases in intelligence tests, knowledge versus process, and the uses and misuses of intelligence tests, each of which we consider in turn.

Heredity-Environment

Arthur Jensen (1969) sparked a lively and at times hostile debate when he presented his thesis that intelligence is primarily inherited. Jensen believes that environment and culture play only a minimal role in intelligence. Jensen examined a number of studies of intelligence, many of which involved comparisons of identical and fraternal twins. Remember that identical twins have identical genetic endowments, so their IQs should be similar. Fraternal twins and ordinary siblings are less similar genetically, so their IQs should be less similar. Jensen found support for his argument in these studies. Studies with identical twins produced an average correlation of .82; studies with ordinary siblings produced an average correlation of .50. Note the difference of .32. To show that genetic factors are more important than environmental factors, Jensen compared identical twins reared together with those reared apart; the correlation for those reared together was .89 and for those reared apart it was .78 (a difference of .11). Jensen argued that if environmental influences were more important than genetic influences, then siblings reared apart, who experienced different environments, should have IQs much further apart.

Many scholars have criticized Jensen's work. One criticism concerns the definition of intelligence itself. Jensen believes that IQ as measured by standard intelligence tests is a good indicator of intelligence. Critics argue that IQ tests tap only a narrow range of intelligence. Everyday problem solving, work, and social adaptability, say the critics, are important aspects of intelligence not measured by the traditional intelligence tests used in Jensen's sources. A second criticism is that most investigations of heredity and environment do not include environments that differ radically. Thus, it is not surprising that many genetic studies show environment to be a fairly weak influence on intelligence. Jensen places the importance of heredity's influence at about 80%. The consensus of today's experts on intelligence is that its genetic determination is more likely to be in the 50% range (Plomin, 1989; Plomin, DeFries, & McClearn, in press). For most individuals, this means that modification of present environmental circumstances can change their IQ scores substantially (Weinberg, 1989). While genetic endowment will always influence the individual's intellectual ability, the opportunities we provide adolescents can make a difference.

Japanese Question the Value of IQ Tests

In Japan, intelligence is a private matter. You don't hear people talking about someone being very bright the way we often do in the United States. In Japan, a very high IQ is usually thought of as unrealistic. Some psychologists have claimed that Japanese children have the highest mean IQ in the world and that the gap between them and the rest of the world is growing. Such comments catch the attention of Americans and Europeans but attract little interest in Japan. Faith in hard work and a belief in group achievement help to explain the relative lack of interest in individual differences in intelligence in Japan (Hathaway, 1984).

Social Class, Racial, and Ethnic Comparisons

Some years ago I knocked on the door of a house in a low-income area of the city. The father came to the door and invited me into the living room. It was getting dark outside and no lights were on inside the house. The father excused himself for a minute, then returned with a light bulb, which he screwed into the lamp socket. He said that he could barely pay his monthly mortgage and the electric company had threatened to turn off his electricity, so he was carefully monitoring his family's use of electricity. There were seven children in the family ranging in age from 2 to 16. Neither he nor his wife had completed high school. He worked as a bricklayer when he could find a job and his wife worked in a laundry ironing clothes. The parents wanted their children to have more opportunities than they themselves had had but so far their children were experiencing a life of social disadvantage too. Do adolescents from such families perform more poorly on tests of intelligence than their middle-income counterparts? Are there racial and ethnic differences in intelligence as well?

A consistent finding is that adolescents from low-income or lower-class families average 10–20 points lower than adolescents from middle-income or middle-class families on standardized intelligence tests. However, it is important to consider the dimensions of intelligence when evaluating social class differences. Those dimensions related to academic performance, such as verbal, numerical, and spatial abilities, are more likely to reflect social class differences. Those more closely related to mental abilities such as memory and reasoning are less likely to reveal social class differences (Globerson, 1983).

Racial and ethnic differences in adolescent performance on intelligence tests also exist. For example, in the United States, adolescents in black and Hispanic families score below adolescents from white families on standardized intelligence tests. The most interest in group differences has focused on black-white comparisons. On the average, white American adolescents score 10–15 points higher on standardized intelligence tests than black American adolescents (Anastasi, 1988). Keep in mind, though, that we are talking about average scores. Many black adolescents score higher than many white adolescents because the distributions for black and white adolescents overlap. Estimates indicate that 15%–25% of black adolescents score higher than half of all white adolescents (Shuey, 1966).

While the greatest interest has been in black-white comparisons, patterns of intelligence in Jewish, Chinese, black, and Puerto Rican adolescents suggest some strengths and weaknesses in children from different ethnic backgrounds (Lesser, Fifer, & Clark, 1965). Jewish adolescents scored higher on verbal abilities, lower on reasoning and number, and lower still on space. Chinese adolescents scored low on verbal abilities but higher in number, space, and reasoning. Black adolescents scored higher on verbal abilities and lower on reasoning, space, and number. Puerto Rican adolescents scored lower on verbal abilities and higher on number, space, and reasoning.

How extensively are racial and ethnic differences in adolescents' intelligence influenced by heredity and environment? The consensus is that the available data today do not support a genetic explanation. The consensus is that the available data do not support a genetic interpretation. For example, in recent decades as black Americans have experienced improved social, economic, and educational opportunities, the gap between white and black adolescents has begun to diminish. And when children and adolescents from disadvantaged black families are adopted by more advantaged middle-class families, their scores on intelligence tests more closely resemble national averages for middle-class than lower-class children and adolescents (Scarr, 1989; Scarr & Weinberg, in press).

Are Intelligence Tests Culturally Biased?

Many of the early intelligence tests were culturally biased, favoring urban adolescents over rural adolescents, middle-class adolescents over lower-class adolescents, and white adolescents over minority adolescents. The norms for the early tests were based almost entirely on white, middle-class adolescents, and some of the items themselves were culturally biased. For example, one item on an early test asked what should be done if you find a 3-year-old child in the street—the correct answer was "call the police." Adolescents from impoverished inner city families might not choose this answer if they have had bad experiences with the police; rural adolescents might not choose it since

TABLE 5.1   *The Chitling Intelligence Test*

1. A "gas head" is a person who has a:
    (a) fast-moving car
    (b) stable of "lace"
    (c) "process"
    (d) habit of stealing cars
    (e) long jail record for arson
2. "Bo Diddley" is a:
    (a) game for children
    (b) down-home cheap wine
    (c) down-home singer
    (d) new dance
    (e) Moejoe call
3. If a pimp is uptight with a woman who gets state aid, what does he mean when he talks about "Mother's day"?
    (a) second Sunday in May
    (b) third Sunday in June
    (c) first of every month
    (d) none of these
    (e) first and fifteenth of every month
4. A "handkerchief head" is:
    (a) a cool cat
    (b) a porter
    (c) an Uncle Tom
    (d) a hoddi
    (e) a preacher
5. If a man is called a "blood," then he is a:
    (a) fighter
    (b) Mexican-American
    (c) Negro
    (d) hungry hemophile
    (e) red man, or Indian
6. Cheap chitlings (not the kind you purchase at a frozen-food counter) will taste rubbery unless they are cooked long enough. How soon can you quit cooking them to eat and enjoy them?
    (a) forty-five minutes
    (b) two hours
    (c) twenty-four hours
    (d) one week (on a low flame)
    (e) one hour

Answers: 1.c 2.c 3.e 4.c 5.c 6.c

Note: The Chitling Intelligence Test was not developed to be a formal, standardized test of intelligence, but rather was constructed to provide a sense of how the experiences of minority group individuals differ from those of white individuals and the way these experiences might influence performance on an intelligence test.
Source: Adrian Dove, 1968.

they may not have police nearby. Such items clearly do not measure the knowledge necessary to adapt to one's environment or to be "intelligent" in an inner city minority neighborhood or in rural America (Scarr, 1984). The contemporary versions of intelligence tests attempt to reduce cultural bias.

Even if the content of test items is made appropriate, another problem may exist with intelligence tests. Since many questions are verbal in nature, minority groups may encounter problems understanding the language of the questions (Gibbs & Huang, 1989). Minority groups often speak a language that is very different from standard English. Consequently, they may be at a disadvantage when they take intelligence tests oriented toward middle-class, white children. Cultural bias is dramatically underscored by tests like the one shown in Table 5.1. The items in this test were developed to reduce the cultural disadvantage black adolescents might experience on traditional intelligence tests.

Cultural bias is also dramatically underscored in the life of Gregory Ochoa. When Gregory was a high school student, he and his classmates were given an IQ test. School authorities informed them the test would allow the school to place them in classes appropriate for their skills. Gregory looked at the test questions. He didn't understand many of the words. Spanish was spoken at his home and his English was not very good. Several weeks later Gregory

A 5

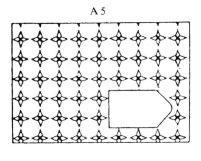

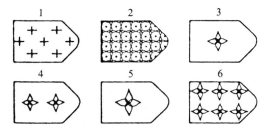

Figure 5.5 The Raven Progressive Matrices Test has no verbal items. Even though this and other nonverbal intelligence tests are designed to be culture fair, researchers find that individuals with more education score higher on them than those with less education.

was placed in a "special" class. Many of the other students had names like Ramirez and Gonzales. The special class was for mentally retarded students. Gregory lost interest in school and eventually dropped out. Subsequently he enrolled in the Navy where he took high school courses, earning enough credits to later attend college. He graduated from San Jose City College as an honor student, continued his education, and became a professor of social work at the University of Washington in Seattle.

Culture-fair tests were devised to reduce cultural bias. Two types of culture-fair tests have been developed. The first includes items that are familiar to individuals from all socioeconomic and ethnic backgrounds, or items that at least are familiar to the individuals who are taking the test. For example, an adolescent might be asked how a bird and a dog are different, on the assumption that virtually all adolescents have been exposed to birds and dogs. The second type of culture-fair test has all the verbal items removed. Figure 5.5 shows a sample item from the Raven Progressive Matrices Test, which exemplifies this approach. Even though tests like the Raven Test are designed to be culture fair, individuals with more education score higher on them than those with less education (Anastasi, 1988).

Culture-fair tests remind us that traditional intelligence tests are probably culturally biased, yet culture-fair tests themselves do not provide a satisfactory alternative. Constructing a truly culture-fair test, one that rules out the role of experience emanating from socioeconomic and ethnic background, has been difficult and may be impossible. Consider, for example, that the intelligence of the Iatmul people of Papua, New Guinea, involves the ability to remember the names of some 10,000 to 20,000 clans; by contrast, the intelligence of the islanders in the widely dispersed Caroline Islands involves the talent of navigating by the stars.

Knowledge Versus Process in Intelligence

The information processing approach we discussed earlier in the chapter raises two interesting questions about adolescent intelligence. What are the fundamental information processing abilities of adolescents? How do these develop?

Few of us would deny that changes in both processing and knowledge occur as we develop. However, a consensus does not exist on something more fundamental. We accumulate knowledge as we grow from being a child to being an adult, but what may be growing is simply a reserve of processing capacity. That is, your greater processing capacity as an adult might be what allows you to learn more. By contrast, possibly your greater processing capacity as an adult is a consequence of your greater knowledge, which allows you to process information more effectively. It is not easy to choose between these two possibilities, and the issue has been called the great **structure-process dilemma** of intelligence (Keil, 1984). That is, What are the mechanisms of intelligence and how do they develop? Does information processing ability change or does knowledge and expertise change? Or do both change?

To make the structure-process dilemma more concrete, consider a simple computer metaphor. Suppose we have two computers, each of which is capable of solving multiplication problems (e.g., 13 × 24, 45 × 21), but one computer works faster than the other. What is the explanation? One possibility is that the faster computer has a greater capacity—that is, core memory—in which to do mental work. This greater core memory, which psychologists refer to as *working memory,* might allow the computer to work on two or more components of a problem at once. Another explanation is that the faster computer might have a greater store of relevant knowledge. Perhaps it has in its data bank (long-term memory) a complete multiplication table up to 99 × 99. The slower computer might have a table up to 12 × 12 (as do most humans). The faster computer need not be fundamentally faster—its subroutines may be relatively slow, but it is able to perform the multiplication task because of knowledge, not because of processing capacity.

Explaining intelligence is similar to explaining the difference between the fast and slow computers—is processing or knowledge responsible for how intelligence changes with age? Based on research on memory, it seems likely that the answer is both (Zembar & Naus, 1985). If so, the essential task becomes one of determining the ways that processing and knowledge interact in the course of intellectual development.

The modern information processing approach does not argue that knowledge is unimportant. Rather, many information processing psychologists believe that attention should be given to the knowledge base generated by intellectual processes. One information processing approach to intelligence that recognizes the importance of both process and knowledge is R. J. Sternberg's (1986, 1988, 1989) model. To learn more about Sternberg's view of intelligence, turn to Perspective on Adolescent Development 5.3.

Analytical Ann, Insightful Todd, and Street-Smart Art

R. J. Sternberg (1986, 1988, 1989) believes every adolescent has three types of intelligence and he calls his view the **triarchic theory of intelligence.** Consider Ann, who scores high on traditional intelligence tests such as the Stanford-Binet and is a star analytical thinker. Consider Todd, who does not have the best test results but has an insightful and creative mind. And consider Art, a street-smart adolescent who has learned how to deal in practical ways with his world, although his scores on traditional intelligence tests are low.

Sternberg calls Ann's analytical thinking and abstract reasoning *componential intelligence;* it is the closest to what we call intelligence in this chapter and what commonly is measured by intelligence tests. Todd's insightful and creative thinking is called *experiential intelligence* by Sternberg. And Art's street smarts and practical know-how is called *contextual intelligence* by Sternberg (see Figure 5.A).

In Sternberg's view of componential intelligence, the basic unit of intelligence is a *component,* simply defined as a basic unit of information processing. Sternberg believes that such components include those used to acquire or store information, to retain or retrieve information, to transfer information, to plan, make decisions, and solve problems, and to carry out problem solving strategies or translate thoughts into performance.

The second part of Sternberg's model focuses on experience. Intelligent individuals have the ability to solve new problems quickly, but also learn how to solve familiar problems in an automatic way so that their minds are free to handle problems that require insight and creativity.

The third part of the model involves practical knowledge—such as how to get out of trouble, how to replace a fuse, and how to get along with people. Sternberg calls this practical knowledge *tacit knowledge.* It includes all of the information about getting along in the world that is not taught in school. Sternberg believes that tacit knowledge is more important for success in life than explicit, or "book," knowledge. Once again we see—in Sternberg's model—the effort to determine the nature of intelligence's faces.

R. J. Sternberg has developed an information processing view of intelligence.

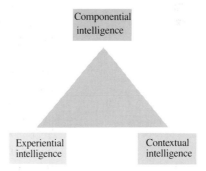

Figure 5.A   Sternberg's triarchic theory of intelligence.

The Use and Misuse of Intelligence Tests

Psychological tests are tools. Like all tools, their effectiveness depends on the knowledge, skill, and integrity of the user. A hammer can be used to build a beautiful kitchen cabinet or it can be used as a weapon of assault. Like a hammer, intelligence tests can be used for positive purposes or they can be badly abused. It is important for both the test constructor and the test examiner to be familiar with the current state of scientific knowledge about intelligence and intelligence tests (Anastasi, 1988).

Even though they have limitations, intelligence tests are among psychology's most widely used tools. To be effective, though, intelligence tests must be viewed realistically. They should not be thought of as a fixed, unchanging indicator of an individual's intelligence. They also should be used in conjunction with other information about the adolescent and not relied upon as the sole indicator of intelligence. For example, an intelligence test should not be used as the sole indicator of whether an adolescent should be placed in a special education or gifted class. The adolescent's developmental history, medical background, performance in school, social competencies, and family experiences should be taken into account too.

The single number provided by many IQ tests can easily lead to stereotypes and expectations about the individual. Many individuals do not know how to interpret the results of an intelligence test, and sweeping generalizations about an individual too often are made on the basis of an IQ score. For example, imagine that you are a teacher in the teacher's lounge on the day after school has started in the fall. You mention a student—Johnny Jones—and a fellow teacher remarks that she had Johnny in class last year; she comments that he was a real dunce and points out that his IQ is 78. You cannot help but remember this information, and it may lead you to think that Johnny Jones is not very bright so it is useless to spend much time teaching him. In this way, IQ scores are misused and stereotypes are formed (Rosenthal & Jacobsen, 1968).

We also have a tendency in our culture to consider intelligence or a high IQ as the ultimate human value. It is important to keep in mind that our value as humans includes other matters—consideration of others, positive close relationships, and competence in social situations, for example. The verbal and problem solving skills measured on traditional intelligence tests are only one part of human competence.

Despite their limitations, when used judiciously by a competent examiner intelligence tests provide valuable information about individuals. There are not many alternatives to intelligence tests. Subjective judgments about individuals simply reintroduce the biases the tests were designed to eliminate.

The Extremes of Intelligence

The atypical adolescent has always been of interest to developmentalists. Intellectual atypicality has intrigued psychologists and drawn them to study mentally retarded, gifted, and creative adolescents.

Biological and Cognitive Processes and Development

held belief that the intellectually gifted are somehow emotionally or socially maladjusted. This belief is based on striking instances of mental disturbances among the gifted. Sir Isaac Newton, Vincent van Gogh, Leonardo da Vinci, Socrates, and Edgar Allan Poe all had emotional problems. But these are exceptions rather than the rule; no relation between giftedness and mental disturbance in general has been found. Recent studies support Terman's conclusion that, if anything, the gifted tend to be more mature and have fewer emotional problems than others.

"Stars" devote tremendous amounts of time to practice and training.

In one investigation individuals with exceptional talents as adults were interviewed about what they believe contributed to their giftedness (Bloom, 1983). The 120 individuals had excelled in one of six fields—concert pianists and sculptors (arts), Olympic swimmers and tennis champions (psychomotor), and research mathematicians and research neurologists (cognitive). They said the development of their exceptional accomplishments required special environmental support, excellent teaching, and motivational encouragement. Each experienced years of special attention under the tutelage and supervision of a remarkable set of teachers and coaches. They also were given extensive support and encouragement from parents. All of these stars devoted exceptional time to practice and training, easily outdistancing the amount of time spent in all other activities combined. Of course, not every parent wants to raise a star, and too many parents develop unrealistic expectations for their offspring, putting unbearable pressure on them and wanting achievement that far exceeds their talents. For every Chris Evert, there are thousands of girls with only mediocre tennis talent whose parents have wanted them to become another "Chris Evert." Such unreal expectations always meet with failure and place adolescents under considerable stress. And all too often parents try to push children and adolescents into activities that bore them rather than excite them (Feldman, 1989; Hennessey & Amabile, 1988).

Creativity

Most parents would like their adolescents to be both gifted *and* creative. Why was Thomas Edison able to invent so many things? Was he simply more intelligent than most individuals? Did he spend long hours toiling away in private? Somewhat surprisingly, when Edison was a young boy his teacher told him that he was too dumb to learn anything! The creative genius of other famous individuals went unnoticed when they were young: Walt Disney was fired from a newspaper job because he did not have any good ideas; Enrico Caruso's music teacher told him that his voice was terrible; and Winston Churchill failed one year of secondary school. One reason such individuals are underestimated is the difficulty of defining and measuring creativity.

The prevailing belief of experts who study intelligence and creativity is that the two are not the same thing (Monroe, 1988; Wallach, 1985; Winner, 1989). One distinction is between **convergent thinking,** which produces one correct answer, and **divergent thinking,** which produces many different answers to the same question (Guilford, 1967). For example, this problem solving task has one correct answer and requires convergent thinking: "How many quarters will you get for sixty dimes?" But this question has many possible answers and requires divergent thinking: "What are some unique things that can be done with a paper clip?" A degree of creativity is needed to answer this question. Other examples of divergent thinking are generated by the following: Name words that belong to a particular class. For example, name as many objects as you can that weigh less than one pound. Even when you are not asked to, do you give divergent answers? For example, if you are asked what things can be done with a paper clip, do you spontaneously generate different categories of use for the paper clip? For more examples of items on tests of creativity turn to Figure 5.6.

Creativity is the ability to think about something in a novel way and to come up with unique solutions to problems. When individuals in the arts and sciences who fit this description are asked what enables them to produce their creative works, they say that they generate large amounts of associative content when solving problems and that they have the freedom to entertain a wide range of possible solutions in a playful manner (Wallach & Kogan, 1965).

R. J. Sternberg (Sternberg, 1988, in press; Sternberg & Davidson, 1986) believes that **insight** is an especially important ingredient of creativity and giftedness. He believes that exceptional intellectual accomplishments—for example, major scientific discoveries, important inventions, and special literary and philosophical works—invariably involve major intellectual insights. Sternberg says that many students classified by secondary schools as gifted are not especially insightful, while many students who are insightful are not classified as gifted. In the extreme case, schools may find insightful adolescents to be "pains in the neck" and actually keep them out of gifted programs because they are perceived as behavior problems.

How strongly is creativity related to intelligence? A certain level of intelligence seems to be required to be creative in most fields, but many highly intelligent individuals (as measured by IQ tests) are not very creative.

Some experts remain skeptical that we will ever fully understand the creative process. Other experts believe that a psychology of creativity is in reach. Most experts do agree that the concept of creativity as spontaneously

Figure 5.6   Sample of items from
Guilford's Test of Creative Thinking.

1. *Sketches:* Add just enough detail to the circle below to make a recognizable object (two examples of acceptable responses are shown).

2. *Word fluency:* Write as many words as you can think of with the first and last letters R_____M ("rim" would be one).

3. *Name grouping:* Classify the following six names in as many different ways as you can (a person might group 1, 3, and 4 together because each has two syllables).
   1. GERTRUDE   2. BILL
   3. ALEX   4. CARRIE
   5. BELLE   6. DON

4. *Making objects:* Using two or more of the forms shown below, make a face. Now make a lamp (examples of good responses are shown).

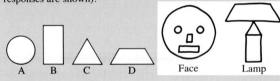

bubbling up from a magical well is a myth. Momentary flashes of insight, accompanied by images, make up only a small part of the creative process. At the heart of the creative process are ability and experience that shape an individual's intentional and sustained effort, often over the course of a lifetime. Based on his own research and analysis of the creativity literature, Daniel Perkins (1984; Gardner & Perkins, 1989) has developed a model that takes into account the complexity of the creativity process. An overview of Perkins' model appears in Perspective on Adolescent Development 5.4. As we learn more about creativity, we come to understand how important it is as a human resource, truly being one of adolescents' wondrous gifts.

Since our last review we have discussed many different ideas about intelligence. A summary of these ideas is presented in Concept Table 5.2.

The Snowflake Model of Creativity

Daniel Perkins describes his view as the *snowflake model of creativity.* Like the six sides of the snowflake, each with its own complex structure, Perkin's model consists of six characteristics common to highly creative individuals. People who are creative may not have all six characteristics, but the more they have, the more creative they tend to be, says Perkins (McAleer, 1989).

The first characteristic is a *strong commitment to a personal aesthetic.* This refers to the drive to impart order, simplicity, meaning, and powerful expression to what is seemingly chaos. For example, Einstein's life was full of circumstances reflecting his powerful motivation for simplicity. Someone once asked him why he used hand soap for shaving instead of shaving cream. He replied that two soaps were too complicated! As part of their personal aesthetic, creative individuals have a high tolerance for complexity or ambiguity, disorganization, and asymmetry. They seem to thrive on the challenge of cutting through chaos and struggling toward a synthesis. In science, for example, the core challenge is often dealing with a maze of ambiguities and coming up with a unique solution.

The second characteristic of creative individuals in Perkins' model is the ability to *excel in finding problems.* Creative individuals spend an unusual amount of time thinking about problems and exploring the options in solving them before they choose which solution to pursue. Creative individuals value good questions because they can produce discoveries and creative answers. A student once asked Nobel laureate Linus Pauling how he came up with good ideas. Pauling said that he developed a lot of ideas and then threw away the bad ones.

The third characteristic in the creative model is *mental mobility,* which allows individuals to find new perspectives and approaches to problems. One example of mental mobility is being able to think in terms of opposites and contraries while seeking a new solution.

The fourth characteristic is a *willingness to take risks.* Accompanying risk taking is the acceptance of failure as part of the creative quest and the ability to learn from failures. Creative geniuses don't always produce masterpieces. Picasso produced more than 20,000 works of art, but much of it was mediocre, for example. The more you produce, the better your chance of creating something important.

The fifth characteristic is *objectivity.* The popular image of creative individuals usually highlights their subjectivity, personal insight, and commitment. But without some objectivity, they would create a private world that is distant from reality. Creative individuals not only criticize their own works, they also seek criticism from others. Contrary to the popular image, the creative individual is not a self-absorbed loner. For example, Perkins has found that for both amateur and professional poets, those who sought feedback produced poetry a panel of experts judged to be superior to the poetry of those who did not seek criticism. Objectivity involves more than luck or talent. It means seeking advice from others and testing ideas in the real world.

The sixth and final characteristic in Perkins' model is a very important one—*inner motivation.* Creative individuals are motivated to produce something for its own sake, not for school grades or money. Their catalyst is the challenge, enjoyment, and satisfaction of the work itself. Researchers have found that individuals ranging from preschool children through adults are more creative when they are internally rather than externally motivated. Work evaluation, competition for prizes, and supervision tend to undermine internal motivation and diminish creativity.

Intelligence

Concept	Processes/Related Ideas	Characteristics/Description
What is intelligence?	Its nature	An abstract concept that is measured indirectly. Psychologists rely on intelligence tests to estimate intellectual processes. Verbal ability and problem solving skills are included in the definition of intelligence. Some psychologists believe the ability to learn from and adapt to everyday life also should be included in the definition. Extensive effort is devoted to assessing intelligence's individual differences—the field that does this assessment is called psychometrics.
The Binet and Wechsler tests	The Binet tests	Alfred Binet developed the first intelligence test, known as the 1905 scale. He developed the concept of mental age, and William Stern developed the concept of IQ. The Binet has been standardized and revised a number of times. The test approximates a normal distribution.
	The Wechsler scales	Besides the Binet, the most widely used intelligence tests. They include the WAIS-R and the WISC-R. These tests provide an overall IQ, verbal and performance IQs, and information about subtests.
Does intelligence have a single nature?	The controversy	Psychologists debate whether intelligence is a general ability or a number of specific abilities. Spearman's two-factor theory and Thurstone's multiple-factor theory state that a number of specific factors are involved, as does Gardner's model. Current thinking suggests intelligence involves both general and specific factors.
Aptitude and achievement tests	Their nature	Aptitude tests predict an adolescent's ability to learn a skill or his or her future performance. Achievement tests assess what an adolescent already knows. The distinction between these tests is sometimes blurred. The SAT has ingredients of both.
Controversies and issues in intelligence	Heredity-environment	Jensen's argument that intelligence is primarily due to heredity sparked a lively and at times bitter debate. Intelligence is influenced by heredity but not as strongly as Jensen envisioned.
	Social class, race, and ethnic comparisons	Differences exist between social classes, races, and ethnic groups, but the evidence suggests they are not genetically based. In recent decades, as blacks have experienced more opportunities, the gap in black-white differences has been diminishing.
	Cultural bias in intelligence testing	Early tests favored middle-class, white, urban adolescents. Current tests try to reduce this bias. Culture-fair tests are an alternative to traditional tests but most psychologists believe they cannot replace the traditional tests.
	Knowledge versus process	The mechanisms of intelligence and its development are both those of changing information processing abilities and changing expertise and knowledge. Sternberg's triarchic model emphasizes three dimensions of intelligence: componential, experiential, and contextual.

(continued on next page)

Intelligence *(continued)*

Concept	Processes/Related Ideas	Characteristics/Description
	Uses and misuses of intelligence tests	Despite limitations, when used by a judicious examiner tests can be valuable tools for determining individual differences in adolescent intelligence. The tests should be used with other information about the adolescent. IQ scores can produce unfortunate stereotypes and expectations. Ability tests can be used to divide adolescents into homogeneous groups, but periodic testing should be done. Intelligence or a high IQ is not necessarily the ultimate human value.
Extremes of intelligence	Mental retardation	A mentally retarded adolescent has a low IQ, usually below 70 on traditional IQ tests, and has difficulty adapting to everyday life. Different classifications of mental retardation exist. The two main causes of retardation are organic and cultural-familial.
	Giftedness and creativity	We defined a gifted adolescent as one with well-above-average intelligence (an IQ of 120 or more) and/or superior talent for something. We defined creativity as the ability to think about something in a novel or unusual way and to come up with unique solutions to problems. Insight may be especially important in understanding creativity and giftedness although as reflected in Perkin's snowflake model, creativity involves much more than insight.

Summary

I. The Information Processing Perspective

Information processing is concerned with how individuals analyze the many sources of information in the environment and make sense of these experiences. This perspective focuses on how information gets into the mind, how it is stored and transformed, and how it is retrieved to think and to solve problems. In comparison to other approaches, the information processing approaches provide details about what is going on during mental activity. Information processing psychologists may try to write a computer program to represent the steps needed to solve a problem. They sometimes rely on computers to tell them how the human mind works—an area referred to as artificial intelligence.

II. Attention and Memory

Two ways adolescents can use attention are selective attention and divided attention. Adolescents are superior to children at both types of attention. Memory is the retention of information over time—it can be divided into short-term and long-term memory. Strategies, or control processes, improve adolescent memory, especially organization. Increases in storage space, as well as in the speed and efficiency of information processing, are likely involved in the superiority adolescent memory to child memory.

III. Cognitive Monitoring

Cognitive monitoring refers to the process of taking stock of what one is doing currently, what will be done next, and how effectively mental activity is unfolding. Parents, teachers, and peers can be effective sources for improving the adolescent's cognitive monitoring.

IV. Information Processing and Education

The information processing perspective needs to be applied more widely to adolescent education. This is especially true as we move further into the information age. Researchers are working on a menu of information processing skills that can be taught, but as yet we do not have a stepwise, developmental curriculum of information processing.

V. What Is Intelligence?

Intelligence is an abstract concept that is measured indirectly. Psychologists rely on intelligence tests to estimate intellectual processes. Verbal ability, problem solving skills, and the ability to learn from and adapt to life's everyday experiences are important aspects of intelligence. Extensive effort is devoted to assessing intelligence's individual differences—the field involved in this assessment is called psychometrics.

VI. The Binet and Wechsler Tests

Alfred Binet developed the first intelligence test, known as the 1905 scale. He developed the concept of mental age, and William Stern developed the concept of IQ. The Binet has been standardized and revised a number of times. The test approximates a normal distribution. Besides the Binet, the most widely used intelligence tests are the Wechsler scales. They include the WAIS-R and the WISC-R. These tests provide an overall IQ, verbal and performance IQs, and information about subtests.

VII. Does Intelligence Have a Single Nature?

Psychologists debate whether intelligence is a general ability or a number of specific abilities. Spearman's two-factor theory and Thurstone's multiple-factor theory, as well as Gardner's model, stress that intelligence is made up of a number of factors. Current thinking suggests that intelligence involves both a general factor and specific factors.

VIII. Aptitude and Achievement Tests

Aptitude tests predict an adolescent's ability to learn a skill or his or her future performance. Achievement tests assess what an adolescent already knows. The distinction between these tests is often blurred. The SAT has ingredients of both.

IX. Controversies and Issues in Intelligence

Among the main controversies and issues in intelligence are those involving heredity-environment, social class, race, and ethnic comparisons, cultural bias in intelligence testing, knowledge versus process, and uses and misuses of intelligence tests.

X. Extremes of Intelligence

The extremes of intelligence focus on mental retardation, giftedness, and creativity.

Key Terms

artificial intelligence 161
lective attention 162
divided attention 163
memory 163
short-term memory 163
long-term memory 163
strategies 164
cognitive monitoring 165
individual differences 169
psychometrics 169
intelligence 169

mental age (MA) 170
intelligence quotient (IQ) 170
normal distribution 170
Wechsler scales 171
two-factor theory 174
multiple-factor theory of intelligence 174
aptitude test 174
achievement test 174
culture-fair tests 180

structure-process dilemma 181
triarchic theory of intelligence 183
mental retardation 185
organic retardation 186
cultural-familial retardation 186
gifted 186
convergent thinking 188
divergent thinking 188
creativity 188
insight 188

Biological and Cognitive Processes and Development

Suggested Readings

Anastasi, A. (1988): *Psychological testing* (6th ed.). New York: Macmillan.
This widely used text on psychological testing provides extensive information about test construction, test evaluation, and the nature of intelligence testing.

Baron, J. B., & Sternberg, R. J. (Eds.). (1987). *Teaching thinking skills: Theory and practice.* New York: W. H. Freeman.
This book presents essays by ten eminent psychologists, educators, and philosophers that portray the current state of knowledge about critical thinking skills. It offers various exercises and strategies that can be performed both inside and outside the classroom to enhance adolescents' critical thinking skills.

Fancher, R. E. (1985). *The intelligence men: Makers of the IQ controversy.* New York: W. W. Norton.
Fancher's book includes an extensive portrayal of the history of intelligence testing—many insights and detailed descriptions of the lives of the intelligence test makers are provided.

Gardner, H., & Perkins, D. (Eds.) (1989). *Art, mind, and education.* Ithaca, NY: University of Illinois Press.
An excellent collection of up-to-date ideas on creativity. Special attention is given to education's role in art.

Horowitz, F. D., & O'Brien, M. (Eds.). (1985). *The gifted and the talented* Washington, D.C.: The American Psychological Association.
This volume pulls together what we currently know about the gifted and the talented. Experts have contributed chapters on the nature of the gifted and the diverse topics involved.

Siegler, R. (1983). Information processing approaches to development. In P. H. Mussen (Ed.), *Handbook of child psychology* (Vol. 3, 4th ed.). New York: Wiley.
The information processing perspective approach is described, along with many ideas about how researchers evaluate the nature of information processing skills.

The Contexts of Adolescent

Development

Man is a knot, a web, a
mesh into which relation-
ships are tied.

Saint-Exupéry

on Mitchell is a 10-year-old black boy. His father works as an officer at a bank and his mother is a teacher. He has two younger sisters—Rena, age 5, and Martha, age 7. His parents have worked hard to provide a good life for themselves and their children. They encourage Don and his sisters to work hard in school and to listen carefully to what their teachers say. The Mitchells could be characterized as achievement-oriented, serious parents. They spend considerable time monitoring Don's academic and social world. The Mitchells recently moved to a predominantly white, middle-class neighborhood in a suburb of Houston, Texas. Don's parents believe the schools are better there than in the urban area in the north where they previously lived.

When we look at Don at the age of 14, we find that he is in the ninth grade of his junior high school. He is an excellent basketball player and is the leading scorer on his junior high school team. He is one of the most popular boys in his junior high school and over the course of his early adolescence seems to have gradually adapted to living in a predominantly white area. He has three close friends, two who are black and one who is white. The two black friends also play on the basketball team, and the white friend lives next door to him. Don's parents still monitor his academic and social world closely—"sometimes too closely," says Don. His mother was recently transferred to his school and is teaching eighth-grade English—Don frankly would have preferred it if his mother had stayed at the school where she had been teaching. Conflict between Don and his parents seems to have increased somewhat during the last several years, but most of the conflict is neither prolonged nor intense. Don is pushing to become a more independent individual and his parents are still trying to get him to conform to their high standards.

At age 17 Don is a junior in high school and has become the leading scorer on his high school basketball team. College coaches are already talking with him about a possible college scholarship. Don's parents are very proud of him—he has successfully managed to juggle the demands of sports and a rather rigorous set of classes in school. He has an A− average. Don's parents have recognized that he is now capable of making more mature decisions, so they feel comfortable in "letting loose" more than they did in the junior high school years. Still, Don has done some things they consider wrong—last summer, he and several of his friends went on a drinking binge one night. It was 3 a.m. and they didn't know where he was. At 3:30 a.m. Don and his friends finally realized they had better go home, even if they weren't sober. Don's parents were not very understanding. He wishes they would realize that you don't become an adult overnight; they don't seem to recognize that going from childhood to adulthood is a very long, gradual process and that adolescents are going to fall on their faces more than once during this time. Still, Don says he doesn't think he is going to stay out drinking until 3:00 or 4:00 in the morning any more, and when he drinks he is going to do it more moderately and be very careful that his parents do not find out.

What about his little sisters? They are now 12 and 14 years old. The night Don came home from his night of drinking, the commotion woke them up and they listened from the stairway as their parents yelled at Don in the living room. The next day they teased him about it—he didn't think it was very funny, especially since he wasn't feeling too well. Don's sisters are close to each other—Martha, the 14-year-old, is dating someone steadily, and she and her sister talk about boys a lot. Still, their relationship contains a mixture of attachment and conflict. They sometimes fight about wearing each other's clothes or taking things from each other's rooms, but they still share many intimate conversations. They, too, have done well in school, although they have not been as popular as Don. They seem to sense that their father, in particular, caters to Don more than to them.

Conflict between the two girls and their parents, particularly their mother, seems to have escalated in the last year. Both girls show a strong inclination to spend more time on the weekends with their peers than they used to. Last Saturday night, Martha's boyfriend was spending some time with his friends, and Martha couldn't find anything to do. She was mad at her sister and didn't want to spend Saturday night at home. She told her mother: "What a boring place this is—I never have anything to do!" Several minutes later, Don walked by and told everyone what a great time he was looking forward to—after having been grounded for three months for his drinking episode, he had the family car to take his girlfriend out. His 14-year-old sister took a swipe at him, but missed, as he walked out the door. If she couldn't have any fun tonight, she didn't want anyone else in the family to have any either.

When we follow Don's sisters into their later adolescent years they are still doing well in school, and are getting ready to go away to college. Their mother says she doesn't think she could stand it if they stayed at home and went to school nearby! The sisters are proud of their older brother now—he is a college basketball star, and they don't have to contend with him on a daily basis, as they did several years ago. Like Don, they seem to conflict with their parents less as they grow older, although they still complain that their mother "sticks her nose" in their business too often.

The Family

It is not enough for parents to understand children. They must accord children the privilege of understanding them.

Milton Saperstein, Paradoxes of Everyday Life, *1955*

Hal's Adolescent Independence

*I*n my mind, I always dreamed of the day I would have teenagers. Young boys would pinch me in the swimming pool and exclaim, "Gee, ma'am, I'm sorry, I thought you were your sensuous daughter, Dale."

The entire family would gather around the piano and sing songs from the King Family album. And on Friday nights, we'd have a family council meeting to decide what flavor of ice cream their father, Ozzie, would bring home from the ice cream parlor.

It never worked out that way. Our teenagers withdrew to their bedrooms on their thirteenth birthday and didn't show themselves to us again until it was time to get married. If we spoke to them in public, they threatened to self-destruct within three minutes.

Heaven knows, we tried to make contact. One day when I knew our son Hal was in his bedroom, I pounded on the door and demanded, "Open up! I know you are in there staring at your navel."

The door opened a crack and I charged into my son's bedroom shouting, "Look Hal, I'm your mother. I love you. So does your father. We care about you.

We haven't seen you in months. All we get is a glimpse of the back of your head as you slam the door, and a blurred profile as the car whizzes by. We're supposed to be communicating. How do you think I feel when the TV set flashes on the message, 'IT'S ELEVEN O'CLOCK. DO YOU KNOW WHERE YOUR CHILDREN ARE?' I can't even remember *who* they are."

"I'm not Hal," said the kid, peeling a banana. "I'm Henny. Hal isn't home from school yet."

Another time I thought I saw Hal race for the bathroom and bolt the door.

"I know this isn't the place to talk," I shouted through the keyhole, "but I thought you should know we're moving next week. I'm sliding the new address under the door and certainly hope you can join us. I wouldn't have brought it up, but I thought you'd become anxious if you came home and the refrigerator and the hot water were gone."

A note came slowly under the door. It read, "I'll surely miss you. Yours very truly, Hartley."

Finally, my husband and I figured out the only way to see Hal was to watch him play football. As we shivered in the stands, our eyes eagerly searched the satin-covered backsides on the bench. Then, a pair of familiar shoulders turned and headed toward the showers.

"Hey, Hal," said his father, grabbing his arm. "Son of a gun. Remember me? I'm Father."

"Father who?" asked the boy.

"You're looking great, Hal. I remember the last time I saw you. You were wearing that little suit with the duck on the pocket. Your mother tells me you're going to be joining us when we move."

"You have me confused, sir," said the boy. "I'm not Hal, I'm Harry."

"Aren't you the guy I saw poking around our refrigerator the other night? And didn't you go with us on our vacation last year?"

"No sir, that was Harold. Incidentally, could you give me a lift to your house? I'm spending the night with Hal."

We thought we saw Hal a few times after that. Once when we were attending a movie and they announced a car bearing our license number had left its parking lights on, a rather thin boy raced up the aisle, but we were never sure.

Another time at a father-son banquet, someone noticed a resemblance between my husband and a boy who hung on the phone all night mumbling, "Aw c'mon, Wilma," but that was also indefinite.

One day in the mail I received a package of graduation pictures and a bill for $76. It was worth it. "Look, dear," I said to my husband, "it's Hal." Our eyes misted as we looked at the clear-skinned boy with the angular jaw and the sideburns that grew down to his jugular vein. It made spotting him at graduation a snap.

"Son of a gun," said his father, punching him on the arm, "if you aren't a chip off the old block, Henny."

"Hartley," I corrected.

"Harry," interjected a mother at my elbow.

"Harold," interjected another voice.

"I'm Hal," said the boy graduate, straightening his shoulders and grimacing.

"Hal who?" we all asked in unison.

(Excerpts from "Hal's Adolescent Independence" from Just Wait Till You Have Children of Your Own, *by Erma Bombeck and Bill Keane. Copyright 1971 by Erma Bombeck and Bill Keane. Reprinted by permission of Doubleday, a division of Bantam, Doubleday, Dell Publishing Group, Inc.)*

ortunately, most parents interact more with their adolescents than those in Erma Bombeck's description. An important contemporary theme of family processes in adolescence is that both autonomy and attachment are involved in the adolescent's successful adaptation to the world. Historically, because so much emphasis has been placed on adolescent autonomy, adolescent attachment to parents has been given too little attention. Our extensive tour of family processes in adolescence takes us not only through information about autonomy and attachment, but also focuses on the nature of family processes, parenting techniques and parent-adolescent conflict, sibling relationships, and the changing family in a changing society.

The Nature of Family Processes

Among the important considerations in studying adolescents and their families are reciprocal socialization, mutual regulation, and the family system, how adolescents construct relationships and how such relationships influence the development of social maturity, and social and historical influences on the family.

Reciprocal Socialization, Mutual Regulation, and the Family as a System

For many years, the socialization process between parents and adolescents was viewed as a one-way affair. Adolescents were considered to be the products of their parents' socialization techniques. In contrast, the socialization process between parents and their adolescents is now viewed as reciprocal—adolescents socialize parents just as parents socialize adolescents. This process is called **reciprocal socialization.** To get a better feel for how reciprocal socialization works, consider two situations, the first emphasizing the impact of growing up in a single-parent home (parent influences), the second a talented teenage ice skater (adolescent influences). In the first situation, the speaker is 14-year-old Robert:

> I never have seen my father. He never married my mother, and she had to quit school to help support us. Maybe my mother and I are better off that he didn't marry her because he apparently didn't love her . . . but sometimes I get very depressed about not having a father, particularly when I see a lot of my friends with their fathers at ball games and such. My father still lives around here, but he has married, and I guess he wants to forget about me and my mother. . . . A lot of times I wish my mother would get married and I could at least have a stepfather to talk with about things and do things with me.

The Contexts of Adolescent Development

In the second situation, the speaker is 13-year-old Kathy:

> "Mother, my skating coach says that I have a lot of talent, but it is going to take a lot of lessons and travel to fully develop it." Her mother responds, "Kathy, I just don't know. We will have to talk with your father about it tonight when he gets home from work." That evening, Kathy's father tells his wife, "Look, in order to do that for Kathy I will have to get a second job, or you will have to get a job. There is no way we can afford what she wants with what I make."

In reciprocal socialization, the interaction of parents and adolescents can be symbolized as a dance or a dialogue in which successive actions of the partners are closely coordinated. This coordinated dance or dialogue can assume the form of mutual synchrony (each individual's behavior depends on the partner's previous behavior), or it can be reciprocal in a more precise sense—the actions of the partners can be matched, as when one partner imitates the other or there is mutual smiling (Cohn & Tronick, 1988; Rutter & Durkin, 1987).

As a social system, the family can be thought of as a constellation of subsystems defined in terms of generation, gender, and role (Hooper & Hooper, in press). Divisions of labor among family members define particular subunits, and attachments define others. Each family member is a participant in several subsystems—some dyadic (involving two people), some polyadic (involving more than two people). The father and adolescent represent one dyadic subsystem, the mother and father another. The mother-father-adolescent represent one polyadic subsystem (Vuchinich, Emery, & Cassidy, 1988).

An organizational scheme that highlights the reciprocal influences of family members and family subsystems is shown in Figure 6.1 (Belsky, 1981). As can be seen by following the arrows in the figure, marital relations, parenting, and adolescent behavior can have both direct and indirect effects on each other. An example of a direct effect is the influence of the parent's behavior on the adolescent. An example of an indirect effect is how the relationship between the spouses mediates the way a parent acts toward the adolescent. For example, marital conflict might reduce the efficiency of parenting, in which case marital conflict would have an indirect effect on the adolescent's behavior.

In one investigation, 44 adolescents were observed either separately with their mother and father (dyadic settings) or in the presence of both parents (tradic setting) (Gjerde, Block, & Block, 1985). The presence of the father improved mother-son relationships, but the presence of the mother decreased the quality of father-son relations (see Figure 6.2). This may have occurred because the father takes the strain off the mother by controlling the adolescent or because the mother's presence reduces father-son interaction, which may not be high in many instances.

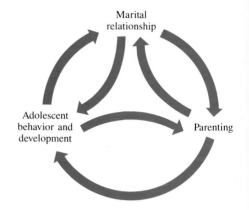

Figure 6.1   Interaction between the adolescent and her parents: Direct and indirect effects.

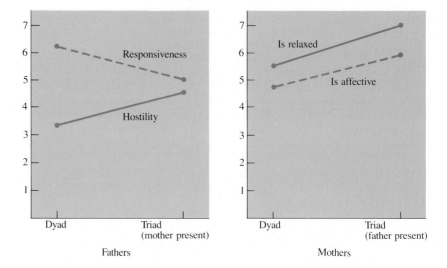

Figure 6.2   Second-order effects: Parent-adolescent relationships in dyadic (without the other parent present) and triadic (with both parents present) situations.

The Construction of Relationships

Recently, developmentalists have shown an increased interest in understanding how we construct relationships and carry them forward in time. Psychoanalytic theorists always have been interested in how this process works in families. However, the current rendition of this process is virtually stripped of psychosexual stage terminology and also is not confined to the first five years of life, as has been the case in classical psychoanalytic theory. The current ideas about the construction of relationships have been influenced by psychology's cognitive revolution and by conceptual and research interest in the nature of attachment (Bowlby, 1969, 1988, 1989; Duck, 1989; Hartup, 1989; Hazen & Shaver, 1987; Sroufe, 1988). Three important aspects of this **developmental construction view** of relationships are continuity and coherence, close relationships and the wider social world, and carrying forward relationships (Sroufe & Fleeson, 1985), each of which we consider in turn.

Changes in the infant's, child's, and adolescent's behavior do occur, but through all of this change there exists some continuity and systemization as well. There is continuity, for instance, to such close relationships as that between the mother and the child over time. Some infants, children, and adolescents learn over the course of 10–20 years that their caregiver will be emotionally available; others come to expect their caregiver not to be very available. What goes on in the close relationships between caregivers and the child/adolescent leads the adolescent to construct a picture of relationships with social objects, as we see next.

Our experiences in close relationships, especially with parents, serve as bases or resources that allow us to function independently in the wider social world and affect how we construct relationships with others. Developmentalists have argued that a secure attachment to parents during infancy promotes

The Contexts of Adolescent Development

the infant's exploration of the environment, a positive sense of self, and socially competent behavior (Bowlby, 1989; Sroufe, 1985, in press). Much less emphasis has been given to attachment in adolescence, but connectedness and attachment to parents serve as important bases or resources for exploration of the world and identity during adolescence as well (Allen & Hauser, 1989; Cooper & Ayers-Lopez, 1985; Cooper & Grotevant, 1989; Koback & Sceery, 1988; Santrock & Sitterle, 1985). A healthy exploration of the widening social world is enhanced when adolescents sense that parents are there when needed. More about the connected worlds of parents and adolescents appears later in the chapter.

Close relationships with parents are important in the development of the adolescent in functioning as models or templates that are carried forward over time to influence the construction of new relationships. Clearly, close relationships do not repeat themselves in an endless fashion over the course of the child's and adolescent's development. And, the quality of any relationship depends to some degree on the specific individual with whom the relationship is formed. However, the nature of earlier relationships that are developed over many years often can be detected in later relationships, both with those same individuals and in the formation of relationships with others at a later point in time. Thus, the nature of parent-adolescent relationships does not depend just on what happens in the relationship during adolescence. Relationships with parents over the long course of childhood are carried forward to influence, at least to some degree, the nature of parent-adolescent relationships. And, the long course of parent-child relationships also could be expected to influence, again at least to some degree, the fabric of the adolescent's peer relationships, friendships, and dating relationships.

In considering the nature of the adolescent's development, it is not only important to evaluate how childhood experiences with parents are carried forward, but it is valuable to look at the nature of intergenerational relationships as well. As the life span perspective has taken on greater acceptance among developmental psychologists, researchers have become interested in the transmission of close relationships across generations (Bengston, 1989; Santrock, 1989; Troll, 1985). The middle generation in three generations is especially important in the socialization process. For example, the parents of adolescents can be studied in terms of their relationships with their own parents, when they were children and presently, and they can be evaluated in regard to the nature of their relationships with their own adolescents, both when they were children and presently. Life span theorists argue that the middle-aged parents of adolescents may feel a strong squeeze when they have to give more help than they receive. Not only are their adolescents reaching the point where they require considerable financial support for college, but their parents, whose generation is living longer than past generations, may require financial support from their middle-aged children. In addition to financial help, their aging parents also may need more comfort and affection than earlier in the life cycle.

Our socialization takes place across generations. Each generation of young people requires access to a range of legitimate opportunities and to long-term support from parents and grandparents who deeply care about them.

The Maturation of the Adolescent and the Maturation of Parents

Mark Twain once reflected, "When I was boy of 14 my father was so ignorant I could hardly stand to have the man around. But when I got to be 21, I was astonished at how much he learnt in 7 years." Mark Twain's comments suggest that maturation is an important theme of parent-adolescent relationships. Not only do adolescents change as they move from childhood to adulthood, but parents undergo change during their adult years. What are the changes in adolescents and their parents that influence the way they interact with each other and the type of relationship they have?

Adolescent Changes

Among the changes in the adolescent that influence parent-adolescent relationships are puberty, expanded logical reasoning and increased idealistic and egocentric thought, violated expectations, changes in schooling, peers, friendship, dating, and movement toward independence. Several recent investigations have shown that conflict between parents and adolescents, especially between mothers and sons, is the most stressful during the apex of pubertal growth (Hill & others, 1985; Steinberg, 1981, 1987, 1988). For example, as shown in Figure 6.3, mothers were less satisfied with their sons' participation in family activities during the apex of pubertal change (Hill & others, 1985). Observations revealed that the father retains his influence over family decision making throughout the pubertal transition and asserts his authority by requiring the son to be obedient. During pubertal change, mothers and sons interrupt each other more and explain themselves less. Toward the end of pubertal

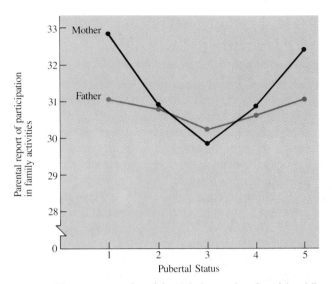

Figure 6.3 Parents' perception of their son's participation in family activities at five points in puberty.

Note: 1 = prepubertal (n=11); 2 = early pubertal (n=34); 3 = apex pubertal (n=33); 4 = postapex pubertal (n = 17); 5 = late pubertal (n=5).

change, sons have grown larger and more powerful. At this time they are less likely to engage in conflict with their mothers probably because their mothers defer to them. More about sex differences and similarities in family relations appears later in the chapter. In sum, the adolescent's pubertal status is related to the nature of parent-adolescent relationships.

In terms of cognitive changes, the adolescent can now reason in more logical ways with parents than in childhood. During childhood, parents may be able to get by with saying, "O.K. That is it. We do it my way or else," and the child conforms. But with increased cognitive skills, adolescents no longer are likely to accept such a statement as a reason for conforming to parental dictates. Adolescents want to know, often in fine detail, why they are being disciplined. Even when parents give what seem to be logical reasons for discipline, adolescents' cognitive sophistication may call attention to deficiencies in the reasoning. Such prolonged bouts of discourse with parents are usually uncharacteristic of parent-child relationships, but are frequent occurrences in parent-adolescent relationships.

In addition, the adolescent's increasing idealistic thought comes into play in parent-adolescent relationships. Parents are now evaluated vis-à-vis what an ideal parent is like. The very real interactions with parents, which inevitably involve some negative interchanges and flaws, are placed next to the adolescent's schema of an ideal parent. And, as part of their egocentrism, adolescents' concerns with how others view them are likely to produce overreactions to parents' comments. A mother may comment to her adolescent daughter that she needs a new blouse. The daughter might respond, "What's the matter? You don't think I have good taste? You think I look gross don't you? Well, you are the one who is gross!" The same comment made to the daughter several years earlier in late childhood probably would have elicited a less intense response.

Another dimension of the adolescent's changing cognitive world related to parent-adolescent relations is the expectations parents and adolescents have for each other (Collins, 1985, 1987; 1989). The rapid changes of puberty make it difficult to use the individual's past behavior as a predicator of future behavior. For example, preadolescent children are often compliant and easy to manage. As they enter puberty, children begin to question or seek rationales for parental demands (Maccoby, 1984). Parents may perceive this behavior as resistant and oppositional because it departs from the child's usual compliant behavior. Parents often respond to the lack of compliance with increased pressure for compliance. In this situation, expectations that were stabilized during a period of relatively slow developmental change are lagging behind the behavior of the adolescent during the period of rapid pubertal change.

What dimensions of the adolescent's social world contribute to parent-adolescent relationships? Adolescence brings with it new definitions of socially appropriate behavior. In our society, these definitions are associated with changes in schooling arrangements—transitions to middle or junior high school. Adolescents are required to function in a more anonymous, larger environment with multiple and varying teachers. More work is required and more initiative and responsibility must be shown to adapt successfully. The school is not the only social arena that contributes to parent-adolescent relationships. Adolescents spend more time with peers than when they were children, and they develop more sophisticated friendships than in childhood. Adolescents also begin to push more strongly for independence. In sum, parents are called on to adapt to the changing world of the adolescent's schooling, peer relations, and push for autonomy (Hill, 1980).

Parental Changes

Parental changes that contribute to parent-adolescent relationships are marital dissatisfaction, economic burdens, career reevaluation and time perspective, and health and body concerns (Hill, 1980). Marital dissatisfaction is greater when the offspring is an adolescent than a child or an adult. A greater economic burden is placed on parents during the rearing of adolescents. Parents may reevaluate their occupational achievement, deciding whether they have met their youthful aspirations of success. Parents may look to the future and think about how much time they have remaining to accomplish what they want. Adolescents, however, look to the future with unbounded optimism, sensing that they have an unlimited amount of time to accomplish what they desire. Health concerns and an interest in body integrity and sexual attractiveness become prominent themes of adolescents' parents. Even when their body and sexual attractiveness are not deteriorating, many parents of adolescents perceive that they are. By contrast, adolescents have reached or are beginning to reach the peak of their physical attractiveness, strength, and health.

Changing Developmental Trajectories: Delayed Childbearing

The changes in adolescents' parents we have described are those that characterize development in middle adulthood. The majority of adolescents' parents either are in middle adulthood or are rapidly approaching middle adulthood. However, in the last two decades the timing of parenthood has undergone some dramatic shifts. Parenthood is taking place earlier for some, later for others than in previous decades. First, there has been a substantial increase in the number of adolescent pregnancies during the 1980s. Second, there has been a simultaneous increase in the number of women who postpone childbearing until their 30s and early 40s. Information about adolescents as parents is discussed in Chapter 12. Here we focus on sociohistorical changes related to postponement of childbearing until the 30s or 40s. Table 6.A shows this increasing trend.

There are many contrasts between becoming a parent in adolescence and becoming a parent 15–30 years later. When childbearing is delayed, considerable progress in occupational and educational domains often has taken place. For both males and females, education usually has been completed and career development is well established (Parke, 1988).

The marital relationship varies with the timing of parenthood onset. In one investigation, couples who began childbearing in their early 20s were compared with those

TABLE 6.A	*Median age at first marriage*	
	1970	**1984**
Men	23.2	25.4
Women	20.8	23.0

who began in their early 30s (Walter, 1986). The late-timed couples had more egalitarian relationships, with men participating in child care and household tasks more often.

Is parent-child interaction different for families who delay having their children until their 30s or 40s? Investigators have found that older fathers are warmer, communicate better, encourage more achievement, and show less rejection with their children than younger fathers. However, older fathers are less likely to place demands on children, are less likely to enforce rules, are less likely to engage in physical play or sports with their children (MacDonald, 1987; Mitteness & Nydegger, 1982; Nydegger, 1975, 1981; Parke & others, 1988). These findings suggest that sociohistorical changes are resulting in different developmental trajectories for many families, trajectories that involve changes in the way marital partners and parents and adolescents interact.

While both adolescents and their parents show a heightened preoccupation with their bodies, the adolescent's outcome probably is more positive. More about the developmental aspects of adolescents' parents appears in Perspective on Adolescent Development 6.1, where we discuss the increase in delayed childbearing.

Sociocultural, Historical Changes

Family development does not occur in a social vacuum. Important sociocultural and historical influences affect family processes. Family changes may be due to great upheavals in a nation such as war, famine, or mass immigration. Or they may be due more to subtle transitions in ways of life. The Great

Depression in the early 1930s had some negative effects on families. During its height, the depression produced economic deprivation, adult discontent, depression about living conditions, marital conflict, inconsistent childrearing, and unhealthy life-styles, especially in the father—heavy drinking, demoralized attitudes, and health disabilities (Elder, 1980).

Some more subtle changes in a culture that have significant influences on the family have been described by Margaret Mead (1978). These changes focus on the longevity of the elderly and their role in the family, the urban and the suburban orientation of families and their mobility, television, and a general dissatisfaction and restlessness. Fifty years ago, the older people who survived were usually hearty and still closely linked to the family, often helping to maintain its existence. As more elderly live to an older age, their middle-aged children have been pressed into a caretaking role for their parents or the elderly parents may be placed in a nursing home. Elderly parents may have lost some of their socializing role in the family during the twentieth century as many of their children moved great distances away.

Many of these family moves were away from farms and small towns to urban and suburban settings. In the small towns and farms, individuals were surrounded by lifelong neighbors, relatives, and friends. Today, neighborhood and extended-family support systems are not nearly as prevalent. Families now move all over the country, often uprooting the child from a school and peer group he or she has known for a considerable length of time. And for many families, it is not unusual for this type of move to occur every year or two, as one or both parents are transferred from job to job.

Television has played a major role in the changing family. Many children who watch television find that parents are too busy working to share this experience with them. Children increasingly have experienced a world their parents are not a part of. Instead of participating in neighborhood peer groups, children have come home after school and plopped down in front of the television set. And television has allowed children and their families to see new ways of life. Lower-class families can look into the family lives of the middle-class more readily by simply pushing a button.

Another subtle change in families has been an increase in general dissatisfaction and restlessness. Women became increasingly dissatisfied with their way of life, placing great strain on marriages. With fewer elders and long-term friends close by to help and advise young people during the initial difficult years of marriage and childbearing, marriages began to fracture at the first signs of disagreement. Divorce has become epidemic in our culture. As women moved into the labor market, men simultaneously became restless and looked for stimulation outside of family life. The result of such restlessness and the tendency to divorce and remarry has produced a hodgepodge of family structures with far greater numbers of single-parent and stepparent families than ever before in history. Later in the chapter, we will have much more to say about such aspects of the changing social world of the adolescent and the family.

The Contexts of Adolescent Development

Parenting Techniques and Parent-Adolescent Conflict

We have seen how the expectations of adolescents and their parents often seem violated as the adolescent changes dramatically during the course of puberty. Many parents see their child moving from a compliant being to someone who is noncompliant, oppositional, and resistant to parental standards. The tendency on the part of parents often is to clamp down tighter and put more pressure on the adolescent to conform to parental standards. Parents often deal with the young adolescent as if they expect the adolescent to become a mature being within the next 10–15 minutes. But the transition from childhood to adulthood is a long journey with many hills and valleys. Adolescents are not going to conform to adult standards immediately. Parents who recognize that adolescents take a long time "to get it right" may well be able to deal more competently and calmly with adolescent transgressions than parents who demand immediate conformity to parental standards. Yet other parents, rather than placing heavy demands on their adolescents for compliance, do virtually the opposite, letting the adolescent do as he or she pleases in a very permissive manner. As we discuss parent-adolescent relationships, we will discover that neither high intensity demands for compliance nor an unwillingness to monitor and be involved in the adolescent's development are likely to be wise parenting strategies. Further, we will look at another misperception that parents of adolescents sometimes entertain. Parents may perceive that virtually all conflict with their adolescent is bad. We will discover that a moderate degree of conflict with parents in adolescence is not only inevitable but may serve a positive developmental function.

Parenting Techniques

Parents want their adolescents to grow into socially mature individuals, and they often feel a great deal of frustration in their role as parents. Psychologists have long searched for ingredients of parenting that will promote competent social development in their adolescents. For example, in the 1930s the behaviorist John Watson argued that parents were too affectionate with their charges. Early research focused on a distinction between physical and psychological discipline, or between controlling and permissive parenting. More recently, there has been greater precision in unraveling the dimensions of competent parenting.

Especially widespread is the view of Diana Baumrind (1971, 1989), who believes that parents should be neither punitive nor aloof from their adolescents, but rather should develop rules and be affectionate with them. She emphasizes three types of parenting that are associated with different aspects of the adolescent's social behavior: authoritarian, authoritative, and laissez-faire (permissive). More recently, developmentalists have argued that permissive parenting comes in two forms—permissive indulgent and permissive indifferent. What are these forms of parenting like?

CHEEVERWOOD

by Michael Fry

Authoritarian parents are restrictive, punitive, exhort the adolescent to follow their directions, respect work and effort, place limits and controls on the adolescent, and offer little verbal give-and-take between the adolescent and the parent. **Authoritarian parenting** is associated with these adolescent behaviors: anxiety about social comparison, failure to initiate activity, and ineffective social interaction.

Authoritative parenting encourages the adolescent to be independent but still places limits and controls on the adolescent's actions. Verbal give-and-take is extensive and parents are warm and nurturant toward the adolescent. Authoritative parenting is associated with the adolescent's social competence, especially self-reliance and social responsibility.

Permissive indifferent parenting is a style in which parents are uninvolved in their adolescent's life. These parents are neglecting and unresponsive. This type of parenting is consistently linked with a lack of self-control on the part of adolescents. **Permissive indulgent parenting** is undemanding but accepting and responsive. These parents are involved in their adolescent's life but allow extensive freedom and do not control negative behavior. Their adolescents grow up learning that they can get by with just about anything. They disregard and flaunt rules. In one family with permissive indulgent parents, the 14-year-old son moved his parents out of their master bedroom suite and claimed it—along with their expensive stereo system and color television—as his. The boy is an excellent tennis player but behaves in the manner of John McEnroe, raving and ranting around the tennis court. He has few friends, is self-indulgent, and has never learned to abide by rules and regulations. Why should he? His parents never made him follow any. In our discussion of parenting styles we have talked about parents who vary on the dimensions of acceptance, responsiveness, demand, and control. As shown in Figure 6.4 four parenting styles—authoritarian, authoritative, permissive indulgent, and permissive indifferent—can be described in terms of these dimensions.

The Contexts of Adolescent Development

Figure 6.4 A four-fold scheme of parenting styles.

	Accepting Responsive Child-centered	Rejecting Unresponsive Parent-centered
Demanding controlling	Authoritative reciprocal High in bidirectional communication	Authoritarian Power assertive
Undemanding low in control attempts	Indulgent	Neglecting, ignoring, indifferent, uninvolved

Several caveats about parenting styles are in order. First, the parenting styles do not capture the important theme of reciprocal socialization and mutual regulation. Keep in mind that adolescents socialize parents, just as parents socialize adolescents. Second, many parents use a combination of techniques rather than a single technique, although one technique may be dominant. While consistent parenting is usually recommended, the wise parent may sense the importance of being more permissive in certain situations, more authoritarian in others, and yet more authoritative in others. Third, most of the data associating authoritative parenting with social competence is based on children, not adolescents.

In a recent investigation, Diana Baumrind (in press) analyzed parenting styles and social competence in adolescence. The comprehensive assessment involved observations and interviews with 139 14-year-old boys and girls and their parents. More than any other factor, the responsiveness of the parents (considerateness and supportiveness, for example) was related to the adolescents' social competence. And when parents had problem behaviors themselves (alcohol problems and marital conflict, for example), adolescents were more likely to have problems and show decreased social competence. More about parenting strategies appears in Perspective on Adolescent Development 6.2.

The Family   215

Between Parent and Teenager and Man, the Manipulator

In his best-selling book *Between Parent and Teenager,* Haim Ginott (1969) details a number of commonsense solutions and strategies for coping with the everyday problems of adolescents. Ginott, in the humanistic tradition, stresses above all else that the key to peaceful coexistence between parents and adolescents is for parents to let go. He says that the adolescent's need is to *not* need parents, and that the parent should resist the need to hold on, even when it seems the most necessary. This attitude, says Ginott, is what parental love for an adolescent is all about.

Relying on catchy phrases like "don't collect thorns" and "don't step on corns," Ginott describes how to let the adolescent become a mature person. Ginott's phrase "don't collect thorns" refers to his belief that parents who constantly detect imperfections in themselves often expect perfection from adolescents. "Don't step on corns" indicates that although all teenagers have a lot of imperfections they are sensitive about (ranging from zits to dimples), they don't need parents to make them acutely aware of such imperfections. Other "Ginottisms" that make sense include the following: "Don't talk in chapters" refers to lecturing rather than sensitive communication; "don't futurize" captures the frequent parental habit of telling the adolescent he or she won't ever amount to anything in the future; "don't violate his privacy" reminds parents that teens need their own territory to develop their sense of autonomy and identity; "don't emulate his language and conduct" warns parents not to use teenage slang—because most teens resent it; and "accept his restlessness and discontent" reminds parents that adolescence is a period of uncertainty and difficulty. Parents can help by not prying into many of their teenagers' affairs.

Other strategies Ginott recommends for parents of adolescents also focus on the parent's struggle to let go of the adolescent. For example, Ginott advises: "Don't push them into popularity battles," "don't push them into early dating," "consider the feelings of the adolescent," and "don't put down their wishes and fantasies." In regard to the first two suggestions, Ginott describes a young girl whose mother constantly prods her to be the most popular girl in school, and another girl whose mother set up a party for boy–girl pairs of twelve-year-olds. This same mother purchased a padded bra for her daughter when the girl was only eleven.

Ginott talks intelligently and simply about many different situations that result in conflict between parents and teenagers—driving, drinking, drugs, sex, and values are but a few of the many topics for which he suggests coping strategies. His descriptions of conversations between adolescents and parents can provide a useful source

"I want to talk to you about the way you're frittering away your life."

"Oh, I know what you're going to say: 'You just don't understand.' Well, I understand this, my friend. You're headed down a dead-end street!"

"I'm talking about a sense of purpose. You've got to look for direction to find direction."

of information about the real world of parents and teenagers. Take a look at some of them and think about whether you would handle them in the way Ginott suggests.

Everett Shostrum, author of *Man, the Manipulator: The Inner Journey from Manipulation to Actualization* (1967), believes that to help teenagers become competent adults, parents have to "let go" when they most want to hold on. Shostrum details conversations between parents and teenagers to illustrate how most parents are not self-actualized in the way they communicate with their teenagers.

Shostrum describes the ways teenagers manipulate their parents and vice versa. Teens say, "You don't love me or you would———." "Everybody else is going," and "I'm going to quit school if you don't———." They play one parent against the other, blackmail, and mope to get what they want from their parents. Parents manipulate by making threats and comparisons: "Bob does better in school than you do," "If you loved me you wouldn't do that," "I'll tell your father when he gets home." Teenagers see interaction with parents as a competition. The game is between the "top dog" (the parent) and the "underdog" (the adolescent). Many encounters with parents end up as minor skirmishes.

Shostrum mentions several specific examples of competitive parent–teen encounters. Steve doesn't want to wear a particular coat his mother tells him he has to wear, and Mary tries to coerce her parents into letting her go out on a date Saturday night. In most cases like these, the parents and the teenagers assume an "I win–you lose" strategy. Shostrum says that the key for parents is to turn such battles into mutual win–win experiences—sharing love and respect for each other's feelings.

The primary goal of the self-actualized parent is to assist rather than inhibit the adolescent in channeling his or her feelings into competent behavior. Parents must recognize that their teenagers are going to try to battle with them and realize that this is the teens' way of trying to adapt to a frustrating world. As part of the actualizing process, parents should create an atmosphere in which teenagers feel comfortable about discussing their true feelings, and in which the parents feel secure about telling the teenager their own feelings as well.

Shostrum goes on to say that teenagers are not as bad as many parents think they are. And, he says, if parents will stay out of the picture, most teenagers will turn into mature, comptent young adults. Above all else, Shostrum says, parents must recognize and accept that the teenager is a manipulating individual trying to become a self-actualizing one.

"I suppose it's my fault. What kind of example have I been, right? Well, I'm not ashamed of the modest success I've had with my materialistic orientation."

"O.K., so I suppose I'm wrong. Put down that paper and tell me how I've failed."

Drawing by Saxon; © 1970 The New Yorker Magazine, Inc.

Parent-Adolescent Conflict

Early adolescence is a time when parent-adolescent conflict escalates beyond parent-child conflict (Montemayor & Hanson, 1985; Steinberg, 1987). This increase may be due to a number of factors we discussed earlier involving the maturation of the adolescent and the maturation of parents: the biological changes of puberty, cognitive changes involving increased idealism and logical reasoning, social changes focused on independence and identity, violated expectations, and physical, cognitive, and social changes in parents associated with middle adulthood. While conflict with parents does increase in early adolescence, it does not reach the tumultuous proportions envisioned by G. Stanley Hall at the beginning of the twentieth century. Rather, much of the conflict involves the everday events of family life such as keeping a bedroom clean, dressing neatly, getting home by a certain time, not talking on the phone forever, and so on. The conflicts rarely involve major dilemmas like drugs and delinquency. In one investigation of 64 high school sophomores, interviews were conducted in their homes on three randomly selected evenings during a three-week period. The adolescents were asked to tell about the events of the previous day, including any conflicts they had with their parents. Conflict was defined as "either you teased your parent or your parent teased you; you and your parent had a difference of opinion; one of you got mad at the other; you and your parent had a quarrel or an argument; or one of you hit the other." During a period of 192 days of tracking the 64 adolescents, an average of 68 arguments with parents was reported. This represents a rate of 0.35 arguments with parents per day or about 1 argument every 3 days. The average length of the arguments was 11 minutes. Most conflicts were with mothers and the majority were between mothers and daughters.

Still, a high degree of conflict characterizes some parent-adolescent relationships. One estimate of the percentage of parents and adolescents who engage in prolonged, intense, repeated, unhealthy conflict is about 1 in 5 families (Montemayor, 1982). While this figure represents a minority of adolescents, it indicates that 4–5 million American families encounter serious, highly stressful parent-adolescent conflict. And, this prolonged, intense conflict is associated with a number of adolescent problems—moving away from home, juvenile delinquency, school dropout rates, pregnancy and early marriage, joining religious cults, and drug abuse (Bachman, Green, & Wirtanen, 1971; Duncan, 1978; Gottlieb & Chafetz, 1977; Kandel, Dessler, & Margulies, 1978; McHenry, Walters, & Johnson, 1979; Ullman, 1982).

While it may be that these problems are caused by the prolonged stress of parent-adolescent conflict, the problems may have originated before the onset of adolescence (Bandura & Walters, 1959). Simply because children are much smaller than parents, parents may be able to suppress oppositional behavior. But by adolescence, increased size and strength may produce an indifference or confrontation with parental dictates. Consider the following circumstance:

Interviewer What sort of things does your mother object to your doing when you are out with your friends?

Boy She don't know what I do.

Interviewer What about staying out late at night?

Boy She says, "Be home at eleven o'clock." I'll come home at one.

Interviewer How about using the family car?

Boy No. I wrecked mine, and my father wrecked his a month before I wrecked mine, and I can't even get near his. And I got a license and everything. I'm going to hot wire it some night and cut out.

Interviewer How honest do you feel you can be to your mother about where you've been and what things you have done?

Boy I tell her where I've been, period.

Interviewer How about what you've done?

Boy No. I won't tell her what I've done. If we're going to have a beer bust, I'm not going to tell her. I'll tell her I've been to a show or something.

Interviewer How about your father?

Boy I'll tell him where I've been, period.

At this point we have discussed a number of ideas about the nature of adolescents and their families. A summary of these ideas is presented in Concept Table 6.1. Now we turn our attention to further information about the lives of adolescents and their families.

Autonomy and Attachment

It has been said that there are only two lasting bequests we can leave our offspring—one is roots, the other wings. These words reflect the importance of attachment and autonomy in the adolescent's successful adaptation to the world. Historically, developmentalists have shown much more interest in autonomy than in attachment during the adolescent period. Recently, interest has heightened in attachment's role in healthy adolescent development. Adolescents and their parents live in a coordinated social world, one involving autonomy *and* attachment. In keeping with the historical interest in these processes, we will discuss autonomy first.

The Nature of Family Processes, Parenting Techniques, and Parent-Adolescent Conflict

Concept	Processes/Related Ideas	Characteristics/Description
The nature of family processes	Reciprocal socialization, mutual regulation, and the family as a system	Adolescents socialize parents, just as parents socialize adolescents. Synchronization and mutual regulation are important dimensions of reciprocal socialization. The family is a system of interacting individuals with different subsystems, some dyadic, others polyadic. Belsky's model describes direct and indirect effects.
	The construction of relationships	Involve continuity and coherence, bases or resources that allow us to function in the wider social world, and carrying forward relationships.
	The maturation of the adolescent and the maturation of parents	The adolescent changes involved include puberty, expanded logical reasoning and increased idealistic and egocentric thought, violated expectations, changes in schooling, peers, friendship, dating, and movement toward independence. Parent changes are associated with mid-life—marital dissatisfaction, economic burdens, career reevaluation and time perspective, and health and body concerns.
	Sociocultural and historical changes	May be due to great upheavals such as war or more subtle changes such as the mobility of families and television.
Parenting techniques and parent-adolescent conflict	Parenting techniques	Authoritarian, authoritative, permissive indifferent, and permissive indulgent are four main categories. Authoritative parenting is associated with adolescents' social competence more than the other styles. Caveats in understanding parenting styles focus on reciprocal socialization, multiple use of techniques, few data collected on adolescents, and adaptation to the maturity of the adolescent.
	Parent-adolescent conflict	Conflict with parents does increase in early adolescence. Such conflict usually is moderate, an increase that can serve the positive developmental function of promoting autonomy and identity.

Autonomy

The increased independence that typifies adolescence is labeled as rebellious by some parents, but in many instances the adolescent's push for autonomy has little to do with the adolescent's feelings toward the parents. Psychologically healthy families will adjust to adolescents' push for independence by treating them in more adult ways and including them more in family decision making. Psychologically unhealthy families will often remain locked into power-oriented parent control and move even more heavily toward an authoritarian posture in their relationships with adolescents.

The Contexts of Adolescent Development

The adolescent's quest for autonomy and a sense of responsibility creates puzzlement and conflict for many parents. Parents begin to see their teenagers slipping away from their grasp. Often the urge is to take stronger control as the adolescent seeks autonomy and responsibility for himself or herself. Heated emotional exchanges may ensue, with either side calling names, making threats, and doing whatever seems necessary to gain control. Parents can become frustrated because they expected their teenager to heed their advice, to want to spend time with the family, and to grow up to do what is right. To be sure, they anticipated that their teenager would have some difficulty adjusting to the changes adolescence brings, but few parents are able to accurately imagine and predict just how strong adolescents' desires will be to be with their peers, and how much they will want to show that it is they, not the parents, who are responsible for their success or failure. As discussed in Perspective on Adolescent Development 6.3, some adolescents show such a strong desire to be away from parents that they leave home.

The Complexity of Autonomy

Trying to define adolescent autonomy is more complex and elusive than it might seem at first. Think about autonomy for a moment. For most individuals, the term connotes self-direction and independence. But what does it really mean? Is it an internal personality trait that consistently characterizes the adolescent's immunity from parental influence? Is it the ability to make responsible decisions for oneself? Does autonomy imply consistent behavior in all areas of adolescent life, including school, finances, dating, and peer relations? What are the relative contributions of peers and other adults to the development of the adolescent's autonomy?

It is clear that adolescent autonomy is *not* a unitary personality dimension that consistently comes out in all behaviors (Hill & Holmbeck, 1986). For example, in one investigation (Psathas, 1957), high school students were asked 25 questions about their independence from their families. Four distinct patterns of adolescent autonomy emerged from analyses of the high school students' responses. One dimension was labeled "permissiveness in outside activities," and was represented by questions such as "Do you have to account to parents for the way you spend your money?" A second dimension was called "permissiveness in age-related activities" and was reflected in questions such as "Do your parents help you buy your clothes?" A third independent aspect of adolescent autonomy was referred to as "parental regard for judgment," indicated by responses to items like "In family discussions, do your parents encourage you to give your opinion?" And a fourth dimension was characterized as "activities with status implications," and was indexed by parental influence on choice of occupation.

Runaways—Youth Who Flee

Her name was Barbara and she came from the hills of West Virginia. She was homely looking, naive, and not very well socialized. A smooth-talking New York pimp told her she was "foxy" and gave her the name "Country Roads." He broke her into a prostitute's life on the streets of New York. One evening she was stabbed to death by a drunk customer who demanded some things of her she didn't want to do.

Sammy was 14 years old, a handsome, blue-eyed blond. An older man in Chicago became a father figure to him, in many ways replacing the father Sammy had never had. The older man was, in fact, one of the first adult males to show considerable interest in Sammy. But after repeated, abusive homosexual assaults, Sammy was found by the police lying unconscious in an alley.

Both Barbara and Sammy were runaways. While many runaways are not exposed to the worst elements of street life, as Barbara and Sammy were, these two examples nevertheless illustrate dangers runaways may encounter. Why do these adolescents run away from their homes? Generally, runaways are very unhappy at home. The reasons many of them leave seem legitimate by almost anyone's standards. When they run away, they usually don't leave a clue to their whereabouts—they just disappear.

The adolescent girl shown here has run away from home. What is it about family relationships that cause adolescents to run away from home? Are there ways our society could better serve adolescent runaways?

Parent Attitudes

There have been a number of investigations focused on the relationship between parental attitudes and the adolescent's development of autonomy. Researchers have attempted to obtain information of this sort through various strategies, including having parents fill out surveys, interviewing adolescents and/or parents about the parents' attitudes and the ways the parents deal with adolescent problems, and actually presenting discussion problems to parents in the presence of their adolescents. To obtain valid information about adolescents, it is necessary to use a variety of information-collecting methods. While many individual studies of parental attitudes and behaviors in relation to adolescent autonomy have included only a limited number of methods, there

Many runaways are from families in which a parent or another adult beats them or sexually exploits them. Their lives may be in danger daily. Their parents may be drug addicts or alcoholics. In some cases, the family may be so poor that the parents are unable to feed and clothe their teenagers adequately. The parents may be so overburdened by their material inadequacies that they fail to give their adolescents the attention and understanding they need. So teenagers hit the streets in search of the emotional and material rewards they are not getting at home.

But runaways are not all from our society's lower class. Teenage lovers, confronted by parental hostility toward their relationship, may decide to run off together and make it on their own. Or the middle-class teenager may decide that he has seen enough of his hypocritical parents—people who try to make him live by one set of moral standards, while they live by a loose, false set of ideals. Another teen may live with parents who constantly bicker. Any of these adolescents may decide that they would be happier away from home.

Running away often is a gradual process, as adolescents begin to spend less time at home and more time on the streets or with a peer group. The parents may be telling them that they really want to see them, to understand them; but runaways often feel they aren't understood at home, and that the parents care much more about themselves (Ek & Steelman, 1988).

Regardless of the causes of the adolescent's decision to run away from home, some provision must be made for his or her physical and psychological well-being. In recent years, nationwide hotlines and temporary shelters for runaways have been established. However, there are still too few of these shelters, and often there is a noted lack of professional psychological help for the runaways at such shelters.

One exception is the temporary shelter in Dallas, Texas, called Casa de los Amigos (house of friends). At the Casa, there is room for 20 runaways, who are provided with the necessities of life as well as medical and legal assistance. In addition, a professional staff of 13 includes counselors and case managers, assisted by VISTA volunteers and high school and college interns. Each runaway is assigned a counselor, and group discussion sessions are held each day to expose the youth to one another's feelings. Whenever possible, the counselors explore the possibility of working with the runaways' families to see if there are ways that all of the family members can learn to help each other in more competent ways than in the past. It is hoped that more centers like Casa de los Amigos will appear in cities around the United States, so that runaways will not meet the fates that Sammy and Barbara encountered. ❧

are some very consistent agreements across different studies that have used different data sources. Parents who adopt authoritarian decision-making strategies in dealing with their adolescent sons and daughters have adolescents who show little autonomy. Whether the adolescents' self-perceptions are sampled, whether their confidence in their decision making is evaluated, or whether their initiative in joining their parents in a mutual decision-making process is observed, the same conclusion about the relationship between adolescent autonomy and parenting strategies is evident (Hill & Steinberg, 1976).

For example, in an investigation of value independence by Strodtbeck (1958), male adolescents and their parents were queried separately about their values. While there were few links between adolescent and parental values, there was a strong association between the father's dominance in the family and the son's belief in his ability to control himself and his world (what is now referred to as an internal locus of control). In a cross-cultural study of adolescents and their families, further documentation was obtained for the relation between authoritarian parenting and lack of autonomy in adolescents (Kandel & Lesser, 1969). It was revealed that the structure of the average American family is much more authoritarian than the structure of a typical family in Denmark. This difference in family structure should indicate that Danish adolescents are generally more autonomous than their American counterparts.

While there is agreement that an authoritarian family structure restricts the adolescent's development of autonomy, there is not as much consistency in pinpointing the parenting practices that increase autonomy. Some investigations have found that a permissive parenting strategy allows the adolescent to become more independent (Elder, 1968). Others suggest that a democratic parenting strategy is best (Kandel & Lesser, 1969). While investigators vary in how they define permissive and democratic parenting techniques, in most instances a permissive strategy generally entails little parental involvement and fewer parental standards. By contrast, a democratic strategy usually consists of equal involvement on the part of parents and adolescents, with the parents having the final authority to set limits on their teenagers. When the overall competence and adjustment of the adolescent is evaluated (rather than just autonomy) an even more clearcut advantage can be attributed to democratic over permissive strategies of parenting.

In summary, adolescence is a period of development when individuals push for autonomy (or the perception that they have control over their behavior) and gradually develop the ability to take that control. This ability may be acquired through appropriate adult reactions to the adolescent's desire for control. At the onset of adolescence, the average person does not have the knowledge to make appropriate or mature decisions in all areas of life. As adolescents push for autonomy, the wise adult will relinquish control in areas where adolescents can make mature decisions and will help them to make reasonable decisions in areas where their knowledge is more limited. Gradually, adolescents will acquire the ability to make mature decisions on their own.

Developmental Views of Autonomy

Two prominent developmental views of autonomy have been proposed, one by David Ausubel, the other by Peter Blos. David Ausubel's theory of adolescent autonomy (Ausubel, Montemayor, & Svajian, 1977) emphasizes the importance of parent–child relationships in the adolescent's growth toward maturity. Ausubel theorizes that parent–child interactions transform the helpless, submissive infant into an independent adult who monitors his or her own life.

During infancy, parents cater to their children's needs and demands. Later, parents expect children to begin to do things for themselves—for example, use the toilet, pick up their toys, control their tempers, and so forth.

However, as they develop cognitively, children begin to realize that they are not completely autonomous from their parents. This perception creates some conflict for children and may lead to a crisis wherein their self-esteem is threatened. One way the child can resolve this conflict is through what Ausubel calls **satellization.** This simply means that children give up their sense of self-power and the perception that they can do everything for themselves. The result is that children accept their dependence on their parents.

However, Ausubel believes that many parents are not capable of developing or maintaining a satellizing relationship with their children. For satellization to occur, children must perceive that their parents love them unconditionally and entrust their care to their parents' hands. Two parenting styles that do not produce satellization are **overvaluation** and **rejection.** When parents overvaluate, they continually interact with their children as if the children are in control. An example is the parent who lives vicariously through the child and hopes that the child will accomplish things he or she didn't—such as becoming a baseball player or a doctor. When parents reject, they view the child as an unwanted part of their existence. The child's needs are served unwillingly and only if necessary. Love and acceptance are absent, or at least are perceived as being absent by the child.

As the child approaches adolescence, satellization is eventually replaced by **desatellization**—breaking away and becoming independent from parents. Total self-rule is not achieved in desatellization. Instead, adolescents achieve a preparatory phase wherein their potential separation from parental rule begins to develop. When final desatellization is reached, individuals have secure feelings about themselves and do not demonstrate the need to prove themselves. They show strong exploratory tendencies and focus their energies on tasks and problem solving rather than self-aggrandizement. The desatellized individual also views failure as a learning situation rather than as a source of frustration.

Other desatellization mechanisms may occur during adolescence that are unlike the competent form of desatellization just described. In many instances, however, the other mechanisms may be preliminary steps in the adolescent's attainment of the final stage of desatellization. One of these preliminary stages is called **resatellization** by Ausubel. In resatellization, the individual's parents are replaced by other individuals or a group. Resatellized individuals abdicate their identities to their spouse's identity, or to the identity of a fraternity, sorority, or other social group. As a permanent solution to self—other relationships, resatellization can be detrimental to the adolescent's development. But as a temporary solution, it can provide a testing ground for the development of a more complete, autonomous form of desatellization (Berzonsky, 1978).

Peter Blos (1962, 1989), borrowing from Margaret Mahler's ideas about the development of independence during early childhood, introduced the concept of individuation to the study of adolescence. Like Mahler, Blos believes

that there is a critical sharpening of the boundaries of the adolescent's self as distinct from others, particularly parents. Sometimes Blos refers to adolescence as the **second individuation crisis,** the first being the striving for independence during the second year of life. During the second individuation, Blos believes it is critical for adolescents to gain difference and distance from parents to transcend infantile ties to them. Individuation during adolescence is defined as a sharpened sense of one's distinctness from others, a heightened awareness of one's self-boundaries. Blos (1967) stresses that individuation in adolescence means that individuals now take increasing responsibility for what they do and what they are, rather than depositing this responsibility on the shoulders of those under whose influence and tutelage they have grown up. Blos' ideas about individuation are reflected in the comments of Debbie, a girl in late adolescence:

> Up to a certain age, I believed everything my parents said. Then, in college, I saw all these new ideas and I said, "Okay, now I'm going to make a new Debbie which has nothing to do with my mother and father. I'm going to start with a clean slate," and what I started to put on it were all new ideas. These ideas were opposite to what my parents believed. But slowly, what's happening is that I'm adding on a lot of the things which they've told me and I'm taking them as my own and I'm coming more together with them. (Josselson, 1973, p. 37)

Debbie's thinking reflects a now commonly held belief about adolescents and their parents. While many adolescents seem to be rejecting their parents and attempting to pull away from them, most adolescents still retain a fundamentally positive, valuing, close, and warm relationship with their parents (e.g., Douvan & Adelson, 1966; Josselson, 1988; Offer, 1969). Indeed, today many adolescents complain that they do not get to spend enough time with their parents, although they often want to spend the time at their own convenience, and wish they had a better relationship with their parents.

A special transition in the development of autonomy takes place when many adolescents leave home and go away to college. The transition from high school to college involves increased autonomy for most individuals. For some, homesickness sets in; for others, sampling the privileges of life without parents hovering around is marvelous. For the growing number of students whose families have been torn by separation and divorce though, moving away can be

The Contexts of Adolescent Development

especially painful. Adolescents in such families may find themselves in the roles of comforter, confidant, and even caretaker of their parents as well as their siblings. In the words of one college freshman, "I feel responsible for my parents. I guess I shouldn't, but I can't help it. It makes my separation from them, my desire to be free of others' problems, my motivation to pursue my own identity more difficult." For yet other students, the independence of being a college freshman is not always as stressful. According to 18-year-old Brian, "Becoming an adult is kind of hard. I'm having to learn to balance my own checkbook, make my own plane reservations, do my own laundry, and the hardest thing of all is waking up in the morning. I don't have my mother there banging on the door."

In one recent investigation, the psychological separation and adjustment of 130 college freshmen and 123 college upperclassmen were studied (Lapsley, Rice, & Shadid, in press). As expected, freshmen showed more psychological dependency on their parents and poorer social and personal adjustment than upperclassmen. Female students also showed more psychological dependency on their parents than male students. Our following discussion reveals in greater detail how it is erroneous to view the development of autonomy apart from connectedness to parents.

Attachment

Adolescents do not simply move away from parental influence into a decision-making world all their own. As adolescents move toward becoming more autonomous individuals, it is healthy for them to continue to be attached to their parents.

Attachment theorists such as John Bowlby (1969, 1989) and Mary Ainsworth (1979, 1988) argue that secure attachment in infancy is central to the development of social competence. **Secure attachment** refers to the positive bond that develops between the infant and the caregiver. The bond is believed to promote healthy exploration of the world because the caregiver provides a secure base to which the infant can return if stress is encountered. By contrast, **insecure attachment** is the relationship between the infant and the caregiver in which the infant either avoids the caregiver or is ambivalent toward her or him. This type of anxious attachment to the caregiver is said to be associated with social incompetence.

In the last decade, developmentalists have begun to explore the possibility that secure attachment is important in the adolescent's development just as it is in the infant's development (Kobak & Sceery, 1988). Just as in infancy and childhood, parents provide an important support system that helps the adolescent to explore in healthy ways a wider, more complex social world full of uncertainties, challenges, and stresses (Cooper & Ayers-Lopez, 1985; Hill & Holmbeck, 1986). Although adolescents show a strong desire to spend more time with their peers, they do not move into a world isolated from parents. In

Adolescents' parent and peer worlds are connected. Parents' choices of neighborhoods, churches, schools, and their own friends influence the pool from which their adolescent children select possible friends.

one investigation, attachment to parents and attachment to peers were assessed (Armsden & Greenberg, 1984). Adolescents who were securely attached to parents also were securely attached to peers; those who were insecurely attached to parents also were more likely to be insecurely attached to peers. And in another investigation, college students who were securely attached to their parents as young children were more likely to have securely attached relationships with friends, dates, and spouses than their insecurely attached counterparts (Hazen & Shaver, 1987). Of course, there are times when adolescents reject this closeness, connection, and attachment as they assert their ability to make decisions and to develop an identity. But for the most part, the worlds of parents and peers are coordinated and connected, not uncoordinated and disconnected.

What are some other ways the worlds of parents and peers are connected? Parents' choices of neighborhoods, churches, schools, and their own friends influence the pool from which their adolescents select possible friends (Cooper & Ayers-Lopez, 1985). For example, choice of schools can lead to differences in grouping policies, academic and extracurricular activities, and classroom organization (open, teacher centered, and so on). In turn, such factors affect which students the adolescent is likely to meet, their purpose in interacting, and eventually who become best friends. For instance, classrooms in which teachers encourage more cooperative peer interchanges have fewer isolates.

Parents may model or coach their adolescents in ways of relating to peers. In one study, parents acknowledged that they recommended specific strategies to their adolescents to help them in their peer relations (Rubin & Sloman,

The Contexts of Adolescent Development

1984). For example, parents discussed with their adolescents ways that disputes could be mediated and how to become less shy. They also encouraged them to be tolerant and to resist peer pressure. Parents also may coach their adolescents in dating strategies. Sometimes these discussions are same sexed, at other times cross sexed. Mothers may instruct their daughters in how to attract a boy or initiate a relationship, and fathers may instruct their daughters about the type of guys to watch out for, and so on.

As can be seen, there is much more connectedness between the family and peer worlds of adolescents than earlier conceptualizations suggested. Throughout adolescence, the worlds of parents and peers work in coordinated ways to influence the adolescent's development. So far in our discussion of families, we have spoken extensively about parent-adolescent relationships. But there is another aspect to the family worlds of most adolescents, which we discuss next—sibling relationships.

Sibling Relationships

Sandra describes to her mother what happened in a conflict with her sister:

> We had just come home from the ball game. I sat down on the sofa next to the light so I could read. Sally (the sister) said, "Get up. I was sitting there first. I just got up for a second to get a drink." I told her I was not going to get up and that I didn't see her name on the chair. I got mad and started pushing her—her drink spilled all over her. Then she got really mad; she shoved me against the wall, hitting and clawing at me. I managed to grab a handful of hair.

At this point, Sally comes into the room and begins to tell her side of the story. Sandra interrupts, "Mother, you always take her side." Sound familiar? Any of you who have grown up with siblings probably have a rich memory of aggressive, hostile interchanges; but sibling relationships have many pleasant, caring moments as well. Adolescent sibling relations include helping, sharing, teaching, fighting, and playing. Adolescents can act as emotional supports, rivals, and communication partners (Vandell, 1987).

More than 80% of American adolescents have one or more siblings—that is, brothers or sisters. Because there are so many possible sibling combinations, it is difficult to generalize about sibling influences. Among the factors to be considered are the number of siblings, age of siblings, birth order, age spacing, and sex of siblings.

In some instances, siblings may be stronger socializing influences on the adolescent than parents are (Cicirelli, 1977). Someone close in age to the adolescent—such as a sibling—may be able to understand the adolescent's problems and be able to communicate more effectively than parents can. In dealing with peers, coping with difficult teachers, and discussing taboo subjects (such as sex), siblings may be more influential in socializing adolescents than parents.

More than 80% of us have one or more siblings. Any of you who have grown up with siblings know that rivalry is a fact of sibling life, as indicated by the arguing over the phone by these two sisters. But remember, sibling life is not all rivalry. Adolescent siblings also share special moments of caring and trust.

Birth order is of special interest both to sibling researchers and to each of us. We want to know the characteristics associated with being born into a particular slot in a family. When differences in birth order are found, they usually are explained by variations in interactions with parents and siblings associated with the unique experiences of being in a particular position in a family. This is especially true of the firstborn child. The oldest child is the only one who does not have to share the parents' love and affection with other siblings—until another sibling comes along. An infant requires more attention than an older child. This means that the firstborn sibling now gets less attention than before the newborn arrived. Does this result in conflict between parents and the firstborn? In one research study, mothers became more negative, coercive, restraining, and played less with the firstborn following the birth of a second child (Dunn & Kendrick, 1982). Even though a new infant requires more attention from parents than does an older child, an especially intense relationship seems to be maintained between parents and firstborns throughout the life cycle. Parents have higher expectations for, put more pressure for achievement and responsibility on, and interfere more with the activities of firstborn than later-born children (Rothbart, 1971).

Given the differences in family dynamics involved in birth order, it is not surprising that firstborns and later-borns have different characteristics. Firstborns are more adult oriented, helpful, conforming, anxious, self-controlled, and less aggressive than their siblings. Parental demands and high standards established for firstborns result in these children excelling in academic and professional endeavors. Firstborns are overrepresented in *Who's Who* and Rhodes scholars, for example. However, some of the same pressures placed on firstborns for high achievement may be the reason they also have more guilt, anxiety, difficulty in coping with stressful situations, and higher admission to child guidance clinics.

What are later-borns like? Characterizing later-borns is difficult because they can occupy so many different sibling positions. For example, a later-born might be the second-born male in a family of two siblings or a third-born female in a famly of four siblings. In two-child families, the profile of the later-born child is related to the sex of his or her sibling. For example, a boy with an older sister is more likely to develop "feminine" interests than a boy with an older brother. Overall, later-borns also usually enjoy better relations with peers than first-borns. Last-borns, who are often described as the "baby" in the family even after they have outgrown infancy, run the risk of becoming overly dependent. Middle-borns tend to be more diplomatic, often performing the role of negotiator in times of dispute (Sutton-Smith, 1982).

The popular conception of the only child is of a "spoiled brat" with such undesirable characteristics as dependency, lack of self-control, and self-centered behavior. But research presents a more positive portrayal of the only child, who often is achievement oriented and displays a desirable personality, especially in comparison to later-borns and children from large families (Falbo & Polit, 1986).

The Contexts of Adolescent Development

The "Only Child" Policy in China

What would it be like to grow up in a world where almost everyone is an only child, where few people really know what it is like to have brothers and sisters, where couples who dare to have two—or worse, three—children are criticized for being selfish? This world can now be glimpsed in Shanghai and several other Chinese cities where the one-child family has become much more prevalent because of the strong motivation to limit population growth in the People's Republic of China. While the policy is still new and its effects not fully examined, China's kindergartens and early elementary school classrooms are being increasingly populated by only children. The changes could stimulate people to look to society for social bonds and services they once depended on families to give them. China's culture is providing a giant laboratory for revealing what a world minus siblings is like. It will be intriguing to follow the outcomes (Huang, 1982; Pines, 1981).

Birth order also is associated with variations in sibling relationships. The oldest sibling is expected to exercise self-control and show responsibility in interacting with younger siblings. When the oldest sibling is jealous or hostile, parents restrain him or her and protect the younger sibling. The oldest sibling is more dominant, competent, and powerful than the younger siblings; the oldest sibling also is expected to assist and teach younger siblings. Indeed, researchers have shown that older siblings are both more antagonistic—hitting, kicking, and biting—and more nurturant toward their younger siblings than vice versa (Abramovitch & others, 1986). There also is something unique about same-sex sibling relationships. Aggression, dominance, and cheating occur more in same-sex relationships than opposite—sex relationships (Minnett, Vandell, & Santrock, 1983).

We have discussed many aspects of adolescents and their families but there still is much more to be said. Especially important is the nature of the changing family in a changing society.

The Changing Family in a Changing Society

More adolescents are growing up in a greater variety of family structures than ever before in history. Many mothers spend the greater part of their day away from their children. More than 1 of every 2 mothers with a child under the age of 5 is in the labor force; more than 2 of every 3 with a child from 6 to

17 years of age is. And the increasing number of children and adolescents growing up in single-parent families is staggering. One estimate indicates that 25% of the children born between 1910 and 1960 lived in a single-parent family at some point during their childhood. However, at least 50% of the individuals born in the 1980s will spend part of their childhood in a single-parent family (Glick & Lin, 1986). Further, about 11% of all American households now are made up of so-called blended families—that is, families with stepparents or cohabitating adults. What are the effects of divorce on adolescents? What are the effects of remarriage on adolescents? What are the effects of working mothers on adolescents? We consider each of these questions in turn.

The Effects of Divorce

Early studies of the effects of divorce on children followed a **father-absence tradition.** Children from father-absent and father-present families were compared, and differences in their development were attributed to the absence of the father. But family structure (such as father present, divorced, and widowed) is only one of many factors that influence the child's adjustment. The contemporary approach advocates evaluating the strengths and weaknesses of the child prior to divorce, the nature of events surrounding the divorce itself, and post-divorce family functioning. Investigators are finding that the availability and use of support systems (baby-sitters, relatives, day-care), an ongoing, positive relationship between the custodial parent and the ex-spouse, authoritative parenting, financial stability, and the child's competencies at the time of the divorce are factors in the child's adjustment (Block, Block, & Gjerde, 1986; Chase-Lansdale & Hetherington, in press; Hetherington, 1988; Hetherington, Cox, & Cox, 1982; Hetherington, Hagan, & Anderson, 1989; Kelly, 1987; Parish, 1987; Santrock & Warshak, 1986; Wallerstein & Kelly, 1980).

Many separations and divorces are highly emotional affairs that immerse the child in conflict. Conflict is a critical aspect of family functioning that seems to outweigh the influence of family structure on the adolescent's development. For example, adolescents in divorced families low in conflict function better than adolescents in intact, never-divorced families high in conflict (Rutter, 1983; Wallerstein, 1989). Although escape from conflict may be a positive benefit for adolescents, in the year immediately following the divorce, the conflict does not decline but increases. At this time, adolescents—especially boys—in divorced families show more adjustment problems than adolescents in intact families with both parents present. During the first year after the divorce, the quality of parenting the adolescent experiences is often poor; parents seem to be preoccupied with their own needs and adjustment—experiencing anger, depression, confusion, and emotional instability—which inhibits their ability to respond sensitively to the adolescent's needs. During the second year after the divorce, parents are more effective in their child-rearing duties, especially with daughters (Hetherington, Cox, & Cox, 1982; Hetherington, Hagan, & Anderson, 1989).

Child Custody in the People's Republic of the Congo

Legal provisions for child custody in the People's Republic of the Congo are typical of many developing countries. As a general rule, since men are in much better economic circumstances than women, with the exception of the very youngest, children are left to the responsibility of the husband in cases of breakdowns in marriage. Only a small portion of the population in poor countries have access to formal law. In most countries the majority of poor people settle child custody matters outside of the formal legal system (Tchibinda & Mayetela, 1983).

Recent evaluations of children six years after the divorce of their parents by Mavis Hetherington and her colleagues (Hetherington, 1988; Hetherington, Hagan, & Anderson, 1989) found that living in a nonremarried mother custody home had long-term negative effects on boys, with deleterious outcomes appearing consistently from preschool to adolescence. No negative effects of divorce on preadolescent girls were found. However, at the onset of adolescence early maturing girls from divorced families engaged in frequent conflict with their mothers, behaved in noncompliant ways, had lower self-esteem, and experienced more problems in heterosexual relations.

The sex of the child and the sex of the custodial parent are important considerations in evaluating the effects of divorce on children. One research study directly compared children living in father-custody and mother-custody families (Santrock & Warshak, 1979, 1986). On a number of measures, including videotaped observations of parent-child interaction, children living with the same-sex parent were more socially competent—happier, more independent, higher self-esteem, and more mature—than children living with the opposite-sex parent. Other research recently has supported these findings (Camara & Resnick, 1987; Furstenberg, 1988).

Support systems are especially important for low-income divorce families (Coletta, 1978; Hetherington, 1988). The extended family and community services may be crucial for low-income divorced families with infants and young children, because the majority of these parents must work full time but still may not be able to make ends meet.

The age of the child at the time of the divorce also needs to be considered. Young children's responses to divorce are mediated by their limited cognitive and social competencies, their dependency on parents, and their

The Effects of Divorce on Female Adolescents' Heterosexual Behavior

Divorce also influences the adolescent's heterosexual behavior. In an investigation by Mavis Hetherington (1972), adolescent girls with absent fathers acted in one of two extreme ways: They either were very withdrawn, passive, and subdued around males or were overly active, aggressive, and flirtatious. The girls who were inhibited, rigid, and restrained around males were more likely to be from widowed homes; those who sought the attention of males, who showed early heterosexual behavior, and who seemed more open and uninhibited around males were more likely to come from divorced homes.

Several examples of the girls' behavior provide further insight. The girls were interviewed by either a male or a female interviewer. Four chairs were placed in the room, including one for the interviewer. Daughters of the widows more often chose the farthest from the male interviewer; daughters of the divorcees more often chose the chair closest to him. There were no differences when the interviewer was female. The girls also were observed at a dance and during activities at a recreation center. At the dance, the daughters of the widows often refused to dance when asked. One widow's daughter spent the entire evening in the restroom. The daughters of the divorcees were more likely to accept the boys' invitation to dance. At the recreation center, the daughters of the divorcees were more frequently observed outside the gym where

TABLE 6.B *The Behavior of Young Adolescent Girls from Divorced, Widowed, and Intact Families at a Recreation Center*

Observational Variable	Father Absent		Group Father Present
	Divorce	Death	
Subject-initiated physical contact and nearness with male peers	3.08	1.71	1.79
Male areas	7.75	2.25	4.71
Female areas	11.67	17.42	14.42

From E. Mavis Hetherington, "Effects of Father Absence on Personality Development on Adolescent Daughters" in *Developmental Psychology,* 7, 313–326, 1972. Copyright 1972 by the American Psychological Association. Reprinted by permission of the publisher and author.

Note: The numbers shown are means. Notice that the daughters of divorcees were more likely to initiate contact with males and spend time in male areas. Notice also that the daughters of the widows were more likely to spend time in female areas of the recreation center.

boys were playing; the daughters of the widows were more frequently observed in traditional female activities, like sewing and cooking (see Table 6.B).

Hetherington (1977) continued to study these girls, following them in late adolescence and early adulthood

restriction to the home or inferior day-care (Hetherington, Hagan, & Anderson, 1989). During the interval immediately following divorce, young children less accurately appraise the divorce situation. These young children may blame themselves for the divorce, may fear abandonment by both parents, and may misperceive and be confused by what is happening (Wallerstein, Corbin, & Lewis, 1988).

The cognitive immaturity that creates extensive anxiety for children who are young at the time of their parents' divorce may benefit the children over time. Ten years after the divorce of their parents, adolescents have few memories of their own earlier fears and suffering or their parents' conflict (Wallerstein, Corbin, & Lewis, 1988). Nonetheless, approximately one-third of these children continue to express anger about not being able to grow up in an intact, never-divorced family. Those who were adolescents at the time of their parents' divorce were more likely to remember the conflict and stress surrounding the divorce some 10 years later in their early adult years. They too expressed

Mavis Hetherington found that adolescent girls from divorced mothers responded differently to males than adolescent girls from widowed and intact families. What behavioral profile did the adolescent girls from divorced families have? Does every adolescent girl from a divorced family show this same profile?

to determine their sexual behavior, marital choices, and marital behavior. The daughters of the divorcees tended to marry younger and select marital partners who were more likely to have poor work histories and drug problems. In contrast, daughters of widows tended to marry males with a more puritanical makeup. In addition, both the daughters of the divorcees and the daughters of the widows reported more sexual adjustment problems than the daughters from the intact homes; for example, the daughters from the homes in which the father was absent had fewer orgasms than daughters from intact homes. The daughters from the intact homes seem to have worked through their relationships with their fathers and were more psychologically free to deal successfully in their relationships with other males. In contrast, the daughters of the divorcees and the daughters of the widows appeared to be marrying images of their fathers.

It should be recognized that findings such as Hetherington's (1972, 1977) may not hold as the woman's role in society continues to change. Also, the findings are from a restricted sample of middle-class families living in one city—the results might not be the same in other subcultures. Nonetheless, Hetherington's results do point to some likely vulnerabilities of adolescent girls growing up in divorced and widowed families.

disappointment at not being able to grow up in an intact family and wondered if their life wouldn't have been better if they had been able to do so.

In sum, large numbers of children are growing up in divorced families. Most children initially experience considerable stress when their parents divorce and they are placed at risk for developing problem behaviors. However, divorce also can remove children from conflicted marriages. Many children emerge from divorce as competent individuals. In recent years, researchers have moved away from the view that single-parent families are atypical or pathological, focusing more on the diversity of children's responses to divorce and the factors that facilitate or disrupt the development and adjustment of children in these family circumstances (Hetherington, Hagan, & Anderson, 1988). More about the effects of divorce on adolescents appears in Perspective on Adolescent Development 6.4, where a classic investigation by Mavis Hetherington (1972) is presented. Pay special attention to the observation of the adolescent's behavior in different social contexts, a strategy we need to follow much more often in our investigation of adolescents and their families.

Stepfamilies

The number of remarriages involving children has steadily grown in recent years, although both the rate of increase in divorce and stepfamilies has slowed in the 1980s. Stepfather families, in which a woman with custody of children in a previous marriage, make up 70% of stepfamilies. Stepmother families make up almost 20% of stepfamilies. A small minority are blends, with both parents bringing children from a previous marriage. A substantial percentage of stepfamilies also produce children of their own.

Research on stepfamilies has lagged behind research on divorced families, but recently a number of investigators have turned their attention to this increasingly common family structure (e.g., Bray, 1988; Furstenberg, 1988; Hetherington, Hagan, & Anderson, 1989; Pasley & Ihinger-Tallman, 1987; Santrock & Sitterle, 1987; Zill, 1988). Following remarriage, children of all ages show a resurgence of problem behaviors. Younger children seem to be able to eventually form an attachment to a stepparent and accept the stepparent in a parenting role. However, the developmental tasks facing adolescents make them especially vulnerable to the entrance of a stepparent. At the time they are searching for an identity and exploring sexual and close relationships outside the family, a nonbiological parent may increase the stress associated with the accomplishment of these important tasks.

Following the remarriage of the custodial parent, a reemergence of emotional upheaval in girls and intensification of problems in boys often take place. Over time, preadolescent boys seem to improve more than girls in stepfather families. Sons who frequently are involved in conflicted, coercive relations with their custodial mothers likely have much to gain from the introduction of a warm, supportive stepfather. In contrast, daughters who frequently have a close relationship with their custodial mothers and considerable independence may find a stepfather disruptive and constraining.

Children's relationships with biological parents are more positive than with stepparents regardless of whether a stepmother or a stepfather family is involved. Stepfathers often have a distant, disengaged relationship with their stepchildren. And as a rule, the more complex the stepfamily the more difficult the children's adjustment. For example, families in which both parents bring children from a previous marriage are associated with the highest level of behavioral problems.

In sum, as with divorce, entrance into a stepfamily involves a disequilibrium in children's lives. Most children initially experience their parent's remarriage as stressful. Remarriage, though, can remove children from stressful single-parent circumstances and provide additional resources for children. Many children emerge from their remarried family as competent individuals. As with divorced families, it is important to consider the complexity of stepfamilies, the diversity of outcomes possible, and the factors that facilitate children's adjustment in stepfamilies (Hetherington, Hagan, & Anderson, 1989; Santrock, Sitterle, & Warshak, 1988).

The Contexts of Adolescent Development

Working Mothers

Because household operations have become more efficient and family size has decreased in America, it is not certain that children with mothers working outside the home actually receive less attention than children in the past whose mothers were not employed. Outside employment—at least for mothers with school-aged children—may simply be filling time previously taken up by added household burdens and more children. It also cannot be assumed that, if the mother did not go to work, the child would benefit from the time freed by streamlined household operations and smaller families. Mothering does not always have a positive effect on the child. The educated, nonworking mother may overinvest her energies in her children, fostering an excess of worry and discouraging the child's independence. In such situations, the mother may inject more parenting than the child can profitably handle. Maternal employment also may encourage involvement of fathers with adolescents (Richards & Duckett, 1989).

As Lois Hoffman (1979; 1989) comments, maternal employment is a part of modern life. It is not an aberrant aspect of it, but a response to other social changes that meets the needs not met by the previous family ideal of a full-time mother and homemaker. Not only does it meet the parent's needs, but in many ways it may be a pattern better suited to socializing children for the adult roles they will occupy. This is especially true for daughters, but for sons too. The broader range of emotions and skills that each parent presents is more consistent with this adult role. Just as the father shares the bread-winning role and the childrearing role with his mother, so the son, too, will be more likely to share these roles. The rigid gender role stereotyping perpetuated by the divisions of labor in the traditional family is not appropriate for the demands children of both sexes will have made on them as adults. The needs of the growing child require the mother to loosen her hold on the child, and this task may be easier for the working woman whose job is an additional source of identity and self-esteem.

While the mother's working is not associated with negative outcomes for children, a certain set of children from working mother families bears further scrutiny—those called latchkey children. They typically do not see their parents from the time they leave for school in the morning until about 6:00 or 7:00 P.M. They are called latchkey children because they are given the key to their home, take the key to school, and then use it to let themselves into the home while their parents are still at work. Latchkey children are largely unsupervised for two to four hours a day during each school week. During the summer months, they may be unsupervised for entire days, five days a week.

Thomas and Lynette Long (1983) interviewed more than 1,500 latchkey children. They concluded that a slight majority of these children had negative latchkey experiences. Some latchkey children may grow up too fast, hurried by the responsibility placed on them (Elkind, 1981). How do latchkey children handle the lack of limits and structure during the latchkey hours? Without

The latchkey experiences of adolescents vary considerably. Some latchkey adolescents live completely unmonitored lives after school and in the summer months, others are involved in structured activities.

limits and parental supervision, it becomes easier for latchkey children to find their way into trouble—possibly abusing a sibling, stealing, or vandalizing. The Longs point out that 90% of the adjudicated juvenile delinquents in Montgomery County, Maryland, are latchkey children. Joan Lipsitz (1983), in testifying before the Select Committee on Children, Youth, and Families, called the lack of adult supervision of children in the afterschool hours one of the nation's major problems today. Lipsitz calls it the "three–six o'clock problem" because it is during this time frame that the Center for Early Adolescence in North Carolina, where she is director, experiences a peak of referrals for clinical help.

But while latchkey children may be vulnerable to problems, keep in mind that the experiences of latchkey children vary enormously, just as do the experiences of all children with working mothers. Parents need to give special attention to the ways their latchkey children's lives can be monitored effectively. Variations in latchkey experiences suggest that parental monitoring and authoritative parenting help the adolescent cope more effectively with latchkey experiences, especially in resisting peer pressure (Galambos & Maggs, 1989; Steinberg, 1986). The degree to which latchkey children are at developmental risk remains unsettled. A positive sign is that researchers are beginning to conduct more fine-grained analysis of adolescents' latchkey experiences in an effort to determine which aspects of latchkey circumstances are the most detrimental and which aspects foster better adaptation (Rodman & others, 1988; Steinberg, 1988).

At this point we have discussed many different aspects of autonomy and attachment, sibling relationships, and the changing family in a changing society. A summary of these ideas is presented in Concept Table 6.2.

Summary

I. Reciprocal Socialization, Mutual Regulation, and the Family as a System
Adolescents socialize parents, just as parents socialize adolescents. Synchronization and mutual regulation are important dimensions of reciprocal socialization. The family is a system of interacting individuals with different

The Contexts of Adolescent Development

Autonomy and Attachment, Sibling Relationships, and the Changing Family in a Changing Society

Concept	Processes/Related Ideas	Characteristics/Description
Autonomy and attachment	Autonomy	Many parents have a difficult time handling the adolescent's push for autonomy. Autonomy is a complex concept with multiple referents. Democratic parenting is associated with adolescent autonomy. The wise parent relinquishes control in areas where the adolescent makes mature decisions and retains more control where immature decisions are made by the adolescent. Two important developmental views of autonomy have been proposed by Ausubel (desatellization) and Blos (individuation).
	Attachment	Adolescents do not simply move away into a world isolated from parents. Attachment to parents increases the probability the adolescent will be socially competent and explore a widening social world in healthy ways. The social worlds of parents and peers are coordinated and connected.
The changing family in a changing society	Divorce	The early father-absence tradition has been supplanted by an emphasis on the complexity of the divorced family, pre- and postdivorce family functioning, and varied response to divorce. Among the factors that influence the adolescent's adjustment in divorced families are conflict, time since divorce, sex of the adolescent and sex of the custodial parent, support systems, and age of the child and adolescent.
	Stepfamilies	Just as divorce produces disequilibrium and stress for adolescents, so does remarriage. Over time, preadolescent boys seem to improve more than girls in stepfather families. Adolescence appears to be an especially difficult time for adjustment to the entrance of a stepparent. Children's relationships with biological parents are consistently better than with stepparents, and children's adjustment is adversely affected the more complex the stepfamily becomes.
	Working mothers	Overall, the mother working full time outside the home does not seem to have an adverse effect on adolescents' development. Neither do latchkey experiences, although parental monitoring and participation in structured activities with competent supervision are important influences on latchkey children's adjustment.

subsystems, some dyadic, others polyadic. Belsky's model describes direct and indirect effects.

II. The Construction of Relationships

The construction of relationships involves continuity and coherence, bases or resources that allow us to function in the wider social world, and carrying forward relationships.

III. The Maturation of the Adolescent and the Maturation of Parents

Adolescent changes involved in understanding parent-adolescent relationships include puberty, expanded logical reasoning and increased idealistic and egocentric thought, violated expectations, changes in schooling, peers, friendship, dating, and movement toward independence. Parent changes are associated with mid-life—marital dissatisfaction, economic burdens, career reevaluation and time perspective, and health and body concerns.

IV. Sociocultural and Historical Changes

These may be due to great upheavals such as war or more subtle changes such as the mobility of families and television.

V. Parenting Techniques

Authoritarian, authoritative, permissive indifferent, and permissive indulgent are four main categories. Authoritative parenting is associated with adolescents' social competence more than the other styles. Caveats in understanding parenting styles focus on reciprocal socialization, multiple use of techniques, few data collected on adolescents, and adaptation to the maturity of the adolescent.

VI. Parent-Adolescent Conflict

Conflict with parents does increase in early adolescence. Such conflict usually is moderate, an increase that can serve the positive developmental function of promoting autonomy and identity.

VII. Autonomy

Many parents have a difficult time handling the adolescent's push for autonomy. Autonomy is a complex concept with multiple referents. Democratic parenting is associated with adolescent autonomy. The wise parent relinquishes control in areas where the adolescent makes mature decisions and retains more control where immature decisions are made by the adolescent. Two important developmental views of autonomy have been proposed by Ausubel (desatellization) and Blos (individuation).

VIII. Attachment

Adolescents do not simply move away into a world isolated from parents. Attachment to parents increases the probability the adolescent will be socially competent and explore a widening social world in healthy ways. The social worlds of parents and peers are coordinated and connected.

IX. Divorce

The early father-absence tradition has been supplanted by an emphasis on the complexity of the divorced family, pre- and postdivorce family functioning, and varied response to divorce. Among the factors that influence the adolescent's adjustment in divorced families are conflict, time since divorce, sex of the adolescent and sex of the custodial parent, support systems, and age of the child and adolescent.

X. Stepfamilies

Just as divorce produces disequilibrium and stress for adolescents, so does remarriage. Over time, preadolescent boys seem to improve more than girls in stepfather families. Adolescence appears to be an especially difficult time for adjustment to the entrance of a stepparent. Children's relationships with biological parents are consistently better than with stepparents, and children's adjustment is adversely affected the more complex the stepfamily becomes.

XI. Working Mothers

Overall, the mother working full time outside the home does not seem to have an adverse effect on the adolescent's development. Neither do latchkey experiences, although parental monitoring and participation in structured activities with competent supervision are important influences on latchkey children's adjustment.

Key Terms

reciprocal socialization 204

developmental construction view 206

authoritarian parenting 214

authoritative parenting 214

permissive indifferent parenting 214

permissive indulgent parenting 214

satellization 225

overvaluation 225

rejection 225

desatellization 225

resatellization 225

second individuation crisis 226

secure attachment 227

insecure attachment 227

father-absence tradition 232

Suggested Readings

Bronstein, P., & Cowan, C. P. (1988). *Fatherhood today: Men's changing role in the family.* New York: Wiley.
A contemporary look at the father's role in families, including chapters on primary caregiving fathers, stepfathers, grandfathers, fathers with custody, as well as prevention and intervention programs for fathers.

Hartup, W. W., & Zubin, R. (1986). *Relationships and development.* Hillsdale, NJ: Erlbaum.
This compendium of articles by leading experts gives insight into the new look in carrying forward relationships in families. Pays special attention to the role of development in family relationships.

Hetherington, E. M., Hagan, M. S., & Anderson, E. R. (1989). Marital transitions: a child's perspective. *American Psychologist, 44,* 303–312.
Hetherington is a leading researcher in the investigation of the effects of divorce on children's development. In this article she and her colleagues review the recent literature on divorce, giving special attention to transitions in divorced and stepparent families.

Journal of Early Adolescence, Spring 1985, vol. 5, no. 1.
The entire issue is devoted to contemporary approaches to the study of families with adolescents. Includes articles by Catherine Cooper and Susan Ayers-Lopez on the connectedness of adolescents and their families, by Raymond Montemayor on parent-adolescent conflict, by John Hill and his colleagues on pubertal status and parent-adolescent relationships, as well as many others.

Maccoby, E. E., & Martin, J. A. (1983). Socialization in the context of the family: Parent-child interaction. In P. H. Mussen (Ed.), *Handbook of child psychology* (Vol. 4, 3rd ed.). New York: Wiley.
An extensive overview of the nature of parent-child relationships.

A man's growth is seen in the successive choirs of his friends.

Ralph Waldo Emerson, 1841

You Jerk!

Y ou jerk, what are you trying to do to me," Jess yelled at his teacher. "I got no use for this school and people like you. Leave me alone and quit hassling me."

Jess is 10 years old and has already had more than his share of confrontations with society. He has been arrested three times for stealing, been suspended from school twice, and has a great deal of difficulty getting along with people in social circumstances. He particularly has difficulty with authority figures. No longer able to cope with his outbursts in class, his teacher recommended that he be suspended from school once again. The principal was aware of a different kind of school she thought might help Jess.

Jess began attending the Manville School, a clinic in the Judge Baker Guidance Center in Boston for learning-disabled and emotionally disturbed children 7–15 years of age. Jess, like many other students at the Manville School, has shown considerable difficulty in interpersonal relationships, since peer relationships become a crucial aspect of development during the elementary school years. Robert Selman (Selman, Newberger, & Jacquette, 1977) has designed a peer therapy program at the Manville School to help students like Jess improve their peer relations in classroom settings, group activities, and sports. The staff at the Manville School has been trained to help peers provide support and encouragement to one another in such group settings.

Structured programs at the Manville School are designed to help adolescents assist one another to become more co-operative, to develop trust, to become leaders, and to understand conformity. Four school activities were developed to improve students' social reasoning skills in these areas.

First, there is a weekly peer problem-solving session in the classroom in which the peers work cooperatively to plan activities and relate problems. At the end of each week the peers evaluate their effectiveness in making improvements in areas like cooperation, conflict resolution, and so forth.

Second, the members of a class, numbering from 6–8 students, plan a series of weekly field trips—for example, going to the movies or visiting historical sites. While the counselor provides some assistance, peer decision making dominates. When each activity is completed, the students discuss how things went and what might have been done to improve social relations with one another on the outings.

Third, Selman recognizes that there are times when students need to get away from a setting where intense frustration is taking place. When students find themselves in highly frustrating circumstances (e.g., angry enough to strike out at a classmate), they are allowed to leave the school room and go to a private "time-out" area of the school to regain their composure. In time-out, students also are given the opportunity to discuss the problems with a counselor who has been trained to help adolescents improve their social reasoning skills.

Fourth, during social studies and current events discussion sessions, students evaluate a number of moral and social issues.

*T*he power of peer relations in adolescent development is recognized in the program you have just read about. When you think back to your adolescent years, many of your most enjoyable moments were spent with peers—on the telephone, at school activities, in the neighborhood, in cars, on dates, at dances, or just fooling around. In this chapter we focus on the nature of peer relations, friendships, adolescent groups, and dating.

The Nature of Peer Relations

What are the peer group's functions? What is the nature of peer popularity, rejection, and neglect? How extensively do adolescents conform to their peers? What is the role of social knowledge and social information processing in peer relations? What strategies do developmentalists use to improve the social skills of adolescents who are having difficulty in peer relations? How do reinforcement, modeling, and social comparison work in peer relations? And what is the relation between the worlds of parent-adolescent relationships and peer relationships? We consider each of these questions in turn.

Peer Group Functions

To many adolescents, how they are seen by peers is the most important aspect of their lives. Some adolescents will go along with anything just to be included as a member of the group. To them, being excluded means stress, frustration, and sadness. Think about Bob, who has no close friends to speak of, in contrast to Steve, who has three close buddies he pals around with all of the time. Sally was turned down by the club at school that she was working to get into for six months, in contrast to Sandra, who is a member of the club and who frequently is told by her peers how "super" her personality is.

Some friends of mine have a daughter who is 13 years old. Last year, she had a number of girlfriends—she spent a lot of time on the phone talking with them and they frequently visited each other's homes. Then her family moved and this 13-year-old girl had to attend a school with a lower socioeconomic mix of students than at her previous school. Many of the girls at the new school feel my friends' daughter is "too good" for them, and because of this she is having difficulty making friends this year. One of her most frequent complaints is, "I don't have any friends. . . .None of the kids at school ever call me. And none of them ever ask me over to their houses. What can I do?"

Peers are children or adolescents who are about the same age or maturity level. Same-age peer interaction serves a unique role in our culture (Hartup, 1983). Age grading would occur even if schools were not age graded and adolescents were left alone to determine the composition of their own societies. After all, one can only learn to be a good fighter among agemates: The bigger guys will kill you, and the little ones are no challenge. One of the most important functions of the peer group is to provide a source of information

Our experiences with peers during adolescence are special. Think back to your own adolescence, to your days at school, to your after school hours, and to your weekends. Chances are you will be able to vividly recall some cherished moments, like those the adolescent card players are experiencing here. What role does these extensive interactions with peers play in the adolescent's development?

about the world outside the family. From the peer group, adolescents receive feedback about their abilities. Adolescents learn whether what they do is better than, as good as, or worse than what other adolescents do. It is hard to do this at home because siblings are usually older or younger.

Children spend an increasing amount of time in peer interaction during middle and late childhood and adolescence (Berndt & Ladd, 1989). In one investigation, children were found to interact with peers 10% of their day at age 2, 20% at age 4, and more than 40% between the ages of 7 and 11. In a typical school day, there were 299 episodes with peers per day (Barker & Wright, 1951). By adolescence, peer relations occupy large chunks of an individual's life. In one investigation (Condry, Simon, & Bronfenbrenner, 1968), over the course of one weekend young adolescent boys and girls spent more than twice as much time with peers as with parents.

What do adolescents do when they are with their peers? In one study, sixth graders were asked what they do when they are with their friends (Medrich & others, 1982). Team sports accounted for 45% of boys' nominations but only 26% of girls'. General play, going places, and socializing were common listings for both sexes. Most peer interactions occur outside the home (although close to home), occur more often in private than public places, and occur more between children of the same sex than the opposite sex.

Are peers necessary for development? When peer monkeys who have been reared together are separated from one another, they become depressed and less advanced socially (Suomi, Harlow, & Domek, 1970). The human development literature contains a classic example of the importance of peers in social development. Anna Freud (Freud & Dann, 1951) studied six children

The Contexts of Adolescent Development

from different families who banded together after their parents were killed in World War II. Intensive peer attachment was observed; the children were a tightly knit group, dependent on one another and aloof with outsiders. Even though deprived of parental care, they became neither delinquent nor psychotic.

Good peer relations may be necessary for normal social development in adolescence. Social isolation, or the inability to "plug in" to a social network, is linked with many different forms of problems and disturbances, ranging from delinquency and problem drinking to depression (Cairns & Cairns, 1989; Dishion & Skinner, 1989). Adolescent social isolates, those individuals who during their teenage years are neither accepted nor rejected by their peers, seem to be particularly vulnerable to problems and disturbances in late adolescence and adulthood. This likely happens because they miss out on a considerable amount of socialization that only comes through association with peers (Hill, 1980). In one investigation (Roff, Sells, & Golden, 1972), very poor peer relations in childhood were linked with abnormal development in late adolescence and youth, including a tendency to drop out of school and engage in antisocial behavior.

Peer Popularity, Rejection, and Neglect

Every adolescent wants to be popular—you probably thought about popularity a lot when you were in junior and senior high school. Teenagers commonly think, "What can I do to have all of the kids at school like me?" "How can I be popular with both girls and guys?" "What's wrong with me? There must be something wrong, or I would be more popular." Sometimes adolescents will go to great lengths to be popular; and in some cases, parents go to even greater lengths to try to insulate their adolescents from rejection and to increase the likelihood that they will be popular. Students show off and cut up because it gets attention and makes their peers laugh. Parents set up elaborate parties, buy cars and clothes for their teens, and drive adolescents and their friends all over in the hope that their sons or daughters will be popular.

Certain physical and cultural factors also affect adolescents' popularity. Adolescents who are physically attractive are more popular than those who are not and, contrary to what some believe, brighter adolescents are more popular than less intelligent ones. Adolescents growing up in middle-class surroundings tend to be more popular than those growing up in lower-class surroundings, presumably in part because they are more in control of establishing standards for popularity (e.g., Hollingshead, 1975). But remember that findings such as these reflect group averages—there are many physically attractive teenagers who are unpopular, and some physically unattractive ones who are very well liked. James Coleman (1980) points out that for adolescents in the average range, there is little or no relation between physical attractiveness and popularity. It is only in the extremes (very attractive and very ugly) that a link between popularity and attractiveness holds. And, with the increase

Ethnic Minority Adolescents' Peer Relations

As ethnic minority children move into adolescence and enter schools with more heterogeneous school populations, they become more aware of their ethnic minority status. Ethnic minority adolescents may have difficulty joining peer groups and clubs in predominantly white schools. However, schools are only one setting in which peer relations take place.

Adolescent peer relations take place in diverse settings—at school, in the neighborhood, and in the community. Ethnic minority adolescents often have two sets of peer relationships, one at school, the other in the community. Community peers are more likely to be from their own ethnic group in their immediate neighborhood. Sometimes they go to the same church and participate in activities together such as Black History Week, Chinese New Year's, or Cinco de Mayo Festival. Because ethnic group adolescents usually have two sets of peers and friends, when researchers ask about their peers and friends, questions should focus on both relationships at school and in the neighborhood and community. Ethnic minority group adolescents who are social isolates at school may be sociometric stars in their segregated neighborhood. Also, because adolescents are more mobile than children, inquiries should be made about the scope of their social networks (Gibbs & Huang, 1989).

in concern for equal treatment of minority groups, lower-class and ethnic group adolescents can be expected to gain in popularity. In addition, popularity may fluctuate—even the adolescent who is very popular with peers may have doubts about his or her ability to maintain popularity. Being popular with peers is an ongoing concern for almost every adolescent.

In recent years, developmentalists have distinguished between two sets of children and adolescents who are not popular with their peers—those who are neglected and those who are rejected (Asher & Parker, in press; Parker & Asher, 1987). **Neglected children,** while they may not have friends, are not especially disliked by their peers. Rejected children are more likely to be disruptive and aggressive than neglected children. And rejected children are more likely to continue to be unaccepted by peers even when they move into a new setting; neglected children seem to get a new social life in new groups. Rejected children say they are lonelier and less happy as well. Rejected children also have more serious adjustment problems, while the risk status of neglected children is less certain.

Peer Conformity

The pressure to conform to peers becomes very strong during the adolescent years. Consider the comments of Kevin, a seventh grader:

> I feel a lot of pressure from my friends to smoke and steal and things like that. My parents do not allow me to smoke, but my best friends are really pushing me to do it. They call me a pansy and a momma's boy if I don't. I really don't like the idea of smoking, but my good friend Steve told me in front of some of our friends, "Kevin, you are an idiot and a chicken wrapped up in one little body." I couldn't stand it any more, so I smoked with them. I was coughing and humped over, but I still said, "This is really fun—yeah, I like it." I felt like I was part of the group.

Also, think about the statement by 14-year-old Andrea:

> Peer pressure is extremely influential in my life. I have never had very many friends, and I spend quite a bit of time alone. The friends I have are older. . . .The closest friend I have had is a lot like me in that we are both sad and depressed a lot. I began to act even more depressed than before when I was with her. I would call her up and try to act even more depressed than I was because that is what I thought she liked. In that relationship I felt pressure to be like her . . . .

These examples show how peer pressure can influence adolescents to act in ways they don't really want to. *Conformity* refers to the act of agreeing with the expressed group opinion when pressed to do so. It also refers to the act of concurring with the rules and social practices of a culture or subculture. The use of slang or jargon, adherence to a dress code, and many behavioral mannerisms reflect conformity.

In thinking about conformity to peer pressure in adolescence, it is important to remember that such conformity can consist of positive or negative circumstances. Teenagers engage in all sorts of negative conformity behavior—they go places in cars with people they are afraid of, use seedy language, steal, vandalize, and make fun of parents and teachers. However, a great deal of peer conformity is not negative and consists of the desire to be involved in the peer world, such as dressing like friends and wanting to spend huge chunks of time with members of a clique. Such circumstances may involve prosocial activities as well, as when clubs raise money for worthy causes.

In one investigation of peer conformity focused on negative, neutral, and positive aspects of conformity, Thomas Berndt (1979) studied 273 3rd-grade through 12th-grade students. Hypothetical dilemmas were presented to the students, requiring them to make choices about conformity with friends on prosocial and antisocial behavior and conformity with parents on neutral and prosocial behaviors. For example, one prosocial item questioned whether students relied on their parents' advice in such situations as deciding about helping at the library or instructing another child to swim. An antisocial question asked a boy what he would do if one of his peers wanted him to help steal some candy.

Notice how similar the dress style of these two adolescent girls is. Think back to your adolescent years for a moment. You probably can remember a number of occasions when you bought clothes that were virtually identical to those of your peers.

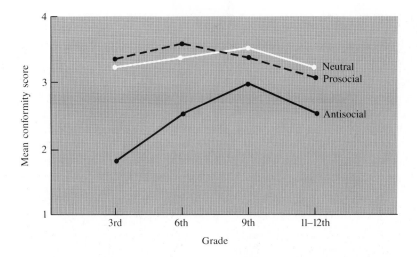

Figure 7.1 Mean scores for peer conformity on different types of behavior. Higher scores indicate greater conformity: The neutral point is 3.5

A neutral question asked a girl if she would follow peer suggestions to engage in an activity she wasn't interested in—for example, going to a movie she didn't want to see.

Some interesting developmental patterns were found in this investigation. In the third grade, parent and peer influences often directly contradicted each other. Since parent conformity is much greater for third-grade children, children of this age are probably still closely tied to and dependent on their parents. However by the sixth grade, parent and peer influences were found to be no longer in direct opposition. Peer conformity had increased, but parent and peer influences were operating in different situations—parents had more impact in some situations, while peers had more clout in others. For example, it was found that parents were more influential in a discussion of political parties, but peers seemed to have more to say when sexual behavior and attitudes were at issue (Hyman, 1959; Vandiver, 1972).

By the ninth grade, parent and peer influences were once again in strong opposition to each other, probably because the increased conformity of adolescents to the social behavior of peers is much stronger at this grade level than at any other. At this time adolescent adoption of antisocial standards endorsed by the peer group inevitably leads to conflict between adolescents and parents. Researchers have also found that the adolescent's attempt to gain independence meets with more parental opposition around the ninth grade than at any other time (Douvan & Adelson, 1966; Kandel & Lesser, 1969).

A stereotypical view of parent-child relationships suggests that parent-peer opposition continues into the late high school and college-age years. But Berndt (1979) found that adolescent conformity to antisocial, peer-endorsed behavior decreases in the late high school years, and greater agreement between parents and peers begins to occur in some areas. In addition, by the 11th and 12th grades, students show signs of developing a decision-making

The Contexts of Adolescent Development

(b)

Most adolescents conform to the mainstream standards of their peers. However, the rebellious or anticonformist adolescent reacts counter to the mainstream peer group's expectations, deliberately moving away from the actions or beliefs they advocate. Two contemporary versions of anticonformist teenagers are the (a) "skinheads" and (b) punks.

(a)

style more independent of peer and parent influence. A summary of peer conformity to antisocial, neutral, and prosocial standards found in Berndt's (1979) study is presented in Figure 7.1.

Other recent research also has focused on a distinction between different kinds of conformity. For instance, Bradford Brown and his colleagues (Brown, Clasen, & Eicher, 1986) have studied peer involvement (the degree of socializing with friends) and misconduct (drug/alcohol use, sexual intercourse, and minor delinquent behavior). Adolescents perceived less peer pressure toward misconduct than peer involvement and also were less willing to follow peers in misconduct. And, males were more likely to accede to antisocial peer pressures than females.

So far, we have looked at how adolescents conform to peer pressure and societal standards. While the majority of adolescents are conformity oriented, some could best be described as independent or rebellious. The truly *independent* or **nonconformist** adolescent knows what the people around him expect, but he doesn't use these expectations to guide his behavior. However, the *rebellious* or **anticonformist** teenager reacts counter to the group's expectations and deliberately moves away from the actions or beliefs they advocate.

In sum, peer pressure is a prominent characteristic of adolescent society. Its power can be seen in almost every dimension of adolescent life—choice of dress, music, language, values, leisure activities, and so on. Parents, teachers, and other adults can help adolescents deal with peer pressure. Donna Clasen and Bradford Brown (1987) offered the following ways this might be accomplished:

> Adolescents need many opportunities to talk with both peers and adults about change in their lives. One 15-year-old pointed out the need to explore his understanding of peer pressure: "Kids need to look at peer pressure and ask, 'Do I want to do this?' Whether the answer is yes or no, they need to ask why."
>
> Peer pressure is often stereotyped as negative. But its positive aspects can be accentuated. One highly visible, national project using constructive peer pressure is Students Against Drunk Driving (SADD), in which students promise themselves, peers, and parents not to drink and drive.
>
> The developmental changes of adolescents may bring forth a sense of insecurity. Young adolescents may be especially sensitive to group norms because of this change and uncertainty. To counter this stress, young adolescents need to experience a number of opportunities for success, both in and out of school, that increase their sense of being in control.

Social Knowledge and Social Information Processing

Recall from our discussion of intelligence in Chapter 5 that a distinction can be made between knowledge and process. In studying cognitive aspects of peer relations the same distinction can be made. It is important to learn about the social knowledge adolescents bring with them to peer relations and it also is helpful to study how adolescents process information during peer interaction.

As children move into adolescence, they acquire more social knowledge. And there is considerable individual variation in how much one adolescent knows about what it takes to make friends, to get peers to like him or her, and so forth. For example, does the adolescent know that giving out reinforcements will increase the likelihood that he or she will be popular? That is, does Mary consciously know that by telling Barbara such things as, "I really like that sweater you have on today," and "Gosh, you sure are popular with the guys," will enhance the likelihood Barbara will want her to be her friend? Does the adolescent know that when others perceive he or she is similar to them, he or she will be liked better by the others? Does the adolescent know that friendship involves sharing intimate conversations and that a friendship likely is improved when the adolescent shares private, confidential information with another adolescent? To what extent does the adolescent know that comforting and listening skills will improve friendship relations? To what extent does the adolescent know what it takes to become a leader? Think back to your adolescent years. How sophisticated were you in knowing about such social matters? Were you aware of the role of nice statements and perceived similarity in determining popularity and friendship? While you may not have been aware of these factors, those of you who were popular and maintained close friendships likely were competent at using these strategies.

One investigation (Dooley, Whalen, & Flowers, 1978) revealed information about the social knowledge of individuals from the ages of 7 to 15. They asked 5th-, 6th-, 8th-, and 10th-grade boys and girls to respond in writing to videotaped, role-played vignettes as though they actually were in contact with the speakers themselves. The videotapes focused on the problems disclosed by males and females aged 7 to 15. The observers were induced to believe that some of the individuals in the videotapes were problem youngsters while others were not. In addition to responding in writing to the videotapes, the boys and girls were asked to rate how often their friends came to talk to them about personal problems.

Compared to younger respondents, the adolescents made more negative statements, gave more advice in general, advised less often to obtain help from a third person, and made fewer disclosures. Female subjects gave more advice, focused on solving problems verbally, and made fewer interpretations than males did. Females shown on the videotapes elicited less advice in general, more advice to change their own thoughts and feelings, and more interpretations than did males. Students portrayed as disturbed on the videotapes were given fewer negatives, more advice to seek third-person help, and more disclosures than students depicted as not disturbed.

Analysis of the advice suggested that the high school students used more instrumental-physical (e.g., "Why don't you try distracting your brother by giving him a game to play with?") and cognitive-affective (e.g., "Put yourself in your brother's shoes," or "You are just going to have to put up with his anger") advice than younger students did. This supports the belief that high school students have more real and self-perceived competence. They have had more experience in coping with problems, are capable of generating more cognitively complex ideas, and are better at finding direct, active solutions to their problems. The decrease in self-disclosure by high school students may indicate increased concern about self-presentation during the high school years.

With regard to the question "What is the best thing you can do when a friend comes to you to talk about a problem?", the most frequent response at the elementary school level was "Try to solve it." However, this was the third most frequent response at the high school level. "Try to help the person understand the problem" was the most frequent response given by junior high students, while "Understand" and "Find out more about the problem" were most frequently the replies of high school students.

From a social cognitive perspective, children and adolescents who are maladjusted likely do not have adequate social cognitive skills necessary for skillful social interaction (Berndt & Ladd, 1989; Dodge & others, 1986; Shantz, 1988; Weissberg, 1988). One investigation explored the possibility that social cognitive skill deficits characterize maladjusted children (Asarnow & Callan, 1985). Boys with and without peer adjustment difficulties were identified and then a number of social cognitive processes or skills were assessed. These included the boy's ability to generate alternative solutions to hypothetical problems, to evaluate these solutions in terms of their effectiveness, to

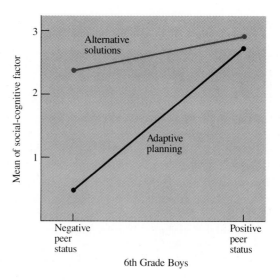

Figure 7.2   Generation of alternative solutions and adaptive planning by negative and positive peer status boys.

describe self-statements, and to rate the likelihood of self-statements. It was found that boys without peer adjustment problems generated more alternative solutions, proposed more assertive and mature solutions, gave less intense aggressive solutions, showed more adaptive planning, and evaluated physically aggressive responses less positively than the boys with peer adjustment problems. For example, as shown in Figure 7.2 negative peer status sixth-grade boys were not as likely to generate alternative solutions and much less likely to adaptively plan ahead than their positive peer status counterparts.

While it is becoming clear that social cognitive knowledge is a very important ingredient of peer relations, as yet we have not developed a precise body of social cognitive knowledge believed to be beneficial to children and adolescents at different developmental levels. However, it seems clear that adolescents who get along better with others, both peers and adults, likely have significantly greater knowledge of social skills than those who are not popular and not well liked.

A peer accidentally trips and knocks a boy's soft drink out of his hand. The boy misinterprets the encounter as hostile, which leads him to retaliate aggressively against the peer. Through repeated encounters of this kind, peers come to perceive the boy as having a habit of acting inappropriately. Kenneth Dodge (1983; Price & Dodge, in press) argues that children go through five steps in processing information about their social world: decoding of social cues, interpretation, response search, selecting an optimal response, and enactment. Dodge has found that aggressive boys are more likely to perceive another child's actions as hostile when the peer's intention is ambiguous. And when aggressive boys search for cues to determine a peer's intention, they respond more rapidly, less efficiently, and less reflectively than nonaggressive children. These are among the social cognitive factors believed to be involved in children's conflicts with each other (Shantz, 1988).

The Contexts of Adolescent Development

Social Skills Training

The development of ideas about social knowledge, communication, and information processing has important implications for improving the social skills of adolescents in peer contexts (Kelly & de Armas, 1989). Let's look more closely at the nature of these social skills training programs. Remember in the prologue to this chapter the peer-oriented school developed by Robert Selman? Selman's approach to helping children and adolescents who have problems with peers is a social cognitive approach that emphasizes social skills training. Other social cognitive strategies are being tried out as well in efforts to improve social skills with peers (Denham & Almeida, 1987). One investigation (Mize, 1985) revealed that teaching children how to ask questions, how to be a leader, how to show support to peers, and how to make appropriate comments to peers was invaluable in getting the children to behave in more socially competent ways during peer interaction. Sophisticated counselor training programs that were designed for adults now are being used with adolescents and children.

It seems that some of the most effective strategies are a conglomerate of processes. For example, in the strategy used by Jacquelyn Mize (1985), not just a single skill or approach was used; rather a combination of strategies were called on to facilitate peer relations. These conglomerate strategies are often referred to as **coaching.** A conglomerate strategy might consist of demonstration or modeling of appropriate social skills, discussion, and reasoning about the social skills, as well as the use of reinforcement for their enactment in actual social situations. In one coaching study, students with few friends were selected and trained in ways to have fun with peers. The "unpopular" students were encouraged to participate fully, to show interest in others, to cooperate, and to maintain communication. A control group of students (who also had few friends) was directed in peer experiences, but was not coached specifically in terms of improved peer strategies. Subsequent assessment revealed that the coaching was effective, with the coached group showing more sociability when observed in peer relationships than their noncoached counterparts (Oden & Asher, 1975).

Other recent efforts to teach social skills also have used conglomerate strategies. In one investigation, middle-school adolescents were instructed in ways to improve their self-control, stress management, and social problem solving (Weissberg, Caplan, & Bennetto, 1988; Weissberg, Caplan, & Sivo, 1989). For example, as problem situations arose, teachers modeled and students practiced six sequential steps: (1) stop, calm down, and think before you act; (2) go over the problem and state how you feel; (3) set a positive goal; (4) think of lots of solutions; (5) plan ahead for the consequences; (6) go ahead and try the best plan. The 240 adolescents who participated in the program improved their ability to devise cooperative solutions to problem situations, and their teachers reported that the students showed improved social relations in the classroom following the program. In another investigation, boys and

Skill-Streaming the Adolescent

A number of strategies for training the social skills of adolescents have been described by Arnold Goldstein and his colleagues in the book *Skill-Streaming the Adolescent* (Goldstein, Sprafkin, Gershaw, & Klein, 1981). These include such behavior management strategies as reinforcement, including social and group reinforcement, punishment, including time-out procedures, modeling, and role playing. A major focus of the book is how such social skills can be trained in the school setting. One particularly helpful set of strategies involves those pertaining to relationship-based techniques.

Psychologists and educators have known for many years that the better the relationship between a helper and a student, the more positive and productive will be the outcome of their interaction. In many instances, relationship-based techniques require the social skills trainer to become aware of broader aspects of the adolescent's life than just those happenings in the classroom. The helper tries to gain some sense of the adolescent's motivation for behaving in a particular way and attempts to respond to the adolescent's needs. One particular strategy that can be beneficial focuses on empathetic encouragement. In using this strategy, trainers show the adolescent that they understand the adolescent's difficulty, and encourage the adolescent to participate as instructed. A series of steps then are followed:

1. The adolescent is offered the chance to explain in detail the problems being encountered while the trainer listens nondefensively.
2. The trainer indicates that she or he understands the adolescent's behavior.
3. If it is appropriate, the trainer indicates that the adolescent's view is a reasonable interpretation or alternative.
4. The trainer restates his or her view with supporting reasons and likely outcomes.
5. The trainer expresses the appropriateness of delaying a resolution of the problem.
6. The trainer encourages the adolescent to try to participate.

An example is the case of Rose, a somewhat temperamental, disruptive adolescent who was very negative about getting involved in the social skills training program, responding by laughing and making mocking gestures. After attempting to ignore such behavior, the trainer finally decided to discuss Rose's behavior in an empathetic manner. Rose was asked to explain why she was acting this way (laughing, mocking). Rose said she

girls in a low-income area of New Jersey were given instruction in social decision making, self-control, and group awareness (Clabby & Elias, 1988). When compared with boys and girls who did not receive the training, the program participants were more sensitive to the feelings of others, more mindful of the consequences of their actions, and better able to analyze problem situations and act appropriately.

To learn more about strategies being used with adolescents who have deficient social skills, read Perspective on Adolescent Development 7.1, where we discuss skill-streaming with adolescents.

thought the skill training was stupid. She said in her family, if she wanted permission for anything she had to wait for a week. At home, then, she simply took what she wanted.

The trainer then told Rose that it is understandable why this skill won't work at home. It might be a skill she would not want to use there. Rose was informed that there might be a lot of situations away from home, such as at school, where the skill could be helpful. She was told that at school there are many times that a student has to ask permission to do certain things, such as leaving the classroom and turning in an assignment late. The trainer indicated that if you just go ahead and do these things without asking permission, you can wind up in a lot of trouble. Rose was told that maybe it would be a good idea to hold off on judging whether this skill involving asking permission was good or bad until she had a chance to try it out. Rose subsequently agreed to try the skill out in a small group and she became reasonably attentive through the remainder of the social skills training session.

Another helpful strategy described by Goldstein and his colleagues (1981) focuses on the elicitation of peer support. To the degree peer group goals are important to the adolescent, peer pressure can be used to the helper's advantage in working with the adolescent. The trainer's task becomes one of structuring the group activity so peer support can be mobilized. The trainer also may elicit specific group support for particular behaviors shown by hesitant or less skilled adolescents in the group.

Consider the following circumstances. The trainer noticed that before and after role-playing strategies, a number of negative comments, jokes, and insults were being hurled around by the adolescents. To deal with these sarcastic rejoinders, the trainer decided to teach the skill called giving a compliment. The trainer made the role-playing task one of giving a true compliment to someone in the class about what they were doing in the class. The adolescents had to think about this for awhile, but eventually were able to compliment each other on their helpfulness, on communicating better, and so forth. When the next skill was taught, the trainer gave the adolescents the task of giving a compliment to each adolescent who had role played.

Through strategies such as those described by Goldstein and his associates (1981), skill-deficient adolescents are being helped to live more socially competent lives and function more maturely in school settings. ❧

Reinforcement, Modeling, and Social Comparison

Other processes involved in influencing the adolescent's peer relations include reinforcement, modeling, and social comparison. Adolescent peer relations are affected by the extent to which the individuals dispense rewards to each other. The members of a peer group who give out the most reinforcements are the ones most likely to receive the most reinforcements in return (Charlesworth & Hartup, 1973). This indicates the reciprocal nature of peer interaction. In one investigation, it was found that training peers to selectively use reinforcement reduced disruptive activity in the classroom (Solomon & Wahler, 1973).

Social comparison is pervasive during the adolescent years. Adolescents are strongly motivated to know where they stand vis a vis others. Are they as attractive as someone else? Are they as good an athlete as someone else? Are they as smart as someone else? And so on.

Peers also are influenced by the model their associates provide (Bandura, 1986; Hartup, 1983; Schunk, 1987). Positive relationships between models and observers enhance the model's effectiveness, as does the extent individuals perceive that models are similar to themselves. Models who are more powerful are imitated more than those who are less powerful. This means that the leaders of the school, captains of the football team and drill team, and president of the student body are more likely to be imitated than those who are not in school leadership positions. In many situations, older adolescents are more likely to be imitated than peers who are the same age as the observer. Because of their age, experience, and knowledge, older adolescents are more likely to be perceived as powerful than same-aged peers of the observer.

In discussing the functions of the peer group earlier in the chapter, it was mentioned that one of the primary functions of the peer group is to provide a means of **social comparison** about one's abilities, talents, characteristics, and the like. Social comparison seems to heighten as boys and girls move from the elementary school years into early adolescence. On a daily basis, it is not unusual to hear comments such as, "I don't like her hair. It is not as natural as yours and mine." And, "What a yucky looking car he has. Mine is much better. Don't you think?" Or, "I got an A on the biology test. What did you get?" Consider also the comments of one individual recalling her girlfriend as a social comparison source:

> "Girlfriends were as essential as mothers . . . girlfriends provided a sense of security, as belonging to any group does . . . (but) a best friend was more complicated: using a friend as a mirror or as a model, expanding your own knowledge through someone else's, painfully acquiring social skills. What little we learned about living with another person in an equal relationship, outside our own families, we learned from our girlfriends" (Toth, 1981, p. 60).

The Contexts of Adolescent Development

Social comparison, of course, can have either negative or positive effects. As adolescents look around their peer world and compare themselves with others, they likely find some things about themselves they like better and others they like less. Adolescents who see themselves more positively than most others likely have higher self-esteem than those who compare themselves more negatively to others. Quite clearly, though, social comparison is a highly motivating aspect of adolescent life, as adolescents strive to find out where they stand vis-à-vis their peers on many different abilities and characteristics (Masters & Smith, 1987; Tessor, Millar, & Moore, 1988).

The Coordinated Worlds of Parents and Peers

As was described in the last chapter, the history of studying adolescents' relationships with their parents and peers has been filled with references to disengagement and disconnectedness with parents and to approach and connectedness to peers. To be sure, adolescents who have problems in their relationships with parents often do try to find a strong identity with the peer group, and adolescents do show a strong motivation to be with peers and develop a sense of independence and identity. However, it is incorrect to assume that movement toward independence and strong peer involvement is not continually linked to parent-adolescent relationships. Even the adolescent who seems to show a complete preoccupation with the world of peers, friendships, and dating cannot be fully understood without knowing the nature of his or her relationships with parents, both in the present and in the past. Parent and peer relations are not opposing forces in many instances. And even when parent and peer relations seem to be in conflict, to understand adolescent development it is important to study how relationships with parents have shaped peer relationships (Parke, 1989).

One investigation revealed how important relationships with parents are in understanding a key dimension of peer relations—friendship. To learn more about this study, turn to Perspective on Adolescent Development 7.2, where we discuss mother-daughter relationships and the adolescent girl's relationships with her girlfriends. Next, we further evaluate more ideas about the nature of adolescents' friendships.

Friendships

My best friend is nice. She's honest, and I can trust her. I can tell her my innermost secrets and know that nobody else will find out about them. I have other friends, too, but she is my best friend. We consider each other's feelings and don't want to hurt each other. We help each other out when we have problems. We make up funny names for people and laugh ourselves silly. We make lists of which boys are the sexiest and which are the ugliest, which are the biggest jerks, and so on. Some of these things we share with other friends, but some we don't.

Mothers, Daughters, and Girlfriends

Martin Gold and Denise Yanof (1985) investigated the relation between adolescent girls' relationships with their mothers and their relationships with their closest girlfriends. They gave questionnaires to 134 high school girls, asking them about mother-daughter affection, democratic treatment by their mothers, and appropriateness of their mothers as models. In addition, they asked the high school girls about the intimacy of their relationships with their closest girlfriends, the mutual influence in these peer relationships, and their identification with their girlfriends.

The results of the study clearly revealed that consideration of their mothers as appropriate models was positively related not only to the girls' identification with their closest girlfriends but to the intimacy of those friendships. This intimacy involved high levels of affection. The general extent to which the girl identified with her mother was significantly related to her identification with her girlfriend(s). Identification with mothers was assessed by such items as the extent to which the girl said she "would like to become like" her mother in regard to such characteristics as career attainment, appearance,

relationships with people, and the like. Identification with a girlfriend(s) was assessed by asking the girl to rate the general extent to which she wanted to be like her girlfriend. Also, the more the girls perceived their mothers treated them in a democratic way, the more likely the girls were to report mutual influence in relationships with their girlfriends.

Gold and Yanof (1985) concluded that these data support a developmental rather than a compensatory model of adolescent relationships. A developmental model suggests that parents, through close, positive relationships with adolescents, influence the adolescent's construction of positive relationships with others. A compensatory model indicates that adolescents immerse themselves in relationships with peers when they lack close, positive relationships with parents. Quite clearly, such data support our argument that connectedness and attachment to parents continue as adolescents form relationships outside of their family, and that the positive nature of parent-adolescent relationships contributes to healthy peer relationships.

Although all adolescents want to be popular with large segments of their age group, they also want to have one or two best friends. Unfortunately, many adolescents do not have a best friend, or even a circle of friends, in whom they can confide. A certain school psychologist always made a practice of asking children and adolescents about their friends. One 12-year-old boy, when asked who his best friend was, replied "My kite." Further discussion revealed that his parents had insulated him from the society of neighborhood peers. Similarly, in one investigation of college-age youth, as many as 1 out of every 3 students surveyed said that they had not found, or were not sure whether they had found, a close, meaningful relationship with a same-sex peer (Katz, 1968).

Why do so many adolescents have difficulty developing a close friendship? Many adolescents may lack the social skills necessary to get and retain friends—such as communication skills. They also may be suspicious of the commitment a friendship entails. An adolescent may ask, "Can I really trust her? Does she really like me for me, or is she just using me?"

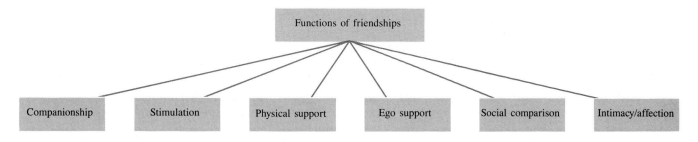

Figure 7.3   The functions of friendships.

The Importance of Friendship

Why are adolescents' friendships important? They serve six functions: companionship, stimulation, physical support, ego support, social comparison, and intimacy/affection (Gottman & Parker, 1987; Parker & Gottman, 1989). Concerning companionship, friendship provides adolescents with a familiar partner, someone who is willing to spend time with them and join in collaborative activities. Concerning stimulation, friendship provides adolescents with interesting information, excitement, and amusement. Concerning physical support, friendship provides time, resources, and assistance. Concerning ego support, friendship provides the expectation of support, encouragement, and feedback that helps the adolescent maintain an impression of himself or herself as a competent, attractive, and worthwhile individual. Concerning social comparison, friendship provides information about where the adolescent stands vis-à-vis others and whether the adolescent is doing okay. Concerning intimacy/affection, friendship provides adolescents with a warm, close, trusting relationship with another individual, a relationship that involves self-disclosure (see Figure 7.3).

Intimacy and Similarity in Friendship

In the context of friendship, what does intimacy mean? It has been defined different ways. For example, it has been defined broadly to include everything in a relationship that makes it seem close or intense. In most research studies, though, **intimacy in friendship** has been defined more narrowly as self-disclosure or sharing of private thoughts. Private or personal knowledge about a friend also has been used as an index of intimacy (Selman, 1980; Sullivan, 1953).

The most consistent finding in the last two decades of research on adolescent friendships is that intimacy is an important feature of friendship (Berndt & Perry, 1990). When young adolescents are asked what they want from a friend or how they can tell someone is their best friend, they frequently say that a best friend will share problems with them, understand them, and listen when they talk about their own thoughts or feelings. When young children talk about their friendships, comments about intimate self-disclosure or mutual understanding are rare. In one recent investigation, friendship intimacy was more prominent in 13–16 year olds than 10–13 year olds (Buhrmester, 1989).

While intimacy in friendships increases during early adolescence, the intimacy is not always positive. During puberty, intimacy in friendships may be affected by increased opposite-sex interests and dating. The disequilibrium created by the transition to and stress of a middle or junior high school also may exacerbate the intimacy of friendship.

Are the friendships of adolescent girls more intimate than the friendships of adolescent boys? When asked to describe their best friends, girls refer to intimate conversations and faithfulness more than boys do. For example, girls are more likely to describe their best friend as "sensitive just like me," or "trustworthy just like me" (Duck, 1975). The assumption behind this gender difference is that girls are more oriented toward interpersonal relationships. Also, intimacy in the friendships of boys may be discouraged because of the fear it will lead to homosexual behavior.

Adolescents also regard loyalty or faithfulness as more critical in friendships than children do (Berndt & Perry, 1990). When talking about their best friend, adolescents frequently refer to the friend's willingness to stand up for them when around other people. A typical comment is "Bob will stick up for me in a fight," "Sally won't talk about me behind my back," or "Jennifer wouldn't leave me for somebody else." In these descriptions adolescents underscore the obligations of a friend in the larger peer group.

Another predominant characteristic of friendship is that throughout the childhood and adolescent years, friends are generally similar—in terms of age, sex, race, and many other factors. Friends often have similar attitudes toward school, similar educational aspirations, and closely aligned achievement orientations. Friends like the same music, wear the same kind of clothes, and prefer the same leisure activities (Berndt, 1982). If friends have different attitudes about schools, one of them may want to play basketball or go shopping rather than doing homework. If one friend insists on completing homework while the other insists on playing basketball, the conflict may weaken the friendship and the two may drift apart.

At this point we have discussed many ideas about the nature of peer relations and friendships. A summary of these ideas is presented in Concept Table 7.1. Next, we consider another aspect of the adolescent's social world—groups.

Adolescent Groups

Think back to your adolescent years. Which groups were you a member of? You probably were a member of both formal and informal groups. You might have been a member of such formal groups as a basketball team or a drill team, Girl Scouts or Boy Scouts, the student council, and so on. And you probably were a member of a more informal group of peers, especially a clique.

Peers and Friends

Concept	Processes/Related Ideas	Characteristics/Description
Peers	Peer group functions	Peers are individuals who are about the same age or maturity level. Two important functions of peers are to provide a means of social comparison and a source of information outside the family.
	Popularity, rejection, and neglect	Listening skills and effective communication, being yourself, being happy, showing enthusiasm and concern for others, and having self-confidence but not being conceited are predictors of peer popularity. Rejected adolescents are at risk for social problems. The risk status of neglected adolescents is less clear.
	Peer conformity	Conformity to antisocial peer standards peaks around the 8th–9th grades, then lessens by the 12th grade. A distinction is made between the nonconformist and the anticonformist.
	Social knowledge and social information processing	Social knowledge and social information processing skills are associated with improved peer relations.
	Social skills training	Conglomerate strategies, referred to as coaching, are often used.
	Reinforcement, modeling, and social comparison	Other processes involved in influencing the adolescent's peer relations.
	The coordinated worlds of parents and peers	While at one time parent and peer worlds were described as disconnected in adolescence, today's view emphasizes their connectedness.
Friends	Functions of friendships	Companionship, stimulation, physical support, ego support, social comparison, and intimacy/affection.
	Intimacy and similarity	Two of the most common characteristics of friendships.

Let's explore the nature of adolescent groups in greater detail by studying how groups are formed, differences between children's groups and adolescent's groups, cultural variations, and cliques.

Group Formation

An assemblage of adolescents is not necessarily a group or a clique. A **group** exists when several adolescents interact with one another on an ongoing basis, sharing values and goals. Norms and status positions are important in group functioning. **Norms** are the standards, rules, and guidelines by which the group abides. **Status positions** are those of greater or lesser power and control within the group.

Years ago social psychologist Muzafer Sherif brought together a group of 11-year-old boys at a summer camp called Robbers Cave in Oklahoma (Sherif & others, 1961). The boys were divided into two groups. Competition between the boys was created by promoting in-groupness. In the first week one group hardly knew the other group existed. One group became known as the Rattlers (a tough and cussing group whose shirts were emblazoned with a snake insignia) and the other as the Eagles.

Near the end of the first week each group learned of the other's existence. It took little time for "we-they" talk to surface ("They had better not be on our ball field." "Did you see the way one of them was sneaking around?") Sherif, who disguised himself as a janitor so he could unobtrusively observe the Rattlers and Eagles, then set up competition between the groups. Baseball, touch football, and tug-of-war were played. Counselors juggled and judged events so the teams were close. Each team perceived the other to be unfair. Raids, burning the other group's flag, and fights resulted. Ethnocentric out-group derogation was observed when the Rattlers and Eagles held their noses in the air as they passed each other. Rattlers described all Rattlers as brave, tough, and friendly and called all Eagles sneaky and smart alecks. The Eagles reciprocated by labeling the Rattlers crybabies.

After in-groupness and competition transformed the Rattlers and Eagles into opposing "armies," Sherif devised ways to reduce hatred between the groups. He tried noncompetitive contact but that did not work. Positive relations between the Rattlers and Eagles were attained only when both groups were required to work cooperatively to solve a problem. Three superordinate goals that required the efforts of both groups were working together to repair the only water supply to the camp, pooling their money to rent a movie, and cooperating to pull the camp truck out of a ditch. All of these dilemmas were created by Sherif.

In addition to recruiting boys for camp to explore the nature of group formation, Sherif has also simply gone out to street corners and hangouts in towns and cities to find out what adolescent groups are like. In one such effort (Sherif & Sherif, 1964), the observers went to a town and began to infiltrate student gathering places. They got to know the adolescents and became their confidants by doing such things as buying them a new basketball when their old ball got a hole in it. After the observers gained the adolescents' acceptance, they began to record information about the conversations and activities of the youth. The strategy was to spend several hours with them and then write down what had transpired.

What do adolescents talk about when they get together regularly on their own volition? The Sherifs (1964) found that in each group of adolescents they studied, much time was spent just "hanging around" together, talking and joking. In addition, many of the groups spent a great deal of time participating in, discussing, or attending athletic events and games. The only exceptions were groups from lower-class neighborhoods.

Cars occupied the minds of many of the group members. Whether they owned cars or not, the adolescent boys discussed, compared, and admired cars. Those who did not own cars knew what kinds they wanted. The boys also discussed the problem of having access to a car so they could go somewhere or take a girl out. The adolescents who did have cars spent tremendous amounts

　　　　The Contexts of Adolescent Development

Cars occupy an important place in the adolescent's status system. Cars were important to the adolescent boys observed by the Sherifs three decades ago. As female adolescents have gained more status and greater freedom, cars have achieved an important status in their lives as well.

of time in and around cars with their buddies. On numerous occasions, the adolescent boys just drove around, looking to see what was going on around town or wanting to be seen by others.

Discussions about girls frequently infiltrated the adolescent boys' conversations. As part of this talk, they focused extensively on sexual activities. They planned, reminisced, and compared notes on girls. Particularly in the middle- and upper-income adolescent groups, looking for opportunities to be with girls and making sure they had dates for the weekend were important group activities.

Much time in every group was spent reflecting on past events and planning for games, parties, and so forth. Thus, despite the fact that the boys just "hung around" a lot, there were times when they constructively discussed how they were going to deal or cope with various events.

Adults were depicted in the adolescents' conversations as a way to obtain needed resources (such as cars, money, and athletic equipment); as figures whose authorization was needed; as obstacles to be overcome; and, occasionally, in terms of obligation.

While the particular activities of the adolescent boys differed from group to group, there was a remarkable similarity in the general nature of the activities of all the groups. All the groups were preoccupied with the pleasure of one another's company, the problems of having places to meet with peers apart from adults, relationships with adult authorities, relationships with the opposite sex, and with the appurtenances of being an adult male (including a car).

Also, in every group the Sherifs studied, the members engaged in some form of deviant behavior not sanctioned by adults. The most common behavior of this type involved alcoholic beverages. In one of the highest socioeconomic groups, the boys regularly drank, sometimes engaged in illicit sexual activities, and set up a boy-girl swimming party at a motel by forging the registration. The party included not only illegal drinking but the destruction of property as well. The boys paid for the property destruction themselves without ever telling their parents what had happened.

Children Groups and Adolescent Groups

Children's groups differ from adolescents' groups in several important ways. The members of children's groups often are friends or neighborhood acquaintances. Their groups usually are not as formalized as many adolescent groups. During the adolescent years, groups tend to include a broader array of members—in other words, adolescents other than friends or neighborhood acquaintances often are members of adolescent groups. Try to recall the student council, honor society, or football team at your junior high school. If you were a member of any of these organizations, you probably remember that they were made up of many individuals and had not met before and that they were a more heterogeneous group than your childhood peer groups. Rules and regulations were probably well defined, and captains or leaders were formally elected or appointed in the adolescent groups.

A well-known observational study by Dexter Dunphy (1963) supports the notion that opposite-sex participation in groups increases during adolescence. In late childhood, boys and girls participate in small, same-sex cliques. As they move into the early adolescent years, the same-sex cliques begin to interact with each other. Gradually, the leaders and high-status members form further cliques based on heterosexual relationships. Eventually, the newly created heterosexual cliques replace the same-sex cliques. The heterosexual cliques interact with each other in large crowd activities too—at dances and athletic events, for example. In late adolescence, the crowd begins to dissolve as couples develop more serious relationships and make long-range plans that may include engagement and marriage. A summary of Dunphy's ideas is presented in Figure 7.4.

Cultural Variations in Adolescent Groups

Whether an adolescent grows up as part of the peer culture in a ghetto or in a middle-class suburban area influences the nature of the groups to which he or she belongs. For example, in a comparison of middle-class and lower-class adolescent groups, lower-class adolescents displayed more aggression toward the low-status members of the group, but showed less aggression toward the president of the class or group than their middle-class counterparts did (Maas, 1954).

In many schools, peer groups are virtually segregated according to race and social class. Where middle- and lower-class students are both included, the middle-class students often assume the leadership roles in formal organizations such as student council, the honor society, fraternity-sorority groups,

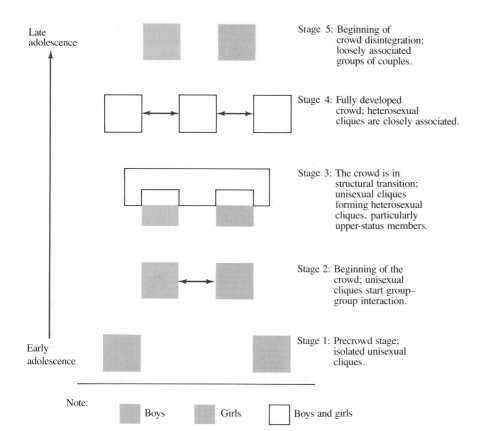

Figure 7.4 Dunphy's stages of group development.

Late adolescence

Stage 5: Beginning of crowd disintegration; loosely associated groups of couples.

Stage 4: Fully developed crowd; heterosexual cliques are closely associated.

Stage 3: The crowd is in structural transition; unisexual cliques forming heterosexual cliques, particularly upper-status members.

Stage 2: Beginning of the crowd; unisexual cliques start group–group interaction.

Stage 1: Precrowd stage; isolated unisexual cliques.

Early adolescence

Note: ▨ Boys   ▨ Girls   ☐ Boys and girls

and so forth. Athletic teams are one type of adolescent group where blacks and lower-class students have been able to gain parity with or surpass middle-class students in achieving status.

Black and white (and lower- and middle-class) students have spent more time with each other during the past two decades than in previous eras, but it has been in the schools rather than in the neighborhoods where the greatest mixture of different backgrounds has occurred. Even when schools are mixed in terms of ethnic and social-class background, it still appears that friendships, cliques, and crowds are more likely to follow social-class and ethnic group lines (Kandel, 1978). It is usually in formal groups such as athletic teams and student council that the greatest mixture of social class and ethnicity occurs.

In some cultures, children are placed in peer groups for much greater lengths of time at an earlier age than they are in the United States. For example, in the Murian culture of eastern India, both male and female children live in a dormitory from the age of 6 until they get married (Barnouw, 1975). The dormitory is seen as a religious haven where members are devoted to work and spiritual harmony. Children work for their parents, and the parents arrange the children's marriages. When the children wed, they must leave the dormitory.

In our discussion of peer groups, we have mentioned adolescent cliques. For example, in describing Dunphy's work, we noted the importance of heterosexual relationships in the evolution of adolescent cliques. Now, we turn our attention in greater detail to the nature of adolescent cliques.

Cliques

Most peer group relationships in adolescence can be categorized in one of three ways: the crowd, the clique, or individual friendships. The largest and least personal of these groups is the **crowd.** The members of the crowd meet because of their mutual interest in activities, not because they are mutually attracted to one another. By contrast, the members of cliques and friendships are attracted to one another on the basis of similar interests and social ideas. **Cliques** are smaller in size, involve greater intimacy among members, and have more group cohesion than crowds. They usually are larger in size and involve less intimacy than friendships.

Allegiance to cliques, clubs, organizations, and teams exerts powerful control over the lives of many adolescents. Group identity often overrides personal identity. The leader of a group may place a member in a position of considerable moral conflict, asking in effect, "What's more important, our code or your parents?" or "Are you looking out for yourself, or for the members of the group?" Labels like "brother" and "sister" sometimes are adopted and used in group members' conversations with one another. These labels symbolize the intensity of the bond between the members and suggest the high status of membership in the group.

One of the most widely quoted studies of adolescent cliques and crowds is that of James Coleman (1961). Students in 10 different high schools were asked to identify the leading crowds in their schools. They also were asked to name the students who were the most outstanding in athletics, popularity, and different activities in the school. Regardless of the school sampled, the leading crowds were likely to be composed of athletes and popular girls. Much less power in the leading crowd was attributed to the bright student. Coleman's finding that being an athlete contributes to popularity for boys was reconfirmed in a more recent investigation by Eitzen (1975).

Think about your high school years—what were the cliques, and which one were you in? While the names of the cliques change, we could go to almost any high school in the United States and find three to six well-defined cliques or crowds. In one recent investigation, six peer group structures emerged: populars, unpopulars, jocks, brains, druggies, and average students (Brown & Mounts, 1989). The proportion of students placed in these cliques was much lower in multi-ethnic schools because of the additional existence of ethnically based crowds.

The exact nature of cliques and crowds depends on the geographical region of the country where the adolescents live. For instance, in towns and cities in Texas, the "kickers" and the "potheads" often create the most controversy. This dichotomy (as well as the dichotomy between groups in most

(a)

(b)

Among the adolescent cliques are the "leathers" or "hoods" (a) and the "collegiates" or "All-American" students (b).

areas) is due to the mixing of cultures—urban and rural, Northern and Southern. The term *kicker* originates from cowboy boots, which were worn mostly by working cowboys. The term has been modified to either "chip kickers" or "cowboys," depending on the purposes of the adolescent using the label. Observers say the kickers may or may not have anything to do with agriculture, but they usually wear cowboy boots, western shirts and jeans, listen to country-and-western music, often drive pickups, and carry around tins of snuff in their hip pockets. The other side of the dichotomy has a wider variety of names, depending on the locale: freaks, potheads, slickers, or thugs. Freaks supposedly prefer rock music, dress in worn-out clothes, and drive "souped-up" cars.

Sociologists say that adolescents growing up in America usually must decide on which culture to go with—whether to be a "roper" or a "doper," an "intellectual" or a "going-steady type" (Hawkins, 1979). This decision often reflects some conflict that exists throughout society—in many instances, the students are making a political statement by siding with one clique or crowd rather than another (the kickers and cowboys are on the right, and potheads are on the left). Policital statements made during adolescence, though, may not be very strong; sometimes they boil down to nothing more than which radio station you listen to or which clothes you buy. The split is fairly easy to see in most high schools. In many instances, the two extreme groupings, such as the "ropers" and the "dopers," are not well integrated into the school system itself and are easily distinguished from students who are making good grades and who are social leaders.

Cliques have been portrayed as playing a pivotal role in the adolescent's maintenance of self-esteem and development of a sense of identity (e.g., Coleman, 1961; Erikson, 1968). Several theoretical perspectives suggest how clique membership might be linked with the adolescent's self-esteem (Brown & Lohr, 1987). In an extension of Erikson's identity development theory, it is argued that virtually all 13–17-year-olds will regard clique membership as highly salient and that self-esteem will be higher among clique members than nonmembers (at least those satisfied with the crowd). The peer group is viewed as a "way station" between relinquishing childhood dependence on parents and adult self-definition, achievement, and autonomy. Group affiliation and acceptance by the clique is seen as important in keeping the adolescent's self-concept positive during this long transition period. Social comparison theory also has implications for understanding clique attachment and self-esteem. It implies that while group members as a whole may have higher self-esteem than nonmembers, there will be differences among group members according to the position of their clique in the peer group status hierarchy. This argument is based on the belief that individuals often compare their own attributes with those of significant others to evaluate the adequacy of their ideas or characteristics (Festinger, 1954).

In one recent investigation, Bradford Brown and Jane Lohr (1987) examined the self-esteem of 221 7th through 12th graders. The adolescents were either associated with one of the five major school cliques or were relatively unknown by classmates and not associated with any school clique. Cliques included the following: jocks (athletically oriented), populars (well-known students who lead social activities), normals (middle-of-the-road students who make up the masses), druggies/toughs (known for illicit drug use or other delinquent activities), and nobodies (low in social skills or intellectual abilities). The self-esteem of the jocks and the populars was highest, while that of the nobodies was the lowest. But one group of adolescents not in a clique had self-esteem equivalent to the jocks and the populars. This group was the independents, who indicated that clique membership was not important to them. Keep in mind that these data are correlational—self-esteem could increase an adolescent's probability of becoming a clique member just as clique membership could increase the adolescent's self-esteem.

So far in our discussion of peers in adolescence, we have discussed the nature of peer relations, friendships, and group behavior. But there is one aspect of peer relations yet to be discussed—dating.

Dating

I met this really neat, good-looking guy, Frank—a college senior. He seemed to like me, but why would a college guy be interested in me, a high school junior, anyway? . . . That guy, Frank, asked me out. I think he is pretty nice, but I'm not sure I want the kind of experience he wants to show me! . . . At

any rate, I said he could pick me up after school. I thought he might not show up because he would be too embarrassed to be seen at the high school. . . . But he came, and we went out for some pizza and talked. He wanted me to go out with him that night, but I told him I had to study, and he should take me home. He did. He keeps calling all the time, and my mother always is saying to me, "Who is that guy that keeps calling you all the time?" (I don't want her to know I'm going out with somebody as old as Frank is.) . . . Frank sure is persistent. I finally agreed to go out with him again. And then I went out with him again, and again. Now, I think I'm falling in love with him. . . . I'm starting to get jealous when he doesn't call me every evening—I think maybe he is out with some girl who is older and a lot more experienced than I am. I sure hope not. . . . Frank is so neat—he is so much more mature than most of the guys in our high school. He is sensitive to my feelings, and doesn't smart off to get attention. . . . But I'm still not sure why he likes me.

While many adolescent boys and girls have social interchanges through formal and informal peer groups, it is through dating that more serious contacts between the sexes occur. Many agonizing moments are spent by young male adolescents worrying about whether they should call a certain girl and ask her out—"Will she turn me down?" "What if she says yes, what do I say next?" "How am I going to get her to the dance? I don't want my mother to take us!" "I want to kiss her, but what if she pushes me away?" "How can I get to be alone with her?" And, on the other side of the coin: "What if no one asks me to the dance?" "What do I do if he tries to kiss me?"

Or, "I really don't want to go with him. Maybe I should wait two more days and see if Bill will call me." Think about your junior high, high school, and early college years. You probably spent a lot of time thinking about how you were going to get a particular girl or boy to go out with you. And many of your weekend evenings were probably spent on dates, or on envying others who had dates. Some of you went steady, perhaps even during junior high school; others of you may have been engaged to be married by the end of high school.

Functions of Dating

Dating is a relatively recent phenomenon. It wasn't until the 1920s that dating as we know it became a reality, and even then its primary role was for the purpose of selecting and winning a mate. Prior to this period, mate selection was the sole purpose of dating, and "dates" were carefully monitored by parents, who completely controlled the nature of any heterosexual companionship. Often, parents bargained with each other about the merits of their adolescents as potential marriage partners and even chose mates for their children. In recent times, of course, adolescents themselves have gained much more control over the dating process; today's adolescents are not as much at the mercy of their parents in regard to whom they go out with. Furthermore, dating has evolved into something more than just courtship for marriage. Dating today serves four main functions for adolescents (Skipper & Nass, 1966):

1. Dating can be a form of recreation. Adolescents who date seem to have fun and see dating as a source of enjoyment and recreation.
2. Dating is a source of status and achievement. Part of the social comparison process in adolescence involves evaluating the status of people one dates—are they the best looking, the most popular, and so forth.
3. Dating is part of the socialization process in adolescence—it helps the adolescent to learn how to get along with others and assists in learning manners and sociable behavior.
4. Dating can be a means of mate sorting and selection—it retains its original courtship function.

Incidence and Age Trends

Most girls in the United States begin dating at the age of 14, while most boys begin sometime between the ages of 14 and 15 (Douvan & Adelson, 1966; Sorenson, 1973). Most adolescents have their first date sometime between the ages of 12 and 16. Less than 10% have a first date before the age of 10, and by the age of 16 more than 90% have had at least one date. More than 50% of the 10th, 11th, and 12th graders in one study averaged one or more dates per week (Dickinson, 1975). About 15% of these high school students dated less than once per month, and about 3 out of every 4 students had gone steady at least once.

Marriage in Traditional and Contemporary China

Family relationships in prerevolutionary China were guided by tradition, religion, and law for 2000 years. A new marriage law was passed in 1980 and took effect in 1981. In traditional China, parents were obligated to arrange a marriage for each child as soon as the child reached marriageable age. Betrothal (engagement to be married) of children was common, in some cases before children were born. In 1950, the communist government prohibited child betrothal and established a minimum marriage age of 20 years for males, 18 years for females. The 1980 law sets even higher marriage age limits—22 years for males, 20 years for females. Late marriage and late childbirth are critical elements in China's effort to control population growth.

Marriage in traditional China was a contract between families rather than a contract between individuals. Personal attraction and love between the bride and groom were considered unnecessary. Arrangement of a marriage involved negotiation of a "bride price," or gifts to be paid to the family of the bride. The 1980 law forbids "mercenary" marriages in which a bride price is paid. In rural areas of China, though, bride price payments are still common.

According to Chinese tradition, a bride was expected to leave her family of origin when she married and become a part of her husband's family. This meant that only sons (and their wives and children) would be available to continue the family's ancestor worship and to provide for parents in old age. Therefore, sons were more valued than daughters. Women were often kept subjugated, subservient, and dependent. While significant strides have been made toward sexual equality in contemporary China, the desire for sons rather than daughters is still strong among many of the Chinese people (Engel, 1984).

Dating and going steady, then, are standard fare on the menu of most teenagers' social relationships. Adolescents who do not date very much may feel left out of the mainstream in their high school and community. Social skills training has been developed for adolescents who have difficulty in peer relations, and programs have been created to improve the ability of the adolescent to obtain a date and to interact more effectively during social relationships with the opposite sex (e.g., Masters & others, 1988; Twentyman & McFall, 1975).

© 1987, BLOOM COUNTY. Washington Post
Writers Group. Reprinted with permission.

Going Steady

At some point in their junior high or high school years, a number of adolescents "go steady" or "go with" each other. Going steady, though, may not mean the same thing to all adolescents. One of my daughter's 13-year-old friends once discussed her history of "going steady." It turned out that in the course of six months she had "gone" with five different boys. In two of those situations, the girl agreed to go steady with the boys over the phone and then broke off the relationships before she even had a date with them!

In one investigation of high school juniors and seniors who were going steady (Schneider, 1966), 75% felt that their relationship involved a commitment to forgo dating other people, and a full 25% felt they were in love. Forty percent had informally agreed to get married, another 40% had considered marriage seriously but had made no commitment, and 20% had not considered marriage at all. The longer the couples had gone steady the more likely they were to consider marriage seriously. For those who had gone steady for only two months, for example, only 3% indicated they planned to get married; while for those who had gone steady for one year or longer, 50% said they planned to get married. Thus, going steady becomes more serious business during high school than junior high school, and the longer a couple goes steady the more likely they are to consider marriage.

Male and Female Patterns

It generally has been believed that females are more strongly oriented toward affection in opposite-sex relationships, while males are more interested in sexual matters. With regard to sexual interest, it does appear that during adolescence, males show a stronger sexual interest than females do, although both males and females show a heightened desire for sexual involvement as the relationship deepens. For example, both male and female adolescents who go steady show a stronger desire for sexual involvement than their counterparts who have only had several dates with the same person (McCabe & Collins, 1979).

With regard to affectional and personality aspects of dating, females show more interest in personality exploration and self-disclosure than males (Douvan & Adelson, 1966; Simon & Gagnon, 1969). However, in one investigation (McCabe & Collins, 1979), both males and females said they begin a dating relationship with an affectional orientation. And as relationships endure, affection often plays a more prominent role.

What Attracts Adolescents to Each Other

Birds of a feather do indeed flock together. One of the most powerful lessons in close relationships is that we like to associate with people who are similar to us. As we already have seen, adolescents' friends are much more like them than unlike them. So it is in dating. Adolescents' dates, as well as their friends, are likely to share similar attitudes, behavior, and characteristics—clothes, intelligence, personality, political attitudes, values, religious attitudes, life-style, physical attractiveness, and so on. In some limited cases and on some isolated characteristics, opposites may attract. For example, an introvert may wish to be with an extrovert, a blond may prefer a brunette, an individual from a low-income background may be attracted to someone with money. But overall, adolescents desire to date individuals with similar rather than opposite characteristics.

Adolescents are motivated to form close relationships with others who are similar to them because similarity provides **consensual validation** of the adolescent's own attitudes and behaviors. That is, if someone else has the same attitudes and behaviors as the adolescent, this supports who the adolescent is. Also, similarity implies that adolescents will enjoy dating another individual because they can participate in mutually satisfying activities, many of which require a partner with similarly disposed behaviors and attitudes (Duck, 1989).

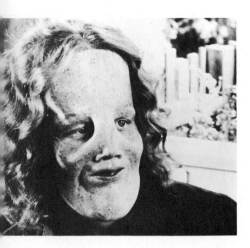

Figure 7.5   Rocky Dennis, as portrayed by Eric Stolz in the movie Mask. Rocky was unloved and unwanted as a young child because of his grotesque features. As his mother and peers got to know him, they became much more attracted to him.

One characteristic deserves special mention—physical attractiveness. How important is physical attractiveness in determining whether adolescents want to date, enjoy dating, or fall in love with someone? In one experiment, college students assumed that a computer had determined their date on the basis of similar interests (Walster & others, 1966). Actually, the dates were randomly assigned. The college students' social skills, physical appearance, intelligence, and personality were measured. Then a dance was set up for the matched partners. At intermission, the partners were asked in private to indicate the most positive aspects of their date that contributed to his or her attractiveness. The overwhelming reason was looks, not other factors such as personality or intelligence. Other research has documented the importance of physical attraction in close relationships (Lerner & Lerner, 1988; Simpson, Campbell, & Berscheid, 1986).

Why do adolescents want to date attractive individuals? As with similarity, it is rewarding to be around physically attractive individuals. It provides adolescents with consensual validation that they too are attractive. As part of the rewarding experience, the adolescent's self-image is enhanced. It also is aesthetically pleasing to look at physically attractive individuals. We also assume that if individuals are physically attractive, they will have other desirable traits that will interest us.

But every adolescent can't date Rob Lowe or Madonna. How do adolescents deal with this in their relationships? While beautiful girls and handsome boys seem to have an advantage, in the end adolescents usually seek out someone at their own level of attractiveness. Most adolescents come away with a reasonably good chance of finding a "good match." Research indicates that the **matching hypothesis** holds up—that is, while adolescents may prefer a more attractive person in the abstract, in the real world they ultimately end up dating someone who is close to their own level of attractiveness (Kalick & Hamilton, 1986).

Several additional points help to clarify the role of physical beauty and attraction in adolescent dating. Much of the research focuses on short-term encounters. Attraction over the course of months and years usually is not evaluated. As relationships endure, physical attraction probably assumes less importance. Rocky Dennis, as portrayed in the movie *Mask,* is a case in point (see Figure 7.5). His peers and even his mother initially wanted to avoid Rocky, whose face was severely distorted. But over the course of his adolescent years, the avoidance turned into attraction as people got to know him.

The criteria for beauty may vary from one culture to another and from one point in history to another. Though attempts are made to arrive at the ultimate criteria for such things as a beautiful female face, beauty is relative. In the 1940s and 1950s, adolescent females aspired to have a Marilyn Monroe body build (a well-rounded, Coke-bottle appearance) and face. By 1970, Twiggy and other virtually anorexic females were what adolescent girls aspired to look like. Now, as we move into the 1990s, the desire for thinness has not ended, but what is considered beautiful is no longer either the pleasingly

The Contexts of Adolescent Development

(a)

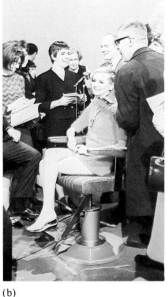
(b)

(c)

Figure 7.6   Changing standards of attractiveness. In the 1940s and 1950s, a Marilyn Monroe body build was ideal (*a*); by the 1970s, the more slender look of Twiggy was popular (*b*); today, a more curvaceous slenderized look like that of Christie Brinkley is considered ideal (*c*).

plump or the very thin but rather a tall stature with moderate curves (see Figure 7.6).

Physical attraction is important in understanding adolescents' attraction for each other. To ignore it and say it does not matter goes against an accumulating body of evidence. To read about how a date's physical attractiveness is more important to some types of males more than others, turn to Perspective on Adolescent Development 7.3.

Romantic Love

Love refers to a vast territory of human behavior. Two main types of love are romantic love and affectionate love. **Romantic love,** also called passionate love or eros, is the type of love that involves passion. It is what we mean when we say we are "in love" with someone, not just "I love" someone. **Affectionate love,** also called companionate love, is the type of love in which we desire to have the other individual nearby and seek the individual's proximity. In affectionate love, we have a deep warmth for the other individual. Psychologists believe that romantic love is especially important in understanding love among adolescents and college students. In one investigation, unattached college males and females were asked to identify their closest relationship. More than half named a romantic partner rather than a parent, sibling, or friend (Berscheid & Snyder, 1988). Well-known love researcher Ellen Berscheid (1985, 1987; Berscheid, Snyder, & Omoto, 1989, in press) believes that sexual desire is vastly neglected in the study of romantic love. When pinned down to say what romantic love truly is, she concluded, "It's about 90 percent sexual desire." Berscheid said that this still is an inadequate answer, but to "discuss romantic

High Self-Monitoring Males and the Company They Wish to Keep

In one investigation, 39 college males were told that they could have a brief coffee date with a female student as part of a study on social interaction (Snyder, Berscheid, & Glick, 1985). The college students were given a self-monitoring questionnaire (see Table 7.A). **Self-monitoring** is the extent to which we are aware of the impressions we make on others and the degree to which we fine tune our performance accordingly (Snyder, 1987). About half of the males were high self-monitors; the other half were low self-monitors. Each student was given 50 file folders with information about potential dates. One page described the female's interests and preferences; another page had a yearbook-type photograph of the female. All of the females were average in appearance and their preferences and interests were normal. As the males looked through the folders, they were observed through a one-way mirror to determine how much time they spent looking at each of the pages. The high and low self-monitors looked at the same number of folders but the high self-monitors spent more time looking at the photographs than did the low self-monitors, who in turn spent more time reading about the females' personal attributes (see Figure 7.A). When asked to describe in their own words the most important characteristic of a date, the high self-monitors were much more likely to talk about physical attractiveness.

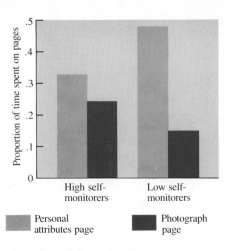

Figure 7.A   Attention to information about potential dates by college males.

In a second study, two more groups of high and low self-monitoring college males were selected. Each student was given the files of two females. One folder contained information about "Kristen," who was physically unattractive but very personable. The other file described "Jennifer," who was very attractive but highly reserved, moody, and more interested in herself than others. The high self-monitoring males were more likely to

love without also prominently mentioning the role sexual arousal and desire plays in it is very much like printing a recipe for tiger soup and leaving out the main ingredient."

The Construction of Dating Relationships

Similarity, physical attractiveness, and sexuality are important ingredients of dating relationships. So is intimacy, which will be discussed in greater detail in Chapter 10. But to fully understand dating relationships in adolescence, we need to know how experiences with family members and peers contribute to the way adolescents construct their dating relationships. Remember the developmental construction view of relationships discussed in the last chapter? One theorist who sees adolescent dating as tied to family relationships is Peter Blos (1962; 1989). At the beginning of adolescence, says Blos, adolescents try

TABLE 7.A   *Measuring self-monitoring*

These statements concern personal reactions to a number of different situations. No two statements are exactly alike, so consider each statement carefully before answering. If a statement is true, or mostly true, as applied to you, circle the T. If a statement is false, or not usually true, as applied to you, circle the F.

1. I find it hard to imitate the behavior of other people.	T F	6. In different situations and with different people, I often act like very different persons.
2. I guess I put on a show to impress or entertain people.	T F	7. I can only argue for ideas I already believe.
3. I would probably make a good actor.	T F	8. In order to get along and be liked, I tend to be what people expect me to be rather than anything else.
4. I sometimes appear to others to be experiencing deeper emotions than I actually am.	T F	9. I may deceive people by being friendly when I really dislike them.
5. In a group of people I am rarely the center of attention.	T F	10. I'm not always the person I appear to be.

Statements 6–10 with responses T F, T F, T F, T F, T F.

Scoring: Give yourself one point for each of questions 1, 5, and 7 that you answered F. Give yourself one point for each of the remaining questions that you answered T. Add up your points. If you are a good judge of yourself and scored 7 or above, you are probably a high self-monitoring individual; 3 or below, you are probably a low self-monitoring individual.

From Mark Snyder, *Journal of Personality and Social Psychology*, 30, 526–537, 1974. Copyright 1974 by the American Psychological Association. Reprinted by permission of the publisher and author.

select Jennifer for a potential date while the low self-monitoring males were more likely to choose Kristen.

Since high self-monitors show so much concern about the self-image they present to others, they are attentive to images presented by potential partners. In other words, high self-monitoring males endorse the statement, "A man is known by the company he keeps." It is not surprising, then, that high self-monitoring college males prefer attractive females as dates.

to separate themselves from the opposite-sex parent as a love object. As adolescents separate themselves, they are very narcissistic. Blos believes this narcissism gives adolescents a sense of strength about themselves. Especially in early adolescence, this narcissistic, self-orientation is likely to produce self-serving, highly idealized, tenuous, and superficial dating relationships.

In the developmental construction view, relationships with parents are carried forward to influence the construction of other relationships, such as dating. Thus, adolescents' relationships with opposite-sex parents, as well as same-sex parents, contribute to adolescents' dating. For example, an adolescent male whose mother has been very nurturant but not smothering, probably feels that relationships with females in a dating relationship will be rewarding. By contrast, the adolescent male whose mother has been cold and unloving toward him likely will perceive that dating relationships with females will be unrewarding.

Adolescents' observations of their parents' marital relationship also probably contribute to their own construction of dating relationships. Consider an adolescent girl who has come from a divorced family and grew up seeing her parents fight on many occasions. Her dating relationships may take one of two turns. She may immerse herself in dating relationships to insulate herself from the stress she has experienced, or she may become aloof and untrusting with males and not wish to become involved heavily in dating relationships. Even when she does date considerably, it may be difficult for her to develop a trusting relationship with males because she has seen promises broken by her parents.

There has been little empirical investigation of the role of parents in influencing the manner in which adolescents construct dating relationships. It may be helpful to recall the investigation of Hetherington (1972, 1977), who found that divorce was associated with a stronger heterosexual orientation of adolescent daughters than with the death of a parent or coming from an intact family. Further, it was suggested that the daughters of divorcees had a more negative opinion of males than did the girls from other family structures. And, it was revealed that girls from divorced and widowed families were more likely to marry images of their fathers than girls from intact families. The argument was made that females from intact families likely have had a greater opportunity to work through relationships with their father and therefore are more psychologically free to date and marry someone different than their fathers.

It also appears that girls are more likely to have their parents involved or interested in their dating patterns and relationships than males. For example, in one investigation (Knox & Wilson, 1981) college females were much more likely than their male counterparts to say their parents tried to influence who they dated during adolescence. They also indicated that it was not unusual for their parents to try to interfere with their dating choices and relationships.

Birth order and sibling relationships also could be expected to be linked with dating relationships. While a number of studies of birth order and attraction in dating have been conducted (Altus, 1970; Critelli & Baldwin, 1979; Toman, 1971), sometimes older siblings are attracted to opposite-sex persons who are younger siblings, while in others they like opposite-sex persons who are also older siblings themselves. Thus, it may be necessary to observe the actual nature of sibling relationships rather than birth order alone to find how sibling relationships influence dating relationships. Nonetheless, it is likely that younger siblings learn a great deal from the triumphs and failings of their older sibling's dating practices. It may be that younger siblings date earlier than older siblings, influenced by the model of their older siblings. And it may be that a younger sibling with an opposite-sex older sibling finds the transition to dating easier, as they have learned much about the opposite sex during their sibling life while growing up. One investigation did reveal that girls often used sibling relationships to their advantage when dealing with parents. Younger siblings pointed to how their older sibling was given dating privileges they had been denied. And, an adolescent would sometimes side with a sibling when the sibling was having an argument with parents in hope that the sibling would do likewise when he or she needed dating privileges parents were denying (Place, 1975).

Peer relationships also are involved in the adolescent's dating relationships. Dunphy's (1963) research, which was discussed earlier in the chapter, found that all large peer crowds were heterosexual and that males in these crowds consistently were older than females. Dunphy also noted the dominant role of the group leader in dating relationships. Both the leaders of large crowds and smaller cliques had a high degree of involvement with the opposite sex. Leaders dated more frequently, were more likely to go steady, and achieved these characteristics earlier than other members of the cliques. Also, leaders were ascribed the task of maintaining a certain level of heterosexual involvement in the peer group. They functioned as confidants and advisors in regard to dating and even put partners together in the case of the "slow learners."

We have discussed many ideas about the nature of adolescent groups and dating. A summary of these ideas is presented in Concept Table 7.2.

Summary

I. Peer Group Functions
Peers are individuals who are about the same age or maturity level. Two important functions of peers are to provide a means of social comparison and a source of information outside the family.

II. Popularity, Rejection, and Neglect
Listening skills and effective communication, being yourself, being happy, showing enthusiasm and concern for others, and having self-confidence but not being conceited are predictors of peer popularity. Rejected adolescents are at risk for social problems. The risk status of neglected adolescents is less clear.

III. Peer Conformity
Conformity to antisocial peer standards peaks around the 8th–9th grades, then lessens by the 12th grade. A distinction is made between nonconformist and anticonformist.

IV. Social Knowledge and Social Information Processing
Social knowledge and social information processing skills are associated with improved peer relations.

V. Reinforcement, Modeling, and Social Comparison
Reinforcement, modeling, and social comparison are processes involved in influencing the adolescent's peer relations.

VI. The Coordinated Worlds of Parents and Peers
While at one time parent and peer worlds were described as disconnected in adolescence, today's view emphasizes their connectedness.

VII. Friends
The functions of friendship include companionship, stimulation, physical support, ego support, social comparison, and intimacy/affection. Intimacy and similarity are two of friendship's most common characteristics.

Adolescent Groups and Dating

Concept	Processes/Related Ideas	Characteristics/Description
Adolescent groups	Group formation	A group exists when several individuals interact with one another on an ongoing basis, sharing values and goals. Norms and status positions are important aspects. Sherif's naturalistic studies documented how adolescents behave in group settings.
	Children groups and adolescent groups	Children's groups are less formal, less heterogeneous, and less heterosexual than adolescent groups. Dunphy found that adolescent group development moves through five stages.
	Cultural variations	More aggression is directed at low-status members in lower-class groups. In many schools, groups are segregated according to race and social class. In formal groups, more mixing of races and social classes occurs.
	Cliques	Are in between friendships and crowds in size and intimacy. Almost every secondary school has three to six well-defined cliques. Membership in certain cliques—jock and populars, for example—is associated with increased self-esteem. Independents also have high self-esteem.
Dating	Functions	Can be a form of recreation, a source of social status and achievement, a setting for learning about close relationships, and can be a means of mate sorting and selection.
	Incidence, age trends, and going steady	Most adolescents date, with girls beginning on the average at 14 and boys at 14–15. Going steady becomes more serious in late adolescence.
	Male and female patterns	Females often show a stronger interest in personality exploration and self-disclosure, males a stronger interest in sexuality.
	What attracts adolescents to each other?	Similarity and physical attraction are important reasons adolescents want to date someone. The matching hypothesis and consensual validation are involved in understanding dating attraction.
	Romantic love	Also called passionate love or eros. Involves sexuality and passion more than affectionate love. Passionate love is especially prominent in adolescents and college students.
	The construction of dating relationships	Relationships with parents, siblings, and peers influence how adolescents construct their dating relationships. Dunphy's study found that group leaders play a role in dating.

VIII. Groups

A group exists when several individuals interact with one another on an ongoing basis, sharing values and goals. Norms and status positions are important aspects of group functioning. Sherif's naturalistic studies documented how adolescents behave in groups. Children's groups are less formal, less heterogeneous, and less heterosexual than adolescent groups. Cultural variations exist in adolescent groups.

IX. Cliques

Cliques are in between friendships and crowds in size and popularity. Almost every secondary school has three to six well-defined cliques. Membership in certain cliques—jocks and populars, for example—is associated with increased self-esteem. Independents also have high self-esteem.

X. Dating

Dating can be a form of recreation, a source of social status and achievement, a setting for learning about close relationships, and can be a means of mate sorting and selection. Most adolescents date, with girls beginning on the average at 14 and boys at 14–15. Females often show a stronger interest in personality exploration and self-disclosure, males a stronger interest in sexuality.

XI. Attraction, Romantic Love, and the Construction of Dating Relationships

Similarity and physical attraction are important reasons adolescents want to date someone. The matching hypothesis and consensual validation are involved in understanding dating attraction. Romantic love, also called passionate love or eros, involves sexuality and passion more than affectionate love. Passionate love is especially characteristic of adolescent and college dating relationships. Relationships with parents, siblings, and peers influence how adolescents construct dating relationships. Dunphy's study found that group leaders play a role in dating.

Key Terms

peers 245
neglected children 248
nonconformist 251
anticonformist 251
coaching 255
social comparison 258

intimacy in friendship 261
group 263
norms 263
status position 263
crowd 268
cliques 268

consensual validation 275
matching hypothesis 276
romantic love 277
affectionate love 277
self-monitoring 278

Suggested Readings

Berndt, T. J., & Ladd, G. W. (1989). *Peer relationships in child development*. New York: Wiley.
   Very up-to-date, authoritative information about the nature of peer relations in childhood and adolescence by two leading researchers.
Duck, S. (1989). *Relating to others*. Chicago: Dorsey Press.
   Valuable information is presented about how individuals construct their relationships, including ideas relevant to dating relationships in adolescence.
Goldstein, A. P., Sprafkin, R. P., Gershaw, N. J., & Klein, P. (1981). *Skill-streaming the adolescent*. Champaign, IL.: Research Press.
   An excellent set of exercises that can be used to improve social skills of adolescents.
Hartup, W. W. (1983). The peer system. In P. H. Mussen (Ed.), *Handbook of child psychology* (Vol. 4, 4th ed.). New York: Wiley.
   A detailed look at the development of peer relations from infancy through adolescence by one of the leading researchers on peer relations.
Journal of Early Adolescence, 5 (1985).
   The entire issue is devoted to friendships in early adolescence.

Schools

The world rests on the breath of the children in the schoolhouse.

The Talmud

From No More "What If" Questions to Authors' Week

Some schools for adolescents are ineffective, others effective. The following excerpts reveal, first, some examples of ineffective middle schools, and second, some effective middle schools.

A teacher sits in the back of the room, her legs up on her desk, asking students questions from a textbook. The students, bored and listless, sit in straight rows facing no one in the front of the room, answering laconically to a blank blackboard. When the principal enters the room, the teacher lowers her legs to the floor. Nothing else changes.

A teacher drills students for a seemingly endless amount of time on prime numbers. After the lesson, not one of them can say why it is important to learn prime numbers.

A visitor asks a teacher if hers is an eighth grade class. "It's called eighth grade," she answers archly, "but we know it's really kindergarten, right class?"

In a predominantly Hispanic school, only the one adult hired as a bilingual teacher speaks Spanish.

In a biracial school, the principal and the guidance counselor cite test scores with pride. They are asked if the difference between the test scores of black and white students is narrowing: "Oh, that's an interesting question!" says the guidance counselor with surprise. The principal agrees. It has never been asked by or of them before.

A teacher in a social studies class squelches several imaginative questions exclaiming, "You're always asking 'what if' questions. Stop asking 'what if'." When a visitor asks who will become president if the president-elect dies before the electoral college meets, the teacher explodes, "You're as bad as they are! That's another 'what if' question!"

These vignettes are from middle schools where life seems to be difficult and unhappy for students. By contrast, consider the following circumstances in effective middle schools:

Everything is peaceful. There are open cubbies instead of locked lockers. There is no theft. Students walk quietly in the corridors. "Why?" they are asked. "So as not to disturb the media center," they answer, which is self-evident to them, but not the visitor who is left wondering. . . . When asked, "Do you like this school?" (They) answer, "No, we don't like it. We love it!"

When asked how the school feels, one student answered, "It feels smart. We're smart. Look at our test scores." Comments from one of the parents of a student at the school are revealing. "My child would have been a dropout." In elementary school, his teacher said to me, "That child isn't going to give you anything but heartaches." He had perfect attendance here. He didn't want to miss a day. Summer vacation was too long and boring. Now he's majoring in communications at the University of Texas. He got here and all of a sudden, someone cared for him. I had been getting notes about Roger every other day, with threats about exclusion.

The young adolescent boy shown here is being given individualized instruction in reading. Think for a moment about the schools you attended as an adolescent. What made them effective or ineffective schools?

Here, the first note said, "It's just a joy to have him in the classroom."

The humane environment that encourages teachers' growth . . . is translated by the teachers . . . into a humane environment that encourages students' growth. The school feels cold when one first enters. It has the institutional feeling of any large school building with metal lockers and impersonal halls. Then one opens the door to a team area and it is filled with energy, movement, productivity, doing. There is a lot of informal relating among students and between students and teachers. Visible from one vantage point are students working on written projects, putting the last touches on posters, watching a film, and working independently from reading kits. . . . Most know what they are doing, can say why it is important, and go back to work immediately after being interrupted.

Authors' Week is yet another special activity built into the school's curriculum that entices students to consider themselves in relation to the rich variety of making and doing in people's lives. Based on student interest, availability, and diversity, authors are invited . . . to discuss their craft. Students sign up to meet with individual authors. They must have read one individual book by the author. . . . Students prepare questions for their sessions with the authors. . . . Sometimes an author stays several days to work with a group of students on his or her manuscript.

Published by permission of Transaction Publishers, from Successful Schools for Young Adolescents, *by Joan Lipsitz. Copyright © 1983 by Transaction Publishers.*

*I*n this chapter we explore many different ideas about schools for adolescents. The main questions we evaluate are the following: What is the nature of schools for adolescents? What transitions take place in adolescents' schooling? How do school size, classroom characteristics, teacher dimensions, and peer relations at school influence adolescents' development? Have schools done a better job of educating middle-class white students than low-income minority group students?

The Nature of Adolescents' Schooling

Today virtually all American adolescents under the age of 16 and most 16–17-year-olds are in school. More than half of all youth continue their education after graduating from high school by attending technical schools, colleges, or universities. Schools for adolescents are vast and varied settings with many functions and diverse makeups.

Functions of Adolescents' Schools

During the twentieth century, schools have assumed a more prominent role in the lives of adolescents. From 1890 to 1920, virtually every state developed laws that excluded youth from work and required them to attend school. In this time frame, a 600% increase in the number of high school graduates occurred (Tyack, 1976). By making secondary education compulsory, the adult power structure placed adolescents in a submissive position and made their move into the adult world of work more manageable. In the nineteenth century, high schools were mainly for the elite, with the educational emphasis on classical, liberal arts courses. By the 1920s educators perceived that the secondary school curriculum needed to be changed. Schools for the masses, it was thought, should not just involve intellectual training but training for work and citizenship (Murphy, 1987). The curriculum of secondary schools became more comprehensive and grew to include general education, college preparatory, and vocational education courses. As the twentieth century unfolded, secondary schools continued to expand their orientation, adding courses in music, art, health, physical education, and other topics. By the middle of the twentieth century, schools had moved further toward preparing students for comprehensive roles in life (Conant, 1959). Today, secondary schools have retained their comprehensive orientation, designed to train adolescents intellectually but in many other ways as well, such as vocationally and socially.

While there has been a consistent trend of increased school attendance for more than 150 years, the distress over alienated and rebellious youth brought up the issue of whether secondary schools actually benefit adolescents. During the early 1970s, three independent panels agreed that high schools contribute to adolescent alienation and actually restrict the transition to adulthood (Brown, 1973; Coleman & others, 1974; Martin, 1976). These

Schools in the Soviet Union

Soviet schools have 10 grades, called forms, which roughly correspond to the 12 grades in American schools. Children begin school at the age of 7 and attend classes 5½ days a week. In the higher forms, students report that they do an average of two to three hours of homework each night. Beginning in the third form, Russian students study both Russian and English. Since most of the Soviet Union's 15 republics have native languages other than Russian, many students study their native language as well. Because of the emphasis on teaching English in their schools, most Soviet citizens under the age of 35 speak at least some English (Cameron, 1988).

prestigious panels argued that adolescents should be given educational alternatives to the comprehensive high school, such as on-the-job community work, to increase their exposure to adult roles and to decrease their sense of isolation from adults. Partially in response to these reports, a number of states lowered the age at which adolescents could leave school from 16 to 14.

Now as we enter the last decade of the twentieth century, the back-to-basics movement has gained momentum, with proponents arguing that the main function of schools should be rigorous training of intellectual skills through subjects like English, math, and science (Cuban, 1988; Kearns, 1988). Advocates of the back-to-basics movement point to the excessive fluff in secondary school curricula, with students being allowed to select from many alternatives that will not give them a basic education in intellectual subjects. Some critics also point to the extensive time spent by students in extracurricular activities. They argue that schools should be in the business of imparting knowledge to adolescents and not be so concerned about their social and emotional lives. Related to the proverbial dilemma of schools' functions is whether schools should include a vocational curriculum in addition to training in basic subjects such as English, math, and science. Critics of the fluff in secondary schools also sometimes argue that the school day should be longer and that the school year should be extended into the summer months. Such arguments are made by critics who believe the main function of schools should be the training of intellectual skills. Little concern for adolescents' social and emotional development appears in these arguments.

Should the main and perhaps only major goal of schooling for adolescents be the development of an intellectually mature individual? Or should schools also focus on the adolescent's maturity in social and emotional development? Should schools be comprehensive and provide a multifaceted curriculum that includes many electives and alternative subjects to a basic core?

Literacy and Secondary School Attendance Around the World

The literacy rate (the ability to read and write) in developing countries more than doubled from 1950 (26%) to 1985 (62%). However, compared to the 98% literacy rate of industrialized nations, it is clear that developing countries face a major task in improving the literacy of their inhabitants. Not only are literacy rates low in developing countries, so is secondary school attendance. Only 36% of adolescents attend secondary schools in developing countries, while 87% of adolescents attend secondary schools in industrialized countries. The improvements that have taken place in literacy and schooling have been uneven in developing countries. Illiteracy is much higher among rural than urban areas, and much higher among females than males. More than two-thirds of the world's illiterate people are female. Consider the situation in India. Less than half of the population in India can read and write. In some of India's states, the female literacy rate is as low as 11%! (MacPherson, 1987; UNICEF, 1986).

These are provocative questions and they continue to be heatedly debated in educational and community circles (Bloome, 1989; Goodlad, 1983; Sizer, 1984; Tharp & Gallimore, 1989). Some education analysts believe secondary schools have become so multifaceted that they are like shopping malls (Powell, Farrar, & Cohen, 1985). The implications of the "shopping mall" analogy for adolescent development are discussed in Perspective on Adolescent Development 8.1.

Should intellectual development be emphasized more than it is even today? Or, should intellectual development be only one of school's functions? Should preparation of the individual for work, a thirst for life-long learning in many areas of life, and social and emotional development also be part of the schooling equation? Patricia Cross (1984) argues that debate about the function of schools produces shifts of emphases much like a swinging pendulum, moving toward basic skills at one point in time, and toward options, frills, or comprehensive training for life at another, and so on back and forth. What we should strive for, though, is not a swinging pendulum but something like a spiral staircase. That is, we might continually be developing more sophisticated ways of fulfilling the varied and changing functions of schools (see Figure 8.1).

The "Shopping Mall" High School

Arthur Powell, Eleanor Farrar, and David Cohen (1985) set out to evaluate the nature of high schools in the United States. They conducted an in-depth examination of 15 diverse high schools across the United States by interviewing students, teachers, and school personnel, as well as observing and interpreting what was happening in the schools. The metaphor of the "shopping mall" high school emerged as the authors tried to make sense out of the data they had collected.

Variety, choice, and neutrality are important dimensions of what is labeled the "shopping mall" high school. Variety appears in the wide range of courses offered (in one school 480 courses in the curriculum!), with something for apparently every student. Variety usually stimulates choice. Choice is often cited as a positive aspect of curricula, but the choice often rests in the hands of students, who, in too many instances, make choices based on ignorance rather than information. The investigators argue that the diversity of individuals, multiple values, and wide range of course offerings combine to produce neutrality. Because they try to accommodate the needs of different student populations, high schools may become neutral institutions that take few stands on the products and services they offer.

The investigators describe the shopping mall high school as possessing "specialty shops" and also having an "unspecial" dimension. Shopping malls usually have a wide range of stores—from large department stores to exclusive boutiques selling a special line of products and catering to a small, select clientele. Like shopping malls, high schools offer a variety of specialities aimed at providing services to students in "high" and "low" tracks.

Students who fall in between—with neither the abilities nor the disabilities to make them unique—make up the domain of the "unspecial." While the unspecial group usually is the largest in number in the school, the allocation of effort and attention to the unspecial usually is the least. Since this difficult-to-define, unspecial group of students lacks strong and influential advocates, minimum requirements may become maximum standards of performance. The investigators stress that the unspecial students may be the forgotten people in high schools, neither "bright" nor "slow," neither driven nor disruptive. They just get through the system on their own, with too little connectedness to each other or to anyone else.

The investigators argue that the shopping mall high school encourages individualization but does not provide personalization. The shopping mall high school offers the freedom to go through school mainly on one's own, which may result in anonymity and increased numbers of unspecial students. In contrast, private schools and speciality shops in the shopping mall high school provide personalization. They offer connections among people, especially between teacher and student, which increases both teacher and student satisfaction.

A criticism of the "shopping mall" high school label is that in choosing to focus on the communalities of high schools, the investigators fail to focus on variations in race, social class, ethnicity, and community history that characterize a high school's uniqueness. Nonetheless, the shopping mall is an intriguing metaphor for America's high schools and provides insight into some general characteristics that have emerged (Santilli & Seidman, 1986).

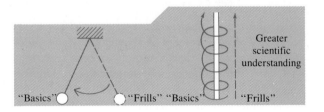

Figure 8.1 The swinging pendulum solution.

Do Schools Make a Difference?

It is justifiable to be concerned about the impact of schools on children and adolescents because of the degree of influence schools have in their lives. By the time students graduate from high school they have accumulated more than 10,000 hours in the classroom. School influences are more powerful today than in past generations because more individuals are in school longer. For example, in 1900, 11.4% of 14–17-year-olds were in school. Today, 94% of the same age group are in school (Smith & Orlosky, 1975).

Children and adolescents spend many years in schools as members of a small society in which there are tasks to be accomplished; people to be socialized and to be socialized by; and rules that define and limit behavior, feelings, and attitudes. The experiences children and adolescents have in this society are likely to have a strong influence in areas such as identity development, belief in one's competence, images of life and career possibilities, social relationships, standards of right and wrong, and conceptions of how a social system beyond the family functions.

It may seem odd even to question whether school has any effect, given the previous statements about the incredible number of hours adolescents spend at school and the diversity of socialization activities taking place in secondary school. But the issue has been raised and has been evaluated from two points of view: (1) Is there a difference between the cognitive performances of those who have gone to school and those who have not? (2) Can schools override the negative effects of poverty? Concerning the first question, there is evidence that schooled children and adolescents do perform differently than the unschooled on a variety of cognitive tasks (Greenfield, 1966; Wagner & Stevenson, 1982). However, we do not yet have a very complete picture of how schooling affects adolescent social development. Research on the second question, regarding poverty, has been extraordinarily controversial. The disagreement is rooted in the work of James Coleman and Christopher Jencks (e.g., Coleman & others, 1966; Jencks & others, 1972). In such investigations, characteristics of schools are compared with family and economic factors as predictors of school achievement and success. Both Coleman and Jencks argue that the evidence supports their belief that schools have little impact on the cognitive devlopment of poverty-stricken students.

But Coleman and Jencks are not without their critics, who fault them on a variety of issues, including the methods they used for collecting their data. One of the most serious criticisms leveled at them is that their analysis is too global, that it was conducted at the level of the school as a whole rather than at the more fine-grained level of everyday happenings in classrooms. In their study of achievement in school and after, the dissenters have compared the effectiveness of schools and classrooms and arrived at the exact opposite conclusion from Coleman and Jencks's (e.g., Brookover & others, 1979; Edmonds, 1979; Klitgaard and Hall, 1975; Rutter & others, 1979). These researchers identify an important idea that we will carry through the remainder

The Contexts of Adolescent Development

of this chapter: namely, that academic and social patterns are intricately interwoven. Schools that produced high achievement in lower-income students were identified not only by particular types of curriculum and time involved in teaching, but by many features of the climate of the school, such as the nature of the teachers' expectations and the patterns of interaction between teachers and students. In other words, various aspects of the school as a social system contributed to the achievement of students in the school.

Additional research focusing on whether schools make a difference in a student's achievement suggests that this question cannot be appropriately addressed unless the extensive variation in schooling is considered. Schools vary even in similar neighborhoods serving similar populations. And they may differ on such dimensions as whether they are integrated or segregated, coed or single sex, parochial or secular, rural or urban, and large or small. Schools are also different in terms of their social climates, educational ideologies, and their concepts of what constitutes the best way to promote the adolescent's development.

Schools' Changing Social Developmental Contexts

The social context differs at the preschool, elementary, and secondary level. The preschool setting is a protected environment, whose boundary is the classroom. In this limited social setting, preschool children interact with one or two teachers, almost always female, who are powerful figures in the young child's life. The preschool child also interacts with peers in a dyadic relationship or in small groups. Preschool children have little concept of the classroom as an organized social system, although they are learning how to make and maintain social contacts and communicate their needs. The preschool serves to modify some patterns of behavior developed through family experiences. Greater self-control may be required in the preschool than earlier in development.

The classroom is still the major context for the elementary school child, although it is more likely to be experienced as a social unit than in the preschool. The network of social expression also is more complex now. Teachers and peers have a prominent influence on children during the elementary school years. The teacher symbolizes authority, which establishes the climate of the classroom, conditions of social interaction, and the nature of group functioning. The peer group becomes more salient, with increased interest in friendship, belonging, and status. And the peer group also becomes a learning community in which social roles and standards related to work and achievement are formed.

As children move into middle or junior high schools, the school environment increases in scope and complexity. The social field is the school as a whole rather than the classroom. Adolescents socially interact with many different teachers and peers from a range of social and ethnic backgrounds. Students are often exposed to a greater mix of male and female teachers. And social behavior is heavily weighted toward peers, extracurricular activities, clubs,

In middle and junior high school, the school environment becomes more complex. The entire school becomes the social world of young adolescents rather than the classroom.

and the community. The student in secondary schools is usually aware of the school as a social system and may be motivated to conform and adapt to the system or challenge it (Minuchin & Shapiro, 1983).

Transitions in Schooling

As children become adolescents and as adolescents develop and then become adults, they experience many transitions in schooling. We have just seen how the social setting changes from preschools through secondary schools. What other aspects of transitions need to be considered? Important considerations involve transitions from elementary school to middle school or junior high school, high school to college, and school to work for noncollege youth, either after completing high school or dropping out of school.

Transition to Middle or Junior High School

The emergence of junior high schools in the 1920s and 1930s was justified on the basis of physical, cognitive, and social changes that characterize early adolescence, as well as on the need for more schools in response to the growing student population. Old high schools became junior high schools and new, regional high schools were built. In most systems, the ninth grade remained a part of the high school in content, although physically separated from it in a 6-3-3 system. Gradually, the ninth grade has been restored to the high school, as many school systems have developed middle schools that include the seventh and eighth grades, or sixth, seventh, and eighth grades. The creation of middle schools has been influenced by the earlier onset of puberty in recent decades. Figure 8.2 reveals the dramatic increase in sixth through eighth grade middle schools and the corresponding decrease in seventh through ninth grade junior high schools.

One worry of educators and psychologists is that junior highs and middle schools have become simply watered-down versions of high schools, mimicking their curricular and extracurricular schedules (Hill, 1980). The critics argue that unique curricular and extracurricular activities reflecting a wide range of individual differences in biological and psychological development in early adolescence should be incorporated into our junior high and middle schools. The critics also stress that too many high schools foster passivity rather than autonomy, and that schools should create a variety of pathways for students to achieve an identity.

The transition to middle school or junior high school from elementary school interests developmentalists, because even though it is a normative experience for virtually all children, the transition can be stressful. It can be stressful because the transition takes place at a time when many changes are occurring simultaneously, including changes in the individual, the family, and the school (Eccles & others, 1989; Hawkins & Berndt, 1985; Hirsch, 1989; Simmons & Blyth, 1987). These changes include puberty and related concerns about body image; the emergence of at least some aspects of formal operational thought, including accompanying changes in social cognition; increased responsibility and independence in association with decreased dependency on parents; change from a small, contained classroom structure to a larger, more impersonal school structure; change from one teacher to many teachers and a small, homogeneous set of peers to a larger, more heterogeneous set of peers; and increased focus on achievement and performance, and their assessment. This list includes a number of negative, stressful features, but there can be positive aspects to the transition. Students are more likely to feel grown up, have more subjects from which to select, have more opportunities to spend time with peers and more opportunities to locate compatible friends, enjoy increased independence from direct parental monitoring, and may be more challenged intellectually by academic work (Hawkins & Berndt, 1985).

When students make the transition from elementary school to middle school or junior high school, they experience the **top-dog phenomenon** (Blyth, Simmons, & Carleton-Ford, 1983). Moving from the top position (the oldest, biggest, and most powerful students in elementary school) to the bottom or lowest position (the youngest, smallest, and least powerful students in middle or junior high school) may create a number of difficulties for the students.

Researchers who have charted the transition from elementary to middle or junior high school find that the first year of middle school or junior high school can be difficult for many students (Douvan & Adelson, 1966; Felner, Ginter, and Primavera, 1982; Gump, 1980; Hawkins & Berndt, 1985; Hirsch & Rapkin, 1987; Simmons & Blyth, 1987). For example, in one investigation of the transition from sixth grade in an elementary school to the seventh grade

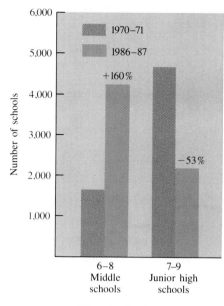

Figure 8.2 The middle school movement.

William M. Alexander & C. Kenneth McEwin from Schools in the Middle: Status & Progress. *Printed June 1989. © National Middle School Association.*

(a)

(b)

The transition from elementary school to middle or junior high school can be stressful. In the last year of elementary school (a), boys and girls are in the "top dog" position as the biggest most powerful students in the school. However, in the first year of middle or junior high school (b), boys and girls are in the "bottom dog" position as the smallest least powerful students in the school.

in a junior high school, adolescents' perceptions of the quality of school life plunged in the seventh grade (Hirsch & Rapkin, 1987). In the seventh grade, students were less satisfied with school, were less committed to school, and liked their teachers less. This drop in school satisfaction occurred regardless of how academically competent the students were.

Might the transition to middle schools be easier for students than the transition to junior high school? It is hard to say. It does guarantee that more girls will experience pubertal change when they are in the large, impersonal context of the middle school. It also will not reduce the number of times adolescents are bottom dogs. And, with the 5-6-7 pattern (another arrangement of middle schools that is being used) boys may be subjected to more stress than in the past because their pubertal change coincides with school change (Entwistle, 1988). The old two-tier system (K–8, 9–12) probably was the best for keeping school transition stress at a minimum because it reduces the number of transitions and because the main transition takes place after many adolescents are already well into puberty.

What kind of experiences might ease the transition from elementary school to middle or junior high school? Schools that provide more support, less anonymity, more stability, and less complexity improve student adjustment during the transition from elementary school to middle or junior high school. For example, in one investigation, 101 students were studied at three points in time: spring of the sixth grade (pretransition), fall of the seventh grade (early transition), and spring of the seventh grade (late transition). Two different schools were sampled, one a traditional junior high school, the other a junior high in which the students were grouped into small teams (100 students, four teachers). The students' adjustment was assessed through self-reports, peer ratings, and teacher ratings. Adjustment dropped during the posttransition. For example, the self-esteem of students was lower in the seventh grade than in the sixth grade. More teacher support was reported by

The Contexts of Adolescent Development

students in the team oriented junior high school, and the nature of friendship also was related to the students' adjustment. Students with greater friendship contact and higher quality of friendship had a more positive perception of themselves and of their junior high school. These data indicate that a supportive, more intimate school environment and friendship can ease the students' stressful school transitions.

What makes a successful middle school? Joan Lipsitz and her colleagues (1984) searched the nation for the best middle schools. Extensive contacts and observations were made. Based on the recommendations of education experts and observations in schools in different parts of the United States, four middle schools were chosen for their outstanding ability to educate young adolescents. What were these middle schools like? The most striking feature was their willingness and ability to adapt all school practices to the individual differences in physical, cognitive, and social development of their students. The schools took seriously the knowledge we have developed about young adolescents. This seriousness was reflected in decisions about different aspects of school life. For example, one middle school fought to keep its schedule of mini-courses on Friday so that every student could be with friends and pursue personal interests. Two other middle schools expended considerable energy on a complex school organization so that small groups of students worked with small groups of teachers who could vary the tone and pace of the school day, depending on students' needs. Another middle school developed an advisory scheme so that each student had daily contact with an adult who was willing to listen, explain, comfort, and prod the adolescent. Such school policies reflect thoughtfulness and personal concern about individuals whose developmental needs are compelling. Another aspect observed was that early in their existence—the first year in three of the schools and the second year in the fourth school—these effective middle schools emphasized the importance of creating an environment that was positive for the adolescent's social and emotional development. This goal was established not only because such environments contribute to academic excellence but also because social and emotional development are intrinsically valued as important in themselves in adolescents' schooling.

Recognizing that the vast majority of middle schools do not approach the excellent schools described by Joan Lipsitz (1984), in 1989 the Carnegie Corporation issued an extremely negative evaluation of our nation's middle schools. In the report, "Turning points: Preparing American youth for the 21st century," the conclusion was reached that most young adolescents attend massive, impersonal schools, learn from seemingly irrelevant curricula, trust few adults in school, and lack access to health care and counseling. The Carnegie report recommends:

- Divide large schools into units of 200–500 students so adolescents can get to know each other and their teachers better.
- Give teachers and administrators more creative power and hire teachers who specialize in working with young adolescents.

- Involve parents and community leaders in middle schools.
- Teach a core academic program aimed at producing students who are literate, understand the sciences, and have a sense of health, ethics, and citizenship.
- Boost students' health and fitness with more in-school programs and help students who need public health care to get it.

In sum, middle schools need a major redesign if they are to be effective in educating young adolescents for becoming competent adults in the 21st century.

Transition from High School to College

Just as the transition from elementary school to middle or junior high school involves change and possible stress, so does the transition from high school to college. In many instances, there are parallel changes in the two transitions. Going from a senior in high school to a freshman in college replays the top-dog phenomenon of going from the oldest and most powerful group of students to the youngest and least powerful group of students that occurred earlier at the beginning of adolescence. For many of you, the transition from high school to college was not too long ago. You may vividly remember the feeling of your first days, weeks, and months on campus. You were called a freshman. Dictionary definitions of *freshmen* describe them not only as being in the first year of high school or college but as novices or beginners. *Senior* not only designates the fourth year of high school or college, but also above others in decision-making power. The transition from high school to college involves moving to a larger, more impersonal school structure, interaction with peers from more diverse geographical and sometimes more diverse ethnic backgrounds, and increased focus on achievement and performance, and their assessment (Belle & Paul, 1989; Upcraft & Gardner, 1989).

But as with the transition from elementary school to middle or junior high school, the transition from high school to college can involve positive features. Students are more likely to feel grown up, have more subjects from which to select, have more time to spend with peers, have more opportunities to explore different life-styles and values, enjoy greater independence from parental monitoring, and may be more challenged intellectually by academic work.

For many individuals, a major change from high school to college is reduced contact with parents. One investigation revealed that going away to college may not only benefit the individual's independence but also improve relationships with parents (Sullivan & Sullivan, 1980). Two groups of parents and their sons were studied. One group of sons left home to board at college, the other group remained home and commuted daily to college. The individuals were evaluated both before they had completed high school and after they were in college. Those who boarded at college were more affectionate toward

their parents, communicated better with them, and were more independent from them than their counterparts who remained at home and attended college.

For the large number of individuals who go directly to college after completing high school, there is a delayed formal entry into the adult world of work. You may remember from Chapter 1 our description of *youth,* a post-high-school age period involving a sense of economic and personal "temporariness" (Kenniston, 1970). For many individuals, going to college postpones career or marriage/family decisions. The major shift to college attendance occurred in the post-World-War-II years, as the GI Bill opened up a college education for many individuals. Since the 1960s, a steady increase in college attendance has occurred.

Students often go to college expecting something special. As one high school student said, "My main concern is that without a college education, I won't have much chance in today's world. I want a better life, which to me, means going to college." While high school students usually approach college with high expectations, their transition from high school to college may be less than ideal. The Carnegie Foundation for the Advancement of Teaching recently completed a study of undergraduate education in the United States (Boyer, 1986). One of the most disturbing findings is the discontinuity between public high schools and institutions of higher learning. Almost half of the prospective college students surveyed said that trying to select a college is confusing because there is no sound basis for making a decision. Many high school seniors choose a college almost blindfolded. Once enrolled, they may not be satisfied with their choice, and may transfer or drop out, sometimes for

TABLE 8.1	Evaluation of Major Sources of College Information by College-Bound High School Seniors and Their Parents (% Agreeing)			
			Students %	Parents %
College representatives at "College Nights"	Relevant		62	65
	Accurate		73	68
High school counselors	Relevant		57	49
	Accurate		70	62
Comparative guides	Relevant		53	50
	Accurate		65	59
College publications	Relevant		32	34
	Accurate		59	49

From the Carnegie Foundation for the Advancement of Teaching, *Survey of the Transition from High School to College, 1984–85.* Reprinted by permission.

the wrong reasons. The transition from high school to college needs to become smoother. As a first step, public schools should take far more responsibility for assisting students in the transition from high school to college. Public high schools could learn considerably from the best private schools, which have always taken this transition seriously, according to the Commission's report. Colleges also need to provide more helpful guidance to prospective students, going beyond glossy brochures and becoming more personalized in their interaction with high school students (Fidler & Hunter, 1989; Gordon, 1989). As an indication of the need for better information about college, Table 8.1 suggests that college representatives, high school counselors, comparative guides, and college publications have a long way to go.

Today's college freshmen appear to be experiencing more stress and depression than in the past, according to a UCLA survey of more than 300,000 freshman at more than 500 colleges and universities (Astin, Green, & Korn, 1989). In 1987, 8.7% of the freshmen reported feeling depressed often; in 1988, the figure rose to 10.5%. Fear of failing in a success-oriented world is frequently given as a reason for stress and depression among college students. The pressure to succeed in college, get an outstanding job, and make lots of money is pervasive, according to many of the students.

High School Dropouts and Noncollege Youth

Dropping out of high school has been viewed as a serious educational and societal problem for many decades. By leaving high school before graduating, many dropouts have educational deficiencies that severely curtail their economic and social well-being throughout their adult lives (Rumberger, 1987). We will study the scope of the problem, the causes of dropping out, and ways to reduce dropout rates.

The Contexts of Adolescent Development

TABLE 8.2   *Dropout Rates by Age, Sex, Race, and Ethnicity: Selected Years, 1968–1984 (percentages)*

Cohort	1968	1978	1980	1982	1984
3 to 34-year-olds	18.3	12.9	12.7	12.7	12.6
White males	17.1	12.2	12.2	12.4	12.5
White females	17.3	12.4	11.9	11.9	11.7
Black males	25.8	17.2	16.5	16.7	15.7
Black females	25.6	16.2	16.2	14.9	15.0
Hispanic males	—	28.1	28.3	26.9	27.0
Hispanic females	—	29.0	27.3	27.3	26.7
18 to 19-year-olds	15.7	16.7	15.7	16.7	15.2
White males	14.3	16.3	16.1	16.6	15.8
White females	14.6	15.0	13.8	14.9	14.0
Black males	23.8	25.8	22.7	26.4	19.7
Black females	24.7	22.8	19.8	18.1	14.5
Hispanic males	—	36.6	43.1	34.9	26.2
Hispanic females	—	39.6	34.6	31.1	26.0
16 to 17-year-olds	7.8	8.8	8.8	7.3	6.8
White males	6.9	9.6	9.3	7.3	7.3
White females	7.6	8.7	9.2	8.0	6.9
Black males	10.1	5.2	7.2	6.4	5.5
Black females	14.2	9.4	6.6	5.5	4.9
Hispanic males	—	15.6	18.1	12.2	13.6
Hispanic females	—	12.2	15.0	15.9	12.7

Note: Dropout rates represent the percent of each cohort who are dropouts. Dropouts are defined as persons of a given cohort who are not enrolled in school in October of the year in question and have not received a high school diploma or an equivalent high school certificate. Source: U.S. Department of the Census. School Enrollment, Current Population Reports, Series P-20, various issues (Washington, D.C.: U.S. Government Printing Office, various years).

Despite the overall decline in high school drop out rates, the school drop out rate remains high in many low income inner city areas.

High School Dropout Rates

While dropping out of high school often has negative consequences for youth, the picture is not entirely bleak (Grant Foundation Commission, 1988). Over the last 40 years, the proportion of adolescents who have not finished high school has decreased considerably. In 1940, more than 60% of all individuals 25–29 years of age had not completed high school. By 1986, this proportion had dropped to less than 14%.

Despite the decline in overall high school dropout rates, a major concern remains the higher dropout rate of minority group and low-income students, especially in large cities (Gibbs & Huang, 1989). While the dropout rates of most minority group students have been declining too, they still remain substantially above those of white students (see Table 8.2 for data on dropout rates for different ages from 1968 to 1984). Note in Table 8.2 that Hispanic dropout rates are the highest and have declined little if at all. Note also that the dropout rate for black students has improved considerably, although overall it still is above that of white students. Dropout rates also are high for native

Americans (fewer than 10% graduate from high school) and certain Hispanic subgroups, especially Cubans and Mexican Americans (LaFromboise, 1989; Ramirez, 1989). The dropout problem is acute for low-income minority group students in large cities, such as Newark, Atlanta, and San Antonio, where minority group students make up more than 90% of the student population. In Chicago, the dropout rate recently was computed to be 50.7% (Hahn, 1987).

Other concerns about problems for high school dropouts focus on increased academic demands by schools and increased educational requirements for jobs. Many states have recently passed legislation to raise academic standards in schools, which can benefit some students, but for those whose commitment to school is weak, the more rigorous requirements could push the dropout rate higher. Also, the increase of new technologies and structural changes in jobs mean that more educational skills will be needed to get these jobs (Levin & Rumberger, in press).

The Causes of Dropping Out

Students drop out of school for many different reasons. In one investigation, almost 50% of the dropouts cited school-related reasons for leaving school, such as not liking school or being expelled or suspended (Rumberger, 1983) (see Table 8.3). Twenty percent of the dropouts (but 40% of the Hispanic students) cited economic reasons for leaving school. One-third of female students dropped out for personal reasons, such as pregnancy or marriage. Other factors associated with dropping out of school include the demographic factors cited earlier, family-related, peer-related, school-related, economic, and individual factors. As we indicated, ethnic and minority group students are more likely to drop out of school than white, Anglo students. Males also are more likely to drop out than females. The factor in family background that is related most strongly to dropping out of school is socioeconomic status—students from low-income families are much more likely to drop out than those from more socioeconomically advantaged families. Peers have not been given much attention in dropout rates, but many dropouts have friends who also are dropouts. School-related factors—poor grades, inferior test scores, and grade retention—are associated with dropping out, as are behavior problems such as truancy and discipline difficulties (Wehlage & Rutter, 1986). Economic factors also affect a student's decision to quit school. In the investigation by Russell Rumberger (1983), about 20% left school because they wanted to or felt they had to work to support their families. And there are many individual factors associated with dropping out. Dropouts have lower self-esteem and less sense of control over their lives than nondropouts. They have poor attitudes toward school and low educational and occupational aspirations. A number of dropouts also leave school to become married or because they are pregnant. As can be seen, a comprehensive model of dropouts needs to address the fact that there are different types of dropouts who leave school for different reasons.

TABLE 8.3 *Primary Reason High School Dropouts Left School, by Sex, Race, and Ethnicity: 1979 (percentage distribution)*

Reason	Males			Females			Total
	White	Black	Hispanic	White	Black	Hispanic	
School-related:							
Poor performance	9	9	4	5	5	4	7
Disliked school	36	29	26	27	18	15	29
Expelled or suspended	9	18	6	2	5	1	7
School too dangerous	1	0	0	2	1	1	1
Economic:							
Desired to work	15	12	16	5	4	7	10
Financial difficulties	3	7	9	3	3	9	4
Home responsibilities	4	4	13	6	8	8	6
Personal:							
Pregnancy	0	0	0	14	41	15	17
Marriage	3	0	3	17	4	15	9
Other	20	21	23	19	11	25	19
TOTAL	100	100	100	100	100	100	100

Note: Data are for persons 14 to 21 years of age.
Source: Rumberger, R. W., "Dropping Out of High School: The Influence of Race, Sex and Family Background." *American Educational Research Journal,* 1983, page 201. Copyright © 1983, American Educational Research Association, Washington, D.C.

Reducing the Dropout Rate and Improving the Lives of Noncollege Youth

In a recent report, *The Forgotten Half: Non-College-Bound Youth in America,* the William T. Grant Foundation Commission on Work, Family, and Citizenship (1988) recommended that reducing the dropout rate and improving the lives of noncollege youth could be accomplished by strengthening schools and bridging the gap between school and work.

Part of the solution lies within schools. Students may work hard through 12 grades of school, attain adequate records, learn basic academic skills, graduate in good standing, and still experience problems in getting started in a productive career. Others may drop out of school because they see little benefit from the type of education they are getting. Although no complete cure-all, strengthening schools is an important dimension of reducing dropout rates. While the education reform movements of the 1980s have encouraged schools to set higher standards for students and teachers, most of the focus has been on college-bound students. But reform movements should not penalize students who will not go to college. One way noncollege-bound youth are being helped is through Chapter 1 of the Education Consolidation and Improvement Act, which provides extra services for low-achieving students. States and communities need to establish clear goals for school completion, youth employment, parental involvement, and youth community service. For example, it should be the goal of every state to reduce the dropout rate to 10% or less by the year 2000.

Community institutions need to break down the barriers between work and school. The adolescent girl shown here is involved in a monitored work experience with an advertising agency. What are other ways community institutions can improve the transition between school and work?

Community institutions, especially schools, need to break down the barriers between work and school. Many youth step off the education ladder long before reaching the level of a professional career, often with nowhere to step next, left to their own devices to search for work. These youth need more assistance than they are now receiving. Among the approaches worth considering are the following:

Monitored work experiences, such as through cooperative education, apprenticeships, internships, pre-employment training, and youth-operated enterprises.

Community and neighborhood services, including voluntary service and youth-guided services.

Redirected vocational education, the principal thrust of which should not be preparation for specific jobs but acquisition of basic skills needed in a wide range of work.

Guarantees of continuing education, employment, or training, especially in conjunction with mentoring programs.

Attacking the High School Dropout Problem

Among the programs currently being implemented to reduce high school dropout rates are summer work enhancement, remedial summer education, an adopt-a-student project, and a cooperative learning venture.

One innovative dropout-prevention program is a joint effort of several New York City agencies and the New York Private Industry Council (Fox, 1988). Inaugurated in the summer of 1986 with 100 students initially, this program includes part-time employment during the school year and two summers, academic and personal counseling, daily remedial reading, writing, and math instruction, and a life-skills course. Computer-assisted instruction also is used, allowing students to begin at any level and learn at their own pace. Students have made impressive strides in improving their academic skills.

In another investigation, low-income high school students who attended remedial education classes while working part-time in summer jobs scored more than half a grade higher on math and reading tests at the end of the summer than a comparison group who worked full-time (Bailen, 1988). Seven-hundred-fifty students aged 14–16 took part in the program in five cities, with funding provided jointly by the federal government and private foundations.

Yet another investigation is designed to keep students in school until they graduate and to help them avoid subsequent unemployment (Anson, 1988). This adopt-a-student program paired 200 underachieving juniors and seniors with mentors from the business community, who helped students plan their futures and counseled them about achieving goals. The participating students were much more likely to be employed or to be continuing their education than similar students who did not take part.

In a final program, the impact of cooperative learning (in which students learn in small groups and the entire group is rated) and of skills training in conflict resolution is being evaluated (Deutsch, 1988). The subjects are inner-city students who dropped out of school and have since enrolled in an alternative high school. Four groups are being given different learning experiences and then compared on the basis of academic achievement, mental health, and social relations. The first group is experiencing cooperative learning, the second is being taught traditionally but is being given conflict resolution training, the third group is experiencing cooperative learning and conflict resolution training, and the fourth group is being taught traditionally. While there are many other programs being implemented to reduce high school dropout rates, these four are an indication of the variety of programs now being evaluated.   ❦

Career information and counseling to expose youth to job
    opportunities and career options as well as to successful role
    models.
School volunteer programs, not only for tutoring but to provide access
    to adult friends and mentors.

Perspective on Adolescent Development 8.2 discusses a number of programs that are currently being implemented to attack the dropout problem.

At this point we have discussed many ideas about the nature of adolescents' schooling and transitions in adolescents' schooling. A summary of these ideas is presented in Concept Table 8.1

The Nature of Schooling and Transitions in Schooling

Concept	Processes/Related Ideas	Characteristics/Description
The nature of adolescents' schooling	Function of schools	In the nineteenth century, secondary schools were for the elite. By the 1920s, they had changed, becoming more comprehensive and training adolescents for work and citizenship as well as intellect. The comprehensive high school remains today, but the function of secondary schools continues to be debated. Some maintain that the function should be intellectual development; others argue for more comprehensive functions.
	Do schools make a difference?	Some sociologists have argued that schools have little impact on adolescents' development. But when researchers have conducted more precise, observational studies of what goes on in schools and classrooms, the effects of schooling become more apparent.
	Schools' changing social developmental contexts	The social context differs at the preschool, elementary, and secondary level, becoming much more expansive for adolescents.
Transitions in schooling	Transition to middle or junior high school	The emergence of junior highs in the 1920s and 1930s was justified on the basis of physical, cognitive, and social changes in early adolescence and the need for more schools in response to a growing student population. Middle schools have become more popular in recent years, and coincide with puberty's earlier arrival. The transition to middle or junior high school coincides with many social, familial, and individual changes in the adolescent's life. The transition involves moving from the top-dog to the bottom-dog position. Successful schools for young adolescents take individual differences in development seriously, show a deep concern for what is known about early adolescence, and emphasize social and emotional development as much as intellectual development. In 1989, the Carnegie Corporation recommended a major redesign of middle schools.
	Transition from high school to college	There are a number of parallels to the transition from elementary to middle or junior high school, including the top-dog phenomenon. An especially important transition for most adolescents is reduced interaction with parents. A special problem today is the discontinuity between public high schools and colleges.
	High school dropouts and noncollege youth	Dropping out has been a serious problem for decades. Many dropouts have educational deficiencies that curtail their economic and social well-being for much of their adult life. Some progress has been made in that dropout rates for most ethnic minority groups have declined in recent decades, although dropout rates for inner city, low-income minorities are still precariously high. Dropping out of school is associated with demographic, family-related, peer-related, school-related, economic, and individual factors. Reducing the dropout rate and improving the lives of noncollege youth could be accomplished by strengthening schools and bridging the gap between school and work.

Schools and Classrooms, Teachers and Peers

Schools and classrooms vary in many dimensions. Among the dimensions that have interested researchers are school size and class size. Classrooms also vary in atmosphere, with some schools being highly structured, others more unstructured. Adolescents' lives in school also involve thousands of hours of interaction with teachers and peers. How do these aspects of schools influence adolescents' development?

School Size and Classroom Size

A number of factors led to the increased size of secondary schools in the United States: increasing urban enrollments, decreasing budgets, and an educational rationale of increased academic stimulation in consolidated institutions (Conant, 1959; Minuchin & Shapiro, 1983). But is bigger really better? No systematic relation between school size and academic achievement has been found, but more prosocial and possibly less antisocial behavior take place in small schools (Rutter & others, 1979). Five hundred has been suggested as an optimal threshold, though experts have set the optimal limit at different points under 1000 students (Garbarino, 1980). Large schools may not provide a personalized climate that allows for an effective system of social control. Students may feel alienated and not take responsibility for their conduct. This may be especially true for unsuccessful students who do not identify with their school and who become members of oppositional peer groups. The responsiveness of the school may mediate the impact of school size on adolescent behavior. For example, in one investigation, low responsive schools (i.e., few rewards for desirable behavior) had higher crime rates than high responsive schools (McPartland & McDill, 1976). While school responsiveness may mediate adolescent conduct, small schools may be more flexible and responsive than larger schools.

Besides the belief that smaller schools provide adolescents with a better education, there also is a belief that smaller classes are better than larger classes. Traditional schools in the United States have about 30–35 students. Analysis of a large number of investigations revealed that as class size increases, achievement decreases (Glass & Smith, 1978). The researchers concluded that a pupil who would score at about the 63rd percentile on a national test when taught individually would score at about the 37th percentile when taught in a class of 40 students. They also concluded that being taught in a class of 20 students versus a class of 40 students is an advantage of about 10 percentile points on national achievement tests in the subject. These researchers also found that the greatest gains in achievement occurred among students who were taught in classes of 15 students or less. In classes of 20–40 students, class size had a less dramatic influence on students' achievement. Although this research has been criticized on methodological grounds, other researchers have reanalyzed the data using different techniques and arrived at the same conclusions (Hedges & Stock, 1983).

Unfortunately, to maximize each adolescent's learning potential, classes must be so small that few schools can afford to staff and house them (Klein, 1985; Slavin, 1989). While class sizes of 15 students or less are not feasible for all subjects, one alternative is to allocate a larger portion of resources to those grade levels or subjects that seem the most critical. For example, some schools are beginning to reduce class size in core academic subjects such as math, English, and science, while having higher class sizes in elective subjects.

Classroom Structure and Climate

The most widely debated aspect of classroom structure and climate in recent years has focused on open versus traditional classrooms. The **open versus traditional classroom** concept is multidimensional. Open classrooms, or open schools, have such characteristics as

free choice by students of activities they will participate in
space flexibility
varied, enriched learning materials
emphasis on individual and small group instruction
the teacher is more a facilitator than a director of learning
students learn to assume responsibility for their learning
multi-age grouping of children
team teaching
classrooms without walls in which the physical nature of the school is more open

Overall, researchers have found that open classrooms are associated with lower language achievement but improved attitudes toward school (Giaconia & Hedges, 1982).

Beyond the overall effects of open versus traditional classrooms, it is important to evaluate how specific dimensions of open classrooms are related to specific dimensions of the adolescent's development. In this regard, researchers have found that individualized instruction (adjusting rate, methods, materials, small group methods) and role of the adolescent (the degree of activity in learning) are associated with positive effects on the adolescent's self-concept (Giaconia & Hedges, 1982).

Characteristics of the adolescent also need to be considered when evaluating the effects of classroom structure and climate. Some adolescents benefit more from structure than others. The importance of both adolescents' characteristics and the treatments or experiences they encounter in classrooms are both represented in the concept of **aptitude-treatment interaction (ATI)**. Aptitude refers to academic potential and personality dimensions on which students differ. Treatment refers to educational techniques—structured versus flexible classrooms, for example (Cronbach & Snow, 1977). Researchers have

found that adolescents' achievement level (aptitude) interacts with classroom structure (treatment) to produce the best learning and most enjoyable learning environment (Peterson, 1977). That is, high-achievement-oriented students usually do well in a flexible classroom and enjoy it; low-achievement-oriented students usually fare worse and dislike the flexibility. The reverse often appears in structured classrooms.

Teachers

Virtually everyone's life is affected in one way or another by teachers. You probably were influenced by teachers as you grew up. One day you may have, or already have, children and adolescents whose lives will be guided by many different teachers. You likely can remember several of your teachers vividly. Perhaps one never smiled, another required you to memorize everything in sight, and yet another always appeared vibrant and encouraged question asking.

Psychologists and educators have tried to compile a profile of a good teacher's personality traits, but the complexity of personality, education, learning, and individuals make this a difficult task. Nonetheless, some teacher traits are associated with positive student outcomes more than others—enthusiasm, ability to plan, poise, adaptability, warmth, flexibility, and awareness of individual differences, for example (Gage, 1965).

Erik Erikson (1968) believes that good teachers should be able to produce a sense of industry, rather than inferiority, in their students. Good teachers are trusted and respected by the community and know how to alternate work and play, study and games, says Erikson. They know how to recognize special efforts and to encourage special abilities. They also know how to create a setting in which adolescents feel good about themselves and know how to handle those adolescents to whom school is not important. In Erikson's (1968) own words, adolescents should be "mildly but firmly coerced into the adventure of finding out that one can learn to accomplish things which one would never have thought of by oneself."

Other recommendations for successful teaching with young adolescents have been offered by Stephanie Feeney (1980). She believes that meaningful learning takes place when the developmental characteristics of the age group are understood, when trust has been established, and when adolescents feel free to explore, to experiment, and to make mistakes. The variability and change that characterizes young adolescents make them a difficult age group to instruct. The student who leans on the teacher one day for help may be strutting around independently the next day. Teachers who work successfully with young adolescents probably have vivid memories of their own adolescence and likely have mastered the developmental tasks of those years. Able to recall their youthful vulnerability, they understand and respect their students' sensitivity to criticism, desire for group acceptance, and feeling of being acutely conspicuous. Successful teachers of adolescents are secure in their own identity

The Contexts of Adolescent Development

and comfortable with their sexuality. Possessing clear values, they use power and authority wisely and are sensitive to their students' feelings. Young adolescents respond best to teachers who exercise natural authority—based on greater age, experience, and wisdom—rather than arbitrary authority or abdication of authority by being pals with the adolescent. Young adolescents need teachers who are fair and consistent, who set reasonable limits, and who realize that adolescents need someone to push against while testing those limits.

Peers

The peer group is an important source of status, friendship, and belonging in the school setting. The peer group also is a learning community in which social roles and standards related to work and achievement are formed. At school, adolescents are with each other for at least six hours per day. The school also provides the locus for many of the adolescent's activities after school and on weekends.

A classic investigation of the association patterns of students was conducted by James Coleman (1961). He found that social structures vary from school to school. In some schools, the association patterns of students are very intense, while in others they are more casual. In small schools, more students are members of various cliques than in large schools, where simple pair relationships occur more frequently. There are even differences in group structures among the large schools. In one suburban school that Coleman studied, the social structure was far more complete and fully developed than in another. Probably because of greater community solidarity, middle-class status, and greater parental interest in the schooling process, many more community functions were carried out in and after school in the first school. Clustering social activities around a school helps to strengthen the social system of the students.

Coleman (1961) analyzed the peer associations of boys and girls separately in small schools. Boys achieved status within their schools in a variety of ways. In some schools, the "all-around boy"—athlete, ladies' man, and to some extent, scholar—achieved status, while in other schools, being either an athlete or a scholar was enough to assure high status.

There was considerable variation in the association patterns of the girls in small schools as well. Elmtown had the largest number of girl cliques, the largest percentage of girls in cliques, and the smallest average clique size. Marketville was the opposite in each of these respects. In Marketville and Maple Grove, middle-class girls from well-educated families formed cliques that dominated social activities, school activities, and adolescent attention. Teachers perceived these cliques as being in control of the student body and as the girls most encouraged by the adults in the community.

Athletic achievement played an important role in the status systems of boys in all ten schools Coleman (1961) studied. Why are athletics so important in the status systems of American high schools? Adolescents identify

strongly with their schools and communities. The identification, in part at least, is due to the fact that the school and the community of adolescents are virtually synonymous. They compete as a school against other schools in athletic contests. So the heroes of the system, those with high status, are the boys who win for the school and the community of adolescents. When they win, the entire school and the entire community of adolescents feel better about themselves.

Because boys have had greater opportunity to participate in interscholastic athletics than girls have, they have been more likely to attain high-status positions in schools. However, in the 1970s the federal government took a big step toward reducing this form of discrimination against female adolescents. Title IX of the 1972 Educational Amendments Act prohibits any educational program from receiving federal funds if sex discrimination is practiced. So far this act has not produced parity for girls and boys in interscholastic athletics, but girls have made greater strides than ever before in participating in interscholastic events.

While research on male athletic participation has produced consistent findings of its high status in schools, research on female athletic participation has produced mixed findings. In one recent investigation, the type of sport females participated in was studied to determine its relation to status in the school (Kane, 1988). One hundred and twenty-one male students were asked to indicate which female athlete they would like to date—one identified with gender-inappropriate sports (such as basketball) or one identified with gender-appropriate sports (like tennis). As predicted, females associated with gender-appropriate sports were accorded more status than females associated with gender-inappropriate sports.

Since the passage of Title IX, female enrollments in previously male-dominated fields such as engineering, law, and business have more than doubled, and reams have been written about sexism in the language, policies, and practices of education. More about gender roles in schools appears later in Chapter 11 (gender roles).

Social Class and Ethnicity in Schools

Sometimes it seems as though the major function of schools has been to train adolescents to contribute to a middle-class society. Politicians who vote on school funding have been from middle-class or elite backgrounds, school board members have often been from middle-class backgrounds, and principals and teachers also have had middle-class upbringing. Critics argue that schools have not done a good job of educating lower-class and ethnic minority children to overcome the barriers that block the enhancement of their position (Holt, 1964; Silberman, 1970).

Social Class

In *Dark Ghetto,* Kenneth Clark (1965) described the ways lower- and middle-class adolescents are treated differently in school. According to Clark's observations, teachers in middle-class schools spend more time teaching students and evaluate students' work more than twice as much as teachers in low-income schools. He observed that teachers in low-income schools made three times as many negative comments to students as teachers did in middle-class schools, who made more positive than negative comments to students. The following observations vividly describe a school in a large urban slum area:

> It is 2 P.M., beginning of the sixth-period class, and Warren Benson, a young teacher, looks around the room. Eight students are present out of thirty. "Where is everybody?" he demands. "They don't like your class," a girl volunteers. Three girls saunter in. Cora, who is playing a cassette recorder, bumps over to her desk in time with the music. She lowers the volume. "Don't mark us down late," she shouts. "We was right here, you mother f———."
> . . . Here you find students from poverty homes, students who can't read, students with drug problems, students wanting to drop out . . .

What are the educational and job aspirations of adolescents from low-income families? Their educational and job *aspirations* are just as high as their counterparts from middle-class families. However, their *expectations* of the educational and career plateaus they will reach are below those of middle-class adolescents (Gribbons & Lohnes, 1964). That is, they want to reach high levels of success, but they do not think they will. However, parents in low-income families can have a significant effect on their adolescents' aspirations. In one investigation, high school boys from low-income families whose parents encouraged them to advance to higher educational and occupational levels did so (Kandel & Lesser, 1969).

Teachers have lower expectations for adolescents from low-income families than for adolescents from middle-class families. A teacher who knows that an adolescent comes from a low-income family may spend less time trying to help the adolescent solve a problem and may anticipate that the adolescent will get into trouble. Teachers may perceive that low-income parents are not

What are the many adjustments involved in the transitions from elementary to middle or junior high school?

interested in helping the adolescent, so they may make fewer efforts to communicate with them. There is evidence that teachers with lower-class origins have different attitudes toward low-income students than teachers with middle-class origins (Gottlieb, 1966). Perhaps because they have experienced inequities themselves, teachers with low-income origins may be more empathetic to the difficulties faced by adolescents from low-income families. When asked to rate the most outstanding characteristics of their lower-class students, middle-class teachers checked lazy, rebellious, and fun-loving. Lower-class teachers checked happy, cooperative, energetic, and ambitious. Teachers from low-income backgrounds perceived the lower-class students' behavior as adaptive; the middle-class teachers viewed the same behaviors as falling short of middle-class standards.

Ethnicity

Martin Luther King once said, "I have a dream that my four little children will one day live in a nation where they will not be judged by the color of their skin but the content of their character." Not only have adolescents from low-income backgrounds had difficulty in schools, so have adolescents from different ethnic minority backgrounds. In most American schools, blacks, Mexican Americans, Puerto Ricans, native Americans, Japanese, and Asian Indians

The Contexts of Adolescent Development

THE CULTURAL WORLDS OF ADOLESCENTS 8.3

A Black Student's View of Public Schools

"Black and Hispanic students have less chance of building strong relationships with teachers because their appearance and behavior may be considered offensive to middle-class white teachers. These students show signs of what white teachers, and some teachers of color, consider disrespect, and they do not get the nurturing relationships that develop respect and dedication. They are considered less intelligent, as can be seen in the proportion of Blacks and Hispanics in lower-level as opposed to upper-level classes. There is less of a teacher-student contact with 'underachievers,' because they are guided into peer tutoring programs. . . . The sad part of the situation is that many students believe that this type of teaching is what academic learning is all about. They have not had the opportunity to experience alternative ways of teaching and learning. From my experience in public school, it appears that many minority students will never be recognized as capable of analytical and critical thinking."

Imani Perry, 15-year-old black student

(*Source:* Perry, 1988)

are minorities. Many teachers have been ignorant of the different cultural meanings non-Anglo adolescents have learned in their communities (Huang & Gibbs, 1989). The social and academic development of minority group students depend on teacher expectations, the teacher's experience in working with adolescents from different backgrounds, the curriculum, the presence of role models in schools for minority students, the quality of relations between school personnel and parents from different ethnic, economic, and educational backgrounds, and the relations between the school and the community (Minuchin & Shapiro, 1983).

Do teachers have lower academic expectations for minority group adolescents? The evidence indicates that teachers look for and reward achievement-oriented behavior in white students more often than in black students (Scott-Jones & Clark, 1986). When teachers praise black students for their academic performance, the praise is often qualified: "This is a good paper. It is better than yesterday's." Also teachers have been found to criticize gifted black students more than gifted white students, possibly because they do not expect intellectual competence in black students (Baron, Tom, & Cooper, 1985).

One of the largest efforts to study ethnicity in schools has focused on desegregation through busing (Bell, 1980). Desegregation attempts to improve the proportions of minority group and white student populations in schools. Efforts to improve this ratio have often involved busing students, usually minority group students, from their home neighborhood to more distant schools. The underlying belief is that bringing different groups together will reduce stereotyped attitudes and improve intergroup relations. But busing tells us nothing about what goes on inside the school once students get there. Minority group adolescents bused to a predominantly white school are often resegregated in the classroom through seating patterns, ability grouping, and tracking systems. Overall, the findings pertaining to desegregation through busing have shown dismal results (Minuchin & Shapiro, 1983).

Improvements in interracial relations among adolescents in schools depend on what happens after students arrive at the school. In one comprehensive national investigation of factors that contribute to positive interracial relations, more than 5,000 5th-grade students and more than 400 10th-grade students were evaluated (Forehand, Ragosta, & Rock, 1976). Multiethnic curricula, projects focused on racial issues, mixed work groups, and supportive teachers and principals led to improved interracial relations.

When the schools of Austin, Texas, were desegregated through extensive busing, the outcome was increased racial tension among blacks, Mexican Americans, and Anglos, producing violence in the schools. The superintendent consulted with Eliot Aronson, a prominent social psychologist, who was a professor at the University of Texas at Austin at the time. Aronson thought it was more important to prevent racial tension than to control it. This led him to observe a number of school classrooms in Austin. What he saw was fierce competition between individuals of unequal status.

Aronson stressed that the reward structure of the classrooms needed to be changed from a setting of unequal competition to one of cooperation among equals, without making any curriculum changes. To accomplish this, he put together the concept of the **jigsaw classroom.** How does this work? Consider a class of 30 students, some Anglo, some black, some Hispanic. The lesson to be learned focuses on Joseph Pulitzer's life. The class might be broken up into five groups of six students each, with the groups being as equal as possible in ethnic composition and academic achievement level. The lesson about Pulitzer's life could be divided into six parts, with one part given to each member of the six-person group. The parts might be paragraphs from Pulitzer's biography, such as how the Pulitzer family came to the United States, his childhood, his early work, and so on. The components are like the parts of a jigsaw puzzle. They have to be put together to form the complete puzzle.

Each student in the group is given an allotted time to study. Then the group meets and each member tries to teach a part to the group. After an hour or so each member is tested on the entire life of Pulitzer, with each member receiving an individual rather than a group score. Each student, therefore, must learn the entire lesson. Learning depends on the cooperation and effort of other members. Aronson (1986) believes this type of learning increases students' interdependence through cooperatively reaching a common goal.

The Contexts of Adolescent Development

The strategy of emphasizing cooperation rather than competition has become a widespread practice in recent years in American education. Earlier in this chapter we mentioned the ongoing evaluation of cooperative learning with dropouts being conducted by Martin Deutsch (1988). A number of research studies reveal that cooperative learning is associated with increased self-esteem, better academic performance, friendships among classmates, and improved interethnic perceptions (Aronson, 1986; Slavin, 1987, 1989b).

Cooperative learning is an important addition to learning strategies, but a caveat about it is offered by esteemed social psychologist Roger Brown (1986). Academic achievement is as much, or more, an individual "sport" as a team "sport." It is individuals who graduate from high school, enter college, and take jobs, not groups. A parent with an advantaged adolescent in a cooperative learning classroom may react with increased ethnic hostility when the adolescent brings home a lower grade than is typical. The adolescent may tell his father, "The teacher is getting us to teach each other. In my group we have this kid named Carlos, who can barely speak English." While cooperative learning is an important strategy for reducing interracial hostility, caution needs to be exercised in its use because of the unequal status of the participants and achievement's individual orientation. Other ways that the educational and achievement orientation of Hispanic students can be improved are described in Perspective on Adolescent Development 8.3.

At this point we have discussed many ideas about schools and classrooms, teachers and peers, and social class and ethnicity. A summary of these ideas is presented in Concept Table 8.2.

The jigsaw classroom and cooperative learning have become popular methods of teaching. What are their strengths and weaknesses?

Schools   317

Helping Hispanic Youth Stay in School and Go to College

The Hispanic population in the United States is increasing more rapidly than any other ethnic minority. Educators are increasingly interested in helping Hispanic adolescents stay in school and succeed in the courses needed for educational and occupational success. As colleges compete to recruit seniors from the small pool of college-eligible and college-ready Hispanics, it is apparent that the pool itself needs to be greatly expanded. Gloria De Necochea (1988) recently described seven strategies to help keep Hispanic adolescents in school and get them ready to go to college:

1. Identify students early for a college preparatory curriculum. As early as the sixth grade, both students and parents need to know about the college preparatory curriculum and the long-term consequences of choices.
2. Give more attention to math and science. Mathematics and science are critical for both college admissions and a range of career options, but these subjects pose big barriers for Hispanic students. Success can be increased by teaching the complex academic language necessary to tackle these subjects effectively. This is especially important in grades 7–9, where algebra—the gatekeeping course for future scientific and technical courses—is taught.
3. Increase school participation. Counselors and teachers can make college-related information more visible throughout the school. Pre-college clubs can be developed. Administrators can invite college representatives, alumni, and individuals in different careers to address students. Critical thinking skills can be stressed. And teachers can occasionally tailor exams to be more like the structure of the SAT and ACT.
4. Expose students to the world of college. College recruiters, faculty, and financial aid officers are important role models and sources of current information. Visits to colleges enable youth to gain first-hand knowledge about campus life (Justiz & Rendon, 1989).
5. Increase workshops. Study skills, assertiveness training, and survival tips can be taught. College-related topics such as "How to choose a college" and "What to say to college admissions officers" should be offered during the senior year.
6. Involve parents. Invitations to all activities should be bilingual and mailed home well in advance of the event. Students can provide child care to increase attendance. Parents should be encouraged to come to workshops and to participate in planning activities.
7. Organize outside support. Better coordination between community organizations and schools could provide a central source for descriptions of available programs at the school and in the community.

Summary

I. Function of Schools

In the nineteenth century, secondary schools were for the elite. By the 1920s, they had changed, becoming more comprehensive and training adolescents for work and citizenship as well as training intellect. The comprehensive high school remains today, but the functions of secondary schools continue to be debated. Some maintain that the function should be intellectual development, others argue for more comprehensive functions, including social and vocational development.

II. The Difference Schools Make and Social Developmental Contexts

Some sociologists have argued that schools have little impact on adolescents' development, but when researchers have conducted more precise observational

Schools and Classrooms, Teachers and Peers, Social Class, and Ethnicity

Concept	Processes/Related Ideas	Characteristics/Description
Schools and classrooms, teachers and peers	School size and classroom size	Smaller is usually better when school size and classroom size are at issue. Recommended maximum secondary-school size ranges from 500–1000. Most class sizes are 30–35 students, but class size of 15 or less benefits student learning.
	Classroom structure and climate	The open classroom concept is multidimensional. Specific dimensions of open and traditional classrooms need to be considered, as well as specific outcomes. Overall, open classrooms are associated with lower language achievement but improved school attitudes. Individualized instruction and role of the adolescent are associated with positive self-concept. Aptitude-treatment interaction also needs to be considered.
	Teachers	Teacher characteristics involve many different dimensions, and coming up with a profile of a competent teacher of adolescents is difficult. Erikson believes that a good teacher creates a sense of industry rather than inferiority. Competent teachers of adolescents are knowledgeable about adolescent development and sensitive to adolescents' needs.
	Peers	At school, adolescents are with each other for at least six hours a day, and the school is a setting for many after-school peer gatherings and weekend activities. Athletics has played a prominent role in the status of males in secondary schools. The role of athletics for girls has yielded more mixed results.
Social class and ethnicity	Social class	Secondary schools have had a strong middle-class orientation rather than lower-class or low-income orientation. Adolescents from low-income families have high achievement aspirations, but do not expect to do as well in education or occupations as middle-class students. Teachers have lower expectations for low-income students, although teachers from lower-class backgrounds see these students' behavior as more adaptive.
	Ethnicity	Many teachers have been ignorant of the different cultural meanings non-Anglo adolescents have learned in their communities. Teachers have lower expectations for minority group adolescents. Desegregation through busing has shown virtually no benefits in reducing interracial tension. What is important to study is what goes on at school after adolescents arrive. Multiethnic curricula, supportive teachers and administrators, and cooperative learning benefit students from minority group backgrounds.

studies of what goes on in schools and classrooms, the effects of schooling become more apparent. The social context differs at the preschool, elementary school, and secondary school levels, becoming much more expansive for adolescents.

III. **Transition to Middle or Junior High School**

The emergence of junior high schools in the 1920s and 1930s was justified on the basis of physical, cognitive, and social changes in early adolescence and the need for more schools in response to growing student populations. Middle schools have become more popular in recent years, and coincide with earlier pubertal development. The transition to middle or junior high school takes place simultaneously with many social, familial, and individual changes in the adolescent's life. The transition involves moving from the top-dog to bottom-dog position. Successful schools for young adolescents take individual differences in development seriously, show a deep concern for what is known about early adolescence, and emphasize social and emotional development as much as intellectual development. In 1989, the Carnegie Corporation recommended a major redesign of middle schools.

IV. Transition from High School to College

There are a number of parallels between the high school-to-college transition and the elementary-to-middle or junior high transition, including the top-dog phenomenon. An especially important transition for most adolescents is reduced interaction with parents. A special problem today is the discontinuity between public schools and colleges.

V. High School Dropouts and Noncollege Youth

Dropping out has been a serious problem for decades. Many dropouts have educational deficiencies that curtail their economic and social well-being for much of their adult life. Some progress has been made in that dropout rates for most ethnic minority groups have declined in recent years, although dropout rates for inner city, low-income minorities remain precariously high. Dropping out of school is associated with demographic, family-related, peer-related, school-related, economic, and individual factors. Reducing the dropout rate and improving the lives of noncollege youth could be accomplished by strengthening schools and bridging the gap between school and work.

VI. Schools and Classrooms

Smaller is usually better when school size and class size are at issue. Recommended maximum secondary school size ranges from 500 to 1000. Most class sizes are 30–35 students, but a class size of 15 or fewer benefits student learning. The open classroom concept is multidimensional. Specific dimensions of open and traditional classrooms need to be considered, as well as specific outcomes. Overall, open classrooms are associated with lower language achievement but improved school attitudes. Individualized instruction and role of the adolescent are associated with positive self-concept. Aptitude-treatment interaction needs to be considered.

VII. Teachers

Teacher characteristics involve many different dimensions, and coming up with a profile of a competent teacher of adolescents is difficult. Erikson believes that a good teacher creates a sense of industry rather than inferiority. Competent teachers of adolescents are knowledgeable about adolescent development and sensitive to adolescents' needs.

VIII. Peers

At school, adolescents are with each other for at least six hours a day, and the school is a setting for many after-school and weekend peer gatherings. Athletics has played a prominent role in the status hierarchy of male adolescents, but findings for the role of athletics in the status hierarchy of females have been more mixed.

IX. Social Class

Secondary schools have had a strong middle-class bias. Adolescents from low-income families have high achievement aspirations, but do not expect to do as well in education and occupations as middle-class students. Teachers have lower expectations for low-income students, although teachers from lower-class backgrounds see these students' behavior as more adaptive.

X. Ethnicity

Many teachers have been ignorant of the different cultural meanings non-Anglo adolescents have learned in their communities. Teachers have lower expectations for minority group adolescents. Desegregation through busing has shown virtually no positive effects in reducing interracial tension. What is important to study is what happens after students arrive at school. Multiethnic curricula, supportive teachers and administrators, and cooperative learning benefit students from minority group backgrounds.

Key Terms

top-dog phenomenon 295
open versus traditional
　classroom 308

aptitude-treatment
　interaction (ATI) 308
jigsaw classroom 316

Suggested Readings

Feeney, S. (1980). *Schools for young adolescents*. Carrboro, NC: Center for Early Adolescence.
　An excellent, easy-to-read overview of what makes a good junior high school teacher.
Harvard Educational Review.
　Go to the library and leaf through the issues of the last three to four years. You'll find a number of articles that address the issues raised in this chapter.
Lipsitz, J. (1984). *Successful schools for young adolescents*. New Brunswick, NJ: Transaction Books.
　Must reading for anyone interested in better schools for young adolescents. Filled with rich examples of successful schools and the many factors that contribute to success in the education of young adolescents.
Minuchin, P. P., & Shapiro, E. K. (1983). "The school as a context for social development." In P. H. Mussen (Ed.), *Handbook of child psychology* (Vol. 4, 4th ed.). New York: Wiley.
　An authoritative, up-to-date review of the role of the school in the adolescent's development by two leading educators. Covers most of the topics in this chapter.
Phi Delta Kappan
　A leading educational journal. Leaf through the 1980s issues to get a feel for controversial, widely debated ideas in secondary education.
Review of Educational Research.
　This journal publishes reviews of educational research. By leafing through the issues of the last several years in your library, you will come across research summaries with references to many of the topics in this chapter.
The William T. Grant Foundation Commission on Work, Family and Citizenship (1988). *The forgotten half: Non-college-bound youth in America*. New York: The William T. Grant Foundation.
　This excellent report on the status of non-college-bound youth in America calls attention to ways our society can help these individuals more effectively make the school-to-work transition.

Culture

Our most basic common link is that we all inhabit this planet. We all breathe the same air. We all cherish our children's future.

John F. Kennedy, address, The American University, 1963

Mustangs and Mascara

As soon as the last bell rings at West High School, Rob rushes to the parking lot, hops into his Mustang convertible, flips the knob on the radio to a high volume, and peels out of the school lot, leaving a trail of rubber. Rob heads for MacDonald's, where he works 25 hours a week so that he can have his own spending money. He is saving to buy a tape deck for his car. Not all high school students drive their own cars, and not all of them are as materially oriented as Rob, but for many adolescents money and cars are highly desired commodities.

Money, cars, and clothes—among other material items—play important roles in the need system of many adolescents. They contribute to the adolescent's identity and self-esteem. Adolescents with their own car or motorcycle achieve a status level in the youth culture beyond that of adolescents without these material goods.

Social scientists suggest that material goods can reflect the adolescent's personality. For example, an adolescent male who dresses casually, lets his hair grow long, and buys a motorcycle probably has a different personality than an adolescent male who dresses conservatively, trims and neatly parts his hair, and drives his mother's car when it is available. The appearances of these two adolescents also are likely to elicit different expectations from their peers and from adults.

Think about your own adolescent years—about the material aspects of the culture . . . wishing for the day you could

Shopping is part of the adolescent culture. Adolescent girls spend more than $9 billion just on back-to-school clothes.

get your driver's license . . . trying to convince your parents you needed a car, or at least needed ready access to their car . . . or if all else failed, at least having a good friend who owned a car so you could cruise around and get where you wanted to go. Think about how much time you spent looking at and trying on clothes. According to *Seventeen* magazine, adolescent girls spend more than $9

billion dollars just on back-to-school clothes. In 1987, adolescents spent $34 billion dollars of their own money, an increase of $4 billion dollars from 1985 levels. Adolescent girls aged 13–15 had $31 a week in allowance and job earnings to spend in 1988 (Rand Youth Poll, 1988). In the same survey, 16–19-year-old girls had $68 a week in pocket money. Because adolescents have virtually no overhead expenses, with the possible exception of an occasional school lunch or bus fare, they spend most of their money on themselves—clothes, cosmetics, snack food, gasoline, cars, and entertainment. Some money may go into savings, but the savings usually goes toward the purchase of a large item. Today's adolescents are a consumer-oriented group, perhaps the most consumer-oriented group ever (Carton, 1988).

There are other aspects of the adolescent's culture to consider—for one, the telephone. The caricature of a phone growing out of an adolescent's ear is not too far-fetched. The telephone plays a special role in the social network of young adolescents, who are not yet old enough to drive. At the time I wrote the first edition of this text, my oldest daughter, Tracy, was 13. Her telephone use went up dramatically at this time. One night I came home about 11 p.m. and asked my wife how her evening had gone. She replied, "Your daughter was on the phone from 7:30 to 10:00—either she was calling her friends, or they were calling her." Many young adolescents spend long hours talking with each other about school, about members of the opposite sex, about friends, about parents, about music, and about clothes. And the telephone comes in handy when the moment comes to ask someone out for a first date—adolescents use the telephone as a "long-distance" communication system to avoid the anxiety of asking in person. ❧

*I*n this chapter we explore many different ideas about the cultural worlds of the adolescent. Our tour of these cultural worlds takes us through information about cultural systems, the settings in which adolescents spend their lives, cross-cultural comparisons, social class, ethnicity, and the media and television.

Cultural Systems

Think about the community you grew up in. What was it like? Was it rural or urban? Were the schools traditional or progressive? What kind of community organizations for youth existed? How much did the townspeople support the school and its athletic teams? What values were emphasized in the community? Were community leaders oriented toward conservative or liberal political philosophy? What kinds of goals were promoted for adolescents—was going to college standard fare, or was the orientation more toward finishing high school and working in town or on the family farm? What were the people like? Were most of them white- or blue-collar workers? Did most people have two cars, take expensive vacations, and send their adolescents off to summer camp? By thinking about and responding to questions such as these, you can get a feel for what a community subculture is like.

Ideas about the nature of adolescence and the techniques used to raise adolescents differ from culture to culture and within the same culture over different time periods (Bruner, 1989; Rogoff & Morelli, 1989; Whiting, 1989; Whiting & Edwards, 1988). The cultural beliefs about adolescents that leaders within a society share have important implications for how adolescents are dealt with.

Governments and political bodies can exert strong influences on the lives of adolescents through decision making based on these beliefs. Consider the different experiences adolescents will have if the leaders of a country decide to wage war against another country (as in the case of Vietnam) and many adolescents are forced to make critical decisions about whether to follow or confront and resist the adult decision makers. Further, consider the experiences of those youth who do go to war compared with youth who grow up in an era when there is a nonaggressive political orientation. In ways such as these, government and political structures can exert a strong influence on youth.

There are many other aspects of the cultural milieu to consider in addition to political structure. We already have analyzed the effects of several important aspects of the cultural milieu—namely, the institutions of family and school, as well as the structure and function of peer groups. Further components of culture that are important to evaluate are the nature of the communities and neighborhoods an adolescent grows up in, as well as the strength of the church within those communities. Other significant cultural forces include television and the other media, which have gained influence over adolescents in recent years. Movies, records, magazines, books, and television provide insight into the lives of adolescents.

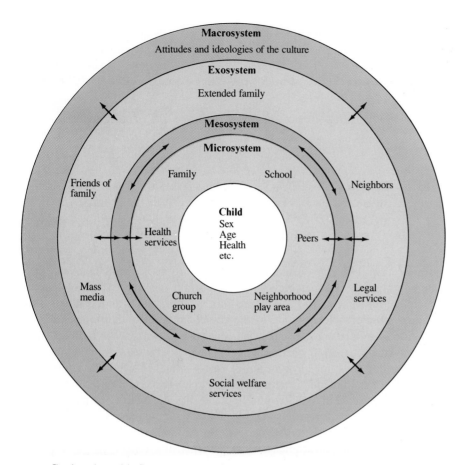

Macrosystem
Attitudes and ideologies of the culture

Exosystem
Extended family

Mesosystem

Microsystem

Friends of family

Family

School

Neighbors

Child
Sex
Age
Health
etc.

Health services

Peers

Mass media

Church group

Neighborhood play area

Legal services

Social welfare services

Figure 9.1 Bronfenbrenner's model is one of the few comprehensive frameworks for understanding the environment's role in the adolescent's development. Notice that the adolescent is placed at the center and that four environmental systems are involved: microsystem, mesosystem, exosystem, and macrosystem.

Sociocultural influences range from the broad-based inputs of culture to the fine-grained inputs of a mother's affectionate hug. A view that captures the sociocultural world's complexity and different levels of analysis has been proposed by Urie Bronfenbrenner (1979, 1987, 1989). Figure 9.1 portrays Bronfenbrenner's model. Notice that the adolescent is placed at the center of the model and that the adolescent's most direct interactions are with the **microsystem**—the setting in which the adolescent lives. These contexts include the adolescent's family, school, peers, and neighborhood. The adolescent is not viewed as a passive recipient of experiences in these settings, but as someone who helps to construct the settings. Most research on sociocultural influences has focused on microsystems, emphasizing parent-adolescent interactions, peer interactions, and school interactions.

The **mesosystem** involves relations between microsystems or connections between contexts. Examples are the relation of family experiences to school experiences, school experiences to church experiences, and family experiences to peer experiences. For example, an adolescent whose parents have rejected

Figure 9.2　(*a*) The peaceful !Kung of Southern Africa. They discourage any kind of aggression; the !Kung are called the "harmless people." (*b*) Hardly harmless, the violent Yanomamo are called the "fierce people." Yanomamo youth are told that manhood cannot be achieved unless they are capable of killing, fighting, and pummeling others.

(a)

(b)

him may have difficulty developing positive relations with his teachers. Developmentalists increasingly believe it is important to observe the adolescent's behavior in multiple settings—such as family, peer, and school contexts—to provide a more complete picture of the adolescent's social development.

Adolescents also experience their environment in a more indirect way. The **exosystem** is involved when experiences in another social setting—in which the adolescent does not have an active role—influence what the adolescent experiences in an immediate context. For example, work experiences may affect a woman's relationship with her husband and the adolescent. She may receive a promotion that requires more travel. This might increase marital conflict and change patterns of parent-adolescent interaction. Another example of an exosystem is the city government, which is responsible for the quality of parks and recreation facilities available to adolescents.

The most abstract level in Bronfenbrenner's analysis of sociocultural influences is the **macrosystem**—the attitudes and ideologies of the culture. People in a particular culture share some broad-based beliefs. The people of Russia have certain beliefs, the people of China have certain beliefs, and so do the people of a South Sea island culture. Consider the !Kung of southern Africa and the Yanamomo Indians of South America. The !Kung are called the "peaceful people." They discourage any kind of aggression on the part of their adolescents and resolve disputes calmly. By contrast, the Yanamomo Indians are called the "fierce people." They teach their sons that manhood cannot be achieved unless they are capable of killing, fighting, and pummelling others. As they grow up, Yanamomo boys are instructed at great length in how to carry out these violent tasks (Figure 9.2 shows the !Kung and Yanamomo).

The Settings in Which Adolescents Spend Their Time

What do adolescents do during a typical week in their lives? Of course, the answer to this question depends on the adolescent's culture. !Kung, Yanamomo, and American adolescents follow very different agendas. Our focus

　The Contexts of Adolescent Development

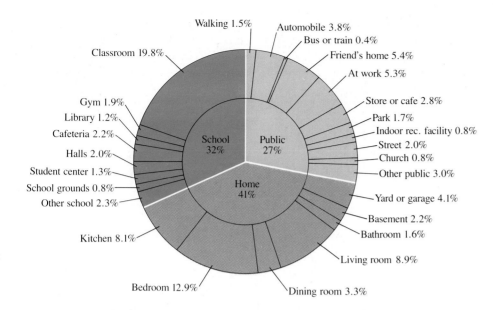

Walking 1.5% Automobile 3.8%
Bus or train 0.4%
Friend's home 5.4%
At work 5.3%
Classroom 19.8%
Store or cafe 2.8%
Gym 1.9%
Park 1.7%
Library 1.2%
Indoor rec. facility 0.8%
Cafeteria 2.2%
Street 2.0%
Halls 2.0%
Church 0.8%
Student center 1.3%
Other public 3.0%
School grounds 0.8%
Other school 2.3%
Yard or garage 4.1%
Basement 2.2%
Kitchen 8.1%
Bathroom 1.6%
Living room 8.9%
Bedroom 12.9%
Dining room 3.3%
School 32% Public 27% Home 41%

Figure 9.3 Where adolescents spend their time. Graph shows the percentage of self-reports in each location (N = 2734). In this and the following figures, one percentage point is equivalent to approximately one hour per week spent in the given location or activity.

here is on the daily activities of American adolescents. Mihaly Csikszentmihalyi and Reed Larson (1984) wanted to know what observers would see if they were privileged to follow adolescents around in their environment. How much time do they spend in educational compared to recreational settings? How much time do they spend with friends compared to adults? These are examples of questions the researchers were interested in answering.

The data that provide the basis for this look into the lives of adolescents were collected in a novel way. Self-reports were made by the adolescents at random times during their lives. All of the subjects carried electronic pagers for one week. A transmitter signaled the adolescents to fill out reports on their experiences from early morning until late at night. This method provided several thousand samples of what adolescents do and where they spend their time. The researchers call their procedure the **experience sampling method.** It is a method of obtaining the thoughts, activities, and feelings of the individual at approximately 40–50 randomly chosen moments in their daily lives.

The community chosen to be studied, of course, cannot be perfectly representative of adolescents everywhere. The community selected for the research, however, did provide a heterogeneous population of adolescents from urban and suburban backgrounds near Chicago. Seventy-five students, with approximately equal numbers of boys and girls, were selected from four school grades, 9th through 12th. Approximately equal numbers came from a lower middle-class background and an upper middle-class sector of the community.

The adolescents' social worlds were studied in terms of where they were, what they were doing, and who they were with at the time of the signals. The paths of adolescents' lives seem to pass through three main locations—home, school, and public places such as parks, buses, supermarkets, and friends' houses. Figure 9.3 reveals where adolescents were when they were beeped.

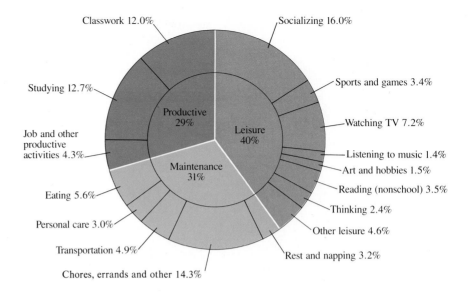

Figure 9.4 What adolescents spend their time doing.

Classwork 12.0%

Socializing 16.0%

Studying 12.7%

Sports and games 3.4%

Job and other productive activities 4.3%

Watching TV 7.2%

Eating 5.6%

Listening to music 1.4%

Personal care 3.0%

Art and hobbies 1.5%

Transportation 4.9%

Reading (nonschool) 3.5%

Thinking 2.4%

Chores, errands and other 14.3%

Other leisure 4.6%

Rest and napping 3.2%

Productive 29%

Leisure 40%

Maintenance 31%

The most prominent location in their lives is their home, although almost one-third of the time they were at school, and more than one-fourth of the time they were in public places. When at home, adolescents spent more time in their bedroom than at any other location in their house. At school, about two-thirds of the time was spent in formal classrooms, but the remainder involved time in fringe areas of classrooms, such as the cafeteria, hallways, and a student center.

What were adolescents doing when they were beeped? Figure 9.4 reveals that 29% of their time was taken up by productive activities, mainly those related to schoolwork. An additional 31% involved various maintenance activities such as eating, resting, bathing, and dressing. The rest of the time adolescents were engaging in other activities, such as talk, sport, and reading, which can be classified primarily as leisure. By far, the largest amount of time spent in a single productive activity was individual studying, which took up 13% of the adolescent's waking hours. The time spent studying by the Chicago adolescents, however, is considerably less than is spent by some technologically strong cultures, such as Japan. In the Chicago sample, combined school and home studying added up to about eleven hours less than the Japanese. And the Japanese spend 69 more days in school each year than their American counterparts. With regard to work, 41% of the adolescents in the Chicago study were employed, with most jobs being in food services, retail sales, and other unskilled areas. The adolescents worked an average of 18 hours per week at their jobs.

Within leisure, the main activity was socializing, which took up approximately one-sixth of waking time. It also was found that adolescents spend about three times as much of their day talking with friends and peers as they do with parents or other adults. And, 13% of talking occurred by phone! The Chicago adolescents were spending far more time socializing and talking than

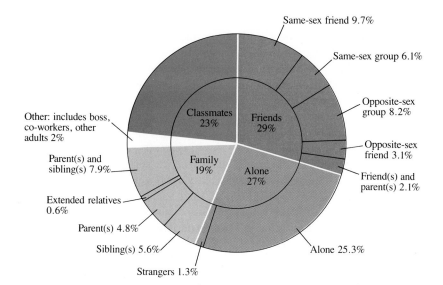

Figure 9.5 People with whom adolescents spend their time.

their counterparts in Japan, Germany, or the Soviet Union. Adolescents watched television as a main activity about one hour per day, but also watched an additional 1.5 hours per day as a secondary activity. About 1.25 hours per day were spent in more active, structured activities such as sports, games, hobbies, reading, and listening to music together.

What percentage of their time do adolescents spend with different people? According to Figure 9.5, adolescents are not often in the company of an adult. During one-fifth of their waking hours, adolescents were with the family and only a portion of this was spent with parents. One-fourth of the day was passed in solitude. A full 50% of the week's waking hours was spent with peers, partly in the classroom, partly outside of class with friends. As adolescents moved from the 9th to the 12th grades, they spent increasing amounts of time with peers.

Cross-Cultural Comparisons

Not every adolescent in every culture is like Rob, the adolescent described in the prologue of this chapter, who rushed out of class, hopped into his Mustang convertible and turned up his radio full blast. Anthropologists have been especially interested in comparing individuals from different cultures.

The Anthropological View

The **anthropological view** focuses on the origins of human beings and cultural influences on their development. Anthropologists believe adolescent behavior may vary from one culture to another in many ways. They also suggest that many cultural variations survive from one generation to the next—are not merely passing thoughts and behaviors. One of the major contributions of anthropologists has been to show similarities and differences between the more industrialized North American and Western European cultures and primitive, less developed cultures. Such investigations are useful in confirming or disconfirming whether theories and data about adolescents are culture-specific or universal in nature.

Early in this century, overgeneralizations about the universal aspects of adolescents were made based on data and experience in a single culture (Havighurst, 1976). For example, it was believed that all adolescents everywhere went through a period of "storm and stress," characterized by self-doubt and conflict. It also was believed that adolescents everywhere encountered extensive, prolonged conflict with the adults of their society. However, when Margaret Mead (1928) visited the island of Samoa, she found that not only were the adolescents of the Samoan culture not experiencing much stress, they generally got along well with the adults in their culture.

Adolescents in Different Cultures

The study of adolescence has emerged in the context of Western industrialized society, with the practical needs and social norms of this culture dominating thinking about adolescents. Consequently, the development of adolescents in Western cultures has evolved as the norm for all adolescents of the human species, regardless of economic and cultural environment. This ethnocentric viewpoint can lead to narrow or erroneous conclusions about the nature of adolescence (Bruner, 1989; Rogoff & Morelli, 1989; Valsiner, 1988). To develop a more cosmopolitan perception of adolescents, let's consider adolescents' achievement behavior and sexuality in different cultures, as well as their rites of passage.

Achievement and Sexuality

Substantial variation crops up when cross-cultural comparisons are made of adolescents' achievement behavior and sexuality. The United States is an achievement-oriented country, and adolescents in the United States are more achievement oriented than adolescents in many other countries. In one investigation of 104 societies, parents in nonindustrialized countries placed a lower value on socializing adolescents for achievement and independence and a higher value on obedience and responsibility than parents in industrialized countries (Barry, Child, & Bacon, 1959). And, in comparisons of Anglo-American adolescents with Mexican and Mexican-American adolescents, Anglo-American adolescents were found to be more competitive and less cooperative. For example, in one investigation, Anglo-American adolescents were more likely to reduce the gains of other students when they could not reach the goals themselves (Kagan & Madsen, 1972). In other investigations, Mexican youth were more family centered, Anglo-American youth more individual centered (Holtzmann, 1982). While some of the comparisons of American adolescents with adolescents from other cultures are encouraging, some experts warn that our culture is too achievement oriented for rearing mentally healthy adolescents (Elkind, 1981). More about the achievement orientation of adolescents appears in Chapter 14.

Culture also plays a prominent role in adolescent sexuality. Some cultures consider sexual pleasure to be normal occurrences for adolescents; others see them as forbidden. Consider the Ines Beag and Mangaian cultures. Ines Beag is a small island off the coast of Ireland. Its inhabitants are among the most sexually repressed in the world. They know nothing about French kissing or hand stimulation of the penis. Sex education does not exist. They believe that after marriage, nature will take its course. The men think that intercourse is bad for their health. Individuals in this culture detest nudity. Only babies are allowed to bathe nude, and adults wash only the parts of their body that extend beyond their clothing. Premarital sex is out of the question. After marriage, sexual partners keep their underwear on during intercourse! It is not difficult to understand why females in the Ines Beag culture rarely, if ever, achieve orgasm (Messinger, 1971).

By contrast, consider the Mangaian culture in the South Pacific. Boys learn about masturbation as early as age 6 or 7. At 13, boys undergo a ritual that introduces them to manhood in which a long incision is made in the penis. The individual who conducts the ritual instructs the boy about sexual strategies, such as how to help his partner achieve orgasm before he does. Two weeks after the incision ceremony, the 13-year-old boy has intercourse with an experienced woman. She helps him to hold back his ejaculation so she can achieve orgasm with him. Soon after, the boy searches for girls to further his sexual experience, or they seek him, knowing that he now is a "man." By the end of adolescence, Mangaians have sex virtually every night.

American adolescents experience a culture more liberal than the Ines Beag but one that does not come close to matching the liberal sexual behavior of the Mangaians. The cultural diversity in the sexual behavior of adolescents is testimony to the power of environmental experiences in determining sexuality. As we move up the animal kingdom, experience seems to take on more power as a determinant of sexuality. While human beings cannot mate in midair like bees or display their plumage as magnificently as peacocks, adolescents can talk about sex with one another, read about it in magazines, and watch it on television and at the movies.

Rites of Passage

Some societies have elaborate ceremonies that signal the adolescent's move to maturity and achievement of adult status. Ceremonies or rituals that mark an individual's transition from one status to another, especially into adulthood, are called **rites of passage.** In many primitive cultures, rites of passage are the avenue through which adolescents gain access to sacred adult practices, to

Nigeria girl, painted for festival dance of "OBITUN" (coming of age).

knowledge, and to sexuality (Sommer, 1978). These rites often involve dramatic practices intended to facilitate the adolescent's separation from the immediate family, especially the mother. The transformation usually is characterized by some form of ritual death and rebirth, or by means of contact with the spiritual world. Bonds are forged between the adolescent and the adult instructors through shared rituals, hazards, and secrets to allow the adolescent to enter the adult world. This kind of ritual provides a forceful and discontinuous entry into the adult world at a time when the adolescent is perceived to be ready for the change.

Africa has been the location of many rites of passage for adolescents, especially sub-Saharan Africa. Under the influence of Western culture, many of the rites are disappearing today, although some vestiges remain. In locations where formal education is not readily available, rites of passage are still prevalent. Perspective on Adolescent Development 9.1 explores gender differences in rites of passage.

The Contexts of Adolescent Development

Josh Maisel's Bar Mitzvah

Aunts, uncles, and cousins from many places came to celebrate Josh Maisel's bar mitzvah. That morning Josh entered Beth Israel Congregration in Waterville, Maine, as a child. He emerged, in the eyes of his faith, a man. Serious duties will replace the weightlessness of his younger years. As a child, Josh had listened to the Scripture and learned. As an adult, Josh is allowed to read from the Torah so that he can pass on his family's faith to a new generation.

Childhood has not been an easy path for Josh. He will never forget the night almost 9 years ago when his parents told him they were going to get a divorce. When asked about his greatest worry as a child, Josh replies, "War. It is scary to think what would happen." But at the mention of his parents' divorce, Josh adds, "Now that I think about it, war looks really small compared to that."

At times Josh imagines what it would be like to be an adult. "I will have to really look after myself and not have somebody looking over my shoulder to be sure I'm doing the right thing," he says. "And I'll have to teach my kids the things I've been taught." (Ludtke, 1988)

(Source: *Time,* August 8, 1988, p. 55.)

This young Jewish boy is shown at his bar mitzvah, a Jewish initiation ceremony that takes place when the boy reaches the age of 13. The bar mitzvah gives the boy adult status in the Jewish religion.

Do we have such rites of passage for American adolescents? We certainly do not have universal formal ceremonies that mark the passage from adolescence to adulthood. Certain religious and social groups do go through initiation ceremonies that indicate an advance in maturity has been reached—the Jewish bar mitzvah, the Catholic Confirmation, and social debuts, for example. School graduation ceremonies come the closest to being rites of passages in today's world. The high school graduation ceremony is especially noteworthy, becoming nearly universal for middle-class adolescents and increasing numbers of adolescents from low-income families (Fasick, 1988). Nonetheless, high school graduation does not result in universal changes—many high school graduates continue to live with their parents, continue to be economically dependent on them, and continue to be undecided about career and life-style directions.

Graduating from high school is one of the few rites of passage in the United States.

Gender Differences in Rites of Passage

The rites of passage in primitive cultures are more directly related to specific pubertal events for females than for males (Sommer, 1978). This probably is due to menarche's role as a pubertal marker, while male pubertal development does not include such a distinctive marker. Also, for boys the rites of passage reflect an introduction to the more ethereal world of spirit and culture, while for girls the rites of passage are more likely to reflect natural phenomena such as menstruation and childbirth.

Themes of death and rebirth are prevalent in the initiation ceremonies of males. Boys frequently are violently removed from their mothers and families by evil-looking masked figures. In the Congo and Loange coastal regions of Africa, boys between the ages of 10 and 12 years are given a potion that makes them lose consciousness. They are then taken into the jungle, circumcised, and ritually buried. When they awake, it is assumed that they have forgotten their past lives (Eliade, 1958).

Circumcision is a prominent practice in rites of passage and has both sexual and spiritual meanings. Circumcision may be done at the onset of puberty for hygienic reasons, to test the endurance of the youth, to reflect symbolic sacrifice, to sanctify procreation, to symbolize incorporation into the community, to represent symbolic castration by a father figure, or to express male envy of women's menstruation (Allen, 1967).

The reproductive capabilities of the female and the onset of menstruation are often the central focus of female rites of passage. As was true for male rites, such ceremonies serve sexual, spiritual, and communal functions. Female rites similar to male rites have been reported in a number of primitive cultures. In such rites, it is not unusual for the girl's clitoris to be removed. In some rites, girls are tortured or scared, while in others they are admired and celebrated (Opler, 1972).

Two frequent themes characterize female initiation rites: a childbirth scenario that is supposed to guarantee fertility and ease of childbirth, and procedures that are designed to ensure the further achievement of cultural standards of beauty and sexual desirability. Information about modes of dress and sexual matters may be passed on during the ceremony, and spirituality is often included by associating femininity with the powers of the moon.

The absence of clear-cut rites of passage make the attainment of adult status ambiguous. Many individuals are unsure whether they have reached adult status or not. In Texas, the age for beginning employment is 15, but there are many younger adolescents and even children who are employed, especially Mexican immigrants. The age for driving is 16, but when emergency need is demonstrated a driver's license can be obtained at 15. Even at age 16, some parents may not allow their son or daughter to obtain a driver's license, believing they are too young for this responsibility. The age for voting is 18, and the age for drinking has recently been raised to 21. Exactly when adolescents become adults in America has not been clearly delineated as it has in some primitive cultures, where rites of passage are universal in the culture.

Social Class

Within countries, subcultures have shared beliefs. The values and attitudes of adolescents growing up in an urban ghetto may differ from those of adolescents growing up in a wealthy suburb, as well as from those of adolescents growing up in Appalachian poverty. Here we investigate what is meant by social class, socioeconomic variations in families, schools, and neighborhoods, and adolescents in poverty.

What Is Social Class?

What is meant when we refer to **social class?** In general, we are speaking about an individual's socioeconomic status and life-style. Along with the labels often come certain connotations. Social stratification carries with it certain inequities. It is generally acknowledged that members of society (1) have occupations that vary in prestige, (2) have different levels of power to influence a community's institutions, (3) have different economic resources, and (4) have different educational and occupational opportunities. These differences in ability to control resources and to participate in society's rewards produce unequal opportunities for adolescents (Hess, 1970; Steinitz & Solomon, 1986).

The number of visibly different social classes depends on the community's size and complexity (Havighurst, 1987). In most investigators' descriptions of social classes there are from two to five. In a five-class structure, upper, upper-middle, lower-middle, upper-lower, and lower-lower classes are delineated. In a two-class structure, lower and middle classes are delineated. Sometimes the lower class is described as working class, blue collar, or low-income; sometimes the middle class is described as managerial class, white collar, or middle-income. Examples of lower-class occupations are factory worker, manual laborer, welfare recipient, and maintenance worker; examples of middle-class occupations are salespeople, managers, and professionals (doctors, lawyers, teachers, accountants, and so on).

Socioeconomic Variations in Families, Schools, and Neighborhoods

The families, schools, and neighborhoods of adolescents have socioeconomic characteristics. Some adolescents have parents who have a great deal of money, work in prestigious occupations, live in attractive houses and neighborhoods, and attend schools where the mix of students is primarily from such middle- and upper-class backgrounds. Other adolescents have parents who do not have very much money, work in less prestigious occupations, do not live in very attractive houses and neighborhoods, and attend schools where the mix of students is mainly from lower-class backgrounds.

Figure 9.6   The reading and television habits of high school students from working-class families.

From "Report of Poll No. 98 of the Purdue Opinion Panel," © 1973, by Purdue Research Foundation, West Lafayette, IN 47907.

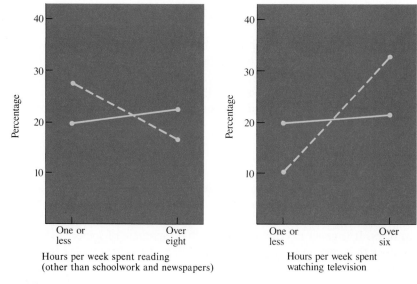

Hours per week spent reading (other than schoolwork and newspapers)

Hours per week spent watching television

——— Students whose mothers had graduated from college (middle class)
- - - Students whose mothers had eleven or fewer years of schooling (working class)

Let's look at one important aspect of the adolescent's intellectual background and see how social class differences in families are involved. Most school tasks require students to use and process language. As part of this language orientation, students often are called on to read efficiently, write effectively, and give competent oral reports. While there is considerable variation within a particular social class, middle-class students are more likely to make use of verbal skills, especially reading, and to enjoy their use more than lower-class students (also called working-class students). As shown in Figure 9.6, working-class students tend to read less and watch television more than middle-class students. While television involves some verbal activity, it is primarily a visual medium; and the working-class adolescents' preference for this medium suggests that they are more interested in visual than verbal experiences, unlike middle-class adolescents (Erlick & Starry, 1973).

The parents of middle-class adolescents likely direct their offspring from very early in the child's development more toward verbal experiences than their lower-class counterparts. For example, Steven Tulkin and Jerome Kagan (1971) observed 30 middle-class and 26 lower-class Caucasian mothers at home with their firstborn, 10-month-old daughters. Social class differences were minimal in physical contact, prohibitions, and nonverbal interactions. By contrast, *every* verbal behavior observed was more frequent among middle-class mothers. They concluded that lower-class mothers were less likely to believe that their infants were capable of communicating with other people. Thus, they felt it was futile to verbally interact with them.

The Contexts of Adolescent Development

Adolescents from the lowest strata of working-class families are of special concern. Economic poverty makes it very difficult for adolescents to successfully make their way in school and life.

A sizable portion of adolescent students from lower-class backgrounds, however, do perform well in school, in many cases better than some middle-class students. In the family background of adolescents from lower-class settings, it is not unusual to find a parent or parents making special efforts and sacrifices to provide the necessary living conditions and support that contribute to enhanced school success.

Turning our attention to schools themselves, schools in low-income neighborhoods often have fewer resources than schools in high-income neighborhoods. The schools in the low-income areas also are likely to have more students with lower achievement test scores, lower rates of graduation, and fewer percentages of students going to college (Garbarino & Asp, 1981). There are some instances, however, where federal aid to schools has provided a context for enhanced learning in low-income areas. The school personnel in schools set in lower-class neighborhoods often is different than in middle-class settings. Younger, less experienced teachers often are the ones who end up with jobs in schools in lower-class neighborhoods, while older, more experienced teachers are more often found in schools in middle-class neighborhoods.

Poverty

Of special concern to psychologists and educators who work with adolescents is the subculture of the poor—those adolescents from the lower strata of working-class families. Although the most noticeable aspect of the poor is their economic poverty, other psychological and social characteristics are present (Hess, 1970). First, the poor are often powerless. In occupations they rarely

Culture   339

are the decision makers. Rules are handed down to them in an authoritarian way. Second, the poor are vulnerable to disaster. They are not likely to be given advance notice when they are laid off from work and usually do not have financial resources to fall back on when problems arise. Third, their range of alternatives is restricted. A limited range of jobs is open to them. Even when alternatives are available, they may not know about them or be prepared to make a wise decision because of inadequate education and inability to read well. Fourth, there is less prestige in being poor. This lack of prestige is transmitted to children early in life. The poor child observes other children who wear nicer clothes and live in more attractive houses.

Currently, one in four children and one in five adolescents is living in poverty. The poverty rate for youth in single-parent, female-headed households is much higher (54%) than for their counterparts in other families (12.5%) (U.S. Bureau of the Census, 1986). In the words of Marian Wright Edelman (1987), president of the Children's Defense Fund,

> The America of the 1980s presents a cruel paradox: While the rich are
> getting rich and often getting more government help, the poor are getting
> poorer and receiving less help. The decline in federal assistance for children
> has made living in poverty a harsher existence for 13 million children, and it
> has crippled the efforts of families to struggle back up out of poverty. (p. 40)

Any society that aspires to be great cannot continue to slash billions of dollars from essential programs for adolescents and their families while poverty rises and nearly half of minority adolescents are unemployed and seeking work. We owe all adolescents, both rich *and* poor, the best we have to give (Conger, 1988; Schorr, 1989).

At this point we have discussed many different ideas about cultural systems, the setting in which adolescents spend their time, cross-cultural comparisons, and social class. A summary of these ideas is presented in Concept Table 9.1.

Ethnicity

We live in an extraordinary time, a time of dramatic changes in social organization and of extensive expansion of information about adolescent development. Nowhere are changes more pronounced than in the rapidly increasing ethnic diversity of America's adolescents (Jones, 1989). Ethnic minority groups—Blacks, Hispanics, Native Americans (American Indians), and Asians—for example, made up slightly more than 20 percent of all children and adolescents under the age of 17 in the United States in 1989. By the year 2000, the percentage will rise to approximately one-third. This changing demographic tapestry promises not only the richness diversity produces but also difficult challenges in extending the American dream to all ethnic minority individuals.

An especially important idea in considering the nature of ethnic minority groups is that not only is there ethnic diversity within a culture, such

The Contexts of Adolescent Development

Cultural Systems, Settings, Cross-Cultural Comparisons, and Social Class

Concept	Processes/Related Ideas	Characteristics/Description
Cultural systems	Culture	A broad concept referring to the behavior patterns, beliefs, values, and other products of humans that are learned and shared by a particular group of people and passed on from one generation to the next.
	Bronfenbrenner's model	He proposes that sociocultural worlds can be divided into microsystems, mesosystems, exosystems, and macrosystems.
Settings	How adolescents spend their time	Adolescents spend more time at home than in other settings. Almost one-third of their time is spent in productive activities, such as schoolwork. They spend considerable time socializing, especially with peers.
Cross-cultural comparisons	Anthropological view	Stresses the origins of human beings and cultural influences on their development.
	Adolescents in different cultures	Anglo-American adolescents are highly achievement oriented compared to adolescents from most cultures. There is considerable variation in adolescent sexuality across different cultures.
	Rites of passage	A ceremony or ritual that marks an individual's transition from one status to another, especially into adulthood. In primitive cultures, rites of passage are often well defined. In contemporary America, rites of passage to adulthood are somewhat ill defined.
Social class	What is it?	An individual's socioeconomic status and life-style. Social stratification involves inequities. The number of social classes varies with the complexity and size of the community. Most analyses involve two to five social classes.
	Socioeconomic variations in families, schools, and neighborhoods	The families, schools, and neighborhoods of adolescents have socioeconomic characteristics that are related to the adolescent's development.
	Poverty	The subculture of the poor is characterized not only by economic poverty but by social and psychological handicaps. Currently, one in five adolescents grows up in poverty. Government assistance to the poor has been reduced.

as the United States, but there also is considerable diversity within each ethnic group. All Black adolescents do not come from low-income families. All Hispanic adolescents are not members of the Catholic church. All Asian adolescents are not geniuses. All American Indian adolescents do not drop out of school. It is easy to make the mistake of thinking about an ethnic minority group and stereotyping its members as all being the same. Keep in mind that as we discuss adolescents from ethnic minority groups each group is heterogeneous (Bronstein & Quina, 1988; Jones, 1989; Trimble, 1989). One of adolescent psychology's challenges is to become more sensitive to race and ethnic origin, and to provide improved services to ethnic minority individuals (Gibbs & Huang, 1989; Pacheco & Valdez, 1989; Sue, 1989).

TABLE 9.1 *Percentages of Adolescents Aged 10–19 from Different Ethnic Backgrounds*

Ethnic Group	Percent of Adolescent Population	Ethnic Group	Percent of Adolescent Population
Caucasian		Asian and Pacific islander	
(Age 10–19)	76.5	(Age 10–19)	1.5
Age 10–14	35.2	Age 10–14	.7
Age 15–19	41.3	Age 15–19	.8
Black		American Indian, Eskimo, and Aleut	
(Age 10–19)	13.7	(Age 10–19)	.8
Age 10–14	6.5	Age 10–14	.4
Age 15–19	7.2	Age 15–19	.4
Hispanic origin			
(Age 10–19)	7.5		
Age 10–14	3.6		
Age 15–19	3.9		

Source: United States Bureau of the Census, 1980, *Detailed Population Characteristics of the United States,* Table 253.

One of the social identities we become acutely aware of during adolescence is our ethnic identity (Phinney, 1989). **Ethnicity** refers to membership in a particular ethnic group. Each of you is a member of one or more ethnic groups and so is every adolescent. Membership in an ethnic group is based on racial, religious, national, and ancestral background. As shown in Table 9.1, adolescents in the United States are members of many different ethnic backgrounds. Notice that black and Hispanic adolescents make up the largest portion of minority group adolescents in the United States. Overall, the percentage of ethnic minority group adolescents has increased in recent decades. In 1970, 11.8% of adolescents were black. By 1980, the figure had reached 13.7%. In 1970, 4.7% of adolescents were of Hispanic origin. By 1980, 7.5% were of Hispanic origin. In 1970, 87% of adolescents were Caucasian. By 1980, that figure decreased to 76.5%. Let's look more closely at adolescents from ethnic minority backgrounds.

Black Adolescents

Black adolescents make up the largest easily visible ethnic minority group. Black adolescents are distributed throughout the social class structure, although they constitute a larger proportion of poor and lower-class individuals than does the majority white group (Gibbs, 1989; McLoyd, 1989). No cultural characteristic is common to all or nearly all blacks and absent in whites, unless it is the experience of being black and the ideology that develops from that experience (Havighurst, 1987).

The majority of black youth stay in school, do not take drugs, do not get married prematurely and become parents, are employed and eager to work, are not involved in crime, and grow up to lead productive lives in spite of social and economic disadvantage. While much of the writing and research about Black adolescents has focused on low-income youth from families mainly re-

The Struggles and Triumphs of Black Children and Adolescents

The 1985 Children's Defense Fund study, "Black and White Children in America: Key Facts," found that black children are twice as likely to:

> have no parent employed.
> live in institutions.

Three times as likely to:

> be poor.
> live with a parent who has separated.
> live in a female-headed family.
> be in foster care.
> die of known child abuse.

Four times as likely to:

> live with neither parent and be supervised by a child welfare agency.

Five times as likely to:

> be dependent on welfare.

Twelve times as likely to:

> live with a parent who never married.

Nonetheless, it is important to keep in mind that millions of black American families are not on welfare, have children who stay in school, stay out of trouble and do not get pregnant, and if they experience difficult times, find a way to overcome their problems. In 1967, Martin Luther King reflected on the black family and gave the following caution. As public awareness of the predicament of the black family increases, there will be danger and opportunity. The opportunity will be to deal fully rather than haphazardly with the problem as a whole, as a social catastrophe brought on by long years of oppression. We need to develop resources to combat the oppression. The danger is that the problems will be attributed to innate black weaknesses and used to justify further neglect and to rationalize continued oppression. In today's world, Dr. King's words still ring true (Edelman, 1987).

siding in inner cities, the majority of black youth do not reside in the ghettos of inner cities. At the heart of the new model of studying black youth is recognition of the growing diversity within black communities in the United States (Bell-Scott & Taylor, 1989).

While prejudice against blacks in some occupations still persists, the proportion of males and females in middle-class occupations has been increasing since 1940. A substantial and increasing proportion of black adolescents are growing up in middle-class families and share middle-class values

and attitudes with white middle-class adolescents. Nonetheless, society's economic structure has changed so that a large underclass of black adolescents live in poverty enshrouded ghettos (Heath, 1989; Wilson, 1989). Thus, two contrasting black subcultures have emerged, one middle class and one composed of individuals below working class, which is sometimes referred to as **underclass.** In the words of Julius Wilson (1978),

> A history of discrimination and oppression created a huge black underclass, and the recent technological and economic revolutions have combined to insure it a permanent status. As the black middle class rides on the wave of political and social changes, benefitting from the growth of employment opportunities in the growing corporate and government sectors of the economy, the black underclass falls behind the larger society in every conceivable respect (p. 21).

The black middle-class subculture graduates from high school and enrolls in college almost to the degree white youth do. The concerns of many middle-class black youth reflect the theme that blacks must continue to fight against racial discrimination. Some of these youth may favor "black studies" programs that have developed in secondary and college curricula. A number of black youth look to their African heritage to develop a sense of racial and cultural identity. Erik Erikson (1968) believes, though, that this positive sense

The Contexts of Adolescent Development

Annie and Tony's Disagreement about Spanish

Annie picked up Spanish when she was a child by spending time with her Mexican grandmother. She says she probably knows more Spanish than all her cousins put together. She often used her second language during her summer job as a long-distance operator. She is currently majoring in journalism at college. Annie says, "I'm really embarrassed that my younger brothers don't speak it. I think they should know it. That's our background, our ancestors." Tony, age 12, seems to take as much pride in not speaking Spanish as Annie does in her fluency. Says Tony, "This is America. I don't talk Spanish. I talk to my grandparents in English. They answer me in Spanish. I don't know what they are saying." Annie shakes her head sadly, "He is embarrassed to use Spanish. I tell him that people pay to learn Spanish. It is important nowadays."

of identity needs to be integrated into the larger culture in which black adolescents participate, a culture dominated by nonblack elements. Erikson believes that for young blacks to achieve a positive, healthy integration into American culture, they should avoid antisocial, angry protests and work toward vocational competence and moral commitment. In this way, black adolescents can earn their rightful place in American society while maintaining their cultural and racial identity. These ideas of Erikson apply to virtually any ethnic minority group, not just blacks.

In the 1960s, black adolescents were described as having a lower self-concept than white adolescents (e.g., Coopersmith, 1967). However, more recent investigations find this not to be true, and in some instances black adolescents perceive themselves more positively than white adolescents (Iheanacho, 1987; Simmons & others, 1978).

Hispanic Adolescents

The number of Hispanics in the United States has increased 30% since 1980 to 19 million (Lacayo, 1988). They now account for almost 8% of the United States population. Most trace their roots to Mexico (63%), Puerto Rico (12%), and Cuba (5%), the rest to Central and South American countries and the Caribbean (Laosa, 1989). By the year 2000 their numbers are expected to swell to 30 million, 15% of the US population. And roughly one-third of all Hispanics in the United States marry non-Hispanics, promising a day when the two cultures will be more intertwined.

The Dreams and Struggles of John David Gutierrez

John David Gutierrez lives in a comfortable house on a treelined street in Austin, Texas. The black hair, the olive skin, the dark eyes reveal the Mexican heritage his grandparents brought to America. His American-born mother and father, fluent in Spanish and English, describe themselves as Mexican Americans. John David, now 13 years old, speaks only English. He says that he is not sure who he is. "I guess I'm Tex-Mex," he says. "Or, I would be happy if you called me American," he quickly follows.

John David has achieved an identity through sports. He has quick reflexes, good speed, and a trim build. At 5 feet 6 inches he is still growing. He plays basketball for a community team, baseball for another community team, and football for his school team. Says John David, "I dream a lot. I want to become a pro baseball player. I try to do the best I can."

John David is young enough to still dream, but he has seen the dreams of two older brothers fail. Abelardo, 24, and Xavier, 20, lost their way during adolescence. John David says that they had a chance but didn't hang tough enough. Abelardo was a good pitcher and had a chance to go to college but did not. Xavier recently told John David not to mess up like he did. He feels he could have made it to the big leagues too. From his brothers, John David has learned how difficult it is to take on adult responsibilities. He reflects, "I don't want to have a family at an early age like my brother has now. Not that soon."

John David also has a different perspective than his parents. They were kept out of the Anglo world as children and adolescents. John David has not grown up as

John David Guitierrez dreams of becoming a professional baseball player. He is a Mexican-American adolescent who describes himself as "Tex-Mex" or American."

an outsider. His grandparents were poor and powerless, but they had the rich hope that America would be better for their children and their grandchildren. That wish came true. The Gutierrez family has the comforts of a middle-class life, but the parents still worry about the hurdles John David has yet to clear, temptations he needs to resist: the prevalence of drugs and alcohol, the growing problem of early sex. His parents hope that the family security they have provided will give him the strength to resist the intense pressures he faces in his effort to reach his dreams (Ludtke, 1988).

By far the largest group of Hispanic adolescents consists of those who identify themselves as having a Mexican origin, although many of them were born in the United States (Ramirez, 1989). Their largest concentration is in the Southwest. They represent more than 50% of the student population in the schools of San Antonio and close to that percentage in the schools of Los Angeles. Mexican Americans have a variety of life-styles and come from a range of socioeconomic statuses—from affluent professional and managerial status to migrant farm worker and welfare recipient in big city barrios. The

Our culture is a melting pot for many ethnic groups. Ethnic minority groups now constitute 20 percent of children and adolescents under the age of 17. By the year 2000, one-third of all school age children in the United States will be from ethnic minority groups. This changing demographic picture promises not only the richness that diversity brings but also many difficult challenges in extending the American dream to all citizens.

life of one Mexican-American adolescent, described in Perspective on Adolescent Development 9.2, vividly reveals the ethnic minority group adolescent's dreams and struggles. While coming from families with diverse backgrounds, Hispanic adolescents have one of the lowest educational levels of any ethnic group in the United States.

Many Hispanic adolescents have developed a new political consciousness and pride in their cultural heritage. Some have fused strong cultural links to Mexican and Indian cultures with the economic limitations and restricted opportunities in the barrio. The politically conscious Mexican-American adolescents call themselves **Chicanos,** individuals who are a product of Spanish-Mexican-Indian heritage and Anglo influences.

Asian-American Adolescents

Asian-American adolescents also are a fast-growing segment of the adolescent population and they too show considerable diversity. In the 1970 census only three Asian-American groups were prominent—Japanese, Chinese, and Philippino. But in the last two decades, there has been rapid growth in three other groups—Koreans, Pacific Islanders (Guam and Samoa), and Vietnamese (Huang, 1989).

Adolescents of Japanese or Chinese origin can be found in virtually every large city. While their grasp of the English language is usually good, they have been raised in a subculture in which family loyalty and family influence are powerful. This has tended to maintain their separate subcultures. The Japanese-American adolescents are somewhat more integrated into the Anglo life-style than are the Chinese-American adolescents. However, both groups have been very successful in school. They tend to take considerable advantage of educational opportunities.

In the last two decades, rapid growth of Asian-American adolescent groups has occurred in the United States. As with other ethnic minority group adolescents, they are a diverse group of adolescents, requiring individual consideration and attention.

Native American Adolescents

Approximately 100,000 American Indian and Eskimo adolescents are scattered in 30 or more tribal groups in about 20 states. About 90% are enrolled in school. About 15,000 are in boarding schools, many of which are maintained by the federal government's Bureau of Indian Affairs. Another 45,000 are in public schools on or near Indian reservations. In these schools, the native American adolescents make up more than 50% of the students. The remaining 30,000 are in public schools where they are an ethnic minority. A growing proportion of native American adolescents have moved to large cities (Havighurst, 1987).

Native American (American Indian) adolescents have experienced an inordinate amount of discrimination. While virtually any minority group experiences some discrimination in being a member of a larger, majority-group culture, in the early years of our country, native Americans were the victims of terrible physical abuse and punishment. Injustices that these 800,000 individuals have experienced are reflected in the lowest standard of living of any ethnic group, the highest teenage pregnancy rate, the highest suicide rate, and the highest school dropout rate of any ethnic group (LaFromboise & Low, 1989).

America: A Nation of Blended Cultures

America has been a great receiver of ethnic groups and continues to be a great receiver. It has embraced new ingredients from many cultures. The cultures often collide and cross-pollinate, mixing their ideologies and identities. Some of the culture of origin is retained, some of it lost, some of it mixed with the American culture. One after another, immigrants have come to America and been exposed to new channels of awareness and in turn exposed Americans to new channels of awareness. Black, Hispanic, Asian American, native American, and other cultural heritages mix with the mainstream, receiving a new content and giving a new content (Gibbs & Huang, 1989).

To describe the way cultures mix, two concepts have been developed. **Acculturation** occurs when members of different cultures interact and the process produces changes in one or both of the cultures. While each culture may retain its "personality," both cultures change through reformulation of the cultures' elements. **Assimilation** (the term has another meaning in Piaget's theory) occurs when the members of one culture become completely absorbed into a more dominant culture. Assimilation has been common in the "melting pot" of American society for many years. More recently, though, many minority cultures have sought to maintain their own identities and standards, yielding an increasing amount of acculturation.

The Contexts of Adolescent Development

Canada

Adolescents in Canada are exposed to some cultural dimensions similar to their counterparts in the United States. Canada has long been economically and culturally tied to the United States. For example, Canadian adolescents are inundated with American mass media: popular magazines, radio, and television. However, the cultural worlds of Canadian adolescents differ in certain ways from the cultural worlds of United States adolescents. In 1971, Canada was officially redefined by the federal government as bilingual (English/French), yet multicultural. Primarily French-speaking individuals reside mainly in Quebec, primarily English-speaking individuals in the other Canadian provinces. While officially Canada is a bilingual nation, it is predominantly the French Canadians who are bilingual. Although Canada's main ethnic ties are British and French, a number of ethnic minorities live in Canada—German (6%), Italian (3%), Ukranian (3%), Scandinavian (2%), Dutch (2%), Indian and Eskimo (1%), and Jewish (1%), for example. While Canada has become more of a multicultural mosaic, it does not come near to being the ethnic melting pot that the United States culture is (Anderson & Frideres, 1981).

Television and the Media

Few developments in society over the last 30 years have had a greater impact on adolescents than television. The persuasion capabilities of television are staggering. As they have grown up, many of today's adolescents have spent more time in front of the television set than with their parents or in the classroom. Other influential media we will consider are radio, records, rock music, and music video.

Television

The messages of television are powerful. What are television's functions? How often do adolescents watch television? How extensively does television violence affect adolescents? What is MTV's role in adolescents' lives? We consider each of these questions in turn.

Television's Functions

Television has been called a lot of things, not all of them good. Depending on one's point of view, it is a "window to the world," the "one-eyed monster," or the "boob tube." Scores on national achievement tests in reading and mathematics, while showing a small improvement recently, have generally been lower than in the past decades—and television has been attacked as one of the reasons. Television may take adolescents away from the printed media and books—one recent study found that children who read books and the printed media watched television less than those who did not (Huston, Siegle, & Bremer, 1983). It is argued that television trains individuals to become passive learners. Rarely, if ever, does television require active responses from the observer. Heavy television use may produce not only a passive learner, but a passive life-style. In one recent investigation of 406 adolescent males, those who watched little television were more physically fit and physically active than those who watched a lot (Tucker, 1987).

Television also can deceive (Huston, Watkins, & Kunkel, 1989). It can teach adolescents that problems are easily resolved and that everything turns out all right in the end. For example, it takes only about 30 to 60 minutes for detectives to sort through a complex array of clues and discover the killer—and they always find the killer. Violence is pictured as a way of life in many shows. It is all right for police to use violence and break moral codes in their fight against evildoers. And the lasting results of violence are rarely brought home to the viewer. An individual who is injured suffers for only a few seconds. In real life, the individual might take months or even years to recover, or perhaps does not recover at all.

But there are some positive aspects to television's influence on adolescents. For one, television presents adolescents with a world that is different from the one in which they live. This means that, through television, adolescents are exposed to a wider variety of views and knowledge than when they are informed only by their parents, teachers, and peers. Before television's advent, adolescents' identification models came in the form of parents or relatives, older siblings and neighborhood peers, famous individuals heard about in conversation or on the radio and read about in the newspaper or magazines, and the film stars seen in the theater, visited no more than twice a week. Many of the identification figures in the past came from family or peers whose attitudes, clothing styles, and occupational objectives were relatively homogenous. The imagery and pervasiveness of television has exposed children and adolescents to hundreds of different neighborhoods, cultures, clothing fashions, career possibilities, and patterns of intimate relationships (Liebert & Sparkin, 1988).

Frequency of Viewing

The 20,000 hours of television watched by the time the American adolescent graduates from high school is far more than the number of hours spent in the classroom and also is more than the number of hours spent interacting with parents. Just how much television do children and adolescents watch? In the surveys of viewing patterns conducted before the 1980s, weekly viewing patterns increased through middle and late childhood, but adolescence was a period of reduced television viewing (Pearl, Bouthilet, & Lazar, 1982). Today's children still watch massive amounts of television—more than 25 hours per week on the average. And, adolescents are watching more television than in earlier years, probably because of the introduction of music television and the accelerated growth of cable television (Singer & Singer, 1987). MTV and other music video channels reflect the first pervasive efforts by the television industry to provide television programming for adolescents. Many young adolescents are now heavy viewers of music television, and even college students have become addicted to some television shows, especially soap operas (Bence, 1989). In contemporary America, all age groups watch at least several hours of television a day.

Television Violence

A special concern is the extent to which children and adolescents are exposed to violence and aggression on television. Up to 80% of prime time shows include violent acts—beatings, shootings, and stabbings, for example. Some psychologists believe television profoundly influences children's and adolescents' aggressive thoughts and behaviors; others believe these suggested effects are exaggerated (Liebert & Sprakin, 1988; McQuire, 1986). Does television violence merely stimulate a child to go out and buy a Darth Vadar ray gun? Or does it trigger an attack on a playmate and increase the number of violent attacks and even murder?

Violence on television is associated with aggression in individuals who watch it. For example, in one investigation the amount of television violence watched by children when they were in elementary school was associated with how aggressive they were at both age 19 and age 30 (Eron, 1987; Huesmann & others, in press; Lefkowitz & others, 1972). In another investigation, long-term exposure to television violence increased the likelihood of aggression in 1,565 boys aged 12 to 17 (Belson, 1978). Boys who watched the most aggression on television were the most likely to commit some violent action, swear, be aggressive in sports, threaten violence toward another boy, write slogans on walls, or break windows. The types of television violence most often associated with aggression were realistic, took place between individuals in close relationships rather than between strangers, and were committed by the "good guys" rather than the "bad guys."

But it is another step to conclude that television violence by itself causes aggression. Adolescents who watch the most violence may be the most aggressive in the first place. Other factors such as poverty and unpleasant life experiences may be culprits too. So far we have not been able to establish a causal link between television and aggression (Freedman, 1984). Like other behaviors, aggression has multiple causes.

MTV has become one of the most popular television shows for adolescents in the 1980s. Why is MTV so popular with adolescents?

Family Influences

How much do parents take an active role in discussing television with their children and adolescents? For the most part, not much. Various aspects of family background and family interaction are associated with television viewing by children and adolescents. Adolescents from lower socioeconomic backgrounds watch more television than adolescents from higher socioeconomic backgrounds (Huston, Siegle, & Bremer, 1983). Also, low parental control and family conflict are associated with increased television viewing by children and adolescents (Price & Feshbach, 1982; Rothschild & Morgan, 1987).

The Media and Music

Anyone who has been around adolescents very long knows that many of them spend huge amounts of time listening to music on the radio, playing records or tapes of their favorite music, or watching music videos on television. Approximately two-thirds of all records and tapes are purchased by the 10–24 age group. And one-third of the nation's 8,200 radio stations aim their broadcast rock music at the pool of adolescent listeners.

The music adolescents enjoy on records, tapes, radio, and television is an important dimension of their culture. Rock music does not seem to be a passing fad. It has now been around for more than 35 years. Recently it has had its share of controversy. Starting in 1983, MTV (the first music video television channel) and music videos in general were targets of debate in the media (Cocks, 1983). About a year later, rock music's lyrics were attacked by the Parents Music Resource Center (PMRC). This group charged in a congressional hearing that rock music's lyrics were dangerously shaping the minds of adolescents in the areas of sexual morality, violence, drugs, and satanism (Cocks, 1985). The national Parent Teacher Association agreed (Cox, 1985). And recently Tipper Gore, a PMRC founder, voiced her views about the dangers of rock music lyrics in a book (Gore, 1987).

How pervasively does rock music affect adolescents? In one investigation, a group of young people waiting in line to attend a punk rock concert by the group *Dead Kennedys* were interviewed (Rosenthal, 1985). More than 90% agreed with the rebellious sentiments expressed in the *Dead Kennedys'* songs, clearly higher than the population as a whole. However, direction of influence cannot be assessed in this case. That is, young people with particular views are attracted to a particular kind of music such as punk. At the same time, it may be these particular young people who pay attention to, comprehend, and are vulnerable to the lyrics' influence.

Motivation, experience, and knowledge are factors in the interpretation of lyrics. In one investigation, preadolescents and adolescents often missed sexual themes in lyrics (Prinsky & Rosenbaum, 1987). Adult organizations such as the PMRC interpret rock music lyrics in terms of sex, violence, drugs, and satanism more than adolescents themselves. In this investigation, it was

The Contexts of Adolescent Development

Songs and Music Videos: Which Stimulates More Imagination?

In one recent investigation, the question of whether music videos provide less imaginative stimulation than songs alone was evaluated (Greenfield & others, 1987). The researchers selected a wide range of songs and types of videos to study. One video told the same story as the song ("Russians," 1985, by *Sting*); one concert video was illustrated with film clips ("When the Going Gets Tough, the Tough Get Going," 1985, by Billy Ocean); one video used video imagery and techniques without telling the song's story ("Take Me Home," 1985, by Phil Collins); and one video was animated and innovative ("How to Be a Millionare," 1985, White & Frye).

Twenty-six fifth and sixth graders from middle-class backgrounds were assigned to one of two experimental conditions: half the class, arbitrarily selected, listened to the four songs on audiotape in the classroom; the other half listened to and viewed the music video in another room. The 11–12-year-old boys and girls answered questions on a sheet after each song. Two key questions were, "If you were going to make a video about the song, what would it be like?" and "If you were to add another verse, what would it be about?" An all-or-none rating system

was used: A particular response was coded either as imaginative or unimaginative. An imaginative response was defined as one containing additional information not previously given during the media presentation of the song. The students who saw the music videos gave less imaginative responses than their counterparts who only listened to audio versions of the songs. The adolescents also were acutely aware of music video's constraining influence on their imagination. Eighty-one percent of the class said the videos made them less imaginative.

The researchers also noticed how easily the videos captured the students' attention. The students never stopped watching the screen until the final song credits were given. By contrast, the audio group became more easily bored. Nonetheless, 56% said they liked to hear songs on the radio rather than watching music videos. Many said that it was because they could do other things while listening to the songs. This reason explains the seeming contradiction between boredom and preference—there were no other activities available in the experimental context of the study.

found that in contrast to these adult groups, adolescents interpreted their favorite songs in terms of love, friendship, growing up, life's struggles, having fun, cars, religion, and other topics in teenage life.

Other recent research has focused on the medium of music video in comparison to other presentations of music (Greenfield & others, 1987). Comparing music videos with audio songs is like comparing the television medium to radio in that music videos and television have been found to detract from imaginative responses (Greenfield & Beagles-Roos, in press). While music video is a compelling medium that attracts attention, it is considered an "easy" medium that requires little mental effort.

It also has been found, as some rock singers have complained, that music video functions to distract attention away from a song's lyrics (Beagles-Roos & Gat, 1983; Greenfield & Beagles-Roos, in press). Perspective on Adolescent Development 9.3 describes a research investigation about this distraction. These

Ethnicity and Television and the Media

Concept	Processes/Related Ideas	Characteristics/Description
Ethnicity	Its nature	Refers to membership in a particular ethnic group based on racial, religious, national, and ancestral background. Black and Hispanic adolescents make up the largest ethnic minority groups in the United States.
	Black adolescents	Make up the largest easily visible ethnic minority group in the United States. They are distributed throughout social class statuses, but constitute a larger portion of low-income individuals than the majority white group. The proportion of blacks in middle-class occupations has increased since 1940. There is no evidence that black adolescents have lower self-concepts than white adolescents.
	Hispanic adolescents	Most trace their roots to Mexico, Puerto Rico, and Cuba. Roughly one-third will marry non-Hispanics. Adolescents of Mexican origin are the largest subgroup of Hispanic adolescents. Their largest concentration is in the Southwest. Hispanics have one of the lowest educational levels of all minority groups. Many Hispanic adolescents have developed a new political consciousness and pride in their cultural heritage.
	Asian-American adolescents	A diverse, fast-growing segment of the adolescent population. Japanese and Chinese are the largest subgroups. Family loyalty is powerful, and they have taken advantage of educational opportunities.
	Native American adolescents	Also called American Indian adolescents, their ethnic group has experienced painful discrimination. Their injustices are reflected in high school dropout rates, high teenage pregnancy rates, and high suicide rates.

investigations are beginning to provide a more thorough understanding of adolescents' responses to rock music, one of the most important media in their culture.

At this point we have discussed a number of ideas about ethnicity and television and the media. A summary of these ideas is presented in Concept Table 9.2.

Summary

I. Cultural Systems

Culture is a broad concept referring to the behavior patterns, beliefs, values, and other products of humans that are learned and shared by a particular group of people and passed on from one generation to the next. Bronfenbrenner developed a model to analyze sociocultural worlds that includes microsystems, mesosystems, exosystems, and macrosystems.

Concept	Processes/Related Ideas	Characteristics/Description
	America: A nation of blended cultures	Black, Hispanic, Asian American, native American and other cultural heritages mix with the mainstream, receiving a new content, giving a new content. Two concepts describing how cultures mix are acculturation and assimilation.
Television and the media	Television	Its functions include providing information and entertainment. Television portrays a world beyond the family, peers, and school. However, television may train adolescents to become passive learners and adopt a passive life-style. By high school graduation, the American adolescent has watched 20,000 hours of television. Adolescent viewing may be increasing because of music videos and cable television. Television violence is associated with adolescents' aggression, but no causal link has been established. Parents rarely take active roles in adolescent television viewing. Adolescents from lower socioeconomic status backgrounds watch more television than their higher socioeconomic status counterparts, and family conflict and low parental control are associated with increased adolescent viewing.
	The media and music	Adolescents are heavy consumers of records, tapes, and rock music. Rock music's lyrics have been controversial. A number of factors influence the power of rock music over an adolescent's thoughts and behavior, and the degree of this power is still unsettled. Music video is a compelling medium. It is attention grabbing and may produce less imaginative responses than audio versions of songs. Rock music does not seem to be a passing fad and is an important dimension of the youth culture.

II. Settings

Adolescents spend more time at home than in other settings. Almost one-third of their time is spent in productive activities, such as schoolwork. They spend considerable time socializing, especially with peers.

III. Cross-Cultural Comparisons

The anthropological view stresses the origins of human beings and cultural influences on their development. Anglo-American adolescents are highly achievement oriented compared to adolescents from most cultures. There is considerable variation in adolescent sexuality across different cultures. Rites of passage are ceremonies that mark an individual's transition from one status to another, especially into adulthood. In primitive cultures, rites of passage are often well defined. In contemporary America, rites of passage to adulthood are ill defined.

IV. Social Class

Social class refers to an individual's socioeconomic status and life-style. Social stratification involves inequities. The number of social classes varies with the complexity and size of the community. Most analyses recognize two to five social classes. The families, schools, and neighborhoods of adolescents have socioeconomic characteristics that are related to the adolescent's development. The subculture of the poor is characterized not only by economic poverty but by social and pyschological handicaps. Currently, 1 in 5 adolescents grows up in poverty. Government assistance to the poor has been reduced.

V. The Nature of Ethnicity

Ethnicity refers to membership in a particular ethnic group based on racial, religious, national, and ancestral background. Black and Hispanic adolescents make up the largest ethnic minority groups in the United States.

VI. Black and Hispanic Adolescents

Black adolescents make up the largest easily visible ethnic minority group in the United States. They are distributed throughout social class statuses, but constitute a larger portion of low-income individuals than the majority white group. The proportion of blacks in middle-class occupations has increased since 1940. There is no evidence that black adolescents have lower self-concepts than white adolescents. Most Hispanic adolescents trace their roots to Mexico, Puerto Rico, and Cuba. Roughly one-third will marry non-Hispanics. Adolescents of Mexican origin are the largest subgroup. Hispanics have one of the lowest educational levels of all minority groups in the United States. Many Hispanic, as well as black, adolescents have developed a political consciousness and pride in their cultural heritage.

VII. Other Ethnic Groups and America as a Nation of Blended Cultures

Asian-American adolescents are a diverse, fast-growing segment of the adolescent population. Japanese and Chinese are the largest subgroups. Family loyalty is powerful and they have taken advantage of educational opportunities. Native American (also called American Indian) adolescents come from a culture that has experienced considerable discrimination. Their injustices are reflected in high school dropout rates, high teenage pregnancy rates, and high suicide rates. Black, Hispanic, Asian American, native American and other cultural heritages mix with the mainstream, receiving a new content and giving a new content. Two concepts describing how cultures mix are acculturation and assimilation.

VIII. Television's Functions and Viewing

Television's functions include providing information and entertainment. Television portrays a world beyond the family, peers, and school. However, television may train adolescents to become passive learners and adopt passive life-styles. By high school graduation, the American adolescent has watched 20,000 hours of television. Adolescent viewing may be increasing because of music videos and cable television.

IX. Television Violence and Family Influences

Television violence is associated with adolescents' aggression, but no casual link has been established. Parents rarely take active roles in adolescent television viewing. Adolescents from lower socioeconomic status backgrounds watch more television than their higher socioeconomic status counterparts. Family conflict and low parental control are associated with increased adolescent viewing.

X. The Media and Music

Adolescents are heavy consumers of records, tapes, and rock music. Rock music's lyrics have been controversial. A number of factors influence the power of rock music over adolescents' thoughts and behavior, and the degree of this power is still unknown. Music video is a compelling medium. It is attention grabbing and may produce less imaginative responses than audio versions of songs. Rock music does not seem to be a passing fad and is an important dimension of the adolescent culture.

Key Terms

microsystem 327
mesosystem 327
exosystem 328
macrosystem 328
experience sampling
    method 329

anthropological view 331
rites of passage 333
social class 338
ethnicity 340

underclass 344
Chicanos 347
acculturation 348
assimilation 348

Suggested Readings

Gibbs, J. T., & Huang, L. N. (Eds.) (1989). *Children of color*. San Francisco: Jossey-Bass.
    An excellent overview of the nature of adolescence in ethnic minority groups. Separate chapters on black adolescents, Mexican American adolescents, American Indian adolescents, Southeast Asia refugee adolescents, Chinese American adolescents, and Puerto Rican adolescents.
Havighurst, R. J. (1987). Adolescent culture and subculture. In V. B. Van Hasselt & M. Hersen (Eds.), *Handbook of adolescent psychology*. New York: Pergamon.
    Information about a number of different ethnic minority adolescents is provided.
Journal of Early Adolescence, 1987, Vol. 7.
    The entire issue of this volume is devoted to the effects of television and the media on adolescent development.
Liebert, R. M., & Sprakin, J. N. (1988). *The early window: Effects of television on children and youth* (3rd ed.). Elmsford, NY: Pergamon.
    An updated account of theory and research focused on the effects of television on children's and adolescents' development.
Schorr, L. B., with Schorr, D. (1988). *Within our reach: Breaking the cycle of disadvantage and despair*. New York: Doubleday/Anchor.
    A penetrating, thought-provoking analysis of poverty in America.
Sommer, B. B. (1988). *Puberty and adolescence*. New York: Oxford University Press.
    Extensive description of rites of passage in primitive cultures.

Social, Emotional, and

Personality Development

> *He who would learn to fly oneday*
> *must learn to stand and walk*
> *and climb and dance:*
> *one cannot fly into flying.*
>
> Friedrich Nietzsche,
> Thus Spake Zarathustra, *1883*

ngela Bliss is 10 years old. When asked to describe herself as a person, she replies that she has blonde hair and blue eyes and that she will be 11 in December. She also says she is a girl, that she likes to play soccer, and that she likes school. Angela hasn't shown much interest in boys yet, although she is in a school system that includes some sex education in the late elementary grades. She goes to church with her parents every Sunday, yet she is rather naive about religion and spiritual matters. Her moral development has progressed to the point where she believes that when people do something wrong they should be punished for it.

Angela is achievement oriented, but is more motivated in English class than in math. She is a somewhat feminine young girl, not much of a tomboy. Her father is the single breadwinner in their family, and her parents have reared her to follow rather traditional sex roles. Angela really hasn't thought much about a future career, but she says she wouldn't mind being a beauty queen.

Frank Martin is also 10 years old. When asked to describe himself as a person, he responds, "I am strong, big for my age, and I have lots of friends. I love sports, and I want to be a professional football player when I grow up." Frank hasn't shown much interest in girls yet, preferring to spend most of his spare time with his male buddies in sports activities or just fooling around the neighborhood. Frank is just an average student and is not very achievement oriented—his father has rewarded him mostly for his accomplishments in sports.

When we reenter Angela Bliss's life at the age of 14 we find that she is now able to describe herself as "a truthful person, reasonably pretty, and well liked by both boys and girls." Her sexual maturation has changed dramatically since we last saw her at the age of 10—she has almost fully matured physically, and she shows a much stronger interest in boys. She still sees herself as being very feminine, and acts accordingly. She has begun to think about religious and spiritual matters and has thought about joining the church she attends. Angela's moral system could best be described as

conventional—she believes rules and regulations should be abided by and that it is morally wrong to violate those rules. She continues to like school, but she is still doing better in English than in math. Angela has started thinking more about a career—she is taking a career education class at her school, and she is considering four or five possible vocations.

When we look at Frank's life at the age of 14 and ask him to once again describe himself as a person, he says, "I am a good football player and I am popular at school. A lot of girls like me, and I have a lot of male buddies as well. We hang around a lot together. Me and my friend Mark are a lot alike—he's good in athletics, neither one of us studies very much, and we usually have a good time." Frank likes girls, and they seem to like him. Almost every night, he says, a girl calls him. Frank sees himself as very masculine—"macho," he says. His moral orientation at age 14 is based on expedience—it's all right to do some things that are not accepted by parents or the police as long as you don't get burned. Frank hasn't thought much about a possible career—he says he is too busy having fun and will think more about a career when the time comes to go to work. Church has never played much part in Frank's life, since neither of his parents go. Last year he did go to a church youth group with one of his buddies, but he went more for social than spiritual reasons.

At age 19, Angela Bliss has just finished her first year of college. She still hasn't decided on an occupation or work she would like to pursue in life. She has given some thought to getting married and raising a family, letting a husband support her. Angela is not exactly sure what she wants from life, but over the last couple of years she has spent a lot of time thinking about it. Her identity has not yet crystalized, but she doesn't sense any need to hurry out into the world and commit herself to a husband or to some type of work at this point. Angela is still very feminine and doesn't really like to be pushed into more "masculine" sex roles—she feels secure in her feminine role.

Angela is still a virgin, but she has been tempted to have intercourse on more than one occasion with the guy she has been dating for eight months. She still shows a conventional orientation toward rules and regulations and believes they should be abided by—it bothered her last month when her roommate cheated on a test. She also believes that moral values are important in relationships. Indeed, for Angela probably the most important aspect of morality is the interdependence that two people develop and the commitment they give to each other. When asked if her personality has changed much during her adolescent years, she responds that she basically is the same old Angela, but that in some ways her personality has gradually changed. She feels more mature now than when she was in junior high—she thinks more before she does something impulsive, and she is more conscientious about her study habits. She also says she is a little more outgoing now than when she was in junior high, but she realizes that how extroverted she is often depends on the situation and whom she is with at the time.

At age 19, Frank Martin has completed high school but elected not to go to college. He has worked for a year in an automobile repair shop—during his last two years of high school he worked part-time there, and worked close to full-time during the summer. Frank is still recognized around town as the guy who intercepted a pass and scored a touchdown to win the state championship in football when he was a junior in high school, and Frank still thinks a lot about his last years of high school and his football stardom. Unfortunately, he injured his knee during his senior year—and this, combined with his deteriorating high school grades, made Frank a rather unattractive candidate for college football. Frank still sees himself as "macho." He lost his virginity when he was 16. In the last six months he has had sex with his steady girlfriend about three or four times a week, and he is unofficially engaged to be married to her. But Frank isn't sure that marriage is what he wants—he says that his fiancée and her parents want the marriage more than he does but that he will probably go along.

The Self and Identity

"Who are you?" said the Caterpillar.
Alice replied, rather shyly, "I—I hardly know, Sir, just at present—at least I know who I was when I got up this morning, but I must have changed several times since then."

Lewis Carroll, Alice in Wonderland, 1865

Groucho Marx: Developing an Identity

G roucho Marx, the famous comedian, and his four brothers left school early to support their family. They were the sons of a lovable and forceful German lady and her handsome, diffident, French-born husband. She looked after her boys and their careers with the ferocity of a mother lion. At times, though, it was a topsy-turvy family. Minnie traveled with the boys while Frenchy stayed home. In the following excerpts, Groucho describes his life as he was growing up, revealing some pieces of his identity:

"I was Sam and Minnie's fourth son. The oldest, Manfred, died of old age. He was three at the time. Leonard and Adolph were the second and third sons. You know them as Chico and Harpo, respectively. Milton (Gummo) and Herbert (Zeppo) would come later.

"The first real job I got was on Coney Island. I sang a song on a beer keg and made a dollar. Later, I sang in a Protestant choir—until they found out what was wrong with it. For that I got a dollar every Sunday. Before long, I had to get a full-time job and leave school. There wasn't enough money to feed five brothers, parents, grandparents, Cousin Polly, Aunt Hannah, and Uncle Julius. That's when I got into the money, making $3.50 a week at the Hepner Wig Company. I lugged the big cans in which the wigs were washed.

"Later, Minnie decided that we brothers should stage our own act. The Four Nightingales toured the country from 1907 to 1910. Because we were a kid act, we traveled at half-fare, despite the fact that we were all around 20. Minnie insisted that we were 13. 'That kid of yours in the dining car is smoking a cigar,' the conductor told her. 'And another one is in the washroom shaving.' Minnie shook her head sadly, 'They grow so fast.'"

"It was around this time that Minnie decided we should move to Chicago, which was more central to the small-time vaudeville circuits we were working. Each of us had a motor scooter. We would travel from town to town, usually with a girl straddling the back. Harpo had a Harley-Davidson, and one day we had a race. We hit a mule. It didn't help the mule any. It was while we were touring that our singing act became intentionally funny. Harpo said in his autobiography that this happened in Ada, Oklahoma. I insist it was Nacogdoches, Texas. Who's right? I am; I'm still living. Another mule disrupted the show, which was being held in an outdoor theatre. We lost most of the audience, and when some of them straggled back, they heard some smart remarks that they took to be funny. We thought we were talking over their heads, but the audience laughed, and a new era began for the Marx brothers."

Reprinted by permission of Macmillan Publishing Company from The Grouchophile *by Groucho Marx. Copyright © 1977 by Julius H. Marx.*

T hese excerpts from Groucho Marx's autobiography reveal some of identity's ingredients—family relationships, the importance of vocational orientation, and the complexity of identity's development over many years. In this chapter, we will discover that Erik Erikson's ideas provide a rich portrayal of identity development. Some experts on adolescence consider Erikson's ideas to be the single most influential theory of adolescent development. For this reason, it is impossible to confine his ideas to a single chapter. Erikson's ideas have been described throughout the book, but it is in this chapter that we devote the most attention to his work. The theme of identity development, the focus of the second part of this chapter, is closely allied with the theme of the self, which is the focus of the first part.

The Self

Adolescents carry with them a sense of who they are and what makes them different from everyone else. They cling to this identity and develop a sense that this identity is becoming more stable. Consider one adolescent male's self-description: "I am male, bright, an athlete, a political liberal, an extravert, and a compassionate individual." And he takes comfort in his uniqueness, "No one else is quite like me. I am 5 feet 11 inches tall and weigh 160 pounds. I grew up in a suburb and attend the state university. I am not married, but one of my friends is. I want to be a sports journalist. I am an expert at building canoes. When I am not studying for exams, I write short stories about sports figures, which I hope to publish someday." Real or imagined, an adolescent's developing sense of self and uniqueness is a motivating force in life. Our exploration of the self in adolescent development looks at the distinction between I and me, cognitive developmental changes, self-concept, and the self and social competence.

I and Me

Early in psychology's history, William James (1890) distinguished the "I" and "me" of the self. "I" is the knower; "me" is the object of what is known. "I" is the active observer; "me" is the observed (the project of the observing process). "I" conveys the sense of independent existence, agency, and volition (i.e., when my eyes close it gets dark; when I burn my hand, it hurts; and so on). Some researchers refer to "I" as the **existential self** and to "me" as the **categorical self.** Development proceeds in a sequence from the existential to the categorical self—from a conception that I am, I exist, to what or who I am (Lapsley & Rice, 1988; Lewis & Brooks-Gunn, 1979).

Cognitive Developmental Changes

In our discussion of cognitive development in Chapter 4, we pointed to a number of cognitive changes that have important implications for adolescents' self-development. These changes include increases in abstract thought, idealism, organization, language sophistication, logical reasoning, perspective taking, and egocentrism. It might be helpful for you to go over ideas about these concepts in your mind or return to Chapter 4 and again read the discussion of cognitive developmental changes in adolescent development. In the process, think about how these cognitive changes might be related to the adolescent's developing sense of self.

To obtain a glimpse of increased abstractness and idealism in adolescents' self-descriptions, consider the comments of the following three individuals:

> *9-year-old boy* (concrete descriptions). My name is Bruce C. I have brown eyes. I have brown hair. I have brown eyebrows. I'm nine years old. I love! sports. I have seven people in my family. I have great! eye site. I have lots! of friends. I live on 1923 Pinecrest Drive. I'm going on ten in September. I'm a boy. I have an uncle that is almost seven feet tall. My school is Pinecrest. My teacher is Mrs. V. I play hockey! I'm almost the smartest boy in the class. I love food! I love fresh air. I love school.

> *11½-year-old girl* (increase in interpersonal descriptions). My name is A. I'm a human being. I'm a girl. I'm a truthful person. I'm not pretty. I do so-so in my studies. I'm a very good cellist. I'm a very good pianist. I'm a little bit tall for my age. I like several boys. I like several girls. I'm old-fashioned. I play tennis. I am a very good musician. I try to be helpful. I'm always ready to be friends with anybody. Mostly I'm good, but I lose my temper. I'm not well liked by some girls and boys. I don't know if boys like me or not.

> *17-year-old girl* (increase in interpersonal descriptions, characteristic mood states, and ideological and belief statements). I am a human being. I am a girl. I am an individual. I don't know who I am. I am Pisces. I am a moody person. I am an indecisive person. I am an ambitious person. I am a big curious person. I am not an individual. I am lonely. I am an American (God help me). I am a Democrat. I am a liberal person. I am a radical. I am conservative. I am a pseudoliberal. I am an atheist. I am not a classifiable person (i.e., I don't want to be). (Montemayor & Eisen, 1977, pp. 317–18)

The onset of formal operational thought allows adolescents to step outside the concrete aspects of their experience and "trip off" on a number of thought excursions about what they would like to be and what they are capable of becoming. By the end of adolescence, individuals have accumulated experiences (sometimes painful ones) that tell them about the accuracy of their idealized images. Gradually, older adolescents modify their self-theories to make them less grandiose, more realistic, and more specific. Older adolescents begin to place boundaries on their self-theories so that they can function more competently and not be saddled with unnecessary disillusionments.

Adolescents also have a more differentiated view of themselves than children do. Children may simply perceive themselves as "good" or "bad." Adolescents perceive themselves in more detailed ways. For example, one adolescent remarked, "I am a good person most of the time, except when my older sister bugs me, when my father won't let me have the car, and when I have to study for a biology test." Adolescents also have a more individuated sense of themselves than children do. This means that adolescents have a more distinct sense of themselves as unique individuals and more readily differentiate themselves from others. Young children tend to label themselves in terms of how similar they are to other children. Adolescents are more likely to describe themselves in terms of differences. Adolescents also have a more stable sense of self than children do. However, in extreme form, stability produces rigidity and unrealistic self-appraisal. Though we say that adolescents have a more stable sense of self than children, this does not imply that self-conceptions do not change during adolescence. They do change; but as adolescents cognitively mature, they become more capable of integrating information into a stable sense of who they are (Hart, Maloney, & Damon, 1987).

The question of how adolescents know that they continue to be themselves despite their transformations in appearance, thoughts, values, and behaviors has intrigued both philosophers and psychologists (Aboud & Ruble, 1987; Chandler & others, 1987). Perceptions of continuity and consistency in different dimensions of the self are thought to be important ingredients of mental health. Adolescents are adaptive beings. They are resilient through the course of their development, but they do not entirely form a new self. In a sense, adolescents change but they remain the same—amidst change is an underlying coherence and stability.

Self-awareness in the form of self-consciousness becomes more prevalent during adolescence (Rosenberg, 1965). Unreflective self-acceptance begins to disappear in early adolescence. What were once unquestioned self-truths become more problematic self-hypotheses, and the search for the truth about one's self is on. Erik Erikson (1968) also calls attention to the adolescent's tortuous self-consciousness. He states that in the effort to discover a coherent, unified self, adolescents are often preoccupied with what they appear to be in the eyes of other people and with the question of how to connect earlier roles and skills with their new, idealized views of themselves and others. Most theorists believe that self-preoccupation begins to dissipate toward the end of adolescence and the beginning of early adulthood.

Some cognitive developmental experts believe it is not until adolescence that individuals begin to develop formal theories about the self. Piaget described the process of searching for self as taking on a scientific air, not unlike a researcher carefully, systematically exploring the answer to a difficult question. David Elkind (1971) says that during adolescence the individual develops a true sense of self. While children are aware of themselves, they are not as

As these two adolescent girls talk with each other, their comments reflect their ability to understand self-other relations. Robert Selman has developed a theory of self-other relations that involves five stages of perspective taking. What would it take for these two girls to interact at Selman's highest stage of perspective taking?

sophisticated as adolescents at looking at themselves from the perspective of another. Adolescents can do this and do engage in a great deal of self-watching. Elkind argues that the characteristic self-consciousness of adolescents results from adolescents' acute concern about how others react to them, a concern that is largely absent in children.

In early adolescence, the individual's self-theory is somewhat tenuous. This is reflected in the self-consciousness and apprehension young adolescents express about how others view them. Like a new scientific theory, the young adolescent's self-theory is especially open to disconfirming data. However, adolescents continually search for new data to help them generate support for their self-theory. Such adolescent events as getting a driver's license and going on a first date are critical components of an adolescent's developing self-theory. After these events take place, the adolescent may think, "I am competent," "I am attractive to others" (Okun & Sasfy, 1977).

A cognitive-developmental sequence of self also has been proposed by Robert Selman (1976, 1980). He has expanded our knowledge of an adolescent's perceptions of self-other relations by describing a sequence of perspective taking. Selman believes that perspective taking moves through a series of five stages, beginning at age 3 and continuing through adolescence. As shown in Table 10.1, these stages range from the egocentric viewpoint of the preschool child to the in-depth perspective taking of the adolescent. To assess the individual's level of perspective taking, Selman individually interviews the adolescent, focusing on such dilemmas as the following:

> Eight-year-old Tom is trying to decide what to buy his best friend, Mike, for his birthday party. By chance, he meets Mike on the street and learns that Mike is extremely upset because his dog, Pepper, has been lost for two weeks. In fact, Mike is so upset he tells Tom, "I miss Pepper so much I never want to look at another dog again." Tom goes off, only to pass a store with a sale on puppies; only two are left and these soon will be gone. (Selman, 1980, p. 94)

Social, Emotional, and Personality Development

TABLE 10.1   *Selman's Stages of Perspective Taking*

Social Role-Taking Stage	Description
Stage 0—Egocentric viewpoint (age range 3 to 6)	Child has a sense of differentiation of self and other but fails to distinguish between the social perspective (thoughts, feelings) of other and self. Child can label other's overt feelings but does not see the cause-and-effect relation of reasons to social actions.
Stage 1—Social-informational role taking (age range 6 to 8)	Child is aware that other has a social perspective based on other's own reasoning, which may or may not be similar to child's. However, child tends to focus on one perspective rather than coordinating viewpoints.
Stage 2—Self-reflective role taking (age range 8 to 10)	Child is conscious that each individual is aware of the other's perspective and that this awareness influences self and other's view of each other. Putting self in other's place is a way of judging other's intentions, purposes, and actions. Child can form a coordinated chain of perspectives, but cannot yet abstract from this process to the level of simultaneous mutuality.
Stage 3—Mutual role taking (age range 10 to 12)	Child realizes that both self and other can view each other mutually and simultaneously as subjects. Child can step outside the two-person dyad and view the interaction from a third-person perspective.
Stage 4—Social and conventional system role taking (age range 12 to 15)	Person realizes mutual perspective taking does not always lead to complete understanding. Social conventions are seen as necessary because they are understood by all members of the group (the generalized other), regardless of their position, role, or experience.

From R. L. Selman, "The Development of Social-Cognitive Understanding: A Guide to Educational and Clinical Practice" in *Moral Development and Behavior: Theory, Research and Social Issues,* edited by Thomas Lickona. Copyright © 1986 Holt, Rinehart & Winston, Inc., New York, NY. Reprinted by permission of Dr. Thomas Lickona.

The dilemma is whether to buy the puppy and how this will influence Mike psychologically. To explore the issue of self-awareness, the interviewer now begins with a general question, such as, "Mike said he never wants to see another puppy again. Why did he say that?" Depending in part on the adolescent's response, the interviewer chooses from a range of questions related to the stages.

The cognitive developmental view has given us a more complete picture of the adolescent's self-development. Next, we look in greater detail at adolescents' self-conceptions, including another theoretical view of the self—that of Carl Rogers.

Self-Concept

An increasing number of clinicians and developmentalists believe that the core of the self—its basic inner organization—is derived from regularities in experience (Kohut, 1977; Sroufe, 1988). Individuals carry forward a history of experiences with caregivers that provide the adolescent with expectations about whether the world is pleasant or unpleasant. And in adolescence, the individual continues to experience the positive or negative affect of social agents. Despite developmental changes and context changes (increased peer contact, a wider social world), an important feature of the self's healthy development is continuity in caregiving and support, especially in the face of environmental challenges and stresses. As children become adolescents, this continuity and support in caregiving gives individuals the confidence to show initiative and to be increasingly the author of their own experiences, which enhances self-pride and self-esteem. Many clinicians stress that difficulties in interpersonal relationships derive from low self-esteem, which in turn derives from a lack of nurturance and support (Bowlby, 1988; Erikson, 1968; Kohut, 1977; Rogers, 1961; Sullivan, 1953). Carl Roger's view has been instrumental in promoting the importance of self-concept in the adolescent's development and the role of nurturance and support in achieving a healthy self-concept.

Carl Roger's View of Self-Concept

Like Sigmund Freud, Carl Rogers (1961, 1980) began his inquiry about human nature with troubled personalities. Rogers explored the human potential for change. In the knotted, anxious, defensive verbal stream of his clients, Rogers concluded that individuals are prevented from becoming who they are.

Rogers believed that most individuals have considerable difficulty accepting their own true feelings, which are innately positive. As children grow up, significant others condition them to move away from these positive feelings. Parents, siblings, teachers, and peers place constraints on the adolescent's behavior. Too often adolescents hear, "Don't do that." "You didn't do that right." "You didn't try hard enough." When adolescents don't do something right, they often get punished. Parents may threaten to take their love away, take privileges away, or sharply criticize and threaten the adolescent. Thus, Rogers believed that adolescents are the victims of conditional personal regard, meaning that love and praise are not given unless the adolescents conform to parental or social standards. The result, says Rogers, is that the adolescent's self-esteem is lowered.

Through the individual's experiences with the world, a self emerges. Rogers did not believe that all aspects of the self are conscious, but he did believe that they are accessible to consciousness. The self is thought of as a whole. It consists of self-perceptions (how attractive I am, how well I get along with others, how good an athlete I am) and the values individuals attach to these perceptions (e.g., good/bad, worthy/unworthy).

Carl Rogers, one of the main figures in the development of the humanistic approach.

Social, Emotional, and Personality Development

Rogers also considered the congruence between the real self, that is, the self as it really is as a result of one's experiences, and the ideal self, which is the self an individual would like to be. The greater the discrepancy between the real self and the ideal self, the more maladjusted the individual will be, said Rogers. To improve their adjustment, adolescents can develop more positive perceptions of their real self, not worry so much about what others want, and increase their positive experiences in the world. In such ways, the adolescent's ideal and real self will be more closely aligned.

Rogers thought that each adolescent should be valued regardless of the adolescent's behavior. Even when the adolescent's behavior is obnoxious, below standards of acceptance, or inappropriate, adolescents need the respect, comfort, and love of others. When these positive behaviors are given without contingency, it is known as **unconditional positive regard.** Rogers strongly believed that unconditional positive regard elevates the adolescent's self-worth and positive self-regard. Unconditional positive regard is directed at the adolescent as a human being of worth and dignity, not to the adolescent's behavior, which might not deserve positive regard (Rogers, 1974).

Rogers also said that each adolescent has a self-actualizing potential that is hard to keep down. Rogers's positive view of the adolescent's development can be seen in his comparison of an individual with a plant he once observed on the coastline of northern California. Rogers was looking at the waves beating furiously against the jagged rocks, shooting mountains of spray into the air. Rogers noticed a tiny palm tree on the rocks, no more than two or three feet high, taking the pounding of the breakers. The plant was fragile and top-heavy. It seemed clear that the waves would crush the tiny specimen. A wave would crunch the plant, bending its slender trunk almost flat and whipping its leaves in a torrent of spray. Yet the moment the wave passed, the plant was erect, tough, and resilient once again. It was incredible that the plant could take this incessant pounding hour after hour, week after week, year after year, all the time nourishing itself, maintaining its position, and growing. In this tiny plant, Rogers saw the human being's tenacity for life, the forward thrust of development, and the ability of a living organism to push into a hostile environment and not only hold its own, but adapt, develop, and become itself. So it is with each adolescent, Rogers (1963) thought. As we develop, Rogers said, each of us has the ability to break through and understand ourselves and our world. We can burst the cocoon and become a butterfly.

Roger's approach has both strengths and weaknesses. His view sensitized psychologists to the importance of self-perceptions, to considering the whole individual and the individual's positive nature, and to the power of self-understanding in improving human relations and communication with others. Some critics point out that while it is well and good to have a positive view of development, at times Rogers's view is almost too optimistic, possibly overestimating the freedom and rationality of individuals. Some critics also argue

TABLE 10.2	*The Self-Image Questionnaire for Young Adolescents*

Scale (item example)

1. Impulse Control
   (I keep an even temper most of the time)

2. Emotional Tone
   (I feel nervous most of the time)

3. Body Image
   (I feel proud of my body)

4. Peer Relationships
   (I think that other people just do not like me)

5. Family Relationships
   (My parents are usually patient with me)

6. Mastery and Coping
   (I am fearful of growing up)

7. Vocational-Educational Goals
   (I enjoy learning new things)

8. Psychopathology
   (I fear something constantly)

9. Superior Adjustment
   (I am a leader in school)

From Anne C. Petersen, et al., "A Self-Image Questionnaire for Young Adolescents (SIQYA): Reliability and Validity Studies" in *Journal of Youth and Adolescence,* 13, p. 100, 1984. Copyright © 1984 Plenum Publishing Corporation, New York, NY. Reprinted by permission of the publisher and author.

that the approach encourages self-love and narcissism. And a major weakness of Rogers's approach is that it is extremely difficult to test scientifically. Verification has come primarily from clinical experiences rather than controlled scientific study. Measurement of self-concept, especially in the global way described by Rogers, has been a difficult task, but as we see next, some progress has been made through recent efforts.

Measuring Self-Concept

While it is recognized that every adolescent has a self-concept and that self-evaluation is an important aspect of adolescent development, psychologists have had a difficult time measuring self-concept (Wylie, 1979; Yardley, 1987). One measure that frequently has been used is the Piers-Harris Scale (Piers & Harris, 1964), which consists of 80 items designed to measure overall self-concept. By responding "yes" or "no" to such items as "I have good ideas," adolescents reveal how they perceive themselves. The Piers-Harris Scale requires 15–20 minutes for completion and can be administered to groups or individuals.

Adolescents' self-perceptions may change according to the situations they are in, although self-concept measures like the Piers-Harris Scale are designed to measure a stable, consistent aspect of personality. And, with self-reporting, it is difficult to determine if adolescents are telling the truth about themselves or describing themselves as they want others to perceive them.

A promising measure of self-concept has been developed by Susan Harter (1982). It is called the **Perceived Competence Scale for Children.** While Harter's scale has not yet been standardized for adolescents, it has important im-

Social, Emotional, and Personality Development

(a)

(b)

(c)

plications for assessing adolescents' self-conceptions. Harter emphasizes the individual's sense of competence across different domains rather than viewing perceived competence as a unitary concept. Three types of skills are assessed on separate subscales: cognitive (academic abilities, memory skills); social (relationships with friends, feelings about self as viewed by others); and physical (athletic abilities, sportsmanship). A fourth subscale, general self-worth (self-confidence, feelings toward self), is independent of any skill domain. One recent investigation of school and peer competence in early adolescence supported treating these as distinct domains rather than lumping them together to obtain an overall measure of self-concept (Cauce, 1987).

Another recent measure of self-concept, one especially designed for young adolescents, is called the Self-Image Questionnaire for Young Adolescents (SIQYA), (Petersen & others, 1984). It is a downward extension of the Offer Self-Image Questionnaire, a widely used measure of older adolescents' self-conceptions, and includes nine separate scales: emotional tone, impulse control, body image, peer relationships, family relationships, mastery and coping, vocational-educational goals, psychopathology, and superior adjustment (see Table 10.2). Adolescents choose the extent to which each of the 98 items describes themselves—from "very well" to "not me at all."

Some assessment experts argue that a combination of several methods should be used in measuring self-concept. In addition to self-reporting, rating of an adolescent's self-concept by others and observations of the adolescent's behavior in various settings could provide a more complete and a more accurate picture of the adolescent's self-concept. Peers, teachers, parents, and even others who do not know the adolescent can be asked to rate the adolescent's self-concept. Adolescents' facial expressions and the extent to which they congratulate or condemn themselves are also good indicators of how they view themselves. For example, adolescents who rarely smile or rarely act happy are revealing something about their self-concept. One recent investigation that

(d)

The Harter Perceived Competence Scale for Children evaluates the individual's perceived competence in four areas: (a) physical, as reflected in such domains as athletic abilities; (b) cognitive, as reflected in such domains as academic abilities; (c) social, as reflected in such domains as relationships with friends; and (d) general self-worth, as reflected in such domains as self-confidence.

TABLE 10.3	*Behavioral Indicators of Self-Concept*	
Positive Indicators	**Negative Indicators**
1. Gives others directives or commands	1. Puts down others by teasing, name calling or gossiping
2. Voice quality is appropriate for situation	2. Gestures are dramatic or out of context
3. Expresses opinions	3. Inappropriate touching or avoids physical contact
4. Sits with others during social activities	4. Gives excuses for failures
5. Works cooperatively in a group	5. Glances around to monitor others
6. Faces others when speaking or being spoken to	6. Brags excessively about achievements, skills, appearance
7. Maintains eye contact during conversation	7. Verbally puts self down; self-depreciation
8. Initiates friendly contact with others	8. Speaks too loudly, abruptly or in a dogmatic tone
9. Maintains comfortable space between self and others	9. Does not express views or opinions, especially when asked
10. Little hesitation in speech, speaks fluently	10. Assumes a submissive stance

Source: Savin-Williams, R. C. & Demo, D. H., Conceiving or misconceiving the self: Issues in adolescent self-esteem.
Journal of Early Adolescence, 3, 121–140. Reprinted with permission of H.E.L.P. Books, Inc.

used behavioral observations in the assessment of self-concept shows some of the positive as well as negative behaviors that can provide clues to the adolescent's self-concept (see Table 10.3) (Savin-Williams & Demo, 1983). By using a variety of methods (such as self-report and behavioral observations) and obtaining information from various sources (such as the adolescent, parents, friends, and teachers), a more accurate construction of the adolescent's self-concept probably will be achieved.

The Self and Social Competence

It is the goal of virtually all parents to rear their adolescents to be socially competent. What does this mean? The term **social competence** has been defined in various ways, reflecting the different perspectives of social theorists' (Dodge & others, 1986). Among the definitions are the following: effective response of the individual to life situations, capacity to interact effectively with the environment, one who is able to make use of environmental and personal resources to achieve developmental outcomes. Even Socrates had a definition for social competence: "Those who manage well the circumstances they encounter daily."

Let's consider further the thinking of Everett Waters and Alan Sroufe (1983), who believe that environmental and personal resources are key dimensions of social competence. Resources in the environment are those things that can support or develop an adolescent's ability to coordinate emotion, cognition, and behavior both in the service of short-term adaptation and long-term developmental progress. Adult social agents, especially parents, are important environmental resources throughout childhood and adolescence. From early childhood on, the range of potential environmental resources expands. Friends, peers, teachers, counselors, coaches, neighborhood youth directors, ministers, and many others are important environmental resources in adolescence.

TABLE 10.4 *The Ingredients of Social Competence: Martin Ford's Model*

	Type of Goal	
Defining Issue	**Self-Assertive Goals**	**Integrative Goals**
Identity:	Individuality	Belongingness
Control:	Self-determination	Social responsibility
Social comparison:	Superiority	Equity
Resource distribution:	Resource acquisition	Resource provision

From M. Ford, "A Living Systems Conceptualization of Social Intelligence: Outcomes, Processes, and Developmental Change" in *Advances in the Psychology of Human Intelligence*, Vol. 3, 1986, edited by R. J. Sternberg. Copyright © 1986 Lawrence Erlbaum Associates, Inc., Hillsdale, NJ. Reprinted by permission.

Resources within the adolescent are another important part of social competence. The possibilities range from specific skills and abilities to general constructs, such as self-esteem. Delay of gratification, ego resiliency (adaptation, flexibility), and self-control are important strengths of the socially competent adolescent. Need for achievement (the motivation to do something well) also is an important aspect of being socially competent, especially in the achievement-oriented American society. The entire class of constructs labeled *self, self-esteem, self-concept,* and the like denotes important resources in the adolescent. Keep in mind that both environmental resources and resources within the adolescent have been referenced to a particular developmental level. For example, dependency is a positive characteristic early in infancy but is more likely to be associated with social incompetence in adolescence.

The ideas of Martin Ford (1986, 1987) emphasize that social competence involves both individual and social goals. Thus, social competence is not entirely a property of the adolescent or solely a property of the social world. Rather, the most competent adolescents accomplish both individual and social goals. Ford believes that social competence consists of four defining issues, each of which has an individual (or self-assertive) and a social (or integrative) goal (see Table 10.4). The four defining issues are identity, control, social comparison, and resource distribution.

Regarding identity, the self-assertive task is to develop and express one's individuality. Examples of this type of social competence are a unique behavioral style or an unusual pattern of interests. The self-assertive adolescent also may have a strongly endorsed set of social values and a clear, stable set of self-conceptions. The self-assertive nature of the adolescent would not depend on other individuals or on groups for self-definition. The integrative aspect of identity development is belongingness. It involves efforts to create, maintain, or enhance the identity of the social units of which the adolescent is a part. The units might be small and intimate, as in the adolescent's family or close friendships, or large and abstract, such as an ethnic group. Ford believes the emphasis should be on active engagement of the social environment to create situations that will enhance the self-assertive and belongingness aspects of identity.

Regarding the second issue, control, self-determination is the self-assertive goal, social responsibility the integrative goal. Adolescents who are making progress in self-determination are beginning to establish and maintain personal control over their life circumstances and regain control of it when it is lost. Social responsibility is attained by accepting legitimate and necessary types of social control. The control is exercised to some degree through society's broad rules, such as the prohibition of certain immoral or illegal actions (e.g., violence and theft) and through regulation of conduct in social contexts, such as the classroom and the neighborhood. Social control also is developed through formal obligations to personal rules, such as being a student and later being an employee. Social control also is established by informal obligations involving social contracts with friends, relatives, and others. Thus, social responsibility occurs in situations when duties are upheld, commitments are kept, and roles are fulfilled. Social responsibility also is reflected in such characteristics as dependability, trustworthiness, and integrity.

The third issue in Ford's model of social competence is social comparison. When adolescents compare themselves to others, the self-assertive consequence is the sense that they are better or higher on some relevant dimension than the other individual or reference group. Since superiority is relative rather than absolute, self-assertiveness occurs most often in competitive situations. In these situations, a high social status is achieved through social assignment or social accident. Superiority also is achieved through commerce with peers, since individuals who are dissimilar (e.g., adults), usually do not provide the best basis for meaningful comparison. The integrative aspect of social comparison is equity, an important interest of group leaders such as teachers, parents, and employers, who need to be concerned about demands for fair, unbiased treatment. Equity can occur in relationships with siblings, peers, and friends, where powerful norms about sharing and fairness are important for maintaining a positive quality in the relationship. Equity also may be demonstrated in relationships with dissimilar others, such as adolescents who are disadvantaged (those who have less money, lower intelligence, and so on).

The fourth and final issue in Ford's social competence model is resource allocation. Adolescents need to be competent at resource allocation. Alternatively, resource provision may be needed to improve the functioning of other individuals and social groups. The resources might be goods and possessions, such as food, clothing, or money. The resources might also be assistance, advice, or cognitive validation. Since social resources are usually distributed through friendships, and social support networks developed through mutual give-and-take, resource acquisition and provision often can be attained in the same context. Indeed, the adolescent's unwillingness to provide resources reciprocally to others may make it difficult for the adolescent to acquire resources.

In sum, Ford (1986, 1987) argues that adolescents who maintain and promote the functioning of themselves and others are more socially competent than those who do not. His view appropriately recognizes that social competence involves both internal, self, self-assertive dimensions and external, social, environmental dimensions. Both Ford's model and that of Waters and Sroufe capture this dual nature of social competence.

The Self

Concept	Processes/Related Ideas	Characteristics/Description
I and me	Their nature	"I" is the knower; "me" is the object of what is known. "I" also is known as the existential self, "me" as the categorical self.
Cognitive developmental changes	Overview of adolescent cognitive changes	Increased abstract thought, idealism, organization, language sophistication, logical reasoning, perspective taking, and egocentrism. By the end of adolescence, idealistic self-theories have become somewhat less grandiose and more realistic.
	Other changes	Adolescents have more differentiated, individuated, and stable self-conceptions than children. Self-awareness in the form of self-consciousness becomes more prevalent in adolesence. Some cognitive developmental experts believe it is not until adolescence that individuals develop formal theories about the self. The young adolescent's self-theory is somewhat tenuous. As individuals go through adolescence, they search for information to confirm or disconfirm their self-theory.
	Selman's cognitive developmental view	Robert Selman proposed five stages of perspective taking, beginning with the egocentric viewpoint in early childhood and ending with in-depth perspective taking in adolescence.
Self-concept	Rogers's view	Adolescents are the victims of conditional personal regard. The result is that their self is not valued. The self is the core of the adolescent's development. It includes the real self and the ideal self. Rogers advocates unconditional positive regard to enhance adolescents' self-conceptions. Rogers's approach sensitized us to the importance of adolescents' self-conceptions, but critics stress that the view is too optimistic, too global, and too unscientific.
	Measuring self-concept	Measuring self-concept is a difficult task. Harter's Perceived Competence Scale for Children is a promising measure, but it has not yet been standardized for adolescents. The SIQYA (Self-Image Questionnaire for Young Adolescents) also provides information about different dimensions of the self. A multimethod assessment of self-concept may be the best strategy.
The self and social competence	What is social competence and how is the self involved?	Social competence has been defined in varied ways. The definition of Waters and Sroufe and that of Ford emphasizes its internal, self, self-assertive dimensions and its external, social, environmental dimensions. Ford believes social competence consists of four main issues: identity, control, social comparison, and resource distribution.

At this point we have discussed a number of ideas about the self. A summary of these ideas appears in Concept Table 10.1. In our discussion of the self in adolescence, we have seen that identity is an important aspect of the self and social competence. Next, we explore the nature of adolescent identity development in more detail.

HARTLAND—"Reprinted with special permission of King Features Syndicate, Inc."

Identity

Who am I? What am I all about? What am I going to do with my life? What is different about me? How can I make it on my own? Not usually considered during childhood, these questions surface as common, virtually universal, concerns during adolescence. Adolescents clamor for solutions to these questions that revolve around the concept of identity. Our exploration of identity begins by focusing on Erik Erikson's ideas about identity and the life cycle. Then we describe the four statuses of identity, developmental stages, identity and gender, family influences, and identity's measurement. We conclude by investigating the relation of identity to intimacy.

Erikson's Ideas on Identity

That today we believe identity is a key concept in understanding the lives of adolescents is a result of Erik Erikson's masterful thinking and analysis.

Revisiting Erikson's Views on Identity and the Life Cycle

You may remember from Chapter 2 that Erikson (1950, 1968) believes identity versus identity confusion is the fifth of life's eight stages, occurring at about the same time as adolescence. At this time go over Erikson's eight stages in your mind. If they are not clear to you, return to Chapter 2 and review them.

During adolescence, world views become important to the individual, who enters what Erikson calls a **psychological moratorium**—a gap between childhood security and adult autonomy. Numerous identities can be drawn from the surrounding culture. As adolescents explore and search the culture's identity files, they may experiment with different roles. The youth who successfully copes with these conflicting identities emerges with a new sense of self that is both refreshing and acceptable. Adolescents who do not successfully resolve this identity crisis suffer what Erikson calls identity confusion.

This confusion takes one of two courses: individuals withdraw, isolating themselves from peers and family; or they may lose their identity in the crowd.

Erikson's ideas about identity development represent one of the most important statements about adolescent development and reveal rich insights into adolescents' thoughts and feelings, so try to read one or more of his original writings. A good starting point is *Identity: Youth and Crisis* (1968). Other works that portray identity development are *Young Man Luther* (1962) and *Gandhi's Truth* (1969)—the latter won a Pulitzer Prize. A sampling of Erikson's writings from these books is presented in Perspective on Adolescent Development 10.1.

Personality and Role Experimentation

Two core ingredients of Erikson's ideas on identity are personality and role experimentation. As we indicated earlier, Erikson believes that adolescents face an overwhelming number of choices and at some point during youth enter a period of psychological moratorium. During this moratorium, they try out different roles and personalities before they reach a stable sense of self. They may be argumentative one moment, cooperative the next moment. They may dress neatly one day, sloppily the next day. They may like a particular friend one week, despise the friend the next week. This personality experimentation is a deliberate effort on the part of adolescents to find out where they fit in the world.

As they gradually come to realize that they will be responsible for themselves and their own lives, adolescents search for what those lives are going to be. Many parents and other adults, accustomed to having children go along with what they say, may be bewildered or incensed by the wise cracks, the rebelliousness, and the rapid mood changes that accompany adolescence. It is important for these adults to give adolescents the time and the opportunities to explore different roles and personalities. In turn, most adolescents eventually discard undesirable roles.

There are literally hundreds of roles for adolescents to try out, and probably just as many ways to pursue each role. Erikson believes that by late adolescence, vocational roles are central to identity's development, especially in a highly technological society like the United States. Youth who have been well trained to enter a work force that offers the potential of reasonably high self-esteem will experience the least stress during the development of identity. Some youth have rejected jobs offering good pay and traditionally high social status, choosing intead to work in situations that allow them to be more genuinely helpful to their fellow humans, such as in the Peace Corps, in mental health clinics, or in schools for children from low-income backgrounds. Some youth prefer unemployment to the prospect of working at a job they feel they would be unable to perform well or at which they would feel useless. To Erikson, this attitude reflects the desire to achieve a meaningful identity through being true to oneself, rather than burying one's identity in that of the larger society.

Hitler, Luther, and Gandhi—The Development of Their Identity

Erik Erikson is a master at analyzing famous individuals' lives and discovering historical clues about their identity formation. Erikson also developed ideas for his view of identity development by analyzing the developmental history of clients in his clinical practice. Erikson (1968) believes that an individual's developmental history must be carefully scrutinized and analyzed to obtain clues about identity. He also believes that the best clues for understanding the world's history appear in the composite of individual life cycles. In the excerpts that follow, Erikson analyzes the lives of Adolf Hitler, Martin Luther, and Mahatma Gandhi.

About Hitler, Erikson (1962) commented,

I will not go into the symbolism of Hitler's urge to build except to say that his shiftless and brutal father had consistently denied the mother a steady residence; one must read how Adolf took care of his mother when she wasted away from breast cancer to get an inkling of this young man's desperate urge to cure. But it would take a very extensive analysis, indeed, to indicate in what way a single boy can daydream his way into history and emerge a sinister genius, and how a whole nation becomes ready to accept the emotive power of that genius as a hope of fulfillment for its national aspirations and as a warrant for national criminality. . . .

The memoirs of young Hitler's friend indicate an almost pitiful fear on the part of the future dictator that he might be nothing. He had to challenge this possibility by being deliberately and totally anonymous; and only out of this self-chosen nothingness could he become everything. (Erikson, 1962, pp. 108–109)

But while the identity crisis of Adolf Hitler led him to turn toward politics in a pathological effort to create a world order, the identity crisis of Martin Luther in a different era led him to turn toward theology in an attempt to deal systematically with human nothingness or lack of identity:

In confession, for example, he was so meticulous in the attempt to be truthful that he spelled out every intention as well as every deed; he splintered relatively acceptable purities into smaller and smaller impurities; he reported temptations in historical sequence, starting back in childhood; and after having confessed for hours, would ask for special appointments in order to correct previous statements. In doing this, he was obviously both exceedingly compulsive and, at least unconsciously, rebellious. . . .

At this point, we must note a characteristic of great young rebels: their inner split between the temptation to surrender and the need to dominate. A great young rebel is torn between, on the one hand, tendencies to give in and fantasies of defeat (Luther used to resign himself to an early death at times of impending success), and the absolute need, on the other hand, to take the lead, not only over himself but over all the forces and people who impinge on him. (Erikson, 1968, pp. 155–157)

And in his Pulitzer Prize winning novel on Mahatma Gandhi's life, Erikson (1969) describes the personality formation of Gandhi during his youth:

Straight and yet not stiff; shy and yet not withdrawn; intelligent and yet not bookish; willful and yet not stubborn; sensual and yet not soft. . . . We must try to reflect on the relation of such a youth to his father

Other important role choices involve sexuality (including decisions on dating, marriage, and sexual behavior), gender roles, politics, religion, and moral values. For example, many adolescents have been indoctrinated in the religious beliefs of their parents. By late adolescence, youth come to understand that they can make their own decisions about religion. The same can be said of political identity. Most children report that they adopt their parents'

Hitler in elementary school. He is in the center of the top row.

What did Erikson believe were some of the key ingredients in Mahatma Gandi's developing of identity?

because the Mahatma places service to the father and the crushing guilt of failing in such service in the center of his adolescent turbulence. Some historians and political scientists seem to find it easy to interpret this account in psychoanalytic terms; I do not. For the question is not how a particular version of the Oedipal complex "causes" a man to be both great and neurotic in a particular way, but rather how such a young person . . . manages the complexes which constrict other men. (Erikson, 1969, p. 113)

In these passages, the workings of an insightful, sensitive mind is shown looking for a historical perspective on personality development. Through analysis of the lives of such famous individuals as Hitler, Luther, and Gandhi, and through the thousands of youth he has talked with in person, Erikson has pieced together a descriptive picture of identity development.

political choices. By late adolescence, however, individuals are more likely to make political choices independent of their parents. Unfortunately, some adolescents consistently and deliberately adopt choices opposite those of their parents as a means of stating their independence. This oppositional behavior does not represent a mature form of identity.

The American Indian's Quest for Identity: Isn't It Enough To Be?

The Hopi Indians are a quiet, thoughtful people, who go to great lengths not to offend anyone. In a pueblo north of Albuquerque, a 12-year-old boy speaks: "I've been living in Albuquerque for a year. The Anglos I've met, they're different. I don't know why. In school, I drew a picture of my father's horse. One of the other kids wouldn't believe that it was ours. He said, 'You don't really own that horse.' I said, 'It's a horse my father rides, and I feed it every morning.' He said, 'How come?' I said, 'My uncle and my father are good riders, and I'm pretty good.' He said, 'I can ride a horse better than you, and I'd rather be a pilot.' I told him I never thought of being a pilot."

The 12-year-old Indian boy continues, "Anglo kids, they won't let you get away with anything. Tell them something, and fast as lightning and loud as thunder, they'll say, 'I'm better than you, so there!' My father says it's always been like that."

The Indian adolescent is not really angry or envious of the white adolescent. Maybe he is in awe of his future power; maybe he fears it. And the white adolescent can't keep from wondering somehow, in some way, that he has missed out on something, and may end up "losing" (Coles, 1986).

The following words of an American Indian vividly capture some important ingredients of the 12-year-old boy's interest in a peaceful identity:

Rivers flow. The sea sings.
Oceans roar. Tides rise.
Who am I?
A small pebble on a giant shore;
Who am I
To ask who I am?
Isn't it enough to be.

The Complexity of Erikson's Theory

The development of an integrated sense of identity is a long, complex, and difficult task. Adolescents are expected to master many different roles in the American culture. It is the rare, perhaps nonexistent, adolescent who does not have serious doubts about handling at least some of these roles competently. The complexity of Erikson's view of identity involves at least seven dimensions (Bourne, 1978): genetic, adaptive, structural, dynamic, subjective or experiential, psychosocial reciprocity, and existential status.

With regard to the genetic dimension, Erikson describes identity development as a developmental product or outcome that incorporates the individual's experiences over the first five stages of development. Identity development reflects the way the adolescent has resolved prior stages such as trust vs. mistrust, autonomy vs. doubt, initiative vs. guilt, and industry vs. inferiority.

With regard to the adaptive dimension, the adolescent's identity development can be viewed as an adaptive accomplishment or achievement. Identity is the adaptation of adolescents' special skills, capacities, and strengths to the society in which they live.

With regard to the structural dimension, identity confusion is a breakdown in time perspective, initiative, and ability to coordinate present behavior toward future goals. This kind of breakdown implies a structural deficit.

With regard to the dynamic dimension, Erikson believes that identity formation begins where the usefulness of identification ends. It arises from childhood identifications with adults but absorbs them in new configurations, which in turn are dependent on society's roles for youth.

With regard to the subjective dimension of identity, Erikson believes that the individual senses an inner feeling of cohesiveness or lack of assuredness.

With regard to the dimension of reciprocity, Erikson emphasizes the mutual relationship of adolescents with their social world and community. Identity development is not just an intrapsychic self-representation, but involves relationships with people, community, and society.

And with regard to the existential dimension, Erikson thinks that adolescents seek the meaning to their life as well as the meaning of life in general, much like an existential philosopher.

Some Contemporary Thoughts about Identity

Contemporary views of identity development suggest several important considerations. First, identity development is a lengthy process, in many instances a more gradual, less cataclysmic transition than Erikson's term *crisis* implies. Second, as we just indicated, identity development is extraordinarily complex (Marcia, 1980, 1987). Identity formation neither begins nor ends with adolescence. It begins with the appearance of attachment, the development of a sense of self, and the emergence of independence in infancy, and reaches its final phase with a life review and integration in old age. What is important about identity development in adolescence, especially late adolescence, is that for the first time physical development, cognitive development, and social development advance to the point at which the individual can sort through and synthesize childhood identities and identifications to construct a viable path toward adult maturity. Resolution of the identity issue at adolescence does not mean that identity will be stable through the remainder of life. An individual who develops a healthy identity is flexible and adaptive, open to changes in society, in relationships, and in careers. This openness assures numerous reorganizations of identity's contents throughout the identity-achieved individual's life.

Identity formation does not happen neatly and it usually does not happen cataclysmically. At the bare minimum, it involves commitment to a vocational direction, an ideological stance, and a sexual orientation. Synthesizing the identity components can be a long and drawn out process, with many negations and affirmations of various roles and faces. Identity development gets done in bits and pieces. Decisions are not made once and for all, but have to be made again and again. And the decisions may seem trivial at the time: whom to date, whether or not to break up, whether or not to have intercourse, whether or not to take drugs, whether or not to go to college or finish high school and get a job, which major, whether to study or to play, whether or not to be politically active, and so on. Over the years of adolescence, the decisions begin to form a core of what the individual is all about as a human being, what is called his or her identity.

The Four Statuses of Identity

James Marcia (1966, 1980, 1987) analyzed Erikson's theory of identity development and concluded that four identity statuses, or modes of resolution, appear in the theory: identity diffusion, identity foreclosure, identity moratorium, and identity achievement. The extent of an adolescent's commitment and crisis is used to classify the individual according to one of the four identity statuses. **Crisis** is defined as a period during which the adolescent is choosing among meaningful alternatives. Most researchers now use the term *exploration* rather than *crisis,* although in the spirit of Marcia's original formulation, we will refer to crisis. **Commitment** is defined as the extent to which the adolescent shows a personal investment in what he or she is going to do.

In **identity diffusion,** adolescents have not yet experienced a crisis (i.e., they have not explored meaningful alternatives) or made any commitments. Not only are they undecided upon occupational or ideological choices, they also are likely to show little interest in such matters. In **identity foreclosure,** adolescents have made a commitment but have not experienced a crisis. This occurs most often when parents simply hand down commitments to their adolescents, more often than not in an authoritarian way. In these circumstances, adolescents have not had adequate opportunities to explore different approaches, ideologies, and vocations on their own. In **identity moratorium,** adolescents are in the midst of a crisis but their commitments either are absent or are only vaguely defined. These adolescents are searching for commitments by actively questioning alternatives. In **identity achievement,** adolescents have undergone a crisis and have made a commitment. A summary of Marcia's four statuses of identity is presented in Table 10.5.

The identity status approach has come under sharp criticism by some researchers and theoreticians (Blasi, 1988; Cote & Levine, 1988a,b, 1989; Lapsley & Power, 1988; Lerner, 1981). They believe the identity status approach distorts and trivializes Erikson's notions of crisis and commitment. For

Social, Emotional, and Personality Development

TABLE 10.5 *The Four Statuses of Identity*

Position on occupation and ideology	Identity Status			
	Identity moratorium	Identity foreclosure	Identity diffusion	Identity achievement
Crisis commitment	Present	Absent	Absent	Present
	Absent	Present	Absent	Present

example, concerning crisis, Erikson emphasized the youth's questioning of the perceptions and expectations of one's culture and developing an autonomous position with regard to one's society. In the identity status approach these complex questions are dealt with by simply evaluating whether a youth has thought about certain issues and considered alternatives. Erikson's idea of commitment loses the meaning of investing one's own self in certain lifelong projects, and is interpreted simply as having made a firm decision or not. Others still believe the identity status paradigm is conceptually related to Erikson's theory and merits further research attention (Waterman, 1988).

Developmental Changes

Early adolescents are primarily in identity confusion or identity moratorium. There are at least three aspects of the young adolescent's life that are important in identity formation (Marcia, 1987). Young adolescents must establish confidence in parental support, develop a sense of industry, and gain a self-reflective perspective on their future.

Some researchers believe the most important identity changes take place in late adolescence. For example, in one investigation, the most significant identity status changes occurred between the ages of 18 and 21 (Meilman, 1979). The college years may be especially important in identity development. During the college years, individuals move in the direction of identity achievement (Marcia, 1987; Waterman & Waterman, 1971, 1972).

Comparisons often are made between less advanced (diffusion, foreclosure) and more advanced (moratorium, achievement) identity statuses. Researchers have found that the changes from less advanced to more advanced identity statuses are related to personality development (more advanced moral development and an inner focus on control) and to social cognitive development (maturity in social thinking processes). For example, in one recent investigation, identity-achieved youth were more likely to reveal information about their self to others than were youth in the other three identity statuses (Adams, Abraham, & Markstrom, 1987).

Some researchers believe important changes in identity take place in the high school and college years. Examine your own life for a moment. What kind of changes have taken place in your identity during your high school and college years?

Identity and Gender

Is the identity development of the adolescent male the same as that of the adolescent female? In the 1960s and 1970s, researchers were finding gender differences during both the high school and college years. For example, in one investigation, vocational identity was more central to the identity formation of adolescent males, affiliative identity to the identity formation of adolescent females (LaVoie, 1976).

In the 1980s, though, research revealed a different pattern of results when the identity development of males and females was compared (Waterman, 1982). There now are fewer gender differences in identity than the earlier studies suggested. As females assumed a stronger vocational identity in the 1970s and 1980s, assessment of adolescent females' identity suggested an identity more similar to that of males. Gender similarities in vocational choice, religious beliefs, political ideology, and gender role attitudes are appearing more often now than in the past. In one recent investigation of seventh graders, females were even more likely than males to explore alternative roles (Streitmatter, 1987).

Family Influences on Identity

Parents are important figures in the adolescent's development of identity. Catherine Cooper and Harold Grotevant (Cooper & Grotevant, 1989; Grotevant & Cooper, 1985) highlight the power of both connectedness to parents and the presence of a family atmosphere that promotes individuation in the adolescent's identity development. **Connectedness** is reflected in mutuality and permeability. Mutuality refers to the adolescent's sensitivity to and respect for others' views. Permeability refers to openness and responsiveness to others' views. Mutuality provides adolescents with support, acknowledgement, and

The adolescent's positive development of identity is related both to connectedness with parents and individuation.

respect for their own beliefs; permeability lets the adolescent sense how to manage the boundaries between the self and others. **Individuation** has two main components—separateness and self-assertion. Separateness is seen in the expressions of how distinctive the self is from others. Self-assertion is involved in the adolescent's expression of his or her personal point of view and in taking responsibility for communicating this clearly. Parents who have both a connectedness with their adolescents and who promote individuation encourage the adolescent's development of identity. As with social competence, with identity we see the importance of thinking about both an individual orientation and a social or relationship orientation. More about Grotevant and Cooper's ideas on the family processes involved in identity development appear in Perspective on Adolescent Development 10.2. In sum, a current theme in identity development research is the role parents play (O'Brien, 1989; Papini, Barnett, Clark, & Micka, 1989).

Measuring Identity

Identity is as difficult to measure as self-concept—if not more difficult. Until recently, even though experts recognized the importance of identity as an integrative concept in adolescence, there was little empirical research about identity. Much of what we knew was based on clinical case studies and psychobiographies (such as Erikson's analysis of Hitler's identity development). Some experts question whether the process of identity formation is spelled out in sufficient detail to permit empirical studies to be derived from Erikson's formulation (Hill, 1983). While empirical documentation of the developmental course of identity development is still sketchy, a number of recent efforts have been directed at improving the assessment of identity (Grotevant & Adams, 1984; Hart, Maloney, & Damon, 1987; Marcia, 1987).

Carol and Janet, Individuated and Nonindividuated Family Experiences

Family experiences play an important role in the adolescent's development of identity. When involved in a family planning activity, Carol's father said, "I think probably what we all ought to do is decide the things that we want to do, each one of us individually. And, then maybe we'll be able to reconcile from that point . . . Let's go ahead and take a few minutes to decide where we'd like to go and what we would like to do. And, maybe we'll be able to work in everything everybody wants to do in these fourteen days. Okay?" In this planning of a two-week vacation, Carol, her mother, and her father all were active and involved, displaying humor, candor, spontaneity, and vulnerability. For example, Carol's mother commented, "I think we all have good imaginations," while the father said, "I think that's kind of nice. I think we ought to be a rich gang."

Carol seemed to be aware of her role in the family and of the boundary between the adolescent and parent generations. During her identity interview, she said, "I have a say, but not a deciding vote in family decisions." Carol's identity exploration rating . . . was very high. A distinctive quality of her identity exploration was that she experienced her parents as providing room for her to explore beyond their own experiences or needs. For ex-

ample, she reported that both parents felt that religion had been forced on them as children, so they decided not to force it on her. Consequently, she had been able to explore several religions as possible alternatives with her friends. In the domain of friendship, Carol had maintained a relationship with a girl who had been a close friend, but who later became involved with drugs and turned against her parents. Carol had been able to maintain this relationship and see how it differed from her other close friendships without compromising her own standards. Her parents were concerned about this friendship, but they trusted Carol and permitted her to work through this situation. In a comparable pattern, Carol's score of fifteen on the Role-Taking Task was also very high. She achieved the highest reciprocal level score by clearly coordinating the perspective of two characters in her story and by elaborating both their external and psychological states.

In contrast, the family of Janet, the firstborn of two, reflected nonindividuated spousal and parent-child relationships with few disagreements, self-assertions that largely coincided with the family's point of view, and frequent expressions of connectedness. The ratio of agreements to disagreements between mother and father

The Extended Measure of Ego Identity Status (Grotevant & Adams, 1984) is being used increasingly as a measure of adolescents' identity development. It consists of 64 items reflecting the presence or absence of commitment in both ideological and interpersonal content domains. The ideological domain includes items about occupation, religion, politics, and philosophical life-style. The interpersonal domain includes items about friendship, dating, recreation, and gender roles. Individuals answer the extent to which they agree or disagree with an item (1 = strongly disagree; 6 = strongly agree). Adolescents may be classified into an ideological identity status, an interpersonal identity status, or both. Marcia's four identity statuses are used for these classifications. While identity's measurement has been elusive, researchers are developing improved methods of assessing it. Even with its measurement problems, the concept of identity—especially the search for self—seems to capture one of adolescence's most important themes.

(sixteen) was unusually high, suggesting a marked imbalance between expression of individuality and connectedness. In addition, Janet disagreed with her father only once, and he never disagreed with her, whereas she was responsive to him twenty-nine times, and he was responsive to her ten times. Enmeshment in this family's interaction was illustrated in the first five utterances on the Family Interaction Task:

Mother: Where shall we go?
Father: Back to Spain.
Mother: Back to Spain.
Janet: Back to Spain.
Sister: Back to Spain.

When Janet's father later asked for more suggestions, she said, "And then, I don't . . . I mean, you go on, Dad, 'cause I don't know . . . what else."

Janet's low identity exploration rating of thirteen may reflect a lack of exploration of issues outside the consensual family beliefs. In this family, in which signs of individuated spousal and parent-child relationships were less evident, the necessity for agreement and connectedness among family members and the family members' excessive involvement in each other's identity appeared to hinder the adolescent's development of individual ideas regarding career, dating, and other issues. With regard to career choice, Janet commented, "I'm having a hard time deciding what to do. It would be easier if they would tell me what to do, but of course I don't want that."

Janet's low role-taking score of nine suggests a lack of ability to express both separate and reciprocal points of view. While telling her story, Janet commented, "I don't know what the others are thinking, because I'm thinking of it only as if I'm the girl." Perhaps the nonindividuated communication patterns that Janet observed in her parents' relationship and that she participated in with her father inhibited her ability both to engage in identity exploration and to coordinate different perspectives.

In these excerpts from the lives of two adolescent girls, we have seen the importance of family interaction in the development of identity. ಜಾ

Identity and Intimacy

As we go through our adolescence, youth, and early adulthood, most of us are motivated to successfully juggle the development of an identity, intimacy, and a sense of independence. What is the nature of intimacy's development? How complex is the link between identity and intimacy? How do we juggle the motivation for intimacy and the motivation for identity and independence?

Intimacy

Erik Erikson (1968) believes that intimacy should come after individuals are well on their way to establishing a stable and successful individual identity. Intimacy is another life crisis in Erikson's scheme—if intimacy is not developed in early adulthood, the individual may be left with what Erikson calls

Erik Erikson believes that it is important to resolve the identity vs. identity confusion crisis before the intimacy vs. isolation crisis. What are some of the problems that might develop if the intimacy crisis is experienced prior to successful resolution of the identity crisis?

isolation. Intimacy versus isolation is the sixth stage in Erikson's eight-stage life cycle perspective, corresponding roughly to the early adulthood years. Erikson (1968) refers to intimacy in both sexual relationships and friendships:

> As the young individual seeks at least tentative forms of playful intimacy in friendship and competition, in sex play and love, in argument and gossip, he is apt to experience a peculiar strain, as if such tentative engagement might turn into an interpersonal fusion amounting to a loss of identity and requiring, therefore, a tense inner reservation, a caution in commitment. Where a youth does not resolve such a commitment, he may isolate himself and enter, at best, only stereotyped and formalized interpersonal relations; or he may, in repeated hectic attempts and dismal failures, seek intimacy with the most improbable of partners. For where an assured sense of identity is missing, even friendships and affairs become desperate attempts at delineating the fuzzy outlines of identity by mutual narcissistic mirroring; to fall in love means to fall in love with one's mirror image, hurting oneself and damaging the mirror. (p. 167)

Social, Emotional, and Personality Development

An inability to develop meaningful relationships with others can be harmful to an individual's personality. It may lead individuals to repudiate, ignore, or attack those who frustrate them. Such circumstances account for the shallow, almost pathetic attempts of youth to merge themselves with a leader. Many youths want to be apprentices or disciples of leaders and adults who will shelter them from the harm of the "outgroup" world. If this fails, and Erikson believes that it must, sooner or later the individuals recoil into a self-search to discover where they went wrong. This introspection sometimes leads to painful depression and isolation and may contribute to a mistrust of others and restrict the willingness to act on one's own initiative.

There are different styles of intimate interaction. One classification suggests five styles: intimate, preintimate, stereotypes, pseudointimate, and isolated (Orlofsky, Marcia, & Lesser, 1973). In the **intimate style** the individual forms and maintains one or more deep and long-lasting love relationships. The **preintimate style** involves mixed emotions about commitment; this ambivalence is reflected in a strategy of offering love without obligations or long-lasting bonds. The **stereotyped style** consists of superficial relationships that tend to be dominated by friendship ties with same-sex rather than opposite-sex individuals. The **pseudointimate style** involves maintenance of long-lasting heterosexual attachment with little or no depth or closeness. And the **isolated style** encompasses withdrawal from social encounters and little or no intimate attachment to same- or opposite-sex individuals. Occasionally, the isolate shows signs of developing interpersonal relationships, but usually the interactions are stressful. In one investigation, intimate and preintimate individuals were more sensitive to their partners' needs and were more open in their friendships than individuals who were categorized according to the other three intimacy statuses (Orlofsky, 1976).

Intimacy, like identity, is a global concept and encompasses many different dimensions. And there are many different social pressures on intimacy in our society (Blyth & Foster-Clark, 1987). First, there is widespread pressure for females to display intimacy. In addition, there are social pressures that may affect intimacy, among them fear of homosexuality and incest. There also are social pressures that encourage greater levels of intimacy with individuals of the opposite-sex who are potential and acceptable romantic partners (Reis & others, 1985). In addition to social pressures arising from sexuality, nurturance also is involved in intimacy. Nurturance involves support and protection of the other. And, finally, there also are social pressures to be more intimate with others with whom we have something in common or who may be appropriate role models. Remember our discussion of dating in Chapter 7, where we concluded that birds of a feather do indeed flock together.

Complexity in the Link between Identity and Intimacy
Not only the nature of intimacy itself but the link between identity and intimacy can be complex (Meacham & Santilli, 1982). One issue raised is what happens when identity foreclosure occurs. Possibly the individual progresses

to the point of experiencing, but not resolving, the crisis of intimacy versus isolation. Any of several resolutions is then possible. For example, this new crisis may be unresolvable until the individual returns to and successfully resolves the identity crisis. Such a sequence is compatible with Erikson's belief that the crises may be experienced out of order but must be resolved in a universal order. A second possibility is that the individual may resolve the intimacy crisis and then move forward to the generativity versus stagnation crisis. Finally, a third possibility is that, after resolving the intimacy crisis, the individual may return to the identity crisis. The three possible paths would be then, respectively: intimacy (unresolved), identity, intimacy, and generativity; intimacy and generativity; or intimacy, identity, and generativity. Other sequences are possible, but these three provide some indication of the variation in which individuals may experience and resolve the identity and intimacy crises. For example, there is some evidence that females experience the crisis of intimacy before identity (Douvan & Adelson, 1966; Fischer, 1981).

Intimacy, Identity, and Independence

As we develop through adolescence and early adulthood, we usually do have an intimate relationship with another individual. An important aspect of this relationship is the commitment of the individuals to each other. At the same time, individuals show a strong interest in independence and identity (McAdams, 1988; Selman, 1989).

Independence is a related aspect of developing an identity. At the same time individuals are trying to establish an identity, they face the difficult task of coping with increased independence from their parents, developing an intimate relationship with another individual, and increasing their friendship commitments, while also being able to think for themselves and do things without always relying on what others say or do. The extent to which young people have begun to develop autonomy has important implications for maturity. The young person who has not sufficiently moved away from parental ties may have difficulty in both interpersonal relationships and in a career. Consider the mother who overprotects her daughter, continues to support her financially, and does not want to let go of her. The daughter may have difficulty developing mature intimate relationships and she may have career difficulties. When a promotion comes up that involves more responsibility and possibly more stress, she may turn it down. When things do not go well in her relationship with a young man, she may go crying to her mother.

The balance between, on the one hand, intimacy and commitment to others and, on the other hand, independence and identity is delicate. These dimensions of development are not necessarily opposite ends of a continuum— some individuals are able to experience a healthy independence and commitment to others along with an intimate relationship. These dimensions also may

Social, Emotional, and Personality Development

fluctuate with social and historical change. For example, in today's world, females exhibit a stronger motivation for independence than in past decades. Also keep in mind that intimacy and commitment, and independence and identity, are worked and reworked throughout the adolescent and adulthood years.

At this point we have discussed many ideas about identity. A summary of these ideas is presented in Concept Table 10.2.

Summary

I. I and Me

"I" is the knower, "me" is the object of what is known. "I" also is known as the existential self, "me" as the categorical self.

II. Overview of Cognitive Developmental Changes

Cognitive developmental changes related to the self involve increases in abstract thought, idealism, organization, language sophistication, logical reasoning, perspective taking, and egocentrism. By the end of adolescence, idealistic self-descriptions have become somewhat less grandiose and more realistic.

III. Other Cognitive Changes and Selman's View

Adolescents have more differentiated, individuated, and stable self-conceptions than children. Self-awareness in the form of self-consciousness becomes more prevalent in adolescence. Some cognitive developmental experts believe it is not until adolescence that individuals develop formal theories about the self. The young adolescent's self-theory is somewhat tenuous. As individuals go through adolescence, they search for information to confirm or disconfirm their self-theory. Robert Selman proposed five stages of perspective taking, beginning with the egocentric viewpoint in early childhood and ending with in-depth perspective taking in adolescence.

IV. Rogers's View of Self-Concept

Adolescents are victims of conditional personal regard. The result is that their self is not valued. The self is the core of the adolescent's development. It includes the real self and the ideal self. Rogers advocates unconditional positive regard to enhance adolescents' self-conceptions. Rogers's approach sensitized us to the importance of adolescents' self-conceptions, but critics stress that the view is too optimistic, too global, and too unscientific.

V. Measuring Self-Concept

Measuring self-concept is a difficult task. Harter's Perceived Competence Scale for Children is a promising measure but it has not yet been standardized for adolescents. The SIQYA (Self-Image Questionnaire for Young Adolescents) also provides information about dimensions of the self. A multimethod assessment of self-concept may be the best strategy.

Identity

Concept	Processes/Related Ideas	Characteristics/Description
Erikson's ideas on identity	Revisiting Erikson's views on identity and the life cycle	Erikson argues that identity versus identity confusion is the fifth stage in the human life cycle, occurring at about the time of adolescence. At this time, individuals enter a psychological moratorium.
	Personality and role experimentation	Two core ingredients of Erikson's ideas on identity. There are literally hundreds of roles for individuals to explore and many ways to pursue each role. In technological societies such as the United States, the vocational role is especially important.
	The complexity of Erikson's theory	Involves genetic, adaptive, structural, dynamic, subjective or experiential, psychosocial reciprocity, and existential status dimensions.
	Some contemporary thoughts about identity	Identity development is a lengthy process, in many cases more gradual than Erikson implied. Identity development is extraordinarily complex. Identity development gets done in bits and pieces. For the first time in development, individuals during adolescence are physically, cognitively, and socially mature enough to synthesize their lives and pursue a viable path toward adult maturity.
The four statuses of identity and developmental changes	The four statuses	Marcia proposed four identity statuses—identity diffusion, identity foreclosure, identity moratorium, and identity achievement—that are based on crisis (exploration) and commitment. Some experts believe the identity status approach oversimplifies Erikson's ideas.
	Developmental changes	Some experts believe the main identity changes take place in late rather than early adolescence. Older adolescents and college students are more likely to be identity achieved. Developmental changes in identity are related to personality and social cognitive changes.

VI. The Self and Social Competence

Social competence has been defined in various ways. The definitions of Waters and Sroufe and of Ford emphasize its internal, self, self-assertive dimensions and its external, social, environmental dimensions. Ford believes social competence consists of four main issues: identity, control, social comparison, and resource distribution.

VII. Revisiting Erikson's Views and Personality and Role Experimentation

Erikson argues that identity versus identity confusion is the fifth stage in the human life cycle, occurring at about the time of adolescence. At this time, individuals enter a psychological moratorium. Two core ingredients of Erikson's theory of identity are personality and role experimentation. There

Concept	Processes/Related Ideas	Characteristics/Description
Identity and gender, family influences	Identity and gender	In the 1960s and 1970s, researchers were finding gender differences in identity, but today those differences have turned into similarities, especially in the area of vocational roles.
	Family influences	Parents are important figures in the adolescent's identity development. Identity development is promoted by a combination of individuation and connectedness.
Measuring identity	Its difficulty	Identity is a global concept and its measurement has been problematic. The Extended Measure of Ego Identity Status is being used increasingly as an indicator of identity development.
Identity, intimacy, and independence	Intimacy	Erikson believes that identity should come before intimacy. His sixth stage is intimacy versus isolation, which he believes should be resolved during early adulthood. Five styles of intimate interaction have been proposed: intimate, preintimate, stereotyped, pseudointimate, and isolated. There are many social pressures on intimacy in our society.
	Complexity in the link between identity and intimacy	Three possible paths are: intimacy (unresolved), identity, intimacy, and generativity; intimacy and generativity; intimacy, identity, and generativity.
	Intimacy, identity, and independence	The balance between, on the one hand, intimacy and commitment to others and, on the other hand, independence and identity is delicate. These important dimensions are worked and reworked throughout our adolescent and adult years.

are literally hundreds of roles for individuals to explore and many ways to pursue each role. In technological societies like the United States, the vocational role is especially important.

VIII. The Complexity of Erikson's Theory and Some Contemporary Thoughts on Identity

The complexity involves genetic, adaptive, structural, dynamic, subjective or experiential, psychosocial reciprocity, and existential status dimensions. Identity development is a lengthy process, in many cases more gradual than Erikson envisioned. Identity development is extraordinarily complex. It is done in bits and pieces. For the first time in development, individuals during adolescence are physically, cognitively, and socially mature enough to synthesize their lives and pursue a viable path toward adult maturity.

IX. The Four Statuses of Identity and Developmental Changes

Marcia proposed four identity statuses—identity diffusion, identity foreclosure, identity moratorium, and identity achievement—that are based on crisis (exploration) and commitment. Some experts believe the identity status approach oversimplifies Erikson's ideas. Some experts also believe the main identity changes take place in late rather than early adolescence. Older adolescents and college students are more likely to have achieved identity. Developmental changes in identity are related to personality and social cognitive changes.

X. Identity and Gender, Family Influences

In the 1960s and 1970s, researchers were finding gender differences in identity; but today those differences have turned into similarities, especially in the area of vocational roles. Parents are important figures in the adolescent's identity development. Identity development is promoted by a combination of individuation and connectedness.

XI. Measuring Identity

Identity is a global concept and its measurement has been problematic. The Extended Measure of Ego Identity Status is increasingly being used as an indicator of identity development.

XII. Identity, Intimacy, and Independence

Erikson believes that identity should come before intimacy. His sixth stage is intimacy versus isolation, which he believes should be resolved in early adulthood. Five styles of intimate interaction are: intimate, preintimate, stereotyped, pseudointimate, and isolated. There are many social pressures on intimacy in our society. Three possible paths in the complex link between identity and intimacy are: intimacy (unresolved), identity, intimacy, and generativity; intimacy and generativity; intimacy, identity, and generativity. The balance between, on the one hand, intimacy and commitment to others and, on the other hand, independence and identity is delicate. These important dimensions are worked and reworked throughout our adolescent and adult years.

Key Terms

existential self 365
categorical self 365
unconditional positive
   regard 371
Perceived Competence
   Scale for Children 372
social competence 374
psychological
   moratorium 378
crisis 384

commitment 384
identity diffusion 384
identity foreclosure 384
identity moratorium 384
identity achievement 384
connectedness 386

individuation 387
intimate style 391
preintimate style 391
stereotyped style 391
pseudointimate style 391
isolated style 391

Suggested Readings

Erikson, E. H. (1969). *Gandhi's truth.* New York: W. W. Norton.
   In this Pulitzer-Prize-winning novel, Erikson weaves an insightful picture of Gandhi's development of identity.

Ford, M., & Ford, D. (Eds.). (1987). *Humans as self-constructing living systems.* Hillsdale, NJ: Erlbaum.
   This book provides an extensive interpretation of social competence, including Martin Ford's model of social competence in terms of self-assertive and integrative criteria.

Harter, S. (1983). Developmental perspectives on the self-system. In P. H. Mussen (Ed.), *Handbook of child psychology* (Vol. 4, 4th ed.). New York: Wiley.
   A thorough overview of the development of the self, particularly in terms of its development during childhood. Provides extensive information about self-concept and self-esteem.

Honess, T., & Yardley, K. (1987). *Self and identity: Perspectives across the lifespan.* London: Routledge & Kegan Paul.
   This excellent volume includes articles by leading theorists and researchers who study the development of the self and identity.

Lapsley, D., & Power, F. C. (1988). *Self, ego, and identity.* New York: Springer-Verlag.
   An up-to-date authoritative treatment of issues involved in the nature of the self and identity by leading scholars.

Selman, R. L. (1980). *The growth of interpersonal understanding.* New York: Academic Press.
   Presents considerable detail about Selman's developmental theory of perspective taking and self-development. Includes information about clinical implications for helping children with problems.

Gender Roles

It is fatal to be man or woman pure and simple; one must be woman-manly or man-womanly.

Virginia Woolf

Mary Smith of 1955 and Tracy McKinley of 1990

*T*he year is 1955 and the conversation is with a 16-year-old girl, Mary Smith. "What are your plans when you finish high school?" Mary replies, "I am going steady with someone I really love and we plan to get married in the summer after I finish high school. I'm a sophomore and he is a junior so he is going to get a job for a year before we get married. I would like to have a baby about a year after we are married. I can't wait. Marrying Tom and having a baby are all I can think about. We plan to set up housekeeping and I will stay home with the baby. We want to live here and have no plans to leave."

"What do you think the man's role and the woman's role should be in a relationship?" Mary responds, "Well, I think a man should be dominant and be the provider. He should make most of the decisions but he should allow the woman to make everyday decisions about the home and children. A man should be good to a woman but she should try to please him the best she can. It's been that way with my parents and I think it works out best that way."

The year is now 1990, some 35 years later, and the conversation is with a 16-year-old girl, Tracy McKinley. "What are your plans when you finish high school?" Tracy replies, "I plan to go to college. Right now I'm looking seriously at several large universities in the West and the Northeast. I want to be an electrical engineer or a computer analyst. I probably will go to graduate school after college. Marriage and a family aren't in my plans. I imagine I might get married when I'm about 30 years old, but that definitely would be the earliest. If I have children, I want to continue my career with as little interruption as possible."

"What do you think the man's role and the woman's role should be in a relationship?" Tracy responds, "I think they should be equal. Completely equal, no ifs, ands, or buts. Why should it be any different? I'm a human being, so are all other females, and so are all other males. I know there still are some girls who want a male to be macho and dominant. I just don't understand that. It just doesn't make sense. Those girls must not have thought very much about what life is all about. Sure I want to date guys that are handsome and strong, but I expect them to be extremely nice, warm, and caring toward me at the same time. At my high school, there are a few guys that fit this description, but they are the exception rather than the rule. My mother tells me that in her day there were even fewer. Some guys have trouble handling my assertiveness. They want a girl who makes them think they are great and builds up their ego. Hey, my ego needs building up too and it is important to me to stand up for my rights. Still, I can be feminine and affectionate toward the right guy, if he is what I want."

*H*ow the gender times have changed. The Tracy McKinleys were few and far between in 1955. The Mary Smiths are still around in 1990 but their ranks have been dramatically reduced. This chapter is about gender, about our world as females and males. Among the questions we explore are: How can gender roles be classified? What are the biological, cognitive, and social influences on gender roles? Are there many gender differences, or are most that we consider differences actually stereotypes? What is the course of gender role development?

Gender Role Classification

Nowhere in an adolescent's social and personality development have more sweeping changes occurred in recent years than in the area of gender roles. **Gender roles** are social expectations of how we should act, think, and feel as males and females. How can we classify gender roles?

Masculinity, Femininity, and Androgyny

At a point not too long ago, it was accepted that boys should grow up to be masculine and that girls should grow up to be feminine, that boys are made of frogs and snails and puppy dogs' tails and that girls are made of sugar and spice and all that's nice. Today, diversity characterizes adolescents' gender roles and the feedback they receive from their culture. A girl's mother might promote femininity, the girl might be close friends with a tomboy, and the girl's teachers at school might encourage her assertiveness.

In the past, the well-adjusted male was expected to be independent, aggressive, and powerful; the well-adjusted female was expected to be dependent, nurturant, and unpowerful. By the mid-1970s, though, the landscape of gender roles was changing. Many females were unhappy with the label "feminine" and felt stigmatized by its association with characteristics such as passivity and unassertiveness. Many males were uncomfortable with being called "masculine" because of its association with such characteristics as insensitivity and aggressiveness.

Many lay people as well as developmentalists believed that something more than "masculinity" and "femininity" was needed to describe the change in gender roles that was taking place. The byword became **androgyny,** meaning the combination of masculine and feminine characteristics in the same individual (Bem, 1977; Spence & Helmreich, 1978). The androgynous adolescent might be a male who is assertive (masculine) and nurturant (feminine), or a female who is dominant (masculine) and sensitive to others' feelings (feminine).

Table 11.1 provides examples of items from a widely used measure of gender roles—the Bem Sex Role Inventory. To see whether you are androgynous or not, rate yourself on the items in Table 11.1. The androgynous individual is simply a male or a female who has a high degree of both feminine

TABLE 11.1   *Are You Androgynous?*

The following items are from the Bem Sex-Role Inventory. To find out whether you score as androgynous on it, first rate yourself on each item, on a scale from 1 (never or almost never true) to 7 (always or almost always true).

1. self-reliant	16. strong personality	31. makes decisions easily	46. aggressive
2. yielding	17. loyal	32. compassionate	47. gullible
3. helpful	18. unpredictable	33. sincere	48. inefficient
4. defends own beliefs	19. forceful	34. self-sufficient	49. acts as a leader
5. cheerful	20. feminine	35. eager to soothe hurt	50. childlike
6. moody	21. reliable	feelings	51. adaptable
7. independent	22. analytical	36. conceited	52. individualistic
8. shy	23. sympathetic	37. dominant	53. does not use harsh
9. conscientious	24. jealous	38. soft-spoken	language
10. athletic	25. has leadership abilities	39. likable	54. unsystematic
11. affectionate	26. sensitive to the needs of	40. masculine	55. competitive
12. theatrical	others	41. warm	56. loves children
13. assertive	27. truthful	42. solemn	57. tactful
14. flatterable	28. willing to take risks	43. willing to take a stand	58. ambitious
15. happy	29. understanding	44. tender	59. gentle
	30. secretive	45. friendly	60. conventional

SCORING:

(a) Add up your ratings for items 1, 4, 7, 10, 13, 16, 19, 22, 25, 28, 31, 34, 37, 40, 43, 46, 49, 55, and 58. Divide the total by 20. That is your masculinity score.

(b) Add up your ratings for items 2, 5, 8, 11, 14, 17, 20, 23, 26 29, 32, 35, 38, 41, 44, 47, 50, 53, 56, and 59. Divide the total by 20. That is your femininity score.

(c) If your masculinity score is above 4.9 (the approximate median for the masculinity scale) and your femininity score is above 4.9 (the approximate femininity median), then you would be classified as androgynous on Bem's scale.

From Janet S. Hyde, *Half the Human Experience: The Psychology of Women,* 3d ed. Copyright © 1985 D.C. Heath and Company, Lexington, MA. Reprinted by permission.

and masculine characteristics. No new characteristics are used to describe the androgynous individual. An individual can be classified as masculine, feminine, or androgynous. A fourth category, **undifferentiated,** also is used in gender role classification. This category describes an individual who has neither masculine nor feminine characteristics. The four classifications of gender roles are shown in Figure 11.1.

Debate still flourishes on what components ought to make up the masculine and feminine categories. Because these are combined to make up the androgyny category, the composition of masculinity and femininity is crucial to what it means to be androgynous. This raises an important issue in psychology. When a concept or construct is developed and evaluated, it is critical to pin down the dimensions of the concept. Specifying the dimensions of a concept in a logical, organized, and empirical way is one of psychology's great lessons. Unfortunately, in the case of androgyny, this lesson has sometimes been lost. In many cases, the concept of androgyny has been based on a hodgepodge of stereotypical ideas, especially those of college students, about personality differences between males and females (Downs & Langlois, 1988; Gill & others, 1987; Ford, 1986).

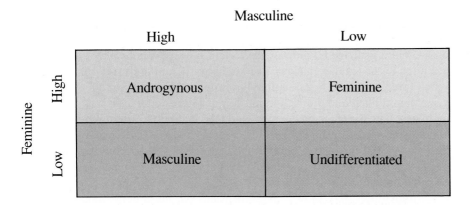

Figure 11.1   The four classifications of gender roles.

Adding to the complexity of determining whether an individual is masculine, feminine, or androgynous is the individual's developmental level (Maccoby, 1987). A four-year-old boy would be labeled masculine if he enjoyed and frequently engaged in rough-and-tumble play, if he preferred to play with blocks and trucks, and if he tended to play outdoors in the company of other boys during free-play periods at his preschool. A four-year-old girl would be labeled feminine if she liked to wear dresses, played with dolls and art materials, and did not get into fights. At age 10, a masculine boy would be one

Gender Role Socialization in Egypt

In recent decades, roles assumed by males and females in the United States are believed to have become increasingly similar, that is, androgynous. In some countries, gender roles have remained more gender specific than in the United States. Egypt is one example. The division of labor between Egyptian males and females is pronounced—Egyptian males are socialized to work in the public sphere, females in the private world of home and childrearing. The Islamic religion dictates that the man's duty is to provide for his family, the woman's duty to care for her family and household (Dickerscheid & others, 1988). Any deviations from this traditional gender role orientation is severely disapproved of. Many cultures around the world socialize children and adolescents to behave, think, and feel in gender specific ways. Kenya and Nepal are two other cultures where children and adolescents are brought up along very strict gender specific guidelines (Munroe, Himmin, & Munroe, 1984). While in the United States and other Western cultures, many parents are rearing their children and adolescents to be more androgynous, this gender role orientation has not touched the lives of people in many of the world's nations.

who engaged in active sports, avoided girls, and was not especially diligent about his schoolwork. At age 10, a feminine girl would be one who had one or two close girlfriends, did not try to join boys' sports or play groups, paid attention to the teacher in class, liked to baby-sit, and preferred romantic television fare. At age 15, a masculine boy would be one who excelled in spatial-visual tasks, liked and did well in math, was interested in cars and machinery, and knew how to repair mechanical gadgets. At age 15, a feminine girl would be more interested in English and history than math or science and would wear lipstick and makeup. These examples are not exhaustive but they give the flavor of how the characteristics of masculinity and femininity depend to some degree on developmental status.

Individuals may show some dimensions but not others among the set of stereotyped masculine and feminine attributes (Maccoby & Jacklin, in press). Also, different aspects of the cluster may take on more or less importance at different ages. For example, two attributes—sexually attractive and gentle-kind-considerate-nurturant—are probably involved in the concept of femininity at all ages, but the sexual aspect probably is dominant in adolescence, while the second component may emerge most strongly in adulthood when many women are involved in the care of children.

According to Martin Ford (1986), greater specification of gender roles is accomplished by describing masculinity in terms of self-assertion and femininity in terms of integration. **Self-assertion** includes such components as leadership, dominance, independence, competitiveness, and individualism. **Integration** includes such components as sympathy, affection, and understanding. An androgynous individual would be high on both self-assertion and integration. Sandra Gill and her colleagues (1987) believe greater specification in gender roles is accomplished by describing masculinity in terms of an instrumental orientation and femininity in terms of an expressive orientation. An **instrumental orientation** is concerned with the attainment of goals and an emphasis on the individual's accomplishments. An **expressive orientation** is concerned with facilitating social interaction, interdependence, and relationships. In the descriptions by Ford and by Gill and her colleagues, we find the same dual emphasis on the self and social relations that is also proposed as the best way to describe social competence. Remember that in Chapter 10 we described the most socially competent adolescents as those who are both individually and socially oriented, and who have both internal and external resources. So it is with androgynous adolescents. They are both self-assertive and integrative, instrumental and expressive.

Are Androgynous Adolescents the Most Competent?

Which adolescents are the most competent? Adolescents who are undifferentiated are the least competent. They are the least socially responsible, have the least self-control, and receive the poorest grades in school (Ford, 1986). This category is not well understood by psychologists and few adolescents are classified this way. But what about the majority of adolescents, those who are either masculine, feminine, or androgynous—which group is the most competent?

This is not an easy question to answer because the dimensions of androgyny and the dimensions of competence are not clearly spelled out in research on the issue. In many instances androgynous adolescents are the most competent, but a key point involves the criteria for competence. If the criteria involve self-assertion and integration or an instrumental and an expressive orientation, then androgynous adolescents are more competent. However, if the criteria for competence primarily involve self-assertion or an instrumental orientation, then a masculine gender role is favored; if they primarily involve integration or an expressive orientation, then a feminine gender role is preferred. For example, masculine individuals might be more competent in school achievement, work, and sports, while feminine adolescents might be more competent in relationships and helping.

The self-assertive and instrumental dimensions of gender roles have been more highly valued in our culture than the integrative or expressive dimensions. When psychologists have assessed the relation of gender roles to competence, their criteria for competence have included twice as many self-assertive and instrumental items as integrative and expressive ones. A disturbing outcome of such cultural standards and research bias is that masculine dimensions are perceived to mean competence. We need to place a higher value on the integrative and expressive dimensions of our own lives and our adolescents' lives and give these dimensions adequate weight in our assessment of competence.

Biological and Cognitive Influences

How much does biological heritage determine adolescents' gender roles? What cognitive factors are involved in adolescents' gender roles? We consider each of these questions in turn.

Biological Influences

One of Freud's basic assumptions is that human behavior and history are directly related to reproductive processes. From this assumption arises the belief that sexuality is essentially unlearned and instinctual. Erikson (1968) extended this argument, claiming that the psychological differences between males and females stem from anatomical differences. Erikson argued that—because of genital structure—males are more intrusive and aggressive, females more inclusive and passive. Erikson's belief has become known as *"anatomy is destiny."* Critics of the anatomy-is-destiny view believe that Erikson has not given experience adequate importance. They argue that males and females are more free to choose their gender role than Erikson allows. In response to the critics, Erikson has modified his view, saying that females in today's world are transcending their biological heritage and correcting society's overemphasis on male intrusiveness.

Biology's influence on gender roles also involves sex hormones, which we learned about in Chapter 3. These are among the most powerful and subtle chemicals in nature. Remember that these hormones are controlled by the brain's master gland, the pituitary. In females, hormones from the pituitary carry messages to the ovaries and produce the hormone estrogen. In males, the pituitary messages travel to the testes where the sex hormone androgen is manufactured.

The secretion of androgen from the testes of the young male fetus (or the absence of androgen in the female) completely controls sexual development in the womb. If enough androgen is produced, as happens with a normal developing boy, male organs and genitals develop. In instances where the hormone level is imbalanced (as in a developing male with insufficient androgen, or a female exposed to excess androgen), the genitals are intermediate between male and female. Such individuals are referred to as **hermaphrodites** (Money, 1965, 1987).

Although estrogen is the dominant sex hormone in females, while androgen is dominant in males, each individual's body contains both hormones. The amount of each hormone varies from one individual to the next. For example, a boy's bass voice is the result of more androgen than another boy with a tenor voice (Durden-Smith & Desimone, 1983). As we move from animals to humans, hormonal control over sexual behavior is less dominant. For example, when the testes of the male rat are removed (castration), sexual behavior declines and eventually ceases. In humans, castration produces much greater variation in sexual behavior.

No one argues about the presence of genetic, biochemical, and anatomical differences between the sexes. Even psychologists with a strong environmental orientation acknowledge that boys and girls will be treated differently because of their physical differences and their different roles in reproduction. The importance of biological factors is not at issue. What is at issue is the directness or indirectness of their effects on social behavior (Huston, 1983). For example, if a high androgen level directly influences the central nervous system, which in turn produces a higher activity level, then the effect is more direct. By contrast, if a high level of androgen produces strong muscle development, which in turn causes others to expect the children to be good athletes and in turn leads them to participate in sports, then the biological effect is more indirect.

While virtually everyone thinks that adolescents' behavior as males and females is due to an interaction of biological and environmental factors, an interactionist position means different things to different people (Hinde, 1989; Maccoby, 1987; Money, 1987). For some it suggests that certain environmental conditions are required to make preprogrammed dispositions appear. For others it suggests that the same environment will have different effects depending on the adolescent's predispositions. For yet others it means that adolescents shape their environments, including their interpersonal environment, as well as vice versa. Processes of influence and counterinfluence unfold over time. Throughout development, males and females actively construct their own version of acceptable masculine and feminine behavior patterns. As we see next, cognitive factors play an important role in this active construction.

Cognitive Influences

Among the ways that cognitive factors influence gender role development are self-categorization, language, and gender schema, each of which we consider in turn.

Lawrence Kohlberg (1966) argued that to have an idea of what is masculine or feminine, a child must be able to categorize objects into these two groups—masculine and feminine. According to Kohlberg, the categories become relatively stable by the age of 6. That is, by the age of 6, children have a fairly definite idea of which category is theirs. Further, they understand what is entailed in belonging to one category or the other and seldom fluctuate in their category judgments. From Kohlberg's perspective, this self-categorization is the impetus for gender role development. Kohlberg reasons that gender role development proceeds in the following sequence: I am a boy, I want to do boy things; therefore, the opportunity to do boy things is rewarding. Having acquired the ability to categorize, children strive toward consistency in the use of the categories and their actual behavior. The striving for consistency forms the basis for gender role development (Carter, 1989; Martin, 1989; Ruble, 1987).

Others have expanded on Kohlberg's cognitive theme. One proposal suggests that initially there is a period of undifferentiated gender role concepts among infants; then comes a period of adopting very rigid, conventional gender roles at some point in the preschool and elementary school years (Pleck, 1975). This rigidity is thought to peak in the early adolescent years as males strive to be the very best male possible and girls strive to be the very best female

How Good Are Girls at Wudgemaking If the Wudgemaker Is "He"?

In one investigation, the following description of a fictitious, gender-neutral occupation, wudgemaker, was read to third- and fifth-grade children, with repeated reference either to *he, they, he or she,* or *she* (Hyde, 1984):

Few people have heard of a job in factories, being a wudgemaker. Wudges are made of oddly shaped plastic, and are an important part of video games. The wudgemaker works from a plan or pattern posted at eye level as *he or she* puts together the pieces at a table while *he or she* is sitting down. Eleven plastic pieces must be snapped together. Some of the pieces are tiny, so that *he or she* must have good coordination in *his or her* fingers. Once all eleven pieces are put together, *he or she* must test out the wudge to make sure that all of the moving pieces move properly. The wudgemaker is well paid, and must be a high school graduate, but *he or she* does not have to have gone to college to get the job. (Hyde, 1984, p. 702)

One-fourth of the children were read the story with *he* as the pronoun, one-fourth with *they,* one-fourth with *he or she* (as shown), and one-fourth with *she.* The children were asked to rate how well women could do the job of wudgemaking and also how well they thought men could perform the job. As shown in figure 11.A, ratings of how well women could make wudges were influenced by the pronoun used; ratings were lowest for *he,* inter-

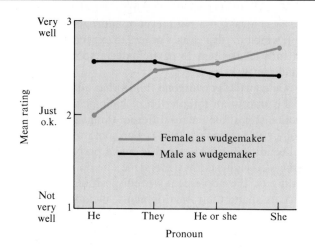

Figure 11.A   Mean ratings of how well women and men would do as wudgemakers, according to pronouns used in the description.

mediate for *they* and *he or she,* and highest for *she.* This suggests that the use of the gender-neutral *he,* compared to other pronouns, influences children's conceptions of how competent males and females are in our society. ✍

possible. Then at some point later in development, often not until the adult years, a stronger androgyny orientation emerges (Block, 1973; Pleck, 1975).

Gender roles also are present in the language children and adolescents use and encounter. The nature of the language they hear most of the time is sexist. That is, the English language contains sex bias, especially in the use of "he" and "man" to refer to everyone (Leinbach & Hort, 1989; O'Donnel, 1989). For example, in one recent investigation, mothers and their 1–3-year-old children looked at popular children's books, such as "The Three Bears," together (DeLoache, Cassidy, & Carpenter, 1987). The Three Bears were almost always referred to as boys: 95% of all characters of indeterminate gender were referred to by mothers as males. By adolescence, boys and girls have been bathed in sexist language. More about children's and adolescents' experiences with sexist language is presented in Perspective on Adolescent Development 11.1.

How might this 17-year-old high school student's hobby choice of flying remote-controlled airplanes reflect gender schema's influence?

An important theme in the cognitive approach to adolescents' gender roles is that the adolescent's mind is set up to perceive and organize information according to a network of associations called a schema. A **schema** is a cognitive structure, a network of associations that organizes and guides an individual's perception. A **gender schema** organizes the world in terms of female and male. The developing individual invariably learns society's definitions of femaleness and maleness. In most cultures, these definitions involve a sprawling network of sex-linked associations, which encompass not only features directly related to female and male persons—such as anatomy, reproductive function, division of labor, and personality attributes—but also features more remotely or metaphorically related to sex, such as an abstract shape's angularity or roundedness and the periodicity of the moon. No other dichotomy of life's experiences seems to have as many features linked to it as does the distinction between being male and being female (Bem, 1985, 1987).

As a real-life example of gender schema's influence on adolescents, consider a 17-year-old high school student deciding which hobby to try out from among the many available possibilities. The student could ask about how expensive each possibility is, whether it can be done in cold weather, whether or not it can be done during the school week, whether it will interfere with studying, and so on. But the adolescent also is likely to look at the hobby through the lens of gender and ask: What sex is the hobby? What sex am I? Do they match? If so, I will consider the hobby further. If not, I will reject it. This student may not be consciously aware of his or her gender's schema's influence on the decision of which hobby to pursue. Indeed, in many of our everyday encounters we are not consciously aware of how gender schema affects our behavior.

Cognitive factors contribute to our understanding of adolescents' active construction of their gender role, but gender role development has already started before individuals reach a stable sense of gender identity. For example,

Gender Role Components and Biological and Cognitive Influences

Concept	Processes/Related Ideas	Characteristics/Description
Gender role classification	Masculinity, femininity, and androgyny	Gender roles focus on society's expectations for males and for females. Recent interest has emphasized the concept of androgyny, the belief that competent individuals have both masculine and feminine characteristics. The four gender role classifications are: masculine, feminine, androgynous, and undifferentiated. Specification of the dimensions of masculinity, femininity, and androgyny has not always been consistent. Conceptualizing masculine dimensions as self-assertive and instrumental and feminine dimensions as integrative and expressive provides greater specification of gender roles. Developmental considerations also are important.
	Are androgynous adolescents more competent?	Controversy surrounds this question. In answering this question it is important to specify not only the criteria for androgyny but also the criteria for competence. Masculine dimensions have been more valued in our culture, and the criteria for competence also have followed this pattern. In contexts in which both self-assertive or instrumental and integrative or expressive characteristics are required for competence, androgynous individuals are more competent.
Biological and cognitive influences	Biological	Freud's and Erikson's theories promote the idea that anatomy is destiny. Hormones influence sexual development, although not as pervasively in humans as in animals. Today's psychologists are all interactionists when biological and environmental influences on gender roles are considered. However, interaction means different things to different people.
	Cognitive	Cognitive factors are involved in adolescents' active construction of their gender roles; two such cognitive factors are self-categorization and language development. An important theme in the cognitive approach is that the adolescent's mind is set up to perceive and organize information according to a network of associations involving male and female. This is called a gender schema.

2-year-old boys choose masculine toys even before they are aware such toys are more appropriate for them than for girls (Blakemore, LaRue, & Olejnik, 1979). The gender schema approach emphasizes the active cognitive construction of gender roles but also accepts that societies determine which schema are important and the associations that are involved.

At this point we have discussed a number of ideas about gender role classification and biological and cognitive influences. A summary of these ideas is presented in Concept Table 11.1.

Social, Emotional, and Personality Development

(a)

(b)

Mothers (a) are less likely than fathers (b) to be given responsibility for seeing that adolescents conform to existing cultural norms, especially boys.

Social Influences

In our culture, adults discriminate between the sexes shortly after the infant's birth. The "pink and blue" treatment may be applied to boys and girls before they leave the hospital. Soon afterward, differences in hair styles, clothes, and toys become obvious. Adults and peers reward these differences throughout development. And boys and girls learn gender roles through imitation or observational learning by watching what other people say and do. In recent years, the idea that parents are the critical socialization agents in gender role development has come under fire (Huston, 1983). Parents are only one of many sources through which the individual learns gender roles. Culture, schools, peers, the media, and other family members are others. Yet it is important to guard against swinging too far in this direction, because—especially in the early years of development—parents are important influences on gender role development.

Parent Influences

Parents, by action and example, influence their children's and adolescents' gender role development. In the psychoanalytic view, this stems primarily from the son's or daughter's identification with the same-sex parent. The son or daughter is motivated to be like and emulate the parent of the same sex. In the social learning view, boys and girls are motivated to imitate the behavior patterns of nurturant, powerful models. In reality, both mothers and fathers are psychologically important for children's and adolescents' gender roles. Mothers are consistently given responsibility for nurturance and physical care; fathers are more likely to engage in playful interaction and be given responsibility for seeing that boys and girls conform to existing cultural norms. And

Gender Roles

whether or not they have more influence on them, fathers are more involved in socializing their sons than their daughters (Lamb, 1986). Fathers seem to play an especially important part in gender role development—they are more likely to act differently toward sons and daughters than mothers are (Huston, 1983).

Many parents encourage boys and girls to engage in different types of play and activities (Lewis, 1987). Girls are more likely to be given dolls to play with during childhood and, when old enough, are more likely to be assigned baby-sitting duties. Girls are encouraged to be more nurturant and emotional than boys, and fathers are more likely to engage in aggressive play with their sons than their daughters. As adolescents increase in age, parents permit boys more freedom than girls, allowing them to be away from home and stay out later without supervision. Parents placing severe restrictions on their adolescent sons has been found to be especially disruptive to the adolescent's development (Baumrind, 1989).

Peer Influences

Parents provide the earliest discrimination of gender roles in development, but, before long, peers join the societal process of responding to and modeling masculine and feminine behavior. Children who play in sex-appropriate activities tend to be rewarded for doing so by their peers. Those who play in cross-sexed activities tend to be criticized by their peers or left to play alone. Children show a clear preference for being with and liking same-sex peers (Maccoby, 1989; Maccoby & Jacklin, in press), and this tendency usually becomes stronger during the middle and late childhood years (Hayden-Thomson, Rubin, & Hymel, 1987). After extensive observations of elementary school playgrounds, two researchers characterized the play settings as "gender school," pointing out that boys teach one another the required masculine behavior and enforce it strictly (Luria & Herzog, 1985). Girls also pass on the female culture and mainly congregate with one another. Individual "tomboy" girls can join boys' activities without losing their status in the girls' groups, but the reverse is not true for boys, reflecting our society's greater sex-typing/pressure for boys.

Peer demands for conformity to gender role become especially intense during early adolescence. While there is greater social mixing of males and females during early adolescence, in both formal groups and in dating, peer pressure is strong for the adolescent boy to be the very best male possible and for the adolescent girl to be the very best female possible.

School and Teacher Influences

In a recent Gallup poll, 80% of the respondents agreed that the federal government should promote educational programs intended to reduce such social problems as poverty and unequal educational opportunities for minorities and females (Gallup & Clark, 1987). Discriminatory treatment involving gender involves all ability groups, but in many cases the stereotypically lower-valued

(a)   (b)

group (by sex, by race, and so on) is treated similarly to the lower-valued ability group. For example, girls with strong math abilities frequently are given fewer quality instructional interactions from teachers than their male counterparts (Eccles, MacIver, & Lange, 1986). And, minority females are given fewer teacher interactions than other females, who are given fewer than black males, who are given fewer than white males (Sadker, Sadker, & Klein, 1986).

In a recent research study, researchers were trained in an observation system to collect data in more than a hundred fourth-, sixth-, and eighth-grade classrooms (Sadker & Sadker, 1986). At all three grade levels, male students were involved in more interactions than female students, and male students were given more attention from teachers. Male students also were given more remediation, more criticism, and more praise than female students.

Historically, education in the United States has been male defined rather than gender balanced. In many instances, traditional male activities, especially white male activities, have been the educational norm. Although females mature earlier, are ready for verbal and math training at a younger age, and have control of small-motor skills earlier than males, educational curricula have been constructed mainly to mirror the development of males. Decisions about the grade in which students should read *Huckleberry Finn,* do long division, or begin to write essays are based primarily on male developmental patterns. Some experts believe that this state of educational affairs means that some girls may become bored or give up, with most girls learning simply to hold back, be quiet, and smile (Shakeshaft, 1986).

Three trends in sex equity education research have been identified (Klein, 1988). First, there is a trend toward greater investigation of subtle discrimination and stereotyping. Much of the sex equity research and initial sex equity policies in the 1970s focused on identifying and putting an end to overt discrimination and stereotyping. By 1981, it was noted that while some progress

Historically, in the United States, math education has favored male adolescents. Today more female adolescents are taking math classes than in the past, but experts argue that we have a long way to go before there is gender fairness in math education.

had been made toward equity in areas of overt sex discrimination such as athletics and college admissions, many subtle types of sex discrimination and stereotyping, such as sex bias in classroom interactions, still remained. Sex equity researchers are now calling attention to sex discrimination and stereotyping in less visible problem areas such as home economics, foreign language, visual arts, and sex education (Klein, in press; Spencer, 1986; Thompson, 1986; Sandell, Collins, & Sherman, 1985).

A second trend in sex equity education research is a shift toward male- and female-valued educational outcome goals. In addition to assisting females in achieving parity with males, researchers and policymakers are focusing more on the development of skills associated with females (Belenky & others, 1986; Tetreault, 1986). For example, placing more value on skills such as writing and human relations, areas in which females excel, can change the content covered in many standardized academic achievement tests. This type of change could improve females' achievement test scores, self-esteem, and job prospects.

A third trend in sex equity education research is an increased emphasis on sex equity outcomes. Much of the initial sex equity education research focused on identifying inequities or problems. Once researchers understand how far we are from attaining sex equity goals, they can emphasize the effectiveness of various sex equity solutions in reaching these goals. For example, researchers have found that girls' participation and achievement in mathematics becomes more equal to boys' through the use of multiple strategies that include anxiety reduction, "hands on" math instructional experiences, career awareness activities, "girl-friendly" classrooms, and role models (Eccles, MacIver, & Lange, 1986; Stage & others, 1985).

Believing that rigid gender roles may be detrimental to both males and females, a number of educators and psychologists have developed materials and created courses to teach androgyny to children and adolescents. Details

Social, Emotional, and Personality Development

about two efforts to teach children and adolescents to be more androgynous and the ethical issues involved are presented in Perspective on Adolescent Development 11.2.

Media Influences

As we've described, adolescents encounter male and female roles in their everyday interactions with parents, peers, and teachers. But the messages carried by television about what is appropriate or inappropriate for males may be an important influence on gender roles as well (Morgan, 1987).

A special concern is the way females are pictured on television. In the 1970s, it became apparent that television was portraying females in less competent ways than males. For example, about 70% of the prime-time characters were males, men were more likely to be shown in the work force, women were more likely to be shown as housewives and in romantic roles, men were more likely to appear in higher status jobs and in a greater diversity of occupations, and men were presented as more aggressive and constructive (Sternglanz & Serbin, 1974).

In the 1980s, television networks have become more sensitive to how males and females are portrayed on television shows. Many programs now focus on divorced families, cohabitation, and women in high-status roles. Even with the onset of this type of programming, researchers continue to find that television portrays males as more competent than females (Durkin, 1985). In one recent investigation, young adolescent girls indicated that television occupations are more extremely stereotyped than real-life occupations (Wroblewski & Huston, 1987).

Gender role stereotyping also appears in the print media. In magazine advertising, females are more likely to appear in advertisements for beauty products, cleaning products, and home appliances, while males are more likely to appear in advertisements for cars, liquor, and travel. As with television programs, females are being portrayed as more competent in advertisements than in the past, but advertisers have not yet given them equal status with men.

Gender Stereotyping and Differences

How pervasive is gender role stereotyping? What are the real differences in gender role behavior? What is the nature of gender roles in matters related to achievement? Each of these questions we consider in turn.

Gender Role Stereotyping

Gender role stereotypes are broad categories that reflect our impressions and beliefs about males and females. All stereotypes, whether based on gender, race, or other groupings, refer to an image of what the typical member of a

Can and Should Androgyny Be Taught to Children and Adolescents in School?

In one investigation (Kahn & Richardson, 1983), 10th–12th-grade students from three high schools in British Columbia were given a twenty-unit course in gender roles. Students analyzed the history and modern development of male and female gender roles and evaluated the function of traditionally accepted stereotypes of males and females. The course centered on student discussion supplemented by films, videotapes, and guest speakers. The materials included exercises to heighten awareness of one's own attitudes and beliefs, role reversal of typical gender role behavior, role play of difficult work and family conflict circumstances, and assertiveness training for direct, honest communication.

A total of 59 students participated in the gender role course. To determine whether the course changed the adolescents' gender role orientation, these students were compared to 59 students from the same schools who did not take the gender role course. Prior to the start of the course, all students were given the Bem Sex Role Inventory. No differences between the two groups were found at that time. After the students completed the course, they and the control group were given the Attitudes Toward Women Scale (Spence & Helmreich, 1972). Scores on this measure can range from 25 (highly traditional) to 100 (highly liberal). As shown in Table 11.A, in schools 1 and 2 the students who took the gender role course had more liberal attitudes about the female's role in society than students who did not take the course. In these schools, the students were primarily girls who chose to take the course as an elective. In school 3, students who took the gender role course actually had more conservative attitudes toward the female's role in society than those who did not. The gender role class in school 3 was required and was made up almost equally of males and females.

Another attempt to produce a more androgynous gender role orientation in students also met with mixed results (Guttentag & Bray, 1976). The curriculum lasted for one year and was implemented in the kindergarten,

TABLE 11.A	Gender Role Attitudes Related to the Woman's Role in Society Following a High School Course on Gender Roles Emphasizing Androgyny	

School	Groups	
	Experimental (Took Gender Role Course)	Control (Did Not Take Course)
1	83.3	75.6
2	85.3	73.9
3	68.8	76.2

From S. E. Kahn and A. Richardson, "Evaluation of a Course in Sex Roles for Secondary School Students," in *Sex Roles, A Journal of Research,* 9, 431–440, 1983. Copyright © 1983 Plenum Publishing Corporation, New York, NY. Reprinted by permission of the publisher and author.

fifth, and ninth grades. It involved books, discussion materials, and classroom exercises. The program was most successful with the fifth graders and least successful with the ninth graders, who actually displayed a boomerang effect of more rigid gender role orientation. The program's success varied from class to class, seeming to be most effective when the teacher produced sympathetic reaction in the peer group. However, some classes ridiculed and rejected the curriculum.

Ethical concerns are aroused when the program involves teaching children to depart from socially approved behavior patterns, especially when there is no evidence of extreme sex typing in the groups of children to whom the interventions are applied. The advocates of androgyny programs believe that traditional sex typing is psychologically harmful for all children and that it has prevented many girls and women from experiencing equal opportunity. While some people believe androgyny is more adaptive than either a traditional masculine or feminine pattern, it is not possible to ignore the imbalance within our culture that values masculinity more than femininity (Huston, 1983; Hyde, 1988).

TABLE 11.2 *Adjectives that Describe Possible Gender Differences*

What are the differences in the behavior and thoughts of boys and girls? For each of the adjectives below, indicate whether you think it *best* describes boys or girls—or neither—in our society. Be honest and follow your first impulse.

	Girls	Boys
Verbal skills	☐	☐
Sensitive	☐	☐
Active	☐	☐
Competitive	☐	☐
Compliant	☐	☐
Dominant	☐	☐
Math skills	☐	☐
Suggestible	☐	☐
Social	☐	☐
Aggressive	☐	☐
Visual-spatial skills	☐	☐

particular social category is like. The world is extremely complex. Every day we are confronted with thousands of different stimuli. The use of stereotypes is one way we simplify this complexity. If we simply assign a label (such as the quality of softness) to someone, we then have much less to consider when we think about the individual. However, once labels are assigned they are remarkably difficult to abandon, even in the face of contradictory evidence. Do you think you have a set of gender role stereotypes? Table 11.2 provides a brief exercise in understanding gender role behavior. Record your answers on a separate sheet so you can check them later when they are discussed.

Many stereotypes are so general that they are very ambiguous. Consider the stereotypes "masculine" and "feminine." Diverse behaviors can be called on to support each stereotype, such as scoring a touchdown or growing facial hair for "masculine" and playing with dolls or wearing lipstick for "feminine." The stereotype may be modified in the face of cultural change. At one point in history, muscular development may be thought of as masculine; at another point it may be a more lithe, slender physique. The behaviors popularly agreed upon as reflecting a stereotype also may fluctuate according to socioeconomic and ethnic groups. For example, a lower socioeconomic group might be more likely than higher socioeconomic groups to include "rough and tough" as part of a masculine stereotype.

Even though the behaviors that are supposed to fit the stereotype often do not, the label itself can have significant consequences for the individual. Labeling an individual "homosexual," "queer," or "sissy" can produce dire social consequences in terms of status and acceptance in groups, even if the individual so labeled is not homosexual, queer, or sissy. Regardless of their

One of the most consistent differences between males and females is the greater aggression of males. This difference was found in the early 1970s. It continues to be found in recent investigations.

accuracy, stereotypes can produce tremendous emotional upheaval in individuals and undermine their own opinions about themselves and their status (Martin & Little, 1989; Mischel, 1970).

Gender Differences

How well did you do with adjectives in Table 11.2? According to a classic review of gender differences in 1974, Eleanor Maccoby and Carol Jacklin concluded that boys have better math skills, have superior visual-spatial ability (the kind of skills an architect would need to design a building's angles and dimensions), and are more aggressive, while girls have better verbal abilities. Recently, Eleanor Maccoby (1987) revised her conclusion about several gender role dimensions. She commented that the accumulation of research evidence suggests that boys now are more active than girls, and she is less certain that girls have greater verbal ability than boys, mainly because boys score as high as girls on the verbal part of the Scholastic Aptitude Test (SAT).

Evidence is accumulating that some gender differences are vanishing, especially in the area of verbal abilities (Feingold, 1988; Hyde & Linn, 1988; Jacklin, 1989). In a recent analysis, Alan Feingold (1988) evaluated gender differences in cognitive abilities on two widely used tests—the Differential Aptitude Test and the SAT—from 1947 to 1983. Girls scored higher than boys on scales of grammar, spelling, and perceptual speed; boys scored higher on measures of spatial visualization, high school mathematics, and mechanical aptitude. No gender differences were found on verbal reasoning, arithmetic, and reasoning about figures. Gender differences declined precipitously over the years. One important exception to the rule of vanishing gender differences is the well-documented gender gap at the upper levels of performance on high school mathematics, which has remained constant over three decades.

As can be seen, few data about gender differences seem to be cast in stone. As our culture has changed, so have some of our findings about gender differences and similarities. As our expectations and attitudes for boys and girls have become more similar, in many areas gender differences are vanishing.

But gender differences are not vanishing in all areas, as indicated by the differences that still persist in the area of math (Ducey, 1989). One area of special concern related to math and science involves computer ability. In two novels, *Turing's Man* (Bolter, 1984) and *The Second Self* (Turkle, 1984), technology overwhelms humanity. In both stories, females are portrayed as not having integral roles in this technological, computer culture. One character notes, "There are few women hackers. This is a male world" (Turkle, 1984). Unfortunately, both boys and girls are socialized to associate computer programming with math skills, and programming is typically taught in math departments by males. Male-female ratios in computer classes range from 2:1 to 5:1, although computers in offices tend to be used equally by females and males. Males also have more positive attitudes toward computers. It is hoped that Turkle's male computer hacker will not serve as the model for the future's computer users (Lockheed, 1985; Miura, 1987).

Social, Emotional, and Personality Development

Achievement

For some areas of achievement, gender differences are so large they can best be described as nonoverlapping. For example, no major league baseball players are female, and 96% of all registered nurses are female. In contrast, many measures of achievement-related behaviors yield no gender differences. For example, girls show just as much persistence at tasks. The question of whether males and females differ in their expectations for success at various achievement tasks is not yet settled (Eccles, 1987).

Because females are often stereotyped as less competent than males, incorporation of gender role stereotypes into a child's self-concept could lead girls to have less confidence than boys in their general intellectual abilities. This could lead girls to have lower expectations for success at difficult academic and vocational activities. It also could lead girls to expect to have to work harder to achieve success at these activities than boys expect to have to work. Evidence supports these predictions (Eccles, Harold-Goldsmith, & Miller, 1989). Either of these beliefs could keep girls from selecting demanding educational or vocational options, especially if these options are not perceived as important or interesting.

Gender roles also could produce different expectations of success depending on the gender stereotyping of the activity. Both educational programs and vocational options are gender stereotyped in our culture. Many high-level professions, especially those that are math-related and scientific/technical, are thought to be male activities. In contrast, teaching below the college level, working in clerical and related support jobs, and excelling in language-related courses are thought to be female activities by both children and adults (Eccles, 1987; Eccles & Hoffman, 1984; Huston, 1983). Incorporating these beliefs into self-concept could cause girls to have lower expectations for success in male-typed activities and higher expectations for success in female-typed activities. This pattern could lead girls to select female-typed activities over male-typed activities. Some support for this perspective has been found (Eccles, 1987). At times, though, researchers have found no gender differences in achievement expectations.

An intriguing view about gender roles and achievement argues that on the basis of an instrumental-achievement (male) versus expressive-affiliation (female) dichotomy, we might expect male superiority in achievement patterns. This is not always the case. In an investigation by Lloyd Lueptow (1984), adolescent girls had both higher levels of achievement value orientations and higher levels of academic achievement than did adolescent boys. It may be that achievement is a stronger component of the female gender role than the male gender role. Or, it may be that a distinction is necessary between achievement based on excellence and accomplishment (a stronger focus of females) and achievement based on assertion and aggressive competition (a stronger focus of males). That is, females may be stronger achievers, males stronger competitors. Since researchers often have neglected this distinction, it may be that the achievement orientation of females has been underestimated. More about gender and achievement appears in Chapter 14, where we focus on gender and career development.

Male-female ratios in computer classes range from 2-1 to 5-1.

Gender Role Development

While some gender typing occurs in the first several years of life, it is difficult to assess. During the age period from 18 months to 3 years children start expressing considerable interest in gender-typed activities and classify themselves according to gender. From 3 to 7 years of age, children begin to acquire an understanding of gender constancy and increasingly enjoy being with same-sex peers. During early childhood, young children also tend to make grand generalizations about gender roles. For example, 3-year-old William accompanied his mother to the doctor's office. A man in a white coat walked by and William said, "Hi, Doc." Then a woman in a white coat walked by and William greeted her, "Hi, nurse." William's mother asked him how he knew which individual was a doctor and which was a nurse. William replied, "Because doctors are daddies and nurses are mommies." As Piaget warned, young children are so sure of their thoughts, yet so often inaccurately understand the world. William's "nurse" turned out to be his doctor and vice versa (Carper, 1978).

In the middle childhood years, two divergent trends in gender roles take place. Children increase their understanding of culturally defined expectations for males and females, and simultaneously the behavior and attitudes of boys increasingly reflects masculine gender typing. However, during the middle childhood years, girls do not show an increased interest in feminine activities. Many girls even begin to show a stronger preference for masculine activities, a finding that has appeared in research studies conducted from the 1920s to the present.

During adolescence the individual's gender role development becomes wrapped in sexuality. As puberty proceeds, young adolescents increasingly think of themselves and other adolescents as sexual beings. Many of these thoughts are uncertain and idealistic. Adolescents also give more abstract definitions of gender roles. The abstractness and idealism of their thoughts lead adolescents to think about what an ideal male and an ideal female are like. Inevitably, adolescents compare themselves and others to these ideal standards. Individuals the adolescent does not know personally, such as media stars, are more likely to approach the ideal standard. As their bodies are flooded with sex hormones and they think about what the ideal male and female are like, adolescent males strive to be the very best male possible and adolescent females strive to be the very best female possible. Adolescence also is a time when males and females focus more attention on integrating vocational and life-style choices (Aneshensel & Rosen, 1980). A special concern for older adolescents is whether to combine career and family interests.

At this point we have discussed a number of ideas about social influences on gender roles, gender stereotyping and differences, and the development of gender roles. A summary of these ideas is presented in Concept Table 11.2.

Social, Emotional, and Personality Development

Social Influences, Gender Stereotyping and Differences, and Gender Role Development

Concept	Processes/Related Ideas	Characteristics/Description
Social influences	Parent influences	Parents, by action and example, influence gender role development. Mothers and fathers often play different roles—mothers more nurturant and responsible for physical care, fathers more playful and demanding. Fathers are more likely than mothers to act differently toward sons and daughters.
	Peer influences	Peers are especially adept at rewarding gender-appropriate behavior. Strong same-sex peer preference is shown in elementary school; in adolescence, more cross-sexed mixing occurs, as sexuality and dating become more prominent interests. Peer demands for conforming to gender become intense during early adolescence.
	School and teacher influences	Historically, in the United States, education has been male-defined rather than gender-balanced. Males receive more attention and teacher interaction in schools. Current trends focus on investigation of subtle sex discrimination and stereotyping, male- and female-valued educational goals, and increased emphasis on sex equity outcomes. One major focus has been on teaching androgyny in schools, which has met with mixed results.
	The media	Despite improvements, television still portrays males as more competent than females. So does advertising.
Gender stereotyping and differences	Gender role stereotypes	These are broad categories that reflect our impressions and beliefs about males and females. Because stereotypes are broad categories, diverse behaviors can be called on to support the stereotype.
	Gender differences	In the 1970s it was concluded that boys have better math skills, have superior visual-spatial ability, and are more aggressive, while girls have better verbal abilities. Today's conclusions suggest that boys are more active, and the differences in verbal abilities has virtually vanished. The other differences—math, visual-spatial ability, and aggression—still persist, although continued cultural change may chip away at these differences.
	Achievement	The question of whether males and females differ in their expectations for success is not yet settled. An often neglected distinction is that females may be more achievement oriented, males more competitive and assertive.
Gender role development	Its nature	From 18 months to 3 years, children begin to express considerable interest in gender role activities and classify themselves according to gender. From 3 to 7 years, children begin to acquire an understanding of gender constancy and increasingly enjoy being with same-sex peers. During middle childhood, children understand more about culturally defined expectations about males and females, and the behavior of boys becomes increasingly masculine. During adolescence, sexuality becomes a more prominent part of gender roles, interpretation of gender roles is more abstract and idealistic, males and females are motivated to be the very best representative of their respective sex, and there are greater career and life-style considerations.

Summary

I. Masculinity, Femininity, and Androgyny

Gender roles are society's expectations for males and for females. Recent interest has emphasized the concept of androgyny, the belief that competent individuals have both masculine and feminine characteristics. The four gender role classifications are masculine, feminine, androgynous, and undifferentiated. Specification of the dimensions of masculinity, femininity, and androgyny has not always been consistent. Conceptualizing masculine dimensions as self-assertive and instrumental and feminine dimensions as integrative and expressive provides greater specification. Developmental considerations also are important.

II. Are Androgynous Adolescents More Competent?

Controversy surrounds the question of whether androgynous adolescents are more competent. In answering this question it is important to specify not only the criteria for androgyny but also the criteria for competence. Masculine dimensions have been more valued in our culture and the criteria for competence also have followed this pattern. In contexts in which both self-assertive or instrumental and integrative or expressive characteristics are required for competence, androgynous individuals are more competent.

III. Biological Influences

Freud's and Erikson's theories promote the idea that anatomy is destiny. Hormones influence sexual development, although not as pervasively in humans as in animals. Today's psychologists are all interactionists when biological and environmental influences on gender roles are considered. However, interaction means different things to different people.

IV. Parent Influences

Parents, by action and by example, influence gender role development. Mothers and fathers often play different roles—mothers more nurturant and responsible for physical care, fathers more playful and demanding. Fathers are more likely to act differently toward sons and daughters than mothers are.

V. Peer Influences

Peers are especially adept at rewarding gender-appropriate behavior. Strong same-sex peer preference is shown during elementary school; in adolescence, more cross-sexed mixing occurs, as sexuality and dating become more prominent interests. Peer demands for conforming to gender become intense during adolescence.

VI. School and Teacher Influences

Historically, in the United States, education has been male defined rather than gender balanced. Males receive more attention and teacher interaction in schools. Current trends focus on investigation of subtle sex discrimination and stereotyping, male and female valued educational goals, and increased emphasis on sex equity outcomes. One major focus has been on teaching androgyny in schools, which has met with mixed results.

VII. The Media

Despite improvements, television still portrays males as more competent than females. So does advertising.

VIII. Gender Role Stereotypes

These are broad categories that reflect our impressions and beliefs about males and females. Because stereotypes are broad categories, diverse behaviors can be called on to support the stereotypes.

IX. Gender Differences

In the 1970s it was concluded that boys have better math skills, have superior visual-spatial ability, and are more aggressive, while girls are better at verbal abilities. Today's conclusions suggest that boys are more active, and the difference in verbal abilities has virtually vanished. The other differences—math, visual-spatial ability, and aggression—still persist, although continued cultural change may chip away at these differences.

X. Achievement

The question of whether males and females differ in their expectations for success is not yet settled. An often neglected distinction is that females may be more achievement oriented, males more competitive and assertive.

XI. Gender Role Development

From 18 months to 3 years, children begin to express considerable interest in gender role activities and classify themselves according to gender. From 3 to 7 years, children begin to acquire an understanding of gender constancy and increasingly enjoy being with same-sexed peers. During middle childhood, children understand more about culturally defined expectations for males and females, and the behavior of boys becomes increasingly masculine. During adolescence, sexuality becomes a more prominent part of gender roles, interpretation of gender roles is more abstract and idealistic, males and females are motivated to be the very best representative of their respective sex, and there are greater career and life-style considerations.

Key Terms

gender roles 401
androgyny 401
undifferentiated 402
self-assertion 404

integration 405
instrumental orientation 405
expressive orientation 405

hermaphrodites 406
schema 409
gender schema 409

Suggested Readings

Bem, S. L. (1985). Androgyny and gender schema theory: Conceptual and empirical integration. In T. B. Sonderegger (Ed.), *Nebraska symposium on motivation*. Lincoln, NE: University of Nebraska Press.
Bem, a leading androgyny expert, describes her views on androgyny and gender schema.

Feingold, A. (1988). Cognitive gender differences are disappearing. *American Psychologist, 43,* 95–103.
Recent information about cognitive gender differences is presented, suggesting that many of the differences are vanishing.

Huston, A. C. (1983). Sex-typing. In P. H. Mussen (Ed.), *Handbook of child psychology* (Vol. 4, 4th ed). New York: Wiley.
A lengthy, comprehensive review of what is known about gender role development.

Hyde, J. S. (1985). *Half the human experience* (3rd ed.). Lexington, MA: D.C. Heath.
An excellent overview of female gender role development.

Reinisch, J. M., Rosenblum, L. A., & Sanders, S. A. (Eds.). (1987). *Masculinity/feminity.* New York: Oxford University Press.
An outstanding collection of articles by leading experts such as Eleanor Maccoby, John Money, and Jacqueline Eccles. Includes a special section of papers on the development of gender roles.

Sexuality

If we listen to boys and girls at the very moment they seem most pimply, awkward and disagreeable, we can penetrate a mystery most of us once felt heavily within us, and have now forgotten. This mystery is the very process of creation of man and woman.

Colin Mcinnes, The World of Children

The Mysteries and the Curiosities of Adolescent Sexuality

I am 16 years old and I really like this one girl. She wants to be a virgin until she marries. We went out last night and she let me go pretty far, but not all the way. I know she really likes me too, but she always stops me when things start getting hot and heavy. It is getting hard for me to handle. She doesn't know it but I'm a virgin too. I feel I am ready to have sex. I have to admit I think about having sex with other girls too. Maybe I should be dating other girls.

Frank C.

I'm 14 years old. I have a lot of sexy thoughts. Sometimes just before I drift off to sleep at night I think about this hunk who is 16 years old and plays on the football team. He is so gorgeous and I can feel him holding me in his arms and kissing and hugging me. When I'm walking down the hall between classes at school, I sometimes start daydreaming about guys I have met, and wonder what it would be like to have sex with them. Last year I had this crush on the men's track coach. I'm on the girls' track team so I saw him a lot during the year. He hardly knew I thought about him the way I did, although I tried to flirt with him several times.

Amy S.

Is it weird to be a 17-year-old guy and still be a virgin? Sometimes I feel like the only 17-year-old male on the planet who has not had sex. I feel like I am missing out on something great, or at least that's what I hear. I'm pretty religious and I sometimes feel guilty when I think about sex. The thought runs through my mind that maybe it is best to wait until I'm married, or at least, until I have a long-term relationship that matters a lot to me.

Tom B.

I'm 15 years old and I had sex for the first time recently. I had all of these expectations about how great it was going to be. He didn't have much experience either. We were both pretty scared about the whole thing. It was all over in a hurry. My first thought was, "Is that all there is?" It was a very disappointing experience.

Claire T.

Adolescent sexual experiences are often a mixed blessing, full of exciting, arousing moments, but also full of confusing, conflicting moments.

uring adolescence, the lives of males and females become wrapped in sexuality. In Chapter 3, we studied the biological basis of sexual maturation, including the timing of these changes and the hormones involved. Here we focus on the sexual attitudes and experiences of adolescents. Adolescence is a time of sexual exploration and experimentation, of sexual fantasies and sexual realities, of incorporating sexuality into one's identity. Adolescents have an almost insatiable curiosity about sexuality's mysteries. Adolescents continually think about whether they are sexually attractive, whether they will grow more, whether anyone will love them, whether their penis or vagina is too small or oddly shaped, and whether it is normal to have sex. Sexual experiences can be enjoyable for some adolescents, painful for others. For most adolescents, they are both enjoyable *and* painful. The curiosity, imagination, expectations, and fantasies adolescents harbor about sex are often extremely enjoyable moments of their lives. The actual sexual experiences of adolescents can be enjoyable too, but the immaturity, disappointment, and pain that may be involved make adolescent sexuality an ambiguous world. At a time when sexual identity is a major developmental task of adolescence, the adolescent is confronted with conflicting sexual values and messages. The majority of adolescents manage eventually to develop a mature sexual identity, but for most there are periods of vulnerability and confusion along life's sexual journey. Our coverage of adolescent sexuality includes sexual attitudes and behavior, sexually transmitted diseases, adolescent pregnancy, and sex education.

Sexual Attitudes and Behavior

The terrain of sexual activity and sexual choices for adolescents includes heterosexual attitudes and behavior, homosexual attitudes and behavior, self-stimulation, and the use of contraceptives. We consider each of these topics in turn.

Heterosexual Attitudes and Behavior

How extensively have heterosexual attitudes and behavior changed in the twentieth century? What sexual scripts do adolescents follow? Are some adolescents more vulnerable to irresponsible sexual behavior than others?

Adolescent Heterosexual Behavior—Trends and Incidence

Had you been a college student in 1940 you probably would have had a different attitude toward many aspects of sexuality than you do today, especially if you are a female. A review of college students' sexual practices and attitudes from 1900 to 1980 reveals two important trends (Darling, Kallen, & Van-Dusen, 1984). First, the percentage of youth reporting that they have had

Figure 12.1 Percentages of college youth reporting having sexual intercourse at different points in the twentieth century. Two lines are drawn for males and two for females. The lines represent the best two fits through the data for males and the data for females of the many studies surveyed.

From C. A. Darling, et al., "Sex in Transition, 1900–1984" in Journal of Youth and Adolescence, *13, 385–399, 1984. Copyright © 1984 Plenum Publishing Corporation, New York, NY. Reprinted by permission of the publisher and author.*

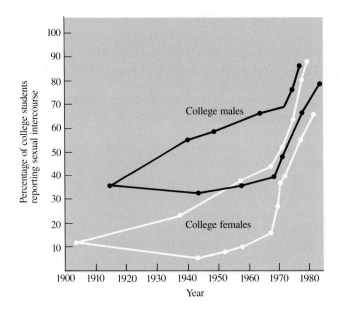

Source: National Research Council, *Risking the Future: Adolescent Sexuality, Pregnancy, and Childbearing.* Washington, D.C.; National Academy Press, 1987, Table 2.6.

TABLE 12.1 *Percent of Young People Sexually Active at Specific Ages*

Age	Women %	Men %
15	5.4	16.6
16	12.6	28.7
17	27.1	47.9
18	44.0	64.0
19	62.9	77.6
20	73.6	83.0

sexual intercourse has dramatically increased. Second, the percentage of females reporting that they have had sexual intercourse has increased more rapidly than for males, although the initial base for males was greater (see Figure 12.1). These changes suggest movement away from a double standard that says it is more appropriate for males to have sexual intercourse than females.

Large portions of American adolescents are sexually active. Table 12.1 shows that by age 18, 44% of adolescent females and 64% of adolescent males are sexually experienced (National Research Council, 1987). Other surveys indicate that almost 4 of 5 individuals among 17–19-year-olds experience sexual intercourse at least once (e.g., Zelnik & Kantner, 1980). While the gap is closing, males still are more sexually experienced at an earlier age than females. Black adolescent females are more sexually active than their white counterparts. Approximately 2 of 3 black adolescent females, but slightly less than 1 of 2 white adolescent females, report having sexual intercourse at least once.

Social, Emotional, and Personality Development

Sexual Attitudes in Cross-Cultural Perspective

In the recent cross-cultural investigation by Daniel Offer and his colleagues (1988), the sexual attitudes of adolescents in 10 countries were sampled: Australia, Bangladesh, Hungary, Irael, Italy, Japan, Taiwan, Turkey, and the United States. Adolescents in two countries—Turkey and Taiwan—showed extremely conservative attitudes toward sex. In traditional cultures such as Turkey and Taiwan, adolescents feel very uncomfortable about sex and feel extremely anxious about it. Nonetheless, in all of the countries studied, having a boyfriend or a girlfriend was viewed as important by the adolescents, especially in West Germany (where 82% rated this important compared to only 73% of the United States adolescents).

Among younger adolescents, surveys indicate that 5%–17% of girls 15 years and younger have had sexual intercourse. Among boys the same age, the range is 16%–38% (Gilgun, 1984; Jessor & Jessor, 1975; National Research Council, 1987; Ostrov & others, 1985). At age 13, boys also show earlier experience with sexual intercourse than girls—12% versus 5% (Dreyer, 1982). The pressure on male adolescents in the American society to have sexual intercourse is reflected in these figures, even though male adolescents enter puberty on the average two years later than female adolescents.

In some areas of the country, sexual experiences of young adolescents may be even greater. In an inner city area of Baltimore, 81% of the males at age 14 said they already have engaged in sexual intercourse. Other surveys in inner city, low-income areas also reveal a high incidence of early sexual intercourse (Clark, Zabin, & Hardy, 1984).

Clearly, large portions of America's adolescents are sexually active, but there is a positive note in the most recent data collected about adolescent sexual behavior. While the rate of sexual activity among adolescents increased dramatically in the 1970s, it appears to be stabilizing or decreasing as we enter the last decade of the twentieth century (National Research Council, 1987).

Researchers describe a heterosexual continuum that takes place during adolescence (Broderick & Rowe, 1968). Experiencing sexual intimacy is usually gradual and often follows a specified order of events. Necking comes first, then petting. Next comes intercourse, or in some cases oral sex, which has increased substantially in adolescents in recent years. In an investigation of 10th–12th graders, 25% of the males and 15% of the females who reported not having intercourse reported having oral sex (Newcomer & Udry, 1985). One researcher calls these individuals who have oral sex but not intercourse "experienced beginners" (Sorensen, 1973). More about variations of sexual experiences among adolescents appears in Table 12.2.

Sexuality

TABLE 12.2   *The Heterosexual Activity of American Adolescents*

Group	Total	Boys	Girls	Ages 13–15	Ages 16–19	White	Non-white
1. *Virgins* (adolescents who have not had sexual intercourse)	48%	41%	55%	63%	36%	55%	49%
Sexually inexperienced (virgins with no experience in any type of sexual activity)	22%	20%	25%	39%	9%	25%	23%
Sexual beginners (virgins who have actively or passively experienced some type of sexual activity)	17%	14%	19%	12%	21%	20%	9%
Unclassified virgins (virgins who could not be classified in the above groups	9%	7%	11%	12%	6%	9%	17%
2. *Nonvirgins* (adolescents who have had sexual intercourse one or more times)	52%	59%	45%	37%	64%	45%	51%
Serial monogamists (nonvirgins having a sexual relationship with only one person)	21%	15%	28%	9%	31%	19%	14%
Sexual adventurers (nonvirgins freely moving from one sexual partner to another)	15%	24%	6%	10%	18%	11%	18%
Inactive nonvirgins (nonvirgins who have not had sexual intercourse for more than one year)	12%	13%	10%	15%	10%	11%	14%
Unclassified nonvirgins (nonvirgins who could not be classified in the above groups)	4%	7%	1%	3%	5%	4%	5%
Currently intercourse-experienced (nonvirgins who have had sexual intercourse during the preceding month)	31%	30%	33%	15%	45%	24%	31%
Noncurrent intercourse-experienced (nonvirgins who have not had sexual intercourse during the preceding month)	21%	29%	12%	22%	19%	21%	20%

From R. C. Sorensen, *Adolescent Sexuality in Contemporary America.* Copyright © 1973, World Publishers, New York, NY.

While sexual intercourse can be a meaningful experience for older, more mature adolescents, many adolescents are not prepared to handle sexual experiences, especially in early adolescence. Adolescents may attempt sexual intercourse without really knowing what to do or how to satisfy their partner, leading to frustration and a sense of sexual inadequacy. And many are poorly informed about contraception or fail to use contraceptives.

Adolescent Female and Male Sexual Scripts

As adolescents explore their sexual identities they engage in sexual scripts (Gagnon & Simon, 1973; Gordon & Gilgun, 1987). A **sexual script** is a stereotyped pattern involving role prescriptions for how individuals should sexually behave. The different ways in which females and males are socialized are wrapped up in the sexual scripts adolescents follow. Discrepancies in male-female scripting can cause problems and confusion for adolescents as they work out their sexual identities. Adolescent girls have learned to link sexual intercourse with love. Female adolescents often rationalize their sexual behavior by telling themselves that they were swept away by love. A number of investigators have revealed that adolescent females, more than adolescent males, report being in love as the main reason for being sexually active (e.g., Cassell, 1984). Far more females than males have intercourse with partners they love and would like to marry. Other reasons for having sexual intercourse include giving in to male pressure, gambling that sex is a way to get a boyfriend, curiosity, and sexual desire unrelated to loving and caring. Adolescent males may be aware that their female counterparts have been socialized into a love ethic. They also may know the pressure many of them feel to have a boyfriend. Two classic male lines show how males understand female thinking about sex and love: "You would if you loved me," and "If you really loved me, you would have sex with me." The female adolescent who says, "If you really loved me, you would not put so much pressure on me," shows insight into male sexual motivation.

The adolescent girl shown here learns about sexual scripts of males and females from many different sources, including the romance novel she is reading.

Some experts on adolescent sexuality, though, believe we are moving toward a new norm suggesting that sexual intercourse is acceptable, but mainly within the boundary of a loving and affectionate relationship (Dreyer, 1982). As part of this new norm, promiscuity, exploitation, and unprotected sexual intercourse are more often perceived as unacceptable by adolescents. One variation of the new norm is that intercourse is acceptable in a nonlove relationship, but physical or emotional exploitation of the partner is not (Cassell, 1984). The new norm suggests that the double standard that once existed does not operate as it did. That is, physical and emotional exploitation of adolescent females by males is not as prevalent today as in prior decades.

Other experts on adolescent sexuality are not so sure the new norm has arrived (Gordon & Gilgun, 1987; Morrison, 1985). They argue that remnants of the double standard are unfortunately still flourishing. In most investigations, about twice as many boys as girls report positive feelings about sexual intercourse. Females are more likely to report guilt, fear, and hurt. Adolescent males feel considerable pressure from their peers to have experienced sexual intercourse and to be sexually active. I remember vividly the raunchy conversations that filled our basketball locker room in junior high school. By the end of the ninth grade, I was sure that I was the only virgin on the 15-member team, but of course, there was no way I let my teammates know that. As one young adolescent recently remarked, "Look, I feel a lot of pressure from my buddies to go for the score." Further evidence for the male's physical and emotional exploitation of the female was found in a survey of 432 14–18-year-olds

"Don't encourage him Sylvia."
"THE FAR SIDE cartoon by Gary Larson is reprinted by permission of Chronicle Features, San Francisco."

(Goodchilds & Zellman, 1984). Both male and female adolescents accepted the right of the male adolescent to be sexually aggressive, but let the female set the limits for the male's sexual overtures. Another attitude related to the double standard was the belief that females should not plan ahead to have sexual intercourse but instead be swept up in the passion of the moment, not taking contraceptive precautions. Unfortunately, while we have chipped away at some parts of the sexual double standard, other aspects remain.

Vulnerable Adolescents and Sexuality

Vulnerable adolescents are most likely to show irresponsible sexual behavior (Gordon & Gilgun, 1987). Adolescents who feel inadequate, who do not have adequate opportunities for education and work, and who feel the need to prove something to themselves through sex are at risk for irresponsible sexual behavior. It is not a coincidence that minority group and low-income adolescents use contraceptives less frequently and have higher pregnancy rates than white middle-income adolescents. Minority group and low-income adolescents have less access to information and to services. Their irresponsible behavior and lack of social support can lead to pregnancy, sexually transmitted diseases, and psychological stress.

Adolescents who do not plan to go to college are less likely to postpone having sex than those who do plan to go (Miller & Simon, 1974). Drinking, drug abuse, and truancy also are associated with sexual activity (Jessor & Jessor, 1975). Some investigators consider these behaviors as part of a general pattern of deviance during adolescence (Jessor & Jessor, 1975). Adolescents who depend heavily on their peers and are less involved with their families are more likely to be sexually involved, with male adolescents' dependence on male peers a strong factor in predicting their sexual activity (Jessor & others, 1983). Negative self-conceptions also can be associated with sexual activity. Some sexually active adolescents may be motivated to have sex because of feelings of low self-worth. Some girls are socialized to believe that sex is one of the few ways they can feel worthwhile about themselves. However, using sex to feel reassured about yourself results in exploitation and increased rather than decreased feelings of inadequacy. More information about adolescents who are vulnerable to behaving in sexually irresponsible ways appears later in the chapter when we discuss contraceptive use and pregnancy.

Homosexual Attitudes and Behavior

Both the early and more recent surveys of sexual choice indicate that about 4% of males and about 3% of females are exclusively homosexual (Hunt, 1974; Kinsey, Pomeroy, & Martin, 1948). As many as 10% of adolescents worry about whether or not they are lesbian or gay (Gordon & Gilgun, 1987). Until a few years ago, attitudes toward homosexuality were becoming increasingly permissive. But with the threat of AIDS, future surveys probably will indicate reduced acceptance of homosexuality.

Social, Emotional, and Personality Development

Adolescence may play an important role in the development of homosexuality. In one investigation, participation in homosexual behavior and sexual arousal by same-sex peers in adolescence was strongly related to an adult homosexual orientation (Bell, Weinberg, & Mammersmith, 1981). When interest in the same sex is intense and compelling, an adolescent often experiences severe conflict (Boxer, 1988; Irvin, 1988). The American culture stigmatizes homosexuality—negative labels such as "fags" and "queers" are given to male homosexuals and "lessies" and "dykes" to female homosexuals. The sexual socialization of adolescent homosexuals becomes a process of learning to hide (Herdt, 1988). Some gay males wait out their entire adolescence, hoping that heterosexual feelings will develop. Many female adolescent homosexuals have similar experiences, although same-sex genital contact is not as common as among males. Many adult females who identify themselves as homosexuals considered themselves predominantly heterosexual during adolescence (Bell & others, 1981).

Why are some individuals homosexual whereas others are heterosexual? Speculation about this question has been extensive, but no firm answers are available. Homosexual and heterosexual males and females have similar physical responses during sexual arousal and seem to be aroused by the same type of tactile stimulation. Investigators have found no differences between heterosexuals and homosexuals in terms of a wide range of attitudes, behaviors, and adjustments (Bell & others, 1981; Blumstein & Schwartz, 1983). Recognizing that homosexuality is not a form of mental illness, the American Psychiatric Association discontinued its classification of homosexuality as a disorder, except in those cases in which the individuals consider their sexual orientation to be abnormal.

Heredity, hormonal imbalance, family processes, and chance learning are among the factors proposed as homosexuality's causes. Concerning family processes, it has been argued that a dominant mother and a weak father promote homosexuality. The evidence is far from clear about this proposal. Concerning chance learning, someone may be seduced by an individual of the same sex and subsequently develop a homosexual preference. The most widely adopted view of homosexuality today is that there are a number of ways to become a homosexual, including any of the aforementioned biological and environmental reasons (McWhirter, Reinisch, & Sanders, in press; Money, 1987).

Self-Stimulation

Earlier we indicated that a heterosexual continuum of necking, petting, and intercourse or oral sex characterizes many adolescents' sexual experiences. Substantial numbers of adolescents, though, have sexual experiences outside of this heterosexual continuum through masturbation or same-sex behavior. Most boys have an ejaculation for the first time at about 12–13 years of age (Bell & others, 1981). Masturbation, genital contact with the same-sex or other-sex partner, or a wet dream during sleep are common circumstances for ejaculation.

Masturbation is the most frequent sexual outlet for many adolescents. In one investigation, masturbation was commonplace among adolescents (Haas, 1979). More than two-thirds of the boys and one-half of the girls masturbated once a week or more. Adolescents today do not feel as guilty about masturbation as they once did, although they still may feel embarrassed or defensive about it (Sorensen, 1973). In past eras masturbation was denounced as causing everything from warts to insanity. Today, as few as 15% of adolescents attach any stigma to masturbation (Hyde, 1988).

Contraceptive Use

The following conversation between an adolescent boy and girl reveals a communication pattern that happens far too often (Gordon, 1987).

> *Susan:* Come in.
>
> *Skip:* I'm sorry I'm late, Susan. I had to go to the U store and the library and run around and, you know, all kinds of things and I'm sorry. . . .
>
> *Susan:* Yeah, well I'm glad you came. I called because I want to talk to you.
>
> *Skip:* Yeah. How was your day today?
>
> *Susan:* Oh, all right. Did you get much studying done?
>
> *Skip:* No, I was running around and uh, you know just thinking, sitting around.
>
> *Susan:* Yeah. I've been thinking a lot also. I really want to talk with you about last night. (pause)
>
> *Skip:* Are you sorry or anything?
>
> *Susan:* No, I'm not sorry, I'm just really worried.
>
> *Skip:* (surprise) About what?
>
> *Susan:* You know I'm not using any birth control.
>
> *Skip:* (shock) You're not using any birth control? (pause) No, I didn't know you weren't using any birth control. How was I supposed to. . . . How could you do that?
>
> *Susan:* My mother always told me the man would take care of it.
>
> *Skip:* The man *can* take care of it, but I *wasn't* taking care of it, obviously. It's the woman's responsibility to take care of it, you know that. All women use the pill nowadays.
>
> *Susan:* Not all women use the pill and why is it my responsibility if we're both involved? Besides we never really talked about it and when was I supposed to bring it up, in the middle of . . . I didn't know you were planning to go to bed.
>
> *Skip:* I didn't plan it. Aw, come on, Susan, You don't plan things like that, they just happen.

From Student SECH Advisor Program, Princeton University Health Services, Princeton, New Jersey, Permission granted by Karen A. Gordon, Director of Health Education, 1987.

Social, Emotional, and Personality Development

TABLE 12.3   *The Increased Use of Contraceptives by Adolescents*

Contraceptive Use Status	1976	1979
Always used	29%	34%
Used at first intercourse, but not always	10	15
Not used at first intercourse, but used at some time	26	25
Never used	36	27

Reprinted with permission from *Family Planning Perspectives,* Volume 12, Number 5, 1980.

Susan: We both must have been thinking about it . . . why didn't we say anything? Aren't we supposed to trust each other?

Skip: Sure we trust each other. Aw, come on it's not that, it's just not the kind of thing you talk about. Susan, could you see me going up to you and saying, "Susan are you using any. . . ." I can't say that. I can't say it.

Susan: Skip, I'm really scared. I could be pregnant. What are we going to do? (Looking at each other scared and questioningly)

Only about 1 of 5 unmarried female adolescents who have had sexual intercourse uses birth control pills, and many sexually active adolescents never use any contraceptives whatsoever (Jessor & Jessor, 1975). Even toward the end of adolescence, only 60% of females use some form of contraceptive, and of those who do use contraceptives, their use may be sporadic (Zelnik & Kantner, 1977). Many adolescents are under a complete misconception about when pregnancy is most likely to occur during the menstrual cycle. In one investigation, a majority of adolescents believed that pregnancy risk is greatest during menstruation (Zelnik & Kantner, 1977).

Adolescents are increasing their use of contraceptives, as indicated in Table 12.3 (Zelnik & Kantner, 1980). As the threat of AIDS and other sexually transmitted diseases continues, one of the positive benefits could be increased contraceptive use by adolescents. Unfortunately, the same investigation that found an increased use of contraceptives from 1976 to 1979 found that less effective measures, such as withdrawal, were increasingly being used. The pill and condoms were the most widely used contraceptives (see Table 12.4).

What social and demographic characteristics are related to contraceptive use? The factors most related to poor, inconsistent, or nonuse of contraceptives among adolescents are the following: being under the age of 18; being single and not involved in a steady, committed dating relationship; having intercourse sporadically; being from a low-income family; being black or hispanic; and not having had a previous pregnancy experience (Chilman, 1979). Personality and attitudes also are factors. The failure of sexually active adolescents to use contraceptives is associated with feelings of incompetency, poor coping skills, lack of a future orientation, high anxiety level, poor social adjustment, and having negative attitudes toward contraceptives (Oskamp & Mindick, 1981).

Method	Method First Used		Method Last Used	
	1976	*1979*	*1976*	*1979*
Pill	33%	19%	48%	41%
IUD	2	1	3	2
Diaphragm	0	1	1	4
Condom	36	34	23	23
Douche	3	1	3	2
Withdrawal	18	36	15	19
Rhythm	5	5	4	6

TABLE 12.4   *Types of Contraceptives Used by Urban Adolescents*

Reprinted with permission from *Family Planning Perspectives,* Volume 12, Number 5, 1980.

Sexually Transmitted Diseases

Tammy, age 15, just finished listening to an expert lecture in her health class. We overhear her talking to one of her girlfriends as she walks down the school corridor: "That was a disgusting lecture. I can't believe all the diseases you can get by having sex. I think she was probably trying to scare us. She spent a lot of time talking about AIDS, which I have heard that normal people do not get. Right? I've heard that only homosexuals and drug addicts get AIDS. And, I've also heard that gonorrhea and most other sexual diseases can be cured, so what is the big deal if you get something like that?" Tammy's view of sexually transmitted diseases (formerly called venereal disease or VD)— that they always happen to someone else, that they can be easily cured without any harm done, that they are too disgusting for a nice young person to hear about, let alone get—is common among adolescents. Tammy's view is wrong. Adolescents who are having sex run the risk of getting sexually transmitted diseases. Sexually transmitted diseases are fairly common among today's adolescents. The sexually transmitted diseases adolescents are most likely to encounter are chlamydia, gonorrhea, venereal warts, and herpes, although the greatest scare in recent years has become the epidemic of AIDS (Belfer, Kerner, & Miller, 1988; Brookman, 1988).

Chlamydia affects as many as 10% of all college students. The disease, which is named for the tiny bacterium that causes it, appears in both males and females. Males experience a burning sensation during urination and a mucoid discharge, while females experience painful urination or a vaginal discharge. These signs often mimic gonorrhea; but when penicillin is prescribed for the gonorrhea-like symptoms, the problem does not go away as it would if gonorrhea were the culprit. If left untreated, the disease can infect the entire reproductive tract. Scar tissue may be produced, preventing the female from becoming pregnant. Drugs have been developed to treat this very common sexually transmitted disease and they are very effective.

Another major sexual problem in recent years has focused on a virus called genital herpes. While this disease is more common among young adults (estimates range to as high as 1 in 5 sexually active adults), as many as 1 in 35 adolescents have genital herpes. The first herpes symptom is a vague itching or burning sensation in or near the genital area. Two or three days later, the burning usually turns into a more painful feeling. Shallow, fluid-filled blisters appear on the shaft or tip of the penis in males and on the outer genitalia, vagina, or cervix in females. The first attack is usually the most painful, often accompanied by flu-like symptoms. The severity of the attacks and whether they recur vary from one individual to another, although approximately 70% experience a repeat attack within nine months of the first.

Usually when you catch a virus like measles or chicken pox, your body produces antibodies that try to destroy the invading virus. The antibodies remain in your bloodstream the rest of your life and instantly attack the virus if it reappears. This is the reason we get measles only once. Unfortunately, herpes antibodies do not work this way. Instead, the virus retreats to the nerve cells at the base of the spine, where it can remain dormant anywhere from several weeks to a lifetime. During new attacks, the virus travels down the nerve fibers to the genitalia and produces another crop of painful blisters.

Girls and women with herpes need to be especially cautious, since there is some indication that it is associated with cervical cancer. Females with herpes should have a Pap smear every six months—fortunately, this type of cancer develops slowly and can be detected in an early form. No cure for genital herpes has yet been found. Some of the unanswered questions about herpes are: How is the virus able to persist in the body? Why does it become dormant? What happens when it reactivates? And how does the body finally repress the recurrences?

Far more rare than any other sexually transmitted disease in the adolescent or adult population, **AIDS** (Acquired Immune Deficiency Snydrome) is unrivaled in the fear it has generated among the American public. AIDS is caused by a virus that destroys the body's immune system. Consequently, many germs that would usually not harm someone with a normal immune system can produce devastating results and ultimately death.

In 1981, when AIDS was first recognized in the United States, there were fewer than 60 cases. By November 1986, there were 27,000 cases of AIDS and 15,000 deaths from the disease. By March 1987, there were more than 32,000 cases of AIDS and 20,000 deaths from the disease. Beginning in 1990, according to Dr. Frank Press, president of the National Academy of Sciences, "We will lose as many Americans each year to AIDS as we lost in the entire Vietnam War." Almost 60,000 Americans died in that war. According to federal health officials, 1–1.5 million Americans are now asymptomatic carriers of AIDS—those who are infected with the virus and presumably capable of infecting others but who show no clinical symptoms of AIDS.

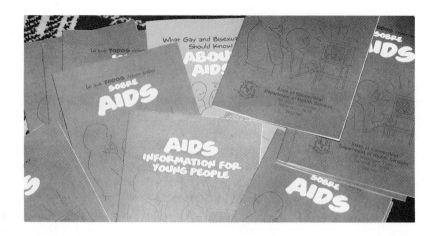

Shown here are pamphlets on AIDS designed for children and adolescents. Awareness of accurate information about AIDS is especially important for our nation's youth, since a number of youth lack adequate knowledge about AIDS.

In a recent survey of 35,239 high school students in 11 states by the Centers for Disease Control in Atlanta, it was revealed that many adolescents are misinformed about AIDS. More than 50% of the adolescents believed that an individual can get AIDS from a blood test. About the same percentage said that AIDS can be contracted from a public toilet. Experts say the disease can be transmitted only by sexual contact, sharing needles, or blood transfusions. More than 90% of the adolescents did know that AIDS can be transmitted through sex and through sharing drug needles. A recent survey of 38,000 Canadian adolescents revealed that the adolescents felt the media is doing a poor job of providing easy to understand information about AIDS (King & others, 1989).

While 90% of AIDS cases continue to occur among homosexual males or intravenous drug users, a disproportionate increase among females who are heterosexual partners of bisexual males or of intravenous drug users has been noted from 1985–1988. This increase suggests that the risk of AIDS may be increasing among heterosexual individuals who have multiple sexual partners (Hein, 1989).

Of special interest to children and adolescents is the controversy surrounding individuals who have contracted the virus. For example, one 13-year-old hemophiliac contracted AIDS while receiving injections of a clotting agent. He was barred from resuming his seventh-grade classes. In another case in another school district, school officials and doctors met with more than 800 concerned parents to defend their decision to admit a 14-year-old AIDS patient to school. Some parents will not let their children attend schools where an identified AIDS patient is enrolled. Others believe children with the disease should not be society's outcasts based on our current knowledge of how the disease spreads (Task Force on Pediatric AIDS, 1989).

AIDS is a lethal threat to adolescents whose sexual activities put them at risk for contracting the disease—especially those who are sexually active with more than one partner and those who are intravenous drug users (Bingham, 1989). Sexually active adolescents—homosexual or heterosexual—can reduce the probability they will contract AIDS by following cer-

Social, Emotional, and Personality Development

Adolescents' Sexual Attitudes and Behavior and Sexually Transmitted Diseases

Concept	Processes/Related Ideas	Characteristics/Description
Sexual attitudes and behavior	Heterosexual attitudes and behavior	There has been a major increase in the number of adolescents reporting having had intercourse, and the proportion of females engaging in intercourse has increased more rapidly than in the case of males. National data indicate that by age 18 44% of females and 64% of males are sexually experienced. Urban inner-city adolescents have even higher incidences. One positive note is that as we enter the 1990s, adolescent sexual activity seems to be stabilizing or dropping off. As we develop our sexual indentities we follow certain sexual scripts, which are different for males and females. Vulnerable adolescents are more likely to show irresponsible sexual behavior.
	Homosexual attitudes and behavior	About 4% of males and 3% of females choose to be exclusively homosexual. About 10% of adolescents worry about whether they are lesbian or gay. Until recently, there was increasing acceptance of homosexuality, but the AIDS epidemic likely is reducing this acceptance. The causes of homosexuality are still unsettled.
	Self-stimulation	Part of the sexual orientation of virtually all adolescents and one of the most frequent sexual outlets. Today's adolescents feel less guilty about masturbation than their counterparts earlier in history.
	Contraceptive use	Possibly due to poor sex education, many adolescents do not use contraceptives. There has been an increase in their use but unfortunately a decreased use of birth control pills and increased use of the withdrawal method. Increased fear of AIDS and education about its consequences should lead to greater use of condoms.
Sexually transmitted diseases	Their nature	Any adolescent who has sex runs the risk of getting a sexually transmitted disease, although many adolescents underestimate their own chances of getting these diseases. Among the sexually transmitted diseases adolescents may get are chlamydia, gonorrhea, venereal warts, herpes, and AIDS.

tain precautions. First, sex with strangers or sex with individuals living in metropolitan locations where AIDS is more prevalent should be engaged in with extreme caution. Second, condoms may provide some protection against the virus, but data are inconclusive on this at this time. Third, a test is now available to determine if an individual has AIDS. Not everyone exposed to the AIDS virus contracts AIDS, but adolescents who test positive for the AIDS virus should refrain from further sexual contacts until their physician informs them otherwise.

At this point we have discussed a number of ideas about sexual attitudes and behavior and about sexually transmitted diseases. A summary of these ideas is presented in Concept Table 12.1.

Adolescent Pregnancy

Angela is 15 years old and she is pregnant. She reflects, "I'm 3 months pregnant. This could ruin my whole life. I've made all of these plans for the future and now they are down the drain. I don't have anybody to talk with about my problem. I can't talk to my parents. There is no way they can understand." Pregnant adolescents were once virtually invisible and unmentionable. But yesterday's secret has become today's national dilemma. Our exploration of adolescent pregnancy focuses on its incidence and nature, its consequences, cognitive factors that may be involved, adolescents as parents, and ways adolescent pregnancy rates can be reduced.

Incidence and Nature of Adolescent Pregnancy

They are of different races and from different places, but their circumstances have the same stressfulness. Each year more than 1 million American adolescents will become pregnant, 4 out of 5 of them unmarried. They represent a flaw in our nation's social fabric. Like Angela, many become pregnant in their early or middle adolescent years, 30,000 of them under the age of 15. In all, this means that 1 of every 10 adolescent females in the United States becomes pregnant each year, with 8 of 10 pregnancies unintended (National Research Council, 1987). As one 17-year-old Los Angeles mother of a 1-year-old son said, "We are children having children." The only bright spot in the adolescent pregnancy statistics is that the adolescent pregnancy rate, after increasing during the 1970s, has leveled off and may even be beginning to decline (National Research Council, 1987).

The adolescent pregnancy rate in the United States is the highest in the Western world. It is more than twice as high as the rates in England, France, or Canada, almost 3 times as high as the rate in Sweden, and 7 times as high as the rate in the Netherlands (Alan Guttmacher Institute, 1981; Jones & others, 1985) (see Figure 12.2). Though American adolescents are no more sexually active than their counterparts in these other nations, they are many more times likely to become pregnant.

Adolescent pregnancy is a complex American problem, one that strikes many sensitive nerves. The subject of adolescent pregnancy touches on many explosive social issues: the battle over abortion rights, contraceptives and the delicate question of whether adolescents should have easy access to them, and the perenially touchy subject of sex education in the public schools.

Dramatic changes have swept through the American culture in the last three decades, changes that involve sexual attitudes and social morals. Adolescents actually gave birth at a higher rate in 1957 than they do today, but that was a time of early marriage, with almost one-fourth of 18–19-year-olds married. The overwhelming majority of births to adolescent mothers in the 1950s occurred within a marriage and mainly involved females 17 years of age and older. Two to three decades ago, if an unwed adolescent girl became

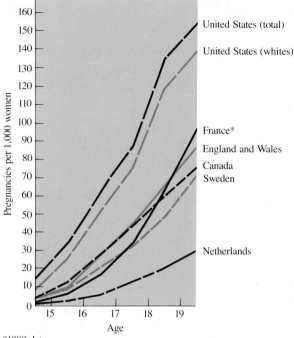

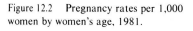
Figure 12.2 Pregnancy rates per 1,000 women by women's age, 1981.

*1980 data.

Note: pregnancies are defined here as births plus abortions; age is the age at outcome.

An International Perspective on Abortion Trends

An estimated 40 million abortions are legally performed each year in the world, or one abortion for every two births. In most countries laws permit induced abortion, but conditions regulating the practice range from limited prohibition to an elective abortion at the request of the pregnant female.

The largest proportion of terminations occurs among females aged 20–34 years. In the early years following the introduction of liberal abortion regulation, the number of females under 20 years of age seeking abortions increased, reaching as high as 30% in some countries such as the United States, Canada, and New Zealand. In Asian countries such as Japan, India, Singapore, Bangladesh, and South Korea, adolescents undergoing abortion make up a small proportion of abortion-seeking females compared to the countries of the West. However, their number is now rising because of increases in the sexual activity of Asian adolescents (Sachdev, 1988).

Adolescent pregnancy has become one of our nation's major problems. How is the world of today's pregnant adolescent different than it was in the 1950s?

pregnant, in most instances her parents had her swiftly married off in a shotgun wedding. If marriage was impractical, the girl would discreetly disappear, the child would be put up for adoption, and the predicament would never be discussed further. Abortion was not a real option for most adolescent females until 1973, when the Supreme Court ruled it could not be outlawed.

In today's world of adolescent pregnancies, a different scenario unfolds. If the girl does not choose to have an abortion (some 45% of adolescent girls do), she usually keeps the baby and raises it without the traditional involvement of marriage. With the stigma of illegitimacy largely absent, girls are less likely to give up their babies for adoption. Fewer than 5% do, compared with about 35% in the early 1960s. But while the stigma of illegitimacy has waned, the lives of most pregnant adolescents are anything but rosy.

Adolescent Pregnancy's Consequences

The consequences of our nation's high adolescent pregnancy rate are cause for great concern. Adolescent pregnancy increases health risks to both the offspring and the mother. Infants born to adolescent mothers are more likely to have low birth weights—a prominent cause of infant mortality as well as of neurological problems and childhood illnesses (Furstenberg, Brooks-Gunn, & Chase-Lansdale, 1989; Hayes, 1987; Schorr, in press). Adolescent mothers often drop out of school, fail to gain employment, and become dependent on welfare. Although many adolescent mothers resume their education later in life, they generally do not catch up with women who postpone childbearing. In the National Longitudinal Survey of Work Experience of Youth, it was found that only half of the 20–26-year-old women who first gave birth at age 17 had completed high school by their 20s (the percentage was even lower for those who gave birth at a younger age) (see Table 12.5) (Mott & Mariglio, 1985). By contrast, among young females who waited until age 20 to have a baby, more than 90% had obtained a high school education. Among the younger adolescent mothers, almost half had obtained a General Equivalency Diploma (GED), which does not often open up good employment opportunities.

Social, Emotional, and Personality Development

TABLE 12.5 *Percent Distribution of Women, Ages 20–26 in 1983, By Type of High School Completion, According to Age at First Birth*

Age at First Birth	Total %	High School Completion by 1983 Diploma %	GED %
15	45	24	21
16	49	28	21
17	53	38	15
18	62	52	10
19	77	68	9
Under 20	90	86	4

Source: Frank L. Mott, William Marsiglio, "Early Childbearing and Completion of High School," *Family Planning Perspectives*, Vol. 17, No. 5, (Sept./Oct. 1985), p. 236, Table 3. © 1985 The Alan Guttmacher Institute.

These educational deficits have negative consequences for the young females themselves and for their children (Kenney, 1987). Adolescent parents are more likely than those who delay childbearing to have low-paying, low-status jobs, or to be unemployed. The mean family income of white females who give birth before age 17 is approximately half that of families in which the mother delays birth until her mid- or late 20s. The difficulties faced by adolescent mothers is clear in the descriptions of three girls in Perspective on Adolescent Development 12.1.

Cognitive Factors in Adolescent Pregnancy

With their developing idealism, ability to think in more abstract and hypothetical ways, young adolescents may get caught up in a mental world far removed from reality, one that may involve a belief that things can't or won't happen to them and that they are omnipotent and indestructible. These cognitive changes have intriguing implications for adolescents' sex education (Lipsitz, 1980). Having information about contraceptives is not enough—what seems to predict whether adolescents will use contraceptives or not is their acceptance of themselves and their sexuality. This acceptance requires not only emotional maturity but cognitive maturity.

Most discussions of adolescent pregnancy and its prevention assume that adolescents have the ability to anticipate consequences, to weigh the probable outcome of behavior, and to project into the future what will happen if they engage in certain acts, such as sexual intercourse. That is, prevention is based on the belief that adolescents have the cognitive ability to approach problem solving in a planned, organized, and analytical manner. However, many adolescents are just beginning to develop these capacities, and others have not developed them at all (Holmbeck, Gasiewski, & Crossman, 1989).

The personal fable we described in Chapter 4 may be associated with adolescent pregnancy. The young adolescent might say, "Hey, it won't happen to me." If the adolescent is locked into this personal fable, she may not respond

Angela, Michelle, and Stephanie: Three Adolescent Mothers

Before the baby arrived, her bedroom was a dimly lit chapel to the idols of rock music. Now the rock posters have been removed and the walls painted white. Angela's room has become a nursery for her 6-week-old son. Angela, who just turned 15, has difficulty thinking of herself as a mother. She feels as young as she was before the baby and also feels that she hasn't grown up any faster. She looks like a typical adolescent girl as she sits in her parents' living room, asking her mother for permission to attend a rock concert, asking if she can buy a pet dog, and complaining that she isn't allowed to do anything. She mentions that last night she couldn't get her homework done because it took her so long to feed the baby. She commented, "When I laid him down, he wanted me to pick him back up." She ponders, "Babies are a giant step in life. I should have thought more about what I was doing. I had no idea what this was going to be like."

It is a hot summer day in San Francisco. Michelle, a 14-year-old black girl, is typing away, practicing her office skills with fervor as beads of sweat trickle down her forehead. She is worried about her future. She feels that she has to get some skills so she can make some money. She is right. In three weeks, Michelle is going to have a baby. She comes from a low-income family. She doesn't know her father's whereabouts and her mother can barely make ends meet. She says that she used to think, "In 10 years I will be 24. Now I think, I'll be 24 and my child will be 10."

In the early afternoon the smells of dirty diapers and grease fill the air in a bleak Minneapolis apartment. The television is tuned to "All My Children." Seventeen-year-old Stephanie has collapsed on the sofa. A few minutes later, above the tone of the television characters' voices, she hears a loud wail. Her 1-month-old baby is hungry. In an adjacent bedroom, her other child, 1½-year-old Joey, is recovering from the flu. Stephanie is one of 10 children herself. She first became pregnant at age 15. She says it was an accident. So was her second baby, she says.

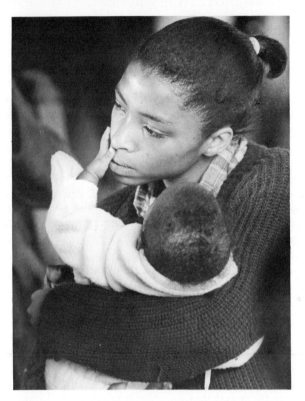

Adolescent pregnancy has become a major national problem. The United States has the highest adolescent pregnancy rate of all Western societies. Why has our nation's adolescent pregnancy rate gotten out of control?

Stephanie complains that she always feels tired. Before Joey's birth, she dropped out of school. She dreamed of being an airline stewardess. Now her hopes are more down to earth. She would like to pay her bills, buy groceries, and be able to live in a house with her own furniture. Says Stephanie, "It has been a long, long time since I had a good time." (Wallis, 1985)

well to a course on sex education that preaches prevention. A developmental perspective on cognition suggests what can be taught in sex education courses for young adolescents.

Late adolescents (18–19 years of age) are to some degree realistic and future oriented about sexual experiences, just as they are about careers and marriage. Middle adolescents (15–17 years of age) often romanticize sexuality. But young adolescents (10–15 years of age) seem to experience sex in a depersonalized way that is filled with anxiety and denial. This depersonalized orientation toward sex is not likely to lead to preventive behavior.

Consider the outcome if the following are combined: the nature of early adolescent cognition, the personal fable, anxiety about sex, gender role definitions about what is masculine and what is feminine, the sexual themes of music, the sexual overtones of magazines and television, and a societal standard that says sex is appropriate for adults but promiscuous for adolescents. That is, our society tells adolescents that sex is fun, harmless, adult, and forbidden. The combination of early physical maturation, risk-taking behavior, egocentrism, the inability to think futuristically, and an ambivalent contradictory culture makes sex difficult for adolescents to handle. Add to this the growing need for adolescents to develop a commitment, especially in a career. Yet youth, especially low-income, minority group youth, face high unemployment rates, which can turn them away from the future and intensively toward the present. Piece together information about early adolescent development, America's sexual ambivalence, and adolescents' vulnerability to economic forces and the result is social dynamite.

Adolescents as Parents

Children of adolescent parents face problems even before they are born. Only 1 of every 5 pregnant adolescent girls receives any prenatal care at all during the important first 3 months of pregnancy. Pregnant adolescents are more likely to have anemia and complications related to prematurity than mothers aged 20–24. The problems of adolescent pregnancy add up to twice the normal risk of delivering a low-birth-weight baby (one that weighs under 5.5 pounds), a category that places that infant at risk for physical and mental deficits (McAnarney, 1988).

Infants who escape the medical hazards of having an adolescent mother may not escape the psychological and social perils. Children born to adolescent mothers do not do as well on intelligence tests and have more behavioral problems than do those born to mothers in their 20s (Broman, 1981; Silver, 1988). Adolescent mothers have less desirable childrearing practices and less realistic expectations for their infants' development than do older mothers (Field & others, 1980; Osofsky, 1989). Said one 18-year-old adolescent mother, "Not long after he was born, I began to resent him. I wouldn't play with him the first year. He didn't talk until he was 2—he would just grunt, I'm sure some of his slow development is my fault. Now I want to make up for it and try to give him extra attention, but he still is behind his age." Other adolescent

An adolescent father and mother shown enjoying their newborn baby. What is the public's perception of adolescent fathers? Is it a myth?

mothers may get excited about having "this little adorable thing" and anticipate that their world with their child will be marvelous. But as the infant demands more and more of their attention and they have to take care of the infant instead of going out on dates, their positive expectations turn sour.

So far we have talked exclusively about adolescent mothers. What role do adolescent fathers play in the adolescent family? The public's perception of the adolescent father is usually of someone irresponsible who rarely if ever is involved in childrearing or support of the adolescent mother. This is a misconception. Researchers have found that adolescent fathers are more willing to participate and do participate more in the adolescent family than is commonly thought (Danziger & Radin, 1989; Parke, Power, & Fisher, 1980; Robinson, 1988). Researchers find that as many as 4 of 5 adolescent fathers have daily contact with their children and that 3 of 4 contribute at least some financial support. However, adolescent fathers need considerable support to assure them of their importance in the adolescent family.

Adolescent fathers have lower incomes, less education, and more children than do men who delay having children until their 20s. One reason for these difficulties is that the adolescent father compounds his problem of getting his girlfriend pregnant by dropping out of school. As soon as he leaves school, the adolescent father moves directly into a low-paying job. Adolescent fathers are saying to themselves, "You need to be a good father. The least you can do is to get a job and provide some support."

Many young fathers have little idea of what a father is supposed to do. They may love their baby but don't know how to behave. Our society has given them few guidelines and few supports. Programs designed to help adolescent fathers are still relatively rare, but they are increasing. One circumstance provides hope. Terry, who is now 21, has a 17-month-old child and is himself the child of adolescent parents. After receiving support from the Teenage Pregnancy and Parenting Project in San Francisco, he is now a counselor there. He reports, "My father was a parent when he was an adolescent. So was my grandfather. I know it will stop with my son" (Stengel, 1985).

Reducing Adolescent Pregnancy

Serious, extensive efforts are needed to help pregnant adolescents and young mothers enhance their educational and occupational opportunities. Adolescent mothers also need extensive help in obtaining competent day care and in planning for the future (Edleman, 1987; Furstenberg, Brooks-Gunn, & Morgan, 1987). The following four recommendations for attacking the high rate of adolescent pregnancy were recently offered by John Conger (1988): sex education and family planning, access to contraceptive methods, the life options approach, and broad community involvement and support, each of which we consider in turn.

We badly need age-appropriate family life education for our nation's adolescents, including sex education that begins in childhood and continues through adolescence. While still a controversial issue, sex education in the schools is favored by a large majority of parents. Much more about sex education is discussed shortly.

In addition to age-appropriate family life and sex education, sexually active adolescents need access to contraceptive methods. These needs often can be fulfilled through adolescent clinics that provide comprehensive, high quality health services. At four of the nation's oldest adolescent clinics in St. Paul, Minnesota, the overall annual rate of first-time pregnancies has dropped from 80 per 1,000 to 29 per 1,000 (Schorr, in press). These clinics offer everything from immunizations to sports physicals to treatment for sexually transmitted diseases. Significantly, they also advise adolescents on contraception and dispense prescriptions for birth control (provided parents have agreed beforehand to allow their adolescents to visit the clinic). An important aspect of the clinics is the presence of individuals trained to understand the special needs and confusions of the adolescent age group.

Better sex education, family planning, and access to contraceptive methods alone will not remedy the adolescent pregnancy crisis, especially for high risk adolescents. Adolescents have to become *motivated* to reduce their pregnancy risk. This motivation will come only when adolescents look to the future and see that they have an opportunity to become self-sufficient and successful (Edelman, 1987). Adolescents need opportunities to improve their academic and career-related skills, job opportunities, life planning consultation, and extensive mental health services.

Finally, for adolescent pregnancy prevention to ultimately succeed we need broad community involvement and support. This support is a major reason for the success of pregnancy prevention efforts in other developed nations where adolescent pregnancy rates, abortion, and childbearing are much lower than ours despite similar levels of sexual activity (Jones & others, 1985; Wallace & Vienonen, 1989). In Holland, as well as other European countries such as Sweden, sex does not carry the mystery and conflict it does in American society. Holland does not have a mandated sex education program, but adolescents can obtain contraceptive counseling at government-sponsored clinics for a small fee. The Dutch media also have played an important role in educating the public about sex through frequent broadcasts focused on birth control, abortion, and related matters. Dutch adolescents do not think about having sex without birth control. Of course, one alternative to contraceptive use is abstention, an especially important consideration for young adolescents.

Sex Education

Swedish adolescents are sexually active at an earlier age than are American adolescents and they are exposed to even more explicit sex on television. However, the Swedish National Board of Education has developed a curriculum that ensures, beginning at age 7, that every child in the country will experience a thorough grounding in reproductive biology and by the age of 10–12 has been introduced to information about various forms of contraceptives. Teachers are expected to handle the subject of sex whenever it becomes relevant, regardless of the subject they are teaching. The idea is to dedramatize and demystify sex so that familiarity will make the individual less vulnerable to unwanted pregnancy and sexually transmitted diseases (Wallis, 1985). American society is not so open about sex education. What are adolescents' sources of sex information? What is the role of schools in sex education?

Sources of Sex Information

One 14-year-old adolescent recently was asked where he learned about sex. He responded, "In the streets." Asked if this was the only place, he said, "Well, I learn some more from *Playboy* and the other sex magazines." What about school, he was asked. He responded, "No, they talk about hygiene, but not much that could help you out." When asked about his parents' contributions, he replied, "They haven't told me one thing."

Parents are an important missing ingredient in the fight against adolescent pregnancy and sexually transmitted diseases. A large majority of adolescents say that they cannot talk freely with their parents about sexual matters. Surveys indicate that about 17% of adolescents' sex education comes from mothers and only about 2% from fathers (Thornburg, 1981). While parents, especially fathers, have been infrequent sources of sex education for adolescents, adolescents report that when they can talk with their parents openly and freely about sex they are *less* likely to be sexually active. Contraceptive use by female adolescents also increases when adolescents report they can communicate about sex with their parents (Fisher, 1987).

TABLE 12.6 *Initial Sources of Sex Information*

	Abortion	Conception	Contraception	Ejaculation	Homosexuality	Intercourse	Masturbation	Menstruation	Petting	Prostitution	Seminal Emissions	Venereal Disease	Totals
Peers	20.6	27.4	42.8	38.9	50.6	39.7	36.3	21.5	59.7	49.7	35.2	28.2	37.1
Literature	32.0	3.2	23.8	22.1	19.4	15.2	25.0	11.2	10.0	26.8	37.4	21.2	21.9
Mother	21.5	49.4	13.1	8.9	7.5	23.8	11.1	41.5	4.5	7.5	4.2	9.4	17.4
Schools	23.7	16.4	16.7	20.7	16.1	7.6	17.5	15.7	9.0	11.7	21.1	36.8	15.2
Experience	.5	.8	1.0	5.2	2.1	7.5	8.0	7.6	14.0	2.0	.7	1.1	5.4
Father	1.0	1.2	2.4	2.6	4.3	3.9	1.3	1.1	2.2	1.0	1.4	2.1	2.2
Minister	1.0	.9	.0	.7	.0	1.0	.0	.7	.2	1.0	.0	.0	.5
Physician	.3	.7	.2	.9	.0	1.3	.8	.7	.4	.3	.0	1.2	.3
Totals	100.0	100.0	100.0	100.0	100.0	100.0	100.0	100.0	100.0	100.0	100.0	100.0	100.0

N = 1152

"Don't know" responses were eliminated from the table. Percentages are on all terms listed as known.
From Thornberg, H. D., "Sources of sex education among early adolescents," *Journal of Early Adolescence*, 1981, 1, p. 174. Reprinted by permission.

In a survey of all 1,152 students at a midwestern high school, students were asked where they learned about various aspects of sex (Thornburg, 1981). As in other investigations, the most common source of sex information was peers, followed by literature, mother, schools, and experience (see Table 12.6). While schools are usually thought of as a main source of sex education, only 15% of the adolescents' information about sex came from school instruction. In one recent study, college students said they got more sex education from reading than any other source (Andre, Frevert, & Schuchmann, 1989).

Sex Education in the Schools

A majority of parents favor sex education in the schools. In a national poll conducted for *Time* magazine, 78% of parents wanted schools to teach sex education, including information about birth control. Despite the majority opinion, sex education remains swirled in controversy. On one side are groups like Planned Parenthood who argue that sex education should be more open and birth control more available as in European countries. On the other side are individuals who believe sex education should be provided by parents and that teaching adolescents about birth control is simply giving them a green light to have sex and be promiscuous. The controversy has led to clashes at school board meetings throughout the nation. In New York City, a program was developed to combat a runaway rate of adolescent pregnancy. Religious groups showed up at a school board meeting with a list of 56 objections. In

"I don't like this A in sex education."
© *Glenn Bernhardt.*

San Juan Capistrano, California, conservative opponents of sex education in the schools appeared at a school board meeting dressed in Revolutionary War clothes. They even brought a cannon with them.

A survey of sex education in the nation's school districts involving cities of 100,000 or more in population found that three-fourths provided some sex education instruction in high school or junior high school, while two-thirds provided it in elementary school (Sonenstein & Pittman, 1984). This does not mean that every school in the district provided sex education or that the instruction was comprehensive and competent. Indeed, most school districts integrated material on sex education into other courses, such as health education, biology, physical education, or home economics.

At the junior or senior high school levels, sex education averaged 6–10 hours of teaching time, with few school districts providing comprehensive programs involving more than 40 hours of instruction. Almost all of the programs covered physiology, sexually transmitted diseases, pregnancy, and parenthood. About three-fourths include pregnancy prevention information, such as contraception, sources of family planning services, and the most likely time for pregnancy to occur. Table 12.7 indicates the grade level at which different topics were most likely to be introduced. The progression is usually from physiological facts to reproductive facts and issues and then to more complicated, value-laden issues.

Sex education programs vary from one school to the next. Many schools have no sex education program at all. Among those that do, a sex education program can range from a well-developed, full semester course on human sexuality to a two-week unit on anatomy and physiology. The most common place for adolescents to be given sex education information is in a 10th-grade biology class. Another factor in quality sex education is the teacher. Most instructors in sex education have majored in biology, health education, home economics, or physical education. Few have extensive coursework in human sexuality (Newton, 1982). While teachers do not need a Ph.D. in human sexuality to be an effective sex education instructor, they should be well trained and knowledgeable about sexuality. They should be willing to admit they do not know the answer to a student's question and to look up the information for the next class. The sex education teacher should be skilled in handling adolescent emotions. Sexuality is a sensitive topic and adolescents need to be helped to feel at ease in discussing sex. One effective sex education program is described in Perspective on Adolescent Development 12.2.

Sex education programs in schools may not by themselves prevent adolescent pregnancy and sexually transmitted diseases. Researchers have found that sex education classes do improve adolescents' knowledge about human sexuality but do not always change their sexual behavior. When sex education programs are combined with contraceptive availability, the pregnancy rates of adolescents are more likely to drop (Wallis, 1985). This has led to the development of *school-linked* rather than school-based approaches to sex education and pregnancy prevention. In one program pioneered by some Baltimore

Social, Emotional, and Personality Development

TABLE 12.7 *Grade-Level Placement of 24 Topics in City Schools*

Grades 5–6

Physical differences*
Changes of puberty

Grades 7–8

Intercourse and pregnancy probability*	Communication with opposite sex*
Most likely time in cycle for pregnancy	Media messages about sex
Pregnancy and childbirth	Resistance to peer pressure for sex
Consequences of teen pregnancy*	Sexual decision making*
Sexually transmitted diseases*	Personal values*
Sexual feelings and attraction*	Masturbation
Communication with parents	

Grades 9–10

Family planning sources	Love relationships and commitment*
Contraceptives	Abortion
Gynecological examination	Homosexuality
Responsibilities of parenthood*	Rape and sexual abuse
Teen marriage*	

*Topic offered by at least 80% of districts.

Source: Freya L. Sonenstein, Karen J. Pittman, "The Availability of Sex Education in Large City School Districts," *Family Planning Perspectives*, Vol. 16, No. 1, (Jan/Feb. 1984), p. 22. © 1984 The Alan Guttmacher Institute.

public schools in cooperation with Johns Hopkins University, family-planning clinics are located adjacent to the schools (Zabin, 1986). They send a nurse and social worker into the schools where they make formal presentations about the services available from the clinics and about sexuality. They also are available to the students for counseling several hours each day. The same health personnel also conduct after-school sessions at the clinics. These sessions involve further counseling, films, and family planning information. The results have been very positive. Students who participated in the programs delayed their first intercourse longer than students in a control group. After 28 months, the pregnancy rate had declined by 30% in the program schools, while it rose 60% in the control group schools. This program demonstrates that a key dimension of pregnancy prevention is the link between information and support services (Kenney, 1987).

At this point we have discussed a number of ideas about adolescent pregnancy and sex education in the schools. A summary of these ideas is presented in Concept Table 12.2.

Postponing Sexual Involvement

Postponing Sexual Involvement is an approach designed for use with 13–15-year-old adolescents. It is aimed at reducing pregnancy by decreasing the number of adolescents who become sexually involved. It was developed in Atlanta, Georgia (Howard, 1983).

This program does not offer factual information about sexual reproduction and it does not discuss family planning. Rather, the program concentrates on social and peer pressures that often lead an adolescent into early sexual behavior. Particular emphasis is placed on building social skills to help adolescents communicate better with each other when faced with sexual pressures.

One main difference between this curriculum and most sex education programs is that it starts with a given value—that is, you should not be having sex at such a young age. Everything in the curriculum is designed to support this argument. Traditional sex education programs invariably have the implicit goal of reducing teenage pregnancy, but they usually include information on birth control and reproduction so that if young adolescents choose to have sex, they can behave in a responsible manner. This curriculum avoids the double message implied in such traditional programs.

The series is divided into four sessions, each 1½ hours long. The first three sessions occur fairly close together, while the fourth session is used as a reinforcement some 3–6 months later. The first session focuses on social pressure, with students given opportunities to explore why they feel adolescents engage in sex at an early age. The reasons they usually give involve various needs, such as to be popular, to hang onto a boyfriend, and so forth. The

leaders then help the adolescents to understand that sexual intercourse will not necessarily fulfill these needs.

The second session presents further information about peer pressure, both in group sessions and in one-on-one sessions. Adolescents are provided with opportunities to become familiar with common pressure statements, and after responses are modeled for them they practice responding in their own words. Session three involves information and exercises about problem solving. It encourages an understanding of limiting physical expression of affection, and through developing and practicing skits provides help in handling difficult sexual situations. As indicated earlier, the fourth session occurs a number of months later and is used to reinforce the ideas in the first three sessions by applying them to new situations.

This series on "how to say no" was designed to provide young adolescents with the ability to bridge the gap between their physical development and their cognitive ability to handle the implications of such development. It was not developed to replace the provision of actual factual information about sexuality and family planning.

It should be pointed out that as part of the Postponing Sexual Involvement Series, some adolescents' parents also are participating. The goal of the parental involvement is to determine the acceptance level both by the community (parents) and the young adolescents themselves, as well as to learn which delivery styles are most effective. For instance, some of the series are being delivered by peers several years older than the adolescents, while others have adult leaders.

Summary

I. Heterosexual Attitudes and Behavior

There has been a major increase in the number of adolescents reporting intercourse, and the proportion of females having intercourse has increased more rapidly than the proportion of males. National data indicate that by age 18, 44% of females and 64% of males are sexually experienced. Urban inner-city adolescents have even higher rates. One positive note is that as we enter

Adolescent Pregnancy and Sex Education in the Schools

Concept	Processes/Related Ideas	Characteristics/Description
Adolescent pregnancy	Incidence and nature	More than 1 million American adolescents become pregnant each year. Eight of ten adolescent pregnancies are unintended. The only bright spot in adolescent pregnancy statistics is that the adolescent pregnancy rate is leveling off or possibly even declining. Our nation's adolescent pregnancy rate is the highest in the Western world. Dramatic changes have swept through the American culture in the last three decades regarding adolescent sexuality and pregnancy.
	Adolescent pregnancy's consequences	Adolescent pregnancy increases health risks for both the mother and the offspring. Adolescent mothers often drop out of school, fail to gain employment, and become dependent on welfare.
	Cognitive factors	The personal fable of adolescents may make pregnancy prevention difficult. The nature of early adolescent cognition, the personal fable, anxiety about sex, gender roles, the sexual themes of music and the media, and a societal standard that says sex is appropriate for adults but not adolescents—all these factors make sex difficult for adolescents to handle.
	Adolescents as parents	The infants of adolescent parents are at risk both medically and psychologically. Adolescent mothers are less effective in rearing their children than older mothers. Adolescent fathers are more involved than the popular stereotype suggests, but many do not know what to do with a baby. Support systems for adolescent fathers are growing but are still far too few. Adolescent fathers have lower incomes, less education, and more children than those who delay having children until their 20s.
	Reducing adolescent pregnancy	This involves sex education and family planning, access to contraceptive methods, the life options approach, and broad community involvement and support.
Sex education	Its nature	America is not as open about sex education as many European countries, such as Sweden, where sex is dedramatized and demystified.
	Sources of sex information	Adolescents get the most information about sex from peers, followed by literature, mother, schools, and experience. Less than 2% comes from fathers.
	Sex education in the schools	A majority of parents favors sex education in the schools, but controversy still swirls around this topic. The majority of American schools provide sex education, but it may be as little as a brief segment of a biology class to as much as a complete course on human sexuality. A promising strategy is to provide school-linked sex education that ties in with community health centers.

the 1990s, the rate of sexual activity seems to be leveling off or even declining. As we develop our sexual identities, we follow certain scripts, which are difficult for males and females. Vulnerable adolescents are more likely to show irresponsible sexual behavior.

II. Homosexual Attitudes and Behavior
About 4% of males and 3% of females choose to be exclusively homosexual. About 10% of adolescents worry about whether they are lesbian or gay. Until recently, there was increasing acceptance of homosexuality, but the AIDS epidemic is likely reducing this acceptance. The causes of homosexuality are unsettled.

III. Self-Stimulation
Part of the sexual orientation of virtually all adolescents and one of the most frequent adolescent sexual outlets is masturbation. Today's adolescents feel less guilty about masturbation than their counterparts earlier in history.

IV. Contraceptive Use
Possibly due to poor sex education, many adolescents do not use contraceptives. There has been an increase in their use, but adolescents' choice of contraceptives has involved decreased use of birth control pills and increased use of the withdrawal method. Increased fear of AIDS and education about its consequences should lead to increased condom use.

V. Sexually Transmitted Diseases
Any adolescent who has sex runs the risk of getting a sexually transmitted disease, although most adolescents underestimate their own chances of getting these diseases. Among the sexually transmitted diseases adolescents may get are chlamydia, gonorrhea, venereal warts, herpes, and AIDS.

VI. Incidence and Nature of Adolescent Pregnancy
More than 1 million American adolescents become pregnant each year. Eight of ten adolescent pregnancies are unintended. The only bright spot in adolescent pregnancy statistics is that the adolescent pregnancy rate is leveling off or slightly dropping. Our nation's adolescent pregnancy rate is the highest in the Western world. Dramatic changes have swept through our American culture in the last three decades regarding adolescent sexuality and pregnancy.

VII. Adolescent Pregnancy's Consequences and Cognitive Factors
Adolescent pregnancy's consequences include health risks for both the mother and the offspring. Adolescent mothers often drop out of school, fail to gain employment, and become dependent on welfare. The personal fable of adolescents makes pregnancy prevention difficult. The nature of early adolescent cognition, the personal fable, anxiety about sex, gender roles, the sexual themes of music and the media, and a societal standard that says sex is appropriate for adults but not adolescents—all these factors make sex difficult for adolescents to handle.

VIII. Adolescents as Parents
The infants of adolescent parents are at risk both medically and psychologically. Adolescent mothers are less effective in rearing their children than older mothers. Adolescent fathers are more involved than the popular stereotype suggests, but many do not know what to do with a baby. Support

systems for adolescent fathers are increasing, but they are still far too few. Adolescent fathers have lower incomes, less education, and more children than those who delay having children until their 20s.

IX. **Reducing Adolescent Pregnancy**

This involves sex education and family planning, access to contraceptive methods, the life options approach, and broad community involvement and support.

X. **Sex Education**

America is not as open about sex education as many European countries, such as Sweden, where sex is dedramatized and demystified. Adolescents get the most sex information from peers, followed by literature, mother, schools, and experience. Less than 2% comes from fathers. A majority of parents favor sex education in the schools, but controversy still swirls around this topic. The majority of American schools provide sex education, but it may be as little as a brief segment of a biology class to as much as a complete course in human sexuality. A promising strategy is to provide school-linked sex education that ties in with community health centers.

Key Terms

sexual script 431   chlamydia 436   AIDS 437

Suggested Readings

Early adolescent sexuality: Resources for parents, professionals, and young people. (1983). Chapel Hill, NC: Center for Early Adolescence, University of North Carolina.
   This compendium of resources provides an excellent annotated bibliography of a wide variety of topics related to sexuality in early adolescence.
Gordon, S., & Gilgun, J. F. (1987). Adolescent sexuality. In V. B. Van Hasselt & M. Hersen (Eds.), *Handbook of adolescent psychology.* New York: Pergamon.
   An excellent chapter on adolescents' sexual choices and what sexuality means to adolescents.
McAnarney, E. R. (1988). Early adolescent motherhood: Crisis in the making? In M. D. Levin & E. R. McAnarney (Eds.), *Early adolescent transitions.* Lexington, MA: D.C. Heath.
   Provides recent information about adolescent mothers, including potential intervention strategies.
Pierce, C., & VanDeVeer, D. (1988). *AIDS.* Belmont, CA: Wadsworth.
   An excellent collection of essays on AIDS is presented, including a general overview of what is known about AIDS and information about ethical issues and public policy involved in AIDS.
Robinson, B. R. (1988). *Teenage fathers,* Lexington, MA: Lexington Books.
   Examines the role of fathers in adolescent pregnancy.

Moral Development, Values, and Religion

It is one of the beautiful compensations of this life that no one can sincerely try to help another without helping himself.

Charles Dudley Warner, 1873

The Morals of a High School Newspaper

F red, a senior in high school wanted to publish a mimeographed newspaper for students so that he could express many of his opinions. He wanted to speak out against the war in Vietnam and against some of the school's rules, like the rule forbidding boys to wear long hair.

When Fred started his newspaper, he asked his principal for permission. The principal said it would be all right if before every publication Fred would turn over all his articles for the principal's approval. Fred agreed and turned in several articles for approval. The principal approved all of them and Fred published two issues of the paper in the next two weeks.

But the principal had not expected that Fred's newspaper would receive so much attention. Students were so excited about the paper that they began to organize protests against the hair regulation and the other school rules. Angry parents objected to Fred's opinions. They phoned the principal, telling him that the newspaper was unpatriotic and should not be published. As a result of the rising excitement, the principal ordered Fred to stop publishing. He gave as a reason that Fred's activities were disruptive to the operation of the school. (Rest, 1986, p. 194)

*T*he story about Fred and his newspaper raises a number of questions, questions that are related to the adolescent's moral development. Should the principal stop the newspaper? When the welfare of the school is threatened, does the principal have the right to give orders to students? Does the principal have the freedom of speech to say "no" in this case? If the principal stopped the newspaper, would he be preventing full discussion of an important problem? Is Fred actually being loyal to his school and patriotic to his country? What effect would stopping the newspaper have on the students' education in critical thinking and judgments? Was Fred in any way violating the rights of others in publishing his own opinions?

This story and the questions that follow it are a common method of investigating adolescents' moral judgments. The strategy is to find out how adolescents think about moral dilemmas. In this chapter we focus extensively on the nature of moral development in adolescence, and we also discuss the nature of values, religion, and cults in adolescence.

What Is Moral Development?

The study of moral development is one of the oldest topics of interest to those who are curious about human nature. And today, people are hardly neutral about moral development. Most have very strong opinions about acceptable and unacceptable behavior, ethical and unethical conduct, and the ways in which acceptable and ethical behaviors can be fostered in adolescents.

Moral development concerns rules and conventions about what people *should* do in their interactions with other people. In studying these rules, developmentalists examine three different domains. First, how do adolescents

What moral dilemmas might crop up for adolescents responsible for the school's newspaper?

reason or *think* about rules for ethical conduct? For example, consider cheating. The adolescent can be presented a story in which someone has a conflict about whether or not to cheat in a particular situation, such as taking an exam in school. The adolescent is asked to decide what is appropriate for the character to do and why. This was the strategy used in the prologue regarding Fred's newspaper. The focus is placed on the reasoning adolescents use to justify their moral decisions (Kahn, 1989).

Second, how do adolescents actually *behave* in moral circumstances? In our example of cheating, the emphasis is on observing the adolescent's cheating and the environmental circumstances that produced and maintain the cheating. Adolescents might be observed through a one-way mirror as they are taking an exam. The observer might note whether they take out "cheat" notes, look at another student's answers, and so on.

Third, how does the adolescent *feel* about moral matters? In the example of cheating, does the adolescent feel enough guilt to resist temptation? If adolescents do cheat, do feelings of guilt after the transgression keep them from cheating the next time they face temptation? In the remainder of our discussion of moral development, we focus extensively on these three facets—thought, action, and feeling.

Moral Thought

How do adolescents think about standards of right and wrong? Piaget had some thoughts about this question. So did Lawrence Kohlberg.

Piaget's Ideas

Interest in how children and adolescents think about moral issues was stimulated by Jean Piaget (1932), who observed and interviewed individuals 4–12 years of age. He watched them play marbles, seeking to learn how they used and thought about the game's rules. He also asked them questions about ethical rules—theft, lies, punishment, and justice, for example. Piaget concluded that boys and girls think in two distinctly different ways about morality, depending on their developmental maturity. The more primitive way of thinking—**heteronomous morality**—is displayed by younger children (4–7 years of age). The more advanced way of thinking—**autonomous morality**—is displayed by older children and adolescents (10 years and older). Children 7–10 years of age are in a transition between the two stages, showing features of both.

What are some of the characteristics of heteronomous morality and autonomous morality? The heteronomous thinker judges the rightness or goodness of behavior by considering the consequences of the behavior, not the intentions of the actor. For example, the heteronomous thinker says that breaking 12 cups accidentally is worse than breaking one cup intentionally while trying to steal a cookie. For the moral autonomist, the reverse is true—the actor's intention assumes paramount importance. The heteronomous thinker also believes that rules are unchangeable and are handed down by all-powerful authorities. When Piaget suggested that new rules be introduced to the game of marbles, the young children resisted. They insisted that the rules had always been the same and could not be changed. By contrast, older children and adolescents—who were moral autonomists—accepted change and recognized that rules are merely convenient, socially agreed upon conventions, and subject to change by consensus.

Heteronomous thinkers also believe in **immanent justice**—that when a rule is broken, punishment will be meted out immediately. They believe that the violation is connected in some automatic or mechanical way to the punishment. Thus, young children often look around worriedly after committing a transgression, expecting inevitable punishment. Researchers continue to verify that immanent justice declines toward the end of the elementary school years (e.g., Jose, 1985). Older children and adolescents—who are moral autonomists—recognize that punishment is socially mediated and occurs only if a relevant person witnesses the wrongdoing and that, even then, punishment is not inevitable.

Piaget believed that as children and adolescents develop, they become more sophisticated in thinking about social matters, especially about the possibilities and conditions of cooperation. Piaget believed that this social understanding comes about through the mutual give-and-take of peer relations. In the peer group—where others have power and status similar to the individual—plans are negotiated and coordinated, disagreements are reasoned about and eventually settled. Parent-child relations—where parents have the power and the child does not—are less likely to advance moral reasoning because rules are often handed down in an authoritarian manner.

Remember that Piaget believed adolescents become formal-operational thinkers. They are no longer anchored to immediate and concrete phenomena but are more logical, abstract, and deductive reasoners. Formal-operational thinkers frequently compare the real to the ideal, create contrary-to-fact propositions, are cognitively capable of relating the distant past to the present, understand their roles in society, in history, and in the universe, and can conceptualize their own thoughts and think about their mental constructs as objects. It is not until about 11–12 years of age that boys and girls spontaneously introduce concepts of belief, intelligence, and faith into definitions of their religious identities.

When children move from the relatively homogeneous grade school neighborhood to more heterogeneous high school and college environments, they are faced with contradictions between the moral concepts they have accepted and happenings in the world outside their family and neighborhood. Adolescents come to recognize that their beliefs are but one of many and that there is a great deal of debate about what is right and what is wrong. Many adolescents start to question their former beliefs, and in the process develop their own moral system. This Piagetian-related view has been referred to as **cognitive-disequilibrium theory** (Hoffman, 1980).

Lawrence Kohlberg, the architect of a provocative cognitive developmental theory of moral development.

Kohlberg's Ideas

The most provocative view of moral development in recent years was crafted by Lawrence Kohlberg (1958, 1976, 1986; Kohlberg & Higgins, 1987). Kohlberg believed that moral development is based primarily on moral reasoning and that it unfolds in a series of stages. Kohlberg arrived at his view after many years of using a unique interview with children and adolescents. In the interview, adolescents are presented with a series of stories in which characters face moral dilemmas. The following is the most widely used Kohlberg dilemma:

In Europe a woman was near death from a special kind of cancer. There was one drug that the doctors thought might save her. It was a form of radium that a druggist in the same town had recently discovered. The drug was expensive to make, but the druggist was charging ten times what the drug cost him to make. He paid $200 for the radium and charged $2,000 for a small dose of the drug. The sick woman's husband, Heinz, went to everyone he knew to borrow the money, but he could only get together $1,000 which is half of what it cost. He told the druggist that his wife was dying and asked him to sell it cheaper or let him pay later. But the druggist said, "No, I discovered the drug, and I am going to make money from it." So Heinz got desperate and broke into the man's store to steal the drug for his wife. (Kohlberg, 1969, p. 379)

This story is one of 11 devised by Kohlberg to investigate the nature of moral thought. After reading the story, the interviewee answers a series of questions about the moral dilemma. Should Heinz have done that? What is right or wrong? Why? Is it a husband's duty to steal the drug for his wife if he can get it in no other way? Would a good husband do it? Did the druggist have the right to charge that much when there was no law actually setting a limit on the price? Why?

Based on the answers individuals gave to this and other moral dilemmas, Kohlberg believed three levels of moral development exist, each of which is characterized by two stages. Each stage also is described in terms of a general structural principle, called the level of sociomoral reflection or perspective. This refers to the point of view taken by the individual in both defining social reality and in choosing moral values. The level of sociomoral reflection is shown in parentheses for each moral stage.

Level 1: Preconventional Moral Reasoning

At the level of **preconventional moral reasoning** the individual shows no internalization of moral values. Morality is truly external to the individual. Adolescents conform to rules imposed by authority figures to avoid punishment or to obtain rewards.

Stage 1. *Punishment and Obedience Orientation* (Egocentric Point of View).
Moral thinking is based on punishments. Adolescents obey because adults tell them to obey. In the Heinz and the druggist story, the adolescent might re-

spond that Heinz should not let his wife die because he would be in big trouble. Or he or she might say that Heinz should not steal the drug because he might get caught and sent to jail.

*Stage 2. **Naive Hedonism or Instrumental Orientation*** (Concrete Individualistic Perspective). Moral thinking is based on rewards and self-interest. Adolescents obey when they want to obey and when it is in their best interest to obey. What is right is what feels good and what is rewarding. Why should Heinz steal the drug? If Heinz gets caught he could give the drug back and they might not give him a long jail sentence. Why shouldn't Heinz steal the drug? The druggist is a businessman and needs to make money.

Level 2: Conventional Moral Reasoning
At the level of **conventional moral reasoning,** internalization is intermediate. The individual abides by certain standards (internal), but they are the standards of others (external). The individual is motivated to obey the rules of others, such as parents, peers, and social groups, to obtain praise recognition for moral behavior or to maintain the social order.

*Stage 3. **Good Boy or Good Girl Orientation*** (Social Relational Perspective). The individual values trust, caring, and loyalty to others as the basis of moral judgments. At this stage, adolescents often adopt their parents' moral standards, seeking to be thought of by their parents as a "good boy" or a "good girl." Why should Heinz steal the drug? Heinz was only doing something that a good husband would do. It shows how much he loves his wife. Why shouldn't Heinz steal the drug? If his wife dies, he can't be blamed for it. It is the druggist's fault. He is the selfish one.

*Stage 4. **Authority and Social-Order Maintaining Morality*** (Member of Society Perspective). Moral judgments are based on understanding the social order, law, justice, and duty. Why should Heinz steal the drug? If you did nothing, you would be letting your wife die. It is your responsibility if she dies. You have to steal it with the idea of paying the druggist later. Why shouldn't Heinz steal the drug? It is always wrong to steal. Heinz will always feel guilty if he steals the drug.

Level 3: Postconventional Moral Reasoning
At the highest level, **postconventional moral reasoning,** morality is completely internalized and not based on others' standards. The individual recognizes alternative moral courses, explores the options, and then decides on a personal moral code.

*Stage 5. **Community Rights versus Individual Rights*** (Prior to Society Perspective). The individual understands that values and laws are relative and that standards may vary from one individual to another. The individual recognizes that laws are important for society but also believes that laws can be changed.

The individual believes that some values, such as liberty, are more important than the law. Stage 5 is a law-creating stage, whereas stage 4 is a law-maintaining stage. In stage 5, the individual asks, Is it moral? as well as, Is it legal? Why should Heinz steal the drug? The law was not set up to take into account these circumstances. Taking the drug may not be completely right, but Heinz should do it. Why should Heinz not steal the drug? At stage 5, the individual invariably argues that Heinz should steal the drug, believing that life takes priority over property rights.

*Stage 6. **Individual Conscience*** (Rational-Moral Perspective). In rare instances, individuals have developed moral standards based on universal human rights. When faced with a conflict between a law and conscience, the individual will always follow his or her conscience, even though the decision might entail personal risk. At stage 6, the moral reasoner values abstract moral principles that are considered universal and binding. The stage 6 reasoner self-consciously uses certain checks on the validity of moral reasoning. For example, "Would you judge this action to be fair if you were in the other person's shoes?" "Would it be right if everyone did X?" Also, at stage 6, trust and community are the preconditions to agreements necessary to protect human rights. At stage 5, the reverse is true: agreements lead to trust and community. And, in stage 6, the intrinsic moral worth and respect of persons is recognized and upheld in the course of resolving a moral dilemma. Again, in stage 6 as in stage 5, Heinz would invariably steal the drug, because by not stealing the drug he would not be recognizing the intrinsic moral worth of a human life.

Kohlberg believed these levels and stages occur in a sequence and are age related: Before age 9, most children reason about moral dilemmas in a preconventional way; by early adolescence, they reason in more conventional ways; and by early adulthood, a small number of individuals reason in post-conventional ways. In a 20-year longitudinal investigation, the uses of stages 1 and 2 decreased. Stage 4, which did not appear at all in the moral reasoning of the 10-year-olds, was reflected in 62% of the moral thinking of the 36-year-olds. Stage 5 did not appear until age 20–22 and never characterized more than 10% of the individuals. Thus, the moral stages appeared somewhat later than Kohlberg initially envisioned, and the higher stages, especially stage 6, were extremely elusive (Colby & others, 1983). Recently, stage 6 was removed from the Kohlberg moral judgment scoring manual, but it still is considered to be theoretically important in the Kohlberg scheme of moral development. A recent review of data from 45 studies in 27 diverse world cultures provided striking support for the universality of Kohlberg's first four stages, although there was more cultural diversity at stages 5 and 6 (Snarey, 1987).

Influences on the Kohlberg Stages

Kohlberg believed that the individual's moral orientation unfolds as a consequence of cognitive development. Children and adolescents construct their moral thoughts as they pass from one stage to the next rather than passively

Social, Emotional, and Personality Development

accepting a cultural norm of morality. Investigators have sought to understand factors that influence movement through the moral stages, among them modeling, cognitive conflict, peer relations, and perspective taking opportunities.

Several investigators have attempted to advance an individual's level of moral development by providing arguments that reflect moral thinking one stage above the individual's established level. These studies are based on the cognitive developmental concepts of equilibrium and conflict. By finding the correct environmental match slightly beyond the individual's cognitive level, a disequilibrium is created that motivates him or her to restructure his or her moral thought. The resolution of the disequilibrium and conflict should be toward increased competence, but the data are mixed on this question. In one of the pioneer studies on this topic, Eliot Turiel (1966) discovered that children preferred a response one stage above their current level over a response two stages above it. However, they actually chose a response one stage below their level more often than a response one stage above it. Apparently the children were motivated more by security needs than by the need to reorganize thought to a higher level. Other studies indicate that individuals do prefer a more advanced stage over a less advanced stage (e.g., Rest, Turiel, & Kohlberg, 1969).

Since the early studies of stage modeling, a number of investigations have attempted to determine more precisely the effectiveness of various forms of stage modeling and arguments (Lapsley, Enright, & Serlin, 1986; Lapsley & Quintana, 1985). The upshot of these studies is that virtually any plus-stage discussion format, for any length of time, seems to promote more advanced moral reasoning. For example, in one investigation (Walker, 1982), exposure to plus-two stage reasoning (arguments two stages above the child's current stage of moral thought) was just as effective in advancing moral thought as plus-one stage reasoning. Exposure to plus-two stage reasoning did not produce more plus-two stage reasoning but rather, like exposure to plus-one stage reasoning, increased the likelihood that the child would reason one stage above his or her current stage. Other research has found that exposure to reasoning only one-third of a stage higher than the individual's current level of moral thought will advance moral thought (Berkowitz & Gibbs, 1983). In sum, current research on modeling and cognitive conflict reveals that moral thought can be moved to a higher level through exposure to models or discussion that are more advanced than the child's or adolescent's.

Like Piaget, Kohlberg believed that peer interaction is a critical part of the social stimulation that challenges individuals to change their moral orientation. Whereas adults characteristically impose rules and regulations on children, the mutual give-and-take in peer interaction provides the child with an opportunity to take the role of another person and to generate rules democratically. Kohlberg stressed that role-taking opportunities can, in principle, be engendered by any peer group encounter. While Kohlberg believed that such role-taking opportunities are ideal for moral development, he also believed that certain types of parent-child experiences can induce the child to

In Kohlberg's theory, peer interaction is critical in developing a more advanced moral orientation. What is it about peer interaction that Kohlberg believes promotes more advanced moral development?

think at more advanced levels of moral thinking. In particular, parents who allow or encourage conversation about value-laden issues promote more advanced moral thought in their children and adolescents. Unfortunately, many parents do not systematically provide their children and adolescents with such role-taking opportunities.

Kohlberg's Critics

Kohlberg's provocative theory of moral development has not gone unchallenged (Kurtines & Gewirtz, in press; Puka, in press). The criticisms involve the link between moral thought and moral behavior, the quality of the research, the care perspective, and societal contributions.

Moral reasons can often be a shelter for immoral behavior. Bank embezzlers and presidents address the loftiest of moral virtues when analyzing moral dilemmas but their own behavior may be immoral. No one wants a nation of cheaters and thieves who can reason at the postconventional level. The cheaters and the thieves may know what is right and what is wrong but still do what is wrong.

Some developmentalists believe more attention should be paid to the way moral development is assessed. For example, James Rest (1976, 1983, 1986, 1988) points out that alternative methods should be used to collect information about moral thinking instead of relying on a single method that requires individuals to reason about hypothetical moral dilemmas. Rest also says that Kohlberg's stories are extremely difficult to score. To help remedy this problem, Rest developed his own measure of moral development, called the Defining Issues Test (DIT) (the story about Fred and the school newspaper in the prologue is one of the moral dilemmas used in Rest's assessment of moral judgment).

Social, Emotional, and Personality Development

TABLE 13.1	Actual Moral Dilemmas Generated by Adolescents		
Story Subject	**7**	**Grade** **9**	**12**
		Percentage	
Alcohol	2	0	5
Civil rights	0	6	7
Drugs	7	10	5
Interpersonal relations	38	24	35
Physical safety	22	8	3
Sexual relations	2	20	10
Smoking	7	2	0
Stealing	9	2	0
Working	2	2	15
Other	11	26	20

From Steven R. Yussen, "Characteristics of Moral Dilemmas Written by Adolescents" in *Developmental Psychology,* 13, 162–163, 1977. Copyright 1977 by the American Psychological Association. Reprinted by permission of the publisher and author.

In the DIT, an effort is made to determine which moral issues individuals feel are more crucial in a given situation by presenting them with a series of dilemmas and a list of definitions of the major issues involved (Kohlberg's procedure does not make use of such a list). In the dilemma of Heinz and the druggist, individuals might be asked whether a community's laws should be upheld or whether Heinz should be willing to risk being injured or caught as a burglar. They might also be asked to list the most important values that govern human interaction. They are given six stories and asked to rate the importance of each issue involved in deciding what ought to be done. Then they are asked to list what they believe are the four most important issues. Rest argues that this method provides a more valid and reliable way to assess moral thinking than Kohlberg's method.

Researchers also have found that the hypothetical moral dilemmas posed in Kohlberg's stories do not match up with the moral dilemmas many children and adults face in their everyday lives (Walker, de Vries, & Trevethan, 1987; Yussen, 1977). Most of Kohlberg's stories focus on the family and authority. However, when one researcher invited adolescents to write stories about their own moral dilemmas, adolescents generated dilemmas that were broader in scope, focusing on friends, acquaintances, and other issues, as well as family and authority (Yussen, 1977). The moral dilemmas also were analyzed in terms of their content. As shown in Table 13.1, the moral issue that concerned adolescents more than any other was interpersonal relationships.

Another criticism of Kohlberg's ideas, one that has been given considerable publicity, is that his view does not adequately reflect connectedness with and concern for others. Carol Gilligan (1982, 1985) argues that Kohlberg's

According to Carol Gilligan, Lawrence Kohlberg placed too much emphasis on the justice perspective in understanding adolescents' moral development. What is the "different voice" Gilligan believes needs to be considered in understanding adolescents' moral development?

theory emphasizes a **justice perspective,** that is, a focus on the rights of the individual. People are differentiated and seen as standing alone in making moral decisions. By contrast, the **care perspective** sees people in terms of their connectedness with others, and the focus is on interpersonal communication. According to Gilligan, Kohlberg has vastly underplayed the care perspective in moral development. She believes this may be because most of his research was with males rather than females. More about Gilligan's belief in the importance of the care perspective in understanding moral development appears in Perspective on Adolescent Development 13.1.

Gilligan also thinks that moral development has three basic levels. She calls Level I preconventional morality, which reflects a concern for self and survival. Level II, conventional morality, shows a concern for being responsible and caring for others. Level III, postconventional morality, shows a concern for self and others as interdependent. Gilligan believes that Kohlberg has underemphasized the care perspective in the moral development of *both* males and females and that morality's highest level for both sexes involves a search for moral equality between oneself and others (Muuss, 1988).

Many critics also argue that moral development is more culture-specific than Kohlberg believes. As Urie Bronfenbrenner and James Garbarino (1976) have observed, moral standards in other cultures are not always consistent with the standards that children and adolescents abide by in the United States. They believe that the more an individual is exposed to different social agents with different sociopolitical views, the more advanced will be the individual's moral development. Their research suggests that individuals who grow up in a culture that is more sociopolitically plural (United States, West Germany) are less likely to be authority oriented and to have more plural ideas about moral dilemmas than their counterparts who grow up in less sociopolitically plural cultures (Poland, Hungary). Bronfenbrenner and Garbarino (1976) also argue that more diverse family styles and more individual freedom within families occur in sociopolitically plural countries such as the United States.

Social, Emotional, and Personality Development

Amy Says They Should Just Talk It Out

The main character in Kohlberg's most widely used dilemma is a male—Heinz. Possibly females have a difficult time identifying with him. Some of the Kohlberg dilemmas are gender neutral, but one is about the captain of a company of marines. The subjects in Kohlberg's original research were all males. Going beyond her critique of Kohlberg's failure to consider females, Gilligan argues that an important voice is not present in his view. Following are two excerpts from responses to the story of Heinz and the druggist, one from 11-year-old Jake, the other from 11-year-old Amy. First, Jake's comments:

> For one thing, human life is worth more than money, and if the druggist only makes $1,000, he is still going to live, but if Heinz doesn't steal the drug, his wife is going to die. (*Why is life worth more than money?*) Because the druggist can get $1,000 later from rich people with cancer, but Heinz can't get his wife again. (Gilligan, 1982, p. 26)

Now Amy's comments:

> Well, I don't think so. I think there might be other ways besides stealing it, like if he could borrow the money or make a loan or something, but he really shouldn't steal the drug—but his wife shouldn't die either. (*Why shouldn't he steal the drug?*) If he stole the drug, he might save his wife then, but if he did, he might have to go to jail, and then his wife might get sicker again, and he couldn't get more of the drug, and it might not be good. So, they should really just talk it out and find some other way to make the money. (Gilligan, 1982, p. 28)

Jake's comments would be scored as a mixture of Kohlberg's stages 3 and 4, but they also include some of the components of a mature level 3 moral thinker. Amy, by contrast, does not fit into Kohlberg's scoring system so well. Jake sees the problem as one of rules and balancing the rights of people. However, Amy views the problem as involving relationships—the druggist's failure to live up to his relationship to the needy woman, the need to maintain the relationship between Heinz and his wife, and the hope that a bad relationship between Heinz and the druggist can be avoided. Amy concludes that the characters should talk it out and try to repair their relationships.

By being exposed to greater diversity and freedom in the culture and in the family, children's and adolescents' moral development should be more advanced.

Moral Reasoning and Social Conventional Reasoning

In recent years there has been considerable interest in whether reasoning about social matters is distinct from reasoning about moral matters (Nucci, 1982; Smetana, 1983, 1985; Turiel, 1977, 1978). Adherents of the belief that social reasoning is distinct from moral reasoning cast their thoughts within a cognitive developmental framework (Enright, Lapsley, & Olson, 1984; Lapsley, Enright, & Serlin, 1986).

The architects of the social reasoning approach argue that conventional rules focus on behavioral irregularities. To control such behavioral improprieties, conventional rules are created. In this manner the actions of individuals can be controlled and the existing social system maintained. Such conventional rules are thought to be arbitrary, with no prescription necessary. For example, not eating food with our fingers is a social conventional rule, as is raising one's hand before talking in class.

By contrast, it is argued that moral rules are not arbitrary and certainly do involve prescription. Furthermore, moral rules are not created through any social consensus but rather are obligatory, virtually universally applicable, and somewhat impersonal (Turiel, 1978). Thus, rules pertaining to lying, stealing, cheating, and physically harming another person are moral rules because violation of these rules affronts ethical standards that exist apart from social consensus and convention. In sum, moral judgments are constructed as concepts of justice, whereas social conventional judgments are structured as concepts of social organization (Lapsley, Enright, & Serlin, 1986).

A review of research on **social conventional reasoning** suggests that the major thrust has been to demonstrate the independence of this form of reasoning apart from moral reasoning and to reveal how even young children make this distinction (Lapsley, Enright, & Serlin, 1986). For example, in two studies children were queried about spontaneously occurring moral and social conventional transgressions (Nucci & Nucci, 1982; Nucci & Turiel, 1978). Children were asked, "If there was no rule in the school about (the observed event), would it be all right to do it?" Approximately 80% of the children at each grade level believed the social conventional act would be appropriate if no rule existed to prohibit it. By contrast, more than 85% of the children at each grade level said that moral transgressions would not be appropriate even if there

Social, Emotional, and Personality Development

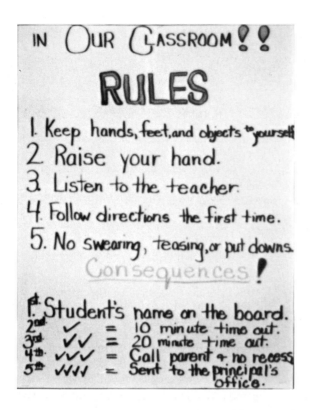

were no rules related to the transgressions. Other research suggests that children are more likely to evaluate actions in the moral domain on the basis of their intrinsic features (such as justice or harm), while social conventional actions are more likely to be interpreted in terms of their regulatory status in a social context (Nucci, 1982). Thus, it seems that actions in the social conventional area are judged wrong only if a social rule exists prohibiting them. By contrast, moral transgressions appear to be judged as universally wrong even in the absence of social consensus.

At this point we have discussed a number of ideas about the nature of moral development, with special attention given to cognitive approaches. A summary of these ideas is presented in Concept Table 13.1.

Moral Behavior

Social learning theory emphasizes the moral behavior of adolescents. The familiar processes of reinforcement, punishment, and imitation have been invoked to explain how and why adolescents learn certain moral behaviors and why their behaviors differ from one another. The general conclusions to be drawn are the same as for other domains of social behavior. When adolescents

The Nature of Moral Development and Moral Thought

Concept	Processes/Related Ideas	Characteristics/Description
What is moral development?	Rules and regulations	Moral development concerns rules and regulations about what people should do in their interaction with other people.
	Components	Moral development's three main domains are thought, behavior, and feeling.
Moral thoughts	Piaget's ideas	Argued that children 4–7 years of age are in the stage of heteronomous morality and from about the age of 10 on are in the stage of autonomous morality. Formal operational thought may undergird changes in the moral reasoning of adolescents.
	Kohlberg's ideas	Proposed a provocative theory of moral development with three levels—preconventional, conventional, and postconventional—and six stages. Increased internalization characterizes movement to levels 2 and 3. Kohlberg's longitudinal data show a relation of the stages to age, although the higher two stages, especially stage 6, rarely appear.
	Influences on the stages	Include cognitive development, imitation and cognitive conflict, peer relations, and perspective taking.
	Critics of Kohlberg	Kohlberg's work has been criticized for overemphasizing cognition and underemphasizing behavior, the questionable quality of the research, for inadequate consideration of the care perspective, and for underestimating culture's role.
	Social conventional reasoning	Moral reasoning pertains to ethical matters, social conventional reasoning to thoughts about social convention and consensus. Moral reasoning is prescriptive, conventional reasoning more arbitrary. Moral reasoning emphasizes justice; social conventional reasoning emphasizes social regulation.

are reinforced for behavior that is consistent with laws and social conventions, they are likely to repeat that behavior. When models who behave "morally" are provided, adolescents are likely to adopt their behavior. And when adolescents are punished for immoral or unacceptable behavior, those behaviors can be eliminated, but at the expense of sanctioning punishment by its very use and of causing emotional side effects for the adolescent.

To these general conclusions, we add several qualifiers. The effectiveness of reinforcement and punishment depends on how consistently they are administered and the schedule that is adopted. The effectiveness of modeling depends on the characteristics of the model (such as power, warmth, uniqueness, and so on) and the presence of cognitive processes such as symbolic codes and imagery to enhance retention of the modeled behavior.

TABLE 13.2 *The Hypocrisy of Adult Moral Models*

Would you:	Percent who said yes, or probably:	Percent who said it is, or probably is, unethical:	Percent who would, or probably would, be more likely to if sure they wouldn't get caught:
Drive away after scratching a car without telling the owner?	44%	89%	52%
Cover for a friend's secret affair?	41%	66%	33%
Cheat on your spouse?	37%	68%	42%
Keep $10 extra change at a local supermarket?	26%	85%	33%
Knowingly buy a stolen color television set?	22%	87%	31%
Try to keep your neighborhood segregated?	13%	81%	8%
Drive while drunk?	11%	90%	24%
Accept praise for another's work?	4%	96%	8%

What kind of adult moral models are adolescents being exposed to in our society? Do such models usually do what they say? Adolescents are especially tuned in to adult hypocrisy, and there is evidence that they are right to believe that many adults display a double standard, their moral actions not always corresponding to their moral thoughts. A poll of 24,000 adults sampled views on a wide variety of moral issues. Eight detailed scenarios of everyday moral problems were developed to test moral decision making. A summary of the adults' responses to these moral dilemmas is shown in Table 13.2. Consider the example of whether the adult would knowingly buy a stolen color television set. More than 20% said they would, even though 87% said that this act is probably morally wrong. And approximately 31% of the adults said that if they knew they would not get caught, they would be more likely to buy the stolen TV. While moral thought is an important dimension of moral development, these data glaringly underscore that what people believe about right and wrong does not always correspond to how they will act in moral situations.

In addition to emphasizing the role of environmental determinants and the gap between moral thought and moral action, social learning theorists also emphasize that moral behavior is situationally dependent. That is, they say that adolescents are not likely to display consistent moral behavior in diverse social settings. In a classic investigation of moral behavior—one of the most extensive ever conducted—Hugh Hartshorne and Mark May (1928–30) observed the moral responses of 11,000 children and adolescents who were given the opportunity to lie, cheat, and steal in a variety of circumstances—at home, at school, at social events, and in athletics. A completely honest or a completely dishonest child or adolescent was difficult to find. Situation-specific moral behavior was the rule. Adolescents were more likely to cheat when their friends pressured them to do so and when the chance of being caught was slim. Other analyses suggest that some adolescents are more likely to lie, cheat, and steal than others, indicating more consistency of moral behavior in some adolescents than in others (Burton, 1984).

We learned in Chapter 2 that in recent years the most popular version of social learning theory has been *cognitive social learning theory*. How can cognitive social learning theory be applied to understanding adolescents' moral development? Walter and Harriet Mischel (1975; Mischel, 1987) distinguish between adolescents' **moral competence**—the ability to produce moral behaviors—and adolescents' **moral performance** of those behaviors in specific situations. Competence or acquisition depends primarily on cognitive-sensory processes; it is the outgrowth of these processes. Competencies include what adolescents are capable of doing, what they know, their skills, their awareness of moral rules and regulations, and their cognitive ability to construct behaviors. Adolescents' moral performance, or behavior, however, is determined by their motivation and the rewards and incentives to act in a specific moral way. Albert Bandura (in press) also believes that moral development is best understood by considering a combination of social and cognitive factors, especially those involving self-control.

In general, social learning theorists have been critical of Kohlberg's view. Among other reasons, they believe he placed too little emphasis on moral behavior and the situational determinants of morality. However, while Kohlberg argued that moral judgment is an important determinant of moral behavior, he, like the Mischels, stressed that the individual's interpretation of both the moral and factual aspects of a situation leads him or her to a moral decision (Kohlberg & Candee, 1979). For example, Kohlberg mentioned that "extramoral" factors, like the desire to avoid embarrassment, may cause the child to avoid doing what he or she believes to be morally right. In sum, both the Mischels and Kohlberg believe that moral action is influenced by a complex of factors. Overall, the findings are mixed with regard to the association of moral thought and behavior (Arnold, 1989), although one recent investigation with college students found that individuals with both high principled moral reasoning and high ego strength were less likely to cheat in a resistance-to-temptation situation than their low-principled and low-ego strength counterparts (Hess, Lonky, & Roodin, 1985).

So far we have seen that both the moral thought and the moral behavior of an individual are important components of moral development. Although psychoanalytic theory has always placed strong faith in the role of feelings in personality development, the emotional aspects of moral development were virtually ignored for many years. Now there is a reemergence of interest in the emotional aspects of moral development. In the next section, we explore this renewed interest.

Moral Feelings and Altruism

In the psychoanalytic account of guilt, individuals avoid transgressing to avoid anxiety. By contrast, an individual with little guilt has little reason to resist temptation. Guilt is responsible for harnessing the id's evil impulses and for maintaining the world as a safe place. In psychoanalytic theory, early childhood is a special time for the development of guilt. According to Freud, it is during this time period that, through identification with parents and parents' use of love withdrawal techniques in discipline, the child turns hostility inward and experiences guilt. The guilt is primarily unconscious and reflects the structure of personality called the superego. Remember also that Erik Erikson believes early childhood has special importance in the development of guilt. His name for the major conflict to be resolved in early childhood is initiative versus guilt.

Erikson (1970) also argues that there are three stages of moral development: specific moral learning in childhood, ideological concerns in adolescence, and ethical consolidation in adulthood. During adolescence, individuals search for an identity. If adolescents become disillusioned with the moral and religious beliefs they acquired during childhood, they are likely to lose, at least temporarily, their sense of purpose and feel that their lives are empty. This may lead to a search for an ideology that will give some purpose to the adolescent's life. For the ideology to be acceptable, it must both fit the evidence and mesh with the adolescent's logical reasoning abilities. If others share this ideology, a sense of community is felt. For Erikson, ideology surfaces as the guardian of identity during adolescence because it provides a sense of purpose, assists in tying the present to the future, and contributes meaning to behavior (Hoffman, 1980).

Returning to the topic of moral feelings, we can point out that they have traditionally been thought of in terms of guilt. But recently substantial interest has developed in empathy's role in moral development (Hoffman, in press). **Empathy** is the ability to understand the feelings of another individual. As we see next, empathy is an important ingredient of the adolescent's altruism.

In studying guilt, cheating, lying, stealing, and resistance to temptation, we are investigating the dark side of morality. Today we recognize that it is important not to dwell too much on the antisocial, negative aspect of moral development. Perhaps we should spend more time evaluating and promoting the positive side of adolescents' morality—their prosocial behavior, altruism, and empathy, for example.

Altruism is an unselfish interest in helping someone. Adolescent acts of altruism are plentiful—the hardworking adolescent who places a $1 bill in the church offering plate each week, car washes, bake sales, and concerts organized to make money to feed the hungry and help mentally retarded children, and the adolescent who takes in a wounded cat and cares for it. How do psychologists account for such frequent bouts of altruism?

Reciprocity and exchange are involved in altruism (Brown, 1986). Reciprocity is found throughout the human world. Not only is it the highest moral principle in Christianity but it is also present in every widely practiced religion in the world—Judaism, Hinduism, Buddhism, and Islam. Reciprocity encourages adolescents to do unto others as they would have others do unto them. Human sentiments are wrapped up in this reciprocity. Trust is probably the most important principle over the long run in adolescent altruism. Guilt surfaces if the adolescent does not reciprocate. Anger may result if someone else does not reciprocate. Not all adolescent altruism is motivated by reciprocity and exchange, but self-other interactions and relationships help us to understand altruism's nature. The circumstances most likely to involve altruism by adolescents are empathetic or sympathetic emotion for an individual in need or a close relationship between the benefactor and the recipient (Batson, in press; Clark & others, 1987; Lerner, 1982). Altruism occurs more often in adolescence than in childhood, although examples of caring for others and comforting someone in distress occur even during the preschool years (Eisenberg, 1987, 1989).

One aspect of considering others is forgiveness, which occurs when the injured person releases the injurer from possible behavioral retaliation. In one recent investigation, individuals from the fourth grade through college and adulthood were asked questions about forgiveness (Enright, Santos, & Al-Mabuk, in press). The adolescents were especially swayed by peer pressure in their willingness to forgive others. Consider one 12-year-old seventh-grade girl's response to Kohlberg's dilemma of Heinz and the druggist:

> *Interviewer:* "*Suppose all of Heinz's friends come to see him and say, 'Please be more mature about this. We want you to be friends with the druggist.' Would it help him to forgive the druggist? Why/why not?*"
> *Girl:* "*Probably, because Heinz would think they wanted him to. They would influence him.*"
> *Another 15-year-old girl:* "*Yes, it would be his friends showing him the outside view. They would help him.*"

The adolescent forgiveness theme that emerged was that the injured party often fails to see the best course of action. Outside aid, especially from friends, helps the harmed person clarify the problem and then forgive.

Emerson once said, "The meaning of good and bad, better and worse, is simply helping or hurting." By developing adolescents' capacity for empathy and altruism, we can become a nation of *good* people who *help* rather than hurt.

Moral Education

More than half a century ago, John Dewey (1933) recognized that whether or not they offer specific programs, schools provide moral education. This moral education includes school and classroom rules, attitudes toward academics and extracurricular activities, the moral orientation of administrators and teachers, and text materials. The pervasive moral atmosphere that characterizes schools is called the **hidden curriculum** by educators. Dewey was right—every school has a moral atmosphere, whether there is a specific moral education program or not. Schools, like families, are settings for moral development. Teachers serve as models of ethical or unethical behavior. Classroom rules and peer relations transmit attitudes about cheating, lying, stealing, and consideration of others. And the school administration, through its rules and regulations, represents a value system to adolescents.

Approaches to moral education can be classified as direct or indirect (Benninga, 1988). **Direct moral education** involves either emphasizing values or character traits during specified time slots or integrating those values or traits throughout the curriculum. **Indirect moral education** involves encouraging students to define their own and others' values and helping them define the moral perspectives that support those values.

In the direct moral education approach, instruction in specified moral concepts can assume the form of example and definition, class discussions and role playing, or rewarding students for proper behavior (Jensen & Knight, 1981). The use of McGuffey Readers during the early part of the twentieth century exemplifies the direct approach. The stories and poems in the readers taught moral behavior and character in addition to academics. A number of contemporary educators advocate a direct approach to moral education. Former U.S. Secretary of Education William Bennett (1986) wrote:

> If a college is really interested in teaching its students a clear lesson in moral responsibility, it should tell the truth about drugs in a straightforward way. This summer our college presidents should send every student a letter saying they will not tolerate drugs on campus—period. The letter should then spell out precisely what the college's policy will be toward students who use drugs. Being simple and straightforward about moral responsibility is not the same as being simplistic and unsophisticated.

Bennett also believes that every elementary and secondary school should have a discipline code, making clear to adolescents and parents what the school expects of them. Then the school should enforce the code.

The most widely adopted indirect approaches to moral education involve values clarification and cognitive moral education. **Values clarification** focuses on helping students clarify what their lives are for and what is worth working for. In values clarification, students are asked questions or presented with dilemmas and expected to respond, either individually or in small groups. The intent is to help students define their own values and to become aware of others' values.

In the following example of values clarification, students are asked to select from among 10 people the 6 who will be admitted to a fallout shelter during World War III:*

Suppose you are a government decision maker in Washington, D.C., when World War III breaks out.

A fallout shelter under your administration in a remote Montana highland contains only enough space, air, food and water for six people for three months, but ten people wish to be admitted.

The ten have agreed by radio contact that for the survival of the human race you must decide which six of them shall be saved. You have exactly thirty minutes to make up your mind before Washington goes up in smoke. These are your choices:

1. A 16-year-old girl of questionable IQ, a high school dropout, pregnant.
2. A policeman with a gun (which cannot be taken from him), thrown off the force recently for brutality.
3. A clergyman, 75.
4. A woman physician, 36, known to be a confirmed racist.
5. A male violinist, 46, who served seven years for pushing narcotics.
6. A 20-year-old black militant, no special skills.
7. A former prostitute, female, 39.
8. An architect, a male homosexual.
9. A 26-year-old law student.
10. The law student's 25-year-old wife who spent the last nine months in a mental hospital, still heavily sedated. They refuse to be separated.

In this exercise, no answers are considered right or wrong. The clarification of values is left up to the individual student. Advocates of the values clarification approach argue that it is value-free. Critics argue that because of its controversial content it offends community standards (Eger, 1981). Critics also say that because of its relativistic nature, values clarification undermines accepted values and fails to stress truth and what is right behavior (Oser, 1986).

Like values clarification, cognitive moral education also challenges direct moral instruction. However, advocates of **cognitive moral education** do not believe that moral education can be value-free. They argue that through more indirect development of students' moral reasoning, values such as democracy and justice will be adopted. The cognitive moral education enthusiasts believe that moral standards should be allowed to develop within students through environmental settings and exercises that encourage more advanced moral thinking. If standards are imposed, they stress, adolescents can never com-

*From C. B. Volkmar, et al., *Values in the Classroom.* Copyright © 1977 Merrill Publishing Company, Columbus, OH. Reprinted by permission of the author.

The whole atmosphere of the school is involved in the adolescent's moral reasoning.

pletely integrate and fully understand moral principles. Only through participation and discussion can adolescents learn to apply the rules and principles of cooperation, trust, community, and self-reliance.

Lawrence Kohlberg's theory of moral development has extensively influenced the cognitive moral education approach. Contrary to what some critics say, Kohlberg's theory is not completely relativistic and it is not completely morally neutral. It clearly treats higher level moral thinking as better than lower level moral thinking. And it stresses that higher level thinking can be stimulated through focused discussion of moral dilemmas. Also, in the 1980s, Kohlberg (1981, 1986) revised his views on moral education by placing more emphasis on the school's moral atmosphere, not unlike John Dewey did many years ago. A summary of Kohlberg's revisionist thinking about moral education can be found in Perspective on Adolescent Development 13.2.

Values, Religion, and Cults

What are adolescents' values like today? How powerful is religion in adolescents' lives? Why do some adolescents run away to join cults? We consider each of these questions in turn.

Values

Adolescents carry with them a set of values that influences their thoughts, feelings, and actions. What were your values like when you were an adolescent? Are the values of today's adolescents changing?

The Just Community and Schools' Moral Atmosphere

In 1974 Kohlberg established the "Just Community," a small school for black and white students from different socioeconomic backgrounds. In the Just Community emphasis was placed on considering realistic issues that arise in school, the nature of moral behavior as well as moral thought, and an active role for teachers as moral advocates.

The Just Community shared with other alternative schools a belief in self-governance, mutual caring, and group solidarity. The goal for moral development was geared toward increasing students' responsibility to the community (stage 4 in Kohlberg's theory) rather than self-principled reasoning. In a recent investigation of the effectiveness of the Just Community—actually named the Cluster School—(Power, 1984), it was found that a more positive orientation toward the community did develop and that students were likely to adhere to the rules they had established. However, although the moral reasoning of the students at the Cluster School did advance, students who simply participated in moral discussion programs advanced their moral reasoning just as much as the students in the Cluster School.

The manner in which Kohlberg set up the Cluster School brings him closer to educators who are concerned with the moral "givens" in life. However, as indicated before, most programs that have included Kohlberg's ideas emphasize the process of moral reasoning rather than a specific moral content. The effectiveness of the programs often varies from school to school and from student to student. Success is usually better at the lower stages (2, 3, and 4) than at postconventional levels (5, 6) (Minuchin & Shapiro, 1983), and better in open schools than in traditional schools (Sullivan, 1975). There is also

some question about the persistence of the effects—how long lasting are the effects of such moral education programs? Usually, assessment takes place immediately after the semester in which moral education is taught, and rarely are there long-term follow-ups.

With the development of the Cluster School in the middle 1970s Kohlberg himself seemed to change his ideas about moral education. Kohlberg (1981) reported that he was not satisfied with the discussion approach to moral education. He realized that attempts to instill principled reasoning about morality in adolescents may be unrealistic because most people do not reach this level of cognitive maturity even in adulthood. And he began to believe that the moral climate of the country was shifting to an emphasis on the self and away from a concern for others in the 1970s. As a consequence, Kohlberg began to show a stronger interest in the school as a social system and in creating moral school communities (Higgins, in press).

A further indication of Kohlberg's belief in the importance of the moral atmosphere of the school is his development of the Moral Atmosphere Interview. This interview poses dilemmas that deal with typically occurring problems in high schools, problems that are likely to involve social responsibility. In a recent investigation (Higgins, Power, & Kohlberg, 1983), the Moral Atmosphere Interview was administered to samples of approximately 20 students from three democratic alternative high schools and three more traditional, authoritarian high schools. Students in the democratic schools perceived the rules of their schools to be more collective and described themselves and their peers as more willing to act responsibly than did students from the traditional schools.

Over the last two decades, although the shift has sometimes been exaggerated, adolescents have shown an increased concern for personal well-being and a decreased concern for the welfare of others, especially the disadvantaged (Astin, Green, & Korn, 1987; Conger, 1981, 1988). As shown in Figure 13.1, today's college freshmen are much more strongly motivated to be very well-off financially and much less motivated to develop a meaningful

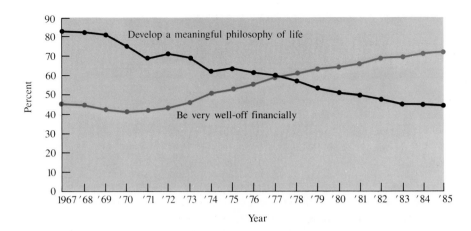

Figure 13.1   Changing freshman life goals, 1967–1985.

philosophy of life than their counterparts from 20 or even 10 years ago. Among high school seniors, increasing numbers are motivated by the chance to earn a considerable amount of money (Johnston, Bachman, & O'Malley, 1986). College and high school students show less interest in the nation's social problems and how they might be resolved than their peers of a decade earlier (Bachman & others, 1987; Astin & others, 1987).

However, two aspects of the values that increased during the 1960s continue to characterize today's youth: self-fulfillment and the opportunity for self-expression (Conger, 1981, 1988). As part of this interest in self, many youth show an increased interest in their physical health and well-being. Greater self-fulfillment and self-expression can be laudable goals for youth, but if they become the only goals, self-destruction, loneliness, or alienation may result. Youth also need to have a corresponding sense of commitment to others' welfare. Encouraging adolescents to develop a stronger commitment to others, in concert with an interest in self-fulfillment, is a major task for our nation as we close the twentieth century.

Religious Beliefs and the Church

Adolescents are more interested in religion and spiritual beliefs than children. Their increasing abstract and idealistic thoughts, as well as their increasing interest in identity, make religion and spiritual matters attractive concerns.

The Development of Religious Concepts

In a series of studies, David Elkind (1978) tested several hundred Jewish, Catholic, and Protestant boys and girls from 5 to 14 years of age. He asked questions such as "Are you a Catholic?" "Is your family Jewish?" "Are all boys and girls in the world Christians?" He also asked questions like, "What is a Jew?" "How do you become a Catholic?" and "Can you be an American and a Protestant (or Jew, or Catholic) at the same time?" The formal-operational thinkers—those who were in early adolescence—had a different

The adolescents shown here are attending a church youth group. What is the nature of the gap between the spiritual interests of adolescents and the role of the traditional church in adolescents' lives?

way of thinking about religious concepts than the concrete-operational thinkers—those in childhood. The formal-operational thinkers were more reflective than their younger counterparts. They no longer looked for manifestations of religious identity in an individual's outward behavior but rather in the evidence of innermost beliefs and convictions. For example, one concrete-operational thinker said that the way you can tell an individual is a Catholic is by whether the person goes to church or not. By contrast, one formal-operational thinker said that you can tell an individual is a Protestant because the person is free to repent and to pray to God.

Another perspective on the development of religious concepts was proposed by James Fowler (1976). He believes late adolescence is especially important in developing a religious identity. Beginning at about age 18, says Fowler, individuals enter a stage called **individuating-reflective faith.** For the first time in their lives, individuals take full responsibility for their religious beliefs. Earlier they relied heavily on their parents' beliefs. During late adolescence, individuals come face to face with personal decisions, evaluating such questions as, "Do I consider myself first, or should I consider the welfare of others first?" "Are the doctrines that have been taught to me absolute, or are they more relative than I have been led to believe?"

Fowler believes there is a close relation between the adolescent's development of moral values and religious values. He also acknowledges that his stage of individuating-reflexive faith is closely related to Kohlberg's level of postconventional morality.

Social, Emotional, and Personality Development

Spiritual Interest and Church Influences

The sociocultural conditions in which adolescents grow up combine with their developing cognitive capacities to influence their religious identity. The formal-operational characteristics of abstract thought and idealism contribute to the adolescent's spiritual interest. Adolescents do show a strong interest in spiritual matters. For example, in one national survey, almost 9 to 10 adolescents said they pray; an even higher percentage said they believe in God or a universal spirit, and only 1 in 1,000 had no religious preference or affiliation (Gallup & Poling, 1980). At the same time, though, many adolescents say that organized religion has little meaning for them and that the church's doctrines are outmoded. In the national poll just mentioned, only 25% said they have a high degree of confidence in organized religion. About 40% said that the honesty and personal ethics of the clergy are average to very low. As we see next, the ethical standards of many cult leaders are also seriously questioned.

Cults

Barb is 17 years old. She grew up in an affluent family and was given all of the material things she wanted. When she was 15, her parents paid her way to Europe and for the last 3 years, she has been attending a private boarding school. Her parents attended a Protestant church on a regular basis, and when Barb was home they took her with them. Six months ago, Barb joined the "Moonies."

There are six unorthodox religious movements that have attracted considerable attention from America's youth: Transcendental Meditation (TM), yoga, the charismatic movement, mysticism, faith healing, and various Eastern religions (Gallup & Poling, 1980). More than 27 million Americans have been touched by these religions, either superficially or deeply. In all, there are more than 2,500 cults in the United States. Two to three million youth and young adults are cult members (Levine, 1984; Swope, 1980). Among the more specific religious cults that have attracted the attention of youth are the Unification Church of Sun Myung Moon (the Moonies), the Divine Light Mission of Maharaj Ji, the Institute of Krishna Consciousness, the Children of God, and the Church of Scientology.

The most recent concerns about cults focus on satanism, or devil worship. The nightmarish tale of human sacrifice that unfolded in the spring of 1989 in Matamoros, Mexico, brought national attention to the increasing prevalence of devil worshiping. Some of bodies in the mass grave had been decapitated. Investigation of the Satanism cult revealed its ties to drugs. The cult's ringleader, Adolpho de Jesus Constanzo, controlled members' lives, getting them to believe that the devil has supernatural, occultlike powers.

Critics of the cults argue that the cult leaders are hypocritical, exploit members to gain wealth, brainwash youth, and develop a hypnoticlike spell over their lives. In some cases, cults have been accused of kidnapping youth and placing them in deprived circumstances to gain control over their minds.

Hari Krisna on the streets of New York City. The Hari Krisna are one of more than 2,500 cults in the United States. Two to three million youth and young adults are cult members.

"We were hoping you'd be home for vacation or whatever Moonies call it when they're not doing what they do."

Drawing by Saxon; © 1967 The New Yorker Magazine. Inc.

Most cults have elaborate training programs in which the cult's preachings are memorized. Cult members are usually required to turn over their wealth to the cult leaders. And cult members are often told that they can associate with or marry only other members of the cult (Galanter, 1989).

Why do some adolescents leave home and become members of a cult? Some experts believe that the failures of organized religion and the church, as well as a weakening of family life, are causes (Gallup & Poling, 1980; Levine, 1984). What kind of youth are most vulnerable to the appeal of cults? Six characteristics have been identified (From G. W. Swope, "Kids and Cults: Who Joins and Why?" in *Media and Methods,* 16:18–21, 1980. Copyright © 1980 American Society of Educators, Philadelphia, PA. Reprinted by permission.):

1. *Idealistic.* Due to the teachings and example of family, religious leaders, peers, educators, and others, there has developed within young people a desire to help others, to improve society, and often to know God better. The cults manipulate this idealism, convincing (their) members that only within their specialized groups can such inclinations be actualized.

2. *Innocent.* Because relationships with religious leaders in the past have been wholesome, the potential recruit naively believes that all who claim to speak in the name of God are sincere and trustworthy. Elmer Gantry and Jim Jones notwithstanding, the trappings of religion are a powerful lure here.

3. *Inquisitive.* On college and high school campuses around the country, intelligent young people, looking for interesting groups to join, are approached by enthusiastic, "together" recruiters who invite them to meetings where, they are told, they will meet other fine young people. It sounds exciting. Discussion, they are assured, will focus on ecology, world problems, religion, ethics, education—anything in which the recruit has shown some interest.

4. *Independent.* Many young people are recruited into cults when they are away from home—independent for the first time. Parents of such students are not always aware of how their children spend evenings and weekends, and often do not learn that they have left college until several weeks or months after they drop out. Backpackers are particular targets for cult recruiters. These young people are often lonely and susceptible to invitations for free meals and fellowship.

5. *Identity-seeking.* Young adults in every generation experience identity crises as they seek to determine their own strengths and weaknesses, their value systems, goals, religious and social beliefs.

6. *Insecure.* Inquisitive young people—looking for new experiences, seeking to clarify their own identities, away from the influence of family, friends, and mentors—develop uneasy feelings of insecurity. Lacking trusted counselors to whom they can turn when upset or disturbed, they are especially vulnerable to smiling, friendly people who show great interest in them and manipulate them through what one cult calls "love bombing."

Moral Behavior, Feelings, and Education; Values, Religion, and Cults

Concept	Processes/Related Ideas	Characteristics/Description
Moral behavior	Its nature	Emphasized by social learning theorists, who focus on the role of reinforcement, punishment, and imitation. Situational variability in moral behavior is stressed. Cognitive social learning theorists emphasize a distinction between moral competence and moral performance.
Moral feelings and altruism	Psychoanalytic view	Individuals avoid transgressing to avoid guilt. Early childhood is a special time for emergence of guilt, which is primarily unconscious. Erikson argues that there are three stages of moral development: specific moral learning in childhood, ideological concerns in adolescence, and ethical consolidation in adulthood.
	Empathy and altruism	Empathy is the ability to understand another's feelings and it promotes altruism, the unselfish interest in helping someone. Reciprocity and exchange are involved in altruism.
Moral education	Hidden curriculum	The pervasive moral atmosphere that characterizes any school, regardless of whether or not there is a specific moral curriculum.
	Direct approaches	Either emphasizing values or character traits during specified time slots or integrating those values or traits throughout the curriculum.
	Indirect approaches	Encouraging students to define their own values and others' values and helping them define the moral perspectives that support those values. Advocated by both values clarification and cognitive moral education. Kohlberg has had a major impact on cognitive moral education.
Values, religion, and cults	Values	Over the last two decades adolescents have shown an increased concern for personal well-being and a decreased concern for the welfare of others.
	Religious beliefs and the church	Both Elkind's and Fowler's views illustrate the increased abstractness in adolescent's thinking that improves their understanding of the nature of religion. Adolescents show a strong interest in spiritual matters but believe that organized religion does not provide them with the spiritual understanding they are seeking.
	Cults	Cult membership in the United States is extensive. It may appeal to adolescents because of weaknesses in organized religion and families.

At this point we have discussed a number of ideas about moral behavior, moral feelings and altruism, moral education, and values, religion, and cults. A summary of these ideas is presented in Concept Table 13.2. We have seen in this chapter that moral and religious values are important aspects of the adolescent's search for identity. In the next chapter, other important ingredients of adolescent identity are discussed—achievement and career development.

Summary

I. What Is Moral Development?

Moral development concerns rules and regulations about what people should do in their interaction with other people. Moral development's three main domains are thought, behavior, and feeling.

II. Piaget's Ideas

Piaget argued that children 4–7 years of age are in the heteronomous stage of morality, and from about the age of 10 on are in the autonomous stage of morality. Formal operational thought may undergird changes in adolescents' moral reasoning.

III. Kohlberg's Ideas

Lawrence Kohlberg proposed a provocative theory of moral development with three levels—preconventional, conventional, and postconventional—and six stages. Increased internalization characterizes movement to levels 2 and 3. Kohlberg's longitudinal data show a relation of stages to age, although the higher two stages, especially stage 6, rarely appear. Influences on the stages include cognitive development, imitation and cognitive conflict, peer relations, and perspective taking. Kohlberg's work has been criticized for overemphasizing cognition and underemphasizing behavior, for the questionable quality of the research, for inadequate consideration of the care perspective, and for underestimating culture's role.

IV. Social Conventional Reasoning

Moral reasoning pertains to ethical matters; social conventional reasoning pertains to thoughts about social convention and consensus. Moral reasoning is prescriptive; conventional reasoning is more arbitrary. Moral reasoning emphasizes justice; social conventional reasoning emphasizes social regulation.

V. Moral Behavior

Social learning theorists emphasize the importance of moral behavior in understanding moral development. They believe moral behavior is influenced by reinforcement, punishment, and imitation. Situational variability in moral behavior is stressed. Cognitive social learning theorists emphasize a distinction between moral competence and moral performance.

VI. Moral Feelings and Altruism

In the psychoanalytic view, individuals avoid transgressing to avoid guilt. Early childhood is a special time for guilt's emergence, which is primarily unconscious. Erikson argues that there are three stages of moral development: specific moral learning in childhood, ideological concerns in adolescence, and ethical consolidation in adulthood. There has been increased interest in empathy and altruism in recent years. Empathy is the ability to understand another's feelings, which promotes altruism, the unselfish interest in helping another. Reciprocity and exchange are involved in many altruistic acts.

VII. Moral Education

There is a hidden curriculum in schools, a moral atmosphere that is pervasive. Direct moral education either emphasizes moral values or character traits during specified time slots or integrates those values or traits throughout the curriculum. Indirect moral education encourages students to define their own values and others' values and helps them define the moral perspectives that support those values. Both values clarification and cognitive moral education (heavily influenced by Kohlberg's theory) are examples of indirect moral education.

VIII. Values, Religion, and Cults

Over the last two decades adolescents have shown an increased concern for personal well-being and a decreased concern for the welfare of others. Both Elkind's and Fowler's views illustrate the increased abstractness in adolescents' thinking that is associated with an interest in religious concepts. Adolescents show a strong interest in religion but believe that organized religion has not provided them with the spiritual understanding they are seeking. Cult membership in the United States is extensive. It may appeal to adolescents because of weaknesses in organized religion and families.

Key Terms

moral development 459
heteronomous morality 460
autonomous morality 460
immanent justice 461
cognitive-disequilibrium theory 461
preconventional moral reasoning 462
punishment and obedience orientation 462
naive hedonism or instrumental orientation 463

conventional moral reasoning 463
good boy or good girl orientation 463
authority and social-order maintaining morality 463
postconventional moral reasoning 463
community rights versus individual rights 463
individual conscience 464
justice perspective 468
care perspective 468
social conventional reasoning 470

moral competence 474
moral performance 474
empathy 475
altruism 475
hidden curriculum 477
direct moral education 477
indirect moral education 477
values clarification 477
cognitive moral education 478
individuating-reflective faith 482

Suggested Readings

Benninga, J. S. (1988, February). An emerging synthesis in moral education. *Phi Delta Kappan,* pp. 415–418.
Outlines the ongoing debate about how to teach morals, ethics, values, or good character in schools.

Gilligan, C. (1982). *In a different voice.* Cambridge, MA: Harvard University Press.
This book advances Gilligan's provocative view that a care perspective is underrepresented in Kohlberg's theory and research.

Lapsley, D. K., Enright, R. D., and Serlin, R. C. (1986). Moral and social education. In J. Worrell and F. Danner (Eds.), *Adolescent development: Issues for education.* New York: Academic Press.
A thorough overview of what is known about moral education and the more recently developed field of social education. Includes thoughtful, detailed comments about the nature of moral and social conventional reasoning.

Lickona, T. (Ed.). (1976). *Moral development and behavior.* New York: Holt, Rinehart & Winston.
Contemporary essays outlining the major theories, research findings, and educational implications of moral development. Included are essays by Kohlberg, Hoffman, Mischel, Aronfreed, Bronfenbrenner, and Rest.

Modgil, S., & Modgil, C. (Eds.). (1986). *Lawrence Kohlberg.* Philadelphia: The Falmer Press.
A number of experts evaluate Kohlberg's theory of moral development. Includes a concluding chapter by Kohlberg.

Achievement, Careers, and Work

Whatever you can do, or dream you can, begin it. Boldness has genius, power, and magic in it.

Johann Wolfgang von Goethe

Cleveland Wilkes

leveland Wilkes's family in Providence, Rhode Island, has never had much money; he and his parents know what unemployment can do to a family. Nevertheless, Cleveland, who is 17, is referred to by his friends as "the Dresser" because of his penchant for flamboyant clothes—especially shoes. What little money Cleveland manages to scrape together is all channeled into maintaining his wardrobe. In conversation, Cleveland may grow quite animated, but he always has time to check the press of his trousers or smooth the wrinkles in his sleeve.

Whole world floats by around here. This here's the whole world, only in miniature, like they call it. There ain't nothin' you can't see on these streets. See more in a month here than a lifetime where the rich folks live, all protected from the big bad world. I ain't saying it's so great over here, ain't saying this would be my first choice for children growing up in this city. I'm only saying where we ain't rich with money we are rich, man, with things happening every second. Only thing we don't have is the thing we need the most of: jobs. Ain't no jobs for us over here. Not a one, man, and I know too, because I been looking for three years, and I ain't all that old. Act old, but I ain't old. Seen things old people seen, but I ain't old. Next week I may be old; next year I sure am fixin' on being old if I don't find no work.

I'd take anything, too, man anything they got for me. That surprise you? Don't surprise me none. You sit in the middle of all this, you ain't got no choice. Like they say, beggars can't be choosy. I ain't about to go begging, except that seems like all I do, specially in the summer. Man, we go to these fat cats sitting there in their offices, you know. "Hey, mister,

you got a job?" "We'll call you. We'll call you." Tell me that or they'll say, "Got your name, Mr. Cleveland, on the top of my list!"

I say to the cat, "Hey, that's cool. You got the only list I ever heard of with my name right at the top. But if you're thinking about me so special, how come you call me Mr. Cleveland when Cleveland's my first name?"

Country got no use for me, folks around here neither. Ain't nobody care too much what happens to us. Tell us, "Ain't you boys got nothing better to do than stand around all day? What you find to talk about all these hours? And ain't you supposed to be in school? Ain't you supposed to be doing this or doing that?" I tell them, "Hey, listen to me turkey. I ain't supposed to be doing nothin' if I don't want to. You hear me? Ain't supposed to be nowhere, helping no one!"

If you want to know what the teenagers on this side of town are doing to pass the time of day, now you got it. We got so many folks here out of work it's enough to blow your mind. I can hear my brain rotting it's been so long I ain't done nothin'. How they let this happen in a country like this, having all these kids walking around the streets, got their hands jammed down in their pockets, head down, like their necks was bent in half? What do folks think these kids gonna do, when they go month after month, year after year without nothing that even smells like a job? Not even no part-time affair. They might get to the point to where they'll waste some kid working for the cleaners, waste the kid and take his job. Folks do it when they ain't got enough food, and they'll start doing it for jobs, too.

his chapter is about achievement, about careers, and about work, three pervasive themes in the life of Cleveland Wilkes.

Achievement

American adolescents live in an achievement-oriented world with standards that tell them success is important. The standards suggest that success requires a competitive spirit, a desire to win, a motivation to do well, and the wherewithal to cope with adversity and persist until obstacles are overcome. Some developmentalists, though, believe we are a nation of hurried, wired people who are raising our youth to become the same way—too uptight about success and failure and far too worried about what we accomplish in comparison to others (Elkind, 1981). In an effort to understand adolescent achievement, this section focuses on the nature of motivation, need for achievement, intrinsic and extrinsic motivation, and achievement in minority group adolescents.

Motivation

Motivation focuses on *why* adolescents behave the way they do. Why is an adolescent hungry? Why is another adolescent studying so hard? Two important dimensions of the "whys" of behavior are activation and direction. First, when adolescents are motivated they do something. Their behavior is activated or energized. If adolescents are hungry, they might go to the refrigerator for a snack. If they are motivated to get a good grade on a test, they might study hard. Second, when adolescents are motivated, their behavior also is directed. Why does an adolescent behave one way when there are several options available? For example, if a father reprimands his son for failing to clean up his room before going out, one adolescent might ignore the reprimand, another adolescent might hurry to clean up the room before departing, and a third adolescent might start a verbal argument. Motivation, thus, involves an attempt to explain how adolescents direct their behavior or, put another way, to explain the specific behaviors they select in certain situations but not others. To summarize, motivation focuses on *why* adolescents behave, think, and feel the way they do, with special consideration of the activation and direction of their behavior.

Psychologists have offered a number of explanations of the "whys" of adolescent behavior. One explanation involves the concept of drive. A **drive** is an aroused state that occurs because of a physiological **need.** An adolescent might have a need for food. The need for food arouses the adolescent's hunger drive. This motivates the adolescent to do something—go to a fast-food restaurant, for example—to reduce the drive and satisfy the need. As a drive becomes stronger, the adolescent is motivated to reduce it. This explanation is known as **drive-reduction theory.**

An important concept in motivation and one that helps us understand the nature of drives is **homeostasis**—the tendency to maintain a balanced equilibrium, or steady state. Literally hundreds of biological states in adolescents' bodies must be maintained within a certain range: temperature, blood-sugar level, potassium and sodium levels, oxygen, and so on. When adolescents dive into an icy swimming pool, their bodies heat up. When adolescents walk out of an air-conditioned room into a summer day's heat, their bodies begin to cool down. These changes occur automatically to restore the body to its optimal state of functioning.

Homeostasis is used to explain both physiological imbalances and psychological imbalances. For example, if an adolescent has not been around friends for a long time, he or she may be motivated to seek their company. If an adolescent has not studied hard for a test in some months, he or she may be aroused to put in considerably more study time. The concepts of drive and homeostasis have played important roles in understanding motivation.

However, psychologists became disenchanted with drive-reduction theory as a comprehensive theory of motivation when it became apparent that individuals are not always motivated to reduce a need. In the 1950s, experiments began to show that in many instances individuals are motivated to seek stimulation (e.g., Butler, 1953). According to R. W. White (1959), rather than always being motivated to reduce biological needs, individuals have **competence motivation** (also called mastery or effectance motivation). This is the motivation to deal effectively with the environment, to do well what is attempted, to process information efficiently, and to make the world a better place. White said we do these things not because they serve biological needs, but because we have an intrinsic (internal) motivation to interact effectively with the environment. Closely related to this idea is achievement motivation, which we discuss shortly.

As psychologists recognized the importance of competence motivation and the environment's role in motivation, they began to describe a number of learned motives in humans. These include the motivation for achievement, the motivation for power, the motivation for affiliation, the motivation for identity, and the motivation for self-actualization. As we see next, self-actualization is viewed as the highest form of motivation in one well-known theory of motivation.

Is getting an A in school more important to a child than eating? If the girl of an adolescent boy's dreams told him that he was marvelous, would that motivate him to throw himself in front of a car for her safety? According to Abraham Maslow (1954, 1971), basic needs have to be satisfied before higher needs can be satisfied. Based on Maslow's **hierarchy of motives,** we would conclude that in most instances children need to eat before they can achieve, and that they need to satisfy their safety needs before their love needs. Maslow believes that humans have five basic needs, which unfold in the following sequence: physiological, safety, love and belongingness, self-esteem, and self-actualization (see Figure 14.1). It is the need for self-actualization that Maslow

Social, Emotional, and Personality Development

has described in the greatest detail. Self-actualization includes everything an individual is capable of being. According to Maslow, self-actualization is possible only after the other needs in the hierarchy are met. Obviously, adolescents cannot be everything they are capable of being if they are hungry all of the time. Among the characteristics of self-actualization are finding self-fulfillment and peace with one's own life, realizing one's full self-potential, and feeling content with that. A self-actualized adolescent has an open manner, is not defensive, loves himself or herself, feels no need to manipulate others or be aggressive toward them, acts in ways that promote moral and ethical principles, and is creative, curious, and spontaneous in interchanges with others.

The idea that humans have a hierarchy of motives is appealing. Maslow's theory stimulates us to think about the ordering of the motives in adolescents' lives. Not everyone, though, agrees on the order in which adolescents satisfy their needs. In some instances the order may be different than Maslow envisioned.

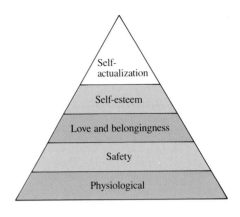

Figure 14.1   Maslow's hierarchy of needs.

Achievement Motivation

Think about yourself and your friends for a moment. Are you more achievement oriented than they are or less so? If we asked you and your friends to tell stories about achievement-related themes, could we actually determine which of you is more achievement oriented?

David McClelland (McClelland & others, 1953) stressed that individuals vary in their motivation for achievement and that we can measure these differences. McClelland called achievement motivation **need for achievement** (or *n* achievement), referring to the individual's motivation to overcome obstacles, desire for success, and the effort expended to seek out difficult tasks and do them well as quickly as possible. To measure achievement, individuals were shown ambiguous pictures that were likely to stimulate achievement-related responses. Then they were asked to tell a story about the picture. Their comments were scored according to how strongly they reflected achievement (McClelland & others, 1953).

A host of studies have correlated achievement-related responses with different aspects of children's and adolescents' experiences and behavior. The findings are diverse, but they do suggest that achievement-oriented adolescents have a stronger hope for success than fear of failure, are moderate rather than high or low risk takers, and persist for appropriate lengths of time in solving difficult problems (Atkinson & Raynor, 1974). Early research indicated that independence training by parents promoted achievement, but more recent research reveals that parents need to set high standards for achievement, model achievement-oriented behavior, and reward adolescents for their achievements to increase achievement (Huston-Stein & Higgens-Trenk, 1978). More about the role of parents in adolescents' achievement orientation appears in Perspective on Adolescent Development 14.1.

Hurried Adolescents

Adolescents who were called "spoiled" a generation ago took longer to grow up and had more freedom and power than they knew how to handle. Today's adolescents are pressured to achieve more, earlier—academically, socially, sexually. These hurried adolescents, as David Elkind (1981) calls them, must contend with a fear of failure, and a feeling that society's promises to them have been broken. Unlike the spoiled adolescents who remain children too long, hurried adolescents grow up too fast, pushed in their early years toward many avenues of achievement.

In adolescence, the symptoms of being hurried become evident, too often taking the form of severe anxiety about academic success. Elkind believes that parent-adolescent contracts—implicit agreements about mutual obligation—can help to alleviate some of this uptightness about achievement. He describes three basic contracts: freedom and responsibility, loyalty and commitment, and achievement and support.

Parents usually give adolescents freedom as long as the adolescents show that they can handle it. In adolescence, though, new types of responsibilities are demanded when individuals begin to date, drive cars, and experiment with drugs. Parents have less control than they did earlier because adolescents can take certain freedoms regardless of parental consent. Yet parents can still set limits and make clear that some freedoms (such as using the family car) will be withdrawn if adolescents transgress.

A second type of parent-adolescent contract involves loyalty and commitment. Parents usually assume that children will be loyal to them, in the sense of preferring them to other adults. In return, parents show commitment to their children in the time they spend with them and in their concern for their children's well-being.

In adolescence, when friendships become more important, parents no longer expect the loyal affection they received when children were young. They do expect, however, that their adolescents will be loyal to their family's values and beliefs. Adolescents, in return, demand that parents not be hypocritical and show commitment to the values they endorse.

A third contract involves achievement and support. Parents demand little in the way of achievement from infants, other than that they learn to sit up, crawl, walk, and talk at appropriate ages. As children grow up and go to school, the achievement-support contract becomes rewritten. Middle-class families expect achievements in academic subjects, extracurricular activities, and social events. Parents reciprocate with affection for good grades, with material support for lessons, instruments, and uniforms, and with transportation to and from friends' homes and various social activities. In adolescence, parental demands for achievement become more intense, as adolescents prepare for adult maturity.

In a society that places emphasis on early achievement, when parents do not couple demands for that achievement with a comparable level of support, there is a disequilibrium in parent-child relations. When the disequilibrium persists, the result is a hurried child or hurried adolescent, achieving ever earlier in adult ways, but also acquiring the tensions that arise from the pressure to achieve. As adolescents, they may be motivated to pay back their parents for what they experienced as childhood inequities. They may come to resent their parents who pushed them to excel in school but who never bothered to look at their work, attend parent conferences, or participate in school functions. They often experience a sense of failure, both in their school performance, and in their ability to meet their parents' expectations. ❧

Attribution Theory and Intrinsic-Extrinsic Motivation

Shakespeare once wrote, "Find out the cause of this effect, or rather say, the cause of this defect, for the effect defective comes by cause."

Attribution theorists have taken Shakespeare's comments to heart. They argue that individuals want to know the causes of people's behavior because the knowledge promotes more effective coping with life's circumstances. **Attribution theory** says that individuals are motivated to discover the underlying causes of behavior as part of the effort to make sense out of the behavior. In a way, attribution theorists say that adolescents are like intuitive scientists, seeking the cause behind what happens.

We can classify the reasons individuals behave the way they do in a number of ways, but one basic distinction stands out above all others—the distinction between internal causes, such as the actor's personality traits or motives, and external causes, which are environmental, situational factors such as rewards or how difficult a task is (Heider, 1958). If adolescents do not do well on a test, do they attribute it to the fact that the teacher plotted against them and made the test too difficult (external cause) or to the fact that they did not study hard enough (internal cause)? The answer to such a question influences how adolescents feel about themselves. If adolescents believe their performance is the teacher's fault, they won't feel as bad as when they do not spend enough time studying.

Adolescents' attributions are not always accurate. The way the human mind sees things suggests that attributions have some built-in bias. Adolescents, as well as adults, tend to overestimate the importance of traits and underestimate the importance of situations when they seek explanations of behavior. This is called the **fundamental attribution error** (Ross, 1977). Also, the attributions of the actor and the observer diverge such that the actor is more likely to choose external causes and the observer internal causes. In these circumstances, the actor is the one who is producing the action to be explained; the observer is the onlooker, who offers a causal explanation of the actor's behavior. Since the actor and the observer often disagree about whether internal or external causes are responsible for the actor's behavior, one of them must be wrong. Based on the fundamental attribution error, we could anticipate that the observer overestimates the internal, trait causes of behavior and underestimates the social, situational causes.

Closely related to the concept of internal and external causes of behavior is the concept of intrinsic and extrinsic motivation. The interest in intrinsic motivation comes from ideas about competence motivation (Harter, 1981; White, 1959), curiosity (Berlyne, 1960), and perceived control (Deci, 1975). **Intrinsic motivation** involves an underlying need for competence and self-determination. By contrast, **extrinsic motivation** involves external factors in the environment, especially rewards. If an adolescent works hard in school because a personal standard of excellence is important, intrinsic motivation is functioning. But if the adolescent works hard in school because the adolescent knows it will bring a higher paying job after graduation, extrinsic motivation is functioning.

An important consideration when motivating an adolescent to do something is whether or not to offer an incentive (Pittman & Heller, 1987; Rotter, 1989). If the adolescent is not doing competent work, is bored, or has a negative attitude, it may be worthwhile to consider incentives to improve motivation. However, if an adolescent already has a strong interest in an activity, no external rewards may be necessary (Lepper, Greene, & Nisbett, 1973).

Intrinsic motivation implies that internal motivation should be promoted and external factors deemphasized. In this way, adolescents learn to attribute the cause of their success and their failure to themselves, especially how much effort they expend. But in reality, achievement is motivated by both internal and external factors. Adolescents are never entirely divorced from their environment. Some of the most achievement-oriented adolescents are those who have *both* a high personal standard for achievement and also are highly competitive. In one investigation, low-achieving boys and girls who engaged in individual goal setting *and* were given comparative information about peers worked more math problems and got more of them correct than their counterparts who experienced either condition alone (Schunk, 1983). Other research suggests that social comparison by itself is not a wise strategy because it places the adolescent in an ego-involved, threatening, self-focused state rather than a task-involved, effortful, strategy-focused state (Nicholls, 1984).

Social, Emotional, and Personality Development

The Achievement and Adjustment of Asian-American Adolescents

Suzanna Kang is a 17-year-old Korean American student at T. C. Williams High School in Alexandria, Virginia. She fits the stereotype of Asian-American students. She is bright, hard-working, and carries a 4.0 grade-point average. Suzanna likes science and math, is headed for a college scholarship, and is very close to her family. Says Suzanna, "I guess I do fit the Asian-American superachiever image, but I know there are many Asian-American children who are not doing so well, especially those who have recently immigrated to this country. Many of them are struggling to learn English." The whiz kid image fits many of the children of Asian immigrant families who arrived in the United States in the late 1960s and early 1970s. Many of these immigrants came from Hong Kong, South Korea, India, and the Philippines. And the image fits many of the more than 100,000 Indochinese (primarily Vietnamese) immigrants who arrived in the United States following the end of the Vietnam war in 1975. Both of these groups included mostly middle- to upper-income professional people who were reasonably well educated and who passed along to their children a strong interest in education and a solid work ethic. For thousands of other Asian Americans—a high percentage of the 600,000 Indochinese refugees who fled Vietnam, Laos, and Cambodia in the late 1970s—the problems are many. Many in this wave of refugees lived in poor surroundings in their homelands. They came to the United States with few skills and little education. They speak little English and have a difficult time finding a decent job. They often share housing with relatives. Adjustment to school is difficult for their children. Some are attracted to gangs and drugs. Some drop out of school. Better school systems use a variety of techniques to help these Asian Americans, including English as a Second Language classes and a range of social services. ✿

Achievement in Minority Group Adolescents

A primary limitation of existing research on minority group achievement is that there has been so little of it. The research literature on achievement has focused heavily on white males. And too often the results of research on minority groups have been interpreted as "deficits" by middle-class, white standards. Rather than characterizing individuals as *culturally different,* many conclusions unfortunately characterize the cultural distinctiveness of blacks, Hispanics, and other minority groups as deficient in some way.

Sandra Graham, UCLA psychologist. Shown here talking with a group of young boys about motivation, Dr. Graham has conducted important research showing that middle-class black children—like their middle-class white counterparts—have high achievement expectations and understand that their failure is often due to lack of effort rather than to lack of luck.

Much of the research on minority group children and adolescents is plagued by a failure to consider socioeconomic status (determined by some combination of education, occupation, and income of parents). In many instances, when race *and* socioeconomic status (also called social class) are investigated in the same study, social class is a far better predictor of achievement orientation than race (Graham, 1986). Middle-class adolescents fare better than their lower-class counterparts in a variety of achievement-related circumstances—expectations for success, achievement aspirations, and recognition of the importance of effort, for example (McAdoo & McAdoo, 1985).

Sandra Graham has conducted a number of investigations that reveal not only stronger social class differences than racial differences but also the importance of studying minority group motivation in the context of general motivation theory (Graham, 1984, 1986, 1987). Her inquiries focus on the reasons black children and adolescents give for their achievement orientation—why they succeed or fail, for example. She is struck by how consistently middle-class black adolescents do not fit our stereotypes of either deviant or special populations. Like their middle-class white counterparts, they have high expectations and understand that failure is usually due to lack of effort rather than luck.

At this point we have studied a number of ideas about adolescent achievement. A summary of these ideas is presented in Concept Table 14.1. Achievement orientation serves as a foundation for the adolescent's career development, the topic we turn to next.

Social, Emotional, and Personality Development

Achievement

Concept	Processes/Related Ideas	Characteristics/Description
Motivation	Its nature	Focuses on why adolescents behave, think, and feel the way they do, with special consideration of the activation and direction of their behavior.
	Different views	Include drive-reduction theory, especially homeostasis, competence motivation, and Maslow's hierarchy of motives.
Achievement motivation	Need for achievement and its correlates	Defined by McClelland as motivation to overcome obstacles, desire for success, and effort expended to seek out difficult tasks and do them well and as quickly as possible. Related to hope for success, moderate risk taking, and appropriate persistence at task, as well as parents' characteristics.
Attribution theory and intrinsic-extrinsic motivation	Attribution theory	Says that individuals are motivated to discover the underlying causes of behavior in their effort to make sense out of the behavior. One basic set of attributions involves internal versus external causes. Attributions are not always accurate, as shown in the fundamental attribution error.
	Intrinsic-extrinsic motivation	Intrinsic motivation involves an underlying need for competence and self-determination. Extrinsic motivation involves external factors in the environment, especially rewards. Some of the most achievement-oriented adolescents are both intrinsically and extrinsically motivated.
Achievement in minority group adolescents	Its nature	Emphasis should be placed on cultural differences rather than cultural deficits. Researchers have shown that social class differences in achievement are greater than racial differences.

Career Development

What are the future occupations of today's adolescents? What theories have been developed to direct our understanding of adolescents' career choices? What roles do exploration, decision making, and planning play in career development? How do sociocultural factors affect career development? What changes have taken place in the career development of females? We consider each of these questions in turn.

Tomorrow's Jobs for Today's Adolescents

For nearly 40 years, the United States Bureau of Labor Statistics has published the *Occupational Outlook Handbook,* a valuable source of career information. The following information comes from the 1988–1989 edition (the handbook is revised every two years). The long-term shift from goods-producing to service-producing employment will continue. By the year 2000, nearly 4 out of 5 jobs will be in industries that provide services—industries such as banking, insurance, health care, education, data processing, and management consulting. Continued expansion of the service-producing sector generates a vision of a work force dominated by cashiers, retail sales workers, and waiters. However, while the service sector growth will create millions of clerical, sales, and service jobs, it also will create jobs for engineers, accountants, lawyers, nurses, and many other managerial, professional, and technical workers. In fact, the fastest-growing careers will be those that require the most educational preparation.

The range of employment growth in various careers will be diverse (see Table 14.1). As indicated in Table 14.1, the greatest growth in jobs will be in the natural, computer, and mathematical sciences—especially strong will be the need for computer and math scientists, largely due to substantial growth in computer and data processing services. There actually will be a decrease in agriculture, forestry, fishing, and related occupations.

Theories of Career Development

Three dominant theories describe the manner in which adolescents make choices about careers—Ginzberg's developmental theory, Super's self-concept theory, and Holland's personality type theory.

Ginzberg's Developmental Theory

In Eli Ginzberg's (Ginzberg, 1972; Ginzberg & others, 1951) **developmental theory of career choice,** children and adolescents are described as going through three career choice stages—fantasy, tentative, and realistic. When asked what they want to be when they grow up, young children may answer "a doctor," "a superhero," "a teacher," "a movie star," "a sports star," or any number of other occupations. In childhood, the future seems to hold almost unlimited opportunites. Ginzberg argues that until about the age of 11, children are in the *fantasy stage* of career choice. From the ages of 11 to 17, adolescents are in the *tentative stage* of career development, a transition from the fantasy stage of childhood to the realistic decision making of young adulthood. He believes that adolescents progress from evaluating their interests (11–12 years of age) to evaluating their capacities (13–14 years of age) to evaluating their values (15–16 years of age). Thinking shifts from less subjective to more realistic career choices at around 17–18 years of age. The period from 17 to 18 years of age through the early 20s is called the *realistic stage* of career choice by Ginzberg. At this time, the individual extensively explores available careers, then focuses on a particular career, and finally selects a specific job within the career (such as family practitioner or orthopedic surgeon within the career of doctor).

Critics have attacked Ginzberg's theory on a number of grounds. For one, the initial data were collected from middle-class youth, who probably had more career options open to them. And, as with other developmental theories (such as Piaget's), the time frames are too rigid. Morever, Ginzberg's theory

Social, Emotional, and Personality Development

TABLE 14.1   *Employment Growth Will Vary Widely by Broad Occupational Group*

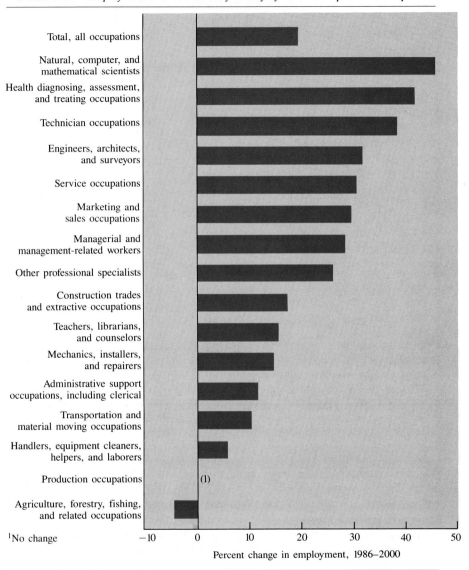

	Percent change in employment, 1986–2000
Total, all occupations	
Natural, computer, and mathematical scientists	
Health diagnosing, assessment, and treating occupations	
Technician occupations	
Engineers, architects, and surveyors	
Service occupations	
Marketing and sales occupations	
Managerial and management-related workers	
Other professional specialists	
Construction trades and extractive occupations	
Teachers, librarians, and counselors	
Mechanics, installers, and repairers	
Administrative support occupations, including clerical	
Transportation and material moving occupations	
Handlers, equipment cleaners, helpers, and laborers	
Production occupations	(1)
Agriculture, forestry, fishing, and related occupations	

¹No change

Percent change in employment, 1986–2000

Source: Occupational Outlook Handbook. U.S. Department of Labor. Bureau of Labor Statistics. April, 1988, Bulletin 2300, P. 12.

does not take into account individual differences—some adolescents make mature decisions about careers (and stick with them) at much earlier ages than specified by Ginzberg. Not all children engage in career fantasies either. In a revision of his theory, Ginzberg (1972) conceded that lower-class individuals do not have as many options available as middle-class individuals do. Ginzberg's general point—that at some point during late adolescence or early adulthood more realistic career choices are made—probably is correct.

Super's Self-Concept Theory

In Donald Super's (1967, 1976) **career self-concept theory,** the individual's self-concepts play a central role. Super believes that it is during adolescence that individuals first construct a career self-concept. He argues that career development consists of five different phases. First, at about 14–18 years of age, adolescents develop ideas about work that mesh with their already existing global self-concept—this phase is called *crystallization.* Between 18 and 22 years of age, they narrow their career choices and initiate behavior that enables them to enter some type of career—this phase is called *specification.* Between 21 and 24 years of age, young adults complete their education or training and enter the world of work—this phase is called *implementation.* The decision on a specific, appropriate career is made between 25 and 35 years of age—this phase is called *stabilization.* Finally, after the age of 35, individuals seek to advance their careers and reach higher-status positions—this phase is called *consolidation.* The age ranges should be thought of as approximate rather than rigid. Super believes that career exploration in adolescence is a key ingredient of the adolescent's career self-concept. He constructed the Career Development Inventory to assist counselors in promoting adolescents' career exploration.

Holland's Personality Type Theory

In John Holland's (1973, 1985, 1987) **personality type theory,** emphasis is placed on the individual's selection of a career that matches his or her personality. Once individuals find a career that fits with their personality, they are more likely to enjoy that particular career and stay in a job for a longer period of time than individuals who work at jobs that are not suitable for their personality. Holland believes there are six basic personality types to be considered when matching the individual's psychological makeup to a career:

> *Realistic.* These individuals show characteristically "masculine" traits. They are physically strong, deal in practical ways with problems, and have very little social know-how. They are best oriented toward practical careers such as labor, farming, truck driving, and construction.
> *Intellectual.* These individuals are conceptually and theoretically oriented. They are thinkers rather than doers. Often they avoid interpersonal relations, and are best suited to careers in math and science.

Social, Emotional, and Personality Development

Social. These individuals often show characteristically "feminine" traits, particularly those associated with verbal skills and interpersonal relations. They are likely to be best equipped to enter "people" professions such as teaching, social work, counseling, and the like.

Conventional. These youth show a distaste for unstructured activities. They are best suited for jobs as subordinates, such as bank tellers, secretaries, and file clerks.

Enterprising. These boys and girls energize their verbal abilities toward leading others, dominating individuals, and selling people on issues or products. They are best counseled to enter careers such as sales, politics, and management.

Artistic. These boys and girls prefer to interact with their world through artistic expression, avoiding conventional and interpersonal situations in many instances. These youth should be oriented toward careers such as art and writing.

If all individuals fell conveniently into Holland's personality types, career counselors would have an easy job. But individuals are more varied and complex than Holland's theory suggests. Even Holland (1987) now admits that most individuals are not pure types. Still, the basic idea of matching the abilities and attitudes of individuals to particular careers is an important contribution to the career field (Brown, 1987). Holland's personality types are incorporated into the Strong-Campbell Vocational Interest Inventory, a widely used measure in career guidance.

Exploration, Decision Making, and Planning

Exploration, decision making, and planning play important roles in adolescents' career choices (Crites, 1989). In countries where equal employment opportunities have emerged—such as the United States, Canada, Great Britain, and France—exploration of various career paths is critical in the adolescent's career development. Adolescents often approach career exploration and decision making with considerable ambiguity, uncertainty, and stress (Fuqua, Blum, & Hartman, 1987; Neimeyer & Metzler, 1987; Schulenberg & others, 1988). Many of the career decisions made by youth involve floundering and unplanned changes. Many adolescents do not adequately explore careers on their own and also receive little direction from guidance counselors at their schools. On the average, it has been found that high school students spend less than three hours per year with guidance counselors, and in some schools the average is even less (National Assessment of Educational Progress, 1976). In many schools, students not only do not know what information to seek about careers, but do not know how to seek it.

Among the important aspects of planning in career development is awareness of the educational requirements for a particular career. In one investigation, a sample of 6,029 high school seniors from 57 different school districts in Texas was studied (Grotevant & Durrett, 1980). Students lacked knowledge about two aspects of careers: (1) accurate information about the educational requirements of careers they desired, and (2) information about the vocational interests predominantly associated with their career choices.

Sociocultural Influences

Not every individual born into the world can grow up to become a nuclear physicist or a doctor—there is a genetic limitation that keeps some adolescents from performing at the high intellectual levels necessary to enter such careers. Similarly, there are genetic limitations that restrict some adolescents from becoming professional football players or professional golfers. But there usually are many careers available to each of us, careers that provide a reasonable match with our abilities. Our sociocultural experiences exert strong influences on career choices from among the wide range available. Among the important sociocultural factors that influence career development are social class, parents and peers, and schools.

Social Class

In the prologue to this chapter, you read about Cleveland Wilkes, who grew up in poverty, and the barriers he faced in career development. Perspective on Adolescent Development 14.2 provides information about an adolescent from a more affluent family and his thoughts about careers and work. Social class is a powerful force in career development. The adolescent growing up in a New York city ghetto family has much less chance of entering a middle-class career than the adolescent whose parents live in an affluent suburb.

The channels of upward mobility open to lower-class youth are largely educational in nature. The school hierarchy from grade school through high school, as well as through college and graduate school, is programmed to orient individuals toward some type of career. Less than a hundred years ago, only eight years of education were believed to be necessary for vocational competence, and anything beyond that qualified the individual for advanced placement in higher status occupations. By the middle of the twentieth century, the high school diploma had already lost ground as a ticket to career success. College rapidly became a prerequisite for entering a higher status occupation. Employers reason that an individual with a college degree is a better risk than a high school graduate or a high school dropout.

Parents and Peers

Parents and peers also are strong influences on adolescents' career choices. Remember our discussion of David Elkind's belief that today's parents are pressuring their adolescents to achieve too much too soon. In some cases,

Social, Emotional, and Personality Development

Bobby Hardwicke's Career Dilemmas

Bobby Hardwicke, whose parents are professionals, attends a private school in the suburbs of Hartford, Connecticut. His home is luxurious, his future prospects (as his parents would say) limitless, and his manner charming. He is 17 years old. Ask Bobby a question and he will first demur, claiming he doesn't have much to say. If you can get him to open up, however, he will go on at length.

No one recognizes what people like me have to go through. I'm sure if you asked most people they'd say the life of a teenager is all fun. Everyone I talk to seems to want to be young again—which is one of the sicknesses of our culture. But no one sees teenagers for what we are. First off, teenagers, or whatever you want to call us, are people. Real, live people. I know that sounds strange, but you can't believe how many times I'm treated like I'm a thing. In stores, or the post office, I'm this one's son, that one's classmate, that one's student.

I'll go to college, although I think now the best thing for me would be to take a year out and work somewhere. I've never really worked—at something real, I mean. Something that would make the slightest difference to anybody. I've studied Latin for two years. I get A's. I get A's in history, European history. Okay, so I've done well, although I think anybody could do well at this place if they were halfway verbal. All the classes are small and we don't have that many exams, so all you have to do, like we always kid each other, is "talk good." "I talk good, Mrs. Arnold, so can I get a good grade now?"

So with all the studying and talking good, you know what I'd really like to do? Carpentry. I'd like to build a house, or fix someone's stairs or porch. Something real.

You know what it is? You go to a good school like this, it costs a lot of money, a whole lot, in fact, and all you think about is doing well so you can get into a good college, and because just going to college these days doesn't mean a thing, you ask yourself "What am I doing? What does any of this matter?" And the answer is, it doesn't matter at all. One course is only meant to get you to the next one, and then the one after that, and none of it makes the slightest bit of difference until you're all done. So you can look back and say, "Well I did it, I passed; so now what?" All school is, you know,

is the great time passer. It's all a big invention to keep kids from becoming anything. What can you become in this society, until you're thirty? You can't do anything real or worthwhile, no matter how many A's you get or how good you talk. Say I learned carpentry, like I learn all the other dilettante things I learn. Where would I get a job? Where do I get any worthwhile job for that matter, regardless of what I know or how well I do in school? And why should I get a job just to get a job? For the experience. That's what people say, for the experience. What experience? So you can learn how boring it is to park cars at a summer carnival place? Or take tickets at a movie theater? Is that supposed to get you anything?

There isn't anything people my age can do that matters in the slightest to anybody in this country unless you're a sensational athlete, and, even then, you have to be a gymnast or a swimmer. This country doesn't have the time or the place or the interest in young people. We're a waste to them, that's all. There isn't a single responsibility I could get at my age which the person giving it could honestly call worthwhile. Anything I could get to do could be done by a billion people; smarter people, dumber people, older, younger, it wouldn't make the slightest bit of difference.

When I'm twenty-five or thirty, I'll probably get jobs. And the jobs I get will be the exact same jobs I could do right now. No difference, except for one thing. When I'm thirty they'll say, "Well, you've worked hard for this, Mr. Hardwicke" or "Dr. Hardwicke, you've earned this, so here's your nice big adult job." But it's a fake. You know what they're really saying? They're really saying, you made it to twenty-five or thirty, so now you get the job and the status or whatever else you're supposed to get. But it's all a lie.

All it is, is a big age thing. From zero to twenty-five, you get the big runaround, the big zilch. From twenty-five on, or thirty—maybe it's getting later and later, for all I know—they let you in. You still don't have any great skills, but you got a few wrinkles. That's what they're looking for—wrinkles, signs of old age. Hey, if I suddenly went bald they'd let me in. I swear they would!

though, adolescents do not get challenged enough by their parents. Consider the 25-year-old female who vividly describes the details of her adolescence that later prevented her from seeking a competent career. From early in adolescence, both of her parents encouraged her to finish high school, but at the same time they emphasized that she needed to get a job to help them pay the family's bills. She was never told that she could not go to college, but both parents encouraged her to find someone to marry who could support her financially. This very bright girl is now divorced and feels intellectually cheated by her parents, who socialized her in the direction of marriage and away from a college education.

From an early age, children see and hear about what jobs their parents have. In some cases, parents even take their children to work with them on jobs. Recently, when we were building our house, the bricklayer brought his two sons to help with the work. They were only 14 years old, yet were already engaging in apprenticeship work with their father.

Unfortunately, many parents want to live vicariously through their son's or daughter's career achievements. The mother who did not get into medical school and the father who did not make it as a professional athlete may pressure their youth to achieve a career status that is beyond the youth's talents.

Many factors influence the parent's role in the adolescent's career development (Bogenschneider, 1989). For one, mothers who work regularly outside the home and show effort and pride in their work probably have strong influences on their adolescents' career development. A reasonable conclusion is that when both parents work and enjoy their work, adolescents learn work values from both parents. Peers also can influence the adolescent's career development. In one investigation, when adolescents had friends and parents with high career standards, they were more likely to seek higher career status jobs, even if they came from low-income families (Simpson, 1962).

School Influences

Schools, teachers, and counselors can exert a powerful influence on adolescents' career development. School is the primary setting where individuals first encounter the world of work. School provides an atmosphere for continuing self-development in relation to achievement and work. And school is the only

Social, Emotional, and Personality Development

Hispanic adolescents at a job fair seeking information about careers. Improving adolescents' awareness of career options and educational requirements is an important agenda for our nation.

institution in our society presently capable of providing the delivery systems necessary for career education—instruction, guidance, placement, and community connections.

A national survey reveals the nature of career information available to adolescents (Chapman & Katz, 1983). The most common single resource was the *Occupational Outlook Handbook* (*OOH*), with 92% of the schools having one or more copies. The second major source was the *Dictionary of Occupational Titles* (*DOT*), with 82% having this book available for students. Less than 30% had no established committee to review career information resources. When students talked to counselors, it was more often about high school courses than about career guidance.

School counseling has been criticized heavily, both inside and outside the educational establishment. Insiders complain about the large number of students per school counselor and the weight of noncounseling administrative duties. Outsiders complain that school counseling is ineffective, biased, and a waste of money. Short of a new profession, several options are possible (William T. Grant Foundation Commission, 1988). First, twice the number of counselors are needed to meet all students' needs. Second, there could be a redefinition of teachers' roles, accompanied by retraining and reduction in teaching loads, so that classroom teachers could assume a stronger role in handling the counseling needs of adolescents. The professional counselor's role in this plan would be to train and assist teachers in their counseling and to provide direct counseling in situations the teacher could not handle. Third, the whole idea of school counselors would be abandoned and counselors would be located elsewhere—in neighborhood social service centers or labor offices, for example. (West Germany forbids teachers to give career counseling, reserving this task for officials in well-developed networks of labor offices.)

The College Board Commission on Precollege Guidance and Counseling (1986) recommends other alternatives. It believes that local school districts should develop broad-based planning that actively involves the home, school, and community. Advocating better-trained counselors, the Commission supports stronger partnerships between home and school to increase two-way communication about student progress and better collaboration among schools, community agencies, colleges, businesses, and other community resources.

Career Development and Gender

There has been a significant increase in the number of females entering careers previously thought to be appropriate only for males. Yet discrimination and inadequate opportunities for education affect the achievement levels of females (Eccles, 1987; Gutek, 1988; Tittle, 1988). Females have diminished the gap between male and female earnings in the 1980s, but significant disparities still exist. The gap is smallest for workers in their 20s, presumably because females and males have had access to similar education and job opportunities in recent years. Overall, the earnings for females who worked fulltime were 70% of those for males in 1986, up from 62% in 1979. More than half the remaining gap is explained by differences in factors such as education and work experience. Females are more than 3 times as likely as males to have had interruptions in their work experience. Forty-seven percent of females between the ages of 21 and 64 had spent 6 months or more without a job since their 21st birthday; only 13% of the males had experienced this gap. Reasons for interruptions included childbearing, child care, illness, disability, and unemployment.

How much progress have females made in moving into professions dominated by males? As shown in Figure 14.2, they have made some progress in the 1980s, but fields such as computer systems analysis, computer programming, electrical engineering, accounting, and law are still male-dominated.

Because females have been socialized to adopt nurturing roles rather than career or achieving roles, traditionally they have not planned seriously for careers, have not explored career options extensively, and have restricted their career choices to careers that are gender-stereotyped (Baumrind, 1989; Diamond, 1988). The motivation for work is the same for both sexes. However, females and males make different choices because of their socialization experiences and the ways that social forces structure the opportunities available to them (Astin, 1984).

As growing numbers of females pursue careers, they are faced with questions involving career and family. Should they delay marriage and childbearing and establish their career first? Or should they combine their career, marriage, and childbearing in their 20s? Some females in the last decade have embraced the domestic patterns of an earlier historical period. They have mar-

Figure 14.2 Females are entering professions such as engineering, once reserved almost exclusively for males.

ried, borne children, and committed themselves to full-time mothering. These "traditional" females have worked outside the home only intermittently, if at all, and have subordinated the work role to the family role.

Many other females, though, have veered from this time-honored path. They have postponed, and even forgotten, motherhood. They have developed committed, permanent ties to the workplace that resemble the pattern once reserved only for males. When they have had children, they have strived to combine a career and motherhood. While there have always been "career" females, today their numbers are growing at an unprecedented rate. More about the paths of two females appears in Perspective on Adolescent Development 14.3. Recent research reveals that high-ability juniors and seniors in college show a strong interest in combining career *and* family (Fassinger, 1985).

The Life and Career Paths of Joanne and Joan

The life paths of Joanne and Joan were very different. Joanne grew up in a typical American family. While her father earned only a modest wage as a repairman, her mother stayed home to rear their 4 children because both parents believed that full-time mothering for the children was more important than additional income. However, they hoped that Joanne would educate herself for a better life. But Joanne was more interested in dating than in schoolwork or in her part-time job at a fast-food restaurant. When she became pregnant at 17, she was happy to marry her boyfriend and to settle down in a role as a full-time mother. Two children, several brief and disenchanting sales jobs, and 10 years later, Joanne still finds satisfaction in full-time mothering. At times she feels financial pressure to give up homemaking for paid work and resents being snubbed when she says her family is her career. But every time she searches the want ads, she vividly remembers how much she disliked her temporary jobs. Since her husband earns enough money to make ends meet, the urge to go to work quickly passes. Instead, Joanne is seriously thinking about having another child.

Joanne's life history reflects the traditional model of female development: An adult woman chooses a domestic life for which she was prepared emotionally and practically since childhood. Approximately 20% of females from a variety of social class and family backgrounds are believed to follow this life course. These females are insulated from events that might steer them away from their expected paths. They are neither pushed out of the home by economic necessity or marital instability nor pulled into the workplace by enticing opportunities. Instead, they remain committed to the domestic role that they assume is the female's proper and natural place in society.

In contrast, consider Joan's path. Like Joanne, Joan assumed as a child that when she grew up she would become married, have children, and live happily ever after as a housewife. She harbored a vague wish to go to college, but her father thought females should not go to college, and as a low-paid laborer he could not afford to send her to college, anyway. Joan worked after high school as a filing clerk and married Frank, a salesman, 2 years later. Within 6 months of the ceremony, she was pregnant and planning to stay home with her young child. But things changed soon after her daughter was born. Unlike Joanne, she became bored and unhappy as a full-time mother. Taking care of the baby was not the ultimate fulfillment for Joan. Motherhood was a mixture of feelings for her— alternately rewarding and frustrating, joyful and depressive. Despite her reluctance to admit these feelings to anyone but herself, a growing sense of emptiness and the need for additional income spurred Joan to look for paid work. She took a job as a bank teller, perceiving it to be a temporary way to boost family income. But the right time to quit never came. Frank's income fell consistently short of their needs, and as his work frustrations mounted, their marriage began to falter. When Frank pressured Joan to have another child, she began to think more seriously about whether she wanted to remain married to Frank. Just when the marriage seemed unbearable, Joan's boss gave her a chance to advance. She accepted the advance and decided to divorce Frank. Today, more than a decade later Joan is dedicated to her career, aspires to upper-level management, and does not plan to remarry or expand her family beyond one child. Joan's life represents an increasingly common pattern among women—one of rising work aspirations and ambivalence toward motherhood. Like their traditional counterparts, these women grew up wanting and preparing for a domestic role, only to find that events stimulated them to move in a different direction. About one-third of women today seem to follow this life pattern. These women are more likely to experience unstable relationships with men, unanticipated opportunities for job advancement, economic squeezes at home, and disappointment with mothering and full-time homemaking. As a consequence, heightened work ambitions replace their earlier home-centered orientation. Although Joanne and Joan experienced similar childhood backgrounds and aspirations, their lives diverged increasingly as they were confronted with the opportunities and restrictions of adolescence, youth, and early adulthood.

Some of the brightest and most gifted females do not have achievement and career aspirations that match their talents. One investigation found that high-achieving females had much lower expectations for success than high-achieving males (Stipak & Hoffman, 1980). In the gifted research program at Johns Hopkins University, many mathematically precocious females did select scientific and medical careers, although only 46% aspired to a full-time career compared to 98% of the males (Fox, Brody, & Tobin, 1979).

To help talented females redirect their life paths, some high schools are using programs developed by colleges and universities. Project CHOICE (Creating Her Options In Career Education) was designed by Case Western University to detect barriers in reaching one's potential. Gifted 11th-grade females received individualized counseling that included interviews with female role models, referral to appropriate occupational groups, and information about career workshops. A program at the University of Nebraska (Kerr, 1983) was successful in encouraging talented female high school students to pursue more prestigious careers. This was accomplished through individual counseling and participation in a "Perfect Future Day," in which girls shared their career fantasies and discussed barriers that might impede their fantasies. Internal and external constraints were evaluated, gender-role stereotypes were discouraged, and high aspirations were applauded. While these programs have short-term success in redirecting the career paths of high-ability females, in some instances the effects fade over time—six months or more, for example. It is important to be concerned about improving the career alternatives for all female youth, however, not just those of high ability.

Work

One of the greatest changes in adolescents' lives in recent years has been the increased number of adolescents who work in some part-time capacity and still attend school on a regular basis. Our coverage of adolescents and work includes information about the sociohistorical context of adolescent work, the advantages and disadvantages of part-time work, bridging the gap from school to work, and an added chance for adolescents in the world of work.

Sociohistorical Context of Adolescent Work

Over the past century, the percentage of youth who work full-time as opposed to those who are in school has decreased dramatically. In the late 1800s, fewer than 1 of every 20 high school-aged adolescents was in school. Today more than 9 of every 10 adolescents receive high school diplomas. In the nineteenth century, many adolescents learned a trade from their father or some other adult member of the community.

One of the most sweeping changes in adolescent lives in the last two decades has been the increasing number of adolescents who go to school full time and work part-time. What are some of the positive and negative benefits of this adolescent style of life? Assume you are the parent of a 15-year-old adolescent who wants to work part-time and go to school full time. How would you respond?

While prolonged education has kept many contemporary youth from holding full-time jobs, it has not kept them from working on a part-time basis while going to school. Most high school seniors have had some work experience. In a national survey of 17,000 high school seniors, 3 of 4 reported some job income during the average school week (Bachman, 1982). For 41% of the males and 30% of the females, this income exceeded $50 a week. The typical part-time job for high school seniors involves 16–20 hours of work per week, although 10% work 30 hours a week or more.

In 1940, only 1 of 25 10th-grade males attended school and simultaneously worked part-time. In the 1970s, the number had increased to more than 1 of every 4. And, in the 1980s, as just indicated, 3 of 4 combine school and part-time work. Adolescents also are working longer hours now than in the past. For example, the number of 14–15-year-olds who work more than 14 hours per week has increased substantially in the last three decades. A

Social, Emotional, and Personality Development

similar picture emerges for 16-year-olds. In 1960, 44% of 16-year-old males who attended school worked more than 14 hours a week, but by the 1980s the figure had increased to more than 60%.

What kinds of jobs are adolescents working at today? About 17% who work do so in restaurants, such as McDonald's, Burger King, and the like, waiting on customers, cleaning up, and so on. Other adolescents work in retail stores as cashiers or salespeople (about 20%), in offices as clerical assistants (about 10%), or as unskilled laborers (about 10%) (Cole, 1981).

Do male and female adolescents take the same type of jobs and are they paid equally? Some jobs are held almost exclusively by male adolescents—busboys, gardners, manual laborers, and newspaper carriers—while other jobs are held almost exclusively by female adolescents—baby-sitters and maids. Male adolescents work longer hours and are paid more per hour than female adolescents (Helson, Elliott, & Leigh, 1989).

Advantages and Disadvantages of Part-Time Work in Adolescence

Does the increase in work have benefits for adolescents? In some cases, yes, in others, no. Ellen Greenberger and Laurence Steinberg (1981) examined the work experiences of students in four California high schools. Their findings disproved some common myths. For example, generally it is assumed that adolescents get extensive on-the-job training when they are hired for work—the reality is that they get little training at all. Also, it is assumed that youths—through work experiences—learn to get along better with adults. However, adolescents reported that they rarely felt close to the adults with whom they worked. The work experiences of the adolescents did help them to understand how the business world works, how to get and how to keep a job, and how to manage money. Working also helped adolescents to learn to budget their time, to take pride in their accomplishments, and to evaluate their goals. But working adolescents often have to give up sports, social affairs with peers, and sometimes sleep. And they have to balance the demands of work, school, family, and peers.

Greenberger and Steinberg asked students about their grade-point averages, school attendance, satisfaction from school, and the number of hours spent studying and participating in extracurricular activities since they began working. They found that working adolescents have lower grade-point averages than nonworking adolescents. More than 1 of 4 students reported that their grades dropped when they began working; only 1 of 9 said that their grades improved. But it was not just working that affected adolescents' grades—more importantly, it was *how long* they worked. Tenth-graders who worked more than 14 hours a week suffered a drop in grades. Eleventh-graders

TABLE 14.2   *Percentages of Unemployed Youths and Adults*

	Whites	Blacks and Other Minorities
Men 20 years and older	5.1	8.3
Women 20 years and older	3.5	10.2
Men 16 to 19 years old	14.1	34.8
Women 16 to 19 years old	13.9	35.9

Source: U.S. Department of Labor. Special Labor Force Report No. 218. (Washington, DC: U.S. Government Printing Office, 1979), p. 9.

worked up to 20 hours a week before their grades dropped. When adolescents spend more than 20 hours per week working, there is little time to study for tests and to complete homework assignments.

In addition to work affecting grades, working adolescents felt less involved in school, were absent more, and said they did not enjoy school as much as their nonworking counterparts. Adolescents who worked also spent less time with their families—but just as much time with their peers—as their nonworking counterparts. Adolescents who worked long hours also were more frequent users of alcohol and marijuana.

Some states have responded to these findings by limiting the number of hours adolescents can work while they are attending secondary school. In 1986, in Pinellas County, Florida, a law was enacted that placed a cap on the previously unregulated hours that adolescents could work while school is in session. The allowable limit was set at 30 hours, which—based on research evidence—is still too high.

The Transition from School to Work

In some cases the media have exaggerated the degree of adolescent unemployment. For example, based on data collected by the U.S. Department of Labor, 9 of 10 adolescents either are in school, working at a job, or both. Only 5% are out of school, without a job, and looking for full-time employment. Most adolescents who are unemployed are not unemployed for long periods of time. Only 10% are without a job for 6 months or longer. The major portion of adolescents who are unemployed are individuals who have dropped out of school.

Certain segments of the adolescent population, however, are more likely to be unemployed than others. For example, a disproportionate percentage of unemployed adolescents are black (Bowman, 1989). As indicated in Table 14.2, the unemployment situation is especially acute for blacks and other minorities

Certain segments of the adolescent population are more likely to be unemployed than others. A disproportionate number of unemployed adolescents are black. Special efforts are needed to help these unemployed adolescents bridge the gap between school and work, such as monitored work experiences.

between the ages of 16 and 19. The job situation has improved for black adolescents—in 1969, 44% of black adolescents were unemployed; today's figures indicate that about one-third are unemployed.

How can adolescents be helped to bridge the gap between school and work? For the adolescent bound for higher education and a professional degree, the education system provides ladders from school to career. Most youth, though, step off the education ladder before reaching the level of a professional career. Often they are on their own in their search for work. Recommendations of how the gap from school to work can be bridged were described briefly in Chapter 8, on schools, but are expanded on here (William T. Grant Foundation Commission, 1988).

Monitored work experiences should be implemented. This includes cooperative education, internships, apprenticeships, pre-employment training, and youth-operated enterprises. These experiences feature opportunities for youth to gain work experience, to be exposed to adult supervisors and models in the workplace, and to relate their academic training to the workplace.

Sandy Bonds

Sandy Bonds was 14 when she first left her mother's home in Maryland. She hitched a ride to Phoenix, where she planned to live with her father and finish high school. When things did not work out there, she moved on to Albuquerque. By the time she decided to settle down in Oregon, Sandy had lived in five different states in four years. She was 18 when she came to a city-operated youth center in Portland looking for help to find a job. Sandy had been out of school for more than two years, but she did not know much about the world of work:

> I've traveled around, but I haven't worked much, you know? 'Cause most of the time, I was livin' with a foster parent or with friends, and they were always tryin' to get me back in school. The only job I can really say I ever had was bein' like a housekeeper for five months for this one family I lived with in Washington. And I worked at Burgerville once for about two days. I always had it in my mind to work, but I didn't have any skills—didn't know what I wanted to work at, you know? I learned how to get by out on the street. But working—I just plain don't know much about it. I don't know what I could do with myself once I had the skills. (Snedeker, 1982)

Community and neighborhood services should be expanded. This includes individual voluntary service and youth-guided services. Youth need experiences not only as workers but as citizens. Service programs not only expose youth to the adult world, but provide them with a sense of the obligations of citizenship in building a more caring and competent society.

Vocational education should be redirected. With few exceptions, the vocational education of adolescents in the 1980s does not prepare youth adequately for specific jobs. However, its hands-on methods can provide students with valuable and effective ways of acquiring skills they will need to be successful in a number of jobs.

Incentives need to be introduced. Low motivation and low expectations for success in the workplace often restrict adolescents' educational achievement. Recent efforts to guarantee postsecondary and continuing education, guaranteed employment, and guaranteed work-related training for students who do well show promise of encouraging adolescents to work harder and be more successful in school.

Career information and counseling need to be improved. A variety of information and counseling approaches can be implemented to expose adolescents to job opportunities and career options. These services can be offered both in school and in community settings. They include setting up career information centers, developing the capacity of parents as career educators, and expanding the work of community-based organizations.

More school volunteers should be used. Tutoring is the most common form of school volunteer activity. However, adults are needed even more generally—as friends, as mentors for opening up career opportunities, and for assisting youth in mastering the dilemmas of living in a stressful time.

Improving education, elevating skill levels, and providing "hands-on" experience will help adolescents bridge the gap between school and work. We need to address the needs of youth if we are to retain the confidence of youth who have been brought up to believe in the promise of the American Dream (Grubb, 1989; Wilson, 1989).

An Added Chance

For most youth over the age of 18 who lack a high school diploma, more traditional schooling is probably not the solution. The following recommendations by the William T. Grant Foundation Commission (1988) describe an expanded array of opportunities for youth who are out of school and out of work.

Intensive academic skills training should be implemented in all employment training programs where they are not currently offered. The *Job Corps* is an intensive intervention that has been extensively evaluated and fine tuned. Though it is not for everyone, evaluations have indicated that the Job Corps increases earnings, enables its graduates to be employed longer, and gives society a net return of $1.46 for every tax dollar invested. *State and local youth corps* currently operate in 14 states and 12 cities. They incorporate various dimensions of the Job Corps experience. Other states and communities operate summer programs. An evaluation of the California Conservation Corps indicated that the work of the Corps provided a positive economic return. *Nonresidential pre-employment training* is accomplished by a number of national organizations that specialize in pre-employment training and basic skills remediation. Their efforts deserve further encouragement and support. *The Job Training Partnership Act's* potential for serving at-risk youth has not been adequately realized. Only 5% of eligible youth are currently being served. The *Armed Forces* also can be used more effectively. Although only 9% of all recruits lack a high school diploma, the proportion is likely to increase dramatically with the changing youth demographics. The Armed Forces should expand

Career Development and Work

Concept	Processes/Related Ideas	Characteristics/Description
Career development	Tomorrow's jobs for today's adolescents	The long-term shift from goods-producing to service-producing employment will continue. In the year 2000, nearly 4 of 5 jobs will be in industries that provide services.
	Theories of career development	Three prominent theories are Ginzberg's developmental theory, Super's vocational self-concept theory, and Holland's personality type theory.
	Exploration, decision making, and planning	Exploration of career options is a critical aspect of career development in countries where equal employment opportunities exist. Many youth flounder and make unplanned career choice changes. Students also need more knowledge about the education and ability requirements of various careers.
	Sociocultural influences	Involve social class, parents and peers, and schools. The channels of opportunity for lower-class youth are largely educational. Many factors influence the parent's role in the adolescent's career development. School counseling has been criticized heavily and recommendations have been made for its improvement.
	Career development and gender	There has been a tremendous influx of females into the labor force in recent years. Females have diminished the pay gap in the 1980s, but a gap still exists. Females also have increased their presence in occupations previously dominated by males. As greater numbers of females pursue careers, they are faced with questions involving both family and career. Special attention needs to be given to the career paths of the brightest and most gifted female adolescents, but not to the exclusion of promoting career exploration and options for all female adolescents.

programs to upgrade the academic and work skills of its members. To obtain maximum effectiveness for added-chance programs, coordination among agencies that serve youth needs to be improved.

At this point we have discussed many aspects of careers and work. A summary of these ideas is presented in Concept Table 14.2.

Summary

I. Motivation
Motivation focuses on why adolescents behave, think, and feel the way they do, with special consideration of the activation and direction of their behavior. Different views include drive-reduction theory, especially homeostasis, and Maslow's hierarchy of motives.

Concept	Processes/Related Ideas	Characteristics/Description
Work	Sociohistorical context	Adolescents are not as likely to hold full-time jobs today as their adolescent counterparts from the nineteenth century. While prolonged education has reduced the number of adolescents holding down full-time jobs, there has been a tremendous increase in the number of adolescents who work part-time and go to school.
	Advantages and disadvantages of part-time work in adolescence	Advantages include learning how the business world works, how to get and how to keep a job, how to manage money, learning to budget time, to take pride in accomplishments, and to evaluate goals. Disadvantages include giving up sports, social affairs with peers, and sometimes sleep, as well as balancing the demands of school, family, peers, and work. Grades, identity with the school, and school participation may be reduced when adolescents work long hours.
	The transition from school to work	In some cases adolescent unemployment has been exaggerated, but certain segments, such as minority group adolescents, face major unemployment problems. We should monitor work experiences, expand community and neighborhood services, redirect vocational education, introduce incentives, improve career information and counseling, and use more school volunteers.
	An added chance	For youth over 18 who lack a high school diploma, we should improve academic skills training in all employment training programs, upgrade the Job Corps, as well as state and local youth corps, continue nonresidential pre-employment training, increase the potential of the Job Training Partnership Act, and use the Armed Forces more effectively.

II. Attribution Theory and Intrinsic-Extrinsic Motivation

Attribution theory says that individuals are motivated to discover the underlying causes of behavior in their effort to make sense out of behavior. One basic set of attributions involves internal versus external causes. Attributions are not always accurate, as shown by the fundamental attribution error. Intrinsic motivation involves an underlying need for competence and self-determination. Extrinsic motivation involves external factors in the environment, especially rewards. Some of the most achievement-oriented adolescents are both intrinsically and extrinsically motivated.

III. Achievement in Minority Group Adolescents

Emphasis should be placed on cultural differences rather than cultural deficits. Researchers have shown that social class differences in achievement are greater than racial differences.

IV. Tomorrow's Jobs for Today's Adolescents

The long-term shift from goods-producing to service-producing employment will continue. In the year 2000, nearly 4 of 5 jobs will be in industries that provide services.

V. Theories of Career Development and Exploration, Decision Making, and Planning

Three prominent theories are Ginzberg's developmental theory, Super's vocational self-concept theory, and Holland's personality type theory. Exploration of career options is a critical aspect of career development in countries having equal employment opportunities. Many youth flounder and make unplanned career choice changes. Students also need to know more about the education and ability requirements of various careers.

VI. Sociocultural Influences

These involve social class, parents and peers, and schools. The channels of opportunity for lower-class youth are largely educational in nature. Many factors influence the parent's role in the adolescent's career development. School counseling has been criticized heavily and recommendations have been made for its improvement.

VII. Sociohistorical Context of Work

Adolescents are not as likely to hold full-time jobs today as their adolescent counterparts of the nineteenth century. While prolonged education has reduced the number of adolescents holding down full-time jobs, there has been a tremendous increase in the number of adolescents who work part-time and go to school.

VIII. Advantages and Disadvantages of Part-Time Work in Adolescence

Advantages include learning how the business world works, how to get and how to keep a job, how to manage money, learning to budget time, to take pride in accomplishments, and to evaluate goals. Disadvantages include giving up sports, social affairs with peers, and sometimes sleep, as well as balancing the demands of family, peers, school, and work. Grades, identity with the school, and school participation may be reduced when adolescents work long hours.

IX. The Transition from School to Work and an Added Chance

In some cases adolescent unemployment has been exaggerated, but certain segments, such as minority group adolescents, face major unemployment problems. We should monitor work experiences, expand community and neighborhood services, redirect vocational education, introduce incentives, improve career information and counseling, and use more school volunteers. For youth over 18 who lack a high school diploma, we should improve academic skills training in all employment training programs, upgrade the Job Corps, as well as state and local youth corps, continue nonresidential pre-employment training, increase the potential of the Job Training Partnership Act, and use the Armed Services more effectively.

Key Terms

motivation 491
drive 491
need 491
drive-reduction theory 491
homeostasis 492
competence motivation 492

hierarchy of motives 492
need for achievement 493
attribution theory 495
fundamental attribution error 496
intrinsic motivation 496

extrinsic motivation 496
developmental theory of career choice 500
career self-concept theory 502
personality type theory 502

Suggested Readings

Ames, R. E., and Ames, C. (Eds.). (1984). *Motivation in education.* New York: Academic Press.
   This book includes many ideas by leading scholars on the topic of achievement orientation. A number of chapters are devoted to ideas on attributions.
Applied Psychology: An International Review, 1988, Vol. 37.
   The entire issue of this journal is devoted to gender and career development. Special attention is given to the current status of female career development.
Career Development Quarterly
   This research journal has many articles that pertain to career development in adolescence. Go to your library and look through the issues of the last several years to get a feel for the kinds of issues that are interesting to researchers who study the nature of career development.
Occupational Outlook Handbook, 1988–89 Edition. (1988). Washington, D.C.: Bureau of Labor Statistics.
   A compendium of tomorrow's jobs for today's adolescents.
The William T. Grant Foundation Commission on Work, Family, and Citizenship (1988). *The forgotten half: Non-college-bound youth in America.* New York: The William T. Grant Foundation.
   Also recommended as reading for Chapter 8, Schools, this report focuses on ways our society can help adolescents at risk for career difficulties. Pay special attention to the transition from school to work and the added chance.

Disturbances, Stress, and Health

There is no easy path
leading out of life,
and few are the easy ones
that lie within it.

Walter Savage Landor,
Imaginary Conversations, *1824*

*R*obert Jones is 12 years old. He just smoked his first marijuana joint with two peers behind his school. Robert has been smoking cigarettes for almost a year now, and sometimes smokes a pack a day. Now he has decided to see what marijuana is like. He feels a little high, but not as much as he thought he would. The next day, Robert and his friends get together during lunch and smoke marijuana again—but this time Robert is not content with just one joint, so he smokes three. This time, he feels the effects more strongly, but he is alert enough to make it to his first afternoon class. The teacher, however, sounds a little fuzzy to him, and the next day he doesn't remember much of what was said in the class.

When we return to Robert's life at age 17, we find that he still is a marijuana user, perhaps best described as a daily user. He is fed up with school and says it doesn't have any meaning for him—about the only thing he enjoys about it is getting to see some of his friends. During the last two years, Robert has taken a curriculum oriented toward training him for work as a mechanic. But he is tired of not having much money— he comes from a lower-income background—so he decides to drop out of school. Robert finds a job with a garage, and he enjoys the money he is now making.

Robert never tried "hard" drugs like heroin, but he has experimented with cocaine and angel dust. He still smokes a pack of cigarettes a day and most days does one or two joints of marijuana, although he has learned not to smoke grass while he is at work. His boss caught him smoking a joint two weeks ago and told him if he ever caught him again he would fire him.

One of Robert's best friends in the seventh grade was Toby Adams. Toby is one of the boys with whom Robert smoked his first joint of marijuana. But while Robert has continued to smoke marijuana on a daily basis, Toby no longer does. He occasionally smokes a joint, but at most smokes about once every three or four weeks, usually at a party. Nonetheless, at 17 Toby is a fairly heavy user of alcohol. He had his first drink back in the seventh grade when one of his friend's older brothers bought them two six-packs of beer. Toby still drinks beer, but he likes vodka as well or better. At least every other weekend, Toby and some of his friends get together and drink—last Saturday night Toby had ten beers, but he is a little envious because his buddy Tom downed twelve.

Toby and Robert no longer hang around together—after the seventh grade they didn't see each other very often. Toby's parents moved to another city where his father had found a better job. Toby's family is middle-class and Toby plans on going to college. His parents know that he drinks; on more than one occasion in the last 6 months he has come home "smashed." The Adamses have tried different ways of handling Toby's drinking problem, but so far none have worked. When he gets out with his friends on weekends, he just can't seem to control his drinking.

Al, the third boy in the pot-smoking session back in the seventh grade, is now 18 years old. He is a junior, old for his class, because he was held back a year in the 10th grade. At the age of 15, Al got into some trouble: he was caught stealing a television from a neighbor's house. Al's arrest for the theft came after a long history of breaking into houses and stealing everything from tape recorders to jewelry. He missed a lot of school that year, and when he was in school, he spent much of his time daydreaming about the excitement he and his friends could get into after school.

In the eighth grade, Al had moved to another neighborhood. His parents had divorced and his mother could not afford to live in the same neighborhood where they had lived for 6 years. She rented a small apartment near her work in the city. His mother often didn't get home until 6:00 or 7:00 in the evening, and on weekends she liked to go out on dates or with one or two girlfriends. Al was virtually left to take care of himself most of the time. His mother was surprised when the police came to the door and revealed to her the many robberies Al had been involved in.

Two years ago Al and his mother moved again when his mother found a better job in another city. Things have gone better for Al in the last year. His mother remarried, and Al's new stepfather seems to care about helping Al. For the first time in years someone monitors whether Al is doing his homework and talks with him about what he is going to make out of his life. Al's grades are not great, but he is no longer flunking, and he even managed to get a B in history last semester. His stepfather has even convinced him to think about going to the local junior college after he graduates from high school. It seems Al's life is finally straightening out.

Problems and Disturbances

They cannot scare me with their empty spaces

Between stars—on stars where no human race is.

I have it in me so much nearer home

To scare myself with my own desert places.

Robert Frost, 1936

527

Annie and Arnie

Some mornings, Annie, a 15-year-old cheerleader, was too drunk to go to school. Other days, she'd stop for a couple of beers or a screwdriver on the way to school. She was tall and blonde and good-looking, and no one who sold her liquor, even at 8:00 in the morning questioned her age. Where did she get her money? From baby-sitting and what her mother gave her to buy lunch. Finally Annie was kicked off the squad for missing practice so often. Soon, she and several of her peers were drinking almost every morning. Sometimes, they skipped school and went to the woods to drink. Annie's whole life began to revolve around her drinking. It went on for 2 years, and during the last summer, anytime she saw anybody she was drunk. After a while, her parents began to detect Annie's problem. But even when they punished her, it did not stop her drinking. Finally, this year, Annie started dating a boy she really likes and who would not put up with her drinking. She agreed to go to Alcoholics Anonymous and has just successfully completed treatment. She has stopped drinking for 4 consecutive months now, and it is hoped that her abstinence will continue.

Arnie is 13 years old. He has a history of committing thefts and physical assaults. The first theft occurred when Arnie was 8—he stole a SONY walkman from an electronics store. The first physical assault took place a year later when he shoved his 7-year-old brother up against the wall, bloodied his face, and then threatened to kill him with a butcher knife. Recently, the thefts and physical assaults have increased. In the last week, he stole a television set and struck his mother repeatedly and threatened to kill her. He also broke some neighborhood streetlights and threatened youths with a wrench and a hammer. Arnie's father left home when Arnie was 3 years old. Until the father left, his parents argued extensively and his father often beat up his mother. Arnie's mother indicates that when Arnie was younger she was able to control his behavior, but in the last several years she has not been able to enforce any sanctions on his antisocial behavior. Because of Arnie's volatility and dangerous behavior, it was recommended that he be placed in a group-home with other juvenile delinquents.

*A*nnie and Arnie are two adolescents whose lives have developed serious problems. Their alcohol and delinquency problems are but two of the many problems and disturbances that can emerge in the adolescent's journey to maturity. Throughout this book we have focused on normal adolescents' development, though there have been many examples of adolescents with problems. In this chapter we look more closely at some of the major problems adolescents can develop. To begin, though, we discuss the nature of abnormality.

The Nature of Abnormality

At various points in history, malevolent gods, demons, witches, vampires, even the moon and planets have been identified as the culprits in adolescents' abnormal behavior. We no longer believe these supernatural forces are responsible for adolescents' disturbances. What do we believe *is* responsible?

Models of Abnormality

Attempts to define abnormality and search for its causes involve examining statistics, biological factors, psychological factors, culture, and experience.

When Ludwig von Beethoven was 6 years old he played concertos and trios at concerts. When Steffi Graf was 17 she already had become the number one women's tennis player in the world. Are these individuals abnormal or deviant? The **statistical approach** defines abnormal behavior as that which deviates substantially from the average. We don't ususaly think of Beethoven as abnormal because he was a musical genius or Graf as deviant because she is a masterful tennis player.

Every adolescent is deviant from another on certain dimensions. The fact that one adolescent likes classical music and her friends do not does not make her abnormal. It is in the areas of social behavior and thought that we look for statistical differences that might underscore abnormality. If an adolescent sits on the floor day after day uttering bizarre, confused statements while staring blankly at the wall, his behavior deviates dramatically from what is commonly displayed by adolescents in our culture.

Sometimes, though, statistical incidences may vary from one culture to another, or from one point in history to another within the same culture. Remember from our discussion of sexuality earlier in the text how the women of the Mangaian culture in the South Sea islands train young adolescent males in sexual techniques. The young males are then encouraged to practice their skills with young adolescent females. In the United States, we would consider such behavior abnormal. In the Mangaian culture it is the norm. Remember also our comments about opinions of masturbation from early in this century. Masturbation was thought to cause everything from warts to insanity, but less than 15% of today's adolescents think masturbation is wrong (Hyde, 1988).

Proponents of the biological approach believe that adolescents' abnormal behavior is due to some malfunctioning of their body. If adolescents are out of touch with reality, or are severely depressed, biological factors are believed to be the culprits. Today special interest focuses on the role of brain processes and drug therapy in understanding and treating adolescents' abnormal behavior. There is also interest in genetic factors.

The forerunner of the biological approach was the **medical model** (also called the disease model). The medical model emphasizes that adolescents' abnormalities are diseases or illnesses precipitated by internal body causes. From this perspective, adolescent abnormalities are called mental *illnesses* and the adolescents afflicted are *patients* in *hospitals* who are treated by *doctors*.

While the biological approach is an important perspective in understanding adolescents' abnormal behavior, many developmentalists believe it underplays psychological and sociocultural factors. Emotional turmoil, inappropriate learning, disordered thoughts, and inadequate relationships are of interest in the psychological and sociocultural approaches. The theories of socialization described in Chapter 2 provide insight about abnormal as well as normal behavior. The psychoanalytic and the behavioral and social learning perspectives contain valuable insights about the psychological and sociocultural determinants of adolescents' abnormalities. Advocates of the psychological and sociocultural approaches criticize the medical model because they believe it encourages labeling of mental disturbances. A label such as "juvenile delinquent" may persist even though the adolescent's behavior is temporary. Also the adolescent may accept the label and then display the abnormal behavior more frequently (Scheff, 1966; Szasz, 1977).

When considering adolescents' behavior, whether abnormal or normal, it is important to remember the complexity of adolescents and the multiple influences on their behavior. Neither the biological approach nor the psychological and sociocultural approaches can independently capture this complexity and the multiple influences (Powers, Hauser, & Kilner, 1989).

Adolescents' abnormal behavior results from an interplay of biological, cognitive, and environmental factors. Current areas of interest in studying biological factors are computer imaging techniques to discover abnormalities in adolescents' brain structure and functioning; the role of neurotransmitters in different mental disturbances; the use of drugs to treat abnormal behavior; and the degree to which disorders are inherited (Pardes & others, 1989).

Among the current areas of interest in studying cognitive factors are the roles of symbolic thought, decision making, planning, imagery, reasoning, memory, and problem-focused coping (Kendall & Watson, 1989). And among the current areas of interest in studying environmental factors are the importance of close relationships, especially family processes, support systems, reward and punishment, and the incidence of mental disturbances in different cultures and subcultures (Bowlby, 1989; Kazdin, 1989; Pinderhughes, 1989; Robins & Regier, 1989; Rogler, 1989).

Types of Adolescent Disturbances

The spectrum of adolescent disturbances is wide. The disturbances vary in their severity, developmental level, sex, and social class. Some of adolescents' disturbances are short lived; others may persist over many years. One

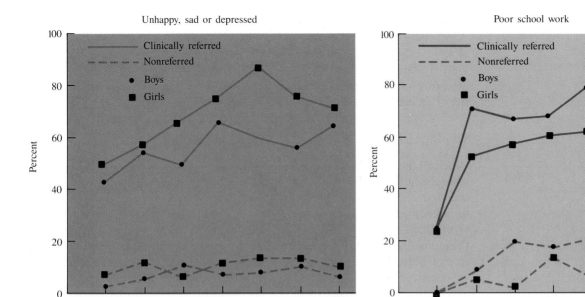

Unhappy, sad or depressed

Poor school work

Figure 15.1 The two items most likely to differentiate between clinically referred and clinically nonreferred children and adolescents.

13-year-old adolescent may show a pattern of acting out behavior that is disruptive to his classroom. When we look at his behavior as a 14-year-old he is assertive and aggressive, but the disruptive behavior has virtually disappeared. Another 13-year-old may show a similar pattern of acting out behavior. When we look at his behavior at age 16 he has been arrested for numerous juvenile offenses and is still a disruptive influence in the classroom.

Some disturbances are more likely to appear at one developmental level than another. For example, fears are more common in early childhood; many school-related problems surface for the first time in middle and late childhood; and drug-related problems become more common in adolescence (Achenbach, 1981). In one recent study, depression, truancy, and drug abuse were more common among older adolescents, while arguing, fighting, and being too loud were more common among younger adolescents (Edelbrock, 1989).

In the large-scale investigation by Thomas Achenbach and Craig Edelbrock (1981), adolescents from a lower-class background were more likely to have problems than those from a middle-class background. Most of the problems reported for adolescents from a lower-class background were undercontrolled, externalizing behaviors—destroying others' things and fighting, for example. These behaviors also were more characteristic of boys than girls. The problems of middle-class adolescents and girls were more likely to be overcontrolled and internalizing—anxiety or depression, for example.

The behavioral problems that most likely caused adolescents to be referred to a clinic for mental health treatment were those in which the adolescents felt unhappy, sad, or depressed, and were not doing well in school (see Figure 15.1). Difficulties in school achievement, whether secondary to other kinds of disturbances or primary problems in themselves, seem to account for most clinical referrals of adolescents (Weiner, 1980).

531

Drugs and Alcohol

Why do adolescents take drugs? How pervasive is adolescent drug use in the United States? What is the nature and effects of various drugs taken by adolescents? What factors contribute to adolescent drug use? These are among the questions we now evaluate.

Why Do Adolescents Take Drugs?

When Sigmund Freud experimented with cocaine he was searching for possible medical uses for the substance, among them a use in eye surgery. He soon found that the drug produced an ecstatic feeling and wrote to his fiancée to inform her of how just a small dose provided lofty, wonderful sensations. Over time Freud stopped taking cocaine, though, because it became apparent that some individuals experienced bad effects from the drug and several died from overdoses.

Since the beginning of history humans have searched for substances that would sustain and protect them and also act on their nervous system to produce pleasurable sensations. Individuals are attracted to drugs because drugs help them to adapt to an ever-changing environment. Smoking, drinking, and taking drugs reduce tension and frustration, relieve boredom and fatigue, and in some cases help adolescents escape the harsh realities of their world (Carroll, 1989). Drugs provide pleasure by giving inner peace, joy, relaxation, kaleidoscopic perceptions, surges of exhilaration, or prolonged heightened sensation. They may be useful in helping some adolescents get along better in their world. For example, amphetamines may help the individual stay awake to study for an exam. Drugs also satisfy adolescents' curiosity—some adolescents take drugs because the are intrigued by sensational accounts of drugs in the media, while others may listen to a popular song and wonder if the drugs described can provide them with unique, profound experiences. Drugs are taken for social reasons also, allowing adolescents to feel more comfortable and enjoy the company of others.

But the use of drugs for personal gratification and temporary adaptation carries a very high price tag: drug dependence, personal and social disorganization, and a predisposition to serious and sometimes fatal diseases (Gawin, 1989). Thus, what is intended as adaptive behavior is maladaptive in the long run. For example, prolonged cigarette smoking, in which the active drug is nicotine, is one of the most serious yet preventable health problems. Smoking has been described by some experts as "suicide in slow motion."

When a **tolerance** for drugs develops, the user needs a greater amount of the drug to produce the same effect. The first time an adolescent takes 5 milligrams of an amphetamine, it produces a rush of energy, but after taking the pill regularly for 6 months, 10 milligrams may be needed to achieve the same energizing effect.

When individuals stop taking drugs, it is not uncommon for them to experience **withdrawal.** The unpleasant effects of withdrawal can include intense

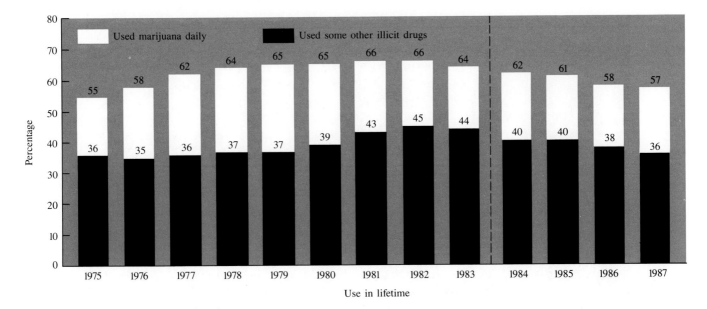

Figure 15.2   Trends in lifetime prevalence of an illicit drug use index.

Source: Illicit Drug Use, Smoking, and Drinking by America's High School Students, College Students, and Young Adults 1975–1979. *Lloyd D. Johnston, Patrick M. O'Malley, and Jerald G. Bachman. National Institute on Drug Abuse, 1982, Rockville, MD, figure 6, p. 54.*

pain and cravings for the drug. This occurs because the individual's body has developed a physical dependency on the drug, also known as addiction (Wise, 1988). In some instances, individuals become psychologically dependent on drugs, using them to cope with problems and stress in their lives. Let's now look at trends in overall drug use by adolescents in the United States.

Trends in Overall Drug Use

The 1960s and 1970s were a time of marked increases in the use of illicit drugs. During the social and political unrest of those years, many youth turned to marijuana, stimulants, and hallucinogens. Increases in alcohol consumption by adolescents during this period also were noted (Robinson & Greene, 1988). More precise data about drug use by adolescents have been collected in recent years.

Each year since 1975, Lloyd Johnston, Patrick O'Malley, and Gerald Bachman, working at the Institute of Social Research at the University of Michigan, have carefully monitored drug use by America's high school seniors in a wide range of public and private high schools. From time to time, they also sample younger adolescents' and adults' drug use.

An encouraging finding from the most recent survey (conducted in 1988) of 16,300 high school seniors is the continued gradual decline in the use of illicit drugs (Johnston, O'Malley, & Bachman, 1989). Nonetheless, the United States still has the highest rate of drug use among the world's industrialized nations. In 1987, 57% of the nation's high school seniors tried an illicit drug other than marijuana (see Figure 15.2). Let's now look at information about some of the specific drugs used by adolescents.

Alcohol abuse is one of adolescents' major problems. Especially disturbing is the high percentage of adolescents who drink heavily. Coupled with driving, excessive drinking by adolescents has led to an excessive number of adolescents who die in automobile accidents.

Alcohol

We usually do not think of alcohol as a drug, but it is an extremely potent one. Alcohol acts upon the body primarily as a depressant and slows down the brain's activities. However, in low doses, alcohol can be a stimulant (Prunell & others, 1987). If used in sufficient quantities it will damage or even kill biological tissues, including muscle and brain cells. The mental and behavioral effects of alcohol include reduced inhibition and impaired judgment. Initially, adolescents feel more talkative and more confident. However, skilled performances, such as driving, become impaired, and as more alcohol is ingested, intellectual functioning, behavioral control, and judgment becomes less efficient. Eventually the drinker becomes drowsy and falls asleep. With extreme intoxication, the drinker may lapse into a coma. Each of these behavioral effects varies with how the adolescent's body metabolizes alcohol, body weight, the amount of alcohol ingested, and whether previous drinking has led to tolerance (Baker, 1988; Cox & Klinger, 1988).

Alcohol is the most widely used drug by adolescents in our society. It has produced many enjoyable moments and many sad ones as well. Alcoholism is the third leading killer in the United States. Each year approximately 25,000 individuals are killed and 1.5 million injured by drunk drivers. In 65% of the aggressive male acts against females the offender has been under the influence of alcohol (Goodman & others, 1986). In numerous instances of drunk driving and assaults on females, the offenders have been adolescents. More than 13 million individuals are classified as alcoholics, many of whom established their drinking habits during adolescence.

Disturbances, Stress, and Health

How extensive is alcohol use by adolescents? During the recent decline in the use of marijuana and other drugs, there appears not to have been a displacement effect in terms of an increase in alcohol use. That is, adolescents do not seem to be drinking more to offset their reduced intake of drugs. Actually, alcohol use by high school seniors has gradually declined—monthly prevalence from 72% in 1980 to 64% in 1988, for example. The prevalence of drinking 5 or more drinks in a row during the prior two-week interval fell from 41% in 1983 to 35% in 1988. There remains a substantial sex difference in heavy adolescent drinking—28% for females versus 46% for males in 1986, although this difference has been diminishing gradually over the last decade. However, data from college students show little drop in alcohol use, and an increase in heavy drinking has occurred—45% in 1986, up 2% from the previous year. Heavy party drinking among college males is common and is becoming more common (Johnston, O'Malley, & Bachman, 1989).

Unfortunately, there are hundreds of thousands of adolescents with a serious drinking problem just like the 15-year-old cheerleader named Annie described in the Prologue. They live in both wealthy suburbs and inner-city housing projects. Annie grew up in a Chicago suburb and said she started drinking when she was 10 because her older brothers always looked like they were having fun when they were doing it. Researchers have found that young adolescents who take drugs are more likely to have older friends than their counterparts who do not take drugs (Blyth, Durant, & Moosbrugger, 1985). Adolescents also have strong expectancies, even more than adults, that alcohol will produce personal effects, such as tension reduction (McLaughlin & Chassin, 1985). It seems common for adolescents to use alcohol to reduce stress and tension in their lives. For adolescent males, a sense of power is also a strong motive.

Adolescent alcohol use also is related to parent and peer relations. Adolescents who drink heavily often come from unhappy homes in which there is a great deal of tension, and also from homes in which parents sanction alcohol use (Barnes, 1984). In one recent investigation, adolescents who were more insecurely attached to their parents were more likely to drink to facilitate social contact than their securely attached counterparts (Kwakman & others, 1988). And the peer group provides the social context for drinking and reinforces adolescent behavior that is learned as part of family socialization practices. The ability of the family to function as a support system seems to be an especially important factor in preventing heavy adolescent drinking.

A strong family support system is clearly an important preventive strategy in reducing alcohol abuse by adolescents. Are there others? Would raising the minimum drinking age have an effect? In one investigation, raising the minimum drinking age did lower the frequency of automobile crashes involving adolescents, but raising the drinking age alone did not seem to reduce alcohol abuse (Wagennar, 1983). Another effort to reduce alcohol abuse involved a school-based program in whch adolescents discussed alcohol-related issues with peers (Wodarski & Hoffman, 1984). At a one-year follow-up, students in the

Alcohol Abuse in Native American Youth

The problem of alcohol abuse in native American youth has grown in recent years. In one national survey, native American youth had a 42% problem-drinking rate compared to 34% for Anglo youth (Donovan & Jessor, 1978). There is not a single, concise answer to the problem of alcohol abuse in native American youth (Watts & Lewis, 1988). It is a complex problem, involving cultural, historical, educational, and economic circumstances. Proposed solutions include elements such as alcohol education and prevention programs that truly involve the local tribal community, programs that involve parents and youth, and economic development programs. Both family and community involvement especially deserve further examination (Edwards & Edwards, 1988; Oetting, Beauvais, & Edwards, 1988).

intervention schools reported less alcohol abuse and had discouraged each other's drinking more often than had students in other schools who had not been involved in the peer discussion of alcohol-related issues. Efforts to help the adolescent with a drinking problem vary enormously. Therapy may include working with other family members, peer-group discussion sessions, and specific behavioral techniques. Unfortunately, there has been little interest in identifying different types of adolescent alcohol abusers and then attempting to match treatment programs to the particular problems of the adolescent drinker. Most efforts simply assume that adolescents with drinking problems are a homogeneous group, and do not take into account the varying developmental patterns and social histories of different adolescents. Some adolescents with drinking problems may be helped more through family therapy, others through peer counseling, and yet others through intensive behavioral strategies, depending on the type of drinking problem and the social agents who have the most influence on the adolescent (Baker, 1988; Finney & Moos, 1979).

Hallucinogens

Hallucinogens—sometimes called psychedelic drugs—modify an individual's perceptual experiences. We will discuss three hallucinogens: marijuana, LSD, and the recent designer drug MDMA.

    LSD stands for the chemical lysergic acid diethylamide. Bodily effects may include dizziness, nausea, and tremors; perceptual effects may include hallucinations or misperceptions of time; emotional and cognitive effects may

Disturbances, Stress, and Health

(a)

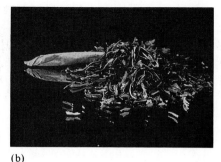
(b)

(c)

include rapid mood swings or impaired attention and memory. Use of LSD was higher in the late 1960s and early 1970s than today. In 1975, more than 7% of high school seniors had used LSD within the last 12 months; in the late 1980s use has averaged slightly less than 5%.

Marijuana, a milder hallucinogen than LSD, comes from the hemp plant, *Cannabis sativa,* which originated in central Asia but is now grown in most parts of the world. Marijuana is made of the hemp plant's dry leaves. Its dried resin is known as hashish (see Figure 15.3). The active ingredient in marijuana is THC, which stands for the chemical delta-9-tetrahydrocannabinol. This ingredient does not resemble the chemicals of other psychoactive drugs and the brain processes affected by marijuana remain mostly uncharted. Because marijuana metabolizes slowly, its effects may be present over the course of several days (Gong & others, 1988; Morgan, 1988).

The physical effects of marijuana include increases in pulse rate and blood pressure, reddening of the eyes, coughing, and dryness of the mouth. Chronic marijuana use also is harmful to the lungs (Fligiel & others, 1988). When marijuana is used daily in heavy amounts it can impair the human reproductive system and may be involved in some birth defects. Psychological effects include a mixture of excitatory, depressive, and hallucinatory characteristics, making it difficult to classify the drug. Marijuana can produce spontaneous unrelated ideas; distorted perceptions of time and place can occur; verbal behavior may increase or cease to occur at all; and there may be increased sensitivity to sounds and colors. Marijuana also can impair attention and memory, suggesting that smoking marijuana is not conducive to optimal school performance (Gieringer, 1988).

Marijuana continues to be a controversial drug in the legal realm. In 1968, under California law, possession of marijuana for personal use was a felony carrying a penalty of 1–10 years of prison on first offense and up to life imprisonment on the third offense. That situation changed dramatically in 1976 when a new California law reduced the possession of an ounce or less of marijuana to a misdemeanor with a maximum fine of $100. Laws for marijuana vary from one state to another, and groups such as the National Organization for the Reform of Marijuana Laws (NORML) continue to push for more lenient legal penalities (Mathre, 1988).

Figure 15.3 (*a*) Hemp plants growing in the wild; marijuana is made of the hemp plant's dry leaves. (*b*) Loose marijuana and a rolled joint. (*c*) Hashish, the dried resin of the hemp plant.

Problems and Disturbances

537

The daily smoking rate of adolescents dropped very little in the last half of the 1980s. A full one-third of high school seniors still do not feel there is a great risk associated with smoking.

"I'll tell you one thing. As soon as I'm thirteen I'm gonna stop!"
Reprinted by permission: Tribune Media Services.

Another drug with mildly hallucinogenic qualities is **MDMA,** chemically labeled methyllene dioxy-metaamphetamine, which has become known as one of the "designer drugs." These drugs are made by chemically reengineering an existing controlled substance to create a drug that is currently legal (Beck & Morgan, 1986). MDMA is known by a variety of street names, among them Ecstasy, Adam, and XTC. It has properties related to marijuana and the amphetamines, producing both mild hallucinogenic and strong stimulant effects.

Stimulants

Stimulants increase the activity of the central nervous system. They also increase heart rate, breathing, and temperature, but decrease appetite. Stimulants increase our energy, lessen our fatigue, and lift our mood. Nicotine (the psychoactive ingredient in cigarettes), amphetamines, and cocaine—all stimulants—have been widely used by adolescents.

Cigarette smoking is one of the most serious yet preventable health problems (Miller & Slap, 1989). Smoking is most likely to begin in grades 7 through 9, although sizable portions of youth are still establishing regular smoking habits during high school and college. Since the national surveys by Johnston, Bachman, and O'Malley began in 1975, cigarettes have been the substance most frequently used by high school seniors on a daily basis. While their daily smoking rate did drop considerably between 1977 and 1981 (from 29% to 20%), it has dropped little in the last 5 years (only by another 1.6%). A full one-third of high school seniors still do not feel there is a great risk associated with smoking.

Disturbances, Stress, and Health

Amphetamines are widely prescribed stimulants, sometimes appearing in the form of diet pills. They also are referred to as pep pills or uppers. There has recently been a sizable decrease in amphetamine use among high school seniors, college students, and adults (Johnston, O'Malley, & Bachman, 1989). Since 1982, annual use of amphetamines has fallen from 20% to 13% among high school seniors and from 21% to 10% among college students. However, there has been a sharp increase in the use of over-the-counter stay-awake pills, which usually contain caffeine as their active ingredient. Their annual prevalence has risen from 12% in 1982 to more than 20% in 1986 and 1987. Two other classes of stimulants—"look alikes" and over-the-counter diet pills—actually declined in use in recent years. Still, 40% of females have tried diet pills by the end of their senior year in high school, and 10% have tried them within the last month.

Did you know that cocaine was an ingredient in Coca-Cola? Of course, it has long since been removed from the soft drink. **Cocaine** comes from the coca plant, native to Bolivia and Peru. For many years Bolivians and Peruvians chewed on the plant to increase their stamina. Today cocaine is either snorted, smoked, or injected in the form of crystals or powder. The effect is a rush of euphoric feelings, which eventually wear off and are followed by depressive feelings, lethargy, insomnia, and irritability.

Cocaine is a highly controversial drug. Users claim it is exciting, makes them feel good, and increases their confidence. Yet it is clear that cocaine has potent cardiovascular effects and is potentially addictive. The recent deaths of sports stars, such as University of Maryland basketball player Len Bias, reveal how lethal cocaine can be. When the drug's impact is severe, it can produce a heart attack, a stroke, or a brain seizure. The increase in cocaine-related deaths often is traced to very pure or tainted forms of the drug, which was the case in Bias's death (Gold, Gallanter, & Stimmel, 1987).

How many individuals take cocaine? Figures vary, but estimates range as high as 5 million regular users and 20 million casual users (Smith, 1986). Encouraging news is that in 1987—for the first time in 8 years—there was a significant drop in cocaine use among high school seniors and college students. Eight percent of high school seniors used cocaine at least once a year in 1988, down from 13% annual prevalence in 1986. Cocaine use by college students also declined from 17.1% annual prevalence in 1986 to 10% in 1988. A growing proportion of high school seniors and college students are reaching the conclusion that cocaine use entails considerable, unpredictable risk. Still, the percentage of adolescents and young adults who use cocaine is precariously high. About 1 of every 6 high school seniors has tried cocaine at least once and 1 in 18 has tried crack cocaine specifically. The trends in lifetime, annual, and 30-day prevalence of cocaine use by high school seniors from 1975 to 1987 is shown in Figure 15.4. As can be seen, while a drop in cocaine use occurred in 1987, prevalence is still very high in comparison to use in the 1970s. And for students who drop out of high school, cocaine use is estimated to be higher.

While adolescent drug use among high school seniors has dropped slightly in recent years, the United States still has the highest rate of drug use by adolescents of any industrialized nation. Shown here is a drug dealer selling cocaine to adolescents.

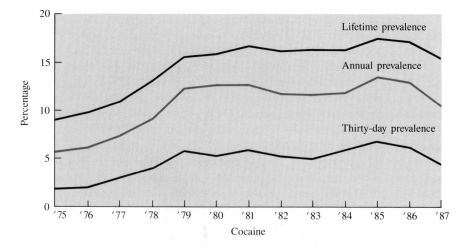

Figure 15.4   Trends in lifetime, annual, and thirty-day prevalence of cocaine.

Source: Illicit Drug Use, Smoking, and Drinking by America's High School Students, College Students, and Young Adults 1975–1979. *Lloyd D. Johnston, Patrick M. O'Malley, and Jerald G. Bachman. National Institute on Drug Abuse, 1982, Rockville, MD, figure 9.E, p. 65.*

A troublesome part of the cocaine story rests in the dangerous shift in how it is administered, due in large part to the advent of crack cocaine—an inexpensive, purified, smokeable form of the drug. The proportion of high school seniors who said they had smoked cocaine more than doubled between 1983 and 1986, from 2.5% to 6%. For the first time, in 1986, seniors were asked specifically about crack use. In 1986 and 1987, 4% said they had used crack cocaine in the prior 12 months. Crack use was especially heavy among noncollege-bound youth in urban settings. Some good news about crack use appeared in the 1988 national survey by Johnston, O'Malley, & Bachman (1989). Use of crack cocaine by high school seniors began to decline—from 4% annual use in 1987 to 3% annual use in 1988.

Depressants

Depressants slow down the activity of the central nervous system. Other than alcohol, which we already have discussed, the depressants most commonly taken by adolescents are barbiturates and Quaaludes. There are more than 2,500 different synthetic barbiturates, divided into two main categories—the "long-acting" barbiturates, dispensed for nighttime use as a sedative or sleep inducer, and the short-acting barbiturates, used in the daytime as tranquilizers to relax highly anxious adolescents. The long-term barbiturates appear to be only moderately addictive, but the short-term ones are very addictive. Taken in large enough doses, the short-term barbiturates produce a sensation similar to alcohol, removing adolescents' inhibitions and relaxing them at the same time. These drugs are especially dangerous when taken with alcohol. Another dangerous combination is the alternation of depressants and stimulants.

Since the initial surveys of drug use by high school seniors, begun in 1975, there has been a decrease in the use of depressants. For example, annual use of barbiturates in 1975 was 10.7%. In 1988 it was only 3.2%. Over the

Disturbances, Stress, and Health

same period of time, tranquilizer use was down from 10.6% to 4.8% annual use. **Quaaludes** (methaqualone) are hypnotic sedatives that have been used by adolescents in recent years. Their use by adolescents peaked in 1981 (7.6% annual use) but has declined since that time (1.3% annual use in 1988).

Heroin

Heroin, a derivative of opium, is a dangerous drug. If taken in sufficient quantities, it can be toxic. Even after just one month of use, an adolescent can become physically addicted to heroin. This means that the adolescent has to continue taking the drug to avoid painful withdrawal symptoms. Heroin is widely perceived by adolescents as having the greatest risk of harm for the user. Its low use reflects this perception—annual use was 1% in 1975 by high school seniors, a percentage that dropped even further by 1988 (to 0.5%).

Inhalants

Inhalants include any aerosol or gaseous fumes, other than smoke, that are inhaled to make the user feel good, high, or intoxicated. The recency of their popularity is indicated by the fact that it was not until 1976 that the Institute of Social Research at the University of Michigan added inhalants to its list of drugs. The two classes of inhalants that have been used most by adolescents are called amyl nitrites, also known as "poppers" and "snappers," and butyl nitrites, known sometimes as "locker room" or "rush." Adolescents usually cannot remember what happened to them while they were intoxicated with the inhalant. Some deaths have been attributed to the use of inhalants, but for the most part, these deaths actually resulted from the youth placing a plastic bag over the head to enhance the effects of the inhalant rather than from the inhalant itself. Use of inhalants by high school seniors has increased in recent years—from slightly more than 6% annual prevalence in 1981 to more than 7% annual prevalence in 1987 (Johnston, Bachman, & O'Malley, 1988). Another drug that has been increasingly used by adolescent males is steroids, the topic of Perspective on Adolescent Development 15.1.

The Role of Parents, Peers, and Schools in Adolescent Drug Use

Most adolescents become drug users at some point in their development, whether limited to alcohol, caffeine, and cigarettes or extended to marijuana, cocaine, and hard drugs. A special concern occurs when adolescents use drugs as a way of coping with stress, which can interfere with the development of competent coping skills and responsible decision making. Researchers have found that when drug use occurs in childhood or early adolescence it has more detrimental long-term effects on the development of responsible, competent behavior than when drug use occurs in late adolescence (Newcomb & Bentler, 1989). By using drugs to cope with stress, young adolescents often enter adult roles of marriage and work prematurely without adequate socioemotional growth and experience greater failure in adult roles.

Parents, peers, and schools play important roles in preventing and reducing drug abuse by adolescents. Earlier we indicated the family's importance as a support system in reducing adolescent drinking. Families do have a very important role in adolescent drug use. In one recent longitudinal investigation, undercontrol by boys at age 4 was related to their drug use in adolescence, and permissive parenting in the families of girls at age 4 was related to their drug use in adolescence (Block & Block, 1988). And in another recent investigation, social support during adolescence substantially reduced drug use (Newcomb & Bentler, 1988). In this study, social support included good relationships with parents, siblings, adults, and peers. Multiple drug use in adolescence was related to drug and alcohol problems, health problems, and family problems in early adulthood. Another researcher found that the greatest use of drugs by adolescents takes place when both the adolescent's parents take drugs (such as tranquilizers, amphetamines, alcohol, or nicotine) and the adolescent's peers take drugs (Kandel, 1974).

Schools are involved in drug use because they frequently are the location where peers initiate and maintain drug use. Schools can play an important role in preventing or reducing drug use—there are few other settings where the adolescent population congregates on such a frequent basis. Although most schools have established policies on drug use, some have gone further and developed drug prevention or intervention programs (Bailey, 1989; Minuchin &

The Anabolic Steroid Crisis

Anabolic steroids are synthetic derivatives of male hormones. Initially, anabolic steroids were prescribed by doctors to help rehabilitate muscles, but more recently they have been prescribed for treating anemia. The current controversy over anabolic steroids focuses on their widespread use to improve athletic performance and develop a better body build.

In a recent investigation of 3,403 male seniors in 46 high schools, 6.6% reported that they had used anabolic steroids (Buckley & others. 1988). That figure translates to an estimated half a million adolescent boys using anabolic steroids in the United States. Nearly half the boys who admitted using steroids said they did so to improve their athletic performance. About 10% said they used steroids to treat sports-related injuries. However, 35% of the users said they did not participate in school sports. And 27% said they took pills or injected the drugs to improve muscular appearance. Almost half of the boys "stacked" the drugs—that is, used more than one steroid at a time. More than one-third started using the drugs by age 15, another one-third by age 16. Approximately 20% got the drugs from a doctor, pharmacist, or a veterinarian; almost two-thirds got them from black market sources such as athletes and coaches.

Why are health experts so concerned about the increased use of anabolic steroids? There are a number of negative side effects associated with the drugs:

1. Hair growth, baldness in females
2. Acne in males and females
3. High blood pressure, clogging of arteries
4. Liver cancer in males and females; prostate cancer in males
5. Increased hostility, aggressiveness, hypertension
6. Breast growth in males; breast cancer and decreased breast size in females
7. Sterility or atrophied testicles in males; menstrual irregularities and enlarged genitals in females

Shapiro, 1983). The most promising school programs are those that have involved comprehensive long-term approaches, not only providing specific information and services, but dealing with the social organization of the school as a whole. Programs that have emphasized detection, discipline, and scare tactics have been the least effective in preventing or reducing drug use by adolescents.

At this point we have discussed many ideas about the nature of abnormality, as well as drugs and alcohol. A summary of these ideas is presented in Concept Table 15.1.

The Nature of Abnormality and Drugs and Alcohol

Concept	Processes/Related Ideas	Characteristics/Description
Nature of abnormality	Models of abnormality	Include the statistical approach, the biological approach and medical model, and psychological and sociocultural approaches. Adolescents' abnormal behavior is the result of an interplay of biological, cognitive, and environmental factors.
	Types of adolescent disturbances	The spectrum of disturbances is wide, varying in severity, developmental level, sex, and social class. Middle-class and female adolescents are more likely to have internalizing problems, lower-class and male adolescents externalizing problems.
Drugs and alcohol	Why do adolescents take drugs?	Drugs have been used since the beginning of human existence for pleasure, for utility, out of curiosity, and for social reasons. Tolerance for many drugs develops, and it is not unusual for users to experience withdrawal when they have taken a drug extensively.
	Trends in overall drug use	The 1960s and 1970s were a time of marked increase in the use of illicit drugs. An encouraging finding is that beginning in the mid-1980s, there was a downturn in illicit drug use by high school seniors. Nonetheless, the United States still has the highest adolescent drug use rate of any industrialized nation.
	Alcohol	Is primarily a depressant; in low dosages can act as a stimulant. It has produced many enjoyable as well as many sad moments for adolescents. Many automobile deaths and aggressive attacks on females are associated with alcohol use. Alcohol is the most widely used drug by adolescents. Alcohol abuse is a major adolescent problem. Alcohol use by the nation's high school seniors has slightly declined in recent years, but heavy drinking is still common. A strong family support system is an important factor in helping adolescents cope with a drinking problem.
	Hallucinogens	Hallucinogens modify an individual's perceptual experiences. These include LSD, marijuana, and MDMA. LSD is the strongest hallucinogen of the three, the latter two being more mildly

Juvenile Delinquency

In the Prologue to this chapter you read about 13-year-old Arnie, who had a history of thefts and physical assaults. Arnie is a juvenile delinquent. What is a juvenile delinquent? What causes juvenile delinquency? What is delinquency's developmental course? What types of interventions have been used to prevent or reduce delinquency? We consider each of these questions in turn.

Concept	Processes/Related Ideas	Characteristics/Description
Drugs and alcohol (continued)	Hallucinogens (continued)	hallucinogenic. Marijuana use has declined substantially among adolescents in the 1980s. It still is a controversial drug in the legal realm. MDMA is one of the designer drugs.
	Stimulants	Increase the activity of the central nervous system. Nicotine, amphetamines, and cocaine are three stimulants widely used by adolescents. Cigarette smoking (nicotine is the active drug) has declined but, in view of its health hazards, remains a dangerous adolescent habit (most smoking habits are formed during adolescence). There has been a decrease in amphetamine use, although there has been a sharp increase in the use of over-the-counter stay-awake pills. Cocaine is a highly controversial drug. Its use by high school seniors dropped for the first time in 8 years in 1987, but a dangerous form of the drug—crack cocaine, which is smoked—is increasingly used.
	Depressants	Slow down the central nervous system's activity. The 1980s has seen a decline in their use by adolescents. Barbiturates, tranquilizers, and Quaaludes are commonly used depressants.
	Heroin	A derivative of opium, and a dangerous drug. Adolescents understand this and rarely take it. Even after just one month's use, heroin can become physically addictive.
	Inhalants	Include any aerosol or gaseous fumes, other than smoke, that makes the user feel good, high, or intoxicated. The use by adolescents has increased in the 1980s.
	Role of parents, peers, and schools in adolescent drug use	Parents, peers, and schools play important roles in adolescent drug use. Adolescent drug use is related to relationships with parents even in early childhood. Social support—including good relations with parents, siblings, adults, and peers—is associated with reduced drug use. The most promising school approaches are long term, not only providing specific services, but dealing with the social organization of the school as a whole.

What Is Juvenile Delinquency?

The label "juvenile delinquent" is applied to an adolescent who breaks the law or engages in behavior that is considered illegal. Like other categories of disturbance, juvenile delinquency is a broad concept; legal infractions range from littering to murder. Because the youth technically becomes a juvenile delinquent only after judged guilty of a crime by a court of law, official records do not accurately reflect the number of illegal acts committed. Nevertheless, there is still every indication that in the last 10 or 15 years, juvenile delinquency has increased in relation to the number of crimes committed by adults.

Information regarding the number of juvenile delinquents in the United States is sketchy, although FBI statistics suggest that at least 2% of all youths are involved in juvenile court cases. The number of girls found guilty of juvenile delinquency has increased significantly in recent years. Delinquency rates among blacks, other minority groups, and the lower class are particularly high in relation to the overall populations of these groups. However, such groups have less influence than others over the judicial decision-making process in the United States and thus may be judged delinquent more readily than their white, middle-class counterparts (Binder, 1987; Gold, 1987).

Some experts on delinquency believe that in defining delinquency, it is misleading to refer only to delinquency rates based on arrests. For example, one recently devised definition of delinquency is "behavior by a juvenile that is a deliberate violation of the law and is believed by the juvenile to make him or her liable to adjudication if it comes to the attention of a law-enforcement agency" (Gold & Petronio, 1980).

Measuring the pervasiveness of delinquency in adolescence is not as easy as it might seem. First, what constitutes a delinquent act must be defined. Not everyone would agree with the definition we have chosen, for example. Some might argue that the individual is not delinquent until proven so in a court of law. Delinquent behavior has usually been measured through self-reports by adolescents. In most cases care is taken to inform adolescents that their reports are completely confidential. This is clearly important because adolescents are not going to report that they have recently committed a delinquent act if they think their parents, school, or the legal authorities will find out.

What Causes Juvenile Delinquency?

We have seen that it is difficult to both define and measure delinquency. There also is lack of agreement about delinquency's causes. Proposed causes of delinquency have included biological instincts (delinquents at one time were even called "animals in captivity") (Hall, 1904); increased biological drive (McCandless, 1970); onset of sexual urges that increases peer contact and reduces parent-adolescent contact, a circumstance that increases acting-out behavior (Blos, 1962); manifestation of the search for identity (Erikson, 1968); failure in self-control (Ross, 1979); blocked cultural opportunities (Simons & Gray, 1989); and inappropriate family socialization (Patterson & Stouthamer-Loeber, 1984). Let's look in more detail at the roles of identity, self-control, and sociocultural influences.

Identity

Recall from our description of Erik Erikson's theory of development that adolescence is the stage when the crisis of identity versus identity diffusion should be resolved. Not surprisingly, Erikson's ideas about delinquency are linked to the ability of the adolescent to positively resolve this crisis. Erikson believes that at the time the biological changes of puberty are occurring, there are concomitant changes in the social expectations placed on adolescents by family, peers, and schools. These biological and social changes allow for two kinds of integration to occur in the adolescent's personality: (1) the establishment of a sense of consistency in life, and (2) the resolution of role identity, a sort of joining of the adolescent's motivation, values, abilities, and styles with the role demands placed on the adolescent.

Erikson believes that delinquency is characterized more by a failure of the adolescent to achieve the second kind of integration, involving the role aspects of identity. He comments that adolescents whose infant, childhood, or adolescent experiences have somehow restricted them from acceptable social roles or made them feel that they can't measure up to the demands placed on them may choose a negative course of identity development. Erikson describes this as "an identity perversely based on all those identifications and roles, which, at critical stages of development, had been presented to them as most undesirable or dangerous and yet also as most real" (1968, p. 197). Some of these adolescents may take on the role of the delinquent, enmeshing themselves in the most negative currents of the youth culture available to them. By organizing their lives around such a negative identity, they establish a continuity of self from one relationship and situation to another, so that they can imagine how they might behave, think, or feel even in encounters that never occur. Not only does their own behavior become predictable to themselves, but they become capable of predicting how others will act toward them. In this manner the delinquent's self-image and his or her perception of himself or herself in the peer group begin to fuse. As the adolescent finds support for such a delinquent image among peers, who themselves seek reciprocal support, the image is reinforced. Thus, for Erikson, delinquency is an attempt to establish an identity.

Self-Control

Juvenile delinquency also can be described as the failure to develop sufficient behavioral self-control. Some children fail to develop the essential controls that others have acquired during the process of growing up. Most youths have learned the difference between acceptable and unacceptable behavior, but juvenile delinquents have not. They may fail to distinguish between acceptable and unacceptable behavior, or they may have learned this distinction but failed to develop adequate control in using the distinction to guide their behavior. To understand the problem of delinquency, it is thus necessary to study different aspects of the development of self-control—for example, delay of gratification and self-imposed standards of conduct. Failure to delay gratification is related to cheating and to a general lack of social responsibility often revealed in delinquent behavior (Mischel & Gilligan, 1964).

Delinquents also may have developed inadequate standards of conduct. An adolescent about to commit an antisocial act must invoke self-critical thoughts to inhibit the tendency to commit the illegal action. These self-critical standards are strongly influenced by the models the youth experiences. Thus, adolescents whose parents, teachers, and peers exhibit self-critical standards can be expected to develop the self-control needed to refrain from an illegal

The incidence of juvenile delinquency is influenced by the community in which adolescents live. Getting into and staying out of trouble is a prominent feature of the lives of adolescents in some communities, especially low-income areas.

or antisocial act. Others, however, may be exposed to models who praise antisocial acts. For example, adolescents whose peer models praise or engage in antisocial deeds may follow their example, especially if family models of high conduct are lacking.

The expected consequences of negative actions also influence the youth's decision to engage in or refrain from delinquent behavior. When youth expect some sort of reward for delinquent behavior, they are more likely to perform the antisocial act than if they expect punishment. The expected rewards can take many different forms—the acquisition of stolen goods, for example, or high status in the gang or in neighborhood peer groups.

Whether or not adolescents engage in juvenile delinquency may also be affected by the competence they have achieved in different aspects of life. Consider youth who do well in academic subjects at school, who actively participate in socially desirable clubs, or who develop athletic skills. These youth are likely to develop a positive view of themselves and receive reinforcement from others for prosocial behavior. Most delinquents, however, have achieved few ego-enhancing competencies. Antisocial behavior is one way they can demonstrate self-competence and receive reinforcement from the delinquent subculture.

Sociocultural Influences

Among the most important sociocultural influences that have been studied as contributors to juvenile delinquency are social class and community influences, as well as family and peer influences (Henggeler, 1989). Although juvenile delinquency is less exclusively a lower-class problem than it was in the past, some characteristics of the lower-class culture are likely to promote delinquency. The norms of many lower-class peer groups and gangs are antisocial, or counterproductive to the goals and norms of society at large. Getting into and staying out of trouble in some instances becomes a prominent feature of the lives of some adolescents from lower-class backgrounds (Miller, 1958). Status in the peer group may be gauged by how often the adolescent can engage in antisocial conduct, yet manage to stay out of jail. Since lower-class adolescents have less opportunity to develop skills that are socially desirable, they may sense that they can gain attention and status by performing antisocial actions. Being "tough" and "masculine" are high-status traits for lower-class boys, and these traits are often gauged by the adolescent's success in performing delinquent acts and getting away with them.

The nature of a community may contribute to delinquency (Chesney-Lind, 1989). A community with a high crime rate allows the adolescent to observe many models who engage in criminal activities. And adolescents may see these models rewarded for their criminal accomplishments. Such communities often are characterized by poverty, unemployment, and feelings of alienation from the middle class. The quality of schools, funding for education, and organized neighborhood activities are other community factors that may be related to delinquency. Are there caring adults in the schools and neighborhood who can convince the adolescent with delinquent tendencies that education is the best route to success? When family support becomes inadequate, then such community supports take on added importance in preventing delinquency.

Even if adolescents grow up in high crime communities, their peer relations may influence whether they become a delinquent. In one investigation of 500 delinquents and 500 nondelinquents in Boston, Massachusetts, a much higher percentage of the delinquents had regular associations with delinquent peers (Glueck & Glueck, 1950). But even more than peers, family processes have stimulated thinking about delinquency's causes.

While there has been a long history of interest in defining the family factors that contribute to delinquency (Glueck & Glueck, 1950; McCord, McCord, & Gudeman, 1960; Rutter, 1971), the most recent focus has been on the nature of family support and family management practices. Disruptions or omissions in the parents' applications of family support and management practices are consistently linked with antisocial behavior by children and adolescents (Rosenbaum, 1989). These family support and management practices include monitoring the adolescent's whereabouts, using effective discipline for antisocial behavior, calling on effective problem-solving skills, and supporting the development of prosocial skills (Offord & Boyle, 1988).

The parents of delinquents are less skilled in discouraging antisocial behavior than the parents of nondelinquents (Snyder & Patterson, 1987). Parental monitoring of adolescents is especially important in whether an adolescent becomes a delinquent. In one investigation, parental monitoring of the adolescent's whereabouts was the most important family factor in predicting delinquency (Patterson & Stouthamer-Loeber, 1984). "It's 10 P.M., do you know where your children are?" seems to be an important question for parents to answer affirmatively. Family discord and inconsistent and inappropriate discipline also are associated with delinquency.

An important question is whether family experiences cause delinquency, are the consequences of delinquency, or are merely associated or correlated with delinquency (Rutter & Garmezy, 1983). The associations may simply reflect some third factor, such as genetic influences, the result of the disturbing effect of the child's behavior on the family, or may indicate that family stress may produce delinquency through some environmental effect. In a review of research on the family-delinquency link, Michael Rutter and Norman Garmezy (1983) concluded that family influences do have some kind of environmental influence on delinquency. The research by Gerald Patterson and his colleagues (Dishiou, Patterson, & Skinner, 1989; Patterson, DeBarsyhe, & Ramsey, 1989) documents that inadequate parental supervision, involving poor monitoring of adolescents, and inconsistent and inappropriate discipline are key family factors in determining delinquency.

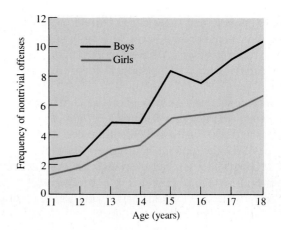

Figure 15.5 Mean frequency of nontrivial incidents committed by boys and girls eleven to eighteen years old.

Developmental Course

The National Survey of Youth (Gold & Reimer, 1975) asked 1,395 adolescents about their delinquent behavior. As indicated in Figure 15.5, the incidence of nontrivial acts rose from the early part to the later part of adolescence. The 18-year-old boys and girls confessed to about 5 times as many nontrivial delinquent acts as the 11-year-olds. Note that there was an acceleration of delinquent acts around the age of 15.

In other research, delinquent trends from adolescence through the beginning of early adulthood were charted (O'Malley, Bachman, & Johnston, 1977). Boys were tracked from the 10th grade through 23 years of age. Acts such as vandalism, theft, assault and threatened assault, shoplifting, armed robbery, and joyriding were considered to be delinquent. These behaviors declined from 16 to 18 years of age, rose at 19, then declined through age 23. In sum, it appears that serious delinquent acts decrease as adolescents make the transition to youth or early adulthood.

Do adolescents who commit serious delinquent acts become tomorrow's criminals? Adolescent delinquency and adult criminal activity are related— that is, adolescents who commit serious delinquent acts are more likely to become adult criminals than adolescents who do not commit serious delinquent acts (Johnston, O'Malley, & Eveland, 1978; Le Blanc & Fréchette, 1989). But the relation is not especially strong. Researchers also find that dropping out of school and illicit drug use increase the probability that the delinquents of adolescents will turn into the criminals of adulthood (Elliott, Huizinga, & Menard, 1989). Overall, though, being a delinquent in adolescence is not a good predictor of being a criminal in adulthood.

Prevention and Intervention

A large book could be filled with just brief descriptions of the varied attempts to reduce delinquency. These attempts include forms of individual and group psychotherapy, family therapy, behavior modification, recreation, vocational

Disturbances, Stress, and Health

training, alternative schools, survival camping and wilderness canoeing, incarceration and probation, "big brothers" and "big sisters," community organizations, and Bible reading (Gold & Petronio, 1980). However, we actually know surprisingly little about what actually does help reduce delinquency, and, for the most part, interventions have not been very successful. If they were successful, we would be seeing reduced delinquency rates, but we are not.

By far the most pervasive effort to reduce delinquency rests in the juvenile justice system. Since about 1900, juveniles have been treated differently than adults by the court system. The underlying belief is that children and adolescents, still in their formative years, are not as fully responsible for their actions as adults are. In this way, delinquency is viewed more as a mental illness than as criminality, and the guilt for the offense is not placed on the individual adolescent. Treatment for delinquents is generally designed to be more curative than punitive.

Nonetheless, in recent years, the juvenile justice system has gradually begun to move away from the developmental distinction that was made at the turn of the century. The Supreme Court's landmark decision in 1967 in the Gault case held that juveniles should be punished for their antisocial behavior, just as adults are punished for theirs (U.S. Supreme Court, 1967). Since that time, the juvenile justice system has begun to resemble the adult system more closely in such areas as right to counsel, rules of evidence, and self-incrimination. And, at the same time, there has been a movement to change the definition of juvenile delinquency so that it matches that for adult crime. If this definition were to become law, then running away from home, truancy from school, or frequenting immoral places, for example, would no longer be matters under the jurisdiction of the judicial system.

Arguments for change in the juvenile-delinquency system are rooted in the belief that the system was created to promote child and adolescent development. These arguments state that the freedom of too many adolescents

Reducing John's Delinquent Behavior

John is a 16-year-old black adolescent who was referred to a therapist by his probation officer for excessive truancy, failing grades, and conflict with his mother. Born out of wedlock to a teenage mother, John had a two-year history of minor deliquent offenses and was suspected of using drugs. His delinquent behavior began soon after the death of his grandmother, who had reared him while his mother worked in a nearby city. John was initially hostile and rude to the therapist. He said he didn't want to be there and was not going to cooperate. He arrived late, hummed songs, leafed through magazines, said he was wasting his time, and sarcastically answered questions in a condescending way.

Following several unproductive sessions, the therapist discovered that John had a collection of classic rock-and-roll records. He was encouraged to talk about the collection, which led to lively discussion of his musical interests and his desire to be a disc jockey. The development of a more positive relationship with John allowed the therapist to explore John's unresolved feelings of grief over the loss of his grandmother, who had been supportive of his schoolwork and interests. The therapist also contacted John's school counselor about creating a work-study plan that would permit John to work part-time at a radio station where he could develop his musical interests (Gibbs, 1989).

has been restricted based on insufficient evidence and for insufficient reasons, that treatment has been more punitive than curative, and that the overall effect of the judicial system has been to increase rather than decrease juvenile delinquency. There is actually good reason to believe that the juvenile judicial system does need to be overhauled, although there is little or no agreement on what should be done. For example, investigations usually show that the judicial system is either ineffective or at best neutral in effect (Gold & Petronio, 1980; Polier, 1989).

As mentioned earlier, there are many programs besides the judicial system that have been designed to reduce delinquency. Some of the programs work better than others. Let's look at one of the successful ones.

One intervention program that was effective in reducing the delinquency rate consisted of an alternative school in Quincy, Illinois (Bowman, 1959). Sixty boys in the eighth grade who were below average in ability and who were not doing well in school were selected for the study and randomly assigned to one of two groups. Forty of the boys were exposed to a curriculum different

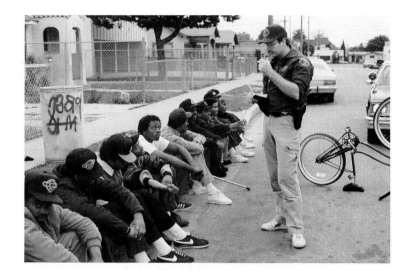

than the conventional one at the school, while the remaining 20 boys continued to attend conventional classes as a control group. The teachers of the two experimental classes were chosen because they seemed to have an interest in and sympathy for adolescents who get in trouble. The classes were small and the delinquents were given considerable individual attention. Student-teacher interaction was informal and friendly. Formal grading was abandoned, and each student was instead evaluated on the basis of his own progress. Discipline was firm but not punitive, and focused on problem solving. At the end of the school term, the students were given the opportunity to return to conventional classrooms. Only two chose to do so.

When compared with the control group of delinquents who remained in a conventional classroom, those in the experimental classrooms showed marked improvement. While they did not do better on standardized achievement tests, they perceived that they were doing better academically and said they now liked school better. Their attendance improved, while those in the control group attended school even less. School and police records documented that the antisocial and delinquency behavior of the experimental-group delinquents decreased by one-third, while the record for the control group tripled. And finally, a follow-up study suggested that the experimental boys made a better transition to the world of work than their control-group counterparts.

While the sources and styles of successful programs for delinquents vary, two themes seem to be dominant: (1) the support of warm, accepting relationships with adults; and (2) the enhancement of the adolescent's self-image as an autonomous and effective individual (Gold & Petronio, 1980).

A recent, special concern in delinquency is escalating gang violence, which is being waged on a level more lethal than ever before. Knives and clubs have been replaced by grenades and automatic weapons, frequently purchased with money made from selling drugs. The lure of gang membership is powerful, especially for children and adolescents who are disconnected from family,

Frog and Dolores

He goes by the name of Frog. He is the cocky prince of the barrio in East Los Angeles. He has street smarts. Frog happily smiles as he talks about raking in $200 a week selling crack cocaine. He proudly details his newly acquired membership in a violent street gang, the Crips. Frog brags about using his drug money to rent a convertible on weekends, even though at less than 5 feet in height he can barely see over the dashboard. Frog is 13 years old.

With the advent of crack, juvenile arrests in New York City tripled from 1983 to 1987 and almost quadrupled in the same time frame in Washington, D.C. Adults who founded the crack trade recognized early on that young adolescents do not run the risk of mandatory jail sentences that courts hand out to adults. Being a lookout is the entry level position for 9- and 10-year-olds. They can make as much as $100 a day warning dealers that police are in the area. The next step up the ladder is as a runner, a job that can pay as much as $300 a day. A runner transports drugs to the dealers on the street from makeshift factories where cocaine powder is cooked into rock-hard crack. And, at the next level, older adolescents can reach the status of dealer. In a hot market like New York City, they can make over $1000 a day.

The escalating drug-related gang violence is difficult to contain or reduce. Police crackdowns across the country seem to have had a minimal impact. In a recent weekend-long raid of drug-dealing gangs in Los Angeles, police arrested 1,453 individuals, including 315 adolescents. Half had to be released for lack of evidence. The Los Angeles County juvenile facilities are designed to house 1,317. Today more than 2,000 adolescents are overflowing their facilities.

Counselors, school officials, and community workers report that it is extremely difficult to turn around the lives of children and adolescents involved in drug-related gang violence. When impoverished children can make $100 a day, it is hard to wean them away from gangs. Federal budgets for training and employment programs, which provide crucial assistance to disadvantaged youth, have been reduced dramatically.

However, in Detroit, Michigan, Dolores Bennett has made a difference. For 25 years, she has worked long hours trying to find things to keep children from low-income families busy. Her activities have led to the creation of neighborhood sports teams, regular fairs and picnics, and an informal job-referral service for the children and youth in her neighborhood. She also holds many casual get-togethers for the youth in her small, tidy yellow frame house. The youth talk openly and freely about their problems and their hopes, knowing that Dolores will listen. Dolores says that she has found being a volunteer to be priceless. On the mantel in her living room are hundreds of pictures of children and adolescents with whom she has worked. She points out that most of them did not have someone in their homes who would listen to them and give them love. Our nation needs more Dolores Bennetts.

school, work, and the community. Children as young as 9–10 years of age cling to the fringes of neighborhood gangs, eager to prove themselves worthy of membership by the age of 12. Once children are members of a gang it is difficult to get them to leave. Recommendations for preventing gang violence include identifying disconnected children in elementary schools and initiating counseling with the children and their families (Calhoun, 1988). More about life in gangs and an effort in Detroit, Michigan, that has made a difference in reducing gang participation appears in Perspective on Adolescent Development 15.2.

Depression and Suicide

Earlier in the chapter, we noted that one of the most frequent characteristics of adolescents referred for psychological treatment is being sad or depressed, especially in the case of girls. What is adolescents' depression like? What is the nature of adolescent suicide?

Depression

In adolescence, the features of depression are mixed with a broader array of behaviors than in adult depression. For example, during adolescence, aggression, school failure, anxiety, antisocial behavior, and poor peer relations are often associated with depression, which makes its diagnosis more difficult (Kendall, Cantwell, & Kazdin, 1989; Matson, 1989; Weiner, 1980). In the following example of an 11-year-old girl, depression is mixed with anxiety and school-related matters:

Elizabeth is a pretty 11-year-old black girl, who was brought to the hospital because she had thrown a book at the school principal. The principal had been trying to find out the reason Elizabeth was crying in the classroom. Elizabeth was restless and confused and could not concentrate for more than a few minutes. She said that people didn't like her, that everybody thought she was ugly. She believed that she had been justified in throwing the book at the principal: "He was bugging me; I was nervous." While Elizabeth's mother was interviewed in another room at the hospital, Elizabeth began to pace up and down, saying that she was feeling hot. She showed someone her clammy, perspiring hands, and began to cry, saying, "I'm dying. Something in my throat doesn't let me breathe. My stomach isn't pumping. People are trying to kill me. I'll die if I stay here. I was normal before I came. Now I am dying. . . ." During the next 3 days, Elizabeth had one or two severe anxiety attacks a day. Between the attacks, she was anxious, restless, and depressed. She did not show any signs of psychosis, in clinical or psychological testings.

The background history obtained on Elizabeth revealed that she had been an insecure, timid, and friendless child since entering school. When Elizabeth was 7 years old, her father had been charged with attempting to seduce a 13-year-old female neighbor; and though the charges had been dismissed, the family was alienated and ostracized from the neighborhood. Elizabeth's father had then deserted the family, leaving Elizabeth, her 13-year-old brother, and her mother with no source of income. Elizabeth's mother was a tense, depressed woman, who felt harassed by the responsibilities of finding a job and caring for her children. Six months before Elizabeth's admission in the hospital, her mother had found a job that kept her away from home from 8:00 A.M. to 6:00 P.M. She had not had time to go over to school when Elizabeth brought a letter from her teacher reporting that Elizabeth seemed very unhappy, that her schoolwork had deteriorated, and that she was frequently

Depression has become so common in our society it has been called the "common cold" of mental disturbances. Depression increases during adolescence, especially among girls.

absent. Elizabeth's mother was now extremely angry at Elizabeth. She explained, "I knew she was sad and hypersensitive, but it was not causing anybody else any problem. Now she has become violent and I can't take that." (Chess & Hassibi, 1979).

Why does depression occur in adolescence? As with other disturbances, biogenetic and socioenvironmental causes have been proposed. As researchers explore the nature of adolescent depression, they have discovered that depression is more likely to appear in adolescence than in childhood and is more likely to appear in girls than in boys (Petersen & Sarigiani, 1989). In one recent study, 14-year-old girls' depression was related to their concern with feeling adequate and a lack of personal meaning in life; by contrast, 14-year-old boys' depression was related to their antisocial and hostile tendencies (Gijerde & Block, 1989).

Some experts argue that understanding adolescent depression requires knowing information about experiences in both adolescence and childhood. For example, John Bowlby (1980, 1989) believes that insecure mother-infant attachment, a lack of love and affection in childrearing, or the actual loss of a parent in childhood creates a negative cognitive set. This schema built up during early experiences causes children to interpret later losses as yet other failures to produce an enduring and close positive relationship. From Bowlby's view, early experiences, especially those involving loss, produce a cognitive schema that is carried forward to influence the way later experiences are interpreted. When these new experiences involve further loss, the loss serves as the immediate precipitant of depression. One recent research investigation revealed that early parent-child relations were associated with adolescent depression, especially for girls (Gjerde, 1985). A lack of affection and emotional support, high control, and a strong push for achievement by parents during early childhood were related to depression among adolescent girls but not boys. Possibly no relation was found for boys because depression occurs more frequently in girls.

Another cognitive view stresses that individuals become depressed because early in their development they acquire a cognitive schema that is characterized by self-devaluation and lack of confidence about the future (Beck, 1973; Clark & Beck, 1989; Kovacs, 1989). These habitual negative thoughts magnify and expand the depressed adolescent's negative experiences. Depressed adolescents, then, may blame themselves far more than is warranted.

One of the environmental factors thought to be important in understanding adolescent depression is **learned helplessness** (Rosehan & Seligman, 1989; Seligman, 1975). When individuals are exposed to stress or prolonged pain over which they have no control, they learn helplessness. In other words, depressed adolescents may be apathetic because they cannot reinstate the rewards they previously experienced. For example, an adolescent girl may not be able to make her boyfriend come back to her.

Disturbances, Stress, and Health

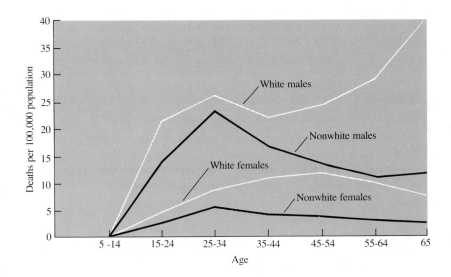

Figure 15.6 Suicides by sex, age, and race in the United States.
Source: U.S. Bureau of the Census, 1980, U.S. Government Printing Office.

Follow-up studies of depressed adolescents indicate that the symptoms of depression experienced in adolescence predict similar problems in adulthood (Garber & others, 1988; Kandel & Davies, 1986). This means that adolescent depression needs to be taken seriously. It does not just automatically go away. Rather, adolescents who are diagnosed as having depression are more likely to experience the problem on a continuing basis in adulthood than adolescents not diagnosed as having depression. And, as we see next, some of the same factors involved in adolescent depression are likely to be involved in adolescent suicide attempts.

Suicide

Suicide is a common problem in our society. Its rate has quadrupled during the last 30 years in the United States; each year about 25,000 individuals take their own lives. Beginning at about the age of 15, the rate of suicide begins to rise rapidly (see Figure 15.6). Suicide accounts for 12% of the mortality in the adolescent and young adult age group (Brent, 1989). Males are about 3 times as likely to commit suicide as females; this may be due to their more active methods for attempting suicide—shooting, for example. By contrast, females are more likely to use passive methods such as sleeping pills, which are less likely to produce death. While males commit suicide more frequently, females attempt it more frequently (Maltsberger, 1988).

Estimates indicate that 6 to 10 suicide attempts occur for every suicide in the general population; for adolescents the figure is as high as 50 attempts for every life taken. As many as 2 in every 3 college students has thought about suicide on at least one occasion; their methods range from drugs to crashing into the White House in an airplane.

TABLE 15.1 *The Early Warning Signs of Suicide Among Adolescents*

1. The adolescent makes suicide threats such as "I wish I was dead"; "My family would be better off without me"; "I don't have anything to live for."

2. A prior suicide attempt, no matter how minor. Four out of five people who commit suicide have made at least one previous attempt.

3. Preoccupation with death in music, art, and personal writing.

4. Loss of a family member, pet, or boyfriend/girlfriend through death, abandonment, breakup.

5. Family disruptions such as unemployment, serious illness, relocation, divorce.

6. Disturbances in sleeping and eating habits, and in personal hygiene.

7. Declining grades and lack of interest in school or activities that previously were important.

8. Dramatic changes in behavior patterns, such as a very gregarious adolescent becoming very shy and withdrawn.

9. Pervasive sense of gloom, helplessness, and hopelessness.

10. Withdrawal from family members and friends; feelings of alienation from significant others.

11. Giving away prized possessions and otherwise getting affairs in order.

12. Series of accidents or impulsive, risk-taking behaviors. Drug or alcohol abuse, disregard for personal safety, taking dangerous dares. (With regard to drug or alcohol abuse, there has been a dramatic increase in recent years in the number of adolescent suicides that are committed while the adolescent is under the influence of alcohol or drugs.)

Reprinted from *Living with 10- to 15-Year-Olds: A Parent Education Curriculum.* Copyright by the Center for Adolescence, Carrboro, N.C. 1982, rev. 1987. Used with permission.

Why do adolescents attempt suicide? There is no simple answer to this important question (Harter & Marold, 1989). It is helpful to think of suicide in terms of proximal and distal factors. Proximal, or immediate, factors can trigger a suicide attempt. Highly stressful circumstances such as the loss of a boyfriend or a girlfriend, failing in class at school, or an unwanted pregnancy can produce a suicide attempt (Blumenthal & Kupfer, 1988; Neiger & Hopkins, 1988). Drugs have been more involved in suicide attempts in recent years than in the past (Rich, Young, & Fowler, 1986).

But distal, or earlier, experiences often are involved in suicide attempts as well. A long-standing history of family instability and unhappiness may be present (Shapiro & Freedman, 1989; Stork, 1989). Just as with adolescent depression, combinations of family experiences are likely to show up as distal factors in suicide attempts. Lack of supportive friendships also may be present (Rubenstein & others, 1989). In a recent investigation of suicide among gifted women, previous suicide attempts, anxiety, conspicuous instability in work and

TABLE 15.2	*What To Do and What Not To Do When You Suspect an Adolescent is Likely to Attempt Suicide*

What to do

1. Ask direct straightforward questions in a calm manner. "Are you thinking about hurting yourself?"
2. Assess the seriousness of the suicidal intent by asking questions about feelings, important relationships, who else the person has talked with, and the amount of thought given to the means to be used. If a gun, pills, rope, or other means have been obtained and a precise plan developed, clearly the situation is dangerous. Stay with the person until some type of help arrives.
3. Be a good listener and be very supportive without being falsely reassuring.
4. Try to persuade the adolescent to obtain professional help and assist him or her in getting this help.

What not to do

1. Do not ignore the warning signs.
2. Do not refuse to talk about suicide if an adolescent approaches you about the topic.
3. Do not react with horror, disapproval, or repulsion.
4. Do not give false reassurances by saying things like, "Everything is going to be okay." Also don't give out simple answers or platitudes like "You have everything to be thankful for."
5. Do not abandon the adolescent after the crisis has gone by or after professional help has commenced.

Reprinted from *Living with 10- to 15-Year-Olds: A Parent Education Curriculum.* Copyright by the Center for Adolescence, Carrboro, N.C. 1982, rev. 1987. Used with permission.

in relationships, depression, or alcoholism also were present in the women's lives (Tomlinson-Keasey, Warren, & Elliott, 1986). These factors are similar to those found to predict suicide among gifted men (Shneidman, 1971).

Genetic factors are associated with suicide just as they are with depression. The closer the genetic relation to someone who has committed suicide, the more likely the individual will commit suicide (Wender & others, 1986). We do not have the complete answers for detecting when an adolescent will attempt suicide or how to prevent suicide (Pfeffer & others, 1988), but the advice offered in Table 15.1 provides valuable information about the early warning signs of suicide among adolescents. Also Table 15.2 provides valuable information about what to do and what not to do when you suspect an adolescent is contemplating suicide.

We have discussed a variety of ideas about juvenile delinquency and adolescent depression and suicide. A summary of these ideas is presented in Concept Table 15.2. In the next chapter, more information about problems and disturbances in adolescence is presented. Among other topics, you will read about eating disorders in adolescence.

Juvenile Delinquency and Depression and Suicide

Concept	Processes/Related Ideas	Characteristics/Description
Juvenile delinquency	What is juvenile delinquency?	A juvenile delinquent is an adolescent who breaks the law or engages in behavior considered illegal. It is a broad concept ranging from littering to murder. Information regarding its incidence is sketchy, but at least 2% of youth are involved in court cases. Measuring delinquency is not an easy task.
	What causes delinquency?	Many different explanations have been given. Erikson's ideas on identity provide a framework for understanding delinquency, as does a view that describes delinquency in terms of a lack of self-control. Important sociocultural factors are social class and community influences, as well as family and peer influences. Considerable attention has been focused on family influences. Parental monitoring is especially important in reducing delinquency.
	Developmental course	The incidence of nontrivial delinquent acts rises as the individual moves from early to late adolescence. A marked increase in their occurrence takes place around 15 years of age. While there is a positive correlation between delinquency and criminal activity in adulthood, the relation is not very strong. Many delinquents do not become criminals.
	Prevention and intervention	The juvenile justice system has not been very effective. Programs that work in reducing delinquency often have two components: (1) support of warm, accepting relationships with adults, (2) enhancement of adolescent's self-image as an autonomous and effective person. A recent special concern is escalating gang violence.
Depression and suicide	Depression	In adolescence, its features often are mixed with school failure, anxiety, antisocial behavior, or poor peer relations, making diagnosis difficult. Biogenetic and socioenvironmental causes have been proposed. Bowlby's developmental construction view, exaggerated self-blame, and learned helplessness are among the explanations of adolescent depression. Depression in adolescence is more frequent among girls than boys.
	Suicide	Its rate has quadrupled in the last 30 years in the United States. Males are more likely to commit suicide; females are more likely to threaten it. There is no simple answer as to why adolescents commit suicide. As with depression, proximal and distal causes probably are involved.

Summary

I. Nature of Abnormality

Models of abnormality include the statistical approach, the biological approach, and psychological and sociocultural approaches. Adolescents' abnormal behavior is the result of an interplay of biological, cognitive, and environmental factors. The spectrum of adolescent problems is wide, varying in severity, developmental level, sex, and social class. Middle-class and female adolescents have more internalizing problems, lower-class and male adolescents more externalizing problems.

II. Reason for Adolescent Drug Use and Trends in Use

Drugs have been used since the beginning of human existence for pleasure, utility, out of curiosity, and for social reasons. Tolerance for many drugs develops, and it is not unusual for users to experience withdrawal when they have taken a drug extensively. The 1960s and 1970s were a time of marked increase in the use of illicit drugs. An encouraging finding is that beginning in the mid-1980s, there was a downturn in illicit drug use by high school seniors. Nonetheless, the United States still has the highest adolescent drug use rate of any industrialized nation.

III. Alcohol

Alcohol is primarily a depressant, but in low dosages it can act as a stimulant. It has produced many enjoyable as well as many sad moments for America's adolescents. Many automobile deaths and male aggressive attacks on females involve alcohol use. Alcohol is the most widely used drug among adolescents. Alcohol abuse is a major adolescent problem. Alcohol use by the nation's high school seniors has slightly declined in recent years, but heavy drinking is common. A strong family support system is an important factor in helping adolescents cope with a drinking problem.

IV. Hallucinogens

Hallucinogens modify an individual's perceptual experiences. Hallucinogens include LSD, marijuana, and MDMA. LSD is the strongest hallucinogen, the latter two being more mildly hallucinogenic. Marijuana use has declined substantially among adolescents in the 1980s. It still is a controversial drug in the legal realm. MDMA is one of the designer drugs.

V. Stimulants and Depressants

Stimulants increase the activity of the central nervous system. Nicotine (the active drug is cigarettes), amphetamines, and cocaine are widely used stimulants by adolescents. Cigarette smoking has declined, but in view of its health hazards remains a dangerous adolescent habit (most smoking habits are formed during adolescence). There has been a decrease in amphetamine use, but there has been a sharp increase in over-the-counter stay-awake pills. Cocaine is a highly controversial drug. Its use by high school seniors dropped for the first time in 8 years in 1987, but a dangerous form of the drug—crack cocaine, which is smoked—is increasingly used. Depressants slow down the central nervous system's activity. The 1980s has seen a decline in their use by adolescents. Barbiturates, tranquilizers, and Quaaludes are commonly used depressants.

VI. Heroin and Inhalants

Heroin, a derivative of opium, is a dangerous drug. Adolescents understand its danger and rarely take it. Even after just one month's use, heroin can be physically addictive. Inhalants include any aerosol or gaseous fumes, other than smoke, that make the user feel good, high, or intoxicated. Their use by adolescents has increased in the 1980s.

VII. Role of Parents, Peers, and Schools in Adolescent Drug Use

Parents, peers, and schools play important roles in adolescent drug use. Adolescent drug use is related to relationships with parents even in early childhood. Social support—including good relations with parents, siblings, adults, and peers—is associated with reduced drug use. The most promising school approaches are long term, not only providing specific services but dealing with the social organization of the school as a whole.

VIII. The Nature of Juvenile Delinquency and Its Causes

A juvenile delinquent is an adolescent who breaks the law or engages in behavior considered illegal. Juvenile delinquency is a broad concept that ranges from littering to murder. Information regarding its incidence is sketchy, but at least 2% of youth are involved in court cases. Measuring delinquency is not an easy task. Many different explanations have been given for delinquency's occurrence. Erikson's ideas on identity provide a framework for understanding delinquency, as does a view that describes delinquency in terms of a failure in self-control. Important sociocultural factors are social class and community influences, as well as family and peer influences. Considerable attention has focused on family influences. Parental monitoring is especially important in reducing delinquency.

IX. Delinquency's Developmental Course and Prevention and Intervention

The incidence of nontrivial delinquent acts rises as the individual moves from early to late adolescence. A marked increase in their occurrence takes place around the age of 15. While there is a positive correlation between delinquency in adolescence and criminal activity in adulthood, the relation is not very strong. Many delinquents do not become criminals. The juvenile justice system has not been very effective. Programs that work in reducing delinquency often have two components: (1) support of warm, accepting relationships with adults, (2) enhancement of adolescent's self-image as an autonomous and effective person. A recent special concern is escalating gang violence.

X. Depression

In adolescence, depression is often mixed with school failure, anxiety, antisocial behavior, or poor peer relations, making diagnosis difficult. Biogenetic and socioenvironmental factors have been proposed. Bowlby's developmental construction view, exaggerated self-blame, and learned helplessness are among the explanations of adolescent depression. Depression in adolescence is more common among girls than boys.

XI. Suicide

Its rate has quintupled in the last 30 years in the United States. Males are more likely to commit suicide; females are more likely to threaten it. There is no simple answer to the question of why adolescents commit suicide. As with depression, proximal and distal factors probably are involved.

Key Terms

statistical approach 529
medical model 530
tolerance 532
withdrawal 532
hallucinogens 536
LSD 536

marijuana 537
MDMA 538
stimulants 538
amphetamines 539
cocaine 539

depressants 540
Quaaludes 541
heroin 541
inhalants 541
learned helplessness 556

Suggested Readings

Blumenthal, S. J., & Kupfer, D. J. (1988). Overview of early detection and treatment strategies for suicidal behavior in young people. *Journal of Youth and Adolescence, 17,* 1–23.
A contemporary, up-to-date overview of what is known about suicide prevention in adolescence.

Coleman, J. (Ed.). (1987). *Working with troubled adolescents.* Orlando, FL: Academic Press.
Includes chapters on adolescent individuation and family therapy, social skills training for adolescents, helping adolescents improve their identity, and suicide.

Johnston, L. D., O'Malley, P. M., & Bachman, J. G. (1988). *Illicit drug use, smoking, and drinking by America's high school students, college students, and young adults, 1975–1987.* Washington, DC: National Institute of Drug Abuse.
A very detailed overview of the findings from the annual surveys of drug use conducted by the Institute of Social Research at the University of Michigan.

Quay, H. C. (Ed.). (1987). *Handbook of juvenile delinquency.* New York: Wiley.
A collection of articles by leading experts about many dimensions of delinquency.

Rutter, M., and Garmezy, N. (1983). Developmental psychopathology. In P. H. Mussen (Ed.), *Handbook of child psychology* (Vol. 4, 4th ed.). New York: Wiley.
This lengthy, highly detailed chapter spells out many important dimensions of the field of developmental psychopathology. Includes considerable discussion of Rutter's and Garmezy's research.

Stress and Health

Look to your health and if you have it value it next to a good conscience; for health is a blessing we mortals are capable of.

Izaak Walton,
The Compleat Angler, 1653

Alan's Stress, Sarah's Obesity, and Brian's Exercise

I never thought it would be so hard to grow up. I feel a lot of pressure. My parents put a lot of pressure on me. They say they don't, but they do. I'm afraid to bring home a "B" on my report card. They want me to be perfect. I feel anxious every day about achieving. I want to be able to get into one of the top colleges, but I don't know if it's worth all of this anxiety and nervous feelings I have inside of me. I don't want to feel this way. Sometimes my heart starts pounding really fast when I get nervous and I'm not always able to settle myself down. I remember when I was in elementary school I was a lot happier. I didn't seem to care as much about what other people thought and I was more fun to be around. The competition for grades wasn't as tough then. In the last several years I've noticed how much more intense the push for good grades is. I wish someone could help me cope better with all of these pressures.

Alan, age 16

Food is a major problem in my life. Let's face it—I'm fat. Fat and ugly. I don't like myself and I know other people don't like me either. I'm only 5 feet 4 inches tall and I weight 166 pounds. I hate being fat but I can't seem to lose weight. In the last year I haven't grown in height but I have gained 20 pounds. Some girls just think they are fat and they really aren't. I heard this one girl talking yesterday about how fat she was. No way. She is about 5 feet tall and probably doesn't weigh over 100 pounds. She should be in my body. It seems like the fatter I get the more I want to eat. I hear about all of these diets, but from what I know, none of them work in the long run. I've thought about going on one hundreds of times, especially right after I've pigged out. But I just get up the next day and start pigging out again. I'm a hopeless case.

Sarah, age 15

A lot of kids in my class are in pitiful physical shape. They never exercise, except in gym class, and even then a lot of them hardly ever break a sweat. During lunch hour, I see some of the same loafers hanging out and smoking a bunch of cigarettes. Don't they know what they are doing to their bodies? All I can say is that I'm glad I'm not like them. I'm on the basketball team and during the season the coach runs us until we are exhausted. In the summer, I still play basketball and do a lot of swimming. Just last month, I started lifting weights. I don't know what I would do without exercise. I couldn't stand to be out of shape.

Brian, age 14

Stress, obesity, and exercise—the themes of Alan's, Sarah's, and Brian's comments, respectively—are issues in the burgeoning interest in adolescents' stress and health. Before turning to detailed discussions on stress and health, we introduce the new approach to preventing illness and promoting health.

The Holistic Health Orientation

Modern life is stressful and leaves its psychological scars on too many adolescents, who, unable to effectively cope, never reach their human potential. The need is not only to find better treatment for mentally disturbed adolescents, but to encourage adolescents to adopt healthier life styles that prevent problems from occurring in the first place.

Around 2600 B.C., Oriental physicians, and later around 500 B.C., Greek physicians, recognized that good habits were essential for good health. Instead of blaming magic or the gods for illness, they realized that human beings are capable of exercising some control over their health. The physician's role was as guide, assisting the patient in restoring a natural and emotional balance.

As we approach the 21st century, once again we have begun to recognize the power of our life styles and psychological states in promoting our health. We are returning to the early Oriental and Greek views that the ultimate responsibility for influencing individuals' health rests with the individuals themselves. The new approach to preventing illnesses and promoting health is a **holistic orientation.** Rather than blaming genes and germs for poor health, this approach recognizes the complex, multidimensional nature of illness and health. Genes and germs might be involved, say the holistic health advocates, but a better understanding of the problem will develop if we know something about psychological factors, life-style, and the nature of the health care delivery system. Interest in the psychological factors involved in illness and the promotion of health led to a new division in 1978 in the American Psychological Association called health psychology (Matarazzo, 1979). **Health psychology,** like the holistic orientation, emphasizes psychology's role in understanding health behavior (Feist & Brannon, 1989). Closely aligned with the holistic orientation and health psychology is the field of **behavioral medicine,** which combines medical and behavioral information to reduce illness and promote health (Garrick & Lowenstein, 1989). The interests of health psychologists are broad. Examples of this breadth include examination of why we do or do not comply with medical advice, how effective media campaigns are in reducing adolescent smoking, psychological factors involved in adolescents' ability to lose weight, and the role of exercise in reducing adolescents' stress. One of health psychology's major concerns is stress, a topic to which we now devote considerable time.

Stress and Coping

Stress is a sign of the times. No one really knows whether today's adolescents experience more stress than their predecessors, but it does seem that their stressors have increased. Among the stress-related questions we evaluate are the following: How are environmental and social factors related to stress? How is stress related to illness and Type-A behavior? How can adolescents cope with stress?

Environmental and Social Factors

Many circumstances, big and small, can produce stress in adolescents' lives. What makes some circumstances more stressful and others less stressful?

Overload, Conflict, and Frustration

Sometimes circumstances become so intense that adolescents no longer can cope. Adolescents are known for their interest in listening to loud music, but when noise remains at a high level for a prolonged period of time—such as a loud siren—the individual's adaptability becomes overloaded at some point. This overload can occur with work too. An adolescent may say, "There are not enough hours in the day to do all I have to do."

The buzzword for overload in today's world is **burnout,** a hopeless, helpless feeling brought on by relentless work-related stress. Burnout leaves its sufferers in a state of physical and emotional exhaustion (Pines & Aronson, 1988). On a number of campuses, college burnout is the most common reason students leave school before earning their degrees, reaching a rate of 25% at some schools. Dropping out of college for a semester or two used to be thought of as a sign of weakness. Now sometimes called "stopping out" because the student fully intends to return, it may be encouraged for some students who are feeling overwhelmed by stress. Before recommending "stopping out" though, most counselors suggest first examining ways the overload could be reduced and possible coping strategies that would allow the student to remain in school. The simple strategy of taking a reduced or better balanced class load sometimes works, for example. Most college counseling services have professionals who can effectively work with students to alleviate the sense of being overloaded and overwhelmed by life (Leafgren, 1989; Rayman & Garig, 1989).

Circumstances not only may overwhelm adolescents but be a source of conflict. Conflict occurs when an adolescent must decide between two or more incompatible stimuli. Three major types of conflicts are approach/approach, avoidance/avoidance, and approach/avoidance. In an **approach/approach conflict,** adolescents are attracted to two stimuli, but have to choose one of them. Should the adolescent go out with the tall, thin, good-looking person or with the rich, more stockily built person? Should the individual decide to take a summer job as a lifeguard or as a salesperson? The approach/approach conflict is the least stressful of the three types because either choice leads to a reasonably positive result.

In an **avoidance/avoidance conflict,** adolescents must choose between two unattractive stimuli. Adolescents want to avoid both, but must choose one. Will the adolescent go to the dentist to have a tooth pulled or endure the toothache? Is the adolescent going to give a presentation in class or not show up and get a zero? Obviously these conflicts are more stressful than the approach/approach conflict. In many instances, adolescents delay their decision about the avoidance/avoidance conflict until the last possible moment.

In an **approach/avoidance conflict,** a single stimulus or circumstance includes both negative and positive aspects. The adolescent really likes a particular individual and even is thinking about getting married. The possibility of steady love and affection is attractive but, on the other hand, marriage at this time might hinder college and a career. The adolescent looks at a menu and faces a dilemma—the double chocolate delight would be sumptuous, but is it worth the extra pound of weight? The adolescent's world is full of approach/avoidance conflicts, and they can be very stressful. In these circumstances, adolescents often vacillate before deciding. As the adolescent approaches decision time, avoidance tendencies usually dominate (Miller, 1959).

Frustration is another circumstance that produces stress for adolescents. **Frustration** refers to any situation in which the individual cannot reach a desired goal. If the adolescent wants something and cannot have it, he or she feels frustrated. The adolescent's world is full of frustrations that build up to make the adolescent's life stressful—not having enough money to buy a car, not getting a good job, not getting an A average, being late for school because of traffic, and not being able to get a date with a particular person. Failures and losses are especially frustrating—for example, not getting grades that are high enough to get into the desired college or losing someone the adolescent is close to through death. Sometimes the frustrations adolescents experience are major life events—as in the divorce of their parents or the suicide of a friend. Others are an accumulation of daily hassles.

Life Events and Daily Hassles

Adolescents can experience a spectrum of stresses, ranging from ordinary to severe. At the ordinary end are experiences that occur in most adolescents' lives and for which there are reasonably well-defined coping patterns. For example, most parents are aware that siblings are jealous of one another and that when one sibling does well at something the other sibling(s) will be jealous. They know how jealousy works and know ways to help adolescents cope with it. More severe stress occurs when children or adolescents become separated from their parents. Healthy coping patterns for this stressful experience are not spelled out well. Some adolescents are well cared for; others are ignored when there is a separation caused by divorce, death, illness, or foster placement (Kreppner, 1989; Sakurai, 1989). Even more severe are the experiences of adolescents who have lived for years in situations of neglect or abuse (Williamson & Borduin, 1989). Victims of incest also experience severe stress, with few coping guidelines.

Most research on stress has focused on negative experiences. As yet we know little about the nature of stress that occurs when adolescents are chosen captain of the team, graduate from high school, or win first place in a science fair. Researchers have found that adults rank these kind of positive experiences as involving low levels of stress for adolescents (Chandler, 1982). Hans Selye (1983), the Austrian-born founding father of stress research, recognized that not all stress is bad for adolescents. Selye called stress's positive features **eustress.**

In many instances, more than one stress occurs at a time in adolescents' lives. Researchers have found that when several stresses are combined, the effects may be compounded (Brenner, 1984; Rutter & Garmezy, 1983; Rutter & Schopler, 1987). For example, in one investigation, Michael Rutter (1979) found that boys and girls who were under two chronic life stresses were four times as likely to eventually need psychological services as those who had to cope with only one chronic stress. A similar multiplier effect was found for boys and girls who experienced more than one short-term strain at a time.

Recently, psychologists have emphasized that life's daily experiences as well as life's major events may be the culprits in stress. Enduring a tense family and living in poverty do not show up on scales of major life events in adolescents' development, yet the everyday pounding adolescents experience in these living conditions can add up to a highly stressful life and eventually psychological disturbance or illness (Compas, 1989; Conger & others, 1989; Greene, 1989; Lazarus & Folkman, 1984; Lempers, Clark-Lempers, & Simons, 1989). In one recent investigation, 16–18-year-old adolescents who experienced the most daily hassles had the most negative self-images (Tolan, Miller, & Thomas, 1988). More about daily hassles, as well as daily uplifts, in adolescents' lives is presented in Perspective on Adolescent Development 16.1.

Stress, Illness, and Type-A Behavior

What do migraine headaches, indigestion, high blood pressure, and hives have in common? They are all stress-related ailments. It has long been known that life's hassles can produce ulcers, asthma, high blood pressure, make skin break out, cause migraine headaches, and generate allergy attacks. The longer stress persists, the more damage it causes to the adolescent's body (Selye, 1974, 1983).

In recent years there has been considerable interest in the **Type-A behavioral pattern**—a cluster of characteristics that includes being excessively competitive, an accelerated pace of ordinary activities, impatience, doing several things at the same time, and an inability to hide that time is a struggle

"You're a Type A just like your father."

Disturbances, Stress, and Health

(a)

(b)

Recently, psychologists have examined the importance of daily hassles, such as fighting with parents (a), and daily uplifts, such as when parents give special positive attention to the adolescent (b), in understanding the nature of adolescent stress.

in life (Friedman & Rosenman, 1974). Most of the research on Type-A behavior has been conducted with adults (Siegman & Dembrowski, in press). Currently, the Type-A behavior cluster is controversial. Some researchers argue that only specific components of the cluster, especially hostility, are linked with coronary disease (Dimsdale, 1988; Williams, 1989). Others still believe the Type-A cluster as a whole is related to cardiovascular disease (Fischman, 1987).

Recent research with children and adolescents does reveal that those with a Type-A behavioral pattern have more illnesses, cardiovascular symptoms, muscle tension, and sleep disturbances (Eagleston & others, in press; Murray & others, 1988; Thoresen & others, 1985). Some researchers have found that Type-A children and adolescents are more likely to have Type-A parents— this association seems to be stronger for fathers and sons than parents and daughters (Eagleston & others, in press; Weidner & others, 1988). In one investigation, when Type-A parents were observed interacting with their sons and daughters, the parents often criticized their failures and compared them to others when evaluating their performance (Eagleston & others, in press). Such stressful family experiences may set the tone for ineffective ways of coping with stress and a tendency to develop cardiovascular symptoms. In other research, the Type-A behavioral pattern was more stable among adolescents than among children (Steinberg, 1986).

Daily Hassles and Daily Uplifts In the Lives of Young Adolescents

It's not the large things that send a man to the madhouse . . . no, it's the continuing series of small tragedies that send a man to the madhouse . . . not the death of his love but a shoelace that snaps with no time left.

Charles Bukowski

Robbie is a sixth-grade boy. He gets punished a lot for doing things wrong, and he also feels that he gets punished a lot even when he doesn't do things wrong. He hasn't been doing that well in school and his father yelled at him last night for not working on his homework. The night before, his mother and father got into a big argument—his mother threw a lamp across the room and broke it. Last week at school, Robbie got into a fight with another kid and was sent to the principal's office for discipline. His best friend moved away two months ago and since that time he hasn't found anyone he likes nearly as well. Robbie's life is filled with daily hassles.

Stephanie is a sixth-grade girl. She gets good marks at school, enjoys playing with her friends, and feels that her teacher is pleased with her. Her parents spend a lot of time with her and last week she enjoyed going out to

---

TABLE 16.A *Percentage of Sample Endorsing Items on the Children's Hassles Scale*

Item Content	Percent Occurrence	Item Content	Percent Occurrence
You had to clean up your room	83	You didn't know the answer when the teacher called on you	58
You felt bored and wished there was something interesting to do	81	Your mother or father didn't have enough time to do something with you	57
You didn't have enough privacy (a time and place to be alone) when you wanted it	54	Your mother or father wasn't home when you expected them	55
Another kid could do something better than you could	75	You didn't have enough privacy (a time and place to be alone) when you wanted it	54
You lost something	73	You were punished for something you didn't do	50
Your brothers and sisters bugged you	73	You didn't do well at sports	45
You got punished when you did something wrong	66	Your teacher was mad at you because of your behavior	44
You didn't like the way you looked and wished you could be different (taller, stronger, better looking)	66	Your mother and father were fighting	43
You had to go to bed when you didn't feel like it	64	When the kids were picking teams you were one of the last ones to be picked	39
Your mother or father forgot to do something they said they would do	62	Your pet died	36
Kids at school teased you	61	Your mother or father was mad at you for getting a bad school report	35
Your mother or father got sick	59	You got into a fight with another kid	35
Your schoolwork was too hard	59	Your best friend didn't want to be your best friend anymore	30

Note: The numbers in the column refer to the percentage of children who indicated that the item made them feel bad.
From A. D. Kanner, et al., "Uplifts, Hassles, and Adaptational Outcomes in Early Adolescents" in *Journal of Early Adolescence*, 7:379, 1987. Copyright © 1987 Sage Publications, Inc., Newberry Park, CA. Reprinted by permission.

dinner with them. Just yesterday her mother took her shopping and bought her a new dress. Stephanie also enjoys talking on the phone with her friends. She plays goalie on her girl's soccer team and two days ago her team won, a victory that moved them into first place in their league.

In a recent research investigation, Allen Kanner and his colleagues (1987) studied the daily hassles and daily uplifts of 232 sixth-grade boys and girls. As shown in Tables 16.A and 16.B, the daily experiences of Robbie and Stephanie are representative of the types of hassles and uplifts young adolescents encounter in their everyday lives. In general, boys and girls reported the same number of hassles and uplifts. The researchers also examined the relation of the hassles and uplifts to the presence of anxiety, depression, distress, self-restraint, perceived support from friends, perceived competence, and general self-worth. The results were in the expected direction: daily hassles were associated with negative outcomes, and daily uplifts were associated with positive outcomes. Uplifts were especially important in contributing to adaptive outcomes.

TABLE 16.B *Percentage of Sample Endorsing Items on the Children's Uplifts Scale*

Item Content	Percent Occurrence	Item Content	Percent Occurrence
You got a good mark at school	95	You made or fixed something by yourself	78
You had a good time playing with your friends	93	You won a game	77
Your teacher was pleased with you	89	You got a present you really wanted	76
You went out to eat	88	You did well at sports	75
There was a school holiday	88	You found something you thought you had lost	73
Your mother or father spent time with you	87	You helped your brother or sister	71
You got a phone call or a letter	87	You made a new friend	68
You had fun joking with the kids at school	83	You played with your pet	64
You learned something new	83	Your mother or father agreed with you that something wasn't your fault	64
You got some new clothes	82	You were helped by your brother or sister	63
Your friends wanted you to be on their team	81	You had a good time at a party	60
Your parents were pleased with a good grade that you got	80	You gave a talk at school that went well	41
You did something special with your mother or father	79		

Note: The numbers refer to the percentage of children who indicated that the item made them feel good.

From A. D. Kanner, et al., "Uplifts, Hassles, and Adaptational Outcomes in Early Adolescents" in *Journal of Early Adolescence,* 7:379, 1987. Copyright © 1987 Sage Publications, Inc., Newberry Park, CA. Reprinted by permission.

Heart Smart

The school is the focus of the Heart Smart intervention. Since 95% of children and adolescents age 5–18 are in school, schools are an efficient context in which to educate individuals about health. Intervention includes training school personnel, curriculum, physical education, a school lunch program, and parent education. Special attention is given to teachers who serve as role models. Teachers who value the role of health in life and who engage in health-enhancing behavior present children and adolescents with positive models for health. Teacher in-service education is conducted by an interdisciplinary team of specialists, including physicians, psychologists, nutritionists, physical educators, and exercise physiologists. The school's staff is introduced to heart health education, the nature of cardiovascular disease, and risk factors for heart disease. Coping behavior, exercise behavior, and eating behavior are discussed with the staff. And a heart smart curriculum is explained. For example, the heart smart curriculum for grade 5 includes the content areas of cardiovascular health (e.g., risk factors associated with heart disease), behavior skills (e.g., self-assessment and monitoring), eating behavior (e.g., the effects of food on health), and exercise behavior (e.g., the effects of exercise on the heart).

The physical education component of Heart Smart involves two-to-four class periods each week to incorporate a "Superkids-Superfit" exercise program. The physical education instructor teaches skills required by the school system, plus aerobic activities aimed at cardiovascular conditioning, including jogging, race walking, interval workouts, rope skipping, circuit training, aerobic dance, and games. Classes begin and end with five minutes of walking and stretching.

The school lunch program serves as an intervention site where sodium, fat, and sugar levels are decreased. Children and adolescents are given reasons why they should eat cardiovascular healthy foods such as a tuna sandwich and why they should not eat cardiovascular unhealthy foods such as a hot dog with chili. The school lunch program includes a salad bar where children and adolescents can serve themselves. The amount and type of snack foods sold on school premises is monitored.

High-risk children and adolescents—those with elevated blood pressure, cholesterol, and weight—are identified as part of Heart Smart. A multidisciplinary team of physicians, nutritionists, nurses, and behavioral counselors work with the high-risk boys and girls and their parents through group-oriented activities and individual-based family counseling. High-risk boys and girls and their parents receive diet, exercise, and relaxation prescriptions in an intensive 12-session program, followed by long-term monthly evaluations.

Extensive assessment is a part of this ongoing program. Short-term and long-term changes in children's and adolescents' knowledge about cardiovascular disease and changes in their behavior are being assessed.

One large-scale investigation, the Bogalusa Heart Study, involves an ongoing evaluation of 8,000 boys and girls in Bogalusa, Louisiana (Downey & others, 1987; Rosenbaum & others, 1987). Observations show the precursors of heart disease begin at a young age, with many children already possessing one or more clinical risk factors—hypertension, obesity, or adverse lipoprotein changes. Based on the Bogalusa Heart Study, a cardiovascular health intervention model for children and young adolescents has been developed. The model is called Heart Smart. An overview of Heart Smart is described in Perspective on Adolescent Development 16.2. Other efforts to improve adolescents' cardiovascular health involve combinations of school curriculum, parental involvement, and more nutritional school food service (Stone, Perry, & Luepker, 1989).

There are many ways to cope with stress in adolescence. Talking with a friend may be especially helpful.

Coping with Stress

How can adolescents cope with stress? In many instances, adolescents can call on more than one strategy at a time. For example, in the course of one day when 13-year-old Tammy's cat died, she constructed a shoe box coffin and ceremonially buried it in the backyard, a favorite television show helped her to keep her mind off the loss for a while, she spoke sadly of the cat at dinner, was distracted by a game of cards with her best friend, then returned to her grieving at bedtime, crying herself to sleep. Most of the time adolescents are not aware of their coping strategies. They simply act without thinking when they are under stress. For example, when his brother went away to college, 12-year-old Kevin responded by playing basketball all day. The concentration got his mind off of his brother's exit and made him feel better, although he was not aware that he was coping with the feeling of loss attached to his brother going away to school.

It is important to determine whether adolescents' coping modes are a way of avoiding or facing stress. Strategies that allow adolescents to go on with their lives without confronting the cause of tension are usually believed to be more useful over the short term. Adaptations that acknowledge and accept the stress are usually believed to be more useful over the long term (Brenner, 1984).

What are some of the ways adolescents avoid stress? Denial, regression, withdrawal, and impulsive acting out are common responses. When adolescents use *denial*, they act as if the stress does not exist. For example, an adolescent may not acknowledge that he is flunking a class. When adolescents use *regression*, they act younger than their age and engage in younger behavior. For example, an adolescent may become dependent or demanding.

Stress and Health 575

Impulsive acting out takes place when adolescents act impulsively, sometimes even flamboyantly, to conceal their stress and hurt. In the long run, this type of coping is virtually guaranteed to be self-destructive.

Withdrawal takes place when adolescents remove themselves either physically or mentally from the stress. They might run away from the stressful environment or become extremely quiet and almost invisible. They might lose themselves in their daydreams to mentally escape. These efforts afford temporary refuge from the stress. *Impulsive acting out* occurs when adolescents act impulsively and sometimes flamboyantly to avoid thinking either of the past or of the consequences of their current actions. They conceal their pain by making others angry at them, seeking easy and quick solutions to their misery. By doing so they draw attention to themselves and momentarily ease their tension. However, in the long run, this coping strategy is virtually guaranteed to be self-destructive.

In contrast to these evasive strategies, there are ways adolescents can accept and face stress. Richard Lazarus (1984) distinguishes between emotion-focused coping and problem-focused coping. In **emotion-focused coping,** adolescents change the way they perceive an encounter and the way they respond emotionally to their difficulties. The different methods of avoidance just described are characteristic of emotion-focused coping. In **problem-focused coping,** adolescents face their problems and try to solve them. For example, if a 17-year-old boy is having trouble in a class, he might go to the counselor's office and get some help in how to study more effectively. He has faced his problem and tried to do something about it. In one recent study, depressed adolescents used more avoidant coping strategies than nondepressed adolescents (Ebata & Moos, 1989).

Lazarus also emphasizes that the adolescents' beliefs about themselves make an important difference in how they handle stress. Especially significant is having a sense of control over events. If adolescents believe they have effective resources for handling demanding encounters, they probably will react with more composure and confidence than they would otherwise. Adolescents' beliefs that they can effectively control their world and have an impact on it is an important contributor to their coping capabilities (Blanchard-Fields & Robinson, 1987).

"Don't worry, be happy" goes the words of the popular tune by Bobby McFerrin, "Cause when you worry, your face will frown, and that will bring everybody down . . ." Is McFerrin's cheerful optimism a good coping strategy? Most of the time adolescents *do* want to avoid negative thinking when handling stress. A positive mood improves our ability to process information more efficiently, makes us more altruistic, and gives adolescents more self-esteem. An optimistic attitude is superior to a pessimistic one in most instances, producing a sense that adolescents are controlling their environment, or what Bandura (1986, 1989) calls self-efficacy. A negative mood increases adolescents' chances of getting angry, feeling guilty, and magnifying our mistakes. Several months before 17-year-old Michael Chang became the youngest male to win the French Open Tennis Championships in 1989, sports psychologist

Jim Loehr (1989) pieced together videotaped segments of the most outstanding points Chang had played during the last year. Chang periodically watched the videotape, always seeing himself winning, never seeing himself making mistakes, and always seeing himself in a positive mood.

For a number of years, seeing reality as accurately as possible was described as the best path to health. Recently though, researchers have found increasing evidence that maintaining some positive illusions about one's self and the world is healthy. Happy people often have falsely high opinions of themselves, give self-serving explanations for events, and have exaggerated beliefs about their ability to control the world around them. (Snyder, 1988; Taylor, 1989; Taylor & others, 1988).

Illusions, whether positive or negative, are related to one's sense of self-esteem. Having too grandiose an idea of yourself or thinking too negatively about yourself both have negative consequences. Rather, the ideal overall orientation may be an optimal margin of illusion in which individuals see themselves as slightly above average. For some individuals, seeing things too accurately can lead to depression. Seeing one's suffering as meaningless and random does not help individuals cope and move forward, even when the suffering is random and meaningless. An absence of illusions may also thwart individuals from undertaking risky and ambitious projects that yield the greatest rewards (Baumeister, 1989).

As much as positive self-illusions can improve the adolescent's quality of life, some cautions are in order. It is easy to fall into the trap of simply becoming extremely positive and ignoring reality. When individuals see that a positive outlook makes their lives better, they may take on unrealistic projects. For example, Napoleon and Hitler probably benefited from an optimal level of self-confidence early in their careers, but as their self-illusion expanded, they tackled grandiose, impossible projects, such as invading Russia, with disastrous consequences.

In some cases, a strategy of **defensive pessimism** may actually work best in handling stress. By imagining negative outcomes individuals prepare for forthcoming stressful circumstances (Norem & Cantor, 1986). Think about the honors students who is absolutely convinced she will flunk the next text, or the nervous host who is afraid her lavish dinner party will fall apart. For these two adolescents, thoughts of failure may not be paralyzing but instead will motivate them to do everything necessary to ensure that things go smoothly. In one recent investigation, negative thinking initiated the following constructive pattern of thoughts and feelings: evaluating negative possibilities; wondering what the future held; psyching up for future experiences so they would be positively experienced; feeling good by sensing that one was prepared to cope with the worst; and forming positive expectations (Showers, 1986). Positive *and* negative thinking, then, are involved in coping with stress.

The Holistic Health Orientation and the Nature of Stress and Coping

Concept	Processes/Related Ideas	Characteristics/Description
The holistic health orientation	Its nature	Instead of linking illness only to a specific cause like genes or germs, recognizes the complex, multidimensional nature of illness and health. Includes focus on psychological factors and life-style.
Stress and coping	Environmental and social factors	Include an understanding of overload, conflict, and frustration, as well as the nature of life events and daily hassles. Sometimes circumstances become so intense they overload adolescents who no longer can cope. Three common forms of conflicts are approach/approach, avoidance/avoidance, and approach/avoidance. Frustration—any situation in which the individual cannot reach a goal—is a common source of stress among adolescents. Adolescents can experience a spectrum of stresses, ranging from ordinary to severe. In many instances more than one stress occurs. Two or more stresses can have multiplier effects. Some approaches to stress focus on major life events. Recently, it has been argued that life's daily hassles and uplifts are important to consider in evaluating adolescents' stress.
	Stress, illness, and Type-A behavior	Stress can be a factor in illnesses, such as migraine headaches, ulcers, asthma, skin problems, allergy attacks, and high blood pressure. The longer stress persists, the more damage it causes to the adolescent's body. Children and adolescents with a Type-A behavioral pattern do have more illnesses, cardiovascular symptoms, muscle tension, and sleep disturbances. Debate focuses on the precise nature of the Type-A components and the role of parents.
	Coping with stress	In many instances adolescents can call on more than one strategy at a time. It is important to determine whether their behavior is a way of avoiding stress or facing it. Lazarus distinguishes between emotion-focused and problem-focused coping, arguing that long-term adaptation is best served by the latter. Most of the time adolescents need to think positively and avoid negative thinking. An optimistic attitude produces a sense of self-efficacy. Positive self-illusions can improve adolescents' lives, but it is important to guard against unrealistic expectations. A strategy of defensive pessimism helps some adolescents cope more effectively. Adults can call on three wise strategies in helping adolescents cope with stress: remove at least one stressor, teach new coping strategies, and show them how to transfer coping strategies to other, more appropriate life circumstances.

How can parents, teachers, and helping professionals most effectively work with adolescents in stressful circumstances? Three intelligent strategies are (1) try to remove at least one stressor, (2) teach new coping strategies, and (3) show adolescents how they can transfer existing coping strategies to other, more appropriate life circumstances (Brenner, 1984).

Based on Michael Rutter's (1979) research focused on multiple effects of stress, it makes sense that removing one stress or hassle can help adolescents feel stronger and more competent. For example, consider Lisa, who had been coming to school hungry each morning. One of her teachers arranged for Lisa to have a hot breakfast at school each morning, which made a big difference in improving her concentration in school. This in turn helped Lisa to suppress for a time her anxieties about her parents' impending divorce.

Adolescents who have a number of coping techniques have the best chance of adapting and functioning competently in the face of stress. By learning new coping strategies, adolescents may feel more competent and their self-confidence may improve. For example, Kim was relieved when a clinical psychologist helped her to anticipate what it would be like to visit her seriously ill sister. She had developed a high level of anxiety about the illness and used the defense mechanism of withdrawal to cope with the anxiety, saying she did not want to see her sister, even though she missed her enormously. Adolescents tend to apply their coping strategies only in the situation in which they are developed. Adults can show adolescents how to use these coping strategies to their best advantage in other situations as well. For example, Jennifer used altruism to cope with her mother's hospitalization for cancer. She coped with separation by mothering her father and her little brother. She also volunteered time to the local chapter of the National Cancer Society.

At this point we have discussed many ideas about the holistic health orientation and the nature of stress and coping. A summary of these ideas is presented in Concept Table 16.1. Now we turn our attention to nutrition and exercise, two important dimensions of health in adolescence.

Health

While we have become a health-conscious nation, aware of the importance of nutrition and exercise in our lives, many of us still smoke, eat junk food, have extra flab hanging around our middle, and spend too much of our lives as couch potatoes. This description fits too many adolescents as well as adults.

Adolescents often reach a level of health, strength, and energy they never will match during the remainder of their lives. Adolescents also have a sense of uniqueness and invulnerability, leading them to think that illness and disorder will not enter their lives. And they possess a time perspective that looks toward the future as having no boundaries, leading them to think they can live forever and recoup any lost health or modify any bad habits they might develop. Given this combination of physical and cognitive factors, is it any wonder that so many adolescents have poor health habits?

Smoking

The year 1988 marked the 75th anniversary of the introduction of Camel cigarettes. Selected magazines surprised readers with elaborate pop-up advertisements for Camels. Camel's ad theme was "75 years and still smokin." Coincidentally, 1988 was also the 75th anniversary of the American Cancer Society.

If 1988 was the year of the camel in the smoking arena, 1989 was the year of the Surgeon General, who with his advisory committee issued a report, *Reducing the Health Consequences of Smoking: 25 Years of Progress*. It was released 25 years after the original warnings that cigarettes are responsible for major health problems, especially lung cancer. Two major themes of the 1989 report are: 1) smoking is an addiction; 2) smoking is increasingly common among low-income, poorly educated individuals who often have psychological problems, such as depression. In the report, new evidence was presented to show that smoking is even more harmful than previously thought. The report estimates that in 1985, for example, cigarette smoking accounted for more than 1/5 of all deaths in the United States—20% higher than previously believed. Thirty percent of all cancer deaths, 21 percent of all coronary heart disease deaths, and 82 percent of all pulmonary disease deaths are attributed to smoking.

At the heart of preventing smoking is a stronger educational and policy effort to keep children and adolescents from starting to use tobacco products. Smoking begins primarily during childhood and adolescence. Adolescent smoking reached its peak in the mid-1970s then began to decline through the mid-1980s. However, rates of adolescent smoking have not dropped since 1984 (Johnston, Bachman, & O'Malley, 1989). In 1988, the proportion of high school seniors who were smokers was 29% with 18% smoking on a daily basis. This means it is important to keep children from initiating smoking, a difficult task since there are fewer restrictions on children's access to cigarettes today than there were in 1964, and the existing restrictions are rarely reinforced (U.S. Public Health Service, 1989).

Traditional school health programs appear to have succeeded in educating adolescents about the long-term health consequences of smoking but have had little effect on adolescent smoking behavior. That is, adolescent smokers know as much about the health risks of smoking as do non-adolescent smokers, but this knowledge has had little impact in reducing their smoking behavior (Miller & Slap, 1989). The need for effective intervention has prompted investigators to focus on those factors that place young adolescents at high risk for future smoking, especially social pressures from peers, family members, and the media.

A number of research teams have developed strategies for interrupting behavioral patterns that lead to smoking (Foon, 1987; Harkens, 1987; Pederson, 1987). In one investigation, high school students were recruited to help seventh grade students resist peer pressure to smoke (McAlister & others, 1980). The high school students encouraged the younger adolescents to resist the influence of high-powered ads suggesting that liberated women smoke by saying, "She is not really liberated if she is hooked on tobacco." The students also engaged in role-playing exercises called "chicken." In these situations, the high school students called the younger adolescents "chicken" for not trying a cigarette. The seventh graders practiced resistance to the peer pressure by saying, "I'd be a real chicken if I smoked just to impress you." Following several sessions, the students in the smoking prevention group were 50% less likely to begin smoking compared to a group of seventh grade students in a neighboring junior high school, even though the parents of both groups of students had the same smoking rate.

The tobacco industry does prey on adolescents' motivation to feel grown up by including "cool" people who smoke in their advertisements—successful young women smoking Virginia Slims cigarettes, handsome Marlboro men in rich surroundings with beautiful women at their side, for example. The advertisements encourage adolescents to associate cigarette smoking with a successful, active life-style. Legislators are working on the introduction of more stringent laws to further regulate the tobacco industry, which are badly needed since smoking is the only industry in America that will have killed 3 million of its best customers between 1964 and the year 2000, according to the 1989 report of the United States Department of Public Health.

Nutrition

The recommended range of energy intake for adolescents takes into account the different needs of adolescents, their growth rate, and level of exercise. As shown in Table 16.1, males have higher energy needs than females. Older adolescent girls also have slightly lower energy needs than younger adolescent girls. Some adolescents' bodies burn energy faster than others. **Basal metabolism rate (BMR)** is the minimum amount of energy an individual uses in a resting state. As shown in Figure 16.1, BMR gradually declines from the beginning of adolescence through the end of adolescence.

Concern is often expressed over adolescents' tendency to eat between meals. The choice of foods is much more important than the time or place of eating. Fresh vegetables and fruits as well as whole-grain products are needed to complement the foods high in energy value and protein adolescents commonly choose (Rees & Mahan, 1988).

A special concern in our culture is the amount of fat in our diet. Many of today's adolescents virtually live on fast-food meals, which contributes to the increased fat levels in their diet. Most fast-food meals are high in protein, especially meat and dairy products. But the average American adolescent does not have to worry about getting enough protein. What should be of concern

TABLE 16.1 *Recommended Dietary Allowances for Energy for Children and Adolescents (kilocalories per day)*

Age	Median*	Range†	Height per cm	Range per cm height
Children				
7–10 yrs	2400	1650–3300	18.2	12.5–25
Males				
11–14 yrs	2700	2000–3700	17.2	12.7–23.6
15–18 yrs	2800	2100–3900	16	12–22.2
Females				
11–14 yrs	2200	1500–3000	14.0	9.6–19.1
15–18 yrs	2100	1200–3000	13.0	7.4–18.4

*Median *is the median energy intake of children of these ages followed in longitudinal growth studies.*
†Range *is the 10th and 90th percentiles of energy intake of children of these ages followed in longitudinal growth studies.*
Source: Food and Nutrition Board, National Research Council: *Recommended Dietary Allowances, 9th ed., Washington, D.C., 1980, National Academy of Sciences.*

Figure 16.1   Basal metabolic rates (BMR) for adolescent females and males.

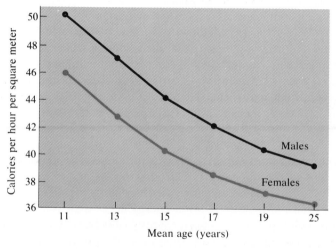

is the vast number of adolescents who consume large quantities of fast foods that not only are high in protein but high in fat. The American Heart Association recommends that the daily limit for calories from fat should be approximately 30%. Compare this figure with the figures in Table 16.2. Clearly, many fast-food meals contribute to excess fat intake by adolescents.

Eating Disorders

A tall, slender 16-year-old girl goes into the locker room of a fitness center, throws her towel across the bench, and looks squarely in the mirror. She yells,

Disturbances, Stress, and Health

TABLE 16.2   *Fat and Calorie Intake of Selected Fast-Food Meals*

Selected Meal	Calories	Percent of Calories from Fat
Burger King Whopper, fries, vanilla shake	1,250	43
Big Mac, fries, chocolate shake	1,100	41
McDonald's Quarter-Pounder with cheese	418	52
Pizza Hut 10-inch pizza with sausage, mushrooms, pepperoni, and green pepper	1,035	35
Arby's roast beef plate (roast beef sandwich, two potato patties, and coleslaw), chocolate shake	1,200	30
Kentucky Fried Chicken dinner (three pieces chicken, mashed potatoes and gravy, coleslaw, roll)	830	50
Arthur Treacher's fish and chips (two pieces breaded, fried fish, french fries, cola drink)	900	42
Typical restaurant "diet plate" (hamburger patty, cottage cheese, etc.)	638	63

From Virginia Demoss, "Good, the Bad and the Edible" in *Runner's World,* June 1980. Copyright Virginia Demoss. Reprinted by permission.

What factors might be responsible for being overweight in adolescence?

"You fat pig. You are nothing but a fat pig." We are a nation obsessed with food, spending extraordinary amounts of time thinking about, eating, and avoiding food. Understanding eating disorders is complex; it involves genetic inheritance, physiological factors, cognitive factors, and environmental experiences (Stunkard, in press). In one recent investigation, girls who in early adolescence felt most negatively about their bodies were more likely to develop eating problems 2 years later (Attie & Brooks-Gunn, 1989). The three most prominent eating disorders are obesity, anorexia nervosa, and bulimia. We consider each of these in turn.

Obesity

Individuals may inherit a tendency to be overweight. Only 10% of children who do not have obese parents become obese themselves; about 40% of children with one obese parent become obese; about 70% of children who have two obese parents become obese themselves. The extent to which this is due to experiences with parents or genes cannot be determined in studies with humans, but research with animals indicates they can be bred to have a propensity for fatness (Blundell, 1984).

Every adolescent has a set point for body weight. **Set point** is the weight maintained when no effort is made to gain or lose weight. The amount of stored fat in your body is an important factor in the set point of your body weight. It seems that when we gain weight the number of fat cells increases, and we may not be able to get rid of them. It is interesting though, that adults who were not obese as children but who became overweight as adults have larger fat cells than their normal weight counterparts—but they do not have more fat cells (VanItallie, 1984). Another biological factor involved is the basal metabolism factor mentioned earlier. Slow metabolism is an important dimension of understanding obesity. Recently, researchers have discovered that individuals with a slow metabolism are most likely to gain weight (Browell & Stein, in press). And, as indicated in Figure 16.1, BMR sharply declines from the beginning to the end of adolescence. During the adult years, BMR drops off much more slowly. To some extent a declining BMR helps explain why there are more fat older adolescents than fat younger adolescents. Scientists are working on drugs they hope will be able to raise the basal metabolism rate of overweight children and adolescents, although as we will see shortly, something else is able to rise metabolic rate and burn calories.

An adolescent's insulin level also is an important factor in eating behavior and obesity. Judy Rodin (1984, 1987) argues that what adolescents eat influences their insulin levels. When adolescents eat complex carbohydrates such as cereals, bread, and pasta, insulin levels go up but fall off gradually. When adolescents consume simple sugars such as candy bars and Cokes, insulin levels rise and then fall, often sharply—producing the sugar low with which many of us are all too familiar.

Glucose levels in the blood also are affected by these complex carbohydrates and simple sugars, and in similar ways. The consequence is that adolescents are more likely to eat within the next several hours after eating simple sugars than after eating complex carbohydrates. And the food adolescents eat at one meal influences how much they will eat at the next meal. So consuming doughnuts and candy bars, in addition to providing only minimal nutritional value, sets up an ongoing sequence of what and how much adolescents crave the next time they eat.

Rodin also believes that exercise is an important part of weight loss and weight maintenance for adolescents. She points out that no matter what an adolescent's genetic background, aerobic exercise increases metabolic rate, which helps to burn calories. Exercise not only burns up calories but continues to raise metabolic rate for several hours *after* the exercise. Exercise actually lowers the body's set point for weight, making it much easier to maintain a lower weight (Bennett & Gurin, 1982).

Many obese adolescents feel that everything would be great in their lives if only they could lose weight. As one adolescent commented, "Losing weight would make my parents happy, my peers at school would like me, and I could concentrate on other things." A typical example is Debby, age 17, who has been obese since she was 12. She comes from a middle-class family in which her parents have pressured her to lose weight, repeatedly sending her to reducing centers and to physicians. One summer, Debby was sent to a diet camp, where she went from 200 to 150 pounds. On returning home, she was terribly disappointed when her parents pressured her to lose more. With increased tension and parental preoccupation with her weight, she gave up all efforts at dieting and her weight rose rapidly. Debby isolated herself and continued her preoccupation with food. Later, clinical help was sought and fortunately Debbie was able to work through her hostility toward her parents and understand her self-destructive behavior. Eventually, she gained a sense of self-control and became willing to reduce for herself and not for her parents or her peers.

Medical personnel and psychologists have become increasingly concerned with the health hazards associated with obesity. Eating patterns established in childhood and adolescence are highly associated with obesity in adulthood—80% of obese adolescents become obese adults. Obesity is estimated to characterize 25% of today's American adolescents (Brone & Fisher, 1988). As we see next, a more infrequent condition has received considerable attention in recent years.

Anorexia Nervosa and Bulimia

Fifteen-year-old Jane gradually eliminated foods from her diet to the point where she subsisted by eating *only* applesauce and eggnog. She spent hours observing her own body, wrapping her fingers around her waist to see if it was getting any thinner. She fantasized about becoming a beautiful fashion model and would wear designer bathing suits. But even when she reached 85 pounds, Jane still felt fat. She continued to lose weight, eventually emaciating herself. She was hospitalized and treated for **anorexia nervosa,** an eating disorder that involves the relentless pursuit of thinness through starvation. Eventually anorexia nervosa can lead to death, as it did for popular singer Karen Carpenter (Casper, 1989).

Anorexia nervosa afflicts primarily females during adolescence and the early adulthood years (only about 5% of anorexics are male) (Travis, in press). Most adolescents with this disorder are white and from well-educated, middle- and upper-income families. Although anorexics avoid eating, they have an intense interest in food. They cook for others, they talk about food, and they insist on watching others eat. Anorexics have a distorted body image, perceiving themselves as beautiful even when they become skeletal in appearance. As self-starvation continues and the fat content of the body drops to a bare minimum, menstruation usually stops. Behavior is often hyperactive (Polivy & Thomsen, 1987).

Numerous causes of anorexia have been proposed, including societal, psychological, and physiological factors (Attie & Brooks-Gunn, in press; Brumberg, 1988). The societal factor most often held responsible is the current fashion image of thinness. Psychological factors include motivation for attention, desire for individuality, denial of sexuality, and a way of coping with overcontrolling parents (Stern & others, 1989). Anorexics sometimes have families that place high demands for achievement on them. Unable to meet their parents' high standards, they feel an inability to control their own lives. By limiting their food intake, anorexics gain some sense of self-control. Physiological causes involve the hypothalamus, which becomes abnormal in a

Anorexia nervosa has become a prominent problem in adolescent females.

number of ways when an adolescent becomes anorexic (Garfinkel & Garner, 1982). But the bottom line is that, at this time, we are uncertain of exactly what causes anorexia nervosa.

An eating disorder related to anorexia nervosa is **bulimia.** Anorexics occasionally follow a binge-and-purge pattern, but bulimics do this on a regular basis. The bulimic goes on an eating binge and then purges by self-induced vomiting or using a laxative. The binges sometimes alternate with fasting and at other times with normal eating behavior. Like anorexia nervosa, bulimia is primarily a female disorder. Bulimia has become prevalent among college women. Some estimates suggest that one in two college women binge and purge at least some of the time. However, recent estimates suggest that true bulimics—those who binge-and-purge on a regular basis—make up less than 2% of the college female population (Stunkard, 1987). Another recent survey of 1,500 high school and university students found a slightly higher incidence of bulimia among college (5%) than high school (4%) students (Howat & Saxton, 1988). While anorexics can control their eating, bulimics cannot. Depression is a common characteristic of bulimics. Bulimia can lead to gastric irritation and chemical imbalance in the body. Many of the causes proposed for anorexia nervosa are offered for bulimia.

Exercise

In 1961, President John F. Kennedy offered the following recommendation: "We are unexercised as a nation. We look instead of play. We ride instead of walk. Our existence deprives us of the minimum physical activity essential for living." While some of today's adolescents are in excellent physical shape, Kennedy's words still apply to the majority of adolescents in the 1980s and 1990s. The 1985 School Fitness Survey tested 18,857 children and adolescents 6–17 years of age on nine fitness tasks. Compared to a similar survey in 1975 there was virtually no improvement on the tasks. For example, 40% of the boys 6–12 years of age could not do more than one pull-up and a full 25% could not do any! Fifty percent of the girls aged 6–17 and 30% of the boys aged 6–12 could not run a mile in less than 10 minutes (which is a slow jog). In the 50-yard dash, the adolescent girls in 1975 were faster than the adolescent girls in 1985.

Some experts believe that television is at least partially to blame for the poor physical shape of our nation's children and adolescents. One investigation, briefly mentioned in Chapter 9, bears mentioning again. Children and adolescents who viewed little television were significantly more physically fit than their counterparts who viewed a lot of television (Tucker, 1987). The more television adolescents watch, the more likely they are to be overweight. No one is quite sure whether it is because adolescents spend their leisure time in front of the television set instead of chasing around the neighborhood or community, or because they tend to eat so much of the junk food they see advertised on television.

Disturbances, Stress, and Health

Training Future Olympic Champions in East Germany and China

East Germany has catapulted to being one of the top medal winners in recent Olympic games. How have they accomplished this lofty status in world athletic competition? East Germany has a national scouting network that evaluates athletic skills in children. Swimming is required in elementary schools, and by the end of the second grade children have to be competent at a minimum of two different swimming strokes. East Germany also has a number of clubs that are open only to outstanding athletes. They provide a special sports education for children with outstanding athletic skills. Children also are placed on special diets. It has been argued that children with promising athletic talent are given certain drugs to enhance their physical development and improve their performance. The muscular body build and deep voice of some of their female athletes suggests there may be drug enhancement of the East German females' development and performance (Childs, 1983; Kirschenbaum, 1976).

China is behind East Germany in garnering Olympic medals, but they are rapidly improving their national athletic status. The Communist Party in China has decided that sports is one of the avenues China can pursue to prove it has arrived in the modern world. China has developed a number of sports schools, which are virtually the only road to Olympic stardom in China. There are precious few neighborhood playgrounds. And there is only one gym for every 3.5 million people! If the athletes excel at one of the large number of sports schools in the country, they are selected for more advanced training at specialized sports schools. For example, at the specialized gymnastics sports school, Shishahai, the day begins at 6 A.M. with breakfast, followed by 4 hours of academic classes and studying until 2:30, 4 grueling hours of training, dinner until 7, more studies from 7:00 to 9:00 and lights out at 9:30. No TVs are allowed in the school, no in-room phones are permitted, and dating is prohibited. Coke, VCRs and Colonel Sanders may have arrived in Beijing, but they aren't to be found at the Shishahai sports school (Reilly, 1988).

Some of the blame falls on the nation's schools, many of which fail to provide physical education class on a daily basis. One recent extensive investigation of behavior in physical education classes at four different schools revealed how little vigorous exercise takes place in these classes (Parcel & others, 1987). Boys and girls moved through space only 50% of the time they were in the classes, and they moved continuously an average of only 2.2 minutes.

The adolescents shown here getting ready to begin a cycling race are benefiting from the exercise in which they participate. Researchers have found that a regular program of exercise not only increases cardiovascular fitness but also increases creativity.

In sum, not only does the adolescent's school week include inadequate physical education classes, but the majority of adolescents do not exercise vigorously even when they are in the physical education classes. Further, while we hear a lot about the exercise revolution among adults, most children and adolescents report that their parents are poor role models when it comes to vigorous physical exercise (Feist & Brannon, 1989).

Does it make a difference if children and adolescents are pushed to exercise more vigorously in school? One recent investigation provided an affirmative answer to this question (Tuckman & Hinkle, 1988). One hundred fifty-four boys and girls were randomly assigned to either three 30-minute running programs per week or to regular attendance in physical education classes. Although the results sometimes varied by sex, for the most part those in the running program had increased cardiovascular health and showed increased creativity. For example, the running-program boys had less body fat, and the running-program girls had more creative involvement in their classrooms.

Earlier in the chapter we discussed ways adolescents can cope with stress. An exciting possibility is that physical exercise might provide a buffer to adolescents' stress. In one recent investigation of 364 females in grades 7–11 in Los Angeles, California, the negative impact of stressful events on health declined as exercise levels increased, suggesting that exercise can be a valuable resource for combating adolescents' life stresses (Brown & Siegel, 1988). In another recent investigation, adolescents who exercised a lot coped more effectively with stress and had more positive identities than adolescents who engaged in little exercise (Grimes & Mattimore, 1989).

In the 4th century B.C., Aristotle commented that the quality of life is determined by its activities. In today's world we know that exercise is one of the principal activities that improves the quality of life, both adolescents' and adults'.

Toward Healthier Adolescents' Lives

In this chapter we have seen that adolescents' health involves far more than simply going to a doctor when they are sick and being treated for disease. We are becoming increasingly aware that adolescents' behavior determines whether they will develop a serious illness and whether they will be healthy (Minkler, 1989). As health psychologists and behavioral medicine specialists examine the lives of adolescents, they believe the next major step in improving the general health of American adolescents will be primarily behavioral, not medical.

What should be our nation's health goals for adolescents? A number of recommendations are being made for the year 2000 (Schwartz & Eriksen, 1989):

> The need to develop preventive services targeting diseases such as cancer, heart disease, unintended pregnancy, and AIDS.
> The need for health promotion, including behavior modification and health education. Stronger programs are urged for dealing with adolescents' smoking, alcohol and drug abuse, nutrition, physical fitness, and mental health.

Health

Concept	Processes/Related Ideas	Characteristics/Description
Smoking	Its nature	In 1989, the Surgeon General released an extensive document with two important themes: 1) smoking is an addiction 2) smoking is increasingly common among low-income, poorly educated people. Traditional school health programs have had little impact on reducing smoking. Current prevention efforts with adolescents focus on coping with social pressures from family, peers, and the media.
Nutrition	Its nature	The recommended range of energy intake for adolescents takes into account their different needs, their growth rate, and their level of exercise. Some adolescents' bodies burn energy faster than others—a key concept is basal metabolism rate. Many adolescents have too much fat in their diet.
Eating disorders	Obesity	Heredity, set point, BMR, insulin level, glucose level in the blood, and exercise are key aspects of understanding the nature of adolescents' obesity. A large percentage of obese adolescents become obese adults.
	Anorexia nervosa and bulimia	Anorexia nervosa is an eating disorder that involves relentless pursuit of thinness through starvation. It especially affects adolescent females. Bulimia involves a binge-and-purge pattern on a regular basis. Societal, psychological, and physiological factors have been proposed as causes of these eating disorders.
Exercise	Its nature	Experts agree that children and adolescents are not getting enough exercise. Television and the nation's schools have been criticized for contributing to the poor exercise patterns of adolescents. Most adolescents also say their parents are poor role models in the realm of exercise. An exciting possibility is that exercise can serve as a buffer for stress.
Toward healthier adolescent lives	Recommendations for the year 2000	Focus on preventive services, health promotion, and special adolescent populations, such as black and Hispanic adolescents.

The need to meet the health problems of special adolescent populations, such as a better understanding of health prevention in black and Hispanic populations.

At this point we have discussed a number of ideas about nutrition, eating disorders, exercise, and healthier life styles for adolescents. A summary of these ideas is presented in Concept Table 16.2.

Summary

I. The Holistic Health Orientation

Instead of linking illness only to germs and genes, this approach recognizes the complex, multidimensional nature of illness and health. This approach includes a focus on psychological factors and life-style.

II. Environmental and Social Factors in Stress

These include an understanding of overload, conflict, and frustration, as well as the nature of life events and daily hassles. Sometimes circumstances become so intense they overload adolescents, who no longer can cope. Three common forms of conflict are approach/approach, avoidance/avoidance, and approach/avoidance. Frustration—any situation in which the individual cannot reach a goal—is a common source of stress among adolescents. Adolescents can experience a spectrum of stresses, ranging from ordinary to severe. Two or more stresses can have multiplier effects. Recently, it has been argued that life's daily hassles and uplifts are important to consider in evaluating adolescent stress.

III. Stress, Illness, and Type-A Behavior

Stress can be involved in illnesses, such as migraine headaches, ulcers, asthma, skin problems, allergy attacks, and high blood pressure. The longer stress persists, the more damage it causes to the adolescent's body. Children and adolescents with a Type-A behavioral pattern do have more illnesses, cardiovascular symptoms, muscle tension, and sleep disturbances. Debate focuses on the precise nature of the Type-A components and the role of parents.

IV. Coping with Stress

In many instances adolescents can call on more than one coping strategy at a time. It is important to determine whether their behavior is a way of avoiding stress or facing it. Lazarus distinguishes between emotion-focused and problem-focused coping, arguing that long-term adaptation is best served by the latter. Most of the time adolescents need to think positively and avoid negative thinking. An optimistic attitude produces a sense of self-efficacy. Positive self-illusions can improve adolescents' lives, but it is important to guard against unrealistic expectations. A strategy of defensive pessimism helps some adolescents cope more effectively. Adults can use three wise strategies in helping adolescents cope with stress: remove at least one stressor, teach new coping strategies, and show them how to transfer coping strategies to other, more appropriate life circumstances.

V. Smoking

In 1989, the Surgeon General released an extensive document with two important themes: 1) smoking is an addiction 2) smoking is increasingly common among low-income, poorly educated people. Traditional school health programs have had little impact on reducing smoking. Current prevention efforts with adolescents focus on coping with social pressures from family, peers, and the media.

VI. Nutrition

The recommended range of energy intake for adolescents takes into account their different needs, their growth rate, and their level of exercise. Some adolescents' bodies burn energy faster than others—a key concept is basal metabolism rate. Many adolescents have too much fat in their diet.

VII. Eating Disorders

Three prominent eating disorders in adolescence are obesity, anorexia nervosa, and bulimia. Heredity, set point, BMR, insulin level, glucose level in the blood, and exercise are key aspects of understanding the nature of obesity in adolescence. A large percentage of obese adolescents become obese adults. Anorexia nervosa involves relentless pursuit of thinness through starvation. Adolescent females are especially susceptible to this eating disorder. Bulimia

Disturbances, Stress, and Health

involves a binge-and-purge pattern on a regular basis. Societal, psychological, and physiological explanations of these eating disorders have been proposed.

VIII. Exercise

Experts agree that children and adolescents are not getting enough exercise. Television and the nation's schools have been criticized for contributing to the poor exercise patterns of adolescents. Most adolescents also say their parents are poor role models in the realm of exercise. An exciting possibility is that exercise can serve as a buffer of stress.

IX. Toward Healthier Adolescents' Lives

Our nation's health goals for adolescents in the year 2000 focus on preventive services, health promotion, and special adolescent populations, such as black and Hispanic adolescents.

Key Terms

holistic orientation 567
health psychology 567
behavioral medicine 567
burnout 568
appoach/approach
    conflict 568
avoidance/avoidance
    conflict 569

approach/avoidance
    conflict 569
frustration 569
eustress 570
Type-A behavioral
    pattern 570
emotion-focused
    coping 576

problem-focused
    coping 576
defensive pessimism 577
basal metabolism rate
    (BMR) 581
set point 583
anorexia nervosa 585
bulimia 586

Suggested Readings

Brenner, A. (1984). *Helping children cope with stress.* Lexington, MA: D.C. Heath.
    An excellent, insightful portrayal of children's and young adolescents' ways of coping with stress. Includes many case examples.

Brone, R. J., & Fisher, C. B. (1988). Determinants of adolescent obesity: A comparison with anorexia nervosa. *Adolescence, 23,* 155–169.
    Describes similarities in the factors contributing to obesity and anorexia nervosa, especially family factors.

Bruch, H., Czyzewski, D., & Suhr, M. A. (1988). *Conversations with anorexics.* New York: Basic Books.
    Fifty years of clinical experience with anorexics are described in this book. Conversations encourage the adolescent to actively explore the past and search for solutions in the present.

Journal of School Health
    This journal includes a number of articles about children's nutrition, health, illness, and exercise. Leaf through the issues of the last several years to get a feel for the type of interventions being used in school settings to improve children's health.

Williams, S. R., & Worthington, B. S. (1988). *Nutrition through the life cycle.* St. Louis, MO: Times Mirror/Mosby.
    This book brings together information about nutrition and eating behavior at different periods in the human life cycle. Separate chapters focus on nutrition in childhood and nutrition in adolescence.

Epilogue

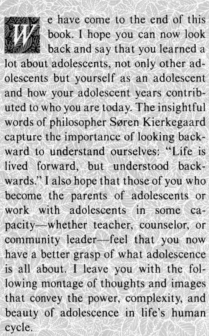

We have come to the end of this book. I hope you can now look back and say that you learned a lot about adolescents, not only other adolescents but yourself as an adolescent and how your adolescent years contributed to who you are today. The insightful words of philosopher Søren Kierkegaard capture the importance of looking backward to understand ourselves: "Life is lived forward, but understood backwards." I also hope that those of you who become the parents of adolescents or work with adolescents in some capacity—whether teacher, counselor, or community leader—feel that you now have a better grasp of what adolescence is all about. I leave you with the following montage of thoughts and images that convey the power, complexity, and beauty of adolescence in life's human cycle.

In no order of things is adolescence the time of simple life. Adolescents feel like they can last forever, think they know everything, and are quite sure about it. They clothe themselves with rainbows and go brave as the zodiac, flashing from one end of the world to the other both in mind and body. In many ways, today's adolescents are privileged, wielding unprecedented economic power. At the same time, they move through a seemingly endless preparation for life. They try on one face after another, seeking to find a face of their own. In their most pimply and awkward moments they become acquainted with sex. They play furiously at "adult games" but are confined to a society of their own peers. They want their parents to understand them and hope that their parents accord them the privilege of understanding them. Their generation of young people is the fragile cable by which the best and the worst of their parents' generation is transmitted to the present. In the end, there are only two lasting gifts parents can leave youth—one is roots, the other is wings.

References

Aboud, F. E., & Ruble, D. N. (1987). Identity constancy in children: Developmental processes and implications. In T. Honess & K. Yardley (Eds.), *Self and identity: Perspectives across the lifespan.* London: Routledge & Kegan Paul.

Abramovitch, R., Corter, C., Pepler, D. J., & Stanhope, L. (1986). Sibling and peer interaction: A final follow-up and comparison. *Child Development, 47,* 217–229.

Achenbach, T. M., & Edelbrock, C. S. (1981). Behavioral problems and competencies reported by parents of normal and disturbed children aged four through sixteen. *Monographs of the Society for Research in Child Development, 46*(1, Serial No. 188).

Adams, G., & Jones, R. (1981). Imaginary audience behavior: A validation study. *Journal of Early Adolescence, 1,* 1–10.

Adams, G. R., Abraham, K. G., & Markstrom, C. A. (1987). The relations among identity development, self-consciousness, and self-focusing during middle and late adolescence. *Developmental Psychology, 23,* 292–297.

Adelson, J. (1979, January). Adolescence and the generalization gap. *Psychology Today,* pp. 33–37.

Adelson, J., & Doehrman, M. J. (1980). The psychodynamic approach to adolescence. In J. Adelson (Ed.), *Handbook of adolescent psychology.* New York: Wiley.

Agnew, N., & Pyke, S. W. (1987). *The science game* (4th ed.). Englewood Cliffs, NJ: Prentice-Hall.

Ainsworth, M. D. S. (1979). Infant-mother attachment. *American Psychologist, 34,* 932–937.

Ainsworth, M. D. S. (1988, August). *Attachments beyond infancy.* Paper presented at the meeting of the American Psychological Association, Atlanta.

Alan Guttmacher Institute. (1981). *Teenage pregnancy: The problem that has not gone away.* New York: Author.

Allen, J. P., & Hauser, S. T. (1989, April). *Autonomy and relatedness in adolescent-family interactions as predictors of adolescent ego development.* Paper presented at the biennial meeting of the Society for Research in Child Development, Kansas City.

Allen, M. R. (1967). *Male cults and secret initiations in Melanesia.* London and New York: Cambridge University Press.

Altus, W. D. (1970). Marriage and order of birth. *Proceedings of the 78th Annual Convention of the American Psychological Association, 5,* 361–362.

Anastasi, A. (1988). *Psychological testing* (6th ed.). New York: Macmillan.

Anderson, A. B., & Frideres, J. S. (1981). *Ethnicity in Canada.* Toronto: Butterworths.

Anderson, J. R. (1985). *Cognitive psychology.* New York: W. H. Freeman.

Andre, T., Frevert, R. L., & Schuchmann, D. (1989). From whom have college students learned what about sex? *Youth and Society, 20,* 241–268.

Aneshensel, C., & Rosen, B. (1980). Domestic roles and sex differences in occupational expectations. *Journal of Marriage and the Family, 42,* 121–131.

Anglin, J. M. (1970). *The growth of word meaning.* Cambridge, MA: MIT Press.

Anson, C. A. (1988). Atlanta's adopt-a-student project. In *William T. Grant Foundation Annual Report*, New York.

Aristotle. (1941). *Rhetorica* (W. R. Roberts, Trans.). In R. McKeon (Ed.), *The basic works of Aristotle*. New York: Random House.

Arlin, P. K. (1984). *Arlin Test of Formal Reasoning*. East Aurora, NY: Slosson Educational Publications.

Armsden, G. G., & Greenberg, M. T. (1984). *The inventory of parent and peer attachment: Individual differences and their relationship to psychological well-being in adolescence*. Unpublished manuscript, University of Washington.

Arnold, M. L. (1989, April). *Moral cognition and conduct: A quantitative review of the literature*. Paper presented at the biennial meeting of the Society for Research in Child Development, Kansas City.

Aronson, E. (1986, August). *Teaching students things they think they know all about: The case of prejudice and desegregation*. Paper presented at the meeting of the American Psychological Association, Washington, DC.

Asarnow, J. R., & Callan, J. W. (1985). Boys with peer adjustment problems: Social cognitive processes. *Journal of Consulting and Clinical Psychology, 53,* 80–87.

Asher, J. (1987, April). Born to be shy? *Psychology Today,* 56–64.

Asher, S. R. (1985, April). *Identification of socially rejected children*. Paper presented at the biennial meeting of the Society for Research in Child Development, Toronto.

Asher, S. R., & Dodge, K. A. (1986). Identifying children who are rejected by their peers. *Developmental Psychology, 22,* 444–449.

Asher, S. R., & Parker, J. G. (in press). The significance of peer relationship problems in childhood. In B. H. Schneider, G. Attili, J. Nadel, & R. P. Weisberg (Eds.), *Social competence in developmental perspective*. Amsterdam: Kluwer Academic Publishing.

Astin, A. W., Green, K. C., & Korn, W. S. (1987). *The American freshman: Twenty year trends*. Los Angeles: UCLA Higher Education Research Institute.

Astin, A. W., Green, K. C., & Korn, W. S. (1989). *The American freshman, 1988*. Unpublished manuscript. Higher Education Institute, UCLA.

Astin, H. S. (1984). The meaning of work in women's lives: A sociopsychological model of career choice and work behavior. *The Counseling Psychologist, 12,* 117–126.

Atkinson, J. W., & Raynor, I. O. (1974). *Motivation and achievement*. Washington, DC: V. H. Winston & Sons.

Attie, I., & Brooks-Gunn, J. (1989). Development of eating problems in adolescent girls: A longitudinal study. *Developmental Psychology, 25,* 70–79.

Attie, I., & Brooks-Gunn, J. (in press). The emergence of eating disorders and eating problems in adolescence: A developmental perspective. *Journal of Child Psychology and Psychiatry and Allied Disciplines.*

Ausubel, D. P., Montemayor, R., & Svajian, P. (1977). *Theories and problems of adolescent development*. New York: Grune & Stratton.

B

Bachman, J. G. (1982, June 28). *The American high school student: A profile based on national survey data*. Paper presented at a conference entitled, "The American High School Today and Tomorrow," Berkeley, CA.

Bachman, J. G., Green, S., & Wirtanen, I. D. (1971). *Youth in transition: Dropping out—problem or symptom?* Ann Arbor, MI.: Survey Research Center, Institute for Social Research.

Bachman, J. G., Johnston, L. P., & O'Malley, P. M. (1987). *Monitoring the future*. Ann Arbor: University of Michigan, Institute of Social Research.

Baer, D. M. (1989, April). *Behavior analysis of human development*. Paper presented at the biennial meeting of the Society for Research in Child Development, Kansas City.

Bailen, M. (1988). Remedial summer program. In *William T. Grant Foundation Annual Report*, New York.

Bailey, G. W. (1989). Current perspectives on substance abuse in youth. *Journal of the American Academy of Child and Adolescent Psychiatry, 28,* 151–162.

Baker, L., & Brown, A. L. (1984). Metacognitive skills and reading. In P. D. Pearson (Ed.), *Handbook of reading research Part 2*. New York: Longman.

Baker, T. B. (1988). Models of addiction. *Journal of Abnormal Psychology, 97,* 115–117.

Baltes, P. B. (1973). Prototypical paradigms and questions in life-span research on development and aging. *The Gerontologist, 113,* 458–467.

Baltes, P. B., Smith, J., Staudinger, V. M., & Sowarka, D. (1988). Wisdom: One facet of successful aging? In M. Perlmutter (Ed.), *Late-life potential*. Washington, DC: Gerontological Association of America.

Bandura, A. (1965). Influence of models' reinforcement contingencies on the acquisition of imitative responses. *Journal of Personality and Social Psychology, 1,* 589–595.

Bandura, A. (1977). *Social learning theory*. Englewood Cliffs, NJ: Prentice-Hall.

Bandura, A. (1986). *Social foundations of thought and action: A social cognitive theory*. Englewood Cliffs, NJ: Prentice-Hall.

Bandura, A. (1989). Social cognitive theory. In R. Vasta (Ed.), *Six theories of child development: Revised formulations and current issues*. Greenwich, CT: JAI Press.

Bandura, A. (in press). Social cognitive theory of moral thought and action. In W. M. Kurtines & J. Gewirtz (Eds.), *Moral behavior and development: Advances in theory, research, and application*. Hillsdale, NJ: Erlbaum.

Bandura, A., & Walters, R. M. (1959). *Adolescent aggression*. New York: Ronald Press.

Barenboim, C. (1981). The development of person perception in childhood and adolescence: From behavioral comparisons to psychological constructs to psychological comparisons. *Child Development, 52,* 129–144.

Barenboim, C. (1985, April). *Person perception and interpersonal behavior*. Paper presented at the biennial meeting of the Society for Research in Child Development, Toronto.

Barker, R., & Wright, H. F. (1951). *One boy's day*. New York: Harper.

Barnes, G. M. (1984). Adolescent alcohol abuse and other problem behaviors: Their relationships and common parental influences. *Journal of Youth and Adolescence, 13*, 329–348.

Barnouw, V. (1975). *An introduction to anthropology.* Vol. 2, *Ethnology.* Homewood, IL: Dorsey Press.

Baron, J. B., & Sternberg, R. J. (1987). *Teaching thinking skills: Theory and practice.* New York: W. H. Freeman.

Baron, R., Tom, D., & Cooper, H. (1985). Social class, race, and teacher expectations. In J. Dusek & G. Joseph (Eds.), *Teacher expectancies.* Hillsdale, NJ: Erlbaum.

Barry, H., Child, I. L., & Bacon, M. K. (1959). Relation of child training to subsistence economy. *American Anthropologist, 61*, 51–63.

Bart, W. M. (1971). The factor structure of formal operations. *The British Journal of Educational Psychology, 41*, 40–77.

Batson, C. D. (in press). Prosocial motivation: Is it ever truly altruistic? In L. D. Berkowitz, (Ed.), *Advances in experimental social psychology.* New York: Academic Press.

Baumeiser, A. A. (1987). Mental retardation: Some conceptions and dilemmas. *American Psychologist, 42*, 796–800.

Baumeister, R. R. (1989). *Masochism and the self.* Hillsdale, NJ: Erlbaum.

Baumrind, D. (1968). Authoritarian vs. authoritative parental control. *Adolescence, 3*, 255–272.

Baumrind, D. (1971). Current patterns of parental authority. *Developmental Psychology Monographs, 4*(1, Pt. 2).

Baumrind, D. (1989, April). *Sex-differentiated socialization effects in childhood and adolescence.* Paper presented at the biennial meeting of the Society for Research in Child Development, Kansas City.

Baumrind, D. (1989). Parenting styles and adolescent development. In J. Brooks-Gunn, R. Lerner, & A. C. Petersen (Eds.), *The encyclopedia of adolescence.* New York: Garland.

Baumrind, D. (in press). Effective parenting during the early adolescent transition. In P. A. Cowan & E. M. Hetherington (Eds.), *Advances in family research* (Vol. 2). Hillsdale, NJ: Erlbaum.

Beagles-Roos, J., & Gat, I. (1983). Specific impact of radio and television on children's story comprehension. *Journal of Educational Psychology, 75*, 128–135.

Beck, A. T. (1973). *The diagnosis and management of depression.* Philadelphia: University of Pennsylvania Press.

Beck, J., & Morgan, P. A. (1986). Designer drug confusion: A focus on MDMA. *Journal of Drug Education, 16*, 287–302.

Beilin, H. (1989a). Piagetian theory. In R. Vasta (Ed.), *Six theories of child development: Revised formulations and current issues.* Greenwich, CT: JAI Press.

Beilin, H. (1989b, April). *Jean Piaget: The old theory and the new.* Paper presented at biennial meeting of the Society for Research in Child Development, Kansas City.

Belenky, M. F., Clinchy, B. M., Goldberger, N. R., & Tarule, J. M. (1986). *Women's ways of knowing: The development of self, voice and mind.* New York: Basic Books.

Belfer, M. L., Kerner, P. K., & Miller, F. B. (1988). AIDS in children and adolescents. *Journal of the American Academy of Child and Adolescent Psychiatry, 27*, 147–151.

Bell, A. P., Weinberg, M. S., & Mammersmith, S. K. (1981). *Sexual preference: Its development in men and women.* New York: Simon & Schuster.

Bell, D. (Ed.). (1980). *Shapes of Brown: New perspectives on school desegregation.* New York: Teachers College Press.

Bell-Scott, P., & Taylor, R. L. (1989). Introduction: The multiple ecologies of black adolescent development. *Journal of Adolescent Research, 4*, 117–118.

Belle, D., & Paul, E. (1989, April). *Structural and functional changes accompanying the transition to college.* Paper presented at the biennial meeting of the Society for Research in Child Development, Kansas City.

Belsky, J. (1981). Early human experience: A family perspective. *Developmental Psychology, 17*, 3–23.

Belson, W. (1978). *Television violence and the adolescent boy.* London: Saxon House.

Bem, S. L. (1977). On the utility of alternative procedures for assessing psychological androgyny. *Journal of Consulting and Clinical Psychology, 45*, 196–205.

Bem, S. L. (1985). Androgyny and gender schema theory: Conceptual and empirical integration. In T. B. Sonderegger (Ed.), *Nebraska symposium on motivation.* Lincoln, NE: University of Nebraska Press.

Bem, S. L. (1987). Masculinity and femininity exist only in the mind of the perceiver. In J. M. Reinisch, L. A. Rosenblum, & S. A. Sanders (Eds.), *Masculinity/femininity.* New York: Oxford University Press.

Bence, P. J. (1989, April). *Adolescent dating behavior and TV soaps: Guided by* The Guiding Light? Paper presented at the biennial meeting of the Society for Child Development, Kansas City.

Bengston, V. L. (1989). The "generation" in the middle: Perceptions of changes in adults' intergenerational relationships. In K. Kreppner & R. M. Lerner (Eds.), *Family systems and life-span development.* Hillsdale, NJ: Erlbaum.

Bennett, W. I., & Gurin, J. (1982). *The dieter's dilemma: Eating less and weighing more.* New York: Basic Books.

Bennett, W. J. (1986). *First lessons: A report on elementary education in American.* Washington, DC: U.S. Government Printing Office.

Benninga, J. S. (1988, February). An emerging synthesis in moral education. *Phi Delta Kappan,* pp. 415–418.

Bereiter, C., & Scardamalia, M. (1982). From conversation to composition: The role of instruction in a developmental process. In R. Glaser (Ed.), *Advances in instructional psychology.* Hillsdale, NJ: Erlbaum.

Berkowitz, M., & Gibbs, J. (1983). Measuring the developmental features of moral discussion. *Merrill-Palmer Quarterly, 29*, 399–410.

Berlyne, D. (1960). *Conflict, arousal, and curiosity.* New York: McGraw-Hill.

Berndt, T. J. (1979). Developmental changes in conformity to peers and parents. *Developmental Psychology, 15*, 608–616.

Berndt, T. J. (1981). Relations between social cognition, nonsocial cognition, and social behavior: The case of friendship.

In J. H. Flavell & L. D. Ross (Eds.), *Social cognitive development.* Cambridge, England: Cambridge University Press.

Berndt, T. J. (1982). The features and effects of friendship in early adolescence. *Child Development, 53,* 1447–1460.

Berndt, T. J., & Ladd, G. W. (1989). *Peer relationships in child development.* New York: Wiley.

Berndt, T. J., & Perry, T. B. (1990). Distinctive features and effects of early adolescent friendships. In R. Montemayor (Ed.), *Advances in adolescent research.* Greenwich, CT: JAI Press.

Berscheid, E. (1985). Interpersonal attraction. In G. Lindzey & E. Aronson (Eds.), *Handbook of social psychology* (Vol. 2, 3rd ed.). New York: Random House.

Berscheid, E. (1987). Some comments on love's anatomy: Or, whatever happened to old-fashioned lust? In R. J. Sternberg & M. L. Barnes (Eds.), *Anatomy of love.* New Haven, CT: Yale University Press.

Berscheid, E., & Snyder, M. (1988). *The measurement of relationship closeness.* Unpublished manuscript, Minneapolis, MN: University of Minnesota.

Berscheid, E., Snyder, M., & Omoto, A. M. (1989). Issues in studying close relationships. In C. Hendrick (Ed.), *Close relationships.* Newbury Park, CA: Sage.

Berscheid, E., Snyder, M., & Omoto, A. M. (in press). The relationship closeness inventory: Assessing the closeness of interpersonal relationships. *Journal of Personality and Social Psychology.*

Berzonsky, M. D. (1978). Formal reasoning in adolescence: An alternative view. *Adolescence, 13,* 279–290.

Bijou, S. W. (1989). Behavior analysis. In R. Vasta (Ed.), *Six theories of child development: Revised formulations and current issues.* Greenwich, CT: JAI Press.

Binder, A. (1987). An historical and theoretical introduction. In H. C. Quay (Ed.), *Handbook of juvenile delinquency.* New York: Wiley.

Bingham, C. R. (1989). AIDS and adolescents: Threat of infection and approaches to prevention. *Journal of Early Adolescence, 9,* 50–66

Blakemore, J. E. O., LaRue, A. A., & Olejnik, A. B. (1979). Sex-appropriate toy preference and the ability to conceptualize toys as sex-role related. *Developmental Psychology, 15,* 339–340.

Blanchard-Fields, F., & Robinson, S. (1987, April). *Controllability and adaptive coping from adolescence through older adulthood.* Paper presented at the biennial meeting of the Society for Research in Child Development, Baltimore.

Blasi, A. (1988). Identity and the development of the self. In D. Lapsley & F. C. Power (Eds.), *Self, ego, and identity: Integrative approaches.* New York: Springer-Verlag.

Blasi, A., & Hoeffel, E. C. (1974). Adolescence and formal operations. *Human Development, 17,* 344–363.

Blazer, D., & others. (1985). Psychiatric disorders: A rural-urban comparison. *Archives of General Psychiatry, 42,* 651–656.

Block, J., & Block, J. H. (1988). Longitudinally foretelling drug usage in adolescence: Early childhood personality and environmental precursors. *Child Development, 59,* 336–355.

Block, J. H. (1973). Conception of sex roles: Some cross-cultural and longitudinal perspectives. *American Psychologist, 28,* 512–516.

Block, J. H., Block, J., & Gjerde, P. (1986). The personality of children prior to divorce: A prospective study. *Child Development, 57,* 827–840.

Bloom, B. S. (1983, April). *The development of exceptional talent.* Paper presented at the biennial meeting of the Society for Research in Child Development, Detroit.

Bloome, D. (1989). *Classrooms and literacy.* Norwood, NJ: Ablex.

Blos, P. (1962). *On adolescence.* New York: Free Press.

Blos, P. (1989). The inner world of the adolescent. In A. H. Esman (Ed.), *International Annals of Adolescent Psychiatry,* Vol. I. Chicago: University of Chicago Press.

Blumenthal, S. J., & Kupfer, D. J. (1988). Overview of early detection and treatment strategies for suicidal behavior in young people. *Journal of Youth and Adolescence, 17,* 1–14.

Blumstein, P., & Schwartz, P. (1983). *American couples: Money, work, sex.* New York: William Morrow.

Blundell, J. E. (1984). Systems and interactions: An approach to the pharmacology of feeding. In A. J. Stunkard & E. Stellar (Eds.), *Eating and its disorders.* New York: Raven Press.

Blyth, D. A., Bulcroft, R., & Simmons, R. G. (1981, August). *The impact of puberty on adolescents: A longitudinal study.* Paper presented at the meeting of the American Psychological Association, Los Angeles.

Blyth, D. A., Durant, D., & Moosbrugger, L. (1985, April). *Perceived intimacy in the social relationships of drug and non-drug using adolescents.* Paper presented at the biennial meeting of the Society for Research in Child Development, Toronto.

Blyth, D. A., & Foster-Clark, F. S. (1987). Gender differences in perceived intimacy with different members of adolescents' social networks. *Sex Roles, 17,* 689–718.

Blyth, D. A., Simmons, R. G., & Carlton-Ford, S. (1983). The adjustment of early adolescents to school transitions. *Journal of Early Adolescence, 3,* 105–120.

Boden, M. A. (1989). *The many faces of AI.* Cambridge, MA: MIT Press.

Bogenschneider, K. (1989, April). *Maternal employment in two-parent intact families, parenting style and adolescents' academic achievement: A process approach.* Paper presented at the biennial meeting of the Society for Research in Child Development, Kansas City.

Bolter, J. D. (1984). *Turing's man.* Chapel Hill, NC: University of North Carolina Press.

Bombeck, E., & Keane, B. (1971). *Just wait till you have children of your own!* New York: Fawcett/Crest.

Bornstein, M. H., & Krasnegor, N. A. (1989). *Stability and continuity in mental development.* Hillsdale, NJ: Erlbaum.

Bourne, E. (1978). The state of research on ego identity: A review and appraisal (Part I). *Journal of Youth and Adolescence, 7,* 223–251.

Bowlby, J. (1969). *Attachment and loss* (Vol. 1). London: Hogarth.

Bowlby, J. (1988). Developmental psychiatry comes of age. *American Journal of Psychiatry, 145,* 1–10.

Bowlby, J. (1989). *Secure attachment.* New York: Basic Books.

Bowman, P. (1989, April). *Job search discouragement among black adolescents: Familial and educational antecedents.* Paper presented at the biennial meeting of the Society for Research in Child Development, Kansas City.

Bowman, P. H. (1959). Effects of a revised school program on potential delinquents. *Annals, 322,* 53–62.

Boxer, A. M. (1988, August). *Developmental continuities of gay and lesbian youth.* Paper presented at the meeting of the American Psychological Association, Atlanta, GA.

Boyer, E. L. (1986, December). Transition from school to college. *Phi Delta Kappan,* pp. 283–287.

Bray, J. H. (1988). The effects of early remarriage on children's development: Preliminary analyses of the developmental issues in stepfamily research project. In E. M. Hetherington & J. D. Arasteh (Eds.), *Impact of divorce, single-parenting, and stepparenting on children.* Hillsdale, NJ: Erlbaum.

Brenner, A. (1984). *Helping children cope with stress.* Lexington, MA: Lexington Books.

Brent, D. A. (1989). Suicide and suicidal behavior in children and adolescents. *Pediatrics in Review, 10,* 269–275.

Broderick, C., & Rowe, G. (1968). A scale of preadolescent heterosexual development. *Journal of Marriage and the Family, 30,* 97–101.

Brofenbrenner, U. (1989, April). *The developing ecology of human development.* Paper presented at the biennial meeting of the Society of Research in Child Development, Kansas City.

Broman, S. (1981). Long-term development of children born to teenagers. In K. G. Scott, T. Field, & E. Robertson (Eds.), *Teenage parents and their offspring.* New York: Grune & Stratton.

Brone, R. J., & Fisher, C. B. (1988). Determinants of adolescent obesity: A comparison with anorexia nervosa. *Adolescence, 23,* 155–169.

Bronfenbrenner, U. (1979). Contexts of child rearing. *American Psychologist, 34,* 844–850.

Bronfenbrenner, U. (1987, August). *Recent advances in theory and design.* Paper presented at the meeting of the American Psychological Association, New York City.

Bronfenbrenner, U. (1989, April). *The developing ecology of human development.* Paper presented at the biennial meeting of the Society for Research in Child Development, Kansas City.

Bronfenbrenner, U., & Garbarino, J. (1976). The socialization of moral judgment and behavior in cross-cultural perspective. In T. Lickona (Ed.), *Moral development and behavior.* New York: Holt, Rinehart & Winston.

Bronstein, P. A., & Quina, K. (Eds.). (1988). *Teaching a psychology of people.* Washington, DC: American Psychological Association.

Brookman, R. R. (1988). Sexually transmitted diseases. In M. D. Levine & E. R. McAnarney (Eds.), *Early adolescent transitions.* Lexington, MA: Lexington Books.

Brookover, W., Beady, C., Flood, P., Schweitzer, J., & Wisenbaker, J. (1979). *School social systems and student achievement: Schools can make a difference.* New York: Praeger.

Brooks-Gunn, J. (1987). Pubertal processes: Their relevance to developmental research. In V. B. Van Hasselt & M. Hersen (Eds.), *Handbook of adolescent psychology.* New York: Pergamon.

Brooks-Gunn, J. (1988). Antecedents and consequences of variations in girls' maturational timing. In M. D. Levine & E. R. McAnarney (Eds.), *Early adolescent transitions.* Lexington, MA: Lexington Books.

Brooks-Gunn, J., & Ruble, D. N. (1982). The development of menstrual-related beliefs and behaviors during early adolescence. *Child Development, 53,* 1567–1577.

Brooks-Gunn, J. & Warren, M. P. (1989, April). *How important are pubertal and social events for different problem behaviors and contexts.* Paper presented at the biennial meeting of the Society for Research in Child Development, Kansas City.

Brooks-Gunn, J., & Warren, M. P. (in press). The psychological significance of secondary sexual characteristics in 9- to 11-year-old girls. *Child Development.*

Broughton, J. (1977). Beyond formal operations: Theoretical thought in adolescence. *Teachers College Record, 79,* 87–96.

Broughton, J. (1983). The cognitive developmental theory of adolescent self and identity. In B. Lee & G. Noam (Eds.), *Developmental approaches to self.* New York: Plenum.

Browell, K., & Stein, L. J. (in press). Metabolic and behavioral effects of weight loss and regain: A review of the animal and human literature. In A. J. Stunkard & A. Baum (Eds.), *Perspectives on behavioral medicine.* Hillsdale, NJ: Erlbaum.

Brown, A. L., & Smiley, S. S. (1977). Rating the importance of structural units of prose passages: A problem of metacognitive development. *Child Development, 48,* 1–8.

Brown, B., & Mounts, N. (1989, April). *Peer group structures in single vs. multiethnic high schools.* Paper presented at the biennial meeting of the Society for Research in Child Development, Kansas City.

Brown, B. B., Clasen, D. R., & Eicher, S. A. (1986). Perceptions of peer pressure, peer conformity dispositions, and self-reported behavior among adolescents. *Developmental Psychology, 22,* 521–530.

Brown, B. B., & Lohr, M. J. (1987). Peer-group affiliation and adolescent self-esteem: An integration of ego-identity and symbolic-interaction theories. *Journal of Personality and Social Psychology, 52,* 47–55.

Brown, D. (1987). The status of Holland's theory of vocational choice. *Career Development Quarterly, 36,* 13–24.

Brown, F. (1973). *The reform of secondary education: Report of the national commission on the reform of secondary education.* New York: McGraw-Hill.

References

Brown, J. D., & Siegel, J. D. (1988). Exercise as a buffer of life stress: A prospective study of adolescent health. *Health Psychology, 7,* 341–353.

Brown, R. (1986). *Social psychology* (2nd ed.). New York: Macmillan.

Brumberg, J. J. (1988). *Fasting girls.* Cambridge, MA: Harvard University Press.

Bruner, J. (1966). *Toward a theory of instruction.* Cambridge, MA: Harvard University Press.

Bruner, J. (1989, April). *The state of developmental psychology.* Paper presented at the biennial meeting of the Society for Research in Child Development, Kansas City.

Bruner, J. S., & Bornstein, M. H. (in press). On interaction. In M. H. Bornstein & I. S. Bruner (Eds.), *Interaction in cognitive development.* Hillsdale, NJ: Erlbaum.

Buchel, F. P. (1988). Training of memory strategies with adolescents and adults in vocational schools. In F. Weinert & M. Perlmutter (Eds.), *Memory development.* Hillsdale, NJ: Erlbaum.

Buckley, W. E., Yesalis, C. E., Friedl, K. E., Anderson, W. A., Streit, A. L., & Wright, J. E. (1988). Estimated prevalence of anabolic steroid use among male high school seniors. *Journal of the American Medical Association, 260,* 3441–3445.

Buhrmester, D. (1989). *Changes in friendship, interpersonal competence, and social adaptation during early adolescence.* Unpublished manuscript, Department of Psychology, UCLA, Los Angeles.

Bukowski, W. M., Newcomb, A. F., & Hoza, B. (1987). Friendship conception among early adolescents: A longitudinal study of stability and change. *Journal of Early Adolescence, 7,* 143–152.

Burbules, N. C., & Linn, M. C. (1988). Response to contradiction: Scientific reasoning during adolescence. *Journal of Educational Psychology, 80,* 67–75.

Burton, R. V. (1984). A paradox in theories and research in moral development. In W. W. Kurtines & J. L. Gewirtz (Eds.), *Morality, moral behavior, and moral development.* New York: Wiley.

Buss, A. H., & Plomin, R. (1987). Commentary. In H. H. Goldsmith, A. H. Buss, R. Plomin, M. K. Rothbart, A. Thomas, S. Chess, R. R. Hinde,

& R. B. McCall, Roundtable: What is temperament? Four approaches. *Child Development, 58,* 505–529.

Butler, R. A. (1953). Discrimination learning by rhesus monkeys to visual-exploration motivation. *Journal of Comparative and Physiological Psychology, 46,* 95–98.

Byrne, D. (1973). *The development of role-taking in adolescence.* Unpublished doctoral dissertation, Harvard University Graduate School of Education.

Byrnes, J. P. (1988a). Formal operations: A systematic reformulation. *Developmental Review, 8,* 66–87.

Byrnes, J. P. (1988b). What's left is closer to right. *Developmental Review, 8,* 385–392.

C

Cairns, R. B., & Cairns, B. D. (1989, April). *Risks and lifelines in adolescence.* Paper presented at the biennial meeting of the Society for Research in Child Development, Kansas City.

Cairns, R. B., & Cairns, B. D. (in press). Social cognition and social networks: A developmental perspective. In D. Pepler & K. Rubin (Eds.), *Aggression in childhood: The Earlcourt symposium.* Hillsdale, NJ: Erlbaum.

Calhoun, J. A. (1988, March). *Gang violence.* Testimony to the House Select Committee on Children, Youth, and Families, Washington, DC.

Callahan, R. (1962). *Education and the cult of efficiency.* Chicago: University of Chicago Press.

Camara, K. A., & Resnick, G. (in press). Interparental conflict and cooperation: Factors moderating children's post-divorce adjustment. In E. M. Hetherington & J. D. Arasteh (Eds.), *Impact of divorce, single-parenting, and stepparenting on children.* Hillsdale, NJ: Erlbaum.

Cameron, D. (1988, February). Soviet schools. *NEA Today,* p. 15.

Capaldi, D. M., & Patterson, G. R. (1989). *The relation of family transitions and disruptions to boys' adjustment problems.* Unpublished manuscript, Oregon Social Learning Center, Eugene, OR.

Carey, S. (1986). *Conceptual change in childhood.* Boston: MIT Press.

Carey, S. (1988). Are children fundamentally different kinds of thinkers and learners than adults? In K. Richardson & S. Sheldon (Eds.), *Cognitive development to adolescence.* Hillsdale, NJ: Erlbaum.

Carkhuff, R. (1969). *Helping and human relations* (Vols. 1 & 2). New York: Holt, Rinehart & Winston.

Carnegie Corporation (1989). *Turning points: Preparing youth for the 21st century.* New York: Carnegie Corporation.

Carper, L. (1978, April). Sex roles in the nursery. *Harper's.*

Carroll, C. R. (1989). *Drugs in modern society* (2nd ed.). Dubuque, IA: Wm. C. Brown.

Carroll, J. B. (1989). Intellectual abilities and aptitudes. In A. Lesgold & R. Glaser (Eds.), *Foundations for a psychology of education.* Hilldale, NJ: Erlbaum.

Carter, D. B. (1989, April). *Gender identity and gender constancy: The roles of cognitive constancies in early gender-role development.* Paper presented at the biennial meeting of the Society for Research in Child Development, Kansas City.

Carton, B. (1988, July 27). Teen buyers: Tracking what's hot. *The Boston Globe,* pp. A1, A13.

Casper, R. C. (1989). Psychodynamic psychotherapy in acute anorexia nervosa and acute bulimia nervosa. In A. H. Esman (Ed.), *International annals of adolescent psychiatry.* Chicago: University of Chicago Press.

Caspi, A., & Elder, G. H. (1989, April). *Turning points in the life course.* Paper presented at the biennial meeting of the society for research in child development, Kansas City.

Cassell, C. (1984). *Swept away: Why women fear their own sexuality.* New York: Simon & Schuster.

Cauce, A. M. (1987). School and peer competence in early adolescence: A test of domain-specific self-perceived competence. *Developmental Psychology, 23,* 287–291.

Chandler, L. A. (1982). *Children under stress*. Springfield, IL: Charles C Thomas.

Chandler, M., Boyes, M., Ball, L., & Hala, S. (1987). The conservation of selfhood: A developmental analysis of children's changing conceptions of self-continuity. In T. Honess & K. Yardley (Eds.), *Self and identity: Perspectives across the lifespan*. London: Routledge & Kegan Paul.

Chapman, W., & Katz, M. R. (1983). Career information systems in secondary schools: A survey and assessment. *Vocational Guidance Quarterly, 31,* 165–177.

Charlesworth, R., & Hartup, W. W. (1973). Positive social reinforcement in the nursery school peer group. *Child Development, 38,* 993–1002.

Chase-Lansdale, P. L., & Hetherington, E. M. (in press). The impact of divorce on life-span development: Short- and long-term effects. In P. B. Baltes, D. L. Featherman, & R. M. Lerner (Eds.), *Life-span development and behavior*. Hillsdale, NJ: Erlbaum.

Chesney-Lind, M. (1989). Girls' crime and woman's place: Toward a feminist model of female delinquency. *Crime and Delinquency, 35,* 5–30.

Chess, S., & Hassibi, M. (1978). *Principles and practices of child psychiatry*. New York: Plenum.

Chess, S., & Thomas, A. (1977). Temperamental individuality from childhood to adolescence. *Journal of Child Psychiatry, 16,* 218–226.

Chess, S., & Thomas, A. (1984). *Origins and evolution of behavior disorders*. New York: Brunner/Mazel.

Childs, D. (1983). *The GDR: Moscow's German ally*. London: G. Allen & Unwin.

Chilman, C. (1979). *Adolescent sexuality in a changing American society: Social and psychological perspectives*. Washington, DC: Public Health Service, National Institute of Mental Health.

Chivian, E., Mack, J., Waletzky, J., Lazaroffi, C., Doctor, S., & Goldening, J. (1985). Soviet children and the threat of nuclear war: A preliminary study. *Journal of Orthopsychiatry, 55,* 484–502.

Cicirelli, V. (1977). Family structure and interaction: Sibling effects on socialization. In M. McMillan & M. Sergio (Eds.), *Child psychiatry: Treatment and research*. New York: Brunner/Mazel.

Clabby, J. G., & Elias, M. J. (1988). Improving social problem-solving and awareness. *William T. Grant Foundation Annual Report,* p. 18.

Clark, D. A., & Beck, A. T. (1989). Cognitive theory and therapy of anxiety and depression. In P. C. Kendall & D. Watson (Eds.), *Anxiety and depression*. San Diego, CA: Academic Press.

Clark, K. (1965). *Dark ghetto*. New York: Harper.

Clark, M. S., Powell, M. C., Ovellette, R., & Milberg, S. (1987). Recipient's mood, relationship type, and helping. *Journal of Personality and Social Psychology, 43,* 94–103.

Clark, S. D., Zabin, L. S., & Hardy, J. B. (1984). Sex, contraception, and parenthood: Experience and attitudes among urban black young men. *Family Planning Perspectives, 16,* 77–82.

Clasen, D. R., & Brown, B. B. (1987). Understanding peer pressure in the middle school. *Middle School Journal, 19,* 21–23.

Cocks, J. (1983, December 26). Sing a song of seeing. *Time,* p. 54.

Cocks, J. (1985, September 30). Rock is a four-letter word. *Time,* pp. 70–71.

Cohn, J. F., & Tronick, E. Z. (1988). Mother-infant face-to-face interaction: Influence is bidirectional and unrelated to periodic cycles in either partner's behavior. *Developmental Psychology, 24,* 396–397.

Colby, A., Kohlberg, L., Gibbs, J., & Lieberman, M. (1983). A longitudinal study of moral judgment. *Monographs of the Society for Research in Child Development, 48*(21, Serial No. 201).

Cole, S. (1981). *Working kids on working*. New York: Lothrop, Lee, & Shephard.

Coleman, J. S. (1961). *The adolescent society*. New York: Free Press.

Coleman, J. S. (1980). The peer group. In J. Adelson (Ed.), *Handbook of adolescent psychology*. New York: Wiley.

Coleman, J. S., Campbell, E. Q., Hobson, C. J., McPartland, J., Mood, A. M., Weinfeld, F. D., & York, R. L. (1966). *Equality of educational opportunity*. Washington, DC: U.S. Government Printing Office.

Coleman, J. S., et al. (1974). *Youth: Transition to adulthood*. Report of the Panel on Youth of the President's Science Advisory Committee. Chicago: University of Chicago Press.

Coles, R. (1970). *Erik H. Erikson: The growth of his work*. Boston: Little, Brown.

Coles, R. (1977). *Eskimos, Chicanos, and Indians*. Boston: Little, Brown.

Coles, R. (1986). *The political life of children*. Boston: Little, Brown.

Coletta, N. D. (1979). *Divorced mothers at two income levels: Stress, support, and child-rearing practices*. Unpublished manuscript, Cornell University.

College Board Commission on Precollege Guidance and Counseling. (1986). *Keeping the options open*. New York: College Entrance Examination Board.

Collins, A. W. (1985, April). *Cognition, affect, and development in parent-child relationships*. Paper presented at the biennial meeting of the Society for Research in Child Development, Toronto.

Collins, W. A. (1987). *Research on the transition to adolescence*. Unpublished manuscript, University of Minnesota.

Collins, W. A. (1989, April). *Parents' relational cognitions and developmental changes in relationships during adolescence*. Paper presented at the biennial meeting of the Society for Research in Child Development, Kansas City.

Compas, B. (1989, April). *Vulnerability and stress in childhood and adolescence*. Paper presented at the biennial meeting of the Society for Research in Child Development, Kansas City.

Conant, J. B. (1959). *The American high school today*. New York: McGraw-Hill.

Condry, J. C., Simon, M. L., & Bronfenbrenner, U. (1968). *Characteristics of peer- and adult-oriented children*. Unpublished manuscript, Cornell University, Ithaca, NY.

Conger, J. J. (1981). Freedom and commitment: Families, youth, and social change. *American Psychologist, 36,* 1475–1484.

Conger, J. J. (1988). Hostages to the future: Youth, values, and the public interest. *American Psychologist, 43,* 291–300.

Conger, R. D., Elder, G. H., Lasley, F., Lorenz, F., Norem, R., & Simons, R. L. (1989, April). *Preliminary findings from the Iowa Youth and Families Project.* Paper presented at the biennial meeting of the Society for Research in Child Development, Kansas City.

Cooper, C. R., & Ayers-Lopez, S. (1985). Family and peer systems in early adolescence: New models of the role of relationships in development. *Journal of Early Adolescence, 5,* 9–22.

Cooper, C. R., & Grotevant, H. D. (1989, April). *Individuality and connectedness in the family and adolescents' self and relational competence.* Paper presented at the biennial meeting of the Society for Research in Child Development, Kansas City.

Cooper, C. R., Grotevant, H. D., & Condon, S. M. (1983). Individuality and connectedness in the family as a context for adolescent identity formation and role-taking skill. In H. D. Grotevant & C. R. Cooper (Eds.), *Adolescent development in the family.* San Francisco: Jossey-Bass.

Coopersmith, S. (1967). *The antecedents of self-esteem.* San Francisco: W. H. Freeman.

Cote, J. E., & Levine, C. (1988a). A critical examination of the ego identity status paradigm. *Developmental Review, 8,* 147–184.

Cote, J. E., & Levine, C. (1988b). On critiquing the identity status paradigm: A rejoinder to Waterman. *Developmental Review, 8,* 209–218.

Cote, J. E., & Levine, C. (1989). *An empirical investigation of the validity of the ego status paradigm.* Unpublished manuscript, University of Western Ontario.

Cottle, T. J. (1979, February). Adolescent voices. *Psychology Today,* pp. 40, 43, 44.

Cowan, P. (1978). *Piaget with feeling.* New York: Holt, Rinehart & Winston.

Cox, T. (Host). (1985, September 29). "At issue" [Television talk show]. Channel 2, Los Angeles.

Cox, W. M., & Klinger, E. (1988). A motivational model of alcohol use. *Journal of Abnormal Psychology, 97,* 168–180.

Cremin, L. (1961). *The transformation of the school.* New York: Knopf.

Critelli, J. W., & Baldwin, A. (1979). Birth order complementarity versus homogamy as determinants of attraction in dating relationships. *Perceptual and Motor Skills, 49,* 467–471.

Crites, J. O. (1989). Career differentiation in adolescence. In D. Stern & D. Eichorn (Eds.), *Adolescence and work.* Hillsdale, NJ: Erlbaum.

Cronbach, L. J., & Snow, R. E. (1977). *Aptitudes and instructional methods.* New York: Irvington.

Cross, K. P. (1984, November). The rising tide of school reform reports. *Phi Delta Kappan,* pp. 167–172.

Csikszentmihalyi, M., & Larson, R. (1984). *Being adolescent.* New York: Basic Books.

Cuban, L. (1988, April). You're on the right track, David. *Phi Delta Kappan,* pp. 571–572.

Curtiss, S. (1978). *Genie.* New York: Academic Press.

D

Damon, A. (1977). *Human biology and ecology.* New York: W. W. Norton.

Damon, W., & Hart, D. (1982). The development of self-understanding from infancy through adolescence. *Child Development, 53,* 841–864.

Danner, F. (1989). Cognitive development in adolescence. In J. Worrell & F. Danner (Eds.), *The adolescent as decision maker.* New York: Academic Press.

Danziger, S. K., & Radin, N. (1989, April). *Absent does not equal uninvolved: Predictors of fathering in teen mother families.* Paper presented at the meeting of the Society for Research in Child Development, Kansas City.

Darling, C. A., Kallen, D. J., & VanDusen, J. E. (1984). Sex in transition, 1900–1984. *Journal of Youth and Adolescence, 13,* 385–399.

Deci, E. (1975). *Intrinsic motivation.* New York: Plenum.

DeFries, J. C., Plomin, R., Vandenberg, S. G., & Kuse, A. R. (1981). Parent-offspring resemblance in cognitive abilities in the Colorado adoption project: Biological, adoption, and control parents and one-year-old children. *Intelligence, 5,* 245–277.

DeLoache, J. S., Cassidy, D. J., & Carpenter, C. J. (1987). The Three Bears are all boys: Mother's gender labeling of neutral picture book characters. *Sex Roles, 17,* 163–178.

Demorest, A., Meyer, C., Phelps, E., Gardner, H., & Winner, E. (1984). Words speak louder than actions: Understanding deliberately false remarks. *Child Development, 55,* 1527–1534.

Dempster, F. N. (1981). Memory span: Sources of individual and developmental differences. *Psychological Bulletin, 89,* 63–100.

Denham, S. A., & Almeida, M. C. (1987). Children's social problem-solving skills, behavioral adjustment, and interventions: A meta-analysis evaluating theory and practice. *Journal of Applied Developmental Psychology, 8,* 391–409.

Deutsch, M. (1988). Use of innovative educational techniques with dropouts. In *William T. Grant Foundation Annual Report,* New York.

Dewey, J. (1933). *How we think: A restatement of the relation of reflective thinking to the educative process.* Lexington, MA: D. C. Heath.

Diamond, E. E. (1988). Women's occupational plans and decisions: An introduction. *Applied Psychology: An International Review, 37,* 97–102.

Dickerscheid, J. D., Schwarz, P. M., Noir, S., & El-Taliawy, T. (1988). Gender concept development of preschool-aged children in the United States and Egypt. *Sex Roles, 18,* 669–677.

Dickinson, G. E. (1975). Dating behavior of black and white adolescents before and after desegregation. *Journal of Marriage and the Family, 37,* 602–608.

Dimsdale, J. E. (1988). A perspective on Type A behavior and coronary heart disease. *The New England Journal of Medicine, 318,* 110–112.

Dishion, T. J., Patterson, G. R., & Skinner, M. L. (1989, April). *Parent monitoring and peer relations in the drift to deviant peers.* Paper presented at the biennial meeting of the Society for Research in Child Development, Kansas City.

Dishion, T. J., & Skinner, M. S. (1989, April). *A process model for the role of peer relations in adolescent social adjustment.* Paper presented at the biennial meeting of the Society for Research in Child Development, Kansas City.

Dodge, K. A. (1983). Behavioral antecedents of peer social status. *Child Development, 54,* 1386–1399.

Dodge, K. A. (1985, April). *Assessment and training of social skills.* Paper presented at the biennial meeting of the Society for Research in Child Development, Toronto.

Dodge, K. A., Pettit, G. S., McClaskey, C. L., & Brown, M. M. (1986). Social competence in children. *Monographs of the Society for Research in Child Development, 51*(2, Serial No. 213).

Dohrenwend, B. P., & Shrout, P. E. (1985). "Hassles" in the conceptualization and measurement of life stress variables. *American Psychologist, 40,* 780–785.

Donovan, J. E., & Jessor, R. (1978). Adolescent problem drinking: Psychosocial correlates in a national sample study. *Journal of Studies on Alcohol, 39,* 1506–1524.

Dooley, D., Whalen, C. K., & Flowers, J. V. (1978). Verbal response styles of children and adolescents in a counseling analog setting: Effects of age, sex, and labeling. *Journal of Counseling Psychology, 25,* 85–95.

Douvan, E., & Adelson, J. (1966). *The adolescent experience.* New York: Wiley.

Downey, A. M., Frank, G. C., Webber, L. S., Harsha, D. W., Virgilio, S. J., Franklin, F. A., & Berenson, G. S. (1987). Implementation of "Heart Smart": A cardiovascular school health promotion program. *Journal of School Health, 57,* 98–104.

Downs, A. C., & Langlois, J. H. (1988). Sex typing: Construct and measurement issues. *Sex Roles, 18,* 87–100.

Dreyer, P. H. (1982). Sexuality during adolescence. In B. B. Wolman (Ed.), *Handbook of developmental psychology.* Englewood Cliffs, NJ: Prentice-Hall.

Ducey, S. (1989, April). *Gender differences in mathematics: Beyond descriptions.* Paper presented at the biennial meeting of the Society for Research in Child Development, Kansas City.

Duck, S. (1989). *Relating to others.* Chicago: Dorsey Press.

Duck, S. W. (1975). Personality similarity and friendship choices by adolescents. *European Journal of Social Psychology, 5,* 351–365.

Duncan, D. F. (1978). Attitudes toward parents and delinquency in suburban adolescent males. *Adolescence, 13,* 365–369.

Dunn, J., & Kendrick, C. (1982). *Siblings.* Cambridge, MA: Harvard University Press.

Dunphy, D. C. (1963). The social structure of urban adolescent peer groups. *Society, 26,* 230–246.

Durden-Smith, J., & Desimone, D. (1983). *Sex and the brain.* New York: Arbor House.

Durkin, K. (1985). Television and sex-role acquisition: 1. Content. *British Journal of Social Psychology, 24,* 101–113.

Dyer, H. S. (1987). The effects of coaching for scholastic aptitude. *NASSP Bulletin, 71,* 46–53.

E

Eagleston, J. R., Kirmil-Gray, K., Thoresen, C. E., Wiedenfield, S. A., Bracke, P., Heft, L., & Arnow, B. (in press). Physical health correlates of Type A behavior in children and adolescents. *Journal of Behavioral Medicine.*

Ebata, A. T., & Moos, R. H. (1989, April). *Coping and adjustment in four groups of adolescents.* Paper presented at the biennial meeting of the Society for Research in Child Development, Kansas City.

Eccles, J. (1987). Gender roles and achievement patterns: An expectancy value perspective. In J. M. Reinisch, L. A. Rosenblum, & S. A. Sanders (Eds.), *Masculinity/femininity.* New York: Oxford University Press.

Eccles, J., & Hoffman, L. W. (1984). Sex roles, socialization, and occupational behavior. In H. W. Stevenson & A. E. Siegel (Eds.), *Research in child development and public policy* (Vol. 1). Chicago: University of Chicago Press.

Eccles, J., MacIver, D., & Lange, L. (1986). *Classroom practices and motivation to study math.* Paper presented at the annual meeting of the American Educational Research Association, San Francisco.

Eccles, J. S., Harold-Goldsmith, R., & Miller, C. L. (1989, April). *Parents' stereotypic beliefs about gender differences and adolescence.* Paper presented at the biennial meeting of the Society for Research in Child Development, Kansas City.

Eccles, J. S., Midgley, C., Feldlaufer, H., Reuman, D., Wigfield, A., & MacIver, D. (1989, April). *Junior high transition: Evidence of a developmental mismatch.* Paper presented at the biennial meeting of the Society for Research in Child Development, Kansas City.

Edelbrock, C. (1989, April). *Self-reported internalizing and externalizing problems in a community sample of adolescents.* Paper presented at the biennial meeting of the Society for Research in Child Development, Kansas City.

Edelman, M. W. (1987). *Families in peril: An agenda for social change.* New York: Alan Guttmacher Institute.

Edmonds, R. (1979). Some schools work and more can. *Social Policy, 9,* 28–32.

Edwards, E. D., & Edwards, M. E. (1988). Alcoholism prevention/treatment and native American youth: A community approach. *Journal of Drug Issues, 18,* 103–114.

Eger, M. (1981). The conflict in moral education: An informal case study. *Public Interest, 63,* 62–80.

Eisenberg, N. (1987). The relation of altruism and other moral behaviors to moral cognition: Methodological and conceptual issues. In N. Eisenberg (Ed.), *Contemporary topics in developmental psychology*. New York: Wiley.

Eisenberg, N. (1989, April). *Sources of variation in prosocial moral reasoning*. Paper presented at the biennial meeting of the Society for Research in Child Development, Kansas City.

Eitzen, D. S. (1975). Athletics in the status system of male adolescents: A replication of Coleman's *The adolescent society*. *Adolescence, 10,* 267–276.

Ek, C. A., & Steelman, L. C. (1988). Becoming a runaway. *Youth and Society, 19,* 334–358.

Elder, G. H. (1968). Democratic parent-youth relations in cross-national perspective. *Social Science Quarterly, 49,* 216–228.

Elder, G. H. (1975). Adolescence in the life cycle. In S. E. Dragastin & G. H. Elder (Eds.), *Adolescence in the life cycle: Psychological change and social context.* New York: Wiley.

Elder, G. H. (1980). Adolescence in historical perspective. In J. Adelson (Ed.), *Handbook of adolescent psychology.* New York: Wiley.

Elder, G. H., & Caspi, A. (in press). Studying lives in a changing society. In A. I. Rabin, R. A. Zucker, S. Frank, and R. Emmons (Eds.), *Study in persons and lives.* New York: Springer.

Eliade, M. (1958). *Birth and rebirth: The religious meaning of initiation in human culture.* New York: Harper & Brothers.

Elkind, D. (1961). Quantity conceptions in junior and senior high school students. *Child Development, 32,* 551–560.

Elkind, D. (1967). Egocentrism in adolescence. *Child Development, 38,* 1025–1034.

Elkind, D. (1971). *Sympathetic understanding of the child six to sixteen.* Boston: Allyn & Bacon.

Elkind, D. (1976). *Child development and education: A Piagetian perspective.* New York: Oxford University Press.

Elkind, D. (1978). Understanding the young adolescent. *Adolescence, 13,* 127–134.

Elkind, D. (1981). *The hurried child.* Reading, MA: Addison-Wesley.

Elkind, D. (1985). Reply to D. Lapsley and M. Murphy's *Developmental Review* paper. *Developmental Review, 5,* 218–226.

Elkind, D., & Bowen, R. (1979). Imaginary audience behavior in children and adolescents. *Developmental Psychology, 15,* 38–44.

Elliott, D. S., Huizinga, D., & Menard, S. (1989). Multiple problem youth: Delinquency, substance abuse, and mental health problems. New York: Springer-Verlag.

Engel, J. W. (1984). Marriage in the People's Republic of China: Analysis of a new law. *Journal of Marriage and the Family, 46,* 947–954.

Englert, C. S., Stewart, S. R., & Hiebert, E. H. (1988). Young writers' use of text structure in expository text generation. *Journal of Educational Psychology, 80,* 143–151.

Enright, R. D., Lapsley, D., & Olson, L. (1984). Moral judgment and the social cognitive development research program. In S. Modgil & C. Modgil (Eds.), *Lawrence Kohlberg: Consensus and controversy.* Slough, England: NFER Press.

Enright, R. D., Levy, V. M., Harris, D., & Lapsley, D. K. (1987). Do economic conditions influence how theorists view adolescents? *Journal of Youth and Adolescence, 16,* 541–559.

Enright, R. D., Santos, M. J. D., & Al-Mabuk, R. (in press). The adolescent as forgiver. *Journal of Adolescence.*

Enright, R. D., Shukla, D., & Lapsley, D. (1980). Adolescent egocentrism in early and late adolescence. *Journal of Youth and Adolescence, 9,* 101–11.

Entwistle, D. R. (1988). Adolescents change schools. *Contemporary Psychology, 33,* 585–586.

Epstein, H. T. (1974). Phrenoblysis: Special brain and mind growth periods. *Developmental Psychobiology, 7,* 217–224.

Epstein, H. T. (1978). Growth spurts during brain development: Implications for educational policy and practice. In J. S. Chall & A. F. Mirsky (Eds.), *Education and the brain.* Chicago: University of Chicago Press.

Epstein, H. T. (1980). EEG developmental stages. *Developmental Psychobiology, 13,* 629–631.

Erikson, E. H. (1950). *Childhood and society.* New York: W. W. Norton.

Erikson, E. H. (1962). *Young man Luther.* New York: W. W. Norton.

Erikson, E. H. (1968). *Identity: Youth and crisis.* New York: W. W. Norton.

Erikson, E. H. (1969). *Gandhi's truth.* New York: W. W. Norton.

Erikson, E. H. (1970). Reflections on the dissent of contemporary youth. *International Journal of Psychoanalysis, 51,* 11–22.

Erikson, E. H. (1980). *Identity and the life cycle.* New York: W. W. Norton.

Erlick, A. C., & Starry, A. R. (1973, June). *Sources of information for career decisions.* Report of Poll No. 98, Purdue Opinion Panel.

Eron, L. D. (1987). The development of aggression from the perspective of developing behaviorism. *American Psychologist, 42,* 435–442.

F

Falbo, T., & Polit, D. F. (1986). A quantitative review of the only-child literature: Research evidence and theory development. *Psychological Bulletin, 100,* 176–189.

Fasick, F. A. (1988). Patterns of formal education in high school as rites of passage. *Adolescence, 23,* 457–468.

Fassinger, R. E. (1985). A causal model of college women's career choice. *Journal of Vocational Behavior, 27,* 123–153.

Faust, M. S. (1977). Somatic development of adolescent girls. *Monographs of the Society for Research in Child Development, 42*(1, Serial No. 169).

Feeney, S. (1980). *Schools for young adolescents: Adapting the early childhood model.* Carrboro, NC: Center for Early Adolescence.

Feingold, A. (1988). Cognitive gender differences are disappearing. *American Psychologist, 43,* 95–103.

Feist, J., & Brannon, L. (1989). *An introduction to behavior and health.* Belmont, CA: Wadsworth.

Feldman, D. H. (1989). Creativity: Proof that development occurs. In W. Damon (Ed.), *Child development today and tomorrow.* San Francisco: Jossey-Bass.

Felner, R. D., Ginter, M., & Primavera, J. (1982). Primary prevention during school transitions: Social support and environmental structure. *American Journal of Community Psychology.* New

Festinger, L. (1954). A theory of social comparison processes. *Human Relations, 7,* 117–150.

Fidler, P. P. & Hunter, M. S. (1989). How seminars enhance student success. In M. L. Upcraft & J. N. Gardner (Eds.), *The freshman year experience.* San Francisco: Jossey-Bass.

Field, J. (1981). Whither quantitative history? A review of some recent work in the economic and social history of education. *Historical Methods, 14,* 85–95.

Field, T. M., Widmayer, S. M., Stringer, S., & Ignatoff, E. (1980). Teenager, lower-class, black mothers and their pre-term infants: An intervention and developmental follow-up. *Child Development, 51,* 426–436.

Finley, M. I. (1985, February 3). [Review of D. B. Davis, *Slavery and human progress.*] *New York Times Book Review,* p. 26.

Finney, J. W., & Moos, R. H. (1979). Treatment and outcome for empirical subtypes of alcoholic patients. *Journal of Consulting and Clinical Psychology, 47,* 25–38.

Fischer, J. L. (1981). Transitions in relationship style from adolescence to young adulthood. *Journal of Youth and Adolescence, 10,* 11–24.

Fischer, K. W. (1980). A theory of cognitive development: The control and construction of hierarchies of skills. *Psychological Review, 87,* 477–531.

Fischer, K. W., Hand, H. H., & Russell, S. (1983). The development of abstractions in adolescence and adulthood. In M. L. Commons, F. A. Richards, & C. Armon (Eds.), *Beyond formal operations.* New York: Praeger.

Fischer, K. W., & Lazerson, A. (1984). *Human development.* San Francisco: W. H. Freeman.

Fischman, S. H. (1987, February). Type A on trial. *Psychology Today,* pp. 42–50.

Fisher, T. D. (1987). Family communication and the sexual behavior and attitudes of college students. *Journal of Youth and Adolescence, 16,* 481–495.

Flavell, J. H. (1979). Metacognition and cognitive monitoring: A new area of psychological inquiry. *American Psychologist, 34,* 906–911.

Flavell, J. H. (1980, Fall). A tribute to Piaget. *SRCD Newsletter.*

Flavell, J. H. (1981). Monitoring social-cognitive enterprises: Something else that may develop in the area of social cognition. In J. H. Flavell & L. Ross (Eds.), *Social cognitive development: Frontiers and possible futures.* New York: Cambridge University Press.

Flavell, J. H. (1985). *Cognitive development* (2nd ed.). Englewood Cliffs, NJ: Prentice-Hall.

Flavell, J. H., Botkin, P. T., Fry, C. L., Wright, J. W., & Jarvis, P. E. (1968). *The development of role-taking and communication skills in children.* New York: Wiley.

Fligiel, S. E. G., Venkat, H., Gong, H., & Tashkin, D. P. (1988). Bronchial pathology in chronic marijuana smokers: A light and electron microscopy study. *Journal of Psychoactive Drugs, 20,* 33–42.

Foon, A. E. (1987). Smoking prevention in programs for adolescents: The value of social psychological approaches. *International Journal of Addiction, 21,* 1017–1029.

Ford, M. (1986). *Androgyny as self-assertion and integration: Implications for psychological and social competence.* Unpublished manuscript, Stanford University, School of Education, Stanford, CA.

Ford, M. E. (1986). A living systems conceptualization of social intelligence: Outcomes, processes, and developmental change. In R. J. Sternberg (Ed.), *Advances in the psychology of human intelligence* (Vol. 3). Hillsdale, NJ: Erlbaum.

Ford, M. E. (1987). Processes contributing to adolescent social competence. In M. E. Ford & D. H. Ford (Eds.), *Humans as self-constructing living systems.* Hillsdale, NJ: Erlbaum.

Forehand, G., Ragosta, J., & Rock, D. (1976). *Conditions and processes of effective school desegregation.* Princeton, NJ: Educational Testing Service.

Fowler, J. W. (1976). Stages in faith: The structural-developmental approach. In T. Hennessy (Ed.), *Values and moral development.* New York: Paulist Press.

Fox, L. H., Brody, L., & Tobin, D. (1979). *Women and mathematics.* Baltimore, MD: Intellectually Gifted Study Group, Johns Hopkins University.

Fox, V. M. (1988). Summer work enhancement program: An evaluation. In *William T. Grant Foundation Annual Report,* New York.

Freedman, J. L. (1984). Effects of television violence on aggressiveness. *Psychological Bulletin, 96,* 227–246.

Fregly, M. J., & Luttge, W. G. (1982). *Human endocrinology: An interactive text.* New York: Elsevier Science.

French, D. C. (in press). Heterogeneity of peer-rejected boys: Aggressive and nonaggressive subtypes. *Child Development.*

Freud, A. (1958). *The ego and the mechanisms of defense.* New York: International Universities Press.

Freud, A. (1958). Adolescence. *Psychoanalytic Study of the Child, 13,* 255–278.

Freud, A. (1966). Instinctual anxiety during puberty. In *The writings of Anna Freud: The ego and the mechanisms of defense.* New York: International Universities Press.

Freud, A., & Dann, S. (1951). Instinctual anxiety during puberty. In A. Freud, *The ego and its mechanisms of defense.* New York: International Universities Press.

Freud, S. (1924). *A general introduction to psychoanalysis.* New York: Boni & Liveright.

Friedman, M., & Rosenman, R. (1974). *Type A behavior and your heart.* New York: Knopf.

Frisch, R., & Revelle, R. (1970). Height and weight at menarche and a hypothesis of critical body weights and adolescent events. *Science, 169,* 397–399.

Fuqua, D. R., Blum, C. R., & Hartman, B. W. (1988). Empirical support for the differential diagnosis of career indecision. *Career Development Quarterly, 36,* 364–373.

Furstenberg, F. F. (1988). Child care after divorce and remarriage. In E. M. Hetherington & J. D. Arasteh (Eds.), *Impact of divorce, single-parenting, and stepparenting on children.* Hillsdale, NJ: Erlbaum.

Furstenberg, F. F., Brooks-Gunn, J., & Chase-Lansdale, L. (1989). Teenaged pregnancy and childbearing. *American Psychologist, 44,* 313–320.

Furstenberg, J. J., Brooks-Gunn, J., & Morgan, S. P. (1987). *Adolescent mothers in later life.* New York: Cambridge University Press.

Furth, H. G., & Wachs, H. (1975). *Thinking goes to school.* New York: Oxford University Press.

G

Gage, N. L. (1965). Desirable behaviors of teachers. *Urban Education, 1,* 85–95.

Gagne, E. D. (1985). *The cognitive psychology of school learning.* Boston: Little, Brown.

Gagne, E. D., Weidemann, C., Bell, M. S., & Ander, T. D. (in press). Training 13-year-olds to elaborate while studying text. *Journal of Human Learning.*

Gagnon, J. H., & Simon, W. (1973). *Sexual conduct.* Chicago: Aldine.

Galambos, N. L., & Maggs, J. L. (1989, April). *The after-school ecology of young adolescents and self-reported behavior.* Paper presented at the biennial meeting of the Society for Research in Child Development, Kansas City.

Galanter, M. (1989). *Cults: Faith, healing, and coercion.* New York: Oxford U. Press.

Gallup, A. M., & Clark, D. L. (1987). The 19th annual Gallup poll of the public's attitude toward the public schools. *Phi Delta Kappan, 69,* 17–30.

Gallup, G., & Poling, D. (1980). *The search for America's faith.* New York: Abington.

Garbarino, J. (1980). Some thoughts on school size and its effects on adolescent development. *Journal of Youth and Adolescence, 9,* 19–31.

Garbarino, J., & Asp, C. E. (1981). *Successful schools and competent students.* Lexington, MA: Lexington Books.

Garber, J., Kriss, M. R., Koch, M., & Lindholm, L. (1988). Recurrent depression in adolescents: A follow-up study. *Journal of the American Academy of Child and Adolescent Psychiatry, 27,* 49–54.

Gardner, H. (1983). *Frames of mind.* New York: Basic Books.

Gardner, H. (1989). Beyond a modular view of mind. In W. Damon (Ed.), *Child development today and tomorrow.* San Francisco: Jossey-Bass.

Gardner, H., & Perkins, D. (Eds.). (1989). *Art, mind, and education.* Ithaca, NY: U. of Illinois Press.

Garfinkel, P. E., & Garner, D. M. (1982). *Anorexia nervosa.* New York: Brunner/Mazel.

Garner, R. (1987). *Metacognition and reading comprehension.* Norwood, NJ: Ablex.

Garrick, T. R., & Loewenstein, R. J. (1989). Behavioral medicine in the general hospital. *Psychosomatics, 30,* 123–134.

Garrison, K. C. (1968). Physiological changes in adolescence. In J. F. Adams (Ed.), *Understanding adolescence.* Boston: Allyn & Bacon.

Gawin, F. (1989). Cocaine dependence. *Annual Review of Medicine, 39.* Palo Alto, CA: Annual Reviews.

Gelman, R., & Baillargeon, R. (1983). A review of some Piagetian concepts. In P. H. Mussen (Ed.), *Handbook of child psychology.* New York: Wiley.

Giaconia, R. M., & Hedges, L. V. (1982). Identifying features of effective open education. *Review of Educational Research, 52,* 579–602.

Gibbs, J. T. (1989). Black American adolescents. In J. T. Gibbs & L. N. Huang (Eds.), *Children of color.* San Francisco: Jossey-Bass.

Gibbs, J. T., & Huang, L. N. (1989). A conceptual framework for assessing and treating minority youth. In J. T. Gibbs & L. N. Huang (Eds.), *Children of color.* San Francisco, CA: Jossey-Bass.

Gieringer, D. H. (1988). Marijuana, driving, and accident safety. *Journal of Psychoactive Drugs, 20,* 93–102.

Gilgun, J. F. (1984). Sexual abuse of the young female in life course perspective (Doctoral dissertation, Syracuse University). *Dissertation Abstracts International, 45,* 3058.

Gill, S., Stockard, J., Johnson, M., & Williams, S. (1987). Measuring gender differences: The expressive dimension and critique of the androgyny scales. *Sex Roles, 17,* 375–400.

Gilligan, C. (1982). *In a different voice.* Cambridge, MA: Harvard University Press.

Gilligan, C. (1985, April). *Response to critics.* Paper presented at the biennial meeting of the Society for Research in Child Development, Toronto.

Ginott, H. (1969). *Between parent and teenager.* New York: Avon Books.

Ginzberg, E. (1972). Toward a theory of occupational choice: A restatement. *Vocational Guidance Quarterly, 20,* 169–176.

Ginzberg, E., Ginzberg, S. W., Axelrad, S., & Herman, J. L. (1951). *Occupational choice.* New York: Columbia University.

Gjerde, P. (1985, April). *Adolescent depression and parental socialization patterns: A prospective study.* Paper presented at the biennial meeting of the Society for Research in Child Development, Toronto.

Gjerde, P. F., & Block, J. (1989, April). *Depressive symptoms and personality in adolescence: A longitudinal perspective on gender differences.* Paper presented at the biennial meeting of the Society for Research in Child Development, Kansas City.

Gjerde, P. F., Block, J., & Block, J. E. (1985). *Parental interactive patterns in dyads and triads: Prospective relationships to adolescent personality characteristics.* Unpublished manuscript, University of California, Berkeley.

Glass, G. V., & Smith, M. L. (1978, September). *Meta-analysis of research on the relationship of class size and achievement.* San Francisco: Far West Educational Laboratory.

Glazer, R. & Bassok, M. (1989). Learning theory and the study of instruction. *Annual Review of Psychology, 40.* Palo Alto, CA: Annual Reviews.

Glick, P. C., & Lin, S. (1986). Recent changes in divorce and remarriage. *Journal of Marriage and the Family, 48,* 737–747.

Globerson, T. (1983). Mental capacity and cognitive functioning: Developmental and social class differences. *Developmental Psychology, 19,* 225–230.

Glueck, S., & Glueck, E. (1950). *Unraveling juvenile delinquency.* Cambridge, MA: Harvard University Press.

Goethals, G. W., & Klos, D. S. (1970). *Experiencing youth.* Boston: Little, Brown.

Gold, M. (1970). *Delinquent behavior in an American city.* Belmont, CA: Brooks/Cole.

Gold, M. (1987). Social ecology. In H. C. Quay (Ed.), *Handbook of juvenile delinquency.* New York: Wiley.

Gold, M., & Petronio, R. J. (1980). Delinquent behavior in adolescence. In J. Adelson (Ed.), *Handbook of adolescent psychology.* New York: Wiley.

Gold, M., & Reimer, D. J. (1975). Changing patterns of delinquent behavior among Americans 13–16 years old, 1967–72. *Crime and Delinquency Literature, 7,* 483–517.

Gold, M., & Yanof, D. S. (1985). Mothers, daughters, and girlfriends. *Journal of Personality and Social Psychology, 49,* 654–659.

Gold, M. S., Gallanter, M., & Stimmel, B. (1987). *Cocaine.* New York: Haworth Press.

Goldsmith, H. H., Buss, A. H., Plomin, R., Rothbart, R., Thomas, A., Chess, S., Hinde, R. A., & McCall, R. B. (1987). Roundtable: What is temperament? Four approaches. *Child Development, 58,* 505–529.

Goldstein, A. P., Sprafkin, R. P., Gershaw, N. J., & Klein, P. (1981). *Skill-streaming the adolescent.* Champaign, IL: Research Press.

Gong, H., Tashkin, M. D., Valentine, J. L., Simmons, M. S., Clark, V. A., & Coulson, A. H. (1988). Sensitivity and specificity of Serum Δ^9-Tetrahydrocannabinol and 11-nor-9-caroxy-Δ^9-Tetrahydrocannabinol by radioimmunoassay in identifying habitual daily smokers of marijuana. *Journal of Psychoactive Drugs, 20,* 103–106.

Goodchilds, J. D., & Zellman, G. L. (1984). Sexual signalling and sexual aggression in adolescent relationships. In N. M. Malamuth & E. D. Donnerstein (Eds.), *Pornography and sexual aggression.* New York: Academic Press.

Goodlad, J. (1983). *A place called school.* New York: McGraw-Hill.

Goodman, R. A., Mercy, J. A., Loya, F., Rosenberg, M. L., Smith, J. C., Allen, N. H., Vargas, L., & Kolts, R. (1986). Alcohol use and interpersonal violence: Alcohol detected in homicide victims. *American Journal of Public Health, 76,* 144–149.

Gordon, K. A. (1976). *Great expectations: Unprotected intercourse scenario.* Princeton, NJ: Princeton University, McCosh Health Center.

Gordon, S., & Gilgun, J. F. (1987). Adolescent sexuality. In V. B. Van Hasselt & M. Hersen (Eds.), *Handbook of adolescent psychology.* New York: Pergamon.

Gordon, V. P. (1989). Origins and purposes of freshman seminar. In M. L. Upcraft & J. N. Gardner (Eds.), *The freshman year experience.* San Francisco: Jossey-Bass.

Gore, T. (1987). *Raising PG kids in an X-rated society.* Nashville, TN: Abingdon Press.

Gottlieb, D. (1966). Teaching and students: The views of Negro and white teachers. *Sociology of Education, 37,* 345–353.

Gottlieb, D., & Chafetz, J. S. (1977). Dynamics of familial, generational conflict and reconciliation. *Youth and Society, 9,* 213–224.

Gottman, J. M., & Parker, J. G. (Eds.). (1987). *Conversations with friends.* New York: Cambridge University Press.

Graham, S. (1984). Communicating sympathy and anger to black and white students: The cognitive (attributional) antecedents of affective cues. *Journal of Personality and Social Psychology, 47,* 40–54.

Graham, S. (1986, August). *Can attribution theory tell us something about motivation in blacks?* Paper presented at the meeting of the American Psychological Association, Washington, DC.

Graham, S. (1987, August). *Developing relations between attributions, affect, and intended social behavior.* Paper presented at the meeting of the American Psychological Association, New York.

Grawbard, S. R. (Ed.). (1988). *The artificial intelligence debate.* Cambridge, MA: MIT Press.

Gray, W. M., & Hudson, L. M. (1984). Formal operations and the imaginary audience. *Developmental Psychology, 20,* 619–627.

Greenberger, E., & Steinberg, L. (1981). *Project for the study of adolescent work: Final report.* Report prepared for the National Institute of Education, U.S. Department of Education, Washington, DC.

Greene, A. L. (1989, April). *Differentiating developmental contributors and contexts of adolescent stress.* Paper presented at the biennial meeting of the Society for Research in Child Development, Kansas City.

Greene, B. (1988, May). The children's hour. *Esquire Magazine,* pp. 47–49.

Greenfield, P., & Beagles-Roos, J. (in press). Television vs. radio: The cognitive impact on different socioeconomic and ethnic groups. *Journal of Communication.*

Greenfield, P. M. (1966). On culture and conservation. In J. S. Bruner, R. R. Oliver, & P. M. Greenfield (Eds.), *Studies in cognitive growth.* New York: Wiley.

Greenfield, P. M., Bruzzone, L., Koyamatsu, K., Satuloff, W., Nixon, K., Brodie, M., & Kingsdale, D. (1987). What is rock music doing to the minds of our youth? A first experimental look at the effects of rock music lyrics and music videos. *Journal of Early Adolescence, 7,* 315–329.

Gribbons, W. D., & Lohnes, P. R. (1964). Relationships among measures of readiness for vocational planning. *Journal of Counseling Psychology, 11,* 13–19.

Grief, E. B., & Ullman, K. J. (1982). The psychological impact of menarche on early adolescent females: A review of the literature. *Child Development, 53,* 1413–1430.

Grimes, B., Mattimore, K. (1989, April). *The effects of stress and exercise on identity formation in adolescence.* Paper presented at the biennial meeting of the Society for Research in Child Development, Kansas City.

Grotevant, H. D., & Adams, G. R. (1984). Development of an objective measure to assess ego identity in adolescence: Validation and application. *Journal of Youth and Adolescence, 13,* 419–438.

Grotevant, H. D., & Cooper, C. R. (1985). Patterns of interaction in family relationships and the development of identity exploration in adolescence. *Child Development, 56,* 415–428.

Grotevant, H. D., & Durrett, M. E. (1980). Occupational knowledge and career development in adolescence. *Journal of Vocational Behavior, 17,* 171–182.

Grubb, W. N. (1989). Preparing youth for work. In D. Stern & D. Eichorn (Eds.), *Adolescence and work.* Hillsdale, NJ: Erlbaum.

Guilford, J. P. (1967). *The nature of human intelligence.* New York: McGraw-Hill.

Gump, P. V. (1980). The school as a social situation. In M. R. Rosenzweig & L. V. Porter (Eds.), *Annual Review of Psychology* (Vol. 31).

Gutek, B. A. (1988). Sex segregation and women at work: A selective review. *Applied Psychology: An International Review, 37,* 103–120.

Guttentag, M., & Bray, H. (1976). *Undoing sex stereotypes: Research and resources for educators.* New York: McGraw-Hill.

Guttentag, R. E. (1984). The mental effort requirement of cumulative rehearsal: A developmental study. *Journal of Experimental Child Psychology, 37,* 92–106.

H

Haas, A. (1979). *Teenage sexuality: A survey of teenage sexual behavior.* New York: Macmillan.

Hahn, A. (1987, December). Reaching out to America's dropouts: What to do? *Phi Delta Kappan,* pp. 256–263.

Hall, G. S. (1904). *Adolescence* (Vols. I & II). Englewood Cliffs, NJ: Prentice-Hall.

Hamburg, B. (1974). Early adolescence: A specific and stressful stage of the life cycle. In G. Coelho, D. A. Hamburg, & J. E. Adams (Eds.), *Coping and adaptation.* New York: Basic Books.

Hamburg, D. A. & Takanishi, R. (1989). Preparing for life: The critical transition of adolescence. *American Psychologist, 44,* 825–827.

Harken, L. S. (1987). The prevention of adolescent smoking: A public health priority. *Evaluation and the Health Profession, 10,* 373–393.

Hart, D., Maloney, J., & Damon, W. (1987). *The meaning and development of identity.* London: Routledge & Kegan Paul.

Harter, S. (1981). A new self-report scale of intrinsic versus extrinsic orientation in the classroom: Motivational and informational components. *Developmental Psychology, 17,* 300–312.

Harter, S. (1982). The perceived competence scale for children. *Child Development, 53,* 87–97.

Harter, S., & Marold, D. (1989, April). *A model of risk factors in adolescent suicide: The mediational role of self-worth.* Paper presented at the biennial meeting of the Society for Research in Child Development, Kansas City.

Hartshorne, H., & May, M. S. (1928–30). *Moral studies in the nature of character: Studies in deceit* (Vol. 1); *Studies in self-control* (Vol. 2); *Studies in the organization of character* (Vol. 3). New York: Macmillan.

Hartup, W. W. (1983). Peer relations. In P. H. Mussen (Ed.), *Handbook of child psychology* (Vol. 4, 4th ed.). New York: Wiley.

Hartup, W. W. (1989). Social relationships and their developmental significance. *American Psychologist, 44,* 120–126.

Hathaway, B. (1984, September). Japanese question the value of IQ tests. *APA Monitor,* pp. 10–11.

Havighurst, R. J. (1976). A cross-cultural view. In J. F. Adams (Ed.), *Understanding adolescence.* Boston: Allyn & Bacon.

Havighurst, R. J. (1987). Adolescent culture and subculture. In V. B. Van Hasselt & M. Hersen (Eds.), *Handbook of adolescent psychology.* New York: Pergamon.

Hawkins, J. A., & Berndt, T. J. (1985, April). *Adjustment following the transition to junior high school.* Paper presented at the biennial meeting of the Society for Research in Child Development, Toronto.

Hawkins, R. (1979, October 29). "Ropers" and "dopers." *Dallas Morning News,* p. 1.

Hayden-Thomson, L., Rubin, K. H., & Hymel, S. (1987). Sex preferences in sociometric choices. *Developmental Psychology, 23,* 558–562.

Hayes, D. (Ed.). (1987). *Risking the future: Adolescent sexuality, pregnancy, and childbearing* (Vol. 1). Washington, DC: National Academy Press.

Hazen, C., & Shaver, P. (1987). Romantic love conceptualized as an attachment process. *Journal of Personality and Social Psychology, 51,* 511–524.

Heath, S. B. (1989). Oral and literate traditions among Black Americans living in poverty. *American Psychologist, 44,* 367–373.

Hedges, L. V., & Stock, W. (1983, Spring). The effects of class size: An examination of rival hypotheses. *American Educational Research Journal,* 63–85.

Heider, F. (1958). *The psychology of interpersonal relations.* New York: Wiley.

Hein, K. (1989). AIDS in adolescence. *Journal of Adolescent Health Care, 10,* 105–135.

Helson, R., Elliot, T., & Leigh, J. (1989). Adolescent antecedents of women's work patterns. In D. Stern & D. Eichorn (Eds.), *Adolescence and work.* Hillsdale, NJ: Erlbaum.

Henderson, N. D. (1982). Human behavior genetics. *Annual Review of Psychology, 33,* 403–440.

Henggeler, S. W. (1989). *Delinquency in adolescence.* Newbury Park, CA: Sage.

Hennessey, B. A., & Amabile, T. M. (1988). The conditions of creativity. In R. J. Sternberg (Ed.), *The nature of creativity.* New York: Cambridge U. Press.

Herdt, G. H. (1988, August). *Coming out processes as an anthropological rite of passage.* Paper presented at the meeting of the American Psychological Association, Atlanta, GA.

Hess, L., Lonky, E., & Roodin, P. A. (1985, April). *The relationship of moral reasoning and ego strength to cheating behavior.* Paper presented at the meeting of the Society for Research in Child Development, Toronto.

Hess, R. D. (1970). Social class and ethnic influences on socialization. In P. H. Mussen (Ed.), *Carmichael's manual of child psychology* (Vol. 2, 3rd ed.). New York: Wiley.

Hetherington, E. M. (1972). Effects of father-absence on personality development in adolescent daughters. *Developmental Psychology, 7,* 313–326.

Hetherington, E. M. (1977). *My heart belongs to daddy: A study of the remarriages of daughters of divorcees and widows.* Unpublished manuscript, University of Virginia.

Hetherington, E. M. (in press). Coping with family transitions: Winners, losers, and survivors. *Child Development.*

Hetherington, E. M., Cox, M., & Cox, R. (1982). Effects of divorce on children and parents. In M. E. Lamb (Ed.), *Nontraditional families.* Hillsdale, NJ: Erlbaum.

Hetherington, E. M., Hagan, M. S., & Anderson, E. R. (1989). Marital transitions: A child's perspective. *American Psychologist, 44,* 303–312.

Hetherington, E. M., Lerner, R. M., & Perlmutter, M. (Eds.). (1989). *Child development in life-span perspective.* Hillsdale, NJ: Erlbaum.

Hiebert, J., & LeFevre, P. (Eds.). (1987). *Conceptual and procedural knowledge: The case of mathematics.* Hillsdale, NJ: Erlbaum.

Higgins, A. (in press). The Just Community approach to moral education: Evolution of the idea and recent findings. In W. M. Kurtines & J. Gewirtz (Eds.), *Moral behavior and development: Advances in theory, research, and application.* Hillsdale, NJ: Erlbaum.

Higgins, A., Power, C., & Kohlberg, L. (1983, April). *Moral atmosphere and moral judgment.* Paper presented at the biennial meeting of the Society for Research in Child Development, Detroit.

Higgins, A. T., & Turnure, J. E. (1984). Distractibility and concentration of attention in children's development. *Child Development, 44,* 1799–1810.

Hill, J. P. (1980a). *Understanding early adolescence: A framework.* Carrboro, NC: Center for Early Adolescence.

Hill, J. P. (1980b). The early adolescent and the family. In M. Johnson (Ed.), *The 79th Yearbook of the National Society for the Study of Education.* Chicago: University of Chicago Press.

Hill, J. P. (1983, April). *Adolescent development.* Paper presented at the biennial meeting of the Society for Research in Child Development, Detroit, MI.

Hill, J. P., & Holmbeck, G. N. (1986). Attachment and autonomy during adolescence. *Annals of Child Development, 3,* 145–189.

Hill, J. P., Holmbeck, G. N., Marlow, L., Green, T. M., & Lynch, M. E. (1985). Pubertal status and parent-child relations in families of seventh-grade boys. *Journal of Early Adolescence, 5,* 31–44.

Hill, J. P., & Steinberg, L. D. (1976, April 26–30). *The development of autonomy in adolescence.* Paper presented at the Symposium on Research on Youth Problems, Fundacion Orbegoza Eizaquirre, Madrid, Spain.

Hinde, R. A. (1989, April). *Differential treatment of particular characteristics in boys and girls.* Paper presented at the biennial meeting of the Society for Research in Child Development, Kansas City.

Hinde, R. A., & Gorebel, J. (1989). The problem of aggression. In J. Gorebel & R. A. Hinde (Eds.). *Aggression and war: Their biological bases.*

Hirsch, B. J. (1989, April). *School transitions and psychological well-being in adolescence: Comparative longitudinal analyses.* Paper presented at the biennial meeting of the Society for Research in Child Development, Kansas City.

Hirsch, B. J., & Rapkin, B. D. (1987). The transition to junior high school: A longitudinal study of self-esteem, psychological symptomatology, school life, and social support. *Child Development, 58,* 1235–1243.

Hoffman, L. W. (1979). Maternal employment: 1979. *American Psychologist, 34,* 859–865.

Hoffman, L. W. (1989). Effects of maternal employment in the two-parent family. *American Psychologist, 44,* 283–292.

Hoffman, M. L. (1980). Moral development in adolescence. In J. Adelson (Ed.), *Handbook of adolescent psychology.* New York: Wiley.

Hoffman, M. L. (in press). Empathy development, moral principles, and action. In W. M. Kurtines & J. Gewirtz (Eds.), *Moral behavior and development: Advances in theory, research, and application.* Hillsdale, NJ: Erlbaum.

Holland, J. L. (1973). *Making vocational choices: A theory of careers.* Englewood Cliffs, NJ: Prentice-Hall.

Holland, J. L. (1985). *Making vocational choices: A theory of vocational personalities and work environments* (2nd ed.). Englewood Cliffs, NJ: Prentice-Hall.

Holland, J. L. (1987). Current status of Holland's theory of careers: Another perspective. *Career Development Quarterly, 36,* 24–30.

Hollingshead, A. B. (1975). *Elmtown's youth and Elmtown revisited.* New York: Wiley.

Holmbeck, G. N., Gasiewski, E., & Crossman, R. (1989, April). *Cognitive development, egocentrism, and adolescent contraceptive knowledge, attitudes and behavior.* Paper presented at the biennial meeting of the Society for Research in Child Development.

Holt, J. (1964). *How children fail.* Belmont, CA: Pitman.

Holtzmann, W. (1982). Cross-cultural comparisons of personality development in Mexico and the United States. In D. Wagner & H. W. Stevenson (Eds.), *Cultural perspectives on child development.* San Francisco: W. H. Freeman.

Hooper, F. H., & Hooper, J. O. (in press). The family as a system of reciprocal relations: Searching for a developmental life-span perspective. In G. Brody & I. E. Siegel (Eds.), *Family research journeys* (Vol. 1). Hillsdale, NJ: Erlbaum.

Howard, M. (1983, March). Postponing sexual involvement: A new approach. *Siecus Report,* pp. 5–6, 8.

Howatt, P. M., & Saxton, A. M. (1988). The incidence of bulimic behavior in a secondary and university school population. *Journal of Youth and Adolescence, 17,* 221–231.

Huang, L. L. (1982). Planned fertility of one-couple one-child policy in the People's Republic of China. *Journal of Marriage and the Family, 44,* 775–784.

Huang, L. N. (1989). Southeast Asian refugee children and adolescents. In J. T. Gibbs & L. N. Huang (Eds.), *Children of color.* San Francisco: Jossey-Bass.

Huang, L. N., & Gibbs, J. T. (1989). Future directions: Implications for research, training, and practice. In J. T. Gibbs & L. N. Huang (Eds.), *Children of color.* San Francisco: Jossey-Bass.

Huesmann, L. R., Eron, L. D., Dubow, E. F., & Seebauer, E. (in press). Television viewing habits in childhood and adult aggression. *Child Development.*

Humphreys, L. G. (1985). A conceptualization of intellectual giftedness. In F. D. Horowitz & M. O'Brien (Eds.), *The gifted and the talented.* Washington, DC: American Psychological Association.

Hunt, K. W. (1970). Syntactic maturity in school children and adults. *Monographs of the Society for Research in Child Development, 35*(1, Serial No. 134).

Hunt, M. (1974). *Sexual behavior in the 1970s.* Chicago: Playboy Press.

Huston, A. C. (1983). Sex-typing. In P. H. Mussen (Ed.), *Handbook of child psychology* (Vol. 4, 4th ed.). New York: Wiley.

Huston, A. C., Siegle, J., & Bremer, M. (1983, April). *Family environment television use by preschool children.* Paper presented at the biennial meeting of the Society for Research in Child Development, Detroit, MI.

Huston, A. C., Watkins, B. A., & Kunkel, D. (1989). Public policy and children's television. *American Psychologist, 44,* 424–433.

Huston-Stein, A., & Higgens-Trenk, A. (1978). Development of females from childhood through adulthood. Career and feminine role orientations. In P. Baltes (Ed.), *Lifespan development and behavior* (Vol. 1). New York: Academic Press.

Hyde, J. S. (1984). Children's understanding of sexist language. *Developmental Psychology, 20,* 697–706.

Hyde, J. S. (1985). *Half the human experience* (3rd ed.). Lexington, MA: D. C. Heath.

Hyde, J. S. (1988). *Half the human experience* (4th ed.). New York: McGraw-Hill.

Hyde, J. S., & Linn, M. C. (1988). Are there sex differences in verbal abilities?: A meta-analysis. *Psychological Bulletin, 104,* 53–69.

Hyman, H. M. (1959). *Political socialization.* New York: Free Press.

I

Iheanacho, S. O. (1987). Minority self-concept: A research review. *Journal of Instructional Psychology, 15,* 3–11.

Inhelder, B., De Caprona, D., & Cornu-Wells, A. (Eds.). (in press). *Piaget today.* Hillsdale, NJ: Erlbaum.

Inoff-Germain, G., Arnold, G. S., Nottelmann, E. D., Susman, E. J., Cutler, G. B., & Chrousos, G. P. (1988). Relations between hormone levels and observational measures of aggressive behavior of young adolescents in family interactions. *Developmental Psychology, 24,* 129–139.

Irvin, F. S. (1988, August). *Clinical perspectives on resilience among gay and lesbian youth.* Paper presented at the annual meeting of the American Psychological Association, Atlanta, GA.

J

Jacklin, C. N. (1989). Female and male: Issues of gender. *American Psychologist, 44,* 127–133.

James, W. (1890). *The principles of psychology.* New York: Dover.

Jencks, C. S., Smith, M., Acland, H., Bane, M. J., Cohen, D., Gintis, H., Heyns, B., & Michelson, S. (1972). *Inequality: A reassessment of the effects of family and schooling in America.* New York: Basic Books.

Jensen, A. R. (1969). How much can we boost IQ and scholastic achievement? *Harvard Educational Review, 39,* 1–123.

Jensen, L. C., & Knight, R. S. (1981). *Moral education: Historical perspectives.* Washington, DC: University Press of America.

Jessor, L., & Jessor, R. (1975). Transition from virginity to nonvirginity among youth: A social-psychological study over time. *Developmental Psychology, 11,* 473–484.

Jessor, R., Costa, F., Jessor, L., & Donovan, J. E. (1983). Time of first intercourse: A prospective study. *Journal of Personality and Social Psychology, 44,* 608–620.

Johnston, L. D. (1973). *Drugs and American youth.* Ann Arbor, MI: Institute of Social Research, University of Michigan.

Johnston, L. D., Bachman, J. G., & O'Malley, P. M. (1986). *Monitoring the future.* Ann Arbor: University of Michigan, Institute of Social Research.

Johnston, L. D., O'Malley, P. M., & Bachman, J. G. (1988). *Illicit drug use, smoking, and drinking by America's high school students, college students, and young adults, 1975–1987.* Washington, DC: National Institute of Drug Abuse.

Johnston, L. D., O'Malley, P. M., & Bachman, J. G. (1989, February 24). *Teen drug use continues decline.* News Release, Institute for Social Research, University of Michigan, Ann Arbor.

Johnston, L. D., O'Malley, P. M., & Eveland, L. K. (1978). Drugs and delinquency: A search for causal connections. In D. G. Kandel (Ed.), *Longitudinal research on drug use: Empirical findings and methodological issues.* Washington, DC: Hemisphere.

Jones, E. R., Forrest, J. D., Goldman, N., Henshaw, S. K., Lincoln, R., Rosoff, J. I., Westoff, C. G., & Wulf, D. (1985). Teenage pregnancy in developed countries: Determinants and policy implications. *Family Planning Perspectives, 17,* 53–63.

Jones, J. M. (1989, August). *Does ethnicity influence behavior? Biculturism in human adaptation.* Paper presented at the meeting of the American Psychological Association, New Orleans.

Jones, L. V. (1984). Black-white achievement differences: Narrowing the gap. *American Psychologist, 39,* 308–315.

Jones, M. C. (1965). Psychological correlates of somatic development. *Child Development, 36,* 899–911.

Jose, P. E. (1985, April). *Development of the immanent justice judgment in moral evaluation.* Paper presented at the biennial meeting of the Society for Research in Child Development, Toronto.

Josselson, R. (1973). Psychodynamic aspects of identity formation in college women. *Journal of Youth and Adolescence, 2,* 3–52.

Josselson, R. (1988). The embedded self: I and thou revisited. In D. K. Lapsley & F. C. Power (Eds.), *Self, ego, and identity: Integrative approaches.* New York: Springer-Verlag.

Justiz, M. J. & Rendon, L. I. (1989). Hispanic students. In M. L. Upcraft & J. N. Gardner (Eds.), *The freshman experience.* San Francisco: Jossey-Bass.

K

Kagan, J. (1984). *The nature of the child.* New York: Basic Books.

Kagan, J. (1987a). Perspectives on infancy. In J. Osofsky (Ed.), *Handbook of Infant Development* (2nd ed.). New York: Wiley.

Kagan, J. (1987b, April). *Temperamental bases for reactions to uncertainty.* Paper presented at the biennial meeting of the Society for Research in Child Development, Baltimore.

Kagan, S., & Madsen, M. C. (1972). Experimental analysis of cooperation and competition of Anglo-American and Mexican children. *Developmental Psychology, 6,* 49–59.

Kahn, P. H. (1989, April). *The components of moral-developmental controversy: Issues and methods.* Paper presented at the biennial meeting of the Society for Research in Child Development, Kansas City.

Kahn, S. E., & Richardson, A. (1983). Evaluation of a course in sex roles for secondary school students. *Sex Roles, 9,* 431–440.

Kail, R., & Pellegrino, J. W. (1985). *Human intelligence.* New York: W. H. Freeman.

Kalick, S. M., & Hamilton, T. E. (1986). The matching hypothesis reexamined. *Journal of Personality and Social Psychology, 51,* 673–682.

Kandel, D., & Lesser, G. S. (1969). Parent-adolescent relationships and adolescence independence in the United States and Denmark. *Journal of Marriage and the Family, 31,* 348–358.

Kandel, D. B. (1974). The role of parents and peers in marijuana use. *Journal of Social Issues, 30,* 107–135.

Kandel, D. B. (1978). Similarity in real-life adolescent friendship pairs. *Journal of Personality and Social Psychology, 36,* 306–312.

Kandel, D. B., & Davies, M. (1986). Adult sequelae of adolescent depressant symptoms. *Archives of General Psychiatry, 43,* 255–262.

Kandel, D. B., Dessler, R. C., & Margulies, R. Z. (1978). Antecedents of adolescent initiation into stages of drug use: A developmental analysis. In D. B. Kandel (Ed.), *Longitudinal research on drug use.* New York: Wiley.

Kane, M. J. (1988). The female athletic role as a status determinant within the social systems of high school adolescents. *Adolescence, 23,* 253–264.

Kanner, A. D., Feldman, S. S., Weinberger, D. A., & Ford, M. E. (1987). Uplifts, hassles, and adaptational outcomes in early adolescents. *Journal of Early Adolescence, 7,* 371–394.

Karplus, R. (1981). Education and formal thought—a modest proposal. In I. Siegel, D. Brodzinsky, & R. Golinkoff (Eds.), *Piagetian theory and research: New directions and applications.* Hillsdale, NJ: Erlbaum.

Katz, P. A. (1968). *No time for youth.* San Francisco: Jossey-Bass.

Kaufmann, A. S., & Flaitz, J. (1987). Intellectual growth. In V. B. Van Hasselt & M. Hersen (Eds.), *Handbook of adolescent psychology.* New York: Pergamon Press.

Kazdin, A. E. (1988). Introduction to special series. *Journal of Consulting and Clinical Psychology, 88,* 3–4.

Kazdin, A. E. (1989). Developmental psychopathology. *American Psychologist, 44,* 180–187.

Kearns, D. T. (1988, April). An education recovery plan for America. *Phi Delta Kappan,* pp. 565–570.

Keating, D. P. (1988). Byrnes' reformulation of Piaget's formal operations: Is what's left what's right? *Developmental Review, 8,* 376–384.

Keating, D. P. (in press). Structuralism, deconstruction, reconstruction: The limits of reasoning. In W. F. Overton (Ed.), *Reasoning, necessity, and logic: Developmental perspectives.* Hillsdale, NJ: Erlbaum.

Keil, F. C. (1984). Mechanisms in cognitive development and the structure of knowledge. In R. J. Sternberg (Ed.), *Mechanisms of cognitive development.* New York: W. H. Freeman.

Kelly, J. A., & de Armas, A. (1989). Social relationships in adolescence: Skill development and training. In J. Worell & F. Danner (Eds.), *The adolescent as decision-maker.* San Diego: Academic Press.

Kelly, J. B. (1987, August). *Children of divorce: Long-term effects and clinical implications.* Paper presented at the meeting of the American Psychological Association, New York City.

Kendall, P. C., Cantwell, D. P., & Kazdin, A. E. (1989). Depression in children and adolescents: Assessment issues and recommendations. *Cognitive Therapy and Research, 13,* 109–146.

Kendall, P. C., & Watson, D. (Eds.). (1989). *Anxiety and depression.* San Diego: Academic Press.

Kenney, A. M. (1987, June). Teen pregnancy: An issue for schools. *Phi Delta Kappan,* pp. 728–736.

Kenniston, K. (1970). Youth: A "new" stage of life. *The American Scholar, 39,* 631–654.

Kenyatta, J. (1965). *Facing Mt. Kenya.* New York: Vintage Books.

Kerr, B. A. (1983). Raising the career aspirations of gifted girls. *Vocational Guidance Quarterly, 32,* 37–43.

Kertzer, D. I. & Schaie, K. W. (Eds.). (1989). *Age structuring in comparative perspective.* Hillsdale, NJ: Erlbaum.

Kett, J. F. (1977). *Rites of passage.* New York: Basic Books.

King, A. J. C., Beazley, R. P., Warren, W. K., Hankins, C. A., Robertson, A. S., & Radford, J. L. (1989). Highlights from the Canada youth and AIDS study. *Journal of School Health, 59,* 139–145.

Kinsey, A. C., Pomeroy, W. B., & Martin, C. E. (1948). *Sexual behavior in the human male.* Philadelphia: Saunders.

Kirschenbaum, J. (1976, July 12). Assembly line for champions. *Sports Illustrated,* pp. 56–65.

Klahr, D. (1989a, April). *Information processing approaches to cognitive development.* Paper presented at the biennial meeting of the Society for Research in Child Development, Kansas City.

Klahr, D. (1989b) Information-processing approaches. In R. Vasta (Ed.), *Six theories of child development: Revised formulations and current issues.* Greenwich, CT: JAI Press.

Klein, K. (1985, April). The research on class size. *Phi Delta Kappan,* pp. 578–580.

Klein, S. S. (1988). Using sex equity research to improve education policies. *Theory into Practice, 27,* 152–160.

Klein, S. S. (in press). Sex equity and gender equity. *Educational Leadership.*

Klitgaard, R. E., & Hall, G. R. (1975). Are there unusually effective schools? *Journal of Human Resources, 10,* 90–106.

Kloba, J. A., & Zimpfer, D. G. (1976). Status and independence as variables in microcounseling training with adolescents. *Journal of Counseling Psychology, 23,* 458–463.

Knox, D., & Wilson, K. (1981). Dating behaviors of university students. *Family Relations, 30,* 255–258.

Kobak, R. R., & Sceery, A. (1988). Attachment in late adolescence: Working models, affect regulation, and representations of self and others. *Child Development, 59,* 135–146.

Kohlberg, L. (1958). *The development of modes of moral thinking and choice in the years 10 to 16.* Unpublished doctoral dissertation, University of Chicago, Chicago, IL.

Kohlberg, L. (1966). A cognitive-developmental analysis of children's sex-role concepts and attitudes. In E. E. Maccoby (Ed.), *The development of sex differences.* Stanford, CA: Stanford University Press.

Kohlberg, L. (1969). Stage and sequence: The cognitive-developmental approach to socialization. In D. A. Goslin (Ed.), *Handbook of socialization theory and research.* Chicago: Rand McNally.

Kohlberg, L. (1976). Moral stages and moralization: The cognitive-developmental approach. In T. Lickona (Ed.), *Moral development and behavior.* New York: Holt, Rinehart & Winston.

Kohlberg, L. (1981). *The philosophy of moral development.* New York: Harper & Row.

Kohlberg, L. (1986). A current statement on some theoretical issues. In S. Modgil & C. Modgil (Eds.), *Lawrence Kohlberg.* Philadelphia: Falmer Press.

Kohlberg, L., & Candee, D. (1979). *Relationships between moral judgment and moral action.* Unpublished manuscript, Harvard University, Cambridge, MA.

Kohlberg, L., & Higgins, A. (1987). School democracy and social interaction. In W. M. Kurtines & J. L. Gewirtz (Eds.), *Moral development through social interaction.* New York: Wiley.

Kohut, H. (1977). *The restoration of the self.* New York: International Universities Press.

Kolb, B., & Whishaw, I. Q. (1988). *Fundamentals of human neuropsychology* (2nd ed.). New York: W. H. Freeman.

Kovacs, M. (1989). Affective disorders in children and adolescents. *American Psychologist, 44,* 209–215.

Kreppner, K. (1989, April). *A longitudinal study of changes in socialization and interaction patterns in families.* Paper presented at the biennial meeting of the Society for Research in Child Development, Kansas City.

Kuhn, D. (1988). Cognitive development. In M. H. Bornstein & M. E. Lamb (Eds.), *Developmental psychology: An advanced textbook* (2nd ed.). Hillsdale, NJ: Erlbaum.

Kulik, J. A., Bangert-Drowns, R. L., & Kulik, C. C. (1984). The effectiveness of coaching for aptitude tests. *Psychological Bulletin, 95,* 179–188.

Kurtines, W. M., & J. Gewirtz (Ed.). (in press). *Moral behavior and development: Advances in theory, research, and application.* Hillsdale, NJ: Erlbaum.

Kwakman, A. M., Zuker, F. A. J. M., Schippers, G. M., & de Wuffel, F. J. (1988). Drinking behavior, drinking attitudes, and attachment relationships of adolescents. *Journal of Youth and Adolescence, 17,* 247–253.

L

Labouvie-Vief, G. (1982). Dynamic development and mature autonomy: A theoretical prologue. *Human Development, 25,* 161–191.

Labouvie-Vief, G. (1986, August). *Modes of knowing and life-span cognition.* Paper presented at the annual meeting of the American Psychological Association, Washington, DC.

Lacayo, R. (1988, July 11). A surging new spirit. *Time,* pp. 46–49.

Ladd, G. W., & Mars, K. T. (1985, April). *Reliability and validity of preschoolers' perceptions of peer behavior.* Paper presented at the biennial meeting of the Society for Research in Child Development, Toronto.

LaFromboise, T. D., & Low, K. G. (1989). American Indian children and adolescents. In J. T. Gibbs & L. N. Huang (Eds.), *Children of color.* San Francisco: Jossey-Bass.

Lamb, M. E. (Ed.). (1986). *The father's role: Applied perspectives.* New York: Wiley.

Lampl, M., & Emde, R. N. (1983). Episodic growth in infancy: A preliminary report on length, head circumference, and behavior. *New directions for child development.* San Francisco: Jossey-Bass.

Landesman, S. & Ramey, C. (1989). Developmental psychology and mental retardation: Integrating scientific principles with treatment practices. *American Psychologist, 44,* 409–415.

Laosa, L. M. (1989, April). *Current research on Hispanic immigration and children's development: Theory and methods.* Paper presented at the biennial meeting of the Society for Research in Child Development, Kansas City.

Lapsley, D. K. (1985). Elkind on egocentrism. *Developmental Review, 5,* 227–236.

Lapsley, D. K. (1989). Continuity and discontinuity in adolescent social cognitive development. In R. Montemayor, G. Adams, & T. Gullota (Eds.), *Advances in adolescence research* (Vol. 2). Orlando, FL: Academic Press.

Lapsley, D. K. (in press). The adolescent egocentrism theory and the "new look" at the imaginary audience and personal fable. In R. M. Lerner, A. C. Petersen, & J. Brooks-Gunn (Eds.), *The encyclopedia of adolescence.* New York: Garland.

Lapsley, D. K., Enright, R. D., & Serlin, R. C. (1985). Toward a theoretical perspective on the legislation of adolescence. *Journal of Early Adolescence, 5,* 441–466.

Lapsley, D. K., Enright, R. D., & Serlin, R. C. (1986). Moral and social education. In J. Worrell & F. Danner (Eds.), *Adolescent development: Issues in education.* New York: Academic Press.

Lapsley, D. K., Milstead, M., Quintana, S. M., Flannery, D., & Buss, R. R. (1986). Adolescent egocentrism and formal operations: Tests of a theoretical assumption. *Developmental Psychology, 22,* 800–807.

Lapsley, D. K., & Murphy, M. N. (1985). Another look at the theoretical assumptions of adolescent egocentrism. *Developmental Review, 5,* 201–217.

Lapsley, D. K., & Power, F. C. (Eds.). (1988). *Self, ego, and identity.* New York: Springer-Verlag.

Lapsley, D. K., & Quintana, S. M. (1985). Recent approaches in children's elementary moral and social education. *Elementary School Guidance and Counseling Journal, 19,* 246–251.

Lapsley, D. K., & Rice, K. G. (1988a). The "new look" at the imaginary audience and personal fable: Toward an integrative model of adolescent ego development. In D. K. Lapsley & F. C. Power (Eds.), *Self, ego, and identity: Integrative approaches.* New York: Springer-Verlag.

Lapsley, D. K., & Rice, K. G. (1988b). History, puberty, and the textbook consensus on adolescent development. *Contemporary Psychology, 33,* 210–213.

Lapsley, D. K., Rice, K. G., & Shadid, G. E. (in press). Psychological separation and adjustment to college. *Journal of Counseling Psychology.*

LaVoie, J. (1976). Ego identity formation in middle adolescence. *Journal of Youth and Adolescence, 5,* 371–385.

Lazarus, R. (1984). On the primacy of cognition. *American Psychologist, 39,* 124–129.

Lazarus, R. S., & Folkman, S. (1984). *Stress, appraisal, and coping.* New York: Springer.

Leafgren, A. (1989). Health and wellness programs. In M. L. Upcraft & J. N. Gardner (Eds.), *The freshman year experience.* San Francisco: Jossey Bass.

Le Blanc, M., & Fréchette, M. (1989). *Male criminal activity from childhood through youth: Multilevel and developmental perspectives.* New York: Springer-Verlag.

Lee, C. B. T. (1970). *The campus scene: 1900–1970.* New York: McKay.

Lefkowitz, M. M., Eron, L. D., Walder, L. O., & Huesmann, L. R. (1972). Television violence and children's aggression: A follow-up study. In G. A. Comstock & E. A. Rubenstein (Eds.), *Television and social behavior* (Vol. 3). Washington, DC: U.S. Government Printing Office.

Lehrer, R., & Yussen, S. R. (1988, April). *Conceptions of computer and human intelligence.* Paper presented at the annual meeting of the American Educational Research Association, New Orleans.

Leinbach, M. D., & Hort, B. (1989, April). *Bears are for boys: "Metaphorical" associations in the young child's gender schema.* Paper presented at the biennial meeting of the Society for Research in Child Development, Kansas City.

Lempers, J. D., Clark-Lempers, D., & Simons, R. L. (1989). Economic hardship, parenting, and distress. *Child Development, 60,* 25–39.

Lepper, M., Greene, D., & Nisbett, R. E. (1973). Undermining children's intrinsic interest with extrinsic rewards. *Journal of Personality and Social Psychology, 28,* 129–137.

Lerner, J. V., Hertzog, C., Hooker, K. A., Hassibi, M., & Thomas, A. (1988). A longitudinal study of negative emotional states and adjustment from early childhood through adolescence. *Child Development, 59,* 356–366.

Lerner, M. J. (1982). The justice motive in human relations and the economic model of man: A radical analysis of facts and fictions. In V. J. Derlega & J. Grzelak (Eds.), *Cooperation and helping behavior.* New York: Academic Press.

Lerner, R. M. (1981). Adolescent development: Scientific study in the 1980s. *Youth and Society, 12,* 251–261.

Lerner, R. M. (1987). A life-span perspective for early adolescence. In R. M. Lerner & T. T. Foch (Eds.), *Biological-psychosocial interactions in early adolescence.* Hillsdale, NJ: Erlbaum.

Lerner, R. M. (1988). Early adolescent transitions: The lore and the laws of adolescence. In M. D. Levine & E. R. McAnarney (Eds.), *Early adolescent transitions.* Lexington, MA: Lexington Books.

Lerner, R. M., & Karabenick, S. A. (1974). Physical attractiveness, body attitudes, and self-concept in late adolescence. *Journal of Youth and Adolescence, 3,* 307–316.

Lerner, R. M., & Lerner, J. V. (1988). Effects of physical attractiveness. *William T. Grant Foundation Annual Report,* p. 21.

Lerner, R. M., Lerner, J. V., & Tubman, J. (1989). Organismic and contextual bases of development in adolescence: A developmental contextual view. In G. R. Adams, R. Montemayor, & T. P. Gullotta (Eds.), *Biology of adolescent behavior and development.* Newbury Park, CA: Sage.

Lesser, G., Fifer, G., & Clark, D. (1965). Mental abilities of children from different social classes and cultural groups. *Monographs of the Society for Research in Child Development, 30*(4, Whole No. 102).

Levin, H. M., & Rumberger, R. W. (in press). Educational requirements for new technologies. *Educational Policy.*

Levine, S. V. (1984, August). Radical departures. *Psychology Today,* pp. 18–27.

Lewis, M. (1987). Early sex-role behavior and school age adjustment. In J. M. Reinisch, L. A. Rosenblum, & S. A. Sanders (Eds.), *Masculinity/femininity.* New York: Oxford University Press.

Lewis, M., & Brooks-Gunn, J. (1979). *Social cognition and acquisition of the self.* New York: Plenum.

Lewis, V. G., Money, J., & Bobrow, N. A. (1977). Idiopathic pubertal delay beyond the age of fifteen: Psychological study of twelve boys. *Adolescence, 12,* 1–11.

Liebert, R. J., & Sprakin, J. N. (1988). *The early window: Effects of television on children and youth* (3rd ed.). Elmsford, NY: Pergamon.

Linn, M. C. (1987). Establishing a research base for scientific education: Challenges, trends, and recommendations. *Journal of Research in Science Teaching, 24,* 191–216.

Lipsitz, J. (1980, March). *Sexual development in young adolescents.* Invited speech given at the American Association of Sex Educators, Counselors, and Therapists.

Lipsitz, J. (1983, October). *Making it the hard way: Adolescents in the 1980s.* Testimony presented at the Crisis Intervention Task Force, House Select Committee on Children, Youth, and Families, Washington, DC.

Lipsitz, J. (1984). *Successful schools for young adolescents.* New Brunswick, NJ: Transaction Books.

Livesley, W. J., & Bromley, D. B. (1973). *Person perception in childhood and adolescence.* New York: Wiley.

Lockheed, M. (1985). Women, girls, and computers: A first look at the evidence. *Sex Roles, 13,* 115–122.

Loehr, J. (1989, May). Personal communication. United States Tennis Association Training Camp, Saddlebrook, FL.

Long, T., & Long, L. (1983). *Latchkey children.* New York: Penguin.

Looney, J. G., & Blotcky, M. J. (1989). Adolescent psychological development revisited. In A. H. Esman (Ed.), *International Annals of Adolescent Psychiatry.* Chicago: University of Chicago Press.

Ludtke, M. (1988, August 8). John David. *Time,* pp. 44–48.

Ludtke, M. (1988, August 8). Josh. *Time,* pp. 55–57.

Lueptow, L. (1984). *Adolescent sex roles and social change.* New York: Columbia University Press.

Luria, A., & Herzog, E. (1985, April). *Gender segregation across and within settings.* Paper presented at the biennial meeting of the Society for Research in Child Development, Toronto.

M

Maas, H. S. (1954). The role of members in clubs of lower-class and middle-class adolescents. *Child Development, 25,* 241–251.

Maccoby, E. E. (1984). Middle childhood in the context of the family. In W. A. Collins (Ed.), *Development during middle childhood.* Washington, DC: National Academy Press.

Maccoby, E. E. (1987, November). Interview with Elizabeth Hall: All in the family. *Psychology Today,* pp. 54–60.

Maccoby, E. E. (1987). The varied meanings of "masculine" and "feminine." In J. M. Reinisch, L. A. Rosenblum, & S. A. Sanders (Eds.), *Masculinity/femininity.* New York: Oxford University Press.

Maccoby, E. E. (1989, August). *Gender and relationships: A developmental account.* Paper presented at the meeting of the American Psychological Association, New Orleans.

Maccoby, E. E., & Jacklin, C. N. (1974). *The psychology of sex differences.* Stanford, CA: Stanford University Press.

Maccoby, E. E., & Jacklin, C. N. (in press). Gender segregation in childhood. In H. Reese (Ed.), *Advances in child development and behavior* (Vol. 20). New York: Academic Press.

MacDonald, K. (1987). Parent-child physical play with rejected, neglected, and popular boys. *Developmental Psychology, 23,* 705–711.

MacPherson, S. (1987). *Five hundred million children.* New York: St. Martin's Press.

Maltsberger, J. T. (1988). *Suicide risk.* New York: Human Sciences Press.

Mandler, J. M. (1983). Representation. In P. H. Mussen (Ed.), *Handbook of child psychology* (Vol. 3, 4th ed.). New York: Wiley.

Marcia, J. (1966). Development and validation of ego-identity status. *Journal of Personality and Social Psychology, 3,* 551–558.

Marcia, J. (1980). Ego identity development. In J. Adelson (Ed.), *Handbook of adolescent psychology.* New York: Wiley.

Marcia, J. (1987). The identity status approach to the study of ego identity development. In T. Honess & K. Yardley (Eds.), *Self and identity: Perspectives across the lifespan.* London: Routledge & Kegan Paul.

Martin, C. L. (1989, April). *Beyond knowledge-based conceptions of gender schematic processing.* Paper presented at the biennial meeting of the Society for Research in Child Development, Kansas City.

Martin, C. L., & Little, J. K. (1989, April). *The acquisition of gender-related knowledge.* Paper presented at the biennial meeting of the Society for Research in Child Development, Kansas City.

Martin, J. (1976). *The education of adolescents.* Washington, DC: U.S. Office of Education.

Martorano, S. (1977). A developmental analysis of performance on Piaget's formal operations tasks. *Developmental Psychology, 13,* 666–672.

Marx, G. (1977). *The Groucho phile.* New York: Pocket Books.

Maslow, A. H. (1954). *Motivation and personality.* New York: Harper & Row.

Maslow, A. H. (1971). *The farther reaches of human nature.* New York: Viking.

Masters, J. C., Burish, T. G., Hollow, S. D., & Rimm, D. C. (1988). *Behavior therapy.* San Diego: Harcourt Brace Jovanovich.

Masters, J. C., & Smith, W. P. (1987). *Social comparison, social justice, and relative deprivation.* Hillsdale, NJ: Erlbaum.

Matarazzo, J. D. (1979). Health psychology: APA's newest division. *The Health Psychologist, 1,* 1.

Mathre, M. L. (1988). A survey on disclosure of marijuana use to health care professionals. *Journal of Psychoactive Drugs, 20,* 117–120.

Matson, J. L. (1989). *Treating depression in children and adolescents.* New York: Plenum.

Mayer, R. (1987). *Educational psychology: A cognitive approach.* Boston, MA: Little, Brown.

McAdams, D. P. (1988). *Power, intimacy, and the life story.* New York: Guilford.

McAdoo, H. P., & McAdoo, J. L. (Eds.). (1985). *Black children: Social, educational, and parental environments.* Beverly Hills, CA: Sage.

McAleer, N. (1989, April). On creativity. *Omni, 11,* pp. 42–44, 98–102.

McAlister, A., Perry, C., Killen, J., Slinkard, L. A., & Maccoby, N. (1980). Pilot study of smoking, alcohol and drug abuse prevention. *American Journal of Public Health, 70,* 719–721.

McAnarney, E. R. (1988). Early adolescent motherhood: Crisis in the making? In M. D. Levine & E. R. McAnarney (Eds.), *Early adolescent transitions.* Lexington, MA: D. C. Heath.

McCabe, M. P., & Collins, J. K. (1979). Sex role and dating orientation. *Journal of Youth and Adolescence, 8,* 407–425.

McCall, R. B., Meyers, E. D., Hartman, J., & Roche, A. F. (1983). Developmental changes in head circumference and mental performance growth rates: A test of Epstein's phrenoblysis hypothesis. *Developmental Psychobiology, 16,* 457–468.

McCandless, B. R. (1970). *Adolescents.* Hinsdale, IL: Dryden Press.

McClelland, D. C., Atkinson, J. W., Clark, R., & Lowell, E. L. (1953). *The achievement motive.* New York: Appleton-Century-Crofts.

McCord, W., McCord, J., & Gudeman, J. (1960). *Origins of alcoholism.* Palo Alto, CA: Stanford University Press.

McHenry, P. C., Walters, L. H., & Johnson, C. (1979). Adolescent pregnancy: A review of the literature. *The Family Coordinator, 28,* 17–28.

McLaughlin, L., & Chassin, L. (1985, April). *Adolescents at risk for future alcohol abuse.* Paper presented at the biennial meeting of the Society for Research in Child Development, Toronto.

McLoyd, V. C. (1989, April). *Facing the future in hard times: Choices, perceptions, and behavior of black adolescents.* Paper presented at the biennial meeting of the Society for Research in Child Development, Kansas City.

McPartland, J. M., & McDill, E. L. (1976). *The unique role of schools in the causes of youthful crime.* Baltimore: Johns Hopkins University Press.

McQuire, W. J. (1986). The myth of mass media effectiveness. In G. Lindzey & E. Aronson (Eds.), *Handbook of social psychology* (Vol. 2, 3rd ed.). New York: Random House.

McWhirter, D. P., Reinisch, J. M., & Sanders, S. A. (in press). *Homosexuality/heterosexuality.* New York: Oxford University Press.

Meacham, J. A., & Santilli, N. R. (1982). Interstage relationships in Erikson's theory: Identity and intimacy. *Child Development, 53,* 1461–1467.

Mead, M. (1928). *Coming of age in Samoa.* New York: William Morrow.

Mead, M. (1978, Dec. 30–Jan 5). The American family: An endangered species. *TV Guide.*

Medrich, E. A., Rosen, J., Rubin, V., & Buckley, S. (1982). *The serious business of growing up.* Berkeley: University of California Press.

Meilman, P. W. (1979). Cross-sectional age changes in ego identity status during adolescence. *Developmental Psychology, 15,* 230–231.

Messinger, J. C. (1971). Sex and repression in an Irish folk community. In D. S. Marshall & R. C. Suggs (Eds.), *Human sexual behavior: Variations in the ethnographic spectrum* (pp. 3–37). New York: Basic Books.

Miller, N. E. (1959). Liberalization of basic S-R concepts: Extension to conflict behavior, motivation, and social learning. In S. Koch (Ed.), *Psychology: A study of science.* New York: McGraw-Hill.

Miller, P. H. (1989). Developmental theories of adolescence. In J. Worrell & F. Danner (Eds.), *The adolescent as decision maker.* New York: Academic Press.

Miller, P. Y., & Simon, W. (1974). Adolescent sexual behavior: Context and change. *Social Problems, 22,* 58–76.

Miller, S. K., & Slap, G. B. (1989). Adolescent smoking: A review of prevalence and prevention. *Journal of Adolescent Health Care, 10,* 129–135.

Miller, W. B. (1958). Lower-class culture as a generating milieu of gang delinquency. *Journal of Social Issues, 14,* 5–19.

Minkler, M. (1989). Health education, health promotion and the open society: An historical perspective. *Health Education Quarterly, 16,* 17–30.

Minnett, A. M., Vandell, D. L., & Santrock, J. W. (1983). The effects of sibling status on sibling interaction: Influence of birth order, age spacing, sex of the child, and sex of the sibling. *Child Development, 54,* 1064–1072.

Minuchin, P. P., & Shapiro, E. K. (1983). The school as a context for social development. In P. H. Mussen (Ed.), *Handbook of child psychology* (Vol. 4, 4th ed.). New York: Wiley.

Mischel, W. (1970). Sex-typing and socialization. In P. H. Mussen (Ed.), *Manual of child psychology* (Vol. 2, 3rd ed.). New York: Wiley.

Mischel, W. (1973). Toward a cognitive social learning reconceptualization of personality. *Psychological Review, 80,* 252–283.

Mischel, W. (1984). Convergences and challenges in the search for consistency. *American Psychologist, 39,* 351–364.

Mischel, W. (1987). *Personality* (4th ed.). New York: Holt, Rinehart & Winston.

Mischel, W., & Gilligan, C. (1964). Delay of gratification, motivation for the prohibited gratification, and responses to temptation. *Journal of Abnormal and Social Psychology, 69,* 411–417.

Mischel, W., & Mischel, H. (1975, April). *A cognitive social-learning analysis of moral development.* Paper presented at the meeting of the Society for Research in Child Development, Denver.

Mitteness, L. S., & Nydegger, C. N. (1982, October). *Dimensions of parent-child relations in adulthood.* Paper presented at the meeting of the American Gerontological Association.

Miura, I. T. (1987). Gender and socioeconomic status differences in middle-school computer interest and use. *Journal of Early Adolescence, 7,* 243–254.

Mize, J. (1985, April). *Social skill training with preschool children: The effects of a cognitive-social learning approach.* Paper presented at the biennial meeting of the Society for Research in Child Development, Toronto.

Money, J. (1965). Psychosexual differentiation. In J. Money (Ed.), *Sex research, new developments.* New York: Holt, Rinehart & Winston.

Money, J. (1987a). Propaedeutics of Diecious G-I/R: Theoretical foundations for understanding dimorphic gender-identity role. In J. M. Reinisch, L. A. Rosenblum, & S. A. Sanders (Eds.), *Masculinity/femininity.* New York: Oxford University Press.

Money, J. (1987b). Sin, sickness, or status? Homosexual gender identity and psychoneuroendocrinology. *American Psychologist, 42,* 384–399.

Monroe, R. (1988). *Creative brainstorms.* New York: Irvington.

Montemayor, R. (1982). The relationship between parent-adolescent conflict and the amount of time adolescents spend with parents, peers, and alone. *Child Development, 53,* 1512–1519.

Montemayor, R., & Eisen, M. (1977). The development of self-conceptions from childhood to adolescence. *Developmental Psychology, 13,* 314–319.

Montemayor, R., & Flannery, D. J. (1989). A naturalistic study of the involvement of children and adolescents with their mothers and friends: Developmental differences in expressive behavior. *Journal of Adolescent Research, 4,* 3–14.

Montemayor, R., & Hanson, E. (1985). A naturalistic view of conflict between adolescents and their parents and siblings. *Journal of Early Adolescence, 5,* 23–30.

Morgan, J. P. (1988). Marijuana metabolism in the context of urine testing for cannabinoid metabolite. *Journal of Psychoactive Drugs, 20,* 107–116.

Morgan, M. (1987). Television, sex-role attitudes, and sex-role behavior. *Journal of Early Adolescence, 7,* 269–282.

Morrison, D. M. (1985). Adolescent contraceptive behavior: A review. *Psychological Bulletin, 98,* 538–568.

Morrow, L. (1988, August 8). Through the eyes of children. *Time,* pp. 32–33.

Mott, F. L., & Marsiglio, W. (1985, September/October). Early childbearing and completion of high school. *Family Planning Perspectives,* p. 234.

Munroe, R. H., Himmin, H. S., & Munroe, R. L. (1984). Gender understanding and sex-role preference in four cultures. *Developmental Psychology, 20,* 673–682.

Murphy, J. (1987). Educational influences. In V. B. Van Hasselt & M. Hersen (Eds.), *Handbook of adolescent psychology.* New York: Pergamon.

Murray, D. M., Matthews, K. A., Blake, S. M., Prineas, R. J., & Gillum, R. F. (1988). Type A behavior in children: Demographic, behavioral, and physiological correlates. In B. G. Melamed & others (Eds.), *Child health psychology.* Hillsdale, NJ: Erlbaum.

Muuss, R. E. (1989). *Theories of adolescence* (15th ed.). New York: Random House.

Muuss, R. E. (1988). Carol Gilligan's theory of sex differences in the development of moral reasoning during adolescence. *Adolescence, 23,* 229–241.

National Assessment of Educational Progress. (1976). *Adult work skills and knowledge* (Report No. 35–COD–01). Denver, CO: Author.

National Research Council. (1987). *Risking the future: Adolescent sexuality, pregnancy, and childbearing.* Washington, DC: National Academy Press.

Neiger, B. L., & Hopkins, R. W. (1988). Adolescent suicide: Character traits of high-risk teenagers. *Adolescence, 23,* 469–475.

Neimark, E. D. (1982). Adolescent thought: Transition to formal operations. In B. B. Wolman (Ed.), *Handbook of developmental psychology.* Englewood Cliffs, NJ: Prentice-Hall.

Neimeyer, G. J., & Metzler, A. (1987). The development of vocational schemas. *Journal of Vocational Behavior, 30,* 16–32.

Nesselroade, J. R., & Baltes, P. B. (1984). Sequential strategies and the role of cohort effects in behavioral development: Adolescent personality (1970–1972) as a sample case. In S. A. Mednick, M. Harway, & K. M. Finello (Eds.), *Handbook of longitudinal research.* New York: Praeger.

Neugarten, B. L., & Datan, N. (1973). Sociological perspectives on the life cycle. In P. B. Baltes & K. W. Schaie (Eds.), *Life-span developmental psychology.* New York: Academic Press.

Neugarten, B. L., & Neugarten, D. A. (1986). Age in the aging society. In A. Pifer & L. Bronte (Eds.), *Our aging society.* New York: W. W. Norton.

Newcomb, M. D., & Bentler, P. M. (1988). Impact of adolescent drug use and social support on problems of young adults: A longitudinal study. *Journal of Abnormal Psychology, 97,* 64–75.

Newcomb, M. D., & Bentler, P. M. (1989). Substance use and abuse among children and teenagers. *American Psychologist, 44,* 242–248.

Newcomer, S. F., & Udry, J. R. (1985). Oral sex in an adolescent population. *Archives of Sexual Behavior, 14,* 41–46.

Newman, D., Griffin, P., & Code, M. (1989). *The construction zone: Working for cognitive change in school.* New York: Cambridge.

Newton, D. E. (1982). The status of programs in human sexuality: A preliminary study. *The High School Journal, 6,* 232–239.

Nicholls, J. G. (1984). Conceptions of ability and achievement motivation. In R. E. Ames & C. Ames (Eds.), *Motivation in education.* New York: Academic Press.

Nichtern, S. (1989). Introduction: The world within the adolescent. In A. H. Esman (Ed.), *International Annals of Adolescent Psychiatry.* Chicago: University of Chicago Press.

Norem, J. K., & Cantor, N. (1986). Anticipatory and post-hoc cushioning strategies: Optimism and defensive pessimism in "risky" situations. *Cognitive Therapy Research, 10,* 347–362.

Nottelmann, E. D., Susman, E. J., Blue, J. H., Inoff-Germain, G., Dorn, L. D., Loriaux, D. L., Cutler, G. B., & Chrousos, G. P. (1987). Gonadal and adrenal hormone correlates of adjustment in early adolescence. In R. M. Lerner & T. T. Foch (Eds.), *Biological-psychological interactions in early adolescence.* Hillsdale, NJ: Erlbaum.

Nottelmann, E. D., Susman, E. J., Inoff, G. E., Dorn, L. D., Cutler, G. B., Loriaux, D. L., & Chrousos, G. P. (1985, May). *Hormone level and adjustment and behavior during early adolescence.* Paper presented at the annual meeting of the American Association for the Advancement of Science, Los Angeles, CA.

Nucci, L. (1982). Conceptual development in the moral and conventional domains: Implications for values education. *Review of Educational Research, 52,* 93–122.

Nucci, L., & Nucci, M. (1982). Children's responses to moral and social conventional transgressions in free-play settings. *Child Development, 53,* 1337–1342.

Nucci, L., & Turiel, E. (1978). Social interactions and the development of social concepts in preschool children. *Child Development, 49,* 400–407.

Nydegger, C. N. (1975, October). *Age and parental behavior.* Paper presented at the meeting of the Gerontological Society of America, Louisville, KY.

Nydegger, C. N. (1981, October). *The ripple effect of parental timing.* Paper presented at the meeting of the American Gerontological Association.

O

O'Brien, R. W. (1989, April). *Family influences on the development of individuation during adolescence.* Paper presented at the biennial meeting of the Society for Research in Child Development, Kansas City.

Occupational Outlook Handbook, 1988–89 Edition. (1988). Washington, DC: Bureau of Labor Statistics.

Oden, S. L., & Asher, S. R. (1975, April). *Coaching children in social skills for friendship making.* Paper presented at the meeting of the Society for Research in Child Development, Denver, CO.

O'Donnel, B. (1989, April). *Altering children's gender stereotypes about adult occupations with nonsexist books.* Paper presented at the biennial meeting of the Society for Research in Child Development, Kansas City.

Oetting, E. R., Beauvasi, F. & Edwards, R. (1988). Alcohol and Indian youth: Social and psychological correlates and prevention. *Journal of Drug Issues, 18,* 87–101.

Offer, D. (1969). *The psychological world of the teenager.* New York: Basic Books.

Offer, D., Ostrov, E., Howard, K. I., & Atkinson, R. (1988). *The teenage world: Adolescents' self-image in ten countries.* New York: Plenum.

Offord, D. R., & Boyle, M. H. (1988). The epidemiology of antisocial behavior in early adolescents, aged 12 to 14. In M. D. Levine & E. R. McAnarney (Eds.), *Early adolescent transitions.* Lexington, MA: Lexington Books.

Okun, M. A., & Sasfy, J. H. (1977). Adolescence, the self-concept, and formal operations. *Adolescence, 12,* 373–379.

Olson, D. R. (1977). From utterance to text: The bias of language in speech and writing. *Harvard Educational Review, 47,* 257–281.

O'Malley, P. M., Bachman, G. G., & Johnston, J. (1977). *Youth in transition. Final report of five years beyond high school: Causes and consequences of educational attainment.* Ann Arbor, MI: Institute of Social Research, University of Michigan.

Opler, M. E. (1972). Cause and effect in Apachean agriculture division of labor, residence patterns, and girls' puberty rites. *American Anthropologist, 74,* 1133–1146.

Orlofsky, J. (1976). Intimacy status: Relationship to interpersonal perception. *Journal of Youth and Adolescence, 5,* 73–88.

Orlofsky, J., Marcia, J., & Lesser, I. (1973). Ego identity status and the intimacy vs. isolation crisis of young adulthood. *Journal of Personality and Social Psychology, 27,* 211–219.

Oser, F. K. (1986). Moral education and values education: The discourse perspective. In M. C. Wittrock (Ed.), *Handbook of research on teaching.* New York: Macmillan.

Oskamp, S., & Mindick, B. (1981). Personality and attitudinal barriers to contraception. In D. Byrne & W. A. Fisher (Eds.), *Adolescents, sex, and contraception.* New York: McGraw-Hill.

Osofsky, J. D. (1989, April). *Affective relationships in adolescent mothers and their infants.* Paper presented at the biennial meeting of the Society for Research in Child Development, Kansas City.

Ostrov, E., Offer, D., Howard, K. I., Kaufman, B., & Meyer, H. (1985). Adolescent sexual behavior. *Medical Aspects of Human Sexuality, 19,* 28, 30–31, 34–36.

Overton, W. (1989). In R. Montemayor, G. Adams, & T. Gullota (Eds.), *Advances in adolescence research.* Orlando, FL: Academic Press.

P

Pacheco, S., & Valdes, L. F. (1989, August). *The present state and future directions of Hispanic psychology.* Paper presented at the meeting of the American Psychological Association, New Orleans.

Papini, D., Barnett, J., Clark, S., & Micka, J. C. (1989, April). *Familial and individual concomitants of adolescent ego identity statuses.* Paper presented at the biennial meeting of the Society for Research in Child Development, Kansas City.

Parcel, G. S., Simons-Morton, G. G., O'Hara, N. M., Baranowski, T., Kolbe, L. J., & Bee, D. E. (1987). School promotion of healthful diet and exercise behavior: An integration of organizational change and social learning theory interventions. *Journal of School Health, 57,* 150–156.

Pardes, H., Kaufmann, C. A., Pincus, H. A., & West, A. (1989). Genetics and psychiatry: Past discoveries, current dilemmas, and future directions. *American Journal of Psychiatry, 146,* 434–443.

Parish, T. S. (1987). Family and environment. In V. B. Van Hasselt & M. Hersen (Eds.), *Handbook of adolescent psychology.* New York: Pergamon Press.

Parke, R. D. (1988). Families in life-span perspective: A multilevel developmental approach. In E. M. Hetherington, R. M. Lerner, & M. Perlmutter (Eds.), *Child development in life-span perspective.* Hillsdale, NJ: Erlbaum.

Parke, R. D. (1989). The role of the family in the development of peer relations. In K. Kreppner & R. M. Lerner (Eds.), *Family systems and life-span development.* Hillsdale, NJ: Erlbaum.

Parke, R. D., MacDonald, K., Beitel, A., & Bhavangri, N. (1988). The interrelationships among families, fathers, and peers. In R. D. Peters (Ed.), *New approaches in family research.* New York: Brunner/Mazel.

Parke, R. D., Power, T. G., & Fisher, T. (1980). The adolescent father's impact on the mother and child. *Journal of Social Issues, 36,* 88–106.

Parker, J. G., & Asher, S. R. (1987). Peer relations and later personal adjustment: Are low accepted children at risk? *Psychological Bulletin, 102,* 357–389.

Parker, J. G., & Gottman, J. M. (1989). Social and emotional development in a relational context: Friendship interaction from early childhood to adolescence. In T. J. Berndt & G. W. Ladd (Eds.), *Peer relations in child development.* New York: Wiley.

Pasley, K., & Ihinger-Tallman, M. (Eds.). (1987). *Remarriage and stepparenting.* New York: Guilford.

Patterson, G. R. (1982). *Coercive family processes.* Eugene, OR: Castalia Press.

Patterson, G. R., DeBarsyshe, B. D., & Ramsey, E. (1989). A developmental perspective on antisocial behavior. *American Psychologist, 44,* 329–335.

Patterson, G. R., Reid, J. B., & Dishon, T. D. (in press). *Antisocial boys.* Eugene, OR: Castalia Press.

Patterson, G. R., & Stouthamer-Loeber, M. (1984). The correlation of family management practices and delinquency. *Child Development, 55,* 1299–1307.

Pearl, D., Bouthilet, L., & Lazar, J. (Eds.). (1982). *Television and behavior: Ten years of scientific progress and implications for the 80s.* Washington, DC: U.S. Government Printing Office.

Pederson, L. L. (1987). Change in variables related to smoking from childhood to late adolescence: An eight year longitudinal study of a cohort of elementary school students. *Canadian Journal of Public Health, 77* (Supplement: 1), 33–39.

Perkins, D. N. (1984, September). Creativity by design. *Educational Leadership,* 18–25.

Perry, I. (1988). A black student's reflection on public and private schools. *Harvard Educational Review, 58,* 332–336.

Peskin, H. (1967). Pubertal onset and ego functioning. *Journal of Abnormal Psychology, 72,* 1–15.

Petersen, A. C. (1979, January). Can puberty come any faster? *Psychology Today,* pp. 45–56.

Petersen, A. C. (1987a, September). Those gangly years. *Psychology Today,* pp. 28–34.

Petersen, A. C. (1987b). The nature of biological-psychosocial interactions: The sample case of early adolescence. In R. M. Lerner & T. T. Foch (Eds.), *Biological-psychosocial interactions in early adolescence.* Hillsdale, NJ: Erlbaum.

Petersen, A. C., & Crockett, L. (1985). Pubertal timing and grade effects on adjustment. *Journal of Youth and Adolescence, 14,* 191–206.

Petersen, A. C., & Sarigiani, P. A. (1989, April). *The development of depression in adolescence: Why more girls?* Paper presented at the biennial meeting of the Society for Research in Child Development, Kansas City.

Petersen, A. C., Schulenberg, J. E., Abramowitz, R. H., Offer, D., & Jarcho, H. D. (1984). A self-image questionnaire for young adolescents (SIQYA): Reliability and validity studies. *Journal of Youth and Adolescence, 13,* 93–111.

Petersen, A. C., & Taylor, B. (1980). The biological approach to adolescence: Biological change and psychological adaptation. In J. Adelson (Ed.), *Handbook of adolescent psychology.* New York: Wiley.

Peterson, P. L. (1977). Interactive effects of student anxiety, achievement orientation, and teacher behavior on student achievement and attitude. *Journal of Educational Psychology, 69,* 779–792.

Pfeffer, C. R., Lipkins, R., Plutchik, R., & Mizruchi, M. (1988). Normal children at risk for suicidal behavior: A two-year follow-up study. *Journal of the American Academy of Child and Adolescent Psychiatry, 27,* 34–41.

Phinney, J. S. (1989). Stages of ethnic identity development in minority group adolescents. *Journal of Early Adolescence, 9,* 34–49.

Piaget, J. (1932). *The moral judgment of the child.* New York: Harcourt Brace Jovanovich.

Piaget, J. (1952). *The origins of intelligence in children.* New York: International Universities Press.

Piaget, J. (1952). Jean Piaget. In C. A. Murchison (Ed.), *A history of psychology in autobiography* (Vol. 4). Worcester, MA: Clark University Press.

Piaget, J. (1954). *The construction of reality in the child.* New York: Basic Books.

Piaget, J. (1967). The mental development of the child. In D. Elkind (Ed.), *Six psychological studies by Piaget.* New York: Random House.

Piaget, J. (1970). Piaget's theory. In P. H. Mussen (Ed.), *Carmichael's manual of child psychology* (Vol. 1, 3rd ed.). New York: Wiley.

Piaget, J. (1972). Intellectual evolution from adolescence to adulthood. *Human Development, 15,* 1–12.

Piers, E. V., & Harris, D. V. (1964). Age and other correlates of self-concept in children. *Journal of Educational Psychology, 55,* 91–95.

Pinderhuges, E. (1989). *Understanding race, ethnicity and power: The key to efficacy in clinical practice.* New York: The Free Press.

Pines, A., & Aronson, E. (1988). *Career burnout: Causes and cures.* New York: The Free Press.

Pines, M. (1981, March). Only isn't lonely (or spoiled or selfish). *Psychology Today,* pp. 15–19.

Pittman, T. S., & Heller, J. S. (1987). Social motivation. *Annual Review of Psychology, 38,* 461–489.

Place, D. M. (1975). The dating experience for adolescent girls. *Adolescence, 38,* 157–173.

Plato. (1968). *The republic.* (B. Jowett, Trans.). Bridgeport, CT: Airmont.

Pleck, J. H. (1975). Masculinity-femininity: Current and alternative paradigms. *Sex Roles, 1,* 161–178.

Plomin, R. (1987). Developmental behavioral genetics and infancy. In J. D. Osofsky (Ed.), *Handbook of infant development.* New York: Wiley.

Plomin, R. (1989). Environment and genes: Determinants of behavior. *American Psychologist, 44,* 105–111.

Plomin, R., DeFries, J. C., & McClearn, G. E. (in press). *Behavioral genetics: A primer* (2nd ed.). New York: W. H. Freeman.

Polier, J. W. (1989). *Juvenile justice in double jeopardy.* Hillsdale, NJ: Erlbaum.

Polivy, J., & Thomsen, L. (1987). Eating, dieting, and body image. In E. A. Blechman & K. D. Brownell (Eds.), *Handbook of behavioral medicine for women.* Elmsford, NY: Pergamon.

Powell, A. G., Farrar, E., & Cohen, D. K. (1985). *The shopping mall high school: Winner and losers in the educational marketplace.* Boston: Houghton Mifflin.

Power, C. (1984). *Moral atmosphere.* Paper presented at the meeting of the American Educational Research Association, New Orleans.

Powers, S. I., Hauser, S. T., & Kilner, L. A. (1989). Adolescent mental health. *American Psychologist, 44,* 200–208.

Price, J., & Feshbach, S. (1982, August). *Emotional adjustment correlates of television viewing in children.* Paper presented at the meeting of the American Psychological Association, Washington, DC.

Price, J. M., & Dodge, K. A. (in press). Reactive and proactive aggression among young children: Relations to peer status and social context dimensions. *Journal of Abnormal Child Psychology.*

Prinsky, L. E., & Rosenbaum, J. L. (1987). Leer-ics or lyrics? *Youth and Society, 18,* 384–394.

Prothrow-Stith, D. (1989). Excerpts from address to the Massachusetts Department of Public Health. *Journal of Adolescent Health Care, 10,* 5–7.

Prunell, M., Boada, J., Feria, M., & Benitez, M. A. (1987). Antagonism of the stimulant and depressant effects of ethanol in rats by naloxone. *Psychopharmacology, 92,* 215–218.

Psathas, G. (1957). Ethnicity, social class, and adolescent independence. *Sociological Review, 22,* 415–523.

Pugh, D. (1983, November 11). Bringing an end to mutilation. *New Statesman,* pp. 8–9.

Puka, B. (in press). Toward the redevelopment of Kohlberg's theory: Preserving essential structure, removing controversial content. In W. M. Kurtines & J. Gewirtz (Eds.), *Moral behavior and development: Advances in theory, research, and application.* Hillsdale, NJ: Erlbaum.

R

Ramirez, O. (1989). Mexican American children and adolescents. In J. T. Gibbs & L. N. Huang (Eds.), *Children of color.* San Francisco: Jossey-Bass.

Rand Youth Poll. (1988). New York: The Rand Corporation.

Rayman, J. R., & Garig, J. W. (1989). Counseling. In M. L. Upcraft & J. N. Gardner (Eds.), *The freshman year experience.* San Francisco: Jossey Bass.

Rees, J. M., & Mahan, M. K. (1988). Nutrition in adolescence. In S. R. Williams & B. S. Worthington-Roberts (Eds.), *Nutrition throughout the life cycle.* St. Louis: Times Mirror/Mosby.

Reilly, R. (1988, August 15). Here no one is spared. *Sports Illustrated,* (7), 70–77.

Reis, H. T., Senchak, M., & Solomon, B. (1985). Sex differences in intimacy of social interaction: Further examination of potential explanations. *Journal of Personality and Social Psychology, 48,* 1204–1217.

Renner, J. W., Stafford, D., Lawson, A., McKinnon, J., Friot, F., & Kellog, D. (1976). *Research, teaching, and learning with the Piaget model.* Norman, OK: University of Oklahoma Press.

Rest, J. R. (1976). New approaches in assessment of moral judgment. In T. Lickona (Ed.), *Moral development and behavior.* New York: Holt, Rinehart & Winston.

Rest, J. R. (1983). Morality. In P. H. Mussen (Ed.), *Handbook of child psychology* (Vol. 3, 4th ed.). New York: Wiley.

Rest, J. R. (1986). *Moral development: Advances in theory and research.* New York: Praeger.

Rest, J. R. (1988, November). *With the benefits of hindsight.* Paper presented at the 13th annual conference of the Association for Moral Education, Pittsburgh, PA.

Rest, J. R., Turiel, E., & Kohlberg, L. (1969). Relations between level of moral judgment and preference and comprehension of the moral judgments of others. *Journal of Personality, 37,* 225–252.

Rich, C. L., Young, D., & Fowler, R. C. (1986). San Diego suicide study. *Archives of General Psychiatry, 43,* 577–582.

Richards, M. H., & Duckett, E. (1989, April). *Maternal employment and young adolescents' time with parents.* Paper presented at the biennial meeting of the Society for Research in Child Development, Kansas City.

Robins, L., & Regier, D. A. (Eds.). (1989). *Psychiatric disorders in America.* New York: The Free Press.

Robinson, B. R. (1988). *Teenage fathers.* Lexington, MA: Lexington Books.

Robinson, D. P., & Greene, J. W. (1988). The adolescent alcohol and drug problem: A practical approach. *Pediatric Nursing, 14,* 305–310.

Robinson, N. M. (1987). Psychology and mental retardation. *American Psychologist, 42,* 791.

Rodin, J. (1984, December). Interview: A sense of control. *Psychology Today,* pp. 38–45.

Rodin, J. (1987, August). *Hunger, taste, and mother: Biobehavioral determinants of eating and its disorders.* Paper presented at the meeting of the American Psychological Association, New York City.

Rodman, H., Pratto, D. J., & Nelson, R. S. (1988). Toward a definition of self-care children: A commentary on Steinberg (1986). *Developmental Psychology, 24,* 292–294.

Roff, M., Sells, S. B., & Golden, M. W. (1972). *Social adjustment and personality development in children.* Minneapolis, MN: University of Minnesota Press.

Rogers, C. R. (1961). *On becoming a person.* Boston: Houghton Mifflin.

Rogers, C. R. (1963). The actualizing tendency in relation to "motives" and consciousness. In M. R. Jones (Ed.), *Nebraska symposium of motivation.* Lincoln, NE: University of Nebraska Press.

Rogers, C. R. (1974). In retrospect: Forty-six years. *American Psychologist, 29,* 115–123.

Rogers, C. R. (1980). *A way of being.* Boston: Houghton Mifflin.

Rogler, L. H. (1989). The meaning of culturally sensitive research in mental health. *American Journal of Psychiatry, 146,* 296–303.

Rogoff, B. (1989). *Apprenticeship in thinking: Cognitive development in a social context.* New York: Oxford U. Press.

Rogoff, B., & Morelli, G. (1989). Perspectives on children's development from cultural psychology. *American Psychologist, 44,* 343–346.

Rosenbaum, J. L. (1989). Family dysfunction and female delinquency. *Crime and Delinquency, 35,* 31–44.

Rosenbaum, P. A., Elston, R. C., Srinivasan, S. R., Webber, L. S., & Berenson, G. S. (1987). Predictive value of parental measures in determining cardiovascular risk factor variables early in life. *Pediatrics, Supplement,* 807–815.

Rosenberg, M. (1965). *Society and the adolescent self-image.* Princeton, NJ: Princeton University Press.

Rosenhan, D. L., & Seligman, M. E. P. (1989). *Abnormal psychology* (2nd ed.). New York: Norton.

Rosenthal, R. (1985). *Lyric cognition and the potential for protest among punk rockers.* Unpublished manuscript, University of Hartford, Hartford, CT.

Rosenthal, R., & Jacobsen, L. (1968). *Pygmalion in the classroom.* New York: Holt, Rinehart & Winston.

Ross, A. O. (1979). *Psychological disorders of children* (2nd ed.). New York: McGraw-Hill.

Ross, D. G. (1972). *G. Stanley Hall: The psychologist as prophet.* Chicago: University of Chicago Press.

Ross, L. (1977). The intuitive psychologist and his shortcomings: Distortions in the attribution process. In L. Berkowitz (Ed.), *Advances in experimental psychology* (Vol. 10). New York: Academic Press.

Rothbart, M. L. K. (1971). Birth order and mother-child interaction. *Dissertation Abstracts, 27,* 45–57.

Rothschild, N., & Morgan, M. (1987). Cohesion and control: Adolescents' relationship with parents as mediators of television. *Journal of Early Adolescence, 7,* 299–314.

Rotter, J. B. (1989, August). *Internal versus external control of reinforcement: A case history of a variable.* Paper presented at the meeting of the American Psychological Association, New Orleans.

Rousseau, J. J. (1962). *The Emile of Jean Jacques Rousseau* (W. Boyd, Ed. and Trans.) New York: Teachers College Press, Columbia University. (Original work published 1762)

Rowe, D. C., & Rodgers, J. E. (1989). Behavioral genetics, Adolescent deviance, and "d": Contributions and issues. In G. R. Adams, R. Montemayor, & T. P. Gulotta (Eds.), *Biology of adolescent behavior and development.* Newbury Park, CA: Sage.

Rubenstein, J., Heeren, T., Housman, D., Rubin, C., & Stechler, G. (1989). Suicidal behavior in "normal" adolescents: Risk and protective factors. *American Journal of Orthopsychiatry, 59,* 59–71.

Rubin, Z., & Mitchell, C. (1976). Couples research as couples counseling. *American Psychologist, 31,* 17–25.

Rubin, Z., & Sloman, J. (1984). How parents influence their children's friendships. In M. Lewis (Ed.), *Beyond the dyad.* New York: Plenum.

Ruble, D. N. (1987). The acquisition of self-knowledge: A self-socialization perspective. In N. Eisenberg (Ed.), *Contemporary topics in developmental psychology.* New York: Wiley.

Rumberger, R. W. (1983). Dropping out of high school: The influence of race, sex, and family background. *American Educational Research Journal, 20,* 199–220.

Rumberger, R. W. (1987). High school dropouts: A review of the issues and evidence. *Review of Educational Research, 57,* 101–121.

Rutter, D. R., & Durkin, K. (1987). Turn-taking in mother-infant interaction: An examination of vocalization and gaze. *Developmental Psychology, 23,* 54–61.

Rutter, M. (1971). Parent-child separation: Psychological effects on the children. *Journal of Child Psychology and Psychiatry, 12,* 233–256.

Rutter, M. (1979). Protective factors in children's response to stress and disadvantage. In M. W. Kent & J. E. Rolf (Eds.), *Primary prevention in psychopathology* (Vol. 3). Hanover, NH: University Press of New England.

Rutter, M. (1983, April). *Influences from family and school.* Paper presented at the meeting of the Society for Research in Child Development, Detroit.

Rutter, M., & Garmezy, N. (1983). Developmental psychopathology. In P. H. Mussen (Ed.), *Handbook of child psychology* (Vol. 4, 4th ed.). New York: Wiley.

Rutter, M., Maughan, B., Mortimore, P., & Ouston, J. (1979). *Fifteen thousand hours: Secondary schools and their effects on children.* Cambridge, MA: Harvard University Press.

Rutter, M., & Schopler, E. (1987). Autism and pervasive developmental disorders: Concepts and diagnostic issues. *Journal of Autism and Developmental Disorders, 17,* 159–186.

S

Sachdev, P. (Ed.). (1988). *International handbook on abortion.* New York: Greenwood Press.

Sadker, M., & Sadker, D. (1986, March). Sexism in the classroom: From grade school to graduate school. *Phi Delta Kappan,* pp. 512–515.

Sadker, M., Sadker, D., & Klein, S. S. (1986). Abolishing misperceptions about sex equity in education. *Theory into Practice, 25,* 219–226.

Sakurai, M. (1989, April). *Risk and resiliency in adolescence: The protective role of relationships.* Paper presented at the biennial meeting of the Society for Research in Child Development, Kansas City.

Salthouse, T. A. (1988). Initiating the formalization of theories of cognitive aging. *Psychology and Aging, 3,* 3–16.

Sandell, R., Collings, G. C., & Sherman, A. (1985). Sex equity in visual arts education. In S. S. Klein (Ed.), *Handbook for achieving sex equity through education.* Baltimore, MD: Johns Hopkins University Press.

Santilli, S. A., & Seidman, I. E. (1986). The shopping mall high school. *Equity and Excellence, 23,* 138–141.

Santrock, J. W. (1989). *Life-span development* (3rd ed.). Dubuque, IA: Wm. C. Brown.

Santrock, J. W., & Bartlett, J. C. (1986). *Developmental psychology.* Dubuque, IA: Wm. C. Brown.

Santrock, J. W., & Sitterle, K. (1985). The developmental world of children in divorced families: Research findings and clinical implications. In D. C. Goldberg (Ed.), *Contemporary marriage.* Homewood, IL: Dorsey Press.

Santrock, J. W., & Sitterle, K. A. (1987). Parent-child relationships in stepmother families. In K. Pasley & M. Ihinger-Tallman (Eds.), *Remarriage and stepparenting.* New York: Guilford.

Santrock, J. W., Sitterle, K. A., & Warshak, R. A. (1988). Parent-child relationships in stepfather families. In P. Bronstein & C. P. Cowan (Eds.), *Fatherhood today.* New York: Wiley.

Santrock, J. W., & Warshak, R. A. (1979). Father custody and social development in boys and girls. *Journal of Social Issues, 35,* 112–125.

Santrock, J. W., & Warshak, R. A. (1986). Development, relationships, and legal/clinical considerations in father-custody families. In M. E. Lamb (Ed.), *The father's role: Applied perspectives.* New York: Wiley.

Santrock, J. W., & Yussen, S. R. (1989). *Child development* (4th ed.). Dubuque, IA: Wm. C. Brown.

Savin-Williams, R. C. (1987). *Adolescence: An ethological perspective.* New York: Springer-Verlag.

Savin-Williams, R. C., & Demo, D. H. (1983). Conceiving or misconceiving the self: Issues in adolescent self-esteem. *Journal of Early Adolescence, 3,* 121–140.

Sax, G. (1989). *Principles of educational and psychological measurement.* (3rd ed.) Belmont, CA: Wadsworth.

Scardamalia, M., Bereiter, C., & Goelman, H. (1982). The role of production factors in writing ability. In M. Nystrand (Ed.), *What writers know: The language, process, and structure of written discourse.* New York: Academic Press.

Scarr, S. (1984, May). Interview. *Psychology Today,* pp. 59–63.

Scarr, S. (1989, April). *Transracial adoption: A unique social experiment to address normative questions in human development.* Discussion at the Biennial Meeting of the Society for Research in Child Development, Kansas City.

Scarr, S., & Kidd, K. K. (1983). Developmental behavior genetics. In P. H. Mussen (Ed.), *Handbook of child psychology* (Vol. 2, 4th ed.). New York: Wiley.

Scarr, S., & Weinberg, R. A. (1976). IQ test performance of black children adopted by white families. *American Psychologist, 31,* 726–739.

Scarr, S., & Weinberg, R. A. (1980). Calling all camps! The war is over. *American Sociological Review, 45,* 859–865.

Scarr, S., & Weinberg, R. A. (in press). The nature-nurture problem revisited: The Minnesota Adoption Studies. In G. Brody & I. Siegel (Eds.), *Family research journeys.* (Vol. 1). Hillsdale, NJ: Erlbaum.

Schaie, K. W. (1977). Quasi-experimental research designs in the psychology of aging. In J. E. Birren & K. W. Schaie (Eds.), *Handbook of the psychology of aging.* New York: Van Nostrand Reinhold.

Scheff, T. J. (1966). *Being mentally ill: A sociological theory.* Chicago: Aldine.

Schiff, A. R., & Knopf, I. J. (1985). The effects of task demands on attention allocation in children of different ages. *Child Development, 56,* 621–630.

Schneider, A. J. (1966). *Measurement of courtship progress of high school upperclassmen currently going steady.* Unpublished dissertation, Pennsylvania State University.

Schorr, L. B. (1989, April). *Within our reach: Breaking the cycle of disadvantage.* Paper presented at the biennial meeting of the Society for Research in Child Development, Kansas City.

Schorr, L. B. (in press). *Within our reach: Breaking the cycle of disadvantage and despair.* New York: Doubleday/Anchor.

Schulenberg, J. E., Shimizu, K., Vondracek, F. W., & Hostetler, M. (1988). Factorial invariance of career indecision dimensions across junior high and high school males and females. *Journal of Vocational Behavior, 33,* 63–81.

Schunk, D. H. (1983). Developing children's self-efficacy and skills: The roles of social comparative information and goal setting. *Contemporary Educational Psychology, 8,* 76–86.

Schunk, D. H. (1987). Peer models and children's behavior change. *Review of Educational Research, 57,* 149–174.

Schwartz, M. A., & Wiggins, O. P. (1986). Systems and structuring of meaning: Contributions to a biopsychosocial medicine. *American Journal of Psychiatry, 143,* 1213–1221.

Schwartz, R., & Eriksen, M. (1989). Statement of the Society for Public Health Education on the national health promotion disease prevention objectives for the year 2000. *Health Education Quarterly, 16,* 3–7.

Scott-Jones, D., & Clark, M. L. (1986, March). The school experiences of black girls: The interaction of gender, race, and socioeconomic status. *Phi Delta Kappan,* pp. 520–526.

Seligman, M. E. P. (1975). *Learned helplessness.* San Francisco: W. H. Freeman.

Selman, R., & Byrne, D. (1974). A structural developmental analysis of levels of role-taking in middle childhood. *Child Development, 45,* 803–806.

Selman, R. L. (1976). Social-cognitive understanding. In T. Lickona (Ed.), *Moral development and behavior.* New York: Holt, Rinehart & Winston.

Selman, R. L. (1980). *The growth of interpersonal understanding.* New York: Academic Press.

Selman, R. L. (1989, April). *Intimacy and autonomy in adolescence.* Paper presented at the biennial meeting of the Society for Research in Child Development, Kansas City.

Selman, R. L., Newberger, C. M., & Jacquette, D. (1977, April). *Observing interpersonal reasoning in a clinic/educational setting: Toward the integration of developmental and clinical child psychology.* Paper

presented at the meeting of the Society for Research in Child Development, New Orleans.

Selye, H. (1974). *Stress without distress.* Philadelphia: Saunders.

Selye, H. (1983). The stress conflict: Past, present, and future. In C. L. Cooper (Ed.), *Stress research.* New York: Wiley.

Sexton, M. A., & Geffen, G. (1979). Development of three strategies of attention in dichotic listening. *Developmental Psychology, 15,* 299–310.

Shakeshaft, C. (1986, March). A gender at risk. *Phi Delta Kappan,* pp. 499–503.

Shantz, C. (1983). The development of social cognition. In P. H. Mussen (Ed.), *Handbook of child psychology* (Vol. 3, 4th ed.). New York: Wiley.

Shantz, C. O. (1988). Conflicts between children. *Child Development, 59,* 283–305.

Shapiro, E. R., & Freedman, J. (1989). Family dynamics of adolescent suicide. In A. H. Esman (Ed.), *International annals of adolescent psychiatry.* Chicago: University of Chicago Press.

Sherif, M., Harvey, O. J., White, B. J., Hood, W. R., & Sherif, C. W. (1961). *Intergroup conflict and cooperation: The Robber's Cave experiment.* Norman, OK: Institute of Group Relations, University of Oklahoma.

Sherif, M., & Sherif, C. W. (1964). *Reference groups: Exploration into conformity and deviation of adolescents.* New York: Harper.

Shneidman, E. S. (1971). Suicide among the gifted. *Suicide and Life-Threatening Behavior, 1,* 23–45.

Shostrum, E. (1967). *Man, the manipulator.* New York: Bantam Books.

Showers, C. (1986, August). *The motivational consequences of negative thinking: Those who imagine the worst try harder.* Paper presented at the annual meeting of the American Psychological Association, Washington, DC.

Shuey, A. (1966). *The testing of Negro intelligence.* New York: Social Science Press.

Siegler, R. S. (in press). Individual differences in strategy choices: Good students, not-so-good students, and perfectionists. *Child Development.*

Siegman, A. W., & Dembrowski, T. (in press). *In search of coronary-prone behavior: Beyond Type-A.* Hillsdale, NJ: Erlbaum.

Silberman, C. E. (1970). *Crisis in the classroom: The remaking of American education.* New York: Random House.

Silver, S. (1988, August). *Behavior problems of children born into early-childbearing families.* Paper presented at the meeting of the American Psychological Association, Atlanta, GA.

Simmons, R. G., & Blyth, D. A. (1987). *Moving into adolescence.* Hawthorne, NY: Aldine.

Simmons, R. G., Brown, L., Bush, D. M., & Blyth, D. A. (1978). Self-esteem and achievement of black and white adolescents. *Social Problems, 26,* 86–96.

Simon, W., & Gagnon, J. H. (1969). On psychosexual development. In D. Goslin (Ed.), *Handbook of socialization theory and research.* Chicago: Rand McNally.

Simons, R. L., & Gray, P. A. (1989). Perceived blocked opportunity as an explanation of delinquency among lower-class black males: A research note. *Journal of Research in Crime and Delinquency, 26,* 90–101.

Simpson, J. A., Campbell, B., & Berscheid, E. (1986). The association between love and marriage: Kephart (1967) twice revisited. *Personality and Social Psychology Bulletin, 12,* 363–372.

Simpson, R. L. (1962). Parental influence, anticipatory socialization, and social mobility. *American Sociological Review, 27,* 517–522.

Singer, D. G., & Singer, J. L. (1987). Introductory comments. *Journal of Early Adolescence, 7,* v–ix.

Singer, J. L. (1984). *The human personality.* San Diego: Harcourt Brace Jovanovich.

Sizer, T. R. (1984). *Horace's compromise: The dilemma of the American high school today.* Boston: Houghton Mifflin.

Skinner, B. F. (1938). *The behavior of organisms: An experimental analysis.* New York: Appleton-Century-Crofts.

Skipper, J. K., & Nass, G. (1966). Dating behavior: A framework for analysis and an illustration. *Journal of Marriage and the Family, 28,* 412–420.

Slavin, R. (1989a). Achievement effects of substantial reductions in class size. In R. Slavin (Ed.), *School and classroom organization.* Hillsdale, NJ: Erlbaum.

Slavin, R. (1989b). Cooperative learning and student achievement. In R. E. Slavin (Ed.), *School and classroom organization.* Hillsdale, NJ: Erlbaum.

Slavin, R. E. (1987). Developmental and motivational perspectives on cooperative learning: A reconciliation. *Child Development, 58,* 1161–1167.

Smetana, J. (1983). Social-cognitive development: Domain distinctions and coordinations. *Developmental Review, 3,* 131–147.

Smetana, J. (1985). Preschool children's conceptions of transgressions: Effects of varying moral and conventional domain-related attributes. *Developmental Psychology, 21,* 18–29.

Smith, B. O., & Orlosky, D. E. (1975). *Socialization and schooling (basics of reform).* Bloomington, IN: Phi Delta Kappa.

Smith, D. E. (1986). Cocaine-alcohol abuse: Epidemiological, diagnostic, and treatment considerations. *Journal of Psychoactive Drugs, 18,* 117–129.

Smith, J., Dixon, R. A., & Baltes, P. B. (in press). Expertise in life planning: A new research approach to investigating aspects of wisdom. In M. L. Commons, J. D. Sinnott, F. A. Richards, & C. Armon (Eds.), *Beyond formal operations II: Comparisons and applications of adolescent and adult models.* New York: Praeger.

Snarey, J. (1987, June). A question of morality. *Psychology Today,* pp. 6–8.

Snedeker, B. (1982). *Hard knocks.* Baltimore, MD: Johns Hopkins University Press.

Snidman, N., & Kagan, J. (1989, April). *Infant predictors of behaviorally inhibited and uninhibited children.* Paper presented at the biennial meeting of the Society for Research in Child Development, Kansas City.

Snyder, M. (1974). Self-monitoring of expressive behavior. *Journal of Personality and Social Psychology, 30,* 526–537.

Snyder, M. (1987). *Public appearances/ Private realities.* New York: W. H. Freeman.

Snyder, M., Berscheid, E., & Glick, P. (1985). Focusing on the exterior and the interior: Two investigations of the initiation of personal relationships. *Journal of Personality and Social Psychology, 48,* 1427–1439.

Solomon, R. W., & Wahler, R. G. (1973). Peer reinforcement control of classroom problem behavior. *Journal of Applied Behavior Analysis, 6,* 49–56.

Sommer, B. B. (1978). *Puberty and adolescence.* New York: Oxford University Press.

Sonenstein, F. L., & Pittman, K. J. (1984, January/February). The availability of sex education in large city school districts. *Family Planning Perspectives,* p. 19.

Sorensen, R. C. (1973). *Adolescent sexuality in contemporary America.* New York: World.

Spearman, C. (1927). *The abilities of man.* New York: Macmillan.

Spence, J. T., & Helmreich, R. (1972). The Attitudes Toward Women Scale. An objective instrument to measure the rights and roles of women in contemporary society. *JSAS Catalog of Selected Documents in Psychology, 2,* 66.

Spence, J. T., & Helmreich, R. L. (1978). *Masculinity and femininity: Their psychological dimensions.* Austin, TX: University of Texas Press.

Spencer, M. L. (1986). Sex equity in bilingual education, English as a second language, and foreign language instruction. *Theory into Practice, 25,* 257–266.

Sroufe, L. A. (1985). Attachment classification from the perspective of infant-caregiver relationships and infant temperament. *Child Development, 56,* 1–14.

Sroufe, L. A. (1988). The role of infant-caregiver attachment in development. In J. Belsky & T. M. Nezworski (Eds.), *Clinical implications of attachment.* Hillsdale, NJ: Erlbaum.

Sroufe, L. A., & Fleeson, J. (1985). Attachment and the construction of relationships. In W. W. Hartup & Z. Rubin (Eds.), *Relationships and development.* Hillsdale, NJ: Erlbaum.

Stage, E. K., Kreinberg, N., Eccles, J., & Becker, J. R. (1985). Increasing the participation and achievement of girls and women in mathematics, science, and engineering. In S. S. Klein (Ed.), *Handbook for achieving sex equity through education.* Baltimore, MD: Johns Hopkins University Press.

Stedman, L., & Smith, M. (1983). Recent reform proposals for American education. *Contemporary Education Review, 2,* 85–104.

Steinberg, L. (1986). Stability (and instability) of Type A behavior from childhood to young adulthood. *Developmental Psychology, 22,* 393–402.

Steinberg, L. (1988). Simple solutions to a complex problem: A response to Rodman, Pratto, and Nelson (1988). *Developmental Psychology, 24,* 295–296.

Steinberg, L. D. (1981). Transformations in family relations at puberty. *Developmental Psychology, 17,* 833–840.

Steinberg, L. D. (1986). Latchkey children and susceptibility to peer pressure: An ecological analysis. *Developmental Psychology, 22,* 433–439.

Steinberg, L. D. (1987). Impact of puberty on family relations: Effects of pubertal status and pubertal timing. *Developmental Psychology, 23,* 451–460.

Steinberg, L. D. (1988). Reciprocal relation between parent-child distance and pubertal maturation. *Developmental Psychology, 24,* 122–128.

Steinitz, V. A., & Solomon, E. R. (1986). *Starting out: Class and community in the lives of working-class youth.* Philadelphia: Temple University Press.

Stengel, R. (1985, December 9). The missing-father myth. *Time*, p. 90.

Stephenson, B., & Wicklund, R. (1983). Self-directed attention and taking the other's perspective. *Journal of Experimental Social Psychology, 19,* 58–77.

Stern, S. L., Dixon, K. N., Jones, D., Lake, M., Nemzer, E., & Sansone, R. (1989). Family environment in anorexia nervosa and bulimia. *International Journal of Eating Disorders, 8,* 25–31.

Sternberg, R. J. (1977). *Intelligence, information processing, and analogical reasoning: The componential analysis of human abilities.* Hillsdale, NJ: Erlbaum.

Sternberg, R. J. (1986). *Intelligence applied.* San Diego: Harcourt Brace Jovanovich.

Sternberg, R. J. (1988). *The triarchic mind.* New York: Viking Penguin.

Sternberg, R. J. (1989). Introduction. In R. J. Sternberg (Ed.), *Advances in the psychology of human intelligence* (Vol. 5). Hillsdale, NJ: Erlbaum.

Sternberg, R. J. (Ed.). (in press). *The nature of creativity.* New York: Cambridge University Press.

Sternberg, R. J., Conway, B. E., Ketron, J. L., & Berstein, M. (1981). People's conceptions of intelligence. *Journal of Personality and Social Psychology, 41,* 37–55.

Sternberg, R. J., & Davidson, J. E. (Eds.). (1986). *Conceptions of giftedness.* New York: Cambridge University Press.

Sternberg, R. J., & Nigro, C. (1980). Developmental patterns in the solution of verbal analogies. *Child Development, 51,* 27–38.

Sternberg, R. J., & Rifkin, B. (1979). The development of analogical reasoning processes. *Journal of Experimental Child Psychology, 27,* 195–232.

Sternglanz, S. H., & Serbin, L. A. (1974). Sex-role stereotyping in children's television programming. *Developmental Psychology, 10,* 710–715.

Stipek, D. J., & Hoffman, J. M. (1980). Children's achievement-related expectancies as a function of academic performance histories and sex. *Journal of Educational Psychology, 72,* 861–865.

Stone, E. J., Perry, C. L., & Luepker, R. V. (1989). Synthesis of cardiovascular behavioral research for youth health promotion. *Health Education Quarterly, 16,* 155–169.

Stork, J. (1989). Suicide and adolescence. In A. H. Esman (Ed.), *International annals of adolescent psychiatry.* Chicago: University of Chicago Press.

Strahan, D. B. (1983). The emergence of formal operations in adolescence. *Transcendence, 11,* 7–14.

Strahan, D. B. (1987). A developmental analysis of formal reasoning in the middle grades. *Journal of Instructional Psychology, 14,* 67–73.

Streitmatter, J. L. (1987). The effect of gender and family status on ego identity development among early adolescents. *Journal of Early Adolescence, 7,* 179–189.

Strodtbeck, F. L. (1958). Family interaction, values, and achievement. In D. C. McClelland, A. L. Baldwin, U. Bronfenbrenner, & F. L. Strodtbeck (Eds.), *Talent and society.* Princeton, NJ: Van Nostrand.

Stunkard, A. J. (1987). The regulation of body weight and the treatment of obesity. In H. Weiner & A. Baum (Eds.), *Eating regulation and discontrol.* Hillsdale, NJ: Erlbaum.

Stunkard, A. J. (in press). Perspectives on human obesity. In A. J. Stunkard & A. Baum (Eds.), *Perspectives on behavioral medicine.* Hillsdale, NJ: Erlbaum.

Styne, D. M. (1988). The physiology of normal and delayed puberty. In M. D. Levine & E. R. McAnarney (Eds.), *Early adolescent transitions.* Lexington, MA: Lexington Books.

Sue, S. (1989). Foreword. In J. T. Gibbs & L. N. Huang (Eds.), *Children of color.* San Francisco: Jossey-Bass.

Sullivan, E. V. (1975). *Moral learning: Findings, issues, and questions.* Paramus, NJ: Paulist/Newman Press.

Sullivan, H. S. (1953). *The interpersonal theory of psychiatry.* New York: W. W. Norton.

Sullivan, K., & Sullivan, A. (1980). Adolescent-parent separation. *Developmental Psychology, 16,* 93–99.

Suomi, S. (1987, April). *Individual differences in rhesus monkey behavioral and adrenocortical responses to social challenge: Correlations with measures of heart rate variability.* Paper presented at the biennial meeting of the Society for Research in Child Development, Baltimore.

Suomi, S. J., Harlow, H. F., & Domek, C. J. (1970). Effect of repetitive infant-infant separations of young monkeys. *Journal of Abnormal Psychology, 76,* 161–172.

Super, D. E. (1967). *The psychology of careers.* New York: Harper & Row.

Super, D. E. (1976). *Career education and the meanings of work.* Washington, DC: U.S. Office of Education.

Susman, E. J., Inoff-Germain, G., Nottelmann, E. D., Cutler, G. B., & Chrousos, G. P. (1987). Hormones, emotional dispositions, and aggressive attributes in young adolescents. *Child Development, 58,* 1114–1134.

Sutton-Smith, B. (1982). Birth order and sibling status effects. In M. E. Lamb & B. Sutton-Smith (Eds.), *Sibling relationships: Their nature and significance across the lifespan.* Hillsdale, NJ: Erlbaum.

Swope, G. W. (1980). Kids and cults: Who joins and why? *Media and Methods, 16,* 18–21.

Szasz, T. (1977). *Psychiatric slavery: When confinement and coercion masquerade as cure.* New York: Free Press.

T

Tanner, J. M. (1970). Physical growth. In P. H. Mussen (Ed.), *Manual of Child Psychology* (Vol. 1, 3rd ed.). New York: Wiley.

Task Force on Pediatric AIDS. (1989). Pediatric AIDS and human immunodeficiency virus infection. *American Psychologist, 44,* 258–264.

Taylor, D. (1985). *Women: A world report.* New York: Oxford University Press.

Taylor, S. (1989, August). *Psychological aspects of chronic illness.* Paper presented at the meeting of the American Psychological Association, New Orleans.

Taylor, S. E., Collins, R., Skokan, L., & Aspinwall, L. (1988, August). *Illusions, reality, and adjustment in coping with victimizing events*. Paper presented at the meeting of the American Psychological Association, Atlanta.

Tchibinda, J., & Mayetela, N. (1983). The rights of the child in the People's Republic of the Congo. In A. Pappas (Ed.), *Law and the status of the child*. New York: United Nations Institute for Training and Research.

Terman, L. (1925). Mental and physical traits of a thousand gifted children. In *Genetic studies of genius* (Vol. 1). Stanford, CA: Stanford University Press.

Tessor, A., Millar, M., & Moore, J. (1988). Some affective consequences of social comparison and reflection processes: The pain and pleasure of closeness. *Journal of Personality and Social Psychology, 54,* 49–61.

Tetreault, M. K. T. (1986). The journey from male-defined to gender balanced education. *Theory into Practice, 25,* 276–283.

Tharp, R. G., & Gallimore, R. G. (1989). *Rousing minds to life*. New York: Cambridge U. Press.

Thomas, A., & Chess, S. (1987). Commentary. In H. H. Goldsmith, A. H. Buss, R. Plomin, M. K. Rothbart, A. Thomas, S. Chess, R. R. Hinde, & R. B. McCall, Roundtable: What is temperament? Four approaches. *Child Development, 58,* 505–529.

Thomas, A., Chess, S., & Birch, H. G. (1968). *Temperament and behavior disorders in children*. New York: New York University Press.

Thomas, A., Chess, S., & Birch, H. G. (1970). The origin of personality. *Scientific American, 233,* 102–109.

Thompson, P. J. (1986). Beyond gender: Equity issues in home economics education. *Theory into Practice, 25,* 276–283.

Thoresen, C. E., Eagleston, J. R., Kirmil-Gray, K., & Bracke, P. E. (1985, August). *Exploring the Type A behavior pattern in children and adolescents*. Paper presented at the meeting of the American Psychological Association, Los Angeles.

Thornburg, H. D. (1981). Sources of sex education among early adolescents. *Journal of Early Adolescence, 1,* 171–184.

Thorndike, R. L., Hagan, E. P., & Sattler, J. M. (1985). *Stanford-Binet* (4th ed.). Chicago: Riverside.

Thurstone, L. L. (1938). *Primary mental abilities*. Chicago: University of Chicago Press.

Tittle, C. K. (1988). Validity, gender research, and studies of the effects of career development interventions. *Applied Psychology: An International Review, 37,* 121–131.

Toepfer, C. F. (1979). Brain growth periodization: A new dogma for education. *Middle School Journal, 10,* 20.

Tolan, P., Miller, L., & Thomas, P. (1988). Perception and experience of types of social stress and self-image among adolescents. *Journal of Youth and Adolescence, 17,* 147–163.

Toman, W. (1971). The duplication theorem of social relationships as tested in the general population. *Psychological Review, 79,* 380–390.

Tomlinson-Keasey, C. (1972). Formal operations in females from 11 to 54 years of age. *Developmental Psychology, 6,* 364.

Tomlinson-Keasey, C., Warren, L. W., & Elliott, J. E. (1986). Suicide among gifted women: A prospective study. *Journal of Abnormal Psychology, 95,* 123–130.

Toth, S. A. (1981). *Blooming*. Boston: Little, Brown.

Travis, C. B. (in press). *Women in health psychology: Mental health issues*. Hillsdale, NJ: Erlbaum.

Trimble, J. E. (1989, August). *The enculturation of contemporary psychology*. Paper presented at the meeting of the American Psychological Association, New Orleans.

Troll, L. (1985). *Development in early and middle adulthood* (2nd ed.). Monterey, CA: Brooks-Cole.

Tucker, L. A. (1987). Television, teenagers, and health. *Journal of Youth and Adolescence, 16,* 415–425.

Tuckman, B. W., & Hinkle, J. S. (1988). An experimental study of the physical and psychological effects of aerobic exercise on schoolchildren. In B. G. Melamed & others (Eds.), *Child health psychology*. Hillsdale, NJ: Erlbaum.

Tulkin, S. R., & Kagan, J. (1971). Mother-child interaction in the first year of life. *Child Development, 43,* 31–41.

Turiel, E. (1966). An experimental test of the sequentiality of developmental stages in the child's moral judgments. *Journal of Personality and Social Psychology, 3,* 611–618.

Turiel, E. (1977). A critical analysis of Kohlberg's contributions to the study of moral thought. *Journal of Social Behavior, 7,* 41–63.

Turiel, E. (1978). Social regulations and domains of social concepts. In W. Damon (Ed.), *New directions for child development: Vol. 1. Social cognition*. San Francisco: Jossey-Bass.

Turkle, S. (1984). *The second self*. Cambridge, MA: Harvard University Press.

Twentyman, C. T., & McFall, R. M. (1975). Behavioral training of social skills in shy males. *Journal of Consulting and Clinical Psychology, 43,* 384–395.

Tyack, D. (1976). Ways of seeing: An essay on the history of compulsory schooling. *Harvard Educational Review, 46,* 355–389.

U

Ullman, C. (1982). Cognitive and emotional antecedents of religious conversion. *Journal of Personality and Social Psychology, 43,* 183–192.

UNICEF. (1986). *The state of the world's children 1987: A summary*. New York: UNICEF.

United States Department of Health and Human Services, Public Health Service (1989). *Reducing the health consequences of smoking: 25 years of progress*. Washington, DC: U.S. Government Printing Office.

United States Supreme Court. (1967). In re Gault. 387 U.S. 1.

Upcraft, M. L., & Gardner, J. N. (1989). *The freshman year experience*. San Francisco: Jossey-Bass.

U.S. Bureau of the Census. (1980). *Social indicators III*. Washington, DC: U.S. Department of Commerce.

U.S. Bureau of the Census. (1986). *Statistical abstract of the United States*. Washington, DC: U.S. Government Printing Office.

Valsiner, J. (Ed.). (1988). *Child development in cultural context.* Toronto: C. J. Hogrefe.

Vandell, D. L. (1987). Baby sister/baby brother: Reactions to the birth of a sibling and patterns of early sibling relations. In F. F. Schachter & R. K. Stone (Eds.), *Practical concerns about siblings.* New York: Haworth Press.

Vandiver, R. (1972). *Sources and interrelation of premarital sexual standards and general liberality and conservatism.* Unpublished doctoral dissertation, Southern Illinois University.

Van Gennep, A. (1969). *The rites of passage.* Chicago: University of Chicago Press.

VanItallie, T. B. (1984). The enduring storage capacity for fat: Implications for treatment of obesity. In A. J. Stunkard & E. Stellar (Eds.), *Eating and its disorders.* New York: Raven Press.

Volkmor, C. B., Pasanella, A. L., & Raths, L. E. (1977). *Values in the classroom.* Columbus, OH: Merrill.

Voss, J. F. (1989). Problem solving and the educational process. In A. Lesgold & R. Glaser (Eds.), *Foundations of a psychology of education.* Hillsdale, NJ: Erlbaum.

Vuchinich, S., Emery, R. E., & Cassidy, J. (in press). Family members as third parties in dyadic family conflict: Strategies, alliances, and outcomes. *Child Development.*

Waddington, C. H. (1957). *The strategy of the genes.* London: Allen & Son.

Wagennar, A. C. (1983). *Alcohol, young drivers, and traffic accidents.* Lexington, MA: D. C. Heath.

Wagner, D. A., & Stevenson, H. W. (1982). *Cultural perspectives on child development.* San Francisco: W. H. Freeman.

Walker, L. (1980). Cognitive and perspective taking prerequisites for moral development. *Child Development, 51,* 131–139.

Walker, L. (1982). The sequentiality of Kohlberg's stages of moral development. *Child Development, 53,* 1330–1336.

Walker, L. J., de Vries, B., & Trevethan, S. D. (1987). Moral stages and moral orientation in real-life and hypothetical dilemmas. *Child Development, 58,* 842–858.

Wallace, H. M., & Vienonen, M. (1989). Teenage pregnancy in Sweden and Finland: Implications for the United States. *Journal of Adolescent Health Care, 10,* 231–236.

Wallach, M. A. (1985). Creative testing and giftedness. In F. D. Horowitz & M. O'Brien (Eds.), *The gifted and the talented.* Washington, DC: American Psychological Association.

Wallach, M. A., & Kogan, N. (1965). *Modes of thinking in young children.* New York: Holt, Rinehart & Winston.

Wallerstein, J. S. (1989). *Second chance.* New York: Ticknor & Fields.

Wallerstein, J. S., Corbin, S. B., & Lewis, J. M. (1988). Children of divorce: A 10-year study. In E. M. Hetherington & J. D. Arasteh (Eds.), *Impact of divorce, single parenting, and stepparenting on children.* Hillsdale, NJ: Erlbaum.

Wallerstein, J. S., & Kelly, J. B. (1980). *Surviving the breakup: How children actually cope with divorce.* New York: Basic Books.

Wallis, C. (1985, December 9). Children having children. *Time,* pp. 78–88.

Walster, E., Aronson, E., Abrahams, D., & Rottman, L. (1966). Importance of physical attractiveness in dating behavior. *Journal of Personality and Social Psychology, 4,* 508–516.

Walter, C. A. (1986). *The timing of motherhood.* Lexington, MA: D.C. Heath.

Waterman, A. S. (1982). Identity development from adolescence to adulthood: An extension of theory and a review of research. *Developmental Psychology, 3,* 341–358.

Waterman, A. S. (1988). Identity status theory and Erikson's theory: Communalities and differences. *Developmental Review, 8,* 185–208.

Waterman, A. S., & Waterman, C. K. (1971). A longitudinal study of changes in ego identity status during the freshman year of college. *Developmental Psychology, 5,* 167–173.

Waterman, A. S., & Waterman, C. K. (1972). Relationship between ego identity status and subsequent academic behavior: A test of the predictive validity of Marcia's categorization for identity status. *Developmental Psychology, 6,* 179.

Waters, E., & Sroufe, L. A. (1983). Social competence as a developmental construct. *Developmental Review, 3,* 79–97.

Watts, T. D., & Lewis, R. G. (1988). Alcoholism and native American youth: An overview. *Journal of Drug Issues, 18,* 69–86.

Wechsler, D. (1949). *Wechsler Intelligence Scale for Children.* New York: Psychological Corporation.

Wechsler, D. (1955). *Wechsler Adult Intelligence Scale Manual.* New York: Psychological Corporation.

Wechsler, D. (1974). *Wechsler Intelligence Scale for Children—Revised.* New York: Psychological Corporation.

Wechsler, D. (1981). *Wechsler Adult Intelligence Scale—Revised.* New York: Psychological Corporation.

Wehlage, G. G., & Rutter, R. A. (1986). Dropping out: How much do schools contribute to the problem? *Teachers College Record, 87,* 374–392.

Weidner, G., Sexton, G., Matarazzo, J. D., Pereira, C., & Friend, R. (1988). Type A behavior in children, adolescents, and their parents. *Developmental Psychology, 24,* 118–121.

Weinberg, R. A. (1989). Intelligence and IQ: Landmark issues and great debates. *American Psychologist, 44,* 98–104.

Weiner, I. B. (1980). Psychopathology in adolescence. In J. Adelson (Ed.), *Handbook of adolescent psychology.* New York: Wiley.

Weissberg, R. P. (1988). Teaching of social skills. *William T. Grant Foundation Annual Report,* p. 18.

Weissberg, R. P., Caplan, M. Z., and Bennetto, L. (1988). *The evaluation of a social competence program with young, urban adolescents.* Unpublished manuscript. New Haven, CT: Yale University Press.

Weissberg, R. P., Caplan, M. Z., & Sivo, P. J. (1989). A new conceptual framework for establishing school-based social competence promotion programs. In L. A. Bond, B. E. Compas, & C. Swift (Eds.), *Prevention in the schools.* Menlo Park, CA: Sage.

Wender, P. H., Kety, S. S., Rosenthal, D., Schulsinger, F., Ortmann, J., & Lunde, I. (1986). Psychiatric disorders in the biological and adoptive families of adopted individuals with affective disorders. *Archives of General Psychiatry, 43,* 923–929.

Wertsch, J. V. (1989). A sociocultural approach to mind. In W. Damon (Ed.), *Child development today and tomorrow.* San Francisco: Jossey-Bass.

White, R. W. (1959). Motivation reconsidered: The concept of competence. *Psychological Review, 66,* 297–333.

White, S. H. (1985, April). *Risings and fallings of developmental psychology.* Paper presented at the biennial meeting of the Society for Research in Child Development, Toronto.

Whiting, B. B. (1989, April). *Culture and interpersonal behavior.* Paper presented at the biennial meeting of the Society for Research in Child Development, Kansas City.

Whiting, B. B., & Edwards, C. P. (1988). *Children of different worlds.* Cambridge, MA: Harvard University Press.

Wicklund, R. (1979). The influence of self-awareness on human behavior. *American Scientist, 67,* 187–193.

Wideck, C., Knefelkamp, L., & Parker, C. (1975). The counselor as a developmental instructor. *Counselor Education and Supervision, 14,* 286–295.

William T. Grant Foundation Commission on Work, Family and Citizenship. (1988, February). *The forgotten half: Non-college-bound youth in America.* New York: William T. Grant Foundation.

Williams, R. B. (1989). *The trusting heart: Great news about Type A behavior.* New York: Random House.

Williamson, J. M., & Borduin, C. (1989, April). *A multivariate examination of adolescent physical abuse, sexual abuse and neglect.* Paper presented at the biennial meeting of the Society for Research in Child Development, Kansas City.

Wilson, A. B. (1989). Dreams and aspirations in the status attainment model. In D. Stern & D. Eichorn (Eds.), *Adolescence and work.* Hillsdale, NJ: Erlbaum.

Wilson, M. N. (1989). Child development in the context of the extended family. *American Psychologist, 44,* 380–385.

Wilson, W. J. (1978). *The declining significance of race.* Chicago: University of Chicago Press.

Winner, E. (1989). Development in the visual arts. In W. Damon (Ed.), *Child development today and tomorrow.* San Francisco: W. H. Freeman.

Wise, R. A. (1988). The neurobiology of craving: Implications for the understanding and treatment of addiction. *Journal of Abnormal Psychology, 97,* 118–132.

Wodarski, J. S., & Hoffman, S. D. (1984). Alcohol education for adolescents. *Social Work in Education, 6,* 69–92.

Wright, M. R. (1989). Body image satisfaction in adolescent girls and boys. *Journal of Youth and Adolescence, 18,* 71–84.

Wroblewski, R., & Huston, A. C. (1987). Televised occupational stereotypes and their effects on early adolescents: Are they changing? *Journal of Early Adolescence, 7,* 283–297.

Wylie, R. C. (1979). *The self-concept: Theory and research on selected topics* (Vol. 2, rev. ed.). Lincoln, NE: University of Nebraska Press.

Y

Yankelovich, D. (1974). *The new morality: A profile of American youth in the 1970s.* New York: McGraw-Hill.

Yardley, K. (1987). What do you mean "Who am I?": Exploring the implications of a self-concept measurement with subjects. In K. Yardley & T. Honess (Eds.), *Self and identity: Psychosocial perspectives.* New York: Wiley.

Youniss, J., & Smollar, J. (1985). *Adolescent relations with mothers, fathers, and friends.* Chicago: University of Chicago Press.

Yussen, S. R. (1977). Characteristics of moral dilemmas written by adolescents. *Developmental Psychology, 13,* 162–163.

Z

Zabin, L. S. (1986, May/June). Evaluation of a pregnancy prevention program for urban teenagers. *Family Planning Perspectives,* p. 119.

Zelnik, M., & Kantner, J. F. (1977). Sexual and contraceptive experiences of young unmarried women in the United States, 1976 and 1971. *Family Planning Perspectives, 9,* 55–71.

Zelnik, M., & Kantner, J. F. (1980). Sexual activity, contraceptive use and pregnancy among metropolitan-area teenagers: 1971–1979. *Family Planning Perspectives, 12,* 230–237.

Zembar, M. J., & Naus, M. J. (1985, April). *The combined effects of knowledge base and mnemonic strategies in children's memory.* Paper presented at the biennial meeting of the Society for Research in Child Development, Toronto.

Zigler, E. F. (1987, August). *Issues in mental retardation research.* Paper presented at the meeting of the American Psychological Association, New York City.

Zigler, E. F., & Farber, E. A. (1985). Commonalities between the intellectual extremes: Giftedness and mental retardation. In F. D. Horowitz & M. O'Brien (Eds.), *The gifted and the talented.* Washington, DC: American Psychological Association.

Zill, N. (1988). Behavior, achievement, and health problems among children in stepfamilies: Findings from a national survey of child health. In E. M. Hetherington & J. D. Arasteh (Eds.), *Impact of divorce, single-parenting, and stepparenting on children.* Hillsdale, NJ: Erlbaum.

Glossary

A

abstract relations The ability of the adolescent to coordinate two or more abstract ideas. (p. 145)

accommodation In Piaget's theory of cognitive development, the act of modifying a current mode or structure of thought to deal with new features of the environment. (p. 58)

acculturation Occurs when members of different cultures interact, and the process produces changes in one or both of the cultures. (p. 348)

achievement test A measure designed to evaluate what has been learned or what skills have been mastered. (p. 174)

adolescence The period of transition between childhood and adulthood, consisting of biological/physical, cognitive, and social/emotional/personal changes. (p. 28)

adolescent generalization gap Widespread generalizations based on information about a limited group of adolescents. (p. 23)

adoption study An examination and comparison of the biological and adopted parents of adopted children to determine the importance of heredity on behavior. (p. 93)

affectionate love Also called companionate love. It involves the desire to have the other individual nearby and to seek the individual's proximity. (p. 277)

AIDS Sexually transmitted disease caused by a virus that destroys the body's immune system. (p. 437)

altruism Selfless concern for the welfare of others. Altruistic behavior includes sharing, contributing to worthy causes, and helping others. (p. 475)

amphetamines Synthetic stimulants that are usually available in the form of pills. Amphetamines are often used by students to maintain high levels of performance for short periods of time. (p. 539)

anal stage Freud's second stage of development, occurring from approximately one-and-a-half to three years of life; pleasure involves the anus. (p. 48)

androgens Sex hormones that are primarily involved in the development of male sex characteristics. (p. 106)

androgyny A gender-role orientation in which the person incorporates both masculine and feminine aspects into his or her behavior. (p. 401)

anorexia nervosa An eating disorder, primarily in females, that leads to self-starvation. (p. 585)

anthropological view Stresses the scientific study of the origin of human beings and cultural influences on their development. Anthropologists believe that the adolescent's behavior may vary from one culture to another in ways the individual would have difficulty recognizing. (p. 331)

anticonformist A rebellious adolescent who reacts counter to the group's expectations and deliberately moves away from the actions or beliefs that they advocate. (p. 251)

approach/approach conflict Conflict we experience when we have to choose between two attractive stimuli. (p. 568)

approach/avoidance conflict Conflict we experience when a single stimulus circumstance includes both negative and positive aspects. (p. 569)

aptitude test A measure designed to predict an individual's ability to learn a skill or to predict what the individual can accomplish with training. (p. 174)

aptitude-treatment interaction (ATI) A field of educational research that determines the best learning conditions for a particular student by considering the interaction between the student's abilities and various teaching methods. (p. 308)

artificial intelligence The branch of computer science devoted to creating computers capable of handling complicated tasks that require some "thinking." (p. 161)

assimilation In Piaget's theory, the act of incorporating a feature of the environment into an existing mode or structure of thought. (p. 58)

assimilation Occurs when the members of one culture become completely absorbed into a more dominant culture. The term has another meaning in Piaget's theory. (p. 348)

attribution theory Theory that views individuals as cognitive beings who attempt to understand the causes of their own and others' behavior. (p. 495)

authoritarian parenting A style of parenting having a restrictive, punitive orientation, and placing limits and controls on the child. There is little verbal give and take between the child and the parent. This form of parenting is linked with the following social behaviors of the child: an anxiety about social comparison, failure to initiate activity, and ineffective social interaction. (p. 214)

authoritative parenting A form of parenting that encourages the child to be independent, but still places limits, demands, and controls on his or her actions. There is extensive verbal give and take, and parents demonstrate a high degree of warmth and nurturance toward the child. This form of parenting

is associated with social competence on the part of the child, particularly self-reliance and social responsibility. (p. 214)

authority and social-order maintaining morality Fourth stage of Kohlberg's theory of moral development, in which moral judgement is based on understanding the social order. (p. 463)

autonomous morality According to Piaget, the more advanced way of thinking, displayed by older children and adolescents. (p. 460)

autonomy vs. shame and doubt Erikson's second stage of development, in which children may develop the healthy attitude that they are capable of independent control of their actions, or the unhealthy attitude of shame because they are incapable or doubt that they are capable of such control. (p. 55)

avoidance/avoidance conflict Conflict we experience when we must choose between two unattractive stimuli. (p. 569)

basal metabolism rate (BMR) The minimum amount of energy a person uses in a state of rest. (p. 581)

behavioral contract A signed agreement that spells out what involved parties need to do to help to facilitate behavior modification. (p. 64)

behavior genetics The discipline concerned with the degree and nature of the heredity basis of behavior. (p. 93)

behavioral medicine Follows a philosophy similar to the holistic orientation and health psychology; combines medical and behavioral information to reduce illness and promote health. (p. 567)

biological processes Changes in the individual's physical nature. (p. 26)

bulimia A binge-and-purge syndrome that occurs primarily in females and is marked by periods of very heavy eating followed by self-induced vomiting. (p. 586)

burnout Today's buzzword for stress overload; a hopeless feeling brought on by relentless work-related stress. (p. 568)

C

canalization The narrow track or path that marks the development of some characteristics in genetic development. (p. 93)

career self-concept theory View that the individual's self-concept plays a central role in career development. Career development consists of five different phases: crystallization, specification, implementation, stabilization, and consolidation. (p. 502)

care perspective An approach to moral development proposed by Gilligan in which people are viewed in terms of their connectedness with other people, and the focus is on their communication with others. (p. 468)

case study An in-depth look at an individual, used primarily by clinical psychologists. (p. 72)

categorical self Refers to the "me", the object of what is known, the observed. (p. 365)

Chicanos The politically conscious Mexican-American adolescents who are a product of Spanish-Mexican-Indian heritage and Anglo influences. (p. 347)

chlamydia Sexually transmitted disease appearing in both males and females. (p. 436)

cliques Peer groups that are smaller in size than a crowd, involve greater intimacy among members, and have more group cohesion. Members of a clique are attracted to one another on the basis of similar interests and social ideals. (p. 268)

coaching A conglomerate of strategies used to facilitate peer relations, possibly consisting of demonstration or modeling, discussion and reasoning, as well as reinforcement of appropriate skills. (p. 255)

cocaine A stimulant, taken in the form of either crystals or powder, which provides increased feelings of stamina, enhanced mental capabilities, excitability, and occasionally hallucinations. (p. 539)

cognitive-disequilibrium theory A Piagetian-related view of moral development in which individuals may start to question and sometimes reject their former beliefs and, in the process, may develop their own moral system. (p. 461)

cognitive monitoring The process of taking stock of what one is currently doing, what will be done next, and how effectively the mental activity is unfolding. (p. 165)

cognitive moral education Advocates of cognitive moral education believe that through development of students' moral reasoning, values such as democracy and justice will be adopted. They argue that moral standards should be allowed to develop within students through environmental settings and exercises that encourage more advanced moral thinking. (p. 478)

cognitive processes Changes in the individual's thought, intelligence, and language. (p. 26)

cognitive social learning theory The contemporary version of social learning theory developed by Mischel and Bandura, which stresses that environment-behavior relations are mediated by cognitive factors. (p. 66)

cohort effect Effects due to an individual's time of birth or generation but not to age. (p. 77)

commitment Refers to the extent to which the adolescent shows a personal investment in what he or she is going to do. (p. 384)

community rights vs. individual rights The fifth stage of Kohlberg's theory of moral development. The individual in this stage understands that values and laws are relative and that standards may vary from one individual to another. (p. 463)

competence motivation Also called mastery motivation. The motivation to deal effectively with the environment, to be competent and do well what is attempted, to process information efficiently, and to change the world in hope of making it better. (p. 492)

concrete operational stage The third stage in Piagetian theory, approximately seven to eleven years old, during which children acquire mental operations that allow for abstractions to some attributes of reality, such as number and substance. These operations can only be applied to concrete events. (p. 59)

connectedness Method of identity achievement reflected in mutuality and permeability in which the adolescent is sensitive to and respects the view of others, and is open and responsive to the view of others. (p. 386)

consensual validation Motivation for the adolescent to form close relationships with others who are similar to him or her in attitude and behavior; provides a confirmation of who he or she is. (p. 275)

conservation The ability to recognize that the length, number, mass, quantity, area, weight, and volume of objects and substances do not change even when transformations alter their appearance. (p. 128)

continuity of development A gradual, cumulative change from conception to death. Stresses connection between points in development. (p. 33)

control group A comparison group in an experiment that serves as a baseline against which the effects found in the manipulated condition can be compared. (p. 75)

conventional moral reasoning The second level in Kohlberg's theory of moral development in which the child's internalization of moral values is intermediate. He or she abides by certain standards of other people, such as parents (stage three) or the rules of society (stage four). (p. 463)

convergent thinking Thinking that goes toward one correct answer, characteristic of the thinking that most intelligence tests elicit. (p. 188)

correlational strategy A technique used to determine how strongly two or more events or characteristics are related. (p. 74)

correlation coefficient Used to describe the degree of association between two variables. (p. 74)

creativity A difficult term to define: one definition is the ability to think about something in a novel and unusual way, and to come up with unique solutions to problems. (p. 188)

crisis Erikson's term for the feelings of confusion and conflict the individual experiences when confronted with numerous identities during identity development. (p. 384)

cross-sectional approach A study in which individuals of different ages are tested at the same time. (p. 76)

crowd The largest and least personal of peer group relationships. The members of the crowd meet because of their mutual interest in activities, not because of mutual attraction to each other. (p. 268)

cultural-familial retardation Mental retardation that is due to environmental experiences and culture, with no evidence of organic brain dysfunction. Most individuals with this type of retardation have an IQ between fifty and seventy. (p. 186)

culture-fair test Tests designed to reduce cultural bias in intelligence tests. (p. 180)

defense mechanism The means by which the ego resolves conflicts between its demands for reality and the id's wishes; defense mechanisms protect the ego and reduce conflict. (p. 46)

defensive pessimism A strategy which helps adolescents to cope in some stressful circumstances. By imagining negative outcomes, they may be able to prepare for forthcoming stressful situations. (p. 577)

dependent variable A variable that is influenced by the effects of the independent variable; it depends on what happens to the subjects in the experiment. (p. 75)

depressants Drugs that slow down the central nervous system. (p. 540)

desatellization Process by which the adolescent begins breaking away and becomes independent from parents. Final desatellization results in secure feelings about the self, strong exploratory tendencies, and the focusing of energies on tasks and problem solving. (In Ausubel's theory). (p. 225)

development The pattern of movement or change that begins at conception and continues throughout the life cycle. (p. 26)

developmental construction view Refers to the construction of relationships that has been influenced by psychology's cognitive revolution and by conceptual and research interest in the nature of attachment. (p. 206)

developmental theory of career choice The idea that children and adolescents go through three career choice stages: fantasy, tentative, and realistic. (p. 500)

direct moral education Emphasizes values or character traits during specified time slots or integrates those values or traits throughout the curriculum. (p. 477)

discontinuity of development Stresses change in development; one type of discontinuity emphasizes stages in development. (p. 33)

divergent thinking Thinking that produces many different answers to the same question. Guilford believes this form of thinking is closely related to creativity. (p. 188)

divided attention The type of attention required to process several relevant sources of information simultaneously. (p. 163)

dizygotic Fraternal twins or coming from two different eggs and therefore genetically more distant than identical twins. (p. 93)

drive An aroused state that occurs because of a physiological need. Motivates the organism to reduce the tension involved. (p. 491)

drive-reduction theory The view that as a drive becomes stronger, it creates tension, which organisms are motivated to reduce. (p. 491)

E

early adolescence The period of time involving the greatest pubertal change, occurring during the middle or junior high school years. (p. 28)

early adulthood The period that begins in the late teens or early twenties and lasts through the thirties. (p. 28)

early childhood The period from the end of infancy to about five or six years old, roughly corresponding to the period in which the child prepares for formal schooling. (p. 27)

ego The executive branch of personality, according to Freud. The structure of personality that operates according to the demands and constraints of society, including our higher cognitive processes, such as reasoning and problem solving. (p. 45)

egocentrism in adolescence In adolescence, two types of thinking represent the emergence of this thinking style: the imaginary audience and the personal fable. Adolescent egocentrism involves belief that others are as interested in himself or herself as much as he or she is; also involves sense of personal uniqueness and indestructability. (p. 146)

emotion-focused coping Lazarus's description of an approach in which an individual responds to stress in an emotional manner, such as through defensive appraisal. (p. 576)

empathy The ability to sense the feelings of another person. (p. 475)

epigenetic principle Erikson's concept that anything has a ground plan, out of which the parts arise, each having a special time of ascendency, until all of the parts have arisen to form a functioning whole. (p. 53)

erogenous zone Freud's concept which states that at each stage of development, pleasure is experienced in one part of the body more than others. (p. 47)

estradiol A hormone associated with breast, uterine, and skeletal development in girls during puberty. (p. 106)

estrogens Sex hormones that are primarily involved in the development of female sex characteristics. (p. 106)

ethnicity The condition of belonging to a particular ethnic group, membership being based on racial, religious, national, and ancestral background. (p. 340)

eustress Selye's term for the positive features of stress. (p. 570)

existential self Refers to the "I", the knower, the active observer. (p. 365)

exosystem Refers to settings in which the adolescent does not participate although important decisions that affect the adolescent's life are made in these settings. (p. 328)

experience sampling method A method of obtaining the thoughts, activities, and feelings of the individual through

approximately forty to fifty randomly chosen moments in their daily lives. (p. 329)

experiment A carefully regulated setting in which one or more of the factors believed to influence studied behavior are manipulated, and all others are held constant. (p. 75)

experimental group The group whose experience is being manipulated in an experiment. (p. 75)

experimental strategy Based on the use of the experiment, a strategy that allows us to precisely determine the causes of behavior. (p. 75)

expressive orientation Concerned with facilitating social interaction, interdependence, and relationships. (p. 405)

extrinsic motivation Behavior that is influenced by external environment, especially rewards. (p. 496)

F

father-absence tradition Method of studying the effect of divorce on children and adolescents that compares children from father-absent and father-present families, and attributes differences in development to the absence of the father, especially in the first five years of the child's life. (p. 232)

fixation Occurs when an individual becomes stuck at a particular stage of development because his or her needs are under- or overgratified. (p. 47)

formal operational stage In Piaget's model, this appears between eleven and fifteen years of age when the individual is believed to achieve the most advanced form of thought possible. The most important feature characterizing this stage is the development of abstract thought. (p. 59)

frustration Any situation in which an individual cannot reach a goal. (p. 569)

fundamental attribution error The tendency to overestimate the importance of traits and to underestimate the importance of situations when we seek explanations of behavior. (p. 496)

gender roles The social expectations of how we should act and think as females and males. (p. 401)

gender schema Cognitive structure that organizes the world in terms of male and female. (p. 409)

generativity vs. stagnation The seventh conflict in Erikson's theory of development. This stage is positively resolved if an adult assists the younger generation in developing and leading useful lives. (p. 55)

genital stage Freud's fifth stage of development, lasting from the onset of puberty throughout adulthood. A time of sexual reawakening where the source of pleasure now becomes someone outside the family. (p. 52)

genotype The special arrangement of chromosomes and genes each person has inherited that make him or her unique. (p. 91)

gifted Describes an individual with well-above-average intelligence and/or a superior talent for something. (p. 186)

gonadal Refers to the sex glands. (p. 106)

gonadotropin A hormone released by the pituitary gland, which stimulates the gonads (ovaries or testes). (p. 106)

good boy or good girl orientation Stage three of Kohlberg's theory of moral development. In this stage the individual values trust, caring, and loyalty to others as the basis of moral judgements. (p. 463)

group Several adolescents interacting with one another on an ongoing basis, sharing values and goals. (p. 263)

hallucinogens Drugs that produce hallucinations or distortions of reality. (p. 536)

health psychology Follows a philosophy similar to the holistic orientation and behavioral medicine; emphasizes psychology's role in understanding health behavior. (p. 567)

heritability A mathematical estimate of the degree to which a particular characteristic is genetically determined. (p. 94)

hermaphrodites Individuals with genitals that are intermediate between male and female. (p. 406)

heroin A derivative of opium, heroin is highly addictive and can be toxic. Perceived by adolescents as having the greatest risk of harm for the user. (p. 541)

heteronomous morality According to Piaget, the more primitive way of thinking displayed by younger children. (p. 460)

hidden curriculum Refers to the pervasive moral atmosphere that characterizes schools. (p. 477)

hierarchy of motives Maslow's view of motivation which states that some motives, such as physiological, have to be satisfied before others, such as self-esteem. Highest motive is self-actualization. (p. 492)

historical time The timing of major historical events in the life of the individual. (p. 32)

holistic orientation An approach that recognizes the multidimensional nature of illness and health, including an emphasis on life-style, psychological factors, and the nature of the health care delivery system. (p. 567)

homeostasis The body's tendency to maintain an equilibrium or steady state. (p. 492)

horizontal décalage Refers to the fact that similar abilities to conserve different quantities do not appear at the same time. (p. 128)

hormones The secretions of endocrine glands, which are powerful chemical substances that regulate bodily organs. (p. 105)

hypothalamic-pituitary-gonadal axis Aspect of the endocrine system that is important in puberty and involves the interaction of the hypothalamus, the pituitary gland, and the sex glands. (p. 105)

hypothalamus A structure in the higher portion of the brain important in the regulation of hunger, temperature, emotional control, and other visceral functions. (p. 105)

hypotheses Assumptions that can be tested to determine their accuracy. (p. 44)

hypothetical-deductive reasoning Ability to entertain many possibilities and test many solutions in a planful way when faced with having to solve a problem. An important aspect of logical thought in the formal operational stage. (p. 130)

id The reservoir of psychic energy and instincts that perpetually press us to satisfy our basic needs. The id is a structure of personality in Freud's theory. (p. 45)

identity achievement Adolescents who have undergone a crisis and made a commitment. To reach the identity achieved status, it is necessary for the adolescent to first experience a crisis, then make an enduring commitment. (p. 384)

identity diffusion Adolescents who have not experienced any crisis, explored any meaningful alternatives, or made any commitments. (p. 384)

identity foreclosure Adolescents who have made a commitment but have not experienced a crisis. (p. 384)

identity moratorium Adolescents in the midst of a crisis, but their commitments are either absent or vaguely defined. (p. 384)

identity vs. identity confusion Erikson's fifth stage of psychological development. The adolescent may become confident and purposeful, or may develop an ill-defined identity. (p. 55)

imaginary audience The egocentric belief that others are as preoccupied with the adolescent's behavior as he or she is with himself or herself. (p. 146)

immanent justice The belief that when a rule is broken, punishment will be meted out immediately. (p. 461)

implicit personality theory The public's or layperson's conception of how personality traits go together in an individual. (p. 148)

independent variable The manipulated or influential factor in an experiment that can be changed independently of other factors. (p. 75)

indirect moral education Encourages students to define their own and others' values and helps them define the moral perspectives that support those values. (p. 477)

individual conscience The sixth and last stage of Kohlberg's theory of moral development. Rarely attained stage in which individuals have developed moral standards based on universal human rights. (p. 464)

individual differences The consistent, stable way individuals differ from each other. (p. 169)

individuating-reflective faith Fowler's stage; this occurs at about eighteen years of age, when individuals, for the first time in their lives, take full responsibility for their religious beliefs. (p. 482)

individuation The formation of the individual's personal identity, which includes the development of one's sense of self and the forging of a special place for oneself within the social order. Adolescents develop a more distinct view of themselves as unique persons and more readily differentiate themselves from others than they did as children. (p. 387)

industry vs. inferiority Erikson's fourth stage of psychological development. The school-aged child may develop a capacity for work and task-directedness, or may view himself or herself as inadequate. (p. 55)

infancy The period of development from birth to eighteen or twenty-four months, a time of extreme dependence upon adults. (p. 27)

information processing approach The theory of cognition that is concerned with the processing of information. It involves such processes as attention, perception, memory, thinking, and problem solving. (p. 59)

inhalants Any aerosol or gaseous fumes, other than smoke, that are inhaled to make the user feel good, high, or intoxicated. Use of inhalants by adolescents seem to be increasing. (p. 541)

initiative vs. guilt Erikson's third crisis of psychological development, occurring during the preschool years. The child may develop a desire for achievement or he or she may be held back by self-criticism. (p. 55)

insecure attachment Refers to the relationship between parents and children in which children either avoid the caregiver or are ambivalent toward her. This type of anxious attachment to the caregiver is believed to be associated with incompetent behavior on the part of the child. (p. 227)

insight Sudden awareness of solution to a problem, believed to be an important aspect in understanding creativity and giftedness. (p. 188)

instrumental orientation Concerned with the attainment of goals and emphasizing the individual's accomplishments. (p. 405)

integration Refers to components such as sympathy, affection, and understanding. (p. 405)

integrity vs. despair Erikson's final stage of development, corresponding approximately to late adulthood. It involves looking back and evaluating what we have accomplished in our lives. (p. 56)

intelligence Verbal ability, problem-solving skills, and the ability to learn from and adapt to the experiences of everyday life. (p. 169)

intelligence quotient (IQ) An index of an individual's performance on a standardized test of intelligence relative to the performance of others of the same age. It consists of the mental age, divided by the chronological age, and multiplied by 100. (p. 170)

interviews A session at which questions are asked of an individual, usually in a face-to-face manner. (p. 72)

intimacy in friendship Self-disclosure or sharing of private thoughts in a relationship. (p. 261)

intimacy vs. isolation Erikson's sixth stage of psychosocial development. The young adult may achieve a capacity for honesty and close relationships, or be unable to form these ties and a feeling of isolation may result. (p. 55)

intimate style An individual who has been able to form and maintain one or more deep and longlasting love relationship(s). (p. 391)

intrinsic motivation Refers to behavior that is motivated by an internal need for competence and self-determination. Also referred to as mastery and competence motivation. (p. 496)

inventionist view The view that the concept of adolescence is the result of sociohistorical occurrences. (p. 17)

isolated style An individual who withdraws from social encounters and fails to form an intimate relationship with members of the same or opposite sex. (p. 391)

jigsaw classroom Classroom structure that emphasizes cooperation. Adolescents are divided into groups with equal ethnic composition and academic achievement levels, and lessons are divided among these groups with one part being given to each member of the group. The components are like parts of a jigsaw puzzle in that they have to be put together to form the complete lesson. (p. 316)

justice perspective An approach to moral development in which people are differentiated and seen as standing alone. The focus is on the rights of the individual, that is, justice. (p. 468)

laboratory A controlled setting in which many of the complex factors of the "real world" are removed. (p. 71)

late adolescence The period that refers to the latter half of the second decade of life, approximately from the ages sixteen to twenty-two. (p. 28)

late adulthood The period that lasts from approximately sixty to seventy years of age until death. (p. 29)

latency stage Freud's fourth stage of development, corresponding approximately to the elementary school years. The child represses sexual urges and focuses on intellectual and social skills. (p. 52)

learned helplessness View of depression proposing that adolescents who are exposed to stress, prolonged pain, or loss over which they have no control learn to become helpless. (p. 556)

life time Perspective of time in the life cycle that is based heavily in the biological timetable, governing the sequence of changes in the process of growing up. (p. 31)

longitudinal approach A study in which individuals are tested and then retested after a period of years. (p. 77)

long-term memory The retention of information for an indefinite period of time. (p. 163)

LSD Stands for the chemical lysergic acid diethylamide, a powerful hallucinogen. (p. 536)

M

macrosystem Refers to the attitudes and ideologies of the culture. (p. 328)

marijuana A milder hallucinogen than LSD, which comes from the hennep plant. Its active ingredient is THC. (p. 537)

matching hypothesis The theory that while we may prefer a more attractive partner in the abstract, in reality we end up choosing someone who is close to our own level of attractiveness. (p. 276)

maturation The pattern of change or movement that has been associated more with changes that are dictated by the genetic blueprint rather than by environmental experiences. (p. 29)

MDMA A "designer drug" with mildly hallucinogenic qualities. (p. 538)

medical model View of abnormality that cites some physical malfunctioning as the cause of the problem. (p. 530)

memory Cognitive process in which we retain information over time. (p. 163)

menarche The first menstruation in pubertal females. (p. 104)

mental age (MA) An individual's level of mental development relative to others. (p. 170)

mental retardation The individual has a low IQ, usually below seventy on a traditional test of intelligence, and also

has difficulty adapting to the course of everyday life. (p. 185)

mesosystem Refers to linkages between microsystems or connectiveness between contexts, such as the relation of family experiences to school experiences. (p. 327)

metaphor An implied comparison between two ideas that is conveyed by the abstract meaning, contained in the words used to make the comparison. (p. 138)

microsystem Refers to contexts in which the adolescent has face-to-face interactions with others who are influential in his or her life. (p. 327)

middle adulthood The period of development beginning at about thirty-five to forty-five years and exited between fifty-five to sixty-five years of age. (p. 29)

middle and late childhood The period extending from about six to eleven years of age, roughly corresponding to the elementary school years. (p. 27)

monozygotic A term referring to identical twins meaning that they come from the same egg. (p. 93)

moral competence Knowledge or moral rules and conventions about what people should do in their interactions with others. (p. 474)

moral development The acquisition of rules and conventions about what people should do in their interactions with others. (p. 459)

moral performance Actual moral behavior. (p. 474)

motivation The desires, needs, and interests that energize the organism and direct it toward a goal. (p. 491)

multiple-factor theory of intelligence Thurstone's view that we have seven primary mental abilities: verbal comprehension, number ability, word fluency, spatial visualization, associative memory, reasoning, and perceptual speed. (p. 174)

N

naive hedonism or instrumental orientation Second stage in Kohlberg's theory of moral development. In this stage moral

thinking is based on rewards and self-interest. (p. 463)

naturalistic observation Observing behavior in "real world" settings without manipulating or controlling the situation. (p. 72)

nature-nurture controversy The debate about the degree behavior and development are influenced by genes and environment. (p. 31)

need A physical deprivation that involves a physiological state. (p. 491)

need for achievement McClelland's concept of a generalized motive to do well what we attempt, to succeed, to persist with effort at achievement tasks, and to overcome obstacles to success. (p. 493)

neglected children Children who are not necessarily disliked by their peers, even though they often do not have many friends. (p. 248)

nonconformist An independent adolescent who knows what people around him expect, but does not use these expectations to guide his behavior. (p. 251)

normal distribution Also called the normal curve. A symmetrical distribution of scores on a graph, in which a majority of the cases fall in the middle range of possible scores and fewer scores appear toward the ends of this range. (p. 170)

norms The standards, rules, and guidelines by which the group abides. (p. 263)

O

Oedipus complex A condition that exists when a young child develops an intense desire to replace the parent of the same sex and enjoy the affections of the opposite-sex parent. (p. 49)

open vs. traditional classroom Open classroom concept involves setting that offers free choice of activities, space flexibility, varied learning materials, individual instruction, self-responsibility by students, multiage grouping of children, team teaching, and classrooms without walls. Opposite of traditional classroom setting. (p. 308)

operant conditioning A type of learning described by Skinner in which the individual operates or acts on his environment, and what happens to him, in turn, controls his behavior. The individual's behavior is determined by its consequences. Behavior followed by a positive stimulus is likely to recur, while behavior followed by a negative stimulus is not as likely to recur. (p. 65)

operations Intellectual activities or processes which reflect what one does with information. In Piaget's theory, mental actions or representations that are reversible. (pp. 59, 127)

oral stage Freud's first stage of development, corresponding approximately to the first year of life; pleasure focuses on the mouth. (p. 48)

organic retardation Mental retardation that is due to some organic factor, such as genetic or brain damage. Organic refers to the tissues or organs of the body, so there is some physical damage that causes organic retardation. (p. 186)

overvaluation Parenting style in which the parents continually interact with their child, as if the child was in control. (p. 225)

P

peers Refers to adolescents who are about the same age or the same behavioral level. (p. 245)

Perceived Competence Scale for Children Instrument to assess adolescents' self-worth and perceived competence in social, cognitive, and physical domains. (p. 372)

permissive indifferent parenting A style of parenting in which the parents are very uninvolved in their children's lives, but allow them considerable freedom to regulate their own behavior, taking a nonpunitive stance. These parents are rejecting as well as undemanding, and the result is usually a lack of self-control on the part of the child. (p. 214)

permissive indulgent parenting A style of parenting in which the parents are highly involved in their children's lives, but allow them considerable freedom and

do not control their negative behaviors. This type of parenting is associated with children's impulsivity, aggressiveness, lack of independence, and inability to take responsibility. (p. 214)

personal fable Type of adolescent egocentrism that refers to the adolescent's sense of personal uniqueness and indestructability. (p. 146)

personality type theory Refers to the idea that competent career choice occurs when the individual's selection of a career matches his or her personality. (p. 502)

perspective taking The ability to understand that other people have feelings and perceptions that are different from one's own. (p. 147)

phallic stage Freud's third stage, corresponding to the preschool years with pleasure focusing on the genitals. (p. 49)

phenotype The observed and measurable characteristics of individuals including physical characteristics such as height, weight, eye color, and skin pigmentation; also includes psychological characteristics such as intelligence, creativity, and social tendencies. (p. 91)

pleasure principle Always seeking pleasure and avoiding pain; the way the id works. (p. 45)

polygenic inheritance A complex form of genetic transmission involving the interaction of many different genes to produce certain traits. (p. 92)

postconventional moral reasoning The highest level of morality in Kohlberg's theory of moral development in which moral values are completely internalized and not based on the standards of others. The moral code that is adopted may be among the principles generally accepted by the community (stage five) or it may be more individualized (stage six). (p. 463)

pragmatics Rules of language pertaining to the social context and how people use language in conversation. (p. 144)

preconventional moral reasoning The first and lowest level in Kohlberg's theory. No internalization of morality occurs here. Moral thought follows the belief that morality is determined by the external environment, particularly rewarding and punishing circumstances. (p. 462)

preintimate style An individual who has mixed emotions about commitment. It is reflected in the tendency to offer love without any obligations or longlasting bonds. (p. 391)

prenatal period The time of development represented from conception to birth. It is a period of tremendous growth. (p. 27)

preoperational stage In Piagetian theory, the stage of thought that lasts from about two to seven years of age, and follows the sensorimotor period. Although logical thought is present, there are several "flaws", such as egocentrism, that limit the individual. (p. 59)

problem-focused coping Lazarus's description of an approach in which an individual faces his or her problems and tries to solve them. (p. 576)

pseudointimate style An individual who appears to be maintaining a longlasting heterosexual attachment, while the relationship actually has little depth or closeness. (p. 391)

psychological moratorium A gap between childhood security and adult autonomy. (p. 378)

psychometrics The field that involves the assessment of individual differences, involving the use of paper-and-pencil tests. (p. 169)

puberty The period of development during which the individual becomes capable of reproduction. This period is usually linked with the onset of adolescence, a time of rapid change to maturation. (p. 104)

punishment A consequence that decreases the probability that a behavior will occur. (p. 65)

punishment and obedience orientation First stage of Kohlberg's theory of moral development in which moral thinking is seen as being based on punishment. (p. 462)

Q

Quaaludes Hypnotic sedatives that are chemically synthesized and sometimes used in conjunction with cocaine to bring the user down. (p. 541)

questionnaire Similar to a highly structured interview, except the respondent reads the question and marks an answer on paper. (p. 72)

R

reaction formation A defense mechanism that expresses an unacceptable impulse by transforming it into its opposite. (p. 47)

reaction range The limits within which the environment can modify genetic inheritance. (p. 92)

reality principle The way the ego operates. The ego takes into account the constraints and demands of reality. (p. 45)

reciprocal socialization A view of the socialization process as a mutual interaction between parents and the adolescent. The adolescent socializes the parent just as the parent socializes the adolescent. (p. 204)

regression A defense mechanism which characterizes behavior from a previous developmental level. (p. 47)

reinforcement A consequence that increases the probability that a behavior will occur. (p. 65)

rejection Parenting view of the child as an unwanted part of the parents' existence, wherein the child's needs are served unwillingly and only if necessary, and love and acceptance are absent or at least are perceived as being absent by the child. (p. 225)

repression The most powerful and pervasive defense mechanism, according to Freud. It works to push unacceptable id impulses out of awareness and back into our unconscious mind. (p. 46)

resatellization A preliminary step in the adolescent's attainment of the final stage of desatellization in which the individual's parents are replaced by other individuals or a group. (p. 225)

rites of passage Pubertal rites that are the avenue through which adolescents gain access to sacred adult practices, to knowledge, and to sexuality. The formal initiation ceremony associated with entry into adolescence in some cultures. (p. 333)

romantic love Also called passionate love or eros. It is the type of love that involves passion. (p. 277)

S

satellization Process by which the child gives up his or her sense of self-power and the perception that he or she can do everything for himself or herself and accepts dependence on his or her parents. (p. 225)

satire A literary work in which irony, derision, or wit in any form is used to expose folly or wickedness. (p. 138)

schema A cognitive structure. A network of associations that organizes and guides an individual's perception. (p. 409)

scientific method An approach to obtain accurate information by following a number of steps: identify and analyze a problem, collect data, draw conclusions, and formulate or revise theories. (p. 70)

second individuation crisis This is a critical sharpening of boundaries of the adolescent's self as distinct from others, particularly parents, in an attempt to transcend infantile ties to them and develop self-responsibility. (p. 226)

secure attachment A positive bond that develops between the child/adolescent and caregiver, which promotes the healthy exploration of the world because the caregiver provides a secure base the child/adolescent can return to if stressors are encountered. (p. 227)

selective attention What happens when people focus on processing relevant information by ignoring the presence of irrelevant information. (p. 162)

self-assertion Refers to components such as leadership, dominance, independence, competitiveness, and individualism. (p. 404)

self-monitoring The extent to which we are aware of the impression we make on others and the degree to which we fine-tune our performance accordingly. (p. 278)

sensorimotor stage The earliest stage of thought in Piaget's model of cognitive development, lasting from birth to about two years of age. This stage extends from simple reflexes through the use of primitive symbols as the means of coordinating sensation and action. (p. 59)

sequential approach A study in which cross-sectional design is combined with a longitudinal design. (p. 78)

set point The weight an individual can maintain when no effort to gain or lose is expended. (p. 583)

sexual script Stereotyped pattern involving role prescriptions for how individuals should sexually behave. (p. 431)

short-term memory The retention of recently encountered information or information retrieved from long-term memory for a brief period of time, usually about fifteen to thirty seconds. (p. 163)

social class Categorization of people based on similarities in economic resources, power, prestige, education, and style of life, which determines socioeconomic status (SES). (p. 338)

social cognition Field of thinking and reasoning that focuses on how people conceptualize and reason about their social world—the people they watch and interact with, the relationships with those people, and the groups in which they participate. Also includes how individuals reason about themselves in relation to others. (p. 144)

social comparison The seeking out of others within a peer group to evaluate our reactions, abilities, talents, and characteristics. (p. 258)

social competence Effective response of the individual to life situations. Capacity to interact effectively with the environment. (p. 374)

social conventional reasoning Refers to thoughts about social consensus and convention, as opposed to moral reasoning, which stresses ethical matters. (p. 470)

social information processing A nondevelopmental perspective of social cognition that focuses on the processing of social memories, social problem solving, and social decision making. Valuable in examining how the adolescent processes social information. (p. 145)

social learning theory An approach to psychology which emphasizes the social, environmental determinants of behavior. Contemporary version emphasizes cognitive mediation of environment-behavior connections. (p. 66)

social processes Changes in the individual's relationships with other people, emotions, and personality. (p. 26)

social time The role of social, cultural processes in development; the dimension of time in the life cycle that underlies the age-grade system of a particular society. This is characterized in some societies by rites of passage. (p. 32)

stability-change issue How consistently people behave over time; the degree to which an individual can either become an older rendition of an early existence or develop into someone different. (p. 33)

standardized tests Measures that require individuals to answer a series of written or oral questions. The person's answers usually are totaled to yield a single score, and this score is compared to the scores of a large group of similar people. (p. 73)

statistical approach View of abnormality as substantial deviation from the average. (p. 529)

status position Positions of more or less power and control in a group. (p. 263)

stereotype A broad category that reflects impressions about people, including ourselves. (p. 22)

stereotyped style An individual who has superficial relationships that tend to be dominated by friendship ties with same-sex rather than opposite-sex individuals. (p. 391)

stimulants Drugs that increase central nervous system activity. (p. 538)

storm and stress The view of adolescence proposed by Hall that sees adolescence as a turbulent time, charged with conflict and full of contradiction, with wide swings in mood and emotion. (p. 15)

strategies Learning activities that are under the learner's conscious control. Sometimes they are also called control processes. (p. 164)

structure-process dilemma The basic issue of what the mechanisms of intelligence are and how they develop, whether by expanding information processing abilities (process), growing knowledge and expertise (structure), or both. (p. 181)

sublimation A defense mechanism that causes a socially useful course of action to replace a distasteful one. (p. 47)

superego The moral branch of personality, according to Freud, similar to our "conscience." (p. 46)

testosterone A hormone associated with the development of external genitals, increase in height, and voice change in boys during puberty. (p. 106)

theories General beliefs that help to explain observed data or facts and to make predictions. (p. 44)

thyroid gland The gland that interacts with the pituitary to influence growth. (p. 107)

tolerance A condition that occurs when a drug user needs a greater amount of the drug to produce the same effect as before. (p. 532)

top-dog phenomenon Moving from the top position (in elementary school, as the oldest, biggest, and most powerful students in the school) to the lowest position (in middle or junior high school, as the youngest, smallest, and least powerful group of students). (p. 295)

triarchic theory of intelligence Sternberg's view that intelligence consists of three dimensions: componential intelligence, experiential intelligence, and practical intelligence. (p. 183)

trust vs. mistrust Erikson's first stage of development, corresponding approximately to the first year of life. In this bipolar conflict, the infant develops either a trust in him or herself and the world, or a sense of mistrust. (p. 53)

twin study An examination of particular behavior patterns or characteristics between monozygotic and dizygotic twins to determine the relative importance of heredity and environment. (p. 93)

two-factor theory Spearman's view that we have both general intelligence and a number of specific intelligences. (p. 174)

Type-A behavioral pattern A cluster of characteristics: excessively competitive, an accelerated pace of ordinary activities, impatience, thinking about doing several things at once, hostility, and an inability to hide the fact that life is a struggle, thought to be related to the incidence of heart disease. (p. 570)

unconditional positive regard Roger's term for how we should behave toward someone to increase their self-worth. Positive behavior shown toward an individual with no contingencies attached. (p. 371)

underclass The poverty subculture of low-income Black individuals. (p. 344)

undifferentiated Refers to adolescents who perceive themselves as neither masculine nor feminine in gender role orientation. (p. 402)

values clarification Helps students clarify what their lives are for and what is worth working for. (p. 477)

Wechsler scales Individual intelligence tests developed by David Wechsler. They provide information not only about overall intelligence, but about nonverbal and verbal intelligence as well. (p. 171)

wisdom Broad interpretive knowledge. (p. 135)

withdrawal Highly unpleasant body effects that result from ceasing to take a drug any longer. The unpleasant effects can involve intense pain and cravings for the drug. (p. 532)

Y

youth The transitional period between adolescence and adulthood; a time of an extended sense of economic and personal "temporariness." (p. 28)

Credits

Chapter 6

Figure 6.2: From data presented by Per F. Gjerde, "A Family Systems Perspective on Parent-Adolescent Interaction: Second-Order Effects and Sex Differences on Family Interaction," 1985. Unpublished Manuscript, P. 20, University of California, Berkeley. Used with Permission. **Figure 6.3:** Source: Hill, J. P., Holmbeck, G. N., Marlow, L., Green, T. M., & Lynch, M. E. "Pubertal Status and Parent-Child Relations in Families of Seventh-Grade Boys," *Journal of Early Adolescence,* 5, 31–44. Reprinted with permission of H.E.L.P. Books, Inc. **Figure 6.4:** From E. E. Maccoby and J. A. Martin, "Socialization in the Context of the Family: Parent-Child Interaction" in *Handbook of Child Psychology,* 4th ed., Vol. 4, edited by P. H. Mussen. Copyright © 1983 John Wiley & Sons, Inc. Reprinted by permission of John Wiley & Sons, Inc., New York, NY.

Chapter 7

Figure 7.2: From J. R. Asarnow and J. W. Callan, "Boys with Peer Adjustment Problems: Social Cognitive Processes" in *Journal of Consulting and Clinical Psychology,* 53, 80–87, 1985. Copyright 1985 by the American Psychological Association. Reprinted by permission of the publisher and author. **Figure 7.4:** From Dexter C. Dunphy, "The Social Structure of Urban Adolescent Peer Groups" in *Sociometry,* Vol. 26, 1963. Copyright © 1963 American Sociological Association, Washington, DC. Reprinted by permission. **Figure 7.A:** From Mark Snyder, et al., "Focusing on the Exterior and Interior: Two Investigations of the Initiation of Personal Relationships" in *Journal of Personality and Social Psychology,* 48, 1427–1439, 1985. Copyright © 1985 by the American Psychological Association. Reprinted by permission of the publisher and author.

Chapter 9

Figure 9.1: J. Garbarino from Kopp/ Krakow, *The Child,* © 1982, Addison-Wesley Publishing Co., Inc., Reading, Massachusetts. Fig. 12.1. Reprinted with permission. **Figures 9.3, 9.4, and 9.5:** From *Being Adolescent: Conflict and Growth in the Teenage Years,* by Mihaly Csikszentmihalyi and Reed Larson. Copyright © 1984 by Basic Books, Inc. Reprinted by permission of Basic Books, Inc., Publishers.

Chapter 11

Figure 11.A: From Janet S. Hyde, "Children's Understanding of Sexist Language" in *Developmental Psychology,* 20, 703, 1984. Copyright © 1984 by the American Psychological Association. Reprinted by permission of the publisher and author.

Chapter 12

Figure 12.2: Reprinted with permission from *Family Planning Perspectives,* Volume 17, Number 2, 1985.

Chapter 13

Figure 13.1: From *The American Freshman: Twenty Year Trends* (p. 23) by A. W. Astin, K. C. Green, and W. S. Korn, 1987, Los Angeles: University of California at Los Angeles, Higher Education Research Institute. Reprinted by permission.

Chapter 15

Poem, page 527: Copyright 1936 by Robert Frost and renewed 1964 by Lesley Frost Ballantine. Reprinted from THE POETRY OF ROBERT FROST edited by Edward Connery Lathem, by permission of Henry Holt and Company, Inc. **Figure 15.1:** From T. Achenbach and C. S. Edelbrock, "Behavioral Problems and Competencies Reported by Parents of Normal and Disturbed Children Aged Four through Sixteen" in *Monographs of the Society for Research in Child Development,* 46, No. 1, 1981. Copyright © 1981 The Society for Research in Child Development, Inc. Reprinted by permission. **Figure 15.5:** From M. Gold and R. J. Petronis, "Delinquent Behavior in Adolescence" in *Handbook of Adolescent Psychology,* edited by J. Adelson. Copyright © 1980 John Wiley & Sons, Inc. Reprinted by permission of John Wiley & Sons, Inc., New York, NY. **Excerpt, page 555:** From S. Chess and M. Hassibi, *Principles and Practices of Child Psychiatry.* Copyright © 1978 Plenum Publishing Corporation, New York, NY. Reprinted by permission of the publisher and author.

Chapter 16

Figure 16.1: From Lee L. Langley, *Physiology of Man.* Copyright © 1971 Van Nostrand Reinhold, New York, NY. Reprinted by permission of the author.

PHOTOS

Table of Contents

Page vii: © David W. Hamilton/The Image Bank; **page viii:** © Kay Chernush/The Image Bank; **page x:** © 1985 Nick Pavloff/ The Image Bank; **page xiii:** © Dann Coffey 1987/The Image Bank; **page xvi:** Mel Di Giacomo/The Image Bank.

All Cultural Boxes

Grant V. Faint/The Image Bank.

Section Openers

Section I: © David W. Hamilton/The Image Bank; **Section II:** © Kay Chernush/The Image Bank; **Section III:** © 1985 Nick Pavloff/The Image Bank; **Section IV:** © Dann Coffey 1987/The Image Bank; **Section V:** Mel Di Giacomo/The Image Bank.

Chapter 1

Chapter Opener: Alan Carey/The Image Works; **pp. 16, 20a:** Historical Pictures Service; **p. 20b:** © Topham/The Image Works; **p. 20c:** © Joe Munroe/Photo Researchers, Inc.; **p. 20d:** © Jean-Claude Lejeune; **p. 20e:** James L. Shaffer; **Fig 1.2 (top to bottom):** © Dr. Landrum Shettles; © Helena Frost/Frost Publishing Group, Ltd.; © Jean-Claude Lejeune; © James L. Shaffer; © Nancy Anne Dawe; © Steve Elmore/Tom Stack & Associates; © Tom Lippert/Instock; **p. 34a:** David Grossman; **p. 34b:** James L. Shaffer.

Chapter 2

Chapter Opener: Jan Doyle; **p. 42:** UPI/ Bettman News Photos; **p. 43:** Courtesy Dr. Andrew Schwebel; **pp. 48, 50a:** Alan Carey/ The Image Works; **p. 50b:** James L. Shaffer; **p. 50c:** Rohn Engh/The Image Works; **p. 50d:** Jim Cronk Photographic Illustratations; **p. 50e:** © Bob Daemmrich/ The Image Works; **p. 54a, b:** H. Armstrong Roberts, Inc.; **p. 54c:** © Michael Siluk; **p. 54d:** Benser/Zefa/H. Armstrong Roberts; **p. 54e:** P. Buddle/H. Armstrong Roberts;

p. 54f: J. Moss/H. Armstrong Roberts;
p. 54g: H. Armstrong Roberts; p. 54h: Blair
Seitz; p. 58 top: H. Armstrong Roberts;
bottom: James L. Shaffer; p. 59 top: © Alan
Carey/The Image Works; bottom: © James
Carroll; p. 63: Jane Reed, Harvard Univ.
News Office; p. 64: James L. Shaffer; p. 66:
© Albert Bandura.

Chapter 3

Chapter Opener: Andy Levin; p. 94: © Rob
Nelson/Picture Group; p. 97: Bob Coyle;
p. 62: James L. Shaffer; p. 109: Donald
Dietz/Stock Boston, p. 114: Jill Cannefax/
EKM-Nepenthe.

Chapter 4

Chapter Opener: Peter Runyon/The Image
Bank; p. 129: Mark Antman/The Image
Works; p. 137: James L. Shaffer; p. 146:
© Alan Carey/The Image Works; p. 150:
© Martin Benjamin/The Image Works.

Chapter 5

Chapter Opener: Butch Martin/The Image
Bank; p. 160: © 1989 Pat McKay,
Flashback; p. 165: © Arvind Garg 1987/
Photo Researchers, Inc.; p. 175 left: Wide
World Photos; right: Historical Picture
Service; p. 176: © Joseph Szabo/Photo
Researchers, Inc.; p. 183: Courtesy Robert
J. Sternberg; p. 185 left: Jan Doyle; p. 185
right: Jean-Claude Lejeune.

Chapter 6

Chapter Opener: © Richard Hutchings/
Photo Researchers, Inc.; p. 208: James L.
Shaffer; p. 215: Harriet Gans/© The Image
Works; p. 222: © Kevin Horan/Picture
Group; p. 228 left: © Alan Carey/The
Image Works; p. 228 right–p. 235: James G.
White; p. 238: Bob Daemmrich/The Image
Works.

Chapter 7

Chapter Opener: Mel Di Giacomo/The
Image Bank; p. 246: © David R. Frazie/
Photo Researchers, Inc.; p. 249: © Tony
Savino/The Image Works; p. 251 left:
© Mark Richards/The Picture Group; right:
© Topham/The Image Works; p. 258:
© Thomas Craig/Lightwave; p. 265: © 1987

David H. Wells; p. 269 left: © Alan Carey/
The Image Works; right: James L. Shaffer;
p. 271: Photo Researchers, Inc.; p. 276:
Courtesy of The Academy of Motion Picture
Arts and Sciences; Fig. 7.6a: Courtesy of
The Academy of Motion Picture Arts and
Sciences; b: AP/Wide World Photos, Inc.;
c: Movie Star News.

Chapter 8

Chapter Opener: © Bob Daemmrich/The
Image Works; p. 287: © Alan Carey/The
Image Works; p. 294: Jeff Greenberg; p. 296
both: James L. Shaffer; p. 299: © Howard
Dratch/The Image Works; p. 301: Jack
Spratt/The Image Works; pp. 304, 309:
James L. Shaffer; p. 312: James G. White;
p. 314: Jean-Claude Lejeune; p. 317: James
L. Shaffer.

Chapter 9

Chapter Opener: Gio Barto/The Image
Bank; p. 324: James L. Shaffer; Fig. 9.2a, b:
Anthro-Photo; p. 334: George Holton/Photo
Researchers, Inc.; p. 335 top: © Blair Seitz/
Photo Researchers, Inc.; p. 335 bottom:
Michael Siluk; p. 339: R. Mayer/
H. Armstrong Roberts, Inc.; p. 344: Bob
Daemmrich/The Image Works; p. 346:
Eddie Adams/TIME Magazine; p. 347: Jan
Doyle; p. 348: Photo Researchers, Inc.;
p. 352: James L. Shaffer.

Chapter 10

Chapter Opener: Mel Di Giacomo/The
Image Bank; p. 368: © Dion Ogust/The
Image Works; p. 370: Nat'l Library of
Medicine; p. 373a: © Alan Carey/The
Image Works; b: © '87 by Blair Seitz;
c: James G. White Photography; d:
© Michael Siluk; p. 381 left: The Bettman
Archives; right: Historical Pictures Service;
p. 386: Dan Chidester/The Image Works;
p. 387: The Image Bank; p. 390: James L.
Shaffer.

Chapter 11

Chapter Opener: Gio Barto/The Image
Bank; p. 409: Dwedric Hill/The Image
Works; p. 411 left: Howard Dratch/The
Image Works; right: Jeff Greenberg; p. 413
left: Jan Doyle; right: James L. Shaffer;

p. 414: Jeff Greenberg; pp. 418, 419: James
L. Shaffer.

Chapter 12

Chapter Opener: Ellis Herwig/Stock Boston;
p. 427: © 1989 Jim Cronk/Photographic
Illustrations; p. 431: Jeff Greenberg; p. 438:
Jan Doyle; p. 442: Jeff Greenberg; p. 444:
© Mauree Fennelli/Photo Researchers, Inc.;
p. 446: © Michael Siluk.

Chapter 13

Chapter Opener: James L. Shaffer; p. 459:
© David M. Grossman; p. 462: Prof.
Lawrence Kohlberg, Harvard University;
p. 466: H. Armstrong Roberts; pp. 468, 471:
James L. Shaffer; p. 479: Jan Scherr/
Jeroboam, Inc.; p. 482: © Michael Siluk;
p. 483: © Esaias Baitel Rapho/Photo
Researchers, Inc.

Chapter 14

Chapter Opener: © 1988 Mike & Carol
Werner/Comstock; p. 495: Jeff Greenberg;
p. 498: Courtesy Dr. Sandra Graham;
p. 507: © Bob Daemmrich/The Image
Works; Fig. 14.2: James L. Shaffer; p. 512:
H. Armstrong Roberts, Inc.; p. 515:
© Michael Siluk.

Chapter 15

Chapter Opener: © 1987 Alan Carey/The
Image Works; p. 534: Jeff Greenberg; Fig.
15.3a–c: Drug Enforcement Administration;
p. 538: Jeff Greenberg; p. 539: © Michael
Siluk; p. 541: H. Armstrong Roberts, Inc.;
p. 548: Jeff Greenberg; p. 551: Comstock;
p. 553: Gamma-Liaison © Jean-Marc
Giboux; p. 556: James L. Shaffer.

Chapter 16

Chapter Opener: Mel Di Giacomo/The
Image Bank; p. 571 both: James L. Shaffer;
p. 575: © Elizabeth Crews/The Image
Works; p. 576: James L. Shaffer; p. 583:
© Robert Kalman; p. 585: Susan
Rosenberg/Photo Researchers, Inc.; p. 588:
Jan Doyle; p. 593: Keith Lanpher,
Photographer.

Name Index

Chase-Lansdale, P. L., 232, 442
Chassin, L., 535
Chesney-Lind, M., 548
Chess, S., 34, 95, 96, 556
Child, I. L., 332
Childs, D., 587
Chilman, C., 435
Chivian, E., 24
Chrousos, G. P., 73, 105, 106–7
Cicirelli, V., 229
Clabby, J. G., 256
Clark, D., 178
Clark, D. A., 556
Clark, D. L., 412
Clark, K., 313
Clark-Lempers, D., 570
Clark, M. L., 315
Clark, M. S., 476
Clark, R., 493
Clark, S., 387
Clark, S. D., 429
Clark, V. A., 537
Clasen, D. R., 251, 252
Clinchy, B. M., 414
Cocks, J., 352
Cohen, A. K., 16
Cohen, D., 292
Cohen, D. K., 290, 291
Cohn, J. F., 205
Colby, A., 464
Cole, M., 142
Cole, S., 513
Coleman, J. S., 247, 268, 270, 288, 292, 311
Coles, R., 43, 56, 382, 470
Coletta, N. D., 233
College Board Commission on Precollege
    Guidance and Counseling, 508
Collins, A. W., 210
Collins, G. C., 414
Collins, J. K., 275
Collins, R., 577
Compas, B., 570
Conant, J. B., 288, 307
Condon, S. M., 389
Condry, J. C., 246
Conger, J. J., 340, 447, 480, 481
Conger, R. D., 570
Conway, B. E., 169
Cooper, C. R., 207, 227, 228, 386, 389
Cooper, H., 315
Coopersmith, S., 345
Corbin, 234
Corter, C., 231
Costa, F., 432
Cote, J. E., 384
Coulson, A. H., 537

Couper, 207
Cowan, P., 131, 136
Cox, M., 232
Cox, R., 232
Cox, T., 352
Cox, W. M., 534
Cremin, L., 18
Critelli, J. W., 280
Crites, J. O., 503
Crockett, L., 118
Cronbach, L. J., 308
Cross, K. P., 290
Crossman, R., 443
Csikszentmihalyi, M., 72, 329
Cuban, L., 289
Curtiss, S., 73
Cutler, G. B., 73, 105, 106–7

Damon, A., 100
Damon, W., 147, 367, 387
Dann, S., 246
Danner, F., 136
Danziger, S. K., 446
Darling, C. A., 427
Datan, N., 31
Davidson, J. E., 188
Davies, M., 557
DeBaryshe, B. D., 70, 549
Deci, E., 496
DeFries, J. C., 96, 177
DeLoache, J. S., 408
Dembrowski, T., 571
Demo, D. H., 374, 374 (Table 10.3)
Demorest, A., 140, 141
Demoss, V., 583 (Table 16.2)
Dempster, F. N., 163
De Necochea, G., 318
Denham, S. A., 255
Desimone, D., 406
Dessler, R. C., 218
Deutsch, M., 305, 317
de Vries, B., 467
Dewey, J., 477
de Wuffel, F. J., 535
Diamond, E. E., 508
Dickerscheid, J. D., 404
Dickinson, G. E., 272
Dimsdale, J. E., 571
Dishion, T. J., 70, 247, 549
Dixon, K. N., 585
Dixon, R. A., 135
Doctor, S., 24

Dodge, K. A., 253, 254, 374
Doehrman, M., 48
Domek, C. J., 246
Donovan, J. E., 432, 534
Dooley, D., 253
Dorn, L. D., 105, 106–7
Douvan, E., 226, 250, 272, 275, 295, 392
Dove, A., 180 (Table 5.1)
Downey, A. M., 574
Downs, A. C., 402
Dreyer, P. H., 429, 431
Dubow, E. F., 351
Ducey, S., 418
Duck, S., 206, 262, 275
Duckett, E., 237
Duncan, D. F., 218
Dunn, J., 230
Dunphy, D. C., 266, 281
Durant, D., 535
Durden-Smith, J., 406
Durkin, K., 205, 415
Durrett, M. E., 504
Dyer, H. S., 176

Eagleston, J. R., 571
Ebata, A. T., 576
Eccles, J. S., 295, 413, 414, 419, 508
Edelbrock, C., 531
Edelman, M. W., 340, 343, 447
Edmonds, R., 292
Edwards, C. P., 326
Edwards, E. D., 534
Edwards, M. E., 534
Edwards, R., 534
Eger, M., 478
Eicher, S. A., 251
Eisen, M., 366
Eisenberg, N., 476
Eitzen, D. S., 268
Ek, C. A., 223
Elder, G. H., 17, 32, 212, 224, 570
Eliade, M., 336
Elias, M. J., 256
Elkind, D., 133, 135, 138, 146, 147, 152,
    237, 333, 367, 481, 485, 490, 494
Elliott, D. S., 550
Elliott, J. E., 559
Elliott, T., 513
Elston, R. C., 574
El-Taliawy, T., 404
Emde, R. N., 103
Emery, R. E., 205

Engel, J. W., 273
Englert, C. S., 140
Enright, R. D., 17, 18, 19 (Table 1.1), 32,
    147, 465, 469, 470, 476
Entwistle, D. R., 296
Epstein, H. T., 99, 102, 103
Erikson, E. H., 42, 52–57, 60 (Fig. 2.3), 68,
    114, 135, 270, 344, 367, 370, 378,
    379, 380–81, 383, 389, 390, 394, 395,
    406, 410, 475, 485, 546, 547, 560, 588
Erickson, M., 588
Erlick, A. C., 338
Eron, L. D., 351
Eveland, L. K., 550

Falbo, T., 230
Family Planning Perspectives, 435 (Table
    12.3), 436 (Table 12.4)
Farber, E. A., 186
Farrar, E., 290, 291
Fasick, F. A., 335
Fassinger, R. E., 509
Faust, M. S., 107, 109
Feeney, S., 310
Feingold, A., 418
Feist, J., 567, 588
Feldlaufer, H., 295
Feldman, D. H., 187
Feldman, S. S., 572 (Table 16.A), 573
    (Table 16.B)
Felner, R. D., 295
Feria, M., 534
Feshbach, S., 352
Festinger, L., 270
Fidler, P. P., 300
Field, J., 17
Field, T. M., 445
Fifer, G., 178
Finley, M. I., 17
Finney, J. W., 534
Fischer, J. L., 392
Fischer, K. W., 138, 139, 141, 145
Fischman, S. H., 571
Fisher, C. B., 585
Fisher, T., 446
Fisher, T. D., 448
Flaitz, J., 133
Flannery, D., 72, 147
Flavell, J. H., 58, 133, 144, 147, 150, 151,
    152
Fleeson, J., 206
Fligiel, S. E. G., 537

Flood, P., 292
Flowers, J. V., 253
Folkman, S., 570
Foon, A. E., 581
Ford, M., 375, 375 (Table 10.4), 376, 402,
    404, 405
Ford, M. E., 572 (Table 16.A), 573 (Table
    16.B)
Forehand, G., 316
Forrest, J. D., 440, 448
Foster-Clark, F. S., 391
Fowler, J., 482, 485
Fowler, R. C., 558
Fox, L. H., 511
Fox, V. M., 305
Frank, G. C., 574
Franklin, F. A., 574
Fréchette, M., 550
Freedman, J., 558
Freedman, J. L., 351
Fregly, M. J., 106
Freud, A., 49, 114, 246
Freud, S., 45–47, 46, 60 (Fig. 2.3), 68, 410,
    475
Frevert, R. L., 449
Frideres, J. S., 349
Friedl, K. E., 543
Friedman, M., 571
Friot, F., 137
Frisch, R., 101, 105
Fuqua, D. R., 503
Furstenberg, F. F., 233, 236, 442
Furstenberg, J. J., 447
Furth, H. G., 128

Gage, N. L., 310
Gagne, E., 166
Gagnon, J. H., 275, 431
Galambos, N. L., 238
Galanter, M., 484, 539
Gallimore, R. G., 290
Gallup, A. M., 412
Gallup, G., 483, 484
Garbarino, J., 307, 339, 468
Garber, J., 557
Gardner, H., 140, 141, 174, 175, 189, 191
Gardner, J. N., 298
Garfinkel, P. E., 586
Garig, J. W., 568
Garmezy, N., 549, 570
Garner, D. M., 586
Garrick, T. R., 567

Garrison, K. C., 109
Gasiewski, E., 443
Gat, I., 353
Gawin, F., 532
Geffen, G., 162
Gelman, R., 142
Gerner, R., 165
Gershaw, N. J., 256
Gewirtz, J., 466
Giaconia, R. M., 308
Gibbs, J. T., 179, 248, 301, 315, 342, 348,
    464, 465, 552
Gieringer, D. H., 537
Gilgun, J. F., 429, 431, 432
Gill, S., 402, 405
Gilligan, C., 467, 469, 547
Gillum, R. F., 571
Ginott, H., 216
Ginter, M., 295
Gintis, H., 292
Ginzberg, E., 500–502, 518
Ginzberg, S. W., 500
Gjerde, P. F., 205, 232
Glass, G. V., 307
Glazer, R., 166
Glick, P. C., 232, 278
Globerson, T., 178
Glueck, E., 549
Glueck, S., 549
Goelman, H., 140
Goethals, G. W., 126
Gold, M., 260, 546, 550, 551, 552, 553
Gold, M. S., 539
Goldberger, N. R., 414
Golden, M. W., 247
Goldening, J., 24
Goldman, N., 440, 448
Goldsmith, H. H., 96
Goldstein, A. P., 256
Gong, H., 537
Goodchilds, J. D., 432
Goodlad, J., 290
Goodman, R. A., 534
Gordon, K. A., 434
Gordon, S., 431, 432
Gordon, V. P., 300
Gore, T., 352
Gorebel, J., 31
Gottlieb, D., 218, 314
Gottman, J. M., 35, 261
Graham, S., 498
Graubard, S. R., 161
Gray, P. A., 546
Gray, W. M., 147
Green, K. C., 300, 480, 481

Green, S., 218
Green, T. M., 208
Greenberg, M. T., 228
Greenberger, E., 513
Greene, A. L., 570
Greene, B., 90
Greene, D., 496
Greene, J. W., 533
Greenfield, P. M., 292, 353
Gribbons, W. D., 313
Grief, E. B., 114
Griffin, P., 142
Grimes, B., 588
Grotevant, H. D., 207, 386, 387, 388, 389, 504
Grubb, W. N., 517
Gudeman, J., 549
Guilford, J. P., 188
Gump, P. V., 295
Gurin, J., 584
Gutek, B. A., 508
Guttentag, M., 416
Guttentag, R. E., 163

Haas, A., 434
Hagan, E. D., 171
Hagan, M. S., 232, 233, 234, 235, 236
Hahn, A., 302
Hala, S., 367
Hall, G. S., 14, 15, 16, 17, 18, 25, 114, 218, 292, 546
Hamburg, B., 112
Hamburg, D. A., 28
Hamilton, T. E., 276
Hand, H. H., 145
Hankins, C. A., 438
Hanson, E., 218
Hardy, J. B., 429
Harken, L. S., 581
Harlow, H. F., 246
Harold-Goldsmith, R., 419
Harris, D., 32
Harris, D. V., 372
Harsha, D. W., 574
Hart, D., 147, 367, 387
Harter, S., 372, 496, 558
Hartman, B. W., 503
Hartman, J., 103
Hartshorne, H., 473
Hartup, W. W., 206, 245, 257, 258
Harvey, O., 263
Hassibi, M., 556
Hathaway, B., 182

Hauser, S. T., 207, 530
Havighurst, R. J., 332, 338, 342, 348
Hawkins, J. A., 295
Hawkins, R., 269
Hayden-Thomson, L., 412
Hayes, D., 442
Hazen, C., 206, 228
Heath, S. B., 344
Hedges, L. V., 307, 308
Heeren, T., 558
Heft, L., 571
Heider, F., 495
Hein, K., 438
Heller, J. S., 496
Helmreich, R. L., 401, 416
Helson, R., 513
Henggeler, S. W., 548
Hennessey, B. A., 187
Henshaw, S. K., 440, 448
Herdt, G. H., 433
Herman, J. L., 500
Herzog, E., 412
Hess, L., 474
Hess, R. D., 338, 339
Hetherington, E. M., 28, 232, 233, 234, 235, 236, 280
Heyns, B., 292
Hiebert, E. H., 140
Hiebert, J., 134
Higgens-Trenk, A., 493
Higgins, A., 462–69, 480
Higgins, A. T., 162
Hill, J. P., 17, 23, 112, 208, 210, 221, 223, 227, 247, 295, 387
Himmin, H. S., 404
Hinde, R. A., 31, 407
Hinkle, J. S., 588
Hirsch, B. J., 295, 296
Historical Statistics of the United States, 19 (Table 1.2)
Hobson, C. J., 292
Hoeffel, E. C., 150
Hoffman, J. M., 511
Hoffman, L., 237
Hoffman, L. W., 419
Hoffman, M. L., 461, 475
Hoffman, S. D., 535
Holland, J. L., 502–3, 518
Hollingshead, A. B., 247
Hollow, S. D., 273
Holmbeck, G. N., 208, 221, 227, 443
Holt, J., 313
Holtzmann, W., 332
Hood, W. R., 263
Hooper, F. H., 205

Hooper, J. O., 205
Hopkins, R. W., 558
Hort, B., 408
Hostetler, M., 503
Housman, D., 558
Howard, K. I., 23, 429
Howard, M., 452
Howat, P. M., 586
Huang, L. N., 179, 231, 248, 301, 315, 347, 348
Hudson, L. M., 147
Huesmann, L. R., 351
Huizinga, D., 550
Humphreys, L. G., 186
Hunt, K. W., 140
Hunt, M., 432
Hunter, M. S., 300
Huston, A. C., 350, 352, 407, 411, 412, 415, 416, 419
Huston-Stein, A., 493
Hyde, J. S., 402 (Table 11.1), 408, 416, 418, 434, 529
Hyman, H. M., 250
Hymel, S., 412

Ignatoff, E., 445
Iheanacho, S. O., 345
Ihinger-Tallman, M., 236
Inoff-Germain, G., 73, 105, 106–7
Irvin, F. S., 433

Jacklin, C. N., 404, 412, 418
Jacobsen, L., 184
James, W., 365
Jarcho, H. D., 372
Jencks, C. S., 292
Jensen, A. R., 177, 191
Jensen, L. C., 477
Jessor, L., 429, 432, 435
Jessor, R., 429, 432, 435, 534
Johnson, C., 218
Johnson, M., 402, 405
Johnston, J., 550
Johnston, L., 533, 535
Johnston, L. D., 481, 538, 539, 540, 542, 550, 580
Jones, D., 585
Jones, E. R., 440, 448
Jones, J. M., 341

Lowell, E. L., 493
Lowenstein, R. J., 567
Loya, F., 534
Ludtke, M., 335, 346
Luepker, R. V., 574
Lueptow, L., 419
Lunde, I., 559
Luria, A., 412
Luttge, W. G., 106
Lynch, M. E., 208

M

Maas, H. S., 266
MacAdoo, J. L., 498
Maccoby, E. E., 210, 403, 404, 407, 412, 418
Maccoby, N., 581
MacDonald, K., 211
MacIver, D., 295, 413, 414
Mack, J., 24
MacPherson, S., 290
Madsen, M. C., 332
Maggs, J. L., 238
Mahan, M. K., 581
Mahler, M., 225
Maloney, J., 367, 387
Maltsberger, J. T., 557
Mammersmith, S. K., 433
Mandler, J. M., 134
Marcia, J., 383, 384, 385, 387, 388, 391, 394
Margulies, R. Z., 218
Markstrom, C. A., 385
Marlow, L., 208
Marold, D., 558
Marsiglio, W., 442, 443 (Table 12.5)
Martin, C. E., 432
Martin, C. L., 407, 418
Martin, J., 288
Martorano, S., 133
Marx, G., 364
Maslow, A. H., 492
Masters, J. C., 259, 273
Matarazzo, J. D., 567, 571
Mathre, M. L., 537
Matson, J. L., 555
Matthews, K. A., 571
Mattimore, K., 588
Maughan, B., 292, 307
May, M., 473
Mayer, R., 165
Mayetela, N., 233
McAdams, D. P., 392

McAdoo, H. P., 498
McAleer, N., 190
McAlister, A., 581
McAnarney, E. R., 445
McCabe, M. P., 275
McCall, R. B., 103
McCandless, B. R., 546
McClaskey, C. L., 253, 374
McClearn, G. E., 96, 177
McClelland, D. C., 493, 499
McCord, J., 549
McCord, W., 549
McDill, E. L., 307
McEwin, C. K., 295
McFall, R. M., 273
McHenry, P. C., 218
McKinnon, J., 137
McLaughlin, L., 535
McLoyd, V. C., 342
McPartland, J. M., 292, 307
McQuire, W. J., 351
McWhirter, D. P., 433
Meacham, J. A., 391
Mead, M., 212, 332
Medrich, E. A., 246
Meilman, P. W., 385
Menard, S., 550
Mercy, J. A., 534
Messinger, J. C., 333
Metzler, A., 503
Meyer, C., 140, 141
Meyer, H., 429
Meyers, E. D., 103
Michelson, S., 292
Micka, J. C., 387
Midgley, C., 295
Milberg, S., 476
Millar, M., 259
Miller, 436
Miller, C. L., 419
Miller, L., 570
Miller, N. E., 548, 569
Miller, P. H., 67
Miller, P. Y., 432
Miller, S. K., 538, 580
Milstead, M., 147
Mindick, B., 435
Minkler, M., 588
Minnett, A. M., 231
Minuchin, P. P., 294, 307, 315, 316, 480, 542
Mischel, H., 474
Mischel, W., 66, 145, 418, 474, 547
Mitchell, C., 78
Mitteness, L. S., 211

Miura, I. T., 418
Mize, J., 255
Mizruchi, M., 559
Money, J., 119, 406, 407, 433
Monroe, R., 188
Montemayor, R., 72, 218, 224, 366
Mood, A. M., 292
Moore, J., 259
Moos, R. H., 534, 576
Moosbrugger, L., 535
Morelli, G., 326, 332
Morgan, J. P., 537
Morgan, M., 352, 415
Morgan, P. A., 538
Morgan, S. P., 447
Morrison, D. M., 431
Morrow, L., 8
Mortimore, P., 292, 307
Mott, F. L., 442, 443 (Table 12.5)
Mounts, N., 268
Munroe, R. H., 404
Munroe, R. L., 404
Murphy, J., 288
Murphy, M. N., 147
Murray, D. M., 571
Muuss, R. E., 12, 468

N

Nass, G., 272
National Assessment of Educational Progress, 503
National Research Council, 428 (Table 12.1), 440, 582 (Table 16.1)
Naus, M. J., 182
Neiger, B. L., 558
Neimark, E. D., 132, 133
Neimeyer, G. J., 503
Nelson, R. S., 238
Nemzer, E., 585
Nesselroade, J. R., 78
Neugarten, B. L., 31
Neugarten, D. A., 31
Newcomb, M. D., 542
Newcomer, S. F., 429
Newman, D., 142
Newton, D. E., 450
Nicholls, J. G., 496
Nichtern, S., 45
Nigro, C., 163
Nisbett, R. E., 496
Nixon, K., 353
Noir, S., 404
Norem, J. K., 577

Norem, R., 570
Nottelman, E. D., 73, 105, 106–7
Nucci, L., 469, 470, 471
Nucci, M., 470
Nydegger, C. N., 211

Subject Index

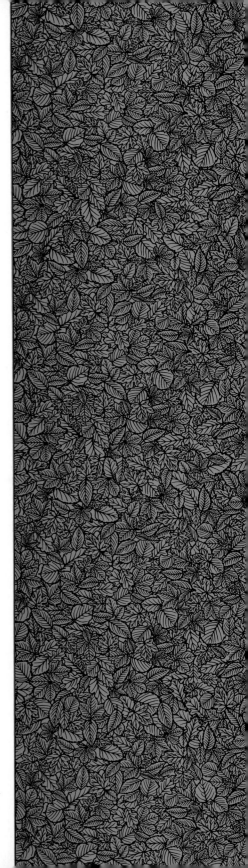

avoidance/avoidance conflict, 569
  divorce and, 232
  parent/adolescent, 218–19
  stress and, 568–69
Conformity, 249–52
  anticonformist, 251
  nonconformist, 251
  parental and peer influences, 250–51
  toward misconduct, 251
Connectedness, in family relationships, 386–87
Conscience, 464
Conservation, Piagetian, 128
Contextual intelligence, 183
Continuity of development, 33
Contraception, 434–35, 447
Control group, 75
Conventional moral reasoning, 463
Convergent thinking, 188
Conversational skills, adolescent's understanding of, 141
Cooperative learning, 317
Coping
  defense mechanisms, 575
  emotion-focused coping, 576
  negative versus positive thinking, 576–77
  problem-focused coping, 576
  self-concept and, 576
  self-illusions and, 577
Correlational strategy
  to research, 74–75
  situations for use of, 76
Correlation coefficient, 74–75
Crack, 540
Creativity, 187–90
  definition of, 188
  divergent thinking, 188
  insight and, 188
  relationship to intelligence, 188
  snowflake model, 190
Cross-cultural approach
  achievement, 332–33
  anthropological view, 331–32
  moral development, 468–69
  rites of passage, 333–36
  sexuality, 333, 429
Cross-sectional approach, to research, 76–77
Crowd, 268
Cults
  concerns about, 483
  types of, 483
  vulnerability to, 484
Cultural bias in testing, 179–81
Cultural-familial retardation, 186
Cultural identity, 56

Culture
  cross-cultural studies, 331–36
  effect on family, 211–12
  ethnicity and, 340–48
  forces of, 326–28
  groups and, 266–67
  model for culture/adolescent interaction, 327–28
  music, impact of, 352, 354
  social class and, 337–40
  study of typical day for teenager, 329–31
  television, impact of, 349–52
  See also individual topics
Culture-fair tests, 180–81

D

Dating, 270–81
  attraction and, 275–77
  family relationships, influence of, 278–81
  functions of, 272
  going steady, 274–75
  incidence and age trends, 272–73
  male versus female patterns, 275
  peer relationships, influence of, 281
  romantic love, 277–78
  self-monitoring and, 278, 279
  sibling relationships, influence of, 280
Defense mechanisms, 46–47, 575
  role in adolescent adjustment, 48–49
  types of, 46–47
Defining Issues Test (DIT), 466
Denial, 575
Dependent variable, 75
Depressants, 540–41
Depression, 531, 555–57
  causes of, 556
  cognitive view of, 556
  learned helplessness, 556
  See also Suicide
Desatellization, 225
Development
  periods of, 27–29
  scope of, 26
  See also Adolescent development
Developmental construction view, relationships, 206
Developmental theory of career choice, 500–501
Direct moral education, 477
Discontinuity of development, 33
Divergent thinking, creativity and, 188
Divided attention, 163
Divorce, 232–35
  adjustment of child, influences in, 232

age of child and, 233–35
  conflict, impact of, 232
  dating relationships, influence on, 280
  sex of child and parent and, 233, 234–35
Drive, 491
Drive-reduction theory, motivation, 491
Drop-outs, 300–302
  minority students, 301–2
  programs for, 305
  reasons for dropping out, 302
  reducing rate, 303–5
Drug abuse. See Substance abuse
Dyzygotic, 93

E

Early adulthood, period of, 28–29
Early childhood, period of, 27
Early and late maturers, 115–16, 117–18
  academic behavior and, 117
  body image and, 116–17
  complexity in occurrence of, 117–18
  differences in, 115
  health care and, 119
  independence and, 117
  opposite-sex popularity and, 117
  self-concept and, 116
  studies of, 115
Eating disorders
  anorexia nervosa, 585
  bulimia, 586
  obesity, 583–85
Eclectic approach to development, 67–69
Education
  information processing and, 165–67
  Piaget's theory, implications of, 135–36, 137
Educational Amendments Act of 1972, 312
Ego, 46
Egocentrism, 146–47
  imaginary audience phenomenon, 146, 147
  personal fable, 146
  rationale for concept of, 147
Elaboration, cognitive skill, 167
Emile (Rousseau), 12
Emotion-focused coping, 576
Empathy, 475
Enlightenment era, adolescence in, 12–13
Epigenetic principle, Erikson's theory, 53
Erikson's theory, 42, 52–56
  basis of, 52–53
  epigenetic principle in, 53
  identity
    dimensions in, 382, 383

Knowledge versus process, intelligence,
   181–82
Kohlberg's theory
   moral development
      conscience, 464
      conventional moral reasoning, 463
      criticism of, 466–68, 474
      influences on moral stages, 464–65
      moral education, 479
      postconventional moral reasoning,
         463
      preconventional moral reasoning, 462
   social development, 144

L

Language development
   conversational skills, 141
   gender differences, 418
   metaphor, 138
   satire, 138–39
   word functions, 138
   written language, 139–41
Latchkey children, 237–38
Late adolescence, period of, 28
Late adulthood, period of, 29
Latency stage, 52
Learned helplessness, 556
Legislation, turn of the century, 18
Life time, 31
Longitudinal approach, to research, 77–78
Long-term memory, 164
Love
   affectionate love, 277
   romantic love, 277–78
LSD, 536–37
Lymphoid tissues, growth curve for, 100

M

Macrosystem, 328
Males, sexual maturation, 109, 110
   See also Gender differences
Marijuana, 537
Masculinity, 401, 403, 404, 407
Masturbation, 433–34
Matching hypothesis, 276
Maturation, in adolescent development, 29,
   31
Maturity gradients, growth curve and, 100
MDMA, 538

Medical model, of abnormal behavior, 530
Memory
   long-term memory, 164
   short-term memory, 163–64
   working memory, 182
Menarche, 104
   reactions to, 114–15
Mental age (MA), 170
Mental retardation, 185–86
   causes of, 186
   degrees of, 185
Mesosystem, 327
Metaphor, adolescent's understanding of,
   138
Mexican-American adolescents, 346–47
Microsystem, 327
Middle adulthood, period of, 29
Middle Ages, adolescence in, 12
Middle and late childhood, period of, 27
Middle schools
   characteristics of best schools, 297
   recommendations for improvement,
      297–98
Minority adolescents, achievement, 497–98
   See also specific groups
Modeling, 66–67
   behavior and, 66
   interactive view, 66
   parental, 228–29
   peer relations and, 228–29, 258
   social skills training, 255–56
Monozygotic, 93
Moral Atmosphere Interview, 480
Moral behavior
   modeling, 465, 472–73
   moral competence versus moral
      performance, 460, 474
   situational dependency and, 473–74
   social conventional reasoning and,
      469–71
Moral development
   cognitive social learning theory, 474
   cross-cultural approach, 468–69
   justice perspective versus care
      perspective, 468
   Kohlberg's theory, 462–68
   measurement of, 466–67
   nature of, 449–50
   parental influences, 465–66
   peer relations and, 465
   Piaget's theory, 450–51
   See also specific theories
Moral education, 477–79
   cognitive moral education, 478–79
   direct and indirect approach, 477

Kohlberg's influence, 479
   values clarification, 477–78
Moral feelings. See Altruism
Motivation, 491–96
   achievement motivation, 493
   attribution theory, 495–96
   competence motivation, 492
   drive-reduction theory, 491
   hierarchy of motives, 492, 493
   homeostasis and, 492
   intrinsic and extrinsic motivation, 496
MTV, 352
Multiple-factor theory, of intelligence, 174
Music, 352–54
   music videos, 352–53
   rock, impact of, 352–53
Mutual regulation, in family interaction,
   205

N

Native American adolescents
   characteristics of, 348
   drop out rates, 301–2
Nature-nurture controversy
   adolescent development, 31
   heredity-environment issue, 96–98
   intelligence, 177
Need, 491
Negative versus positive thinking, 576–77
Neglected and rejected children, peer
      relations and, 248
Nonconformist, 251
Normal distribution, 170
Norms, group, 263
Nutrition, 581–82
   onset of puberty and, 104

O

Obesity, 583–85
   eating behavior, aspects of, 584
Observation, in scientific method, 71–72
Observational learning. See Modeling
Oedipus complex, 49, 51
Open classrooms, 308
Operant learning, 63–65
   development, view of, 63–64
   reinforcement and punishment in, 64–65
Operations
   mental, 59
   Piagetian, 127
Opposite-sex popularity, early/late
      maturation and, 117

Oral stage, 48
Organic retardation, 186
Organization, cognitive skill, 164
Overevaluation by parent, 225

P

Parent-adolescent relationship
    during apex of pubertal growth, 208
    attachment of adolescent and, 227–29
    autonomy of adolescent and, 220–27
    changes in adolescent and, 208–10
    changes in parent and, 210–11
    conflict, 218–19
    idealism of adolescent and, 209–10
    √parental sex differences and, 208–9
    parenting techniques, 213–15
    self-actualized parents and, 217
    values of parent and, 222–24
    See also Family processes
Parenting techniques, 213–15
    authoritarian parenting, 214, 223–24
    authoritative parenting, 214, 224
    autonomy of adolescent and, 223–24,
        225
    flexibility and, 215
    permissive indifferent parenting, 214,
        224
    permissive indulgent parenting, 214, 224
    popular views, 213, 216–17
    social competency of adolescent and, 215
Parents Music Resource Center (PMRC),
    352
Peer pressure
    conformity and, 250–51
    dealing with, 252
    social knowledge, maladjusted
        adolescents, 253–54
Peer relations
    adolescent groups, 262–70
    career development and peer reactions,
        506
    conformity and, 249, 252
    dating, 270–81
    ethnic minority relations, 248
    friendships, 259–62
    gender role and, 412
    influences in
        modeling, 228–29, 258
        reinforcement, 258
        social knowledge, 252–54
        social skills training, 255–57
    moral development and, 464
    neglected and rejected children and, 248
    parental influences, 228–29, 259, 260

√peer pressure, 251–52
    popularity and, 247–48
    school setting, 311–12
    See also individual topics
√Peer relations, social comparison, 258–59
Peers
    functions of peer group, 245–47
    meaning of, 245
Peer therapy programs, 244
Perceived Competence Scale for Children,
    372
Permissive indifferent parenting, 214, 224
Permissive indulgent parenting, 22, 214
Personal fable, 126, 146
Personality development. *See* Erikson's
    theory; Freud's theory
Personality type theory, 502–3
Perspective taking, 147–48
    self-concept and, 368–69
    stages of, 147–48
Phallic stage, 49
Phenotype, 91–93, 97
Physical attractiveness
    dating and, 276–77
    popularity and, 247
Physical development
    brain growth, 102–3
    growth curves, 99–101
    height/weight increases, 107, 109
    heredity and, 101
Physiological research, in scientific method,
    73
Piaget's theory, 43, 58–59
    accommodation, 58, 133
    adolescent education and, 135–36, 137
    assimilation, 58, 133
    brain data and, 103
    cognitive stages, 59, 60
    concrete operational thought, 127–29,
        133
    conservation in, 128
    criticisms of, 134–35, 142
    formal operational thought, 129–33
        hazards of, 135
        hypothetical-deductive reasoning,
          130–32
        individual differences, 133–34
        phases of, 132
    horizontal decalage in, 128
    "knowing that" versus "knowing how"
        issue, 134
    language development, 138–41
    moral thought, 450–51
        autonomous morality, 460
        formal operational thought and, 461

        heteronomous morality, 460–61
        immanent justice, 461
    operations in, 127
    social cognition and, 150–51
Piers-Harris Scale, 372
Pleasure principle, 45
Polygenetic inheritance, 92–93
Poor
    drop-out rates, 301–2
    problems of, 339–40
Popularity, 247–48
    physical attractiveness and, 247
    unpopular children, 248
Postconventional moral reasoning, 463
Postponing Sexual Involvement Program,
    452
Pragmatics, adolescent's understanding of,
    141
Preconventional moral reasoning, 462
Pregnancy
    abortion, 441, 442
    adolescents as parents, 445–47
    cognitive factors, 443, 445
    consequences of, 442–43
    father and, 446–47
    nature/incidence of, 440
    personal fable and, 443, 445
    prevention strategies, 447–48, 452
Preintimate style, 391
Prenatal period, period of, 27
Preoperational thinking, 59, 127
Problem-focused coping, 576
Problem-solving
    cognitive-monitoring, 164–65
    creative persons and, 188, 190
    intelligence and, 169
    short-term memory and, 163–64
Pseudointimate style, 391
Psychoanalytic theories
    Erikson's theory, 52–56
    evaluation of, 57
    Freud's theory, 45–52
    See also specific theories
Psychological aspects of puberty, body
    image, 112–14, 116–17
Psychological moratorium, 378
Psychometrics, 169
Psychosocial stages, Erikson's theory,
    53–56
Puberty
    determinants of, 104–5
    evaluation of effects of, 118–19
    hormonal changes, 105–7
    individual variation, 111–12

psychological dimensions
    body image, 112, 114, 116–17
    early late/maturation, 115–16, 117–18
    reactions to menarche, 114–15
    sexual maturation, 109, 111
Punishment
    behavioral theory, 64–65
    moral behavior and, 472

Q

Quaaludes, 541
Questionnaires, in scientific method, 72–73

R

Racial/ethnic differences, intelligence issue, 178–79
Reaction formation, 47
Reaction range, 92
Reality principle, 45
Reciprocal socialization, in family interaction, 204–5
Regression, 47, 575
Reinforcement
    behavioral theory, 64–65
    moral behavior and, 472
    peer relations and, 258
Rejection by parent, 225
Relationships
    developmental construction view, 206
    in family, 205–7
Religious beliefs
    cults, 483–84
    development of, 481–83
    sociocultural influences, 483
Religious ceremonies, 335
Repression, 46
Reproductive organs, growth curve for, 99
Resatellization, 225
Research studies
    correlational strategy, 74–75
    cross-sectional approach, 76–77
    ethical issues, 78–80
    experimental strategy, 75–76
    longitudinal approach, 77–78
    scientific methods used, 70–73
    sequential approach, 77–78
Rites of passage
    adult status and, 336
    gender differences, 336
    religious and social ceremonies, 335
    ritual in, 334, 336

Rites of Passage (Kett), 8
Robber's Cave experiment, 263–66
Role experimentation, 379–81
Romantic love, sexual desire and, 277–78
Runaways, 222

S

Satellization, 225
Satire, adolescent's understanding of, 138–39
Schema, 409
Scholastic Aptitude Test (SAT), 176
Schools
    back-to-basics movement, 289
    career development and, 506–8
    classroom structure, 308–9
    class size, 307–8
    cooperative learning, 317
    drop-outs, 300–302
    ethnicity and, 314–18
        desegregation study, 315–16
        jigsaw classroom, 316
    functions of, 289–90
    gender role and, 312, 412
    historical view, 288
    impact of, 292–93
    issues related to, 288–91, 292
    middle schools, 294–98
        characteristics of best schools, 297
        recommendations for improvement, 297–98
    moral education, 477–79, 480
    noncollege youth, 303–4
    peer group, 311–12
    sex education, 449–51
    "shopping mall" high school, 29
    size of secondary schools, 307
    social class and, 313–14, 339
    substance abuse and, 542–43
    teachers, 309–11
    transition to college, 298–300
        choosing college, 299–300
        parental relationships and, 298–99
        stress/depression, 300
    transition to junior high schools, 294–98
        easing transition, 296–97
        stress of, 295
        top-dog phenomenon, 295
Science education, Piaget's theory and, 137
Scientific method
    case studies in, 72–73
    identification of problem, 70
    interviews in, 72

multimeasure/multisource/multicontext approach, 73
    observation in, 71–72
    physiological research in, 73
    questionnaires in, 72
    in research, 70–73
    revising theory and, 70
    standardized tests in, 73
    See also Research studies
Second individuation crisis, 226
Secure attachment, 227, 228
Selective attention, 162
Self-actualization, Roger's view, 371
Self-assertion, gender roles and, 404–5
Self-concept
    behavioral indicators of, 374
    cognitive development and, 366–69
    coping and, 576
    early/late maturation and, 116
    I and me, 365
    measurement of, 372–74
    nurturance and, 370
    perspective-taking and, 368–69
    real-self versus ideal self, 371
    Roger's view, 370–72
    self-awareness, 367
    self-consciousness, 367–68
    social competence and, 374–76
    See also Identity
Self-control, juvenile delinquency and, 547–48
Self-Image Questionnaire for Young Adolescents (SIQYA), 372
Self-monitoring, dating partner and, 278–79
Sensorimotor stage, 59
Sequential approach, to research, 78
Set point, body weight, 583–84
Sex differences. *See* Gender differences
Sex discrimination, 312
Sex education
    school-linked approaches, 450–51
    in schools, 449–51
    sources of, 448–49
Sex equity education, 413–14
Sex hormones, 99, 106–7
    androgens, 106
    estradiol, 106–7
    estrogens, 106
    testosterone, 106–7
Sexuality
    contraception, 434–35, 447
    cross-cultural approach, 333, 429
    homosexuality, 432–33
    masturbation, 433–34
    same-sex sexual behavior, 333